Vietnam, Cambodia & Laos

*Jock O'Tailan, Claire Boobbyer,
John Colet and Andrew Spooner*

**On the morning of the fourth day the dawn light
daubed our faces as we came down the skies of
Cochin-China. As the first rays of the sun burst
through the magenta mists that lay along the
horizon, the empty sketching of the child's painting
book open beneath us received a wash of green.**

Norman Lewis, A Dragon Apparent

CHINA

MYANMAR
(BURMA)

Lai Chau
Lao Cai
Sapa ⭐3
Phongsali
Son La
Luang
Namtha
Dien Bien
Phu
Udom Xai
HANOI □
Haiphong ⭐2
Hoa Binh
Xam Neua
Ninh Binh
Thanh Hoa

Gulf of Tonkin

Luang
Prabang ⭐8
Tran Ninh
Highlands
Plain of Jars
Phonsavanh
Sayaboury
Vang Vieng ⭐7
Nam Ngum
Reservoir
VIENTIANE □
Paksan

LAOS
Thakhek ⭐9
Vinh
Dong Hoi
Quang Tri
Hué
Danang
Hoi An ⭐4

THAILAND

BANGKOK □

Savannakhet
Salavan
Pakse
Boloven
Plateau
Sekong
Attapeu

Samrong
Kulen
Ta Veng ⭐10
O Chum
Bokeo
Quy Nhon
Thkov
Sisophon
Angkor ⭐6
Siem Reap
Stung
Treng
Lumphat
Central
Highlands
Pailin
Battambang
Tonlé Sap
CAMBODIA
Kompong
Thom
Kratie
Buon Ma
Thuot
Moung
Roessei
Pursat
Skon
Snuol
Nha Trang
PHNOM PENH □
Kompong
Speu
Prey
Veng
Mekong
Dalat
Phan Rang
Koh Kong
Takeo
Chhuk
Ho Chi
Minh City
(Saigon) ⭐5
Phan Thiet
Sihanoukville
(Kompong Som)
Kampot
Phu Quoc
Island
Rach Gia
Can Tho
Mekong
Delta
Mui Ne
Vung Tau

VIETNAM

South China Sea

N

100 km
100 miles

Don't miss...

⭐1 **The Old City, Hanoi** ▶▶ p104.

⭐2 **A boat trip on Halong Bay** ▶▶ p114.

⭐3 **Trekking around Sapa** ▶▶ p137.

⭐4 **Hoi An** ▶▶ p167.

⭐5 **Downtown Saigon** ▶▶ p213.

⭐6 **Angkor Wat** ▶▶ p286.

⭐7 **Adventure activities in Vang Vieng** ▶▶ p312.

⭐8 **Luang Prabang** ▶▶ p328.

⭐9 **Kong Lor cave** ▶▶ p372.

⭐10 **Islands of Siphandon** ▶▶ p386.

Vietnam, Cambodia and Laos offer unrivalled attractions in the form of ruins, colonial remnants, stunning scenery, ethnic diversity and exotic food. Their shared history as part of Indochina is still evident in the fading French architecture, the cuisine and the ubiquitous reminders of bloody wars, but it is their distinct differences that render the area such a fantastic travel experience.

In Vietnam, vivid green paddies climb up mountainsides or sit alongside beautiful coastal scenery; feverish Ho Chi Minh City plays noisier, more moneyed brother to the enchanting, romantic capital, Hanoi. Cambodia is home to the magnificent Angkor Wat, the zenith of Southeast Asian architecture, and a multitude of other awe-inspiring monuments. Phnom Penh, the fascinating modern day capital, offers the glistening Royal Palace, eclectic markets and poignant relics of a turbulent past. Laid-back Laos, rousing after years of isolation, provides a beautiful, postcard-like backdrop. From the picturesque gilded temples of the former royal capital, Luang Prabang, to the chilled-out Mekong islands of Siphandon, it's hard not to be inspired by this exquisite country and its charming peoples.

$\rightarrow$

4

Contents

Ho Chi Minh City and the south 206

Cambodia 250

Vientiane and northern Laos 300

5

HANOI

VIENTIANE

BANGKOK

PHNOM PENH

- Bangkok
- Hanoi & around
- Northwest Vietnam
- Central Vietnam
- Ho Chi Minh City & the south
- Cambodia
- Vientiane & northern Laos
- Southern Laos

Southern Laos 366

About the guide

Until recently, backpacking was the preserve of the impecunious student, stretching their pesos/baht/rupees as far as possible, sleeping in cockroach-infested, cell-like rooms and risking food poisoning by eating at the cheapest market stalls they could find. Today's backpackers, however, are different. They still have the same adventurous spirit but they probably don't have endless months to swan around the globe; they're interested in the people, culture, wildlife and history of a region and they're willing to splash out occasionally to ensure that their trip is truly memorable.

Footprint's discover guides are designed precisely for this new breed of traveller. We've selected the best sights, sleeping options, restaurants and a range of adventure activities so that you can have the experience of a lifetime. With over 80 years' experience of writing about travel, we hope that you find this guide easy to use, enjoyable to read and good to look at.

Essentials, the first chapter, deals with practicalities: introducing the region and suggesting where and when to go, what to do and how to get around; we give the lowdown on visas, money, health and transport, and provide overviews of history and culture. The rest of the guide is divided into area-based chapters, colour-coded by country for convenience. At the start of each chapter, a **highlights map** gives an instant overview of the area and its attractions. A star-rating system also gives each area marks out of five for Landscape, Activities, Culture etc. The Costs category refers to value for money in relation to Europe and North America: **$$$$$** is expensive and **$** is very cheap. Follow the cross references on the highlights map to the district that interests you and you'll find a more detailed map, together with a snapshot of the area, showing the amount of time you will need, how to get there and move around, and what to expect in terms of weather, accommodation and restaurants. **Special features** include expert tips, inspiring travellers' tales, suggestions for busting your budget and ideas for going that little bit further.

We use a range of symbols throughout the guide to indicate the following listings information:

- Sleeping
- Eating
- Entertainment
- Festivals
- Shopping
- Activities and tours
- Transport
- Directory

Please note that hotel and restaurant codes, p26 and p29, should only be used as a guide to the prices and facilities offered by the establishment. It is at the discretion of the owners to vary them from time to time.

Footprint feedback We try as hard as we can to make each Footprint guide as up to date as possible but, of course, things always change. If you want to let us know about your experiences – good, bad or ugly – then don't delay, go to www.footprintbooks.com and send in your comments.

The Great Escape

ttle time, sensible budget, **big** adventure

evised by travel experts, this new full-colour series
mbines the very best of the region with stunning
notos, great maps, top tips and budget-busting ideas.

" "

*e guides for intelligent, independently
inded souls.* Indie Traveller

discover

www.footprintbooks.com

Essentials

Lotus blossoms, Mui Ne, Vietnam

Travelling

Where to go

If time is limited, by far the best option is to get an open-jaw flight where you fly into one city and out of another or fly into Bangkok, the cheapest point of entry, and use the **Bangkok Airways** regional 'Discovery Airpass', which includes **Siem Reap Airways** routes and **Lao Airlines** primary routes. **Vietnam Airlines** has a good domestic network, too. Distances are huge in this region and in Cambodia and Laos, especially, roads are not always sealed, making overland journey times lengthy and sometimes tortuous, especially in the wet season. Note that there are strict regulations concerning visas that need to be noted before planning your trip, see Visas, p48.

One week

A one-week trip will require careful planning and prioritizing. Either take internal flights, if you want to cover a lot of ground, or limit yourself to just one area. In Vietnam, fly from energetic and historic **Ho Chi Minh City** to the imperial city of **Hué**, followed by a trip to enchanting **Hoi An** and its beach. Then fly on to cultured **Hanoi**. If the countryside is of more interest, the **Mekong Delta** can be visited in a day trip from Ho Chi Minh City; magical **Halong Bay** can be done in a day/night trip from Hanoi but in order to visit **Sapa**, known for its stunning scenery and hilltribes, you'll have to spend two nights on a train. In Cambodia, up to four days could be spent around the exceptional ruins of **Angkor**, with one day in **Phnom Penh** and one in either the laid-back beaches of **Sihanoukville** or in colonial-inspired **Kampot**. For Laos, fly from Bangkok to **Vientiane** before heading north to wonderfully preserved **Luang Prabang** via **Vang Vieng**. Or fly from Vientiane to **Luang Namtha** to access the interesting trekking region in the north before overlanding it back to Luang Prabang. Alternatively, after visiting Luang Prabang, fly back to Vientiane and on to Pakse for a trip to the tranquil, laid-back **Siphandon** (4000 islands) in the south.

Two weeks

Building on the one-week options, you have the chance to cross a border or two. If you fly into **Ho Chi Minh City** you could see the war relic of the **Cu Chi tunnels** and the fantastical **Cao Dai Temple** before making your way through the **Mekong Delta** (visiting the floating markets at **Can Tho**) to **Phnom Penh**, **Choeung Ek** and onto **Siem Reap (Angkor)** by boat, where you will have more time to visit some of the outlying ruins such as **Koh Ker** and **Beng Melea** and, at a push, the brilliant, clifftop temple of **Preah Vihear**. You could then fly from Siem Reap to **Pakse** for **Wat Phou**, the sublime **Tad Lo** and **Tad Fan falls** and **Siphandon**, or to **Vientiane** to access northern Laos. Alternatively, you could fly to Cambodia first and then fly from either Phnom Penh to Vientiane or Ho Chi Minh City or from Siem Reap to Ho Chi Minh City. If you fly into **Hanoi** you could visit both **Sapa** (by train) and **Halong Bay** and then fly to **Vientiane** in Laos continuing to Siem Reap or Phnom Penh by plane.

One month

With one month you can take things a little more slowly. Having explored **Sapa**, **Dien Bien Phu** and the area around **Mai Chau** in northwest Vietnam you could take an overnight train from **Hanoi** to **Hué**. You could either travel west into

Clockwise from top: Hills and rice paddies around Sapa, northwest Vietnam; Wat Xieng Thong in Luang Prabang, Laos; Angkor Wat, Cambodia.

central Laos here or take the splendid **train journey from Hué to Danang**. Close by is **Hoi An**. From there, travel to coastal **Nha Trang** for its islands or to the quieter, lovely resort of **Mui Ne**. From Nha Trang you could go to **Dalat**, the hub of the Central Highlands and the towns of **Buon Ma Thuot**, **Play Ku** and **Kontum**, then continue by air or overland to **Ho Chi Minh City**, from where a side trip to the unspoilt beaches of **Phu Quoc** is possible. To reach Cambodia, fly on to **Phnom Penh** or **Siem Reap** or go by bus and boat through the **Mekong Delta**. Visit **Angkor** and then, from Phnom Penh, go south to **Sihanoukville** and explore the beaches and outlying islands. A day or two can also be spent visiting **Kampot** and the seaside town of **Kep**, as well as exploring the eerie **Bokor Mountain National Park**. From Phnom Penh you could travel overland to **Siphandon** in southern Laos via Stung Treng. Before heading north take a side trip to the interesting **Boloven Plateau** with its stunning coffee plantations and ubiquitous falls. Overland it to **Thakhek** and do the motorcycle loop around

Top tips

Visiting ethnic minorities: house rules

Scores of different ethnic minority groups inhabit northern Vietnam, the Central Highlands of Vietnam and northern Laos, in particular, and their distinctive styles of dress and age-old rituals may be of special interest to western travellers. If you choose to visit or stay in a minority village, please remember that it is not a human zoo. Etiquette and customs vary between the minorities, but the following are general rules of good behaviour that should be adhered to whenever possible.

✅ Organize your visit through a local villager or a travel agency that supports the village.

✅ Inform yourself of local trekking rules and guidance. See in particular p137 and p344.

✅ Dress modestly and avoid undressing/changing in public.

✅ Ask permission before entering a house.

✅ Ask permission before photographing anyone (old people and pregnant women often object to having their photograph taken). Be aware that villagers are unlikely to pose out of the kindness of their hearts so don't begrudge them the money; for many, tourism is their livelihood.

✅ Buy handicrafts that support local industry.

❌ Avoid sitting or stepping on door sills.

❌ Avoid excessive displays of wealth and do not hand out gifts.

❌ Avoid introducing western medicines.

❌ Do not touch or photograph village shrines.

the limestone scenery of central Laos, visiting the **Kong Lor** River Cave en route. Or fly direct to **Vientiane** in order to catch a flight to **Phonsavanh** and explore the mysterious **Plain of Jars**, then overland it to **Xam Neua** to see the ancient rock formations at **Suan Hin** and the Pathet Lao caves at **Vieng Xai**. A long but interesting overland route will take you west from here via increasingly popular **Nong Khiaw** to **Luang Prabang**, from where you can head north to the trekking areas of **Luang Namtha**, **Muang Sing** and **Phongsali**, or catch a boat up the Mekong towards the Thai border. A flight from Vientiane to Luang Namtha will save two days' travel and from Vientiane to Phongsali, four days' travel.

When to go

Climatically the best time to visit the region is between November and April when it should be dry and not too hot. In the southern part of the region it is warm but not too hot with lovely cool evenings. However, in Cambodia wind-blown dust invades everything at this time of year. In the north of Vietnam and Laos the highlands will be a bit chilly but they should be dry with clear blue skies. However, temperatures in upland areas like the Plain of Jars, the Boloven Plateau and some towns in the north of Laos can drop to below freezing.

From late-March to April the region heats up and temperatures can exceed 40°C. In northern Laos, the months from March through to the first rains in May or June can be very hazy as smoke from burning off the secondary forest hangs in the air. On the worst days this can cause itchiness of the eyes. It also means that views are restricted and sometimes flights are cancelled. Travel on the region's mud and laterite roads is difficult and sometimes impossible by June and July; transport will be slower and may cease altogether in some parts. It is also impossible to do any outdoor activities in June and July because of the rain. However, the area is at its most beautiful then. Travel in the south and Mekong Delta can be difficult at the height of the monsoon (particularly during September, October and November). The central regions and north of Vietnam sometimes suffer tropical storms from May to November. Hué is at its wettest wet from September to January.

Tet, Vietnamese new year, is not really a good time to visit. This movable feast usually falls between late January and March and lasts for about a fortnight. It is the only holiday most Vietnamese get in the year so popular destinations are packed, roads are jammed and, for a couple of days, almost all hotels and restaurants are shut. All hotel prices increase and car hire prices rise by 50% or more. Problems also occur during **Khmer New Year** in Cambodia and **Pi Mai** in Laos, when public transport is full and and hotels booked out in popular places.

Sport and activities

Vietnam and Laos are well known for their wonderful trekking opportunities amid stunning mountainous landscape, which is home to a variety of ethnic minorities. Other activities, such as rafting, kayaking and cycling, are fairly recently established or slowly emerging and are not as developed as they are in a place like Thailand. Safety is always an issue when participating in adventurous sports: make sure you are fully covered by your travel insurance; check the credentials of operators offering adventure activities; and make sure that vehicles and safety equipment are in a good condition. Note that medical care in Cambodia and Laos is very limited, see p36.

Caving

Laos has some of the most extensive and largest caves in the region. Some of the best can be found around Vang Vieng, where caving tourism has been developed. Another highlight is the amazing Kong Lor River Cave in the centre of the country.

★ **Head for**
Vang Vieng ▶▶ *p312* **Tham Kong Lor** ▶▶ *p372*.

ⓘ **Green Discovery**, Vang Vieng, T023-511230, www.greendiscoverylaos.com.

Cycling and mountain biking

Large parts of Vietnam are flat so cycling is a popular activity, although the traffic on the roads can be hazardous. It's therefore recommended that any tour is planned off-road or on minor roads. In Cambodia and Laos, cycling is offered by several tour agencies; Luang Namtha is a popular place to start. Many cyclists prefer to bring their own all-terrain or racing bikes but it's also possible to rent them from tour organizers.

★ **Head for**
Hué ▸▸ *p148* **Dalat** ▸▸ *p187* **Mekong Delta** ▸▸ *p235* **Luang Namtha** ▸▸ *p343*

ⓘ **Asian Trails**, www.asiantrails.net.
Exotissimo, Hanoi, T04-8282150; Ho Chi Minh City, T08-8251723, www.exotissimo.com.
Green Discovery, Luang Namtha, T086-211484, www.greendiscoverylaos.com.
Symbiosis, www.symbiosis-travel.com.

Diving and snorkelling

Underwater adventures are limited in the seas around Vietnam, since much of the coast is a muddy deltaic swamp and, elsewhere, the water is turbid from high levels of soil erosion. In those places where snorkelling and diving is good (Nha Trang, Phu Quoc and Danang) it is only possible for a few months of the year in the dry season only (Nov-Apr). The dive industry in Cambodia is still small and undeveloped, but the coast boasts lots of pristine coral reefs and unexplored areas. There are several dive operators in Sihanoukville.

★ **Head for**
Danang ▸▸ *p172* **Nha Trang** ▸▸ *p193* **Phu Quoc** ▸▸ *p242* **Sihanoukville** ▸▸ *p262*

ⓘ **Rainbow Divers**, Nha Trang, T058-829946, T091-3408146 (mob), www.divevietnam.com.
Scuba Nation Diving Centre, Sihanoukville, T012-604680.

Kayaking

Kayaking in Vietnam is centred around Halong Bay. This World Heritage Site, crammed with islands and grottoes, is a fantastic place to explore by kayak. Head to the Nam Song River at Vang Vieng for kayaking, rafting and tubing in Laos.

★ **Head for**
Halong Bay ▸▸ *p114* **Vang Vieng** ▸▸ *p312*

ⓘ **Buffalo Tours**, Hanoi, T04-8280702; Ho Chi Minh City, T08-8279169, www.buffalotours.com.
Exotissimo, Hanoi, T04-8282150; Ho Chi Minh City, T08-8251723, www.exotissimo.com.
Green Discovery, Vang Vieng, T023-511230, www.greendiscoverylaos.com.
Paddle Asia, www.laosadventure.com.

Kitesurfing and windsurfing

Kitesurfing and windsurfing are found largely in Mui Ne, Vietnam, which offers just about perfect conditions throughout the year. The wind is normally brisk over many days and the combination of powerful wind and waves enables good kite surfers to get airborne for several seconds at a time. Equipment can be rented at many places. Windsurfing is popular in Nha Trang where dive schools offer this and other watersports.

Kayaking at Vang Vieng, Laos

★ Head for
Nha Trang ⇥ *p193* **Mui Ne ⇥** *p197*

ⓘ **Jibe's Beach Club**, Mui Ne, T062-847405, www.windsurf-vietnam.com.

Rock climbing

Laos has stunning karst rock formations, caves and cliffs. Vang Vieng is the hot spot for this activity.

★ Head for
Vang Vieng ⇥ *p312*

ⓘ **Green Discovery**, Vang Vieng, T023-511230, www.greendiscoverlaos.com.

Spas

There are only a handful of authentic spas in Vietnam. The country's top spas are **Six Senses** at the **Ana Mandara** resorts in Dalat, Nha Trang and on an island off Nha Trang. Hotels offering massage, treatments and therapies exist across the region and are good value for money.

★ Head for
Dalat ⇥ *p187* **Nha Trang ⇥** *p193*

Trekking

The main focus for trekking in Vietnam is Sapa but some trekking is also organized around Dalat. Trekking can be done alone or through national or local tour operators. Longer walks will require accommodation. If this means staying with ethnic minorities in homestays this must be done through a tour operator. In Laos, Luang Namtha, Muang Sing and Phongsali all offer trekking in areas inhabited by a diverse range of ethnicities. There are also treks from Luang Prabang and Vang Vieng. For a different perspective on the landscape, **elephant trekking** is possible in Yok Don National Park, Vietnam, and around Vang Vieng and Tad Lo in Laos.

★ Head for
Sapa ⇥ *p134* **Dalat ⇥** *p187* **Yok Don National Park ⇥** *p192* **Phou Khao Khouay ⇥** *p311* **Vang Vieng ⇥** *p312* **Luang Namtha ⇥** *p343* **Muang Sing ⇥** *p344* **Phongsali ⇥** *p348* **Tad Lo ⇥** *p385*

ⓘ T021-212251, www.trekkingcentrallaos.com.

Essentials Travelling Sport & activities

Elephant trekking

Taking a tour

Numerous operators offer organized trips to this region, ranging from a whistle-stop tour of the highlights to specialist trips that focus on a specific destination or activity. The advantage of travelling with a reputable operator is that your transport, accommodation and activities are all arranged for you in advance – particularly valuable if you only have limited time in the region. By travelling independently, however, you can be much more flexible and spontaneous about where you go and what you do. You will be able to explore less visited areas and you will save money, if you budget carefully. On arrival in Vietnam, many travellers hire tour operators to take them on day and week-long trips. These tours cater for all budgets and you will benefit from an English-speaking guide and safe vehicles. Some of the most popular trips include week-long tours around the northwest or into the Mekong Delta. A list of specialist tour operators can be found in Essentials A-Z, p45.

Ecotourism

Since the early 1990s there has been a phenomenal growth in 'ecotourism', which promotes and supports the conservation of natural environments and is also fair and equitable to local communities. While the authenticity of some ecotourism operators needs to be interpreted with care, there is clearly both a huge demand for this type of activity and also significant opportunities to support worthwhile conservation and social development initiatives by this means. **Green Globe** (T020-77304428, www.greenglobe21.com) and the **Centre for Environmentally Sustainable Tourism** (CERT; T01268-795772, www.c-e-r-t.org) now offer advice for travellers on selecting destinations and sites that aim to achieve certain commitments to conservation and sustainable development.

In addition, the **Eco-Tourism Society** (T1-802-447 2121, www.ecotourism.org), **Tourism Concern** (T020-7753 3330, www.tourismconcern.org.uk) and **Planeta** (www.planeta.com) develop and promote ecotourism projects in destinations all over the world and their websites provide details for initiatives throughout Southeast Asia.

For opportunities to participate directly in scientific research and development projects, contact **Earthwatch** (in the US and Canada 1-800-7760188, in the UK T01865-311601, www.earthwatch.org), **Discovery International** (T020-7229 9881, www.discoveryinitiatives.com) and the **Nautilus Institute** (www.nautilus.org), which focuses on issues specifically connected with the environment and sustainability in the Asia-Pacific region. See also How big is your footprint?, on the facing page.

MAGIC
OF THE ORIENT

Vietnam,
Cambodia
& Laos

tailor-made for you by specialists

Magic of the Orient
Tel: 0117 311 6050 www.magicoftheorient.com
Email: info@magicoftheorient.com

Top tips

How big is your footprint?

The benefits of international travel are self-evident for both hosts and travellers: employment, increased understanding of different cultures, business and leisure opportunities. At the same time there is clearly a downside to the industry. Where visitor pressure is high or poorly regulated, adverse impacts to society and the natural environment may occur. In order to ensure your contribution to the host nation is a positive one, follow these guidelines, taken from the Tourism Concern website, www.tourismconcern.org.uk

✅ Learn about the country you're visiting. Start enjoying your travels before you leave by tapping into as many sources of information as you can.

✅ Think about where your money goes – be fair and realistic about how cheaply you travel. Try and put money into local people's hands; drink local beer or fruit juice rather than imported brands, and stay in locally-owned accommodation.

✅ Open your mind to new cultures and traditions. It can transform your holiday experience and you'll earn respect and be more readily welcomed by local people.

✅ Think about what happens to your rubbish: take biodegradable products and a water filter bottle. Be sensitive to limited resources like water, fuel and electricity.

✅ Help preserve local wildlife and habitats by respecting rules and regulations, such as sticking to footpaths, not standing on coral and not buying products made from endangered plants or animals.

✅ Use your guidebook as a starting point, not the only source of information. Talk to local people, then discover your own adventure!

❌ Don't treat people as part of the landscape; they may not want their picture taken. Put yourself in their shoes, ask first and respect their wishes. See also Visiting ethnic minorities: house rules, p12.

Getting there and flying around

Arriving by air

The easiest – and cheapest – way to access the region is via **Bangkok** or **Hong Kong**. Most major airlines have direct flights from Europe, North America and Australasia to these hubs. There are only direct flights to **Vietnam** from Paris and one from the USA. **Vietnam Airlines** has plans to fly direct from the US in 2006. International airports are at Tan Son Nhat Airport (SGN) in **Ho Chi Minh City** and Noi Bai Airport (HAN) in **Hanoi** (also **Danang** for some flights from the rest of Asia). **Cambodia and Laos** are only accessible from within Asia. The most important entry point for Cambodia remains **Phnom Penh** though there are now more flights to **Siem Reap** (REP). Both are connected to Bangkok, Singapore, Hong Kong, Ho Chi Minh City and Vientiane and Pakse in Laos. For Laos, there are direct flights to **Vientiane** from Phnom Penh, Siem Reap, Bangkok, Hanoi and Ho Chi Minh City. There are also flights from Bangkok to **Luang Prabang**. A cheaper option for getting to Laos from Bangkok is to fly to **Udon Thani**, Thailand, about 50 km south of the border at the Friendship Bridge and travel overland from there. For full details, see p305. An alternative route is to fly from Bangkok to **Chiang Rai,** Thailand, before overlanding it to **Chiang Khong** and crossing into northern Laos at **Houei Xai**. From Houei Xai there are flights to Vientiane and boats to Luang Prabang. See regional flights p20. ⯈ *For further details, see Ins and outs sections throughout the guide.*

Flights from Europe

There are direct flights to Vietnam only from Paris, with **Vietnam Airlines/Air France**. These code-shared flights cost from around £350 in low season. **Vietnam Airlines** has an office in the UK at Vista Office Centre, 6th Floor, Tower A, 50 Salisbury Road, Hounslow TW4 6JQ, T0870-2240211, www.vietnamairlines.com. Flights from London and other European hubs go via Bangkok, Singapore, Kuala Lumpur, or Hong Kong. From London to Vietnam takes around 15-24 hours, depending on the length of stopover, and costs from £500 in high season. Airlines include **Cathay Pacific, Thai Airways**, **Singapore Airlines**, **Malaysia Airlines** and **Air France**. It is also possible to fly into Hanoi and depart from Ho Chi Minh City. Check details with flight agents and tour operators (see p20 and p45). The best deals usually involve flying to Bangkok and then on from there to your destination. There are countless airlines flying to Bangkok from Europe and lots of good deals, so shop around. From London airports to Bangkok takes around 12 hours non-stop with prices starting around £350.

Flights from the USA and Canada

There are flights to Vietnam from several major US hubs but these are very expensive (eg, as much as US$4000 from New York in high season). By far the best option is to fly via **Bangkok**, **Taipei** or **Hong Kong** and from there to Vietnam, Cambodia or Laos. The approximate flight time from Los Angeles to **Bangkok** is 21 hours. **United** flies from San Francisco to Vietnam. **Thai**, **Delta**, **Northwest**, **United** and **Canadian** fly to Bangkok from a number of US and Canadian cities.

Flights from Australia and New Zealand

There are direct flights daily (nine hours) to **Bangkok** from all major Australian and New Zealand cities with **Cathay Pacific, Korean Airlines**, **Qantas, Malaysia Airlines**, **Singapore Airlines** and **Thai**, among others. There are direct flights to Vietnam from Adelaide, Melbourne, Sydney, Perth, Auckland and Wellington with **Cathay Pacific, Malaysia Airlines**, **Singapore Airlines** and **Thai** , from around AUS$1200. There is also the option of flying into Hanoi and out of Ho Cho Minh City, or vice versa.

Discount flight agents

Online agents
Discount Airfares Worldwide On-Line, www.etn.nl/discount.htm. A hub of consolidator and discount agent links.
Ebookers, www.ebookers.com. Comprehensive ticket booking website.
Expedia, www.expedia.com. Lots of background information.
International Travel Network/Airlines of the Web, www.itn.net/airlines. Online air travel information and reservations.
Travelocity, www.travelocity.com. Online consolidator.

UK
STA Travel, 86 Old Brompton Rd, London, SW7 3LH, T0870-1606070, www.statravel.co.uk. Specialists in low-cost student/youth flights and tours, also good for student IDs and insurance.

Trailfinders, 194 Kensington High St, London, W8 7RG, T020-7938 3939, www.trailfinders.co.uk.

North America
Air Brokers International, 323 Geary St, Suite 411, San Francisco, CA 94102, T01-800-8833273, www.airbrokers.com.
STA Travel, 5900 Wilshire Blvd, Suite 2110, Los Angeles, CA 90036, T1-800-777 0112, www.sta-travel.com.
Travel CUTS, 187 College St, Toronto, ON, M5T 1P7, T1-800-6672887, www.travel cuts.com. Specialist in student discount fares, IDs and other travel services.

Australia and New Zealand
Flight Centres, 82 Elizabeth St, Sydney, T131600; 205 Queen St, Auckland, T09-309 6171, www.flightcentre.com.au.
STA Travel, 702 Harris St, Ultimo, Sydney, T1300-360960, www.statravelaus.com.au, 10 High St, Auckland, T09-3666673.

... and leaving again
Airport tax International departure tax from Hanoi is US$14 for adults and US$12 from Ho Chi Minh City. Domestic departure tax is included in the price of the flight ticket. In Cambodia the international departure tax is US$25, domestic tax is US$6. In Laos it is US$10 for international; domestic airport tax is 5000 kip.

Regional flights
If you have two weeks or less to spend in the region, it's important to factor in some flights if you want to cover a lot of ground. **Bangkok Airways**, www.bangkokair.com, offers a Discovery Airpass in cooperation with **Siem Reap Airways**, www.siemreapairways.com, and **Lao Airlines**, www.laoairlines.com, which permits several flights within the region at reduced rates. National carriers **Vietnam Airlines**, www.vietnamairlines.com, and **Lao Airlines** also offer regional flights.

Within Vietnam **VA** flies from Hanoi or Ho Chi Minh City to Dien Bien Phu, Hué, Danang, Nha Trang, Dalat, Buon Ma Thuot, Play Ku, Rach Gia and Phu Quoc. It also flies to Phnom Penh, Siem Reap and Bangkok. From Hanoi it flies to Luang Prabang. Flights can subsequently be altered at no cost at VA booking offices, seat availability permitting. Within Vietnam there are two other domestic carriers, **Pacific Airlines**, www.pacificairlines.com.vn, and **Vasco Airlines**.

Royal Phnom Penh Airways, www.thefuturegroup.org/royalphnompenh, flies from Phnom Penh, and **Siem Reap Airways**, www.siemreapairways.com, flies between Siem Reap and the capital. **President Airlines**, www.presidentairlines.com, flies within Cambodia, to Bangkok and Danang. **Silk Air**, www.silkair.net, flies from Phnom Penh to Siem Reap.

Lao Airlines flies to Vientiane, Luang Prabang, Luang Namtha, Phongsali, Xam Neua, Phonsavannh (Xieng Khouang), Savannakhet and Pakse within Laos. It also flies to Hanoi, Ho Chi Minh City and Bangkok. All flights using **Lao Airlines**, whether domestic or international, have to be paid for in US dollars by foreigners. **Lao Airlines** flies three types of aeroplane: French-built *ATR-72s*, and Chinese-built *Y-7s* and *Y-12s*. The latter two are a risk. The most reliable, comfortable and newest machines – the *ATR-72s* – operate on the most popular routes (Vientiane-Bangkok, Vientiane-Luang Prabang, Vientiane-Pakse).

Thai, www.thaiair.com, flies to Ho Chi Minh City, Luang Prabang, Phnom Penh and Vientiane from Bangkok. **Air Asia**, www.airasia.com, and **Nok Air**, www.nokair.com, fly to Udon Thani in northern Thailand for overland connections to Vientiane, see p305. **Air Asia** also flies from Bangkok to Chiang Rai, Hanoi and Phnom Penh. Thai also flies to Chiang Rai. **One-Two-Go**, www.fly12go.com, flies from Bangkok to Chiang Rai.

Getting around by land and river

Vietnam

Open Tour Buses, see below, are very useful and cheap for bridging important towns. Train travel is exciting and overnight journeys are a good way of covering long distances. The Vietnamese rail network extends from Hanoi to Ho Chi Minh City. Many travellers opt to take a tour to reach remote areas because of the lack of self-drive car hire and the dangers and slow speed of public transport.

Boat The Victoria hotel chain, www.victoriahotels-asia.com, operates a service to **Can Tho** from Ho Chi Minh City and from Can Tho to **Chau Doc** but it is only for hotel guests. There are also services from Chau Doc to Phnom Penh, see border box, p241.

Bus Since Highway 1 is so dangerous and public transport buses are poor and slow, most travellers opt for the cheap and regular Open Tour Bus (private minibus or coach) that covers the length of the country. Almost every Vietnamese tour operator/travellers' café listed in this guide will run a minibus service or act as an agent. The ticket is a flexible, one-way ticket from Ho Chi Minh City to Hanoi and vice versa. The buses run daily from their own offices and include the following stops: Ho Chi Minh City, Mui Ne, Nha Trang, Dalat, Hoi An, Hué and Hanoi (eg, Hanoi-Ho Chi Minh City, US$27, Hoi An-Nha Trang US$7). They will also stop off at tourist destinations along the way such as Lang Co, Hai Van Pass, Marble Mountains and Po Klong Garai. You may join at any leg of the journey, paying for one trip or several as you go. The Hanoi to Hué and vice versa is an overnight trip but although you might save on a night's accommodation you are unlikely to get much sleep. Note that bus listings in this guide refer to Open Tours Buses unless otherwise stated.

Car hire Self-drive car hire is not available in Vietnam. It is, however, possible to hire cars with drivers and this is a good way of getting to more remote areas with a group of people. Cars with drivers can be hired for around US$40-70 per day. All cars are modern and air-conditioned. Car hire prices increase by 50% or more during Tet. A standard, air-conditioned modern car including the driver, fuel, road fees and food and accommodation for the driver in and around Hanoi and the north would cost around US$420 for one week. For travelling the length of the country the cost could escalate to around US$1200 for a week including fuel, driver and food and accommodation for the driver or a discount may be offered for a one-way service where a company has multiple branches throughout the country.

Motorbike and bicycle hire Most towns are small enough for bicycles to be an attractive option but if taking in a sweep of the surrounding countryside (touring around the

Central Highlands, for example) then a motorbike will mean you can see more. Motorbikes can be rented easily and are an excellent way of getting off the beaten track. You do not need a driver's licence or proof of motorbike training to hire a motorbike in Vietnam. It is only compulsory for motorcyclists riding on highways to wear helmets. Take time to familiarize yourself with road conditions and ride slowly.

Bicycles can be rented by the day in the cities and are useful for getting out into the countryside. Hotels often have bicycles for hire and there is usually someone willing to lend their machine for a small charge (10,000-15,000d per day). Many travellers' cafés rent out bicycles and motorbikes, the former for around 12,000-15,000d a day, the latter for 90,000-120,000d per day. Motorbikes are hired out with helmets and bicycles with locks. Always park your bicycle or motorbike in a guarded parking place (*gui xe*). Ask for a ticket. The 2000d this costs is worth every dong, even if you are just popping in to the post office to post a letter. It is possible to book bicycles on to trains but this must be done at least two days in advance. The cost, for example from Nha Trang to Danang is US$4.

Motorbike taxi and cyclo Motorcycle taxis, known as *honda ôm* or *xe ôm* – *ôm* means to cuddle – are ubiquitous and cheap. You will find them on most street corners, outside hotels or in the street. With their uniform baseball caps and dangling cigarette, *xe ôm* drivers are readily recognizable. If they see you before you see them, they will shout 'moto' to get your attention. In the north and upland areas the Honda is replaced with the Minsk. The shortest hop would be at least 5,000d. Always bargain though.

Cyclos are bicylce trishaws. Cyclo drivers charge double that of a *xe ôm*. A number of streets in the centres of Ho Chi Minh City and Hanoi are one-way or out of bounds to cyclos, necessitating lengthy detours which add to the time and cost. Do not take a cyclo after dark unless the driver is well known to you or you know the route. It is a wonderful way to get around the Old Quarter of Hanoi, though, and for those with plenty of time on their hands it is not so hazardous in smaller towns.

Taxi Taxis ply the streets of Hanoi and Ho Chi Minh City and other large towns and cities. They are cheap, around 12,000d per km, and the drivers are better English speakers than cyclo drivers. See p119 for an explanation of Vietnamese addresses. Always keep a small selection of small denomination notes with you so that when the taxi stops you can round up the fare to the nearest small denomination. At night use the better known taxi companies rather than the unlicensed cars that often gather around popular nightspots.

Train Vietnam Railways, www.vr.com.vn, runs the 2600-km rail network. With overnight stays at hotels along the way to see the sights, a rail sight-seeing tour from Hanoi to Ho Chi Minh City should take a minimum of 10 days but you would need to buy tickets for each separate journey. The difference in price between first and second class is small and it is worth paying the extra. There are three seating classes and four sleeping classes. The kitchen on the Hanoi-Ho Chi Minh City service serves soups and simple, but adequate, rice dishes (it is a good idea to take additional food and drink on long journeys though). First-class long-distance tickets include the price of meals. Six trains leave Hanoi for Ho Chi Minh City daily and vice versa. The express trains (Reunification Express) take between an advertised 29-39 hours. Most ticket offices have some staff who speak English. Queues can be long and sometimes confusing and some offices keep unusual hours. If you are short of time and short on patience it may well pay to get a tour operator to book your ticket for a small fee. All sleepers should be booked three days in advance.

A cyclo in Ho Chi Minh City (left) and a moped in Laos (right)

Cambodia

There is a basic road network of about 2000 km in total. But this doesn't mean that there are 2000 km of 'roads' in the western sense of the word. Much of the network is in a poor state, and anyone travelling overland – at least those travelling long distances – should be prepared to put up with very long and uncomfortable journeys. In the rainy season expect to be slowed down to a slither by mud. The Khmer-American Friendship Highway (Route 4), which runs from Phnom Penh to Sihanoukville, is entirely tarmacked, as is the NH6 between Siem Reap and Phnom Penh.

Boat All the Mekong towns and settlements around the Tonlé Sap are accessible by boat. It is a very quick and relatively comfortable way of travel and much cheaper than flying. For those on a budget it is the best way to go. Boats are used as a main form of transport in the northeast, generally Phnom Penh to Stung Treng via Kratie, though these can not be guaranteed in the dry season when the water level is low.

Bus and shared taxi There are buses and shared taxis to most parts of the country. Shared taxis (generally Toyota Camrys) or pickups are usually the quickest and most reliable public transport option. The taxi operators charge a premium for better seats and you can buy yourself more space. It is not uncommon for a taxi to fit 10 people in it, including two sitting on the driver's seat. Fares for riding in the back of the truck are half that for riding in the cab. The Sihanoukville run has an excellent and cheap air-conditioned bus service.

Car hire and taxi A few travel agents and hotels may be able to organize self-drive car hire and most hotels have cars for hire with a driver (US$30-50 per day). There is a limited taxi service in Phnom Penh.

Motorbike and bicycle hire Motorbikes can be rented from between US$5 and US$8 per day and around US$1 per day for a bicycle. If riding either a motorbike or bicycle be aware that the accident rate is very high. This is partly because of the poor condition of many of the

5 best

Spectacular journeys

Hanoi to Dien Bien Phu by road, with homestays en route, Vietnam ▸▸ *p131*.

By train along the coast from **Hué to Danang**, Vietnam ▸▸ *p162*.

Along the Mekong by slow boat from **Luang Prabang to Houei Xai**, Laos ▸▸ *p346*.

Xam Neua to Vieng Xai by road, crossing through spectacular mountains, rice terraces and beautiful karst scenery, Laos ▸▸ *p362*.

Along the Nam Hinboun River from **Ban Na Hin to Tham Kong Lor** by boat, Laos ▸▸ *p372*.

cars, trucks and other vehicles on the road; partly because of poor roads; and partly because of horrendously poor driving. If you do rent a motorbike ensure it has a working horn (imperative) and buy some rear-view mirrors so you can keep an eye on the traffic. Wear a helmet (even if using a motodop); it may not be cool but neither is a fractured skull.

Motorbike taxi The most popular and sensible option is the motorbike taxi, known as 'moto'. This costs around the same as renting your own machine and with luck you will get a driver who speaks a bit of English and who knows where he's going. Once you have found a good driver stick with him: handing out the odd drink, a packet of cigarettes or an extra dollar or two is a good investment. Outside Phnom Penh and Siem Reap, do not expect much English from your moto driver.

Laos

Roads are not good, but they are slowly improving. Many have been repaired or upgraded in recent years, making journeys infinitely more comfortable, as well as faster. Quite a few bus, truck, tuk-tuk, *songthaews* (see below) and taxi drivers understand the rudimentaries of English, French or Thai, although some of them (especially tuk-tuk drivers) aren't above forgetting the lowest price you thought you'd successfully negotiated before hopping aboard! It is best to take this sort of thing in good humour. Even so, in order to travel to a particular destination, it is a great advantage to have the name written out in Lao. Many people will not know road names, even if it's the road right outside their front door. However, they will know where all the sights of interest are – for example wats, markets, monuments, waterfalls, etc.

Boat It is possible to take river boats up and down the Mekong and its main tributaries. Boats stop at Luang Prabang, Vientiane, Thakhek and Savannakhet, as well as other smaller towns and villages, but there is no scheduled service and departures may be limited during the dry season. Take food and drink and expect somewhat crowded conditions aboard. The most common riverboats are the *hua houa leim*, with no decks, the hold being enclosed by side panels and a flat roof (note that metal boats get very hot). Speedboats also chart some routes, but are very dangerous and never enjoyable. Prices vary according to size of boat and length of journey.

Bus/truck It is now possible to travel to most areas of the country by bus, truck or *songthaew* (converted pickup truck) in the dry season, although road travel in the rainy season can be tricky if not downright impossible. VIP buses are very comfortable night buses, usually allowing a good sleep during the trip – but watch out for karaoke on board. Robberies have been reported on the night buses so keep your valuables somewhere secure.

In the north, Nissan and Mitsubishi trucks are used as pickups and these are often the fastest form of land-based public transport. On certain long routes, such as Vientiane/Luang Prabang to Xam Neua, big Langjian (Chinese) trucks are sometimes used. These trucks have been colourfully converted into buses with a wooden structure on the back, divided wooden seats and glassless windows. In more remote places (Xam Neua to Vieng Xai, for instance), ancient jeeps are common.

In the south of the country, Japanese-donated buses are used although you may see the occasional shiny Volvo bus. Many roads or parts of road are unsealed, and breakdowns, though not frequent, aren't uncommon either. For some connections you may need to wait a day. During the rainy season (June to December) expect journey times to be longer than those quoted; indeed some roads may be closed altogether.

Car hire This costs anything from US$40-100 per day, depending on the vehicle, with first 150 km free, then US$10 every 100 km thereafter. The price includes a driver. For insurance purposes you will probably need an international driver's permit. Insurance is generally included with car hire but it's best to check the fine print. A general rule of thumb: if you are involved in a car crash, you, the foreigner, will be liable for costs as you have more money.

Motorbike and bicycle hire There are an increasing number of motorcycles available from guesthouses and other shops in major towns. 110cc bikes go for around US$7 a day, while 250cc Hondas are around US$20 per day. Bicycles are available in many towns and are a cheap way to see the sights. Many guesthouses have bikes for rent.

Tuk-tuk The majority of motorized three-wheelers known as 'jumbos' or tuk-tuks are large motorbike taxis with two bench seats in the back. You'll find them in most cities and metropolitan areas; expect to pay around 5000-10,000 kip for a short ride. They can also be hired by the hour or the day to reach destinations out of town.

Sleeping

Vietnam

Accommodation ranges from luxury suites in international five-star hotels and spa resorts to small, family hotels (mini hotels) and homestays with local people in the Mekong Delta and with the ethnic minorities in the Central Highlands and northwest Vietnam. During peak seasons – especially December to March and particularly during busy holidays such as Tet, Christmas, New Year's Eve and around Easter – booking is essential. Expect staff to speak English in all top hotels. Do not expect it in cheaper hotels or in more remote places, although most places employ someone with a smattering of a foreign language.

Private, mini hotels are worth seeking out as, being family-run, guests can expect quite good service. Mid-range and tourist hotels may provide a decent breakfast which is often included in the price. Many luxury and first-class hotels charge extra for breakfast and, on top of this, also charge VAT and service charge. There are some world-class beach resorts in Nha Trang, Mui Ne, Hoi An and Danang. In the northern uplands, in places like Sapa and Mai Chau, it is possible to stay in an ethnic minority house. Bathrooms are basic and will consist of a cold shower and a natural toilet. To stay in a homestay, you must book through a tour operator or through the local tourist office. Homestays are also possible on farms and in orchards in the Mekong Delta. Here, guests sleep on camp beds and share a western bathroom with hot and

Top tips

Sleeping price codes

LL Over US$200 Luxury: mostly found in Bangkok with some in Ho Chi Minh City, Hanoi, Phnom Penh and Siem Reap. Some beach and mountain resorts also fall into this category.

L US$100-199 First class plus: there are a number of hotels in this category found in all the major cities and some smaller ones plus resorts across the region. Laos' top hotels fall into this category. A full range of facilities will be included.

A US$50-99 First class: these hotels are increasingly found in towns across Vietnam but less so in Cambodia and Laos. Hotels in this category should offer reasonable business services, a range of recreational facilities, restaurants and bars, although these services will be more limited in Cambodia and Laos. From this category upwards a 5-10% service and 10% VAT will be added to the bill in Vietnam.

B US$25-49 Tourist class: all rooms will have air-conditioning and an attached bathroom with hot water. Other services should include one or more restaurants, a bar and room service. In Bangkok and Vietnamese beach resorts a swimming pool may be available. Service charges may be added to the bill in Vietnam.

C US$15-24 Economy: rooms should be air-conditioned in Vietnam and Laos but not necessarily in Cambodia and will have attached bathrooms with hot water and western toilets. A restaurant and room service will probably be available.

D US$8-14 Medium budget: air-conditioned rooms quite likely in Vietnam although not necessarily in Cambodia and Laos, also rooms may have an attached bathroom. Toilets should be western-style. Bed linen will be provided, towels perhaps. There may be a restaurant.

E US$4-7 Budget: usually fan-cooled rooms and often shared bathrooms with cold water only and basic facilities. Bathrooms are more likely to have squat toilets. Bed linen should be provided, towels may not be. Rooms are small and facilities few.

F Less than US$4 Dormitory/guesthouse type accommodation, with shared bathroom facilities, squat toilets, fan-cooled and probably cold-water showers. Cleanliness will vary.

cold water. National parks offer everything from air-conditioned bungalows to shared dormitory rooms to campsites where, sometimes, it is possible to hire tents. Visitors may spend a romantic night on a boat in Halong Bay or on the Mekong Delta. Boats range from the fairly luxurious to the basic. Most people book through tour operators.

You will have to leave your passport at hotel reception desks for the duration of your stay. It will be released to you temporarily for bank purposes or buying an air ticket. Credit cards are widely accepted but there is often a 2-4% fee for paying in this manner. Tipping is not expected in hotels in Vietnam. See the box above for details of what to expect within each price category.

Cambodia

With some exceptions hotels have not yet been developed to meet the demand of tourists both in terms of standards or numbers. Many parts of the country still lack accommodation of a reasonable standard. At the budget end of the market most towns, even in less frequently visited areas, have serviceable guesthouses. Phnom Penh has a lot of low-cost guesthouse accommodation, not all of it good, while Siem Reap has a decent range of accommodation. In the rest of the country foreigners are a new phenomenon, so accommodation is geared only to the basic needs of Cambodians away from home.

Laos

Rooms in Laos are rarely luxurious and standards vary enormously. You can end up paying double what you would pay in Bangkok for similar facilities and service. However, the hotel industry is expanding rapidly. There is a reasonable choice of hotels of different standards and prices in Vientiane, Luang Prabang and Pakse and an expanding number of budget options in many towns on the fast-developing tourist trail. First-class hotels exist in Vientiane and Luang Prabang. The majority of guesthouses and hotels have fans and attached bathrooms, although more and more are providing air conditioning where there is a stable electricity supply, while others are installing their own generators to cater for the needs of the growing tourist trade. Smaller provincial towns, having previously had only a handful of hotels and guesthouses – some of them quaint French colonial villas – are now home to a growing number of rival concerns as tourism takes off. In rural villages, people's homes are enthusiastically transformed into bed and breakfasts on demand. While Vientiane may still have little budget accommodation, many towns in the north, such as Vang Vieng, Muang Ngoi, Muang Sing and Luang Namtha, have a large choice of very cheap, and in some cases very good accommodation, including dorm beds. Many tour companies offer home-stay in ethnic minority villages and camping as part of a package tour.

Eating and drinking

Vietnam

Vietnam offers outstanding Vietnamese, French and international cuisine in restaurants that range from first class to humble foodstalls. At either the quality will be, in the main, exceptional. The accent is on local, seasonal and fresh produce and the rich pickings from the sea, along Vietnam's 2000-km coastline will always make it far inland too. You will find more hearty stews in the more remote north and more salad dishes along the coast. All restaurants offer a variety of cuisine from the regions and some specialize in certain types of food – Hué cuisine, Cha Ca Hanoi etc. Pho (pronounced fer), noodle soup, is utterly delicious. Some restaurants add 5% service charge and the government tax of 10% to the bill.

All Vietnamese food is dipped, whether in fish sauce, soya sauce, chilli sauce, peanut sauce or pungent prawn sauce (*mam tom* – avoid if possible) before eating. As each course is served so a new set of dips will accompany. Follow the guidance of your waiter or Vietnamese friends to get the right dip with the right dish.

Locally produced fresh beer is called *bia hoi*. Bar customers have a choice of Tiger, Heineken, Carlsberg, San Miguel, 333, Saigon Beer or Huda. Rice and fruit wines are produced and consumed in large quantities in upland areas, particularly in the north of Vietnam. The Chinese believe that snake wines increase their virility and as such are normally found in areas of high Chinese concentration. Soft drinks and bottled still and sparkling mineral water are widely available. Tea and coffee is widely available. Coffee is drunk with condensed milk.

Cambodia

For a country that has suffered and starved in the way Cambodia has, eating for fun as opposed to eating for survival, has yet to catch on as a pastime. There are some good restaurants and things are improving but don't expect Cambodia to be a smaller version of Thailand, or its cuisine even to live up to the standards of Laos. Cambodian food shows clear links with the cuisines of neighbouring countries: Thailand, Vietnam, and to a lesser extent, Laos. The influence of the French colonial period is also in evidence, most clearly in the availability of good French bread. Chinese food is also available owing to strong business ties between Cambodia and China. True Khmer food is difficult to find and much that the Khmers would like to claim as indigenous food is actually of Thai, French or Vietnamese origin. Curries, soups, rice and noodle-based dishes, salads, fried vegetables and sliced meats all feature in Khmer cooking.

Phnom Penh and Siem Reap have the best restaurants with French, Japanese, Italian and Indian food being available. But those who want to sample a range of dishes and get a feel for Khmer cuisine should head for the nearest market where dishes will be cooked on order in a wok – known locally as a *chhnang khteak*.

International soft drink brands are widely available in Cambodia. Tea is drunk without sugar or milk. Coffee is also served black, or 'crème' with sweetened condensed milk. Bottled water is easy to find and local mineral water too. Fruit smoothies – known locally as *tikalok* – are ubiquitous. Local and imported beers are also available everywhere.

Laos

Lao food is similar to that of Thailand, although the Chinese influence is slightly less noticeable. Lao dishes are distinguished by the use of aromatic herbs and spices such as lemon grass, chillies, ginger and tamarind. The best place to try Lao food is often from roadside stalls or in the markets. The staple Lao foods are *kao niao* (glutinous rice), which is eaten with your hands and fermented fish or *pa dek* (distinguishable by its distinctive smell), often laced with liberal spoons of *nam pa*, fish sauce. Being a landlocked country, most of the fish is fresh from the Mekong. Most of the dishes are variations on two themes: fish and bird. *Laap*, also meaning 'luck' in Lao, is a traditional ceremonial dish made from (traditionally) raw

Chillies in Vietnam and spiders in Cambodia

fish or meat crushed into a paste, marinated in lemon juice and mixed with chopped mint. It is called *laap sin* if it has a meat base and *laap paa* if it's fish based. Beware of *laap* in cheap street restaurants. It is sometimes concocted from raw offal and served cold and should be consumed with great caution.

Restaurant food is, on the whole, hygienically prepared, and as long as street stall snacks have been well cooked, they are usually fine and a good place to sample local specialities. Really classy restaurants are only to be found in Vientiane and Luang Prabang (especially the former). Good French cuisine is available in both cities. Salads, steaks, pizzas and more are all on offer. A better bet in terms of value for money are the Lao restaurants.

Far more prevalent are lower-end Lao and Chinese-Lao restaurants which can be found in every town. Right at the bottom end – in terms of price if not necessarily in terms of quality – are stalls that charge a US$1-2 for filled baguettes or simple single-dish meals.

Soft drinks are expensive as they are imported from Thailand. Bottled water is widely available and produced locally, so it is cheap (about 1000 kip for a litre). *Nam saa*, weak Chinese tea, is free. Imported beer can be found in hotels, restaurants and bars but is not particularly cheap. *Beer Lao* is a light lager (although the alcohol content is 5%). The local brew is rice wine (*lau-lao*) which is drunk from a clay jug with long straws.

Essentials Travelling Eating & drinking

Can Tho market, Mekong Delta

5 best

Unmissable markets

Bac Ha (Vietnam) Witness the gathering of the region's ethnic minorities ▸▸ *p138*.
Can Tho floating market (Vietnam) See vegetables dangling from poles and hear the chatter of bartering traders ▸▸ *p239*.
Psar Thmei (Cambodia) Marvel at the magnificent art deco building ▸▸ *p272*.
Talaat Sao (Laos) Enjoy the biggest market in Laos ▸▸ *p321*.
Luang Prabang night market (Laos) Choose a souvenir from among the colourful array of handicrafts ▸▸ *p340*.

Shopping

Vietnam

Vietnam is increasingly a good destination for shopping. A wide range of designer clothing, silk goods, high quality handicrafts, ceramics and lacquerware are available at excellent value. The main shopping centres are Hanoi, Ho Chi Minh City and Hoi An. Hoi An is the best place to get clothes made. Do not buy any marine turtle products. The majority of shops and markets in Vietnam are open from early in the morning to late at night every day of the week and do not close for lunch. Shops and markets will accept US dollars and Vietnamese dong and most shops also accept credit cards. Export of wood or antiques is banned and anything antique or antique-looking will be seized at customs. In order to avoid this happening you will need to get an export licence from the Customs Department, at 51 Nguyen Van Cu Street, Hanoi, T04-8265260.

Cambodia

Phnom Penh's markets are highly diverting. Cambodian craftsmanship is excellent and whether you are in search of silverware, *kramas* – checked cotton scarves – hand-loomed sarongs or bronze buddhas you will find them all in abundance. A great favourite for its range and quality of antiques, jewellery and fabrics is the **Russian Market** (Psar Tuol Tom Pong). Silverware, gold and gems are available in the **Central Market** (Psar Thmei). *Matmii* – ikat – is also commonly found in Cambodia. It may have been an ancient import from Java and is made by tie-dyeing the threads before weaving. It can be bought throughout the country. Other local textile products to look out for are silk scarves bags and traditional wall-hangings. Colourful *kramas* can be found in local markets across the country and fine woven sarongs in cotton and silk are available in Phnom Penh and Siem Reap. Silk and other textiles products can be bought throughout the country. There has been a strong revival of pottery and ceramics in Cambodia in the last 30 years. Other crafts include bamboo work, wooden panels with carvings of the *Ramayana* and temple rubbings.

Laos

Popular souvenirs from Laos include handicrafts and textiles, which are sold pretty much everywhere. The market is usually a good starting point as are some of the minority villagers. The smaller, less touristy towns will sell silk at the cheapest price (at about 40,000 kip a length). Most markets offer a wide selection of patterns and embroidery though amongst the best places to go are **Talaat Sao** (Vientiane Morning Market) or, behind it, the cheaper **Talaat**

Kudin, which has a textile section in the covered area. If you wish to have something made, most tailors can whip up a simple *sinh* (Lao sarong) in a day but you might want to allow longer for adjustments or other items. **OckPopTok** in Luang Prabang also has a fantastic reputation for producing top-shelf, naturally dyed silk. Vientiane and Luang Prabang offer the most sophisticated line in boutiques, where you can get all sorts of clothes from the utterly exquisite to the frankly bizarre. Those on a more frugal budget will find some tailors who can churn out a decent pair of trousers on Sisavangvong in Luang Prabang and around Nam Phou in Vientiane. If you get the right tailor, they can be much better than those found in Thailand both in terms of price and quality but you do need to be patient and allow time for multiple fittings. It is also a good idea to bring a pattern/picture of what you want.

Silverware, most of it is in the form of jewellery and small pots (though they may not be made of silver), is traditional in Laos. The finest silversmiths work out of Vientiane and Luang Prabang. Chunky antique ethnic-minority jewellery, bangles, pendants, belts and earrings are often sold in markets in the main towns, or antique shops in Vientiane. Craftsmen in Laos are still producing **wood carvings** for temples and coffins. Designs are usually traditional, with a religious theme.

Essentials Travelling Shopping

Clockwise from top: Lao silk; masks in Hanoi; Vietnamese wooden pipes

Accident and emergency

Contact the relevant emergency service and your embassy. Make sure you obtain police/medical records in order to file insurance claims. If you need to report a crime visit your local police station and take a local with you who speaks English.

Vietnam Ambulance T115, Fire T114, Police T113.

Cambodia Ambulance T119 /724891, Fire T118, Police T117/112/012-999999.

Laos Ambulance T195, Fire T190, Police T191.

Children

The region is not particularly geared up for visiting children but there are activities that will appeal to both adults and children alike.

Some attractions in **Vietnam** offer a child's concession. In terms of discounts, **Vietnam Airlines** charges children under 2 10% of the adult ticket price; those aged 2-12 pay 75% of the adult ticket price. The railways allow children under 5 to travel free and charge 50% of the adult fare for those aged 5-10. The Open Tour Bus tickets and tours are likewise free for children under two but those aged 2-10 have to pay half the adult price. Baby needs are to be found in major supermarkets in the major cities. In the remoter regions of the country, such as the north and the Central Highlands and smaller towns, take everything with you.

In **Cambodia** be aware that expensive hotels may have squalid cooking conditions; the cheapest street stall is often more hygienic. Powdered milk is available in provincial centres, although most brands have added sugar. But if taking a baby, breast feeding is strongly recommended. Powdered food can also be bought in some towns – the quality may not be the same as equivalent foods bought in the west, but it is perfectly adequate for short periods. Disposable nappies can be bought in Phnom Penh, but are often expensive.

In **Laos**, disposable nappies can be bought in Vientiane and other larger provincial capitals, but are often expensive.

Public transport may be a problem; long bus journeys are restrictive and uncomfortable. Chartering a car is undoubtedly the most convenient way to travel overland but rear seatbelts are scarce and child seats even rarer.

Customs and duty free

Vietnam

Duty-free allowance is 200 cigarettes, 50 cigars or 150 g of tobacco, 1.5 litres of spirits, plus items for personal use. You cannot import pornography, anti-government literature, photographs or movies nor culturally unsuitable children's toys.

Cambodia

A reasonable amount of tobacco products and spirits can be taken in without incurring customs duty – roughly 200 cigarettes or the equivalent quantity of tobacco, 1 bottle of liquor and perfume for personal use.

Laos

Duty-free allowance is 500 cigarettes, 2 bottles of wine and a bottle of liquor. Laos has a strictly enforced ban on the export of antiquities and all Buddha images.

Disabled travellers

Considering the proportion of the region's population that are seriously disabled, foreigners might expect better facilities and allowances for the immobile. However, some of the more upmarket hotels do have a few designated rooms for the disabled. For those with walking difficulties many of the better hotels do have lifts. Wheelchair access is improving with more shopping centres, hotels and restaurants providing ramps for easy access. Those that are sensitive to noise will find **Vietnam**, for example, at times, almost intolerable. The general situation in **Cambodia** is no better. The Angkor Complex can be a real struggle for disabled or frail persons. The stairs are 90 degrees steep and semi-restoration of areas means that visitors will sometimes need to climb over piles of bricks. Hiring an aide to help you climb stairs and generally get around is a very good idea and can be hired for around US$5-10 a day. In **Laos** pavements are often uneven, there are potholes and missing drain covers galore, pedestrian crossings are ignored, ramps are unheard of, lifts are few and far between and escalators are seen only in magazines.

RADAR, 12 City Forum, 250 City Road, London, EC1V 8AF, T020-72503222.
SATH, 347 Fifth Avenue, Suite 610, New York City, NY 10016, T212 447-7284.

Drugs

Vietnam

Drugs are common and cheap and the use of hard drugs by Vietnamese is a rapidly growing problem. Attitudes towards users are incredibly lax and the worst that will happen is that certain bars and nightclubs may be closed for a few weeks. In such an atmosphere of easy availability and tolerance, many visitors may be tempted to indulge, and to excess, but beware that the end result can be disastrous. Attitudes to traffickers on the other hand are harsh, although the death penalty is usually reserved for Vietnamese and other Asians whose governments are less likely to kick up a fuss.

Cambodia

Drug use is illegal in Cambodia but drugs are a big problem. Many places use marijuana in their cooking and the police seem to be quite ambivalent to dope smokers (unless they need to supplement their income with bribe money, in which case – watch out). The backpacker areas around the lake, Phnom Penh and Sihanoukville are particularly notorious for heavy drug usage by westerners, some of whom have actually died as a result of mistakenly overdosing on heroin. Avoid *yaa baa*, a particularly insidious amphetamine. It has serious side effects and can even be lethal.

Laos

Drug use is illegal and there are harsh penalites ranging from fines through to imprisonment or worse. Police have been known to levy heavy fines on people in Vang Vieng for eating so-called 'happy' foods, see p313, or for being caught in possession of drugs. Note that 'happy' food can make some people extremely sick. Though opium has in theory been eradicated it is still for sale in northern areas and people have died from overdosing. *Yaa baa* is also available here and should be avoided at all costs.

Electricity

Vietnam Voltage 110. Sockets are round 2-pin. Sometimes they are two flat pin. A number of top hotels now use UK 3 square-pin sockets.
Cambodia Voltage 220. Sockets are usually round 2-pin.
Laos Voltage 220, 50 cycles in the main towns. 110 volts in the country; 2-pin sockets are common. Blackouts are common outside Vientiane and many smaller towns are not connected to the

national grid and only have power during the evening.

Embassies and consulates

Vietnamese
Australia, 6 Timbarra Cres, O'Malley Canberra, ACT 2606, T02-6286 6059/2.
Cambodia, 436 Monivong, Phnom Penh, T023-364741.
Canada, 226 Maci Aren St, Ottawa, Ontario, K2P OL6, T1-613 236 0772.
France, R Boileau-75016, Paris, T01-4414 6447.
Laos, That Luang Rd, Vientiane, T021-413409.
South Africa, 87 Brooks St-Brooklyn PO Box 13692 Hartfield 0028, Pretoria, T012-3628119.
Thailand, 83/1 Wireless Rd, Lumpini, Pathumwan, Bangkok 10330, T02-251 5838.
United Kingdom, 12-14 Victoria Rd, London W8 5RD, T020-7937 1912.
USA, 1233, 20th St, N.W. Suite 400 Washington DC, 20036, T1-202 861 0737.

Cambodian
Australia, 5 Canterbury Cres, Deakin, ACT 2600, Australia, T02-6273 1259.
Laos, Thadeua Rd, Vientiane, T021-314950.
New Zealand, see Australia.
Thailand, 185 Rajddamri Rd, Lumpini Patumwan, Bangkok 10330, T02-254 6630.
United Kingdom, 28-32 Wellington Rd, London NW8 9SP, T020-7483 9063.
United States, 4500 16th St NW, Washington DC 20011, T1-202 726 8042; 866 UN Plaza, Suite 420, New York, NY 10017, T1-212 223 0676.
Vietnam, 41 Phung Khac Khoan, Ho Chi Minh City, T08-829 2751; 71A Tran Hung Dao St, Hanoi, T04-825 3788.

Laos
Australia, 1 Dalman Cres, O' Malley Canberra, ACT 2606, T02-864595.
Cambodia, 15-17 Mao Tse Toung Bvd,
Phnom Penh, T023-26441.
France, 74 Ave Raymond-Poincaré 75116 Paris, T01-4553 0298.
Thailand, 502/1 Soi Ramkamhaeng 39, Thanon Pracha Uthit, Wangthonglang, Bangkok 10310, T02-539 6667.
Vietnam, 22 Tran Binh Trong, Hanoi, T04-2854576; 181 Hai Ba Trung, Ho Chi Minh City, T08-8299275.

Gay and lesbian

Vietnam
The Vietnamese are tolerant of homosexuality. There are no legal restraints for 2 people of the same sex co-habitating in the same room be they Vietnamese or non-Vietnamese. There are several bars in central Ho Chi Minh City popular with gays. Cruising in dark streets is not advised. An Asian online resource for gays and lesbians which includes a list of scams and warnings in Vietnam as well as gay-friendly bars in Hanoi and Ho Chi Minh City is www.utopia-asia.com.

Cambodia
Gay and lesbian travellers will have no problems in Cambodia. Men often hold other men's hands as do women, so this kind of affection is nothing short of commonplace. Any kind of passionate kissing or sexually orientated affection in public is taboo – both for straight and gay people. The gay scene is just starting to develop in Cambodia but there is definitely a scene in the making: Linga Bar, Siem Reap, and the Salt Lounge, Phnom Penh, are both gay bars.

Laos
Gay and lesbian travellers should have no problems in Laos. It does not have a hot gay scene and the Lao government is intent on avoiding the mushrooming of the gay and straight sex industry. Officially it is illegal for any foreigner to have a sexual relationship with a Lao person they aren't married to. Openly gay behaviour is contrary to local culture and custom and

visitors, whether straight or gay, should not flaunt their sexuality. Any overt display of passion or even affection in public is taboo. In Vientiane there aren't any gay bars, per se, although there are some bars and clubs where gays congregate. Luang Prabang has a few more gay-orientated options.

Health

See your doctor or travel clinic at least 6 weeks before your departure for general advice on travel risks, malaria and vaccinations. Make sure you have travel insurance, get a dental check (especially if you are going to be away for more than a month), know your own blood group and if you suffer a long-term condition such as diabetes or epilepsy make sure someone knows or that you have a Medic Alert bracelet/necklace with this information on it (www.medicalert.co.uk).

Vaccinations

The following are advised:
BCG It is not known how much protection this vaccination gives the traveller against lung tuberculosis but it is currently advised that people have it in the absence of any better alternative.
Hepatitis A Yes, as the disease can be caught easily from food/water.
Japanese Encephalitis May be advised for some areas, depending on the duration of the trip and proximity to rice growing and pig-farming areas.
Polio Yes, if no booster in last 10 years.
Rabies Advised if travelling to jungle and/or remote areas
Tetanus Yes, if not vaccinated in last 10 years (but after 5 doses you've had enough for life).
Typhoid Yes, if none in last 3 years.
Yellow Fever The disease does not exist in Vietnam, Cambodia or Laos. However, the authorities may wish to see a certificate if you have recently arrived from an endemic area in Africa or South America.

Health risks

Malaria exists in rural areas in **Vietnam**. However, there is no risk in the Red River Delta and the coastal plains north of Nha Trang. Neither is there a risk in Hanoi, Ho Chi Minh City, Danang and Nha Trang. Malaria exists in most of **Cambodia**, except the capital Phnom Penh. Malaria is prevalent in **Laos** and remains a serious disease; about a third of the population contracts malaria at some stage in their lives. The choice of malaria prophylaxis will need to be something other than chloroquine for most people, since there is such a high level of resistance to it. Always check with your doctor or travel clinic for the most up-to-date advice.

Malaria can cause death within 24 hours. It can start as something just resembling an attack of flu. You may feel tired, lethargic, headachy, feverish; or more seriously, develop fits, followed by coma and then death. Have a low index of suspicion because it is very easy to write off vague symptoms, which may actually be malaria. If you have a temperature, go to a doctor as soon as you can and ask for a malaria test. On your return home if you suffer any of these symptoms, get tested as soon as possible, even if any previous test proved negative, the test could save your life.

The most serious viral disease is **dengue fever**, which is hard to protect against as the mosquitos bite throughout the day as well as at night. Bacterial diseases include **tuberculosis** (TB) and some causes of the more common traveller's **diarrhoea**. Each year there is the possibilty that **avian flu** or **SARS** might rear their ugly heads. Check the news reports. If there is a problem in an area you are due to visit you may be advised to have an ordinary flu shot or to seek expert advice. There are high rates of **HIV** in the region, especially among sex workers. **Rabies** and **schistosomiasis** (bilharzia, a water-borne parasite) may be a problem in Laos.

Medical services

Vietnam

Western hospitals exist in Hanoi and Ho Chi Minh City in Vietnam.

International SOS, Central Building, 31 Hai Ba Trung St, Hanoi, T04-934066, www.internationalsos.com/countries/Vietnam/. Open 24 hrs for emergencies, routine and medical evacuation. Dental service too.

Columbia Asia (Saigon International Clinic), 8 Alexander de Rhodes St, Ho Chi Minh City, T8-8238455, (T08-8238888, 24-hr emergency), www.columbiaasia.com. International doctors offering a full range of services.

Cambodia

Hospitals are not recommended anywhere in Cambodia (even at some of the clinics that profess to be 'international'). If you fall ill or are injured the best bet is to get yourself quickly to either Bumrungrad Hospital or Bangkok Nursing Home, both in **Bangkok**. Both hospitals are of an exceptional standard, even in international terms.

Laos

Hospitals are few and far between and medical facilities are poor in Laos. Emergency treatment is available at the Mahosot Hospital and Clinique Setthathirath in Vientiane.

The Australian embassy also has a clinic for Commonwealth citizens with minor ailments (see p326); US$50 per consultation. Better facilities are available in Thailand and emergency evacuation to **Nong Khai** or **Udon Thani** (Thailand) can be arranged at short notice.

Thailand

Aek Udon Hospital, Udon Thani, Thailand T+66 42-342555. A 2½-hr trip from Vientiane.

Bumrungrad Hospital, Soi 3 Sukhumvit, Bangkok, T+66 2-667 1000, www.bumrungrad.com. The best option:

a world-class hospital with brilliant medical facilities.

Nong Khai Wattana General Hospital, T+66 42-465201, is a better alternative to the hospitals in Vientiane and only a 40-min trip from the capital.

Useful websites

www.cdc.cov US Government site which gives excellent advice on travel health and details of disease outbreaks.
www.who.int The WHO Blue Book lists the diseases of the world.
www.fitfortravel.scot.nhs.uk A-Z of vaccine/health advice for each country.
www.btha.org British Travel Health Association (UK). This is the official website of an organization of travel health professionals.

Insurance

Always take out travel insurance before you set off and read the small print carefully. Check that the policy covers the activities you intend or may end up doing. Also check exactly what your medical cover includes, ie ambulance, helicopter rescue or emergency flights back home. Also check the payment protocol. You may have to cough up first before the insurance company reimburses you. It is always best to dig out all the receipts for expensive personal effects like jewellery or cameras. Take photos of these items and note down all serial numbers. You are advised to shop around. **STA Travel** and other reputable student travel organisations offer good value policies. Young travellers from North America can try the **International Student Insurance Service** (ISIS), which is available through **STA Travel**, T1-800-7770112, www.sta-travel.com. Other recommended travel insurance companies in North America include: **Travel Guard**, T1-800-8261300, www.noelgroup.com; **Access America**, T1-800- 2848300; **Travel Insurance Services**, T1-800-9371387; and **Travel**

Assistance International, T1-800-8212828. Older travellers should note that some companies will not cover people over 65 years old, or may charge higher premiums. The best policies for older travellers (UK) are offered by **Age Concern**, T01883-346964.

Internet

Vietnam

Although emailing is now usually easy enough in Vietnam, access to the internet from within Vietnam is restricted as the authorities battle vainly to firewall Vietnam-related topics. Access has greatly improved with broadband available in many places in Hanoi and Ho Chi Minh City. Many travellers' cafés provide email access. Rates are around 100-200d per min in the 2 main cities but more in smaller places.

Cambodia

Cambodia is surprisingly well-connected and most medium-sized to large towns have internet access. Not surprisingly, internet is a lot more expensive in smaller towns, up to a whopping US$5 per hr. In Phnom Penh internet rates are US$1-2 per hr and in Siem Reap should be US$1 per hr or under.

Laos

Internet cafés have been popping up all over Laos over the last few years. The connections are surprisingly good in major centres. Fast, cheap internet is available in Vientiane, Luang Prabang, Vang Vieng and Savannakhet for around 100-200 kip per min. Less reliable and more expensive internet (due to long-distance calls) can be found in Xam Neua, Phonsavanh, Don Khone, Don Deth, Luang Namtha and Udom Xai. Many internet cafés also offer international phone services.

Language

Vietnam

You are likely to find a smattering of English wherever there are tourist services but outside tourist centres communication can be a problem for those who have no knowledge of Vietnamese. Furthermore, the Vietnamese language is not easy to learn. For example, pronunciation presents enormous difficulties as it is tonal. On the plus side, Vietnamese is written in a Roman alphabet making life much easier: place and street names are instantly recognizable. French is still spoken and often very well by the more elderly and educated.

Cambodia

In Cambodia the national language is Khmer (pronounced Khmei). It is not tonal and the script is derived from the southern Indian alphabet. French is spoken by the older generation who survived the Khmer Rouge era. English is the language of the younger generations. Away from Phnom Penh, Siem Reap and Sihanoukville it can be difficult to communicate with the local population.

Laos

Lao is the national language but there are many local dialects, not to mention the ubiquitous languages of the minority groups. Lao is closely related to Thai and, in a sense, is becoming more so as the years pass. Though there are important differences between the languages, they are mutually intelligible – just about. French is spoken, though only by government officials, hotel staff and many educated people over 40. However, most government officials and many shopkeepers have some command of English.

Media

Vietnam

Unlike western newspapers, Vietnamese papers are less interested in what has happened (that is to say, news), preferring instead to report on what will happen or what should happen, featuring stories such as 'Party vows to advance ethical lifestyles' and 'Output of fertilizer to grow 200%'. The English language daily *Vietnam News* is widely available. Inside the back page is an excellent 'What's on'. *The Guide*, a monthly magazine on leisure and tourism produced by the *Vietnam Economic Times*, can be found in tourist centres. Good hotels will have cable TV with a full range of options.

Cambodia

Cambodia has a vigorous English-language press which fights bravely for editorial independence and freedom to criticize politicians. The principal English-language newspapers are the fortnightly *Phnom Penh Post*, which many regard as the best and the *Cambodia Daily*, published 5 times per week. There are also several tourist magazine guides. The **BBC World Servic**e provides probably the best news and views on Asia (available on 100 FM).

Laos

The *Vientiane Times*, www.vientiane times.com, is published 5 days a week and provides quirky pieces of information and some interesting cultural and tourist-based features. Television is becoming increasingly popular as more towns and villages get electricity. The national TV station broadcasts in Lao. In Vientiane **CNN**, **BBC**, **ABC** and a range of other channels are broadcast. Thailand's **Channel 5** gives English subtitles to news. The **Lao National Radio** broadcasts news in English. The **BBC World Service** can be picked up on shortwave.

Money

Vietnam

The unit of currency is the **dong**. The exchange rate at the time of going to press was US$1 = 15,896d; £1 = 27,989d, €1 = 19,251d. Under law, shops should only accept dong but in practice this is not enforced and dollars are accepted almost everywhere. If possible, however, try to pay for everything in dong as prices are usually lower and in more remote areas people may be unaware of the latest exchange rate. Also, to ordinary Vietnamese, 15,000d is a lot of money, while US$1 means nothing. **ATM**s are plentiful in Ho Chi Minh City and Hanoi and can also be found in other major tourist centres, except Sapa, but it is a good idea to travel with US$ cash as a back up. Banks in the main centres will change other major currencies including UK£, HK$, Thai baht, Swiss franc, Euro, Aus $, Sing $ and Can $. **Credit cards** are increasingly accepted, particularly Visa, MasterCard, Amex and JCB. Large hotels, expensive restaurants and medical centres invariably take them but beware a surcharge of between 2.5 and 4.5%. Most hotels will not add a surcharge onto your bill if paying by credit card. Traveller's cheques are best denominated in US$ and can only be cashed in banks in the major towns. Commission of 2-4% is payable if cashing into dollars but not if you are converting them direct to dong.

Cambodia

The **riel** is the official currency though US dollars are widely accepted and easily exchanged. At the time of going to press the exchange rates were US$1 = 3981, £1= 6975, €1 = 5199.

In Phnom Penh and other towns most goods and services are priced in dollars and there is little need to buy riel. In remote rural areas prices are quoted in riel (except accommodation). Money can be exchanged in banks and hotels. US$

traveller's cheques are easiest to exchange – commission ranges from 1 to 3%. Cash advances on credit cards are available. Credit card facilities are limited but some banks, hotels and restaurants do accept them, mostly in the tourist centres.

ANZ Royal Bank has recently opened a number of ATMs throughout Phnom Penh, the first in Cambodia.

Laos

The kip is the official currency. At the time of going to press the exchange rate was US$1 = 10,861, £1 = 19,129, €1 = 13,159. The lowest commonly used note is the 500 kip and the kip tends to shadow the Thai baht but with a rather quaint one week delay. It is getting much easier to change currency and traveller's cheques. Banks are generally reluctant to give anything but kip in exchange for hard currency. US$ and Thai baht can be used as cash in most shops, restaurants and hotels. A certain amount of cash (in US$ or Thai baht) can also be useful in an emergency. Banks include the **Lao Development Bank** and **Le Banque pour Commerce Exterieur Lao (BCEL)**, which change most major international currencies (cash) and traveller's cheques denominated in US$ and pounds sterling. Many of the BCEL branches offer cash advances on Visa/MasterCard. Note that some banks charge a hefty commission of US$2 per TC. While banks will change traveller's cheques and cash denominated in most major currencies into kip, some will only change US$ into Thai baht, or into US dollars cash.

Thai baht are readily accepted in most towns but it is advisable to carry kip in rural areas (buses, for example, will usually only accept kip).

At the time of writing, there was one international ATM (at the **BCEL** bank in Vientiane), but will only dispense a maximum of 700,000 kip at a time. On weekends, the only other options for exchange or obtaining cash are the **BCEL**

booth along the river and the ATM booth across from the Lao Plaza, both in Vientiane.

Payment by credit card is becoming easier – although beyond the larger hotels and restaurants in Vientiane and Luang Prabang do not expect to be able to get by on plastic. American Express, Visa, MasterCard/Access cards are accepted in a limited number of more upmarket establishments. Note that commission is charged by some places on credit card transactions. If they can route the payment through Thailand then a commission is not levied; but if this is not possible, then 3% is usually added.

Many banks will now advance cash on credit cards in Luang Prabang, Vientiane, Pakse, Phonsavanh, Savannakhet and Vang Vieng (not not all cards are accepted at these banks, so it's better to check in advance).

Cost of travelling

Vietnam is better overall value than Cambodia and Laos as it has a better established tourism infrastructure and more competitive services. On a budget expect to pay around US$5-10 per night for accommodation and about the same each day for food. A good mid-range hotel will cost US$10-25. There are comfort and cost levels anywhere from here up to US$200 per night. For travelling many use the Open Tour Buses as they are inexpensive and, by Vietnamese standards, 'safe'. Slightly more expensive are trains followed by planes. The budget traveller will find that a little goes a long way in **Cambodia**. Numerous guesthouses offer accommodation at around US$3-7 a night. Food-wise, the seriously strapped can easily manage to survive healthily on US$4-5 per day, so an overall daily budget (not allowing for excursions) of US$7-9 should be enough for the really cost-conscious. For the less frugally minded, a daily allowance of US$30 should see you relatively well-housed and fed, while at the upper end of the scale, there are, in Phnom Penh and Siem Reap, plenty of restaurants and hotels for those looking for Cambodian-levels of luxury. A mid-range hotel (attached bathroom, hot water and a/c) will normally cost around US$25 per night and a good meal at a restaurant around US$5-10.

The variety of available domestic flights means that the bruised bottoms, dust-soaked clothes and stiff limbs that go hand-in-hand with some of the longer bus/boat rides can be avoided by those with thicker wallets in **Laos**. Note that foreigners pay more than locals for flights in Laos. As the roads improve and journey times diminish in Laos though, buses have emerged above both planes and boats as the preferred (not to mention most reasonably priced) transportation option. Budget accommodation costs US$2-7, a mid-range hotel from US$10-20. Food is very cheap and it is possible to eat well for under US$2 a meal.

Opening hours

Vietnam
Shops Daily 0800-2000. Some stay open for another hour or two, especially in tourist centres. **Banks** Mon-Fri 0800-1600. Some close 1100-1300. **Offices** Mon-Fri 0730-1130, 1330-1630. **Restaurants**, **cafés**, **bars** Daily from 0700 or 0800 although some open earlier. Bars are meant to close at 2400 by law.

Cambodia
Shops Daily from 0800-2000. Some, however, stay open for a further hour or two, especially in tourist centres. Most markets open daily between 0530 and 0600-1700.
Banks Mon-Fri 0800-1600. Some close 1100-1300. Some major branches are open until 1100 on Sat.
Offices Mon-Fri 0730-1130, 1330-1630. **Restaurants**, **cafés** and **bars** Daily from 0700-0800 although some open earlier. Bars are meant to close at 2400 by law.

Laos
Banks Mon-Fri 0830-1600 (some close at 1500).
Offices Mon-Fri 0900-1700; those that deal with tourists open a bit later and also usually over the weekend.
Bars and **nightclubs** Usually close around 2200-2300 depending on how strictly the curfew is being reinforced. In smaller towns, most restaurants and bars will be closed by 2200.

Police and the law

If you are robbed in Vietnam, report the incident to the police (for your insurance claim). Otherwise, the police are of no use whatsoever. They will do little or nothing (apart from log the crime on an incident sheet which you will need for your insurance claim). Vietnam is not the best place to come into conflict with the law. Avoid getting arrested. If you are arrested, however, ask for consular assistance immediately and English-speaking staff. Involvement in politics, possession of political material, business activities that have not been licensed by appropriate authorities, or non-sanctioned religious activities (including proselytizing) can result in detention. Sponsors of small, informal religious gatherings such as bible-study groups in hotel rooms, as well as distributors of religious materials, have been detained, fined and expelled. (Source: US State Department.)

Cambodia
A vast array of offences are punishable in Cambodia, from minor traffic violations through to possession of drugs. If you are arrested or are having difficulty with the police contact your embassy immediately. As the police only earn approximately US$20 a month, corruption is a problem and contact should be avoided, unless absolutely necessary. Most services, including the provision of police reports, will require

paying bribes. Law enforcement is very haphazard, at times completely subjective and justice can be hard to find. Some smaller crimes receiving large penalties while perpetrators of greater crimes often get off Scot free.

Laos

If you are robbed insurers will require you to obtain a police report. The police may try to solicit a bribe for this service. Although not ideal, you will probably have to pay this fee to obtain your report. Laws aren't strictly enforced but when the authorities do prosecute people the penalties can be harsh, ranging from deportation through to prison sentences. If you are arrested seek embassy and consular support. People are routinely fined for drugs possession, having sexual relations with locals (when unmarried) and proselytizing. If you are arrested or encounter police, try to remain calm and friendly. Although drugs are available throughout the country, the police levy hefty fines and punishments if caught.

Post

Vietnam

Postal services are pretty good. Post offices open daily 0700-2100; smaller ones close for lunch.

Cambodia

International service is unpredictable but it is reasonably priced and fairly reliable (at least from Phnom Penh). Only send mail from the GPO in any given town rather than sub POs or mail boxes. **Fedex** and **DHL** also offer services.

Laos

The postal service is inexpensive but delays are common. Contents of outgoing parcels must be examined by an official before being sealed. Incoming mail should use the official title, Lao PDR. EMS (Express Mail Service) is available from main post offices in larger towns. In general, post offices open 0800-1200 and 1300-1700. In provincial areas, **Lao Telecom** is usually attached to the post office. **DHL**, **Fedex** and **TNT** have offices in Vientiane.

Public holidays

Vietnam

1 Jan New Year's Day.
Late Jan-Mar (movable, 1-7th day of the new lunar year) Tet.
3 Feb Founding anniversary of the Communist Party of Vietnam.
30 Apr Liberation Day of South Vietnam and Ho Chi Minh City.
1 May International Labour Day .
19 May Anniversary of the Birth of Ho Chi Minh (This is a government holiday) The majority of state institutions will be shut but businesses in the private sector carry on regardless.
2 Sep National Day.
3 Sep President Ho Chi Minh's Anniversary.

Cambodia

1 Jan National Day and Victory over Pol Pot.
7 Jan Celebration of the fall of the Khmer Rouge in 1979.
8 Mar Women's Day. Processions, floats and banners in main towns.
13-15 Apr Cambodian New Year (Bonn Chaul Chhnam).
17 Apr Independence Day.
Apr/May Visak Bauchea (movable with the full moon), the most important Buddhist festival; a triple anniversary commemorating Buddha's birth, enlightenment and his Paranirvana (state of final bliss).
1 May Labour Day.
9 May Genocide Day.
1 Jun International Children's Day.
18 Jun Her Majesty Preah Akkaek Mohesey Norodom Monineath Sihanouk's Birthday.
Sep (moveable) End of Buddhist 'lent'.
24 Sep Constitution Day.

23 Oct Paris Peace Accord.
30 Oct-1 Nov King's Birthday.
Oct/Nov (moveable) Water Festival
(Bon Om Tuk) or Festival of the
Reversing Current.
9 Nov Independence Day (1953).
10 Dec Human Rights Day.

Laos

1 Jan New Year's Day.
6 Jan Pathet Lao Day. Parades in towns.
20 Jan Army Day.
Jan/Feb (movable) Chinese New Year.
8 Mar Women's Day.
22 Mar People's Party Day.
13-15 Apr Lao New Year. The first
month of the Lao New Year is actually
Dec but it is celebrated in Apr when days
are longer than nights. Statues of the
Buddha (in the 'calling for rain' posture)
are ceremonially doused in water, which
is poured along an intricately decorated
trench (*hang song nam pha*). The small
stupas of sand, decorated with streamers,
in wat compounds are symbolic requests
for health and happiness over the coming
year. The New Year is celebrated with
traditional Lao folksinging (*mor lam*)
and the circle dance (*ramwong*). There
is usually a 3-day holiday.
1 May Labour Day
1 Jun Children's Day
13 Aug Lao Issara (Free Lao Day).
23 Aug Liberation Day.
12 Oct Freedom from the French Day.
2 Dec Independence Day.

Safety

Travel advisories

The US State Department's travel
advisories: **Travel Warnings & Consular
Information Sheets**, www.travel.state.gov
/travel_ warnings.html.
The **UK Foreign and Commonwealth
Office**'s travel warning section,
www.fco.gov.uk/travel/

Vietnam

Do not take any valuables on to the
streets of Ho Chi Minh City as bag and
jewellery snatching is a common and
serious problem. Thieves work in teams,
often with beggar women carrying
babies as a decoy. Beware of people who
obstruct your path (pushing a bicycle
across the pavement is a common ruse);
your pockets are being emptied from
behind. Young men on fast motorbikes
also cruise the central streets of Ho Chi
Minh City waiting to pounce on unwary
victims. The situation in other cities is not
so bad but take care in Nha Trang and
Hanoi. Never go by cyclo in a strange part
of town after dark.

Lone women travellers have fewer
problems than in many other Asian
countries. The most common form of
harassment usually consists of comic and
harmless displays of macho behaviour.

Unexploded ordnance is still a threat in
some areas. It is best not to stray too far
from the beaten track and don't unearth
bits of suspicious metal. Single western
men will be targeted by prostitutes on
street corners, in tourist bars and those
cruising on motorbikes.

Cambodia

Cambodia is not as dangerous as some
would have us believe. The country has
really moved forward in protecting
tourists and violent crimes towards
visitors is comparatively low. Since large
penalties have been introduced for those
who kill or maim tourists, random acts of
violence aren't as common these days.
Safety on the nighttime streets of Phnom
Penh is a problem. Robberies and
hold-ups are common. Many robbers are
armed, so do not resist. As Phnom Penh
has a limited taxi service, travel after dark
poses a problem. Stick to moto drivers
you know. Women are, obviously,
particularly targeted by bag snatchers.
Khmer New Year is known locally as the
'robbery season'. Theft is endemic at this

time of year so be on red alert. A common trick around New Year is for robbers to mess around with tourists (usually throwing water and talcum powder in the eyes) and rob them blind. Leave your valuables in the hotel safe or hidden in your room. Sexual harassment is not uncommon. Many motos/tour guides will try their luck with women but generally it is more macho posturing than anything serious.

Outside Phnom Penh safety is not as much of a problem. Visitors should be very cautious when walking in the countryside, however, as landmines and other unexploded ordnance is a ubiquitous hazard. Stick to well worn paths, especially around Siem Reap and when visiting remote temples. Motorbike accidents have serious fatality rates as they do in Vietnam.

Laos

Crime rates are very low but it is advisable to take the usual precautions. Most areas of the country are now safe – a very different state of affairs from only a few years ago when foreign embassies advised tourists not to travel along certain roads and in certain areas (in particular route 13 between Vientiane and Luang Prabang, and route 7 between Phonsavanh and route 13). Today these risks have effectively disappeared. However, the government will sometimes make areas provisionally off-limits if they think there is a security risk – take heed!

There has been a reported increase in motorcycle drive-by thefts in Vientiane, but these and other similar crimes are still at a low level compared with most countries. If riding on a motorbike or bicycle, don't carry your bag strap over your shoulder – as you could get pulled off the bike if someone goes to snatch your bag. In the Siphandon and Vang Vieng areas, theft seems more common. Use a hotel security box if available.

Road accidents are on the increase. The hiring of motorbikes is becoming more

popular and consequently there are are more tourist injuries.

Be careful around waterways, as drowning is one of the primary causes of tourist deaths. Be particularly careful during the rainy season (May-Sep) as rivers have a tendency to flood and can have extremely strong currents. Make sure if you are kayaking, tubing, canoeing, travelling by fast-boat, etc, that proper safety gear, such as life jackets, is provided. 'Fast-boat' river travel can be dangerous due to excessive speed and the risk of hitting something in the river and capsizing.

Xieng Khouang Province, the Boloven Plateau, Xam Neua and areas along the Ho Chi Minh Trail are littered with bombies (small anti-personnel mines and bomblets from cluster bomb units). There are also numerous, large, unexploded bombs; in many villages they have been left lying around. They are very unstable so DO NOT TOUCH. Only walk on clearly marked or newly trodden paths.

Student travellers

There are discounts available on some **Vietnam Airlines** routes and the train in **Vietnam**. Discount travel is provided to those under 22 and over 60. There are no specific student discounts in **Cambodia** or **Laos**. Anyone in full-time education is entitled to an International Student Identity Card (ISIC Association, Box 9048, 1000 Copenhagen, Denmark, T45-3393 9303). These are issued by student travel offices and travel agencies and offer special rates on all forms of transport and other concessions and services. They sometimes permit free admission to museums and sights, at other times a discount on the admission.

Telephone

Vietnam

To make a domestic call dial 0 + area code + phone number. Note that all numbers in this guide include the 0 and the area code. Most shops or cafés will let you call a local number for 2000d: look for the blue sign 'dien thoai cong cong' (meaning public telephone). All post offices provide international telephone services. The cost of calls has greatly reduced but some post offices and hotels still insist on charging for a minimum of 3 mins. You start paying for an overseas call from the moment you ring even if the call is not answered. By dialling 171 or 178 followed by 0 or 00 to make an international call, it is approximately 30% cheaper. Vietnam's country code is +84; IDD access code is 00; directory enquires 116 or 1080; operator-assisted domestic long-distance calls 103; international directory enquiries 143; Yellow pages 1081. Numbers beginning with 091 or 090 are mobile numbers. Pay-as-you-go sim cards are available.

Cambodia

Landline linkages are so poor in Cambodia that many people and businesses prefer to use mobile phones instead. The 3-digit prefix included in a 9-digit landline telephone number is the area (province) code. If dialling within a province, dial only the 6-digit number. International calls can be made from most guesthouses, hotels and phone booths. Don't anticipate being able to make international calls outside Phnom Penh, Siem Reap and Sihanoukville. Use public MPTC or Camintel card phone boxes dotted around Phnom Penh to make international calls (cards are usually sold at shops near the booth). International calls are expensive, starting at US$4 per minute in Phnom Penh, and more in the provinces. To make an overseas call from Cambodia, dial 007 or 001 + IDD country code + area code minus first 0 + subscriber number. Internet calls are without a doubt the cheapest way to call overseas. Pay-as-you-go sim cards are available. The country code for Cambodia is +855.

Laos

Public phones are available in Vientiane and other major cities. You can also go to **Lao Telecom** offices to call overseas. Phone cards are widely available in most convenient stores. Call 178 in Vientiane for town codes. Most towns in Laos have at least 1 telephone box with IDD facility. The one drawback is that you must buy a phonecard. Because these are denominated in such small units, even the highest-value card will only get you a handful of minutes talk time with Europe. All post offices, telecoms offices and many shops sell phone cards. **Note** If ringing Laos from Thailand, dial 007 before the country code for Laos.

Mobile telephone coverage is now quite good. Pay-as-you-go sim cards are available. International operator: T170. Operator: T16. The international code for Laos is +856. IDD access code: 00.

Time

Vietnam, Cambodia and Laos are 7 hrs ahead of Greenwich Mean Time.

Tipping

Vietnamese do not normally tip if eating in small family restaurants but may tip extravagantly in expensive bars. Foreigners normally leave the small change. Big hotels and some restaurants add 5-10% service charge and the government tax of 10% to the bill. Taxis are rounded up to the nearest 5000d, hotel porters 20,000d. Tipping is rare but appreciated in Cambodia. Neither is it common practice in Laos, even in hotels. However, it is a kind gesture to tip guides and some more expensive restaurants.

Tourist information

Contact details for tourist offices and other information resources are given in the relevant Ins and Outs sections throughout the text.

Vietnam

The national tourist office is **Vietnam National Administration of Tourism**, www.vietnamtourism.com, whose role is to promote Vietnam as a tourist destination rather than to provide tourist information. Visitors to their offices can get some information and maps but are more likely to be offered tours. There are exceptions eg **Saigon Tourist**, www.saigontourist.com. Good tourist information is available from tour operators in the main tourist centres.

Cambodia

Government tourism services are minimal at best. The **Ministry of Tourism**, 3 Monivong Blvd, T023-426876, is not able to provide any useful information or services. The tourism office in Siem Reap is marginally better but will only provide services, such as guides, maps etc, for a nominal fee. In all cases in Cambodia you are better off going through a private operator for information and price.

Laos

The **Laos National Tourism Authority**, Lane Xang, Vientiane, T021-212248, provides maps and brochures. The provincial offices are usually excellent and as long as you are patient they will usually come through with the information you need. There are particularly good tourism offices in Thakhek, Savannakhet, Xam Neua and Luang Namtha. The authority has teamed up with local tour operators to provide a number of ecotourism opportunities, www.ecotourismlaos.com.

Tour operators

For regional tour operators, such as **Asian Trails**, www.asiantrails.com, refer to the Activities and tours listings in the guide.

In the UK

Adventure Company, 15 Turk St, Alton, Hampshire GU34 1AG, T0870-7941009, www.adventurecompany.co.uk.

Audley Travel, 6 Willows Gate, Stratton, Audley, Oxfordshire OX27 9AU, T01869-276219, www.audleytravel.com.

Coromandel, Andrew Brock Travel Ltd, 29A Main St, Lyddington, Oakham, Rutland LE15 9LR, T01572-821330, www.coromandelabt.com. Tailored individual travel to all 3 countries.

Guerba Adventure & Discovery Holidays, Wessex House, 40 Station Rd, Westbury, Wiltshire BA13 3JN, T01373-826611, www.guerba.co.uk.

Magic of the Orient, 14 Frederick Pl, Clifton, Bristol BS8 1AS, T0117-3116050, www.magicoftheorient.com. Tailor-made holidays to the Far East.

Regent Holidays, 15 John St, Bristol BS1 2HR, T0117-9211711, www.regent-holidays.co.uk.

Silk Steps, Deep Meadow, Edington, Bridgwater, Somerset TA7 9JH, T01278-722460, www.silksteps.co.uk.

Steppes Travel, 51 Castle St, Cirencester, Glos GL7 1QD, T01285-880980, www.steppestravel.co.uk. Specialists in tailor-made holidays and small group tours.

Symbiosis Expedition Planning, 3B Wilmot Place, London NW1 9JS, T0845-1232844, www.symbiosis-travel.com.

Trans Indus, Northumberland House, 11 The Pavement, Popes Lane, London W5 4NG, T020-8566 2729, www.transindus.co.uk.

Travel Indochina Ltd, 2nd Floor, Chester House, George St, Oxford

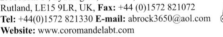

0X1 2AY, T01865-268950, www.travelindochina.co.uk. Small group journeys and tailor-made holidays.

Travelmood, 214 Edgware Rd, London W2 1DH, T0870-001002, www.travelmood.com.

Visit Vietnam (Tennyson Travel), 30-32 Fulham High St, London SW6 3LQ, T020-77364347, www.visitvietnam.co.uk. Also deals with Laos, www.visitasia.co.uk.

In North America
Adventure Center, 1311 63rd St, Suite 200, Emeryville, CA, T1-800 2278747, www.adventurecenter.com.

Global Spectrum, 3907 Laro Court, Fairfax, VA 22031, T1-800 4194446, www.globalspectrumtravel.com. Travel specialists to Southeast Asia.

Hidden Treasure Tours, 162 West Park Av, 2nd Floor, Long Beach, NY 11561, T1-888 8899906 (USA toll free), www.hiddentreasuretours.com.

Journeys, 107 April Drive, Suite 3, Ann Arbor MI 46103, T734-6654407, www.journeys-intl.com.

Myths & Mountains, 976 Tree Court, Incline Village, NV 89451, T1-800 6706984, www.mythsandmountains.com. Organizes travel to all 3 countries.

Nine Dragons Travel & Tours, PO Box 24105, Indianapolis, IN 46224, T1-317-3290350, T1-800 9099050 (USA toll free), www.nine-dragons.com.

In Australia and New Zealand

Intrepid Travel, 360 Bourke St, Melbourne, Victoria 3000, T03-8602 0500, www.intrepidtravel.com.

Travel Indochina, Level 10, HCS House, 403 George St, Sydney, NSW 2000, T02-9244 2133, T1300-367666 (toll free), www.travelindochina.com.au. Small group journeys and tailor-made holidays.

Visas and immigration

30-day tourist visas are granted on arrival in Bangkok.

Vietnam

Valid passports with visas issued by a Vietnamese embassy are required by all visitors, irrespective of citizenship. Visas are normally valid only for arrival by air at Hanoi and Ho Chi Minh City. Those wishing to enter or leave Vietnam by land must specify the border crossing when applying. It is possible to alter the point of departure at immigration offices in Hanoi and Ho Chi Minh City.

The standard tourist visa is valid for one month for 1 entry only. Tourist visas cost £43 (US$76) and generally take 5 days to process. Express visas cost £55 (2 days). If you are planning on staying for a while or making a side trip to Laos or Cambodia with the intention of coming back to Vietnam then a 1-month multiple entry visa, £70 (US$124) will make life much simpler. Visa regulations are ever changing: usually it is possible to extend visas within Vietnam. Travel agencies and hotels will probably add their own mark-up but for many people it is worth paying to avoid the difficulty of making 1 or 2 journeys to an embassy. Visas can be extended for 1 month for US$15-30. Depending on where you are it will take between 1 day and a week. A visa valid for 1 month can only be extended for 1 month.

Essentials Essentials A-Z

Cambodia

Visas for a 30-day stay are available on arrival at Phnom Penh's airport and Siem Reap's airport. Fill in a form and hand over 1 photograph (4 cm x 6 cm). Tourist visas cost US$20 and your passport must be valid for at least 6 months from the date of entry.

Officially, visas are not available on the Lao border. Many people have reported successfully obtaining visas here but don't rely on it. Travellers using the Lao border should try to arrange visa paperwork in advance in either Phnom Penh, Bangkok or Vientiane. The **Cambodian Embassy** in Bangkok, 185 Rajdamri Rd, T+66-2546630, issues visas in 1 day if you apply in the morning, as does the **Consulate General** in Ho Chi Minh City, Vietnam, 41 Phung Khac Khoan, T+84-88292751, and in Hanoi at 71 Tran Hung Dao St, T+84-49424788. In both Vietnam and in Thailand travel agencies are normally willing to obtain visas for a small fee. Cambodia has a few missions overseas from which visas can be obtained.

Travellers leaving by land must ensure that their Vietnam visa specifies Moc Bai or Chau Doc as points of entry otherwise they could be be turned back. You can apply for a Cambodian visa in Ho Chi Minh City and collect in Hanoi and vice versa.

Extensions can be obtained at the 'Department for Foreigners' on the road to the Airport, T023-581558 (passport photo required). Most travel agents arrange visa extensions for around US$40 for 30 days. Those overstaying their visas are fined US$5 per day, although officials at land crossings often try to squeeze out more.

Laos

A 15-day tourist visa (US$30) can be obtained at Vientiane's Wattay Airport, Luang Prabang International Airport and Pakse International Airport, along the Thai border at the Friendship Bridge crossing near Nong Khai/Vientiane and the Lao Bao (Vietnam)/Danasavanh crossing in Savannakhet. 'Overtime fees' are often charged if you enter after 1600 or at a weekend. You will also need a passport photo (sometimes 2).

If you want to stay for longer than 2 weeks, most Lao embassies and consulates (see p34) will issue 30-day visas, US$35. Many visitors to Laos arrange these in a neighbouring country, usually Thailand but also Cambodia and Vietnam, sometimes in as little as a few hours with the required express fees. You generally need to allow 3 working days, although some offer a 1-day express service, with a surcharge. Bangkok is the best place to arrange a 30-day visa in advance either at the Laos embassy (difficult to get to) or through one of the city's many travel agents, who usually only slap a ฿300-500 charge on top of the basic cost. The service can also be provided for a fee by travel agents in Nong Khai and Phnom Penh.

Transit visas (US$15), usually valid for 7-10 days, can be obtained by tourists with a confirmed onward airline ticket. They are available from Lao embassies in Bangkok, Hanoi, Phnom Penh and from Lao consulates in Ho Chi Minh City and Danang. As with regular tourist visas you can pay extra for an 'express' service.

Tourist visa extensions can be obtained from the Lao Immigration Office in the Ministry of the Interior opposite the Morning Market in Vientiane, T021-212529. They can be extended for an additional 15 days at the cost of US$3 per day; you will need one passport photo. Travel agencies in Vientiane and other major centres can also handle this service for you for a fee. Visitors who overstay are charged US$10 for each day beyond the visa's date of expiry on departure.

A sprint through history

Pre history	Archaeological evidence suggests the Mekong Delta and the lower reaches of the river – in modern-day Cambodia – have been inhabited since at least 4000 BC. Between 5000 and 3000 BC, two important Mesolithic cultures occupy North Vietnam: the Hoa Binh and Bac Son. The Vietnamese trace their origins to 15 tribal groups known as the Lac Viet who settle in North Vietnam at the beginning of the Bronze Age. The Khmer in Cambodia adopt and adapt Indian script as well as their ideas about astrology, religion (Buddhism and Hinduism) and royalty (the cult of the semi-divine ruler).
500-200 BC	Dongson culture thrives on the coast of Annam and Tonkin. Squat, bronze, Dongson drums show their makers to have been highly skilled.
200-100 BC	Chinese cultural hegemony over northern Vietnam begins. The Chinese dominate Vietnam until the 10th century.
AD 200-	The kingdom of Champa is the most significant power in southern Vietnam. The kingdom (200-1720) is focused on the ribbon of lowland that runs down the Annamite coast with its various capitals near Danang.
AD 300	The kingdom of Funan – the forerunner of Kambuja – is established on the Mekong by tribal people from South China and becomes the earliest Hindu state in Southeast Asia.
AD 800	Chenla is the immediate predecessor of Kambuja and the great Khmer Empire and is centred in present day southern Laos. Towards the end of the eighth century Water Chenla becomes a vassal of Java's powerful Sailendra Dynasty. This period, from the fall of Funan until the eighth century, is known as the pre-Angkorian period. In 802-835, Jayavarman II (790-850), the Khmer prince, claims independence from Java and founds the Angkor Kingdom to the north of the Tonlé Sap. He declares himself a World Emperor and legitimizes his position by arranging his coronation by a Brahmin priest, declaring himself the first Khmer devaraja, or god-king, a tradition that lasts today. From now on, the reigning monarch is identified with Siva, king of the Hindu gods.
1009-1225	The Ly Dynasty is the first independent Vietnamese dynasty, situated at Thang Long, now Hanoi, and based closely upon the Chinese Confucianist model of government and social relations.
1080	A new kingdom is founded by Jayavarman VI (1080-1107). He never settles at Angkor, living instead in the north.

1112-1150	Suryavarman II becomes the greatest leader of the Angkor Empire. He expands the Khmer Empire and attacks the Cham state relentlessly, eventually defeating the Cham in 1144-1145. He is responsible for the construction of Angkor Wat and Banteay Samre.
1218	Jayavarman VII's extensive building campaign puts pressure on the kingdom's resources; labour is consumed by construction and rice is in short supply. Jayavarman VII dies and the Kambujan Empire falls into progressive decline over the next two centuries.
1353-1368	Fa Ngoum, a Lao prince brought up in the Khmer court of Angkor, consolidates existing principalities to found Lane Xang – the first truly independent Lao kingdom. He makes Luang Prabang the capital and Theravada Buddhism the official religion. He marries the Cambodian king's daughter, Princess Keo Kaengkanya, and is given the Pra Bang (a golden statue, the most revered religious symbol of Laos), by the Khmer court. In 1368, Fa Ngoum is deposed in favour of his son, Samsenthai (1373-1416), who sets up a new administrative system based on the existing city state (muang), nominating governors to each. The system lasts until it is abolished by the communist government in 1975.
1426	Le Loi, together with tactician Nguyen Trai, leads a campaign to remove the Chinese from Vietnamese soil. Following victory against the Ming (1368-1644), Le Loi claims the throne in 1428. The expansion of the Vietnamese state, under the Le Dynasty (1427-1788), follows the decline of the Cham Kingdom. However, this geographical over-extension and the logistical impracticability of ruling from distant Hanoi, leads to the disintegration of the imperial rule. Noble families, locally dominant, challenged the emperor's authority and the Le Dynasty gradually dissolves into internecine strife and regional fiefdoms, namely Trinh in the north and Nguyen in the south.
1434	The royal Khmer court under Ponheayat moves to Phnom Penh.
1471	For more than 1000 years the Cham resist the Chinese and the Vietnamese until 1471 when the Cham suffers a terrible defeat by the Vietnamese.
1520-1571	Under King Pothisarath (1520-1548) Vientiane becomes prominent as a trading and religious centre. Upon his death, Pothisarath's son is crowned Setthathirat and rules until 1571 – the last of the great kings of Lane Xang. He defends invasion from the Burmese and is revered as one of the great Lao kings, having protected the country from foreign domination. After his death Vientiane falls to invading Burmese and is retained under Burmese control for seven years. Finally, the anarchic kingdoms of Luang Prabang and Vientiane are reunified under Nokeo Koumane (1591-1596) and Thammikarath (1596-1622).
1615	The first Jesuits arrive in Vietnam. Alexandre de Rhodes, one of the Jesuit founders of the Paris Foreign Missions Society, converts the Vietnamese writing system (1624-1645) from Chinese characters to Romanized script.

1633   King Souligna Vongsa is crowned king of Laos and brings long awaited peace. The 61 years of his rule are regarded as Lane Xang's golden age. Under him, the kingdom's influence spreads to Yunnan in south China, the Burmese Shan States, Isan in northeast Thailand and areas of Vietnam and Cambodia. Souligna Vongsa marries the Vietnamese emperor's daughter and they agree the borders between the two countries.

1700   Lane Xang splits into three: Luang Prabang under Souligna's grandson, Vientiane under Souligna's nephew and the new kingdom of Champassak was founded in the south. This weakens the country and allows the Siamese and Vietnamese to encroach on Lao lands.

1750   The Khmer royal family in Cambodia has split into pro-Siamese and pro-Vietnamese factions. Between 1794-1811 and 1847-1863, Siamese influence is strongest; from 1835-1837 the Vietnamese are dominant.

1760s   Burmese influence again holds sway in Vientiane and Luang Prabang until the Siamese successfully rampage through Vientiane in 1778. The sacred Buddhas (Phra Ban and Phra Kaeo) are taken as booty back to Bangkok where they remain. King Anou is placed on the Vientiane throne by the Siamese.

1771   The Vietnamese are mired in poverty. There are numerous peasant rebellions, of which the most serious is the Tay Son rebellion. The death of Quang Trung (formerly one of the Tay Son brothers), who had embarked on reforms, paves the way for the establishment of the Nguyen Dynasty in 1802 when Emperor Gia Long ascends to the throne in Hué.

1825   Emperor Minh Mang (reigns 1820-1840) issues an imperial edict outlawing the dissemination of Christianity as a heterodox creed in 1825 but poor Vietnamese see Christianity as a way to break the shackles of their feudal existence.

1827   Following the death of King Rama II of Siam, King Anou of Laos forms an army and marches on Bangkok in 1827. His forces are defeated but the rebellion is considered one of the most daring and ruthless in Siamese history and he is lauded as a war hero back home. King Anou's brief stab at regional power provokes the first US arms shipment to Siam allowing the Siamese to sack Vientiane. This marks America's first intervention in Southeast Asia.

1833   François-Isidore Gagelin of Les Missions Etrangères de Paris (The Paris Foreign Missions Society) becomes the first European priest to be executed in Vietnam.

1840s   The Siamese and Vietnamese fight on Cambodian territory, devastating the country and provoking French intervention. Cambodia loses its independence.

1859   Fearing a peasants' revolt against his anti-Christian policies, Emperor Minh Mang orders a mass execution of Roman Catholics. 25 European priests, 300 Vietnamese priests and 30,000 Vietnamese Roman Catholics are executed between 1848-1860. As a result, the French attack and take Saigon.

1861	The Angkor ruins are rediscovered by French naturalist Henri Mouhot.
1862	Emperor Tu Duc (reigns 1847-1883) signs a treaty ceding the three southern provinces of Vietnam to the French. This paves the way for the eventual seizure by the French of the whole kingdom. The French conquest of the north is motivated by a desire to control trade and the route to what were presumed to be the vast riches of China.
1864-1865	On 17 April King Norodom of Cambodia agrees to French protection believing they will provide military assistance against the Siamese. However, France honours Siam's claim to the western provinces of Battambang, Siem Reap and Sisophon, which Bangkok captured in the late 1600s.
1883-1886	The French force Emperor Tu Duc to sign treaties making Vietnam a French protectorate and, in 1885, the Treaty of Tientsin recognizes the French protectorates of Tonkin (North Vietnam) and Annam (Central Vietnam), to add to that of Cochin China (South Vietnam). In 1884, King Norodom is persuaded by the French governor of Cochin China to sign another treaty that turns Cambodia into a French colony. The establishment of Cambodia as a French protectorate probably saves the country from being apportioned between Siam and Vietnam. France eventually receives reluctant Siamese permission to post a vice consul to Luang Prabang and a year later persuades the Thais to leave Laos. This is the start of colonial rule in Laos. It remains a French protectorate until 1945, when it is briefly occupied by the Japanese. The French see Laos as a resource-rich appendage to Vietnam and colonial administration is relaxed. The Lao king is allowed to stay in Luang Prabang but has little power or influence.
1927-40	Resistance to French colonial rule grows with the rise of Vietnamese nationalism. Quoc Dan Dang (VNQDD), the first nationalist party, is founded in 1927, while the first significant communist group is the Indochina Communist Party (ICP) established by Ho Chi Minh in 1930. Japanese 'occupation' with French consent from 1940 leads to creation of Viet Minh to fight for liberation.
1940s	A small French-educated Lao elite become the core of a typically laid-back Lao nationalist movement.
1945	The Vietnam War starts in September in the south of the country and in 1946 in the north. These years mark the onset of fighting between the Viet Minh (a nationalist organization) and the French. The Viet Minh proclaim the creation of the Democratic Republic of Vietnam on 2 September 1945 when Ho Chi Minh reads out the Vietnamese Declaration of Independence in Hanoi. The French are in no position to respond. Bao Dai, born in 1913, is the 13th and last emperor of the Nguyen Dynasty. The Viet Minh force Bao Dai to relinquish his role in favour of Ho Chi Minh. Japanese forces oust Cambodia's colonial administration and persuade King Norodom Sihanouk to proclaim independence. Following the Japanese surrender in August, the French come back in force. Sihanouk tries to negotiate independence. The French

abolish the absolute monarchy in 1946 although the king remains titular head of state. A new constitution is introduced allowing political activity and a National Assembly is elected. In Laos, the eventual surrender of the Japanese in August gives impetus to the Lao independence movement and independence is declared on 1 September.

1946

France refuses to recognize the new state and crushes the Lao resistance. French rule over Laos is resumed. King Sisavang Vong is crowned the constitutional monarch of the new protectorate. The French and Chinese sign a treaty in March leading to the withdrawal of Chinese forces and Ho Chi Minh concludes a treaty with France in which Vietnam is recognized as a 'free' (the Vietnamese word *doc lap* being translated as free, but not yet independent) state within the French Union and the Indochinese Federation. In November the French seize customs control in Haiphong. The Vietnamese resist and fighting breaks out. In December, the Viet Minh, who cite French provocation, attack the French garrison in Hanoi. For the French, this latter incident marks the beginning of the First Indochina War.

1949-1950

Laos is granted semi-autonomy as an associated state within the French Union. Meanwhile, in Bangkok, the Issara movement forms a government-in-exile. One of the leaders, the Red Prince (Souphanouvong), known for his communist sympathies, is ousted from the movement and joins the Viet Minh.

1951-1954

The French lose their grip on the northern provinces of Laos and grant the country full independence. France signs a treaty of friendship and association with the new royalist government and makes the country a French protectorate. Within a few months of independence civil war breaks out between the royalists and the communist group, the Pathet Lao. France grants Cambodia independence on 9 November 1953 – and Sihanouk returns from self-imposed exile. In 1954, the US, which had been involved in Vietnam since the Second World War, shifts its policy from one of aiding the French colonialists to that of preventing the spread of communism in Asia. From July the US begins pumping military and economic aid to the newly formed government of South Vietnam. Without US military support, the French are defeated in a decisive battle at Dien Bien Phu and, in May 1954, they surrender, effectively marking the end of the French presence in Indochina. At Geneva, Vietnam is divided along the 17th parallel: a communist north – the Democratic Republic of Vietnam (DRV) – and a capitalist south – South Vietnam – with a view to elections in 1956 (these are never held) to reunify the country. The demise of the French in Laos sparks an increase in US involvement in Laos. Weapons are sent to the Royal Lao Army.

1955

Ngo Dinh Diem deposes Bao Dai as head of state of South Vietnam and successfully undermines the strength of the communist party in the south. From 1959 this leads to the north changing its strategy towards one of more overt military confrontation. The north infiltrates about 44,000 sympathisers into the south between 1959-1964, while the number recruited in the south is between 60,000 and 100,000. Sihanouk abdicates in Cambodia and becomes a popular political leader. However, different factions begin to develop at this time, a process which is the root of the conflict in the years to come. As these problems intensify in the late 1960s and the economic situation deteriorates, the popular support base for the Khmer Rouge is put into place. With unchecked population growth, land ownership patterns become skewed, landlessness grows more widespread and food prices escalate. Sihanouk does manage to keep Cambodia out of the war that envelops Laos and Vietnam by following a neutral policy which helps attract millions of dollars of aid to Cambodia. But when civil war breaks out in South Vietnam in the early 1960s, Cambodia's – and Sihanouk's own – survival depends on its outcome. Sihanouk believes the rebels, the National Liberation Front (NLF) (see below), will win and openly backs them. It is an alliance which costs him dear.

1959

The Lao king dies and is succeeded by his son, Sisavang Vatthana. Over the next few years there are a number of unsuccessful attempts to set up a coalition government to bring royalists and communists together.

1959

The Ho Chi Minh Trail is created, allowing supplies and troops to be moved by the North Vietnamese Army from the north to the south, via Laos. See p222.

1960s

Laos is plagued by civil war and coups and is dragged into the Vietnam War. It is subjected to extensive aerial bombing by the US in an attempt to destroy North Vietnamese sanctuaries and rupture the supply lines of the Ho Chi Minh Trail. The air assault becomes known as the 'secret war', see p359. The establishment of the National Liberation Front (NLF) of Vietnam is an important political development towards creating a credible alternative to Diem. Its military wing, the Viet Minh, is now being referred to as the Viet Cong by the US military.

1961

The conflict in Vietnam begins to intensify when the armed forces under the communists' control are unified under the People's Liberation Armed Forces (PLAF). The election of John F Kennedy to the White House coincides with the communists' decision to widen the war in the south. Kennedy dispatches 400 special forces troops and 100 military advisers to Vietnam – in contravention of the 1954 Geneva Accords and begins arming and training the Army of the Republic of Vietnam (ARVN). By the end of 1962 there are 11,000 US personnel in South Vietnam. The US however, shies away from any large-scale, direct confrontation between its forces and the Viet Cong.

1963

At Ap Bac in the Mekong Delta, the communists score their first significant victory in the south. Facing 2000 well-armed ARVN troops, a force of just 300-400 PLAF inflicts heavy casualties (63 ARVN dead and 109 wounded and three Americans dead and eight wounded) and down five helicopters. After this defeat, US advisers conclude that US troops will have to become directly involved if the communists are to be defeated. Some 15,000 people demonstrate at the Xa Loi Pagoda in Saigon in August to denounce the religious discrimination of the Diem regime. Two nights later, ARVN special forces (from Roman Catholic families) raid the pagoda, wounding 30 and killing seven people. Soon afterwards Diem declares martial law, suppressing all opposition, and refuses to hold elections to reunify the country. His brutal brother, Nhu, is appointed to head the security forces and proceeds to terrorize much of Vietnamese society. The pagoda becomes a focus of discontent as several monks commit suicide through self-immolation to protest against the regime. On 2 November, Diem and his brother Ngo Dinh Nhu are assassinated during a US-assisted army coup (the US administration had been behind his rise to power).

1964

It is reported that two American ships, the *USS Maddox* and *USS C Turner Joy*, are attacked without provocation in international waters on the 2 August by North Vietnamese patrol craft. The US responds by bombing shore installations while presenting the Gulf of Tonkin Resolution on 7 August (requesting greater military involvement) to an outraged Congress for approval. Only two Congressmen vote against the resolution. In reality, the *USS Maddox* had been involved in electronic intelligence-gathering while supporting clandestine raids by South Vietnamese mercenaries, well inside North Vietnamese territorial waters. This deception only becomes apparent in 1971 when the *Pentagon Papers*, documenting the circumstances behind the incident, are leaked to the *New York Times* (the *Pentagon Papers* were commissioned by Defence Secretary Robert McNamara in June 1967 and written by 36 Indochina experts).

1965

US President Lyndon Johnson orders the beginning of the air war against the North Vietnamese in March and by June there are 74,000 troops in Vietnam. Government files show Johnson doubts the wisdom of intervention but believes Kennedy made a solemn pledge to help the South Vietnamese. Despite Johnson's reluctance to commit the US to the conflict, events force his hand. He realizes the undisciplined South Vietnamese cannot prevent a Communist victory. The increase in activity forces NLF troops to take refuge inside Cambodia.

1967-1968

The Vietnamese communist leadership in the north decides to escalate the war in the south in order to regain the initiative. On the morning of 1 February 1968, New Year (Tet), 84,000 communist troops – almost all Viet Cong – attack targets in 105 urban centres. The Tet Offensive concentrates American minds. The costs by this time are vast and thousands of men have been killed for a cause which, to many, is becoming less clear by the month.

1969

Negotiations begin in Paris to try and secure an honourable settlement for the USA with regards to Vietnam.

1970

Sihanouk incurs American wrath by allowing North Vietnamese forces to use Cambodian territory as an extension of the Ho Chi Minh Trail. This results in his former army Commander-in-Chief, Marshal Lon Nol, masterminding his removal as Head of State while Sihanouk is in Moscow. Lon Nol abolishes the monarchy and proclaims a republic. On 30 April US President Richard Nixon officially announces Washington's military intervention in Cambodia – although in reality it has been going on for some time. The invasion aims to deny the Vietnamese Communists the use of Sihanoukville port through which 85 per cent of their heavy arms are reaching South Vietnam.

1973	Against the wishes of South Vietnam's President Nguyen Van Thieu, the US signs a treaty on 27 January; the last combat troops leave in March. The North's Central Committee formally decides to abandon the Paris Accord in October. Facing defeat in Vietnam, the US Air Force B-52s begin carpet bombing Communist-controlled areas in Cambodia to enable Lon Nol's inept regime to retain control of the besieged provincial cities. At the same time, the Khmer Rouge increases its military strength dramatically and begins to make inroads into areas formerly controlled by government troops. Officially the rebels represent the Beijing-based Royal Government of National Union of Cambodia (Grunc), headed by the exiled Prince Sihanouk. Unofficially, Grunc's leaders are Pol Pot, Khieu Samphan, Leng Sary and Son Sen – all Khmer Rouge men. A ceasefire is agreed in Laos in February. Power is transferred in April 1974 to yet another coalition government, divided between the Communists and the Royalists. As the US begins its withdrawal from Vietnam, the Pathet Lao gain control over most of the country.
1975	On 1 April, President Lon Nol flees Cambodia to escape the rapidly advancing Khmer Rouge. On 17 April, the victorious Khmer Rouge enter Phnom Penh. Cambodia is renamed Democratic Kampuchea (DK) and Pol Pot starts establishing a radical Maoist-style agrarian society. During the 44-month reign of terror, more than one million people die out of of a population of seven million. Northern Vietnam is ready for the final offensive and on 30 April the communists achieve total victory. With the fall of Saigon and Phnom Penh, opposition to the Pathet Lao crumbles. The capital of Laos is seized, King Savang Vatthana abdicates and the ancient Lao monarchy is abolished, together with King Samsenthai's 600 year old system of village autonomy. Power is transferred peacefully and barely a shot is fired. The appeal to the masses is independence and preservation of Lao culture from the corrosive American influence. The Pathet Lao establish the Lao People's Revolutionary Party (LPRP) and this becomes the only legal political party, with Kaysone Phomvihane as prime minister. All communications with the outside world are cut and socialist transformation begins. Those who do not match up to the Party's scrupulous standards are sent off to re-education camps.
1976-1982	The Socialist Republic of Vietnam is established on 2 July when Vietnam is reunified. It is the beginning of a collective struggle to come to terms with the war, to build a nation and to reinvigorate the economy. Thousands of South Vietnamese are sent to re-education camps, many flee illegally and then legally through the Orderly Departures Programme. Hanoi's determination to oust Pol Pot becomes apparent on Christmas Day 1978 when 120,000 Vietnamese troops invade. By 7 January 1979 they have installed a puppet government and proclaim the foundation of the People's Republic of Kampuchea (PRK). Following the invasion, three main anti-Hanoi factions are formed. In June 1982 they band together to fight the PRK and call themselves the Coalition Government of Democratic Kampuchea (CGDK). They are the Khmer Rouge, the National United Front for an Independent Neutral Peaceful and Co-operative Cambodia (Funcinpec) headed by Prince Sihanouk and the anti-communist Khmer People's National Liberation Front (KPNLF). The three factions unite against the 70,000 troops loyal to the government of President

Essentials About the region A sprint through history

Heng Samrin and Prime Minister Hun Sen (previously a Khmer Rouge cadre). By 1979 food shortages and fear of being sent to re-education camps in Vietnam leads to the exodus of hundreds of thousands of refugees to Thailand. The government is forced to modify its approach and some private enterprise within agriculture is permitted.

1986

The Vietnamese Communist Party launches its economic reform programme, *doi moi*. Although the programme has done much to free up the economy, the party has ensured it retains ultimate political power. Market orientated reforms are also introduced in Laos.

1989

The Vietnamese withdraw from Cambodia. Rebel factions try to take advantage of the supposedly weakened Hun Sen regime in Phnom Penh. The government commits itself to liberalizing the economy and improving the infrastructure to undermine the political appeal of the rebels – particularly that of the Khmer Rouge. The first elections are held in Laos since 1975. All candidates have to be approved by the LPRP. The communists retain power.

1991

The four warring Cambodian factions sign a peace agreement. Later in the year, the factions agree to reduce their armed guerrillas and militias by 70 per cent. The remainder are to be placed under the supervision of the United Nations Transitional Authority in Cambodia (UNTAC), which supervises Cambodia's transition to multi-party democracy. On 14 November Prince Norodom Sihanouk returns to Phnom Penh to an ecstatic welcome, followed, a few days later, by Son Sen, a Khmer Rouge leader. When the Supreme National Council (SNC) finally meet in Phnom Penh at the end of December 1991, it is unanimously decided to rubberstamp the immediate deployment of UN troops to oversee the peace process in the run-up to a general election.

1992

The Khmer Rouge refuses to demobilize their fighters as required by the accord and attempts to gain a foothold in the strategic central province of Kompong Thom in advance of the full deployment of UN peacekeeping forces. The Khmer Rouge – which is by now referred to (in politically neutral parlance) as the Party of Democratic Kampuchea, or the DK – make it as difficult as possible for the UN.

1993

UN workers successfully register 4.7 million out of roughly nine million Cambodians – about 96 per cent of the population above voting age. With a US$2 billion price-tag, this huge operation is the most expensive mission ever undertaken by the UN. The UN is given the task of resettling 360,000 refugees from camps in Thailand and of demobilizing more than a quarter of a million soldiers from the main factions. Khmer Rouge guerrillas launch attacks and start killing ethnic Vietnamese villagers and settlers, sending up to 20,000 of them fleeing into Vietnam. They also begin ambushing and killing UN soldiers and electoral volunteers. The elections give Funcinpec 45 per cent of the vote, the Cambodian People's Party (CPP) 38 per cent and the Liberal Democratic Party (BLDP), 3 per cent. The CPP agrees to join Funcinpec in a power sharing agreement. The new Cambodian constitution ia ratified in September marking the end of UNTAC's involvement in the country. Under the new constitution, Cambodia is to be a pluralistic liberal-democratic country. 70-year-old Sihanouk is crowned King of Cambodia, reclaiming the throne he relinquished in 1955. His son, Norodom Ranariddh, is appointed First Prime Minister and Hun Sen, Second Prime Minister, a situation intended to promote national unity but leads to internal bickering and dissent.

1994-1995 The 1975 US-imposed trade embargo on Vietnam is lifted. In 1995 full normalization of relations resumes. In mid-1994 the Cambodian National Assembly outlaws the Khmer Rouge, offering a six month amnesty to rank-and-file guerrillas. By January 1995, 7000 Khmer Rouge have reportedly defected to the government, leaving somewhere between 5,000 and 6000 hardcore rebels still fighting. The US also lifts a 20-year aid embargo in Laos.

1997 In July the stage is set for Cambodia to join the Association of Southeast Asian Nations (Asean) along with Laos. This is to mark Cambodia's international rehabilitation. But a month before the historic day, Hun Sen mounts a *coup d'état* and ousts Norodom Ranariddh and his party, Funcinpec, from government. The coup is widely condemned. In later elections Hun Sen's Cambodian People's Party win just over 41 per cent while Funcinpec secure 31.7 per cent of the vote and the Sam Rainsy Party, 14.3 per cent.

1998 On 15 April Pol Pot dies in a remote jungle hideout in the north of Cambodia.

1999 Cambodia agrees to set up a tribunal to bring to trial senior leaders of Democratic Kampuchea and those who are most responsible for the serious crimes and violations of Cambodian penal law, international humanitarian law and custom and international conventions recognized by Cambodia committed, during the period from 17 April 1975 to 6 January 1979. It has yet to begin.

2001-2004 The Vietnamese National Assembly finally ratifies a trade treaty with the US in 2001. It leads to a substantial increase in bilateral trade. In 2003 the USA imports US$4.5 billion worth of Vietnamese goods, roughly four times more than it exports to Vietnam. Thousands of ethnic minorities riot in the central highland provinces of Gia Lai and Dac Lac and the army is called in to restore order. All foreigners are banned from the Central Highlands. Violence between ethnic minorities and the Vietnamese government flares in the Central Highlands in 2004 resulting in 'unknown numbers of dead and injured and reports of people missing', according to Amnesty International. The cause is religious freedom and land rights. On October 7 King Sihanouk abdicates. On October 14, the Cambodian Throne Council selects Prince Norodom Sihamoni to succeed Sihanouk as King.

2005 The World Bank approves a loan for the Nam Theun 2 hydroelectric dam project in Laos. The dam is expected to produce electricity for export; there is concern about its environmental and social impact.

Clockwise from top: Don Khone in southern Laos; fishing in Cambodia; sunset on the Mekong Delta

The Mekong

The Mekong River is the heart and soul of mainland Southeast Asia, a sinuous thread that binds Vietnam, Cambodia and Laos geographically, historically, culturally and economically. Indeed, the Mekong – or the Mae Nam Khong (the Mother of Waters) – is the most important geographical feature of mainland Southeast Asia.

The Mekong's origins in eastern Tibet have only been pin-pointed in the last 15-years. From here the giant river plies 4500 km through six countries, cutting through almost the entire length of Laos, dissecting Cambodia, and plunging into Vietnam's Mekong Delta before emptying into the South China Sea. The river is the 12th longest river in the world and is the world's 10th largest by volume of water dispersed into the ocean - 475 km^3.

French explorer Francis Garnier once commented: "without doubt, no other river, over such a length, has a more singular or remarkable character". The Mekong has indeed woven itself into the cultural fabric, shaping the region's history. The river is the one constant from the

Floating village

ancient Funan settlement in the Mekong Delta, through to the Khmer Empire who established its capital at Angkor, relying on the river for transport and agricultural production. After several European expeditions, the French took an interest in the river and the region in the mid 19th century, developing grandiose plans to transform the Mekong into a river highway from China (the plans were thwarted upon discovering that the Mekong could not be traversed). The river later played an integral role in shaping the history during the Vietnam War when it became an important conduit for the running of Viet Cong supplies and was the scene of heavy fighting.

The river has been a major purveyor of culture, ushering in various religions, arts, customs and folklore. The enormous, colourful, boat racing festivals of Vietnam, Cambodia and Laos are staged on the water. Similarly, the annual water festivals in Cambodia and Laos come from deep-rooted traditions stemming from the Mekong and its importance to agricultural production. Nor is the river free from superstition or strange phenomena. In Laos thousands of people gather each year to witness naga fireballs rising from the river's surface. Major arts have also developed from these waters including Vietnam's water puppetry. It also

Background

→ **Vietnam in film**

Few countries have provided so much material for celluloid tales as has Vietnam. In the post-Vietnam War era, American cinema produced some of the most harrowing, soul-searching and cinematically exciting films of the 20th century, as filmakers attempted to explain or come to terms with their country's disastrous involvement in Vietnam. Francis Ford Coppola's **Apocalypse Now** remains the best known and most outstanding of all Vietnam films. In it, Coppola substitutes Vietnam for the Africa of Joseph Conrad's *Heart of Darkness*. **The Deer Hunter**, which stars Robert de Niro charts the horrors experienced by three tough steelworkers who are plunged into the war. Stanley Kubrick's **Full Metal Jacket** (1987) follows GIs from Boot Camp to the Tet Offensive, while **Good Morning Vietnam** (1987) stars Robin Williams as an irreverent DJ working for armed services radio. Oliver Stone's trilogy – **Platoon** (1986), **Born on the Fourth of July** (1989) and **Heaven and Earth** (1993) – is an ambitious attempt to analyze the effects of the war: first through an American soldier serving in Vietnam; second, through an injured veteran adjusting to life after the war, and third, from the perspective of a Vietnamese woman, Le Ly Hayslip, during and after the Indochina conflicts.

The film version of Graham Greene's **The Quiet American** (directed by Phillip Noyce, 2002), a novel of love, war, murder and betrayal set in 1950s Saigon, was the first Hollywood blockbuster to be filmed in Vietnam since the end of the war. The Hotel

provided inspiration in the *Apocalypse Now* mission down the fictional Nung River, said to represent the Mekong.

Today, the Mekong is instrumental in the region's survival, with more than 60 million people in Southeast Asia dependent on the river and its tributaries for their survival. Agricultural production, particularly the farming of rice, the regional staple, relies on the river's annual flood-drought cycle. During the monsoon season the river swells to 30 times its original size , depositing rich sediments along the floodplains and riverbanks, creating a fertilizing effect.

The river is also home to between 770 and 1300 species of freshwater fish, including the world's largest, a giant 300 kg catfish (the size of a grizzly bear) and the endangered Irrawaddy dolphin (numbered at around 80). Fish are also an important part of the Vietnamese, Khmer and Lao diet – constituting 80 per cent of people's protein requirements. Interestingly, all three countries rank the pungent smelling fermented fish sauce as one of their finest delicacies.

Cambodia is particularly reliant on fishing as the swollen Mekong River forces the major tributary, the Tonlé Sap, to reverse its flow from June to September. Each year the Tonlé Sap yields an annual catch of 100,000 tonnes of fish, representing 16 per cent of the country's GDP and making Cambodia's the world's fourth larges catch.

The Mekong has had an undeniable effect on the shaping and livelihood on the Vietnamese, Cambodians and Lao but one has to ask, for how much longer? In the last decade, more than 100 large dam proposals have been tabled for the Mekong basin.

Continental, the social hub of the time, is actually replicated on screen in the facing Hotel Caravelle across Lam Son Square.

In the 1990s French-made films began to represent the colonial era in Vietnam, pre-1954, with a frisson of tension never too far away: **Indochine** (directed by Régis Wargnier, 1993) won acclaim for its beautiful sets and scenery. It is set in the 1930s and captures the vices and flaws of French colonial Vietnam before its demise. **L'Amant** (The Lover, 1992), directed by Jean-Jacques Annaud, charts the relationship of a young French girl with an older, Chinese businessman, while **Scent of Green Papaya** (1993), by Tran Anh Hung, is an account of family relationships in Saigon in the 1950s.

Vietnamese-made films, however, have suffered arrested development. The first Vietnamese film, **On the Same River**, was released in 1959 and follows a couple divided by the 17th parallel in 1954. Post-1975, when the country was reunified, all Vietnamese films were censored at the script stage and those that made it past the censor were state-funded. In 2002, the ministry relaxed its rules but director Le Hoang's **Gai Nhay** (Bar Girls), about sex, drugs and HIV, rocked cinema audiences on its release in 2003. Produced by Ho Chi Minh's Liberation Studios (which is run by the army), the film suited the Vietnamese government as it documented the social evils of prostitution and drug addiction through the grim lives of two working girls, Hoa (My Duyen) and Hanh (Minh Thu).

However, by far the greatest menace is emanating from China, the source of up to 45 per cent of the lower Mekong's water. Without consent and little or no consultation, China has embarked on a massive hydro-dam construction campaign, involving eight new dams, two of which are completed, with a third under way. The dams are already having a detrimental effect upon the Mekong, altering the river's natural ebbs and flows. Chainarong Setthachua, director of South East Asia Rivers Network said that: "Not only is the water the lowest in its history, it is also fluctuating – sometimes up, sometimes down. This comes from dam operations in China." The Mekong River Commission (MRC), the body responsible for overseeing the river agrees, suggesting in some places the Mekong is at its lowest point ever, at rock-bottom levels. In 2004 Cambodia's fish catch dropped by almost 50 per cent. Vietnam, Cambodia and Laos all have a past and present entwined in the mighty Mekong. It is hoped a future in which the river still plays a critical role is possible.

Festivals

Colourful and serious ceremonies take place throughout the lunar calendar in Vietnam. To help you work out on which day these events fall, check out the following websites, which convert the Gregorian calendar to the lunar calendar: http://umunhum.stanford.edu/~lee/chicomp/lunar.html; consult also www.vietnamtourism.com. There are some 30 public holidays celebrated each year in Cambodia. Most are celebrated with public parades and special events to commemorate the particular holiday. The largest holidays also see many

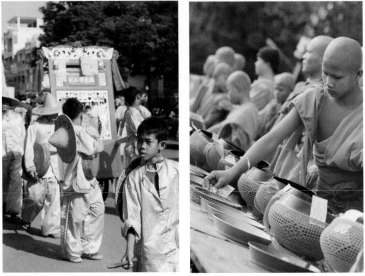

Chinese New Year, Phnom Penh (left); monks collecting alms, Luang Prabang (right)

Khmers – although less than used to be the case – firing their guns, to the extent that red tracer fills the sky. Being of festive inclination, the Lao celebrate New Year four times a year: the international New Year in January, Chinese New Year in January/February, Lao New Year (Pimai) in April and Hmong New Year in December. The Lao Buddhist year follows the lunar calendar, so many of the festivals are movable.

Bangkok

Apr (movable, public holiday) **Songkran** marks the beginning of the Buddhist New Year. It is a 3- to 5-day celebration, with parades, dancing and folk entertainment.

Vietnam

Late Jan-Mar (movable, 1st-7th day of the new lunar year) (29-31 Jan 2006, 18-20 Feb 2007, 7-9 Feb 2008): **Tet** Tet is the traditional new year. The big celebration of the year, the word Tet is the shortened version of tet nguyen dan ('first morning of the new period'). Tet is the time to forgive and forget and to pay off debts. It is also everyone's birthday – everyone adds one year to their age at Tet. Enormous quantities of food are consumed and new clothes are bought.

It is believed that before Tet the spirit of the hearth, Ong Tao, leaves on a journey to visit the palace of the Jade Emperor where he must report on family affairs. To ensure that Ong Tao sets off in good cheer, a ceremony is held before Tet, Le Tao Quan, and during his absence a shrine is constructed (Cay Neu) to keep evil spirits at bay until his return. On the afternoon before Tet, Tat Nien, a sacrifice is offered at the family altar to dead relatives who are invited back to join in the festivities.

Great attention is paid to preparations for Tet, because it is believed that the first week of the new year dictates the fortunes for the rest of the year. The first visitor to the house on New Year's morning should be an influential, lucky and happy person, so families take care to arrange a suitable caller.

Apr (5th or 6th of the 3rd lunar month): **Thanh Minh (New Year of the Dead or Feast of the Pure Light)**. The Vietnamese walk outdoors to evoke the spirit of the dead and family shrines and tombs are cleaned and decorated.

Aug: (movable, 15th day of the 7th lunar month): **Trung Nguyen (Wandering Souls Day)** During this time, prayers can absolve the sins of the dead who leave hell and return, hungry and naked, to their relatives. The Wandering Souls are those with no homes to go to. There are celebrations in Buddhist temples and homes, food is placed out on tables and money is burned.

Sep (movable, 15th day of the 8th month; 6 Oct 2006, 25 Sep 2007, 14 Sep 2008): **Tet Trung Thu (Mid-Autumn Festival)** This festival is particularly celebrated by children. It is based on legend. In the evening families prepare food including sticky rice, fruit and chicken to be placed on the ancestral altars. Moon cakes (egg, green bean, and lotus seed) are baked, lanterns made and painted and children parade through towns with music.

Cambodia

Apr (13-15) **Bonn Chaul Chhnam (Cambodian New Year)** A 3-day celebration to mark the turn of the year when predictions are made for the forthcoming year. The celebration is to show gratitude to the departing demi-god and to welcome the new one. Every household erects a small altar to welcome a new demi-god, filled with offerings of food and drink. Homes are spring cleaned. Householders visit temples and traditional games like boh angkunh and chhoal chhoung are played and festivities are performed.

Oct/Nov (movable) **Bon Om Tuk** (Water Festival or Festival of the Reversing Current) Celebrates the movement of the waters out of the Tonlé Sap with boat races in Phnom Penh. Boat races extend over 3 days with more than 200 competitors but the highlight is the evening gala in Phnom Penh when a fleet of boats, studded with lights, row out

under the full moon. Under the Cambodian monarchy, the king would command the waters to retreat.

Laos

Jan/Feb (movable) **Chinese New Year** Celebrated by Chinese and Vietnamese communities. Many businesses shut down for 3 days.

Apr (13-15) **Pi Mai** Lao New Year. One of the most important annual festivals, particularly in Luang Prabang (see p320). Statues of the Buddha (in the 'calling for rain' posture) are ceremonially doused in water, which is poured along an intricately decorated trench (*hang song nam pha*). The small stupas of sand, decorated with streamers, in wat compounds are symbolic requests for health and happiness over the next year. It is celebrated with traditional Lao folksinging (*mor lam*) and the circle dance (*ramwong*). There is usually a 3-day holiday. 'Sok Dee Pi Mai' (good luck for the New Year) is usually said to one another during this period.

May (movable) **Boun Bang Fai** The rocket festival, is a Buddhist rain-making festival. Large bamboo rockets are built and decorated by monks and carried in procession before being blasted skywards. The higher a rocket goes, the bigger its builder's ego gets. Designers of failed rockets are thrown in the mud. The festival lasts 2 days.

Sep (movable) **Boun Ok Phansa** The end of Buddhist Lent when the faithful take offerings to the temple. It is in the '9th month' in Luang Prabang and the '11th month' in Vientiane, and marks the end of the rainy season. Boat races take place on the Mekong River with crews of 50 or more men and women. On the night before the race small decorated rafts are set afloat on the river.

Nov (movable) **Boun That Luang** Celebrated in all Laos' *thats*, although most enthusiastically and colourfully in Vientiane (see p320).

67

Bangkok

Monkey God on Wat Phra Kaeo

Don't miss...

1. **Grand Palace** ▶▶ *p76.*

2. **Jim Thompson's House** ▶▶ *p80.*

3. **Chatuchak Weekend Market** ▶▶ *p82.*

4. **Thai street food** ▶▶ *p86.*

5. **Tewes Market** ▶▶ *p92.*

A Old City
B Siam Square & Ploenchit Road
C Khaosan Road
D Sukhumvit Road
E Silom & Surawong

| 600 metres |

To Airport & Chatuchak Weekend Market

Thailand's capital is dirty, dynamic, wild and sweaty, a heaving scrum of humanity blended with ancient beauty, booming youth culture and the rituals of a bygone age. The Thais call it the City of Angels but there's nothing angelic about Bangkok. Don't arrive expecting an exotic, languid, dreamy place trapped in a traditional past. What will hit you is the size, pace, endless olfactory/oral cacophony, friendliness of the locals and gridlocked traffic. Some of the old *King and I* romanticism persists. You have the khlongs, palaces and temples but ultimately, what marks Bangkok out from the imaginings of its visitors, is its thrusting modernity in open struggle with the ancient, rural traditions of Thai culture. Neon, steel and glass and futuristic transport rubs shoulders with alms-collecting monks and crumbling teak villas. It's all here: poverty and wealth, smog-filled thoroughfares and backstreets smothered in alluring exotic aromas, cyber cafés and fried-bug-laden barrows. With your senses fully overloaded don't forget the sheer luxury on offer. Bangkok is home to some of the best, and most affordable, hotels in the world. Add the numerous spas, super-hip night life and the diverse range of markets, selling everything from amulets and sarongs to Prada and hi-tech, and your head will be spinning.

Ratings

Landscape
★★

Relaxation
★

Activities
★★★

Culture
★★★★

Costs
$$$-$$

Bangkok

Ins and outs ◉ ▸▸ p94

Getting there

Air Don Muang Airport (BKK), T02-2860190, is around 25 km north of Bangkok. It has two international terminals: Terminal 1 serves Asia, and Terminal 2 the rest of the world. The terminals have banks, currency exchange, post office, left luggage (฿70 per item per day – maximum four months, located between terminals 1 and 2), hotel booking agency, airport information, airport clinic, lost-and-found baggage service, duty-free shops, restaurants and bars. The **Amari Airport Hotel**, T02-5661020, www.amari.com, is linked to the international terminal by a walkway and provides a 'ministay' service for passengers who wish to freshen-up and take a room for up to three hours between 0800 and 1800. Another covered and air-conditioned walkway extends for 500 m, linking the international terminals with the **domestic terminal**. It has a hotel booking counter, post office, currency exchange counters, restaurant and bookshop. A shuttle bus is sometimes available between the terminals; but beware, taxis grossly overcharge for a drive of under 1 km. ▸▸ *For details of onward flights from Don Muang Airport, see Essentials, p20.*

From the airport to the city centre It takes between 30 minutes and one hour to get to central Bangkok from the airport by road, depending on the time of day and the state of the traffic. The elevated expressway can reduce the journey time to 20 minutes but there is a toll.

An air-conditioned **airport bus** operates on three routes every 15 minutes, 0500-2400, ฿70. The **Silom service** (A1) goes to Don Muang Tollway, Din Daeng, Pratunam, Lumpini Park and Silom, stopping at the following hotels: Century, Indra, Anoma, Grand Hyatt, Erawan, Regent, Dusit Thani, and Narai hotels. The **Sanaam Luang service** (A2) goes to Don Muang Tollway, Din Daeng, Victory Monument, Phayathai, Phetburi, Lan Luang, Democracy Monument and Sanaam Luang, stopping at the following hotels: Victory Monument, Siam City Hotel, Soi King Phet, Saphan Khao, Majestic and Rattanakosin. The **Phra Khanong service** (A3) goes to Don Muang Tollway, Din Daeng, Sukhumvit, Ekamai, Phra Khanong, with stops at Amari Building, Ambassador, Delta Grand Pacific, Bang Chan Glass House, Novotel and Soi Ekkamai (Sukhumvit) hotels. Note that return buses have slightly different stops. There is also a **minibus** service, which charge ฿100 to major hotels, ฿50-80 to Khaosan Road, depending on the time of day.

⊘ Getting there International and domestic flights.

◉ Getting around Skytrain, Metro, river taxi, tuk-tuks, taxis and on foot.

⊖ Time required 1-2 days at the beginning or end of your trip

☁ Weather Bangkok is coolest Nov-Feb and hottest in Apr and May. Rainfall is heaviest in Sep.

⊜ Sleeping From outstanding, good-value international hotels to good, cheap guesthouses.

⊘ Eating Plenty of choice across all cuisines and prices.

▲▲ Activities and tours Shopping, massage, boat trips.

★ Don't miss... The unusual Thai street food ▸▸ p86.

The official **taxi** booking service is in the arrivals hall. Official airport limousines have green plates, public taxis have yellow plates; a white plate means the vehicle is not registered as a taxi. There are three sets of taxi/limousine services. First, **airport limos** (before exiting from the restricted area), next **airport taxis** (before exiting from the terminal building), and finally, a **public taxi counter** (outside, on the slipway). The latter are the cheapest. Note that airport flunkies sometimes try to direct passengers to the more expensive 'limousine' service: walk through the barriers to the public taxi desk. If taking a metered taxi, the coupon from the booking desk will quote no fare so ensure that the meter is used and keep hold of your coupon – some taxi drivers try to pocket it – as it details the obligations of taxi drivers.

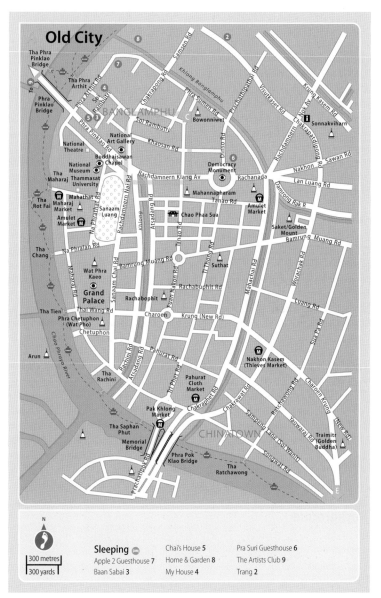

Sleeping 🛏
Apple 2 Guesthouse **7**
Baan Sabai **3**

Chai's House **5**
Home & Garden **8**
My House **4**

Pra Suri Guesthouse **6**
The Artists Club **9**
Trang **2**

A public taxi to downtown should cost roughly ฿250. Tolls on the expressways (฿70, one payment of ฿30 and one of ฿40) are paid on top of the fare on the meter . There is a ฿50 airport surcharge from the airport on top of the meter cost. Don't be surprised if your driver decides to feign that he does not know where to go: it's all part of being a new boy/girl in a new town. Some regular Don Muang visitors recommend going up to the departures floor and flagging down a taxi that has just dropped passengers off. Doing it this way will save you around ฿50 and you should be able to get into town for less than ฿200.

The airport railway station is on the other side of the north-south highway from the airport and is well signposted inside the terminals. There are regular **trains** from here to Bangkok's Hualamphong station. The journey takes 45 minutes and costs ฿5 by ordinary train (third class, the cheapest option). 'Rapid' and 'express' trains (first and second class seats) take the same time but charge a supplementary ฿40-60. ➊ ▶▶ *p94*.

Bangkok Ins & outs

Getting around

Bangkok has the unenviable reputation of having some of the worst traffic in the world, although the **Skytrain** – an elevated railway – along with the new **Metro** have made things a lot easier for those areas of the city they cover. Another alternative to the smog of Bangkok's streets is to hop onboard one of the express **river taxis**, which ply the Chao Phraya River and the network of khlongs (canals) that criss-cross the city. This is often quicker than going by road. **Buses**, with and without air-conditioning, travel to all city sights. If travelling by bus, a bus map of the city – available from most bookshops and hotel gift shops – is an invaluable aid. A **taxi** or **tuk-tuk** ride within the centre should cost ฿50-100. All taxis now have meters. Tuk-tuk numbers are dwindling and the negotiated fares often work out more expensive than a taxi.

Orientation

Begin in the bejewelled beauty of the **Old City**. The charming **Golden Mount** is a short hop to the east, while to the south are the bewildering alleyways and gaudy temples of Bangkok's frenetic **Chinatown**. Head west over the Chao Phraya River to the magnificent spire of **Wat Arun** and the khlongs of **Thonburi**. To the north are the broad, leafy avenues of **Dusit**, the Thai parliament and the King's residence. Carry on east and south and you'll reach modern Bangkok. Mini-boutiques circle **Siam Square**, the Thai centre of youth fashion; **Silom** and **Sukhumvit Roads** are vibrant runs of shopping malls, restaurants and hotels, while the **Chatuchak Weekend Market** in the northern suburbs is one of Asia's greatest markets.

Tourist information

The main offices of the **Tourist Authority of Thailand** (TAT) ⓘ *4 Rachdamnern Nok Av, T02-282 9775, daily 0830-1630*, are supplemented by counters in the arrivals hall at Don Muang (T02-523 8972) and at the Chatuchak Weekend Market (Kamphaeng Phet 2 Rd, T02-2724440). There is also an English-speaking **Tourist Service Centre** ⓘ *T1155, daily 0800- 2400*. A number of good, informative, English-language magazines provide listings of what to do and where to go in Bangkok: *Bangkok Metro*, published monthly (฿100, www.bkkmetro.com) is the well-designed pick of the bunch, covering everything from music and nightlife to sports and fitness, business and children's events. On the internet, see also www.khao-san-road.com.

Background

The official name for Thailand's capital city is Krungthep – phramaha – nakhonbawon – rathanakosin – mahinthara – yutthayaa – mahadilok – phiphobnobpharaat – raatchathaanii – buriiromudomsantisuk. It is not hard to see why Thais prefer the shortened version – Krungthep, or the 'City of Angels'. The name used by the rest of the world – Bangkok – is

Background

→ The Thai Ramayana: the Ramakien

The *Ramakien* – literally the 'Story of Rama' – is an adaptation of the Indian Hindu classic, the *Ramayana*, which was written by the poet Valmiki about 2000 years ago. This 48,000-line epic odyssey, often likened to the works of Homer, was introduced into mainland Southeast Asia in the early centuries of the first millennium. The heroes were simply transposed into a mythical, ancient, Southeast Asian landscape. In Thailand, the *Ramakien* quickly became highly influential, and the name of the former capital of Siam, Ayutthaya, is taken from the legendary hero's city of Ayodhia in the epic. Unfortunately, these early Thai translations of the *Ramayana* were destroyed following the sacking of Ayutthaya by the Burmese in 1767. The earliest extant version was written by King Taksin in about 1775, although Rama I's rather later rendering is usually regarded as the classic interpretation.

In many respects, King Chakri's version closely follows that of the original Indian story. It tells of the life of Ram (Rama), the King of Ayodhia. In the first part of the story, Ram renounces his throne following a long and convoluted court intrigue, and flees into exile. With his wife Seeda (Sita) and trusted companion Hanuman (the monkey god), they undertake a long and arduous journey. In the second part, his wife Seeda is abducted by the evil king Ravana, forcing Ram to wage battle against the demons of Langka Island (Sri Lanka). He defeats the demons with the help of Hanuman and his monkey army, and recovers his wife. In the third and final part of the story – and here it diverges sharply from the Indian original – Seeda and Ram are reunited and reconciled with the help of the gods (in the Indian version there is no such reconciliation). Another difference with the Indian version is the significant role played by the Thai Hanuman – here an amorous adventurer who dominates much of the third part of the epic.

There are also numerous sub-plots which are original to the *Ramakien*, many building upon events in Thai history and local myth and folklore. In tone and issues of morality, the Thai version is less puritanical than the Indian original. There are also, of course, differences in dress, ecology, location and custom.

derived from 17th-century western maps, which referred to the city (or town as it then was) as Bancok, the 'village of the wild plum'. This name was only superseded by Krungthep in 1782, and so the western name has deeper historical roots.

In 1767, Ayutthaya, then the capital of Siam, fell to the marauding Burmese for the second time and it was imperative that the remnants of the court and army find a more defensible site for a new capital. Taksin, the Lord of Tak, chose Thonburi, on the western banks of the Chao Phraya River, far from the Burmese. In three years, Taksin had established a kingdom and crowned himself king. His reign was short-lived; the pressure of thwarting the Burmese over three arduous years caused him to go mad and in 1782 he was forced to abdicate. General Phraya Chakri was recalled from Cambodia and invited to accept the

Background

→ The Emerald Buddha

Wat Phra Kaeo was specifically built to house the Emerald Buddha, the most venerated Buddha image in Thailand. It is carved from green jade (the emerald in the name referring only to its colour) and is a mere 75 cm high, seated in an attitude of meditation.

The image is believed to have been found in 1434 in Chiang Rai, and stylistically belongs to the Late Chiang Saen or Chiang Mai schools. Since then, it has been moved on a number of occasions: to Lampang, Chiang Mai and Laos (both Luang Prabang and Vientiane). It stayed in Vientiane for 214 years before being recaptured by the Thai army in 1778 and placed in Wat Phra Kaeo on 22 March 1784.

The image wears seasonal costumes of gold and jewellery; one each for the hot, cool and the rainy seasons. The changing ceremony takes place three times a year in the presence of the King of Thailand.

Buddha images are often thought to have personalities and the Phra Kaeo is no exception to this. It is said that such is the antipathy between the Pra Bang image in Luang Prabang (Laos, see p333) and the Phra Kaeo that the images can never reside in the same town.

throne. This marked the beginning of the present Chakri Dynasty. In 1782, Chakri (now known as Rama I) moved his capital across the river to Bangkok anticipating trouble from King Bodawpaya who had seized the throne of Burma.

Bangkok is built on unstable land, much of it below sea-level, and floods used to regularly afflict the capital. The most serious were in 1983 when 450 sq km of the city was submerged. Like Venice, Bangkok is sinking by over 10 cm a year in some areas.

Old City and around ⊜🐡🐡💭⛰️😊🐡 ➤ pp83-97

Filled with palaces and temples the Old City is the ancient heart of Bangkok. These days it is the premium destination for the Thai capital's visitors and controversial plans are afoot to change it into a 'tourist zone'. This would strip the area of the usual chaotic charm that typifies Bangkok, moving out the remaining poor people who live in the area and creating an ersatz, gentrified feel.

Wat Pho

Wat Phra Chetuphon (Wat Pho)

ⓘ *Entrance on the south side, www.watpho.com. Daily 0900-1700. ฿20.*

Wat Phra Chetuphon, or Wat Pho, is the largest and most famous temple in Bangkok. The 'Temple of the Reclining Buddha' was built in 1781 and houses one of the largest reclining Buddhas in the country. The soles of the Buddha's feet are decorated with mother-of-pearl, displaying the 108 auspicious signs of the Buddha. The bustling grounds of the wat contains more than 1000 bronze images, mostly rescued from the ruins of Ayutthaya and Sukhothai, while the bot houses the ashes of Rama I. The bot is enclosed by two galleries which house 394 seated bronze Buddha images. Around the exterior base of the bot are marble reliefs telling the story of the abduction and recovery of Ram's wife Seeda from the second section of the *Ramakien* (see p73), as adapted in the Thai poem, 'The Maxims of King Ruang'.

One of Wat Pho's biggest attractions is its role as a respected centre of traditional Thai massage. Thousands of tourists, powerful Thai politicians, businessmen and military officers come here to escape the tensions of modern life. The Burmese destroyed most medical texts when they sacked Ayutthaya in 1776 but, in 1832, to help preserve the ancient medical art, Rama III had what was known about Thai massage inscribed onto a series of stones, which were then set into the walls of Wat Pho. ▲▲ *p93*.

Khaosan Road

Wat Phra Kaeo and Grand Palace

ⓘ *Main entrance is the Viseschaisri Gate, Na Phralan Rd, T02-2220094, www.palaces.thai.net. Ticket office daily 0830-1130 and 1300-1530 except Buddhist holidays when Wat Phra Kaeo is free but the rest of the palace is closed. Tickets ฿250, including a free guidebook to the palace (with plan) plus admission to the Coin Pavilion and to the Vimanmek Palace in the Dusit area (see p80). No photography allowed inside the bot. All labels in Thai. Free guided tours in English throughout the day; personal audio guides in several languages ฿100 (2 hrs). No shorts, short skirts, singlets, sleeveless shirts, flip flops or sandals; plastic shoes and trousers are available for hire near the entrance.*

The Grand Palace is situated on the banks of the Chao Phraya River and is the most spectacular – some might say 'gaudy' – collection of buildings in Bangkok. The complex, which began life in 1782, covers an area of over 1½ sq km and the architectural plan is almost identical to that of the Royal Palace in the former capital of Ayutthaya.

The buildings of greatest interest are clustered around **Wat Phra Kaeo**, or the **Temple of the Emerald Buddha** (see p74). The glittering brilliance of sunlight bouncing off the coloured glass mosaic exterior of Wat Phra Kaeo creates a gobsmacking initial impression for visitors to the complex. Built by Rama I in imitation of the royal chapel in Ayutthaya, Wat Phra Kaeo was the first of the buildings within the Grand Palace complex to be constructed. While it was being erected, the king lived in a small wooden building in one corner of the palace compound.

The ubosoth is raised on a marble platform with a frieze of gilded garudas holding nagas running round the base. Mighty, bronze singhas (lions) act as door guardians. The inlaid mother-of-pearl door panels date from Rama I's reign (late 18th century) while the doors are watched over by Chinese door guardians riding on lions. Inside the temple, the Emerald Buddha peers down on the gathered throng from a lofty, illuminated position above a large golden altar. Facing the Buddha on three sides are dozens of other gilded Buddha images, depicting the enlightenment of the Buddha when he subdues the evil demon Mara, the final temptation of the Buddha and the subjugation of evil spirits.

Around the walls of the shaded **cloister** that encompasses Wat Phra Kaeo, is a continuous mural depicting the *Ramakien* (see p73). There are 178 sections in all, which were first painted during the reign of King Rama I but have since been restored.

Downtown Bangkok

To the north of the ubosoth on a raised platform is the **Royal Pantheon**, with gilded kinarees at the entrance. The Royal Pantheon is only open to the public once a year on Chakri Day, 6 April (the anniversary of the founding of the present Royal Dynasty). On the same terrace there are two gilt stupas built by King Rama I in commemoration of his parents. The **Phra Mondop** (library) was also built by Rama I to house the first revised Buddhist scriptural canon. To the west of the mondop is the large **Golden Stupa** or chedi, with its circular base, in Ceylonese style. To the north of the mondop is a model of Angkor Wat constructed during the reign of King Mongkut (1851-68) when Cambodia was under Thai control. To the north again from the Royal Pantheon is the **Supplementary Library** and two viharns – **Viharn Yod** and **Phra Nak**. The former is encrusted with pieces of Chinese porcelain.

To the south of Wat Phra Kaeo are the buildings of the **Grand Palace**. These are interesting for the contrast that they make with those of Wat Phra Kaeo. Walking out through the cloisters, on your left is the French-style **Boromabiman Hall**, which was completed during the reign of Rama VI. The **Amarinda Hall** has an impressive, airy interior, with chunky pillars and gilded thrones. The **Chakri Mahaprasart** (Palace Reception Hall) stands in front of a carefully manicured garden with topiary. It was built and lived in by King Chulalongkorn (Rama V) shortly after he had returned from a trip to Java and Singapore in 1876 – and it shows: the building is a rather unhappy amalgam of colonial and traditional Thai styles of architecture. Rama V found the overcrowded Grand Palace oppressive and after a visit to Europe in 1897 built himself a new home at Vimanmek (see p80) in Dusit where the present King, Bhumibol, lives in the Chitralada Palace. The Grand Palace is now only used for state occasions.

Next to the Chakri Mahaprasart is the raised **Dusit Hall**, a cool, airy building containing mother-of-pearl thrones. Near the Dusit Hall is a **museum** ① *0900-1600, ฿50*, which has information on the restoration of the Grand Palace, models of the Palace and many more Buddha images. There is also a collection of cannon, mainly supplied by London foundries.

Sanaam Luang and around

To the north of the Grand Palace, across Na Phralan Road, lies the large open space of the Pramane Ground (the Royal Cremation Ground), better known as **Sanaam Luang**. This area was originally used for the cremation of kings, queens and important princes. It is the place in Bangkok to eat charcoal-grilled dried squid and have your fortune told by the *mor duu* (seeing doctors), who sit in the shade of the tamarind trees along the inner ring of the southern footpath. Each *mor duu* has a 'James Bond case' – a black briefcase; having your fortune told costs around ฿30-60 or ฿100 for a full consultation.

North along Na Phrathat Road, on the river side of Sanaam Luang is **Wat Mahathat** (the Temple of the Great Relic) ① *0900-1700*, a temple famous as a meditation centre; walk under the archway marked 'Naradhip Centre for Research in Social Sciences' to reach the wat. At No 24 Maharaj Road a narrow *soi* (lane) leads down towards the river and a large daily **market** selling exotic herbal cures, amulets, clothes and food. At weekends, the market spills out onto the surrounding streets (particularly Phra Chan Road) and amulet sellers line the pavement, their magical and holy talismen carefully displayed.

Banglamphu
Northeast of the National Art Gallery is the district of Banglamphu and the legendary **Khaosan Road**, backpacker haunt and epicentre of Bangkok's travellers' culture.

Golden Mount and around
This area, to the east of the Old City, is where ancient Bangkok begins to give way to the modern thrust of the bewildering 21st-century city. Apart from the Golden Mount there's little reason to hang around here but with the area's history of demonstrations and cries for democracy, it beats a defining pulse in the hearts of most Thais. The Golden Mount itself (also known as the Royal Mount) is an impressive artificial hill nearly 80 m high. The climb to the top is exhausting but worth it for the fabulous views of Bangkok.

Chinatown ○ ↦ *p91*

South of the Old City, Chinatown covers the area from Charoen Krung (or New Road) down to the river. Few other places in Bangkok match Chinatown for atmosphere. The warren of alleys, lanes and tiny streets are cut through with an industrious hive of shops, temples and restaurants. Weird food, neatly arranged mountains of mechanical parts, gaudy temple architecture, gold, flowers and a constant frenetic bustle will lead to many hours of happy wandering. This is an area to explore on foot, getting lost in the many nooks and crannies.

Nakhon Kasem (Thieves' Market)
Nakhon Kasem, strictly speaking Woeng Nakhon Kasem (Thieves' Market), lies between Charoen Krung and Yaowarat Road, to the east of the khlong that runs parallel to Mahachai Road. Its boundaries are marked by archways. As its name suggests, this market used to be the centre for the fencing of stolen goods. It is not quite so colourful today but there remains a number of second-hand and antique shops, such as the Good Luck Antique Shop, which are worth a browse. Among other things, musical instruments, brass ornaments, antique (and not so antique) coffee grinders are all on sale here.

Wat Traimitr (Temple of the Golden Buddha)
① *Traimitr Rd, Chinatown. Daily 0900-1700. ฿20.*
The most celebrated example of the goldsmith's art in Thailand sits within Wat Traimitr (Temple of the Golden Buddha). The Golden Buddha is housed in a small, rather gaudy and unimpressive room. Although the leaflet offered to visitors says the 3 m-high, 700-year-old image is 'unrivalled in beauty', be prepared for disappointment: it's featureless. What makes it special, drawing large numbers of visitors each day, is that it is made of 5½ tonnes of solid gold. Apparently, when the East Asiatic Company was extending the port of Bangkok, they came across a huge stucco Buddha image, which they obtained permission to move.

Wat Arun

However, during the move in 1957, it fell from the crane and the stucco cracked to reveal a solid gold image. During the Ayutthayan period it was the custom to cover valuable Buddha images in plaster to protect them from the Burmese and this particular example had stayed that way for several centuries.

Thonburi and the khlongs 🏠▲🚌 ›› pp83-97

Thonburi is Bangkok's little-known alter ego. Few people cross the Chao Phraya to see this side of the city and, if they do, it is usually only to catch a glimpse from the seat of a speeding *hang yaaw* (long-tailed boat) and then climb the steps of **Wat Arun**. But Thonburi, during the reign of King Taksin, was once the capital of ancient Siam. King Rama I believed the other side of the river – present-day Bangkok – could be more easily defended from the Burmese and so, in 1782, he switched riverbanks.

Exploring the khlongs

One of the most enjoyable ways to see Bangkok is by boat – and particularly by the fast and noisy *hang yaaws*, powerful, lean machines that roar around the river and the khlongs at breakneck speed. There are innumerable tours around the khlongs of Thonburi taking in a number of sights which include the floating market, snake farm and Wat Arun. Boats go from the various piers located along the east bank of the Chao Phraya River. The route skirts past laden rice-barges, squatter communities on public land and houses overhanging the canals. On private tours the first stop is usually the **Floating Market** (Talaat Nam). This is now an artificial, ersatz gathering which exists purely for the tourist industry. The nearest functioning floating market is at Damnoen Saduak (see p82). ▲🚌 ›› *p93 and p94.*

Wat Arun

ⓘ *Daily 0830-1730. ฿20. Water-taxi (A1) from Tha Tien pier (at the end of Thai Wang Rd near Wat Pho) or from Tha Chang (at the end of Na Phralan near Wat Phra Kaeo).*
Facing Wat Pho across the Chao Phraya River is the famous Wat Arun (Temple of the Dawn). The wat stands 81 m high, making it the highest *prang* (tower) in Thailand. It was built in the early 19th century on the site of Wat Chaeng, the Royal Palace complex when Thonburi was briefly the capital of Thailand. Wat Chaeng housed the Emerald Buddha before the image

was transferred to Bangkok. It is said that King Taksin vowed to restore the wat after passing it one dawn. The *prang* is completely covered with fragments of Chinese porcelain and includes some delicate gold and black lacquered doors. The temple is really meant to be viewed from across the river; its scale and beauty can only be appreciated from a distance. The best view of Wat Arun is in the evening from the Bangkok side of the river when the sun sets behind the *prang*.

Dusit area

The present home of the Thai royal family and the administration is located north of Banglamphu in an area of wide, tree-lined boulevards and rationalized spaces, more in keeping with a European city. It is grand but lacks the usual bustling atmosphere found in the rest of Bangkok.

Vimanmek Palace

ⓘ *Just off Rachvithi Road, to the north of the National Assembly, T02-2811569, www.palaces. thai.net. Daily 0900-1600 (last tickets sold at 1500); admission by guided tour only, 1 hr. ฿50, ฿20 for children. Tickets to the Grand Palace include entrance to Vimanmek Palace. Dance shows 1030 and 1400. No shorts or short skirts; sarongs available for hire (฿100, refundable).*

The Vimanmek Palace is the largest golden teakwood mansion in the world, but don't expect to see huge expanses of polished wood – the building is almost entirely painted. It was built by Rama V in 1901 who was clearly taken with western style. It looks like a large Victorian hunting lodge and is filled with china, silver and paintings from all over the world (as well as some gruesome hunting trophies).

East of the Old City ⬤⬤⬤⬤⬤⬤⬤ » pp83-97, maps p81 and p88

Siam Square

A 10-minute walk east along Rama I Road is the biggest and busiest modern shopping area in the city, centred on a maze of tiny boutiques and a covered market known as Siam Square. Head to this area if you want to be at the apex of Thai youth culture and the biggest spread of shopping opportunities in the city. Whether you visit the hi-tech market at Panthip Plaza, the massive MBK complex, the host of upmarket stores at Siam Discovery, pure silk at Jim Thompson's House or the warren of tiny boutiques, you should leave with a big hole in your bank account. Thronged with young people, Siam Square plays host to Bangkok's burgeoning youth culture; weird, experimental fashions, Thai-style fast food and dozens of urban stylists keep the kids entertained. On the corner of Rama 1 and Phayathai Rd is **MBK**, Bangkok's largest indoor shopping area. Crammed with bargains and outlets of every description this is one of the Thai capital's most popular shopping spots.

Jim Thompson's House

ⓘ *Soi Kasemsan Song (2), opposite the National Stadium, Rama I Rd, www.jimthompson.com. Mon-Sat 0900-1630, ฿100, children ฿25 (profits to charity). Shoes must be removed before entering; walking barefoot around the house adds to the appreciation of the cool teak floorboards. Compulsory guided tours around the house and no photography allowed.*

Jim Thompson's House is an assemblage of traditional teak Northern Thai houses, some more than 200 years old, transported here and reassembled. Jim Thompson arrived in Bangkok as an intelligence officer attached to the United States' OSS (Office of Strategic Services) and then made his name by reinvigorating the Thai silk industry after the Second

World War. He disappeared mysteriously in the Malaysian jungle on 27 March 1967 but his silk industry continues to thrive. Jim Thompson chose this site for his house partly because a collection of silk weavers lived nearby on Khlong Saensaep. The house contains an eclectic collection of antiques from Thailand and China, with work displayed as though it was still his home. There is a sophisticated little café attached to the museum as well as a shop selling Jim Thompson products.

Silom and Patpong

Hi-tech, high-rise and clad in concrete and glass, Silom, south of Siam Square, is at the centre of booming Bangkok. Banks, international business and many media companies are based in this area, as is the heart of Bangkok's gay community. Stylish, tacky and sweaty, head down the length of Silom for a full slice of contemporary Bangkok life.

The seedier side of Bangkok life has sadly always been a crowd-puller to the western tourist. Most people flock to the red-light district of **Patpong**, which runs along two lanes (Patpong 1 and 2) linking Silom to Surawong. These streets were transformed from a row of 'tea houses' (brothels serving local clients) into a high-tech lane of go-go bars in 1969 when an American made a major investment. Patpong 1 is the larger and more active of the streets, with a famous market running down the middle at night, and is largely recognized as the eponymous home of Bangkok's notorious girly shows, complete with acrobatic vaginas. Patpong 2 supports cocktail bars, pharmacies and clinics for STDs, as well as a few go-go bars. There are also a few restaurants and bars here. Patpong is also home to a night market infamous for its line in copied designer handbags, some of which are better made than the originals.

Bangkok East of the Old City

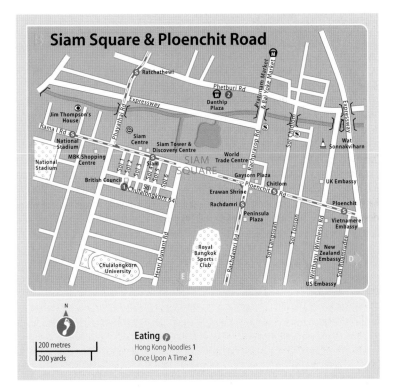

Eating
Hong Kong Noodles **1**
Once Upon A Time **2**

200 metres
200 yards

Damnoen Saduak floating market

Sukhumvit Road

With the **Skytrain** running its length, Sukhumvit Road, east of Siam Square and Silom, has developed into Bangkok's most vibrant strip. Shopping centres, girlie bars, some of the city's best hotels and awesome places to eat have been joined by futuristic nightclubs. The grid of sois that run off the main drag are home to a variety of different communities, including Arab, African and Korean, as well as throngs of westerners.

Around Bangkok

Damnoen Saduak floating market

ⓘ *109 km west of Bangkok, 1½ hrs by bus no 78 from the Southern bus terminal in Thonburi (T02-4355031 for booking) every 40 mins from 0600 (฿30-49); ask the conductor to drop you at Thanarat Bridge in Damnoen Saduak, then either walk down the lane (1½ km) that leads to the market or take a river taxi, ฿10, or a minibus, ฿2. Tour companies also visit the floating market.*
Damnoen Saduak floating market in Ratchaburi Province is (almost) the real thing. Sadly, it is becoming increasingly like the Floating Market in Thonburi (see p79), although it does still function as a legitimate market. Aim to get to Damnoen Saduak between 0800 and 1000, as the market winds down after 1000, leaving only trinket stalls. There are a number of floating markets in the maze of khlongs – Ton Khem, Hia Kui and Khun Phithak – and it is best to hire a *hang yaaw* to explore them (about ฿300 per hr; agree the price before setting out).

Chatuchak Weekend Market

ⓘ *Just off Phahonyothin Road. Take a Skytrain to Mo chit station or Chatuchak Park and Kampaeng Phet Metro stations.*
Chatuchak is a huge conglomeration of 9000 stallholders spread over an area of 12 ha selling virtually everything under the sun. There are antique stalls, basket stalls, textile sellers, carvers and painters along with the usual array of fish sellers, vegetable hawkers, butchers and candlestick makers. At the weekend, the market is officially open from 0900 to 1800 (although in fact it begins earlier around 0700). It's best to go early in the day. Beware of

Sleeping

From humble backstreet digs through to opulent extravagence, Bangkok has an incredible diverse range of hotels, guesthouses and serviced apartments. The best value bargains are often to be had in the luxury sector – you'll find some of the best hotels in the world here, many of which offer their rooms at knock-down prices.

Old City and Banglamphu *p74, map p71*

The guesthouses of Khaosan are cheapish but far more expensive than what you'll find in other parts of the country. Note that rooms facing on to Khaosan Rd tend to be very noisy; the sois off the main road are often quieter, such as Soi Chana Songkhran or Soi Rambutri. Sri Ayutthaya, north of Banglamphu, is emerging as an 'alternative' area for budget travellers. It is a central location, with restaurants and foodstalls nearby, but does not suffer the overcrowding and sheer pandemonium of Khaosan Rd.

A-B Buddy Lodge, 265 Khaosan Rd, T02-6294477, www.buddylodge.com. The luxury pad of Khaosan Rd, Buddy Lodge dominates the far end of a smart shopping arcade. The room decor is quietly opulent, with fridge and TV. There is also a Japanese restaurant, coffee shop and a pool.

Bangkok Listings

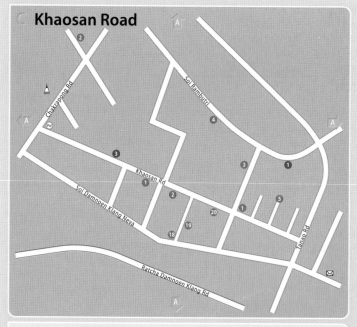

Khaosan Road

Not to scale

Sleeping
Buddy Lodge **5**
Chart Guesthouse **2**
D & D Inn **1**
Sawasdee Bangkok Inn **18**
Sawasdee Krungthep Inn **19**

Siam Oriental **20**
Tuptim B&B **4**

Eating
Bai Bau **1**
D'Rus **3**

Bars & clubs
Lava Club **1**
Sawasdee House **2**
Susie's Pub **3**

A-B Trang Hotel, 99/1 Visutkaset Rd, T02-28221414, www.tranghotelbangkok.com. A/c, restaurant, pool. Friendly mid-range hotel and recommended by regular visitors to Bangkok. It opened way back in 1962 but is still a good establishment at this price.

C-D D&D Inn, 68-70 Khaosan Rd, T02-6290526, ddinn@hotmail.com. Large, purpose-built hotel with lift, tidy a/c rooms, and hot showers. The small, often deserted, swimming pool on the roof offers a fine view, and the small bar alongside makes this an excellent place to start or end the day.

C-D Tuptim Bed and Breakfast, 82 Rambutri St, T02-629153536, info@tuptimb-b.com. Some a/c and en suite shower, but even the shared facilities are exceptionally clean, breakfast included. Very friendly staff.

C-E Chart Guest House, 62 Khaosan Rd, T02-2820171. Very clean airy rooms, cosmopolitan feel, with winding staircase and retro-style bar with movies. Friendly, English-speaking staff.

C-E Siam Oriental, 190 Khaosan Rd, T02-6290312, siam_oriental@hotmail.com. Fine, clean rooms (some a/c), smart tiled corridors, and very friendly staff. Internet facilities downstairs, along with a very popular restaurant. Free safety box.

C-F Baan Sabai, 12 Soi Rongmai, T02-6291599, baansabai@hotmail.com. A large, colonial-style building with a green pillared entrance in front. Although it is not very expensive, it is not the typical backpacker's scene. Rooms are simple but large and airy. Storage is available at ฿10 per bag/suitcase. Occasionally local Thai bands are invited to play here.

C-F Sawasdee Bangkok Inn, 126/2 Khaosan Rd, T02-2801251, sawasdeehotel@yahoo.com. Good value, clean, fair-sized rooms with wooden floors and some with a/c. A vibrant, popular bar, and friendly staff. Free safety deposit, left luggage (฿10/day).

C-F Sawasdee Krungthep Inn, 30 Praathi Rd, T02-6290072. Clean and simple rooms, all with cable TV, lively communal atmosphere. Family rooms available.

D-E My House, 37 Phra Arthit Soi Chana Songkram, T02-2829263. Helpful and friendly management, rooms are very clean and the place maintains excellent standards of cleanliness. Popular, good travel service (minibus to airport every hr).

D-F Chai's House, 49/4-8 Chao Fa Soi Rongmai, last house down Soi Rambutri, so away from the competition, T02-2814901. Some a/c, friendly atmosphere. Rooms are in traditional Thai style, with wood panelling. They vary in size but are clean and the a/c rooms are good value. Balconies and orchid-filled restaurant make it a quiet and relaxing place.

D-F Pra Suri Guesthouse, 85/1 Soi Pra Suri (off Dinso Rd), 5 mins east of Khaosan Rd not far from the Democracy Monument, T/F02-2801428. Fan, restaurant, own bathrooms (no hot water), clean, spacious and quiet, very friendly and helpful family-run travellers' guesthouse with all the services to match.

D-F Tavee, 83 Sri Ayutthaya Rd, Soi 14, T02-2825983. Restaurant, a quiet, relaxed, and respectable place with a small garden and a number of fish tanks. Friendly management – a world away from the chaos of Khaosan Rd. The Tavee family keep the rooms and shared bathrooms immaculately clean and are a good source of information for travellers. Dorms are also available for ฿80 per night. This place has been operating since 1985 and has managed to maintain a very high standard.

E-F Apple 2 Guesthouse, 11 Phra Sumen Rd, T02-2811219. Quite hard to find: if you turn off Phra Arthit Rd, take the soi opposite Baan Chaophraya. If turning off the Phra Sumen Rd, take Trok Kaichee (soi). Very friendly management (run by the same woman for 20 years), this place, with its homely feel and quiet, clean rooms in an old wooden house, remains a firm favourite.

E-F Home and Garden, 16 Samphraya Rd (Samsen 3), T02-2801475. Away from the

Budget busters

LL Metropolitan, 27 South Sathorn Rd T02-6253333, www.metropolitan.como.bz. From its funky members/guest-only bar through to the beautiful, contemporary designer rooms and the awesome restaurants (**Glow** and **Cyan**) this is one of Bangkok's coolest hotels. Bargains can be had when it's quiet.

LL-L Sheraton Grande Sukhumvit, 250 Sukhumvit, T02-6530333, www.sheratongrandesukhumvit.com. Superbly managed business and leisure hotel. Service, food and facilities are impeccable. The roof top garden is an exotic delight and the spa offers some of the best massage in town. The **Rossini** and **Basil** restaurants are also top class. Great location and, if you can afford it, the best place to stay on Sukhumvit.

LL-L Sukhothai, 13/3 South Sathorn Rd, T02-2870222, www.sukhothai.com. A/c, restaurants, pool, beautiful rooms and excellent service. The sleek design might be termed Thai postmodern and it has become a favourite place for the wealthy, hipster crowd, although it is now challenged by the nearby Metropolitan (see above).

L Banyan Tree, 21/100 South Sathorn Rd, T02-6791200, www.banyantree.com. A/c, restaurant, pool. Famous for its luxury spa all rooms are suites with a good location and set back from busy Sathorn Rd.

---

main concentration of guesthouses, down a quiet soi (although the roosters tend to ensure an early start for light sleepers), a small house in a delightful leafy com- pound and with a homely atmosphere. The rooms are a fair size with large windows, some face onto a balcony. Friendly owner, excellent value.

Thonburi and the khlongs *p79*

C-E The Artists Club, 61 Soi Tiem Boon Yang, T02-8620056. Some a/c, run by an artist, this is a guesthouse-cum-studio-cum-gallery buried deep in the khlongs with clean rooms. It makes a genuine alternative with concerts, drawing lessons and other cultural endeavours.

East of the Old City *p80, maps p81, p88 and p86*

In all Bangkok, the Silom area most resembles a western city, with its international banks, skyscrapers, first-class hotels, shopping malls, pizza parlours and pubs. It is also home to one of the world's best-known red-light districts – Patpong.

Sukhumvit is now one of Bangkok's premier centres of accommodation and is a great place for restaurants and nightlife with several good bars and clubs. This is also a good area for shopping for furniture: antique and reproduction.

Soi Ngam Duphli to the east is much the smaller of Bangkok's two main centres of guesthouse accommodation. This area has seen better days but still makes a viable alternative for budget travellers.

A-E New Road Guest House, 1216/1 Charoen Krung Rd, jyskbkk@loxinfo.co.th This Danish-owned place provides a range of accommodation from de luxe rooms to hammocks on the roof. A restaurant serves inexpensive Thai dishes and there's a free fruit buffet breakfast. A bar provides a pool table and darts and there's a small outdoor sitting area.

B-D Atlanta, 78 Sukhumvit Soi 2, T02-2521650, www.theatlantahotel.bizland. com. Basic a/c or fan-cooled rooms. A good large pool and children's pool. Good restaurant (see Eating, p). Prides itself on its literary, peaceful atmosphere. Appears to be the cheapest and is certainly the most appealing hotel in the area at this price, particularly suited for families, writers and dreamers, 24-hr email available.

B-D Charlie's House, Soi Saphan Khu, T02-6798330, www.charlieshouse thailand.com. Helpful owners create a friendly atmosphere and the rooms are carpeted and very clean. This is probably the best place in Soi Ngam Duphli if you are willing to pay that little bit extra. There is a restaurant and coffee corner with good food at reasonable prices.

🍴 Eating

Bangkok is one of the greatest food cities on earth. You could spend an entire lifetime finding the best places to eat in this city that seems totally obsessed with its tastebuds. Many restaurants, especially Thai ones, close early (between 2200 and 2230). Street food can be found across the city and a rice or noodle dish, will cost ฿25-40 instead of a minimum of ฿50 in the restaurants. Some of the best can be found on the roads between Silom and Surawong Rd, Soi Suanphlu off South Sathorn Rd, down Soi Somkid, next to Ploenchit Rd, or opposite on Soi Tonson.

Old City and Banglamphu *p74, map p71*

Travellers' food such as banana pancakes and muesli is available in the guesthouse/ travellers' hotel areas (see above). However, the Thai food sold along Khaosan Rd is some of the worst and least authentic in town, watered down to suit the tastebuds of unadventurous backpackers.

🍴🍷 D'Rus, Khaosan Rd, T02-2810155. It might not look like much from the outside with its bland decor punctuated by Van Gogh prints and slow-moving telly-addict waiters, but the Thai/western food is some of the best in the area.

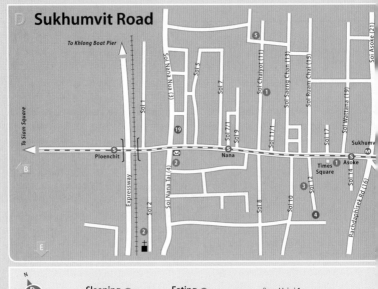

Sleeping 🛏
Atlanta & Restaurant 2
Sheraton Grande
 Sukhumvit 1

Eating 🍴
Cabbages & Condoms 4
Le Dalat Indochine 7
Nasir al-Masri 19

Rang Mahal 1

Bars & clubs 🍸
Bed Supper Club 1

Ψ **Bai Bau**, 146 Rambutri St. Very tasty Thai food, good value in a quiet corner, your best bet for a relaxed authentic meal in a friendly environment.

East of the Old City *p80, maps p81, p88 and p86*

ΨΨΨ-ΨΨ **Anna's Café**, 118 Silom Soi Sala Daeng, T02-6320619, daily 1100-2200. Great Thai-cum-fusion restaurant in a villa off Silom Rd named after Anna of *King & I* fame. Some classic Thai dishes like *larb, nua yaang* and *som tam* along with fusion dishes and western desserts such as apple crumble and banoffee pie.

ΨΨΨ-ΨΨ **Cyan**, Metropolitan, 27 South Sathorn Rd, T02-6253333, www.metropolitan. como.bz. With a menu concocted by one of Asia's leading chefs, Amanda Gale, Cyan is a scintillating dining experience the like of which is not matched in the entire Thai capital. This is international cuisine of the highest order: the almond-fed Serrano ham and Japanese wagyu beef are highlights in a stunning menu. Strangely ignored by wealthy Thais, this is a restaurant at the cutting edge of Bangkok eating, miles ahead of the competition.

ΨΨΨ-ΨΨ **Glow**, Metropolitan, 27 South Sathorn Rd. An organic lunch bar. Feast on spirulina noodles and tuna sashimi, all washed down with fresh beetroot and ginger juice.

ΨΨΨ-ΨΨ **Once Upon a Time**, 32 Phetburi Soi 17 (opposite Panthip Plaza), T02-2528629. Open for lunch and dinner, Tue-Sun. Up-market and inventive Thai cuisine including seafood soufflé in coconut and more traditional dishes such as a delectable duck curry.

ΨΨΨ-ΨΨ **Rang Mahal**, Rembrandt Hotel, Sukhumvit Soi 18, T02-2617107. Best Indian food in town, very popular with the Indian community and spectacular views from the rooftop position, sophisticated, elegant and expensive.

ΨΨΨ-ΨΨ **Zanotti**, 21/2 Sala Daeng Colonnade, Silom Soi Sala Daeng, T02-6360002. Open daily for lunch and

Bangkok Listings

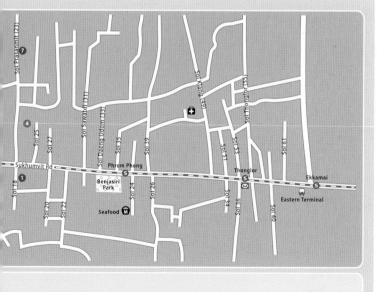

Jools **2**
Ministry of Sound **3**
Narcissus **4**
Q **5**

dinner. Wide-ranging menu including pizza, pasta, risotto dishes, meat and poultry, all served in a renovated, early 20th-century building.

♦♦-♦ **Le Dalat Indochine**, 47/1 Sukhumvit Soi 23, T02-6617967, daily for lunch and dinner. Reputed to serve the best Vietnamese food in Bangkok. Not only is the food good, but the ambience is satisfying too.

♦♦-♦ **Nasir al-Masri**, 4-6 Sukhumvit Soi Nana Nua, T02-2535582. Reputedly the best Arabic food in Bangkok, falafel, taboulie, houmous, frequented by lots of Arabs who come for a taste of home.

♦ **Cabbages and Condoms**, Sukhumvit Soi 12 (around 400 m down the soi). Population and Community Development Association (PDA) Thai restaurant so all proceeds go to this charity. Eat rice in the Condom Room, drink in the Vasectomy Room. Good *tom yam khung* and honey-roast chicken, curries all rather similar, good value. Very attractive courtyard area decorated with fairy lights.

♦ **Hong Kong Noodles**, Chulalongkorn 64. Packed with university students eating the stupendously good *bamii muu deang kio kung sai naam* (noodle soup with red pork and stuffed pasta with shrimp).

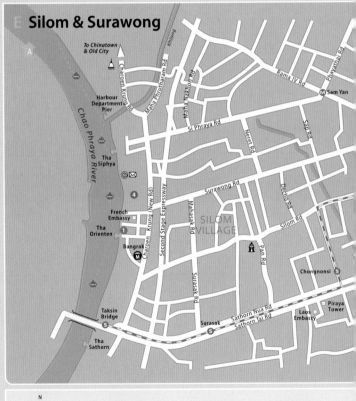

Silom & Surawong

To Chinatown & Old City

Chao Phraya River

Harbour Department Pier

Tha Siphya

Charoen Krung Rd

Maha Phruttharam Rd

Maha Nakhon Rd

Si Phraya Rd

Neret Rd

Rama IV Rd

Phayathai Rd

Sam Yan

Sap Rd

French Embassy

Tha Orienten

Bangrak

Charoen Krung (New Rd)

Second Stage Expressway

Surawong Rd

Mahasak Rd

Surasak Rd

SILOM VILLAGE

Pan Rd

Silom Rd

Decho Rd

Chongnonsi

Taksin Bridge

Surasak

Sathorn Nua Rd

Sathorn Tai Rd

Laos Embassy

Piraya Tower

Tha Sathorn

N

300 metres
300 yards

Sleeping 😴
Banyan Tree 1
Charlie's House 2
Metropolitan & Cyan & Glow Restaurants 3
New Road Guesthouse 4
Sukhothai 5

Eating 🍴
Anna's Café 1
Zanotti 2

🎵 Bars and clubs

The city has some fantastic nightlife – everything from boozy pubs through to uber-trendy clubs. You can listen to decent Jazz and Blues or get into the latest European DJs spinning the hippest beats.

Groovy Map's *Bangkok by Night* (฿120) includes information on bars and dance clubs, the city's gay scene, as well as music venues and drinking spots. Check the Bangkok listing magazines for the latest information on who's spinning and what's opening.

Old City and Banglamphu *p74, map p71*

Lava Club, 249 Khaosan Rd, T02-2816565, daily 2000-0100. Playing a mixture of hip-hop, house and funky tunes, this large and deeply cavernous venue looks not unlike a heavy metal club, decked out as it is in nothing but black with red lava running down the walls and floors.

Sawasdee House, 147 Soi Rambutree, Chakrapong Rd, T02-2818138. Seriously chilled, this is a great place to relax at the end of the day with its airy atmosphere, high ceilings, spaciously arranged and

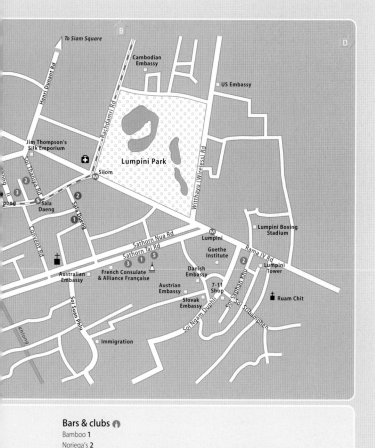

Bars & clubs 🎵
Bamboo **1**
Noriega's **2**
White **3**

comfortable chairs, wooden floorboards, glowing lanterns and friendly staff.

Saxophone, 3/8 Victory Monument, Phayathai Rd, Golden Mount, daily 1800-0300. Series of alternating house bands, including jazz, blues, ska and soul. Another place with a long-standing – and deserved – reputation for delivering the music goods.

Susie's Pub, turn right between Lava Club and Lek GH, 2000-0200. This is the place for a more alternative Thai experience of what it is to go clubbing down Khaosan, as its always absolutely heaving, more with locals than travellers. Top decibel thumping local tunes and all sorts of flashing neon outside announce its presence, but while it might be easy to find, its not always such a simple thing to get in, as there's a seething mass of bodies to negotiate from relatively early on right up until closing.

East of the Old City *p80, maps p81, p88 and p86.*

The greatest concentration of bars in this area are to be found in the 'red light' districts of Patpong.

Bamboo Bar, Oriental Hotel, 48 Oriental Av, T02-2360400. Sun-Thu 1100-0100, Fri-Sat 1100-0200. One of the best jazz venues in Bangkok, classy and cosy with good food and pricey drinks – but worth it if you like your jazz and can take the hit.

Bed Supper Club, 26 Sukhumvit Soi 11, T02-6513537, www.bedsupperclub.com, daily 2000-0200. A futuristic white pod, filled with funky beats, awesome cocktails, superb food, gorgeous designer furniture and hordes of Bangkok's beautiful people. Can be overbearingly stuck-up and incredibly pretentious but is still one of the best spots in Asia to strut your stuff.

Jools Bar, 21/3 Nana Tai, Sukhumvit Soi 4, daily 0900-0100. A favourite watering hole for Brits. Serves classic English food.

Ministry of Sound (MOS), 2 Sukhumvit Soi 12, T02-2295850-3, Mon-Thu and Sun 2200-0200, Fri-Sat 2130-0200. DJs from London and Hong Kong as well as local talent. Music varies through the week. Mon is vodka jelly party, Wed is 70s and 80s night and Sun is urban night.

Narcissus, 112 Sukhumvit Soi 23, T02-2582549, daily 2100-0200. The classy, art deco Narcissus was awarded Metro's Best Nighclub award in 2001. The music here is trance, house and techno and the clientele are office types trying to keep their youth.

Noriega's Bar, 106/108 Soi 4, Silom Rd, T02-2332814, daily 1800-0200. Words like minimalist and Zen spring to mind in this relatively quiet watering hole on an otherwise bustling strip. Live acts on Sat, Sun and Mon nights help cater for the guys and gals this place targets with its promise of booze, broads, bites and blues.

Q Bar, 34 Sukhumvit Soi 11, T02-2523274, www.qbarbangkok.com, daily 1800-0200. Housed in a modern building, it is the reincarnation of photographer David Jacobson's bar of the same name in Ho Chi Minh City. Good beats, great drinks menu and sophisticated layout. Live acid jazz on Sun.

White Bar, 114/15 Silom Soi 4, T01-4823520 (mob), www.whitebar bangkok.com, daily 2000-0200. Plays contemporary dance music, with good guest DJs on Fri and Sat from the UK, New Zealand, Australia and the US. Bit of a concrete bunker, but they dish out very generous cocktail measures.

Gay and lesbian bars and clubs

The hub of Bangkok's gay scene can be found among the clubs, bars and restaurants on Silom, sois 2 and 4. If it's your first time in Thailand, **Utopia Tours**, www.utopia-tours.com, are specialists in organizing gay travel, including tours of Bangkok. Its website also contains a huge amount of listings, contacts and insights for gay and lesbian travellers.

Balcony , 86-8 Silom Soi 4, daily 1700-0200. Cute bar where you can hang out on the venues terraces watching the action below.

DJ Station, Silom Soi 2, www.dj-station.com, daily 2200-0200, ฿100 admission. This is the busiest and largest club on a busy Soi. 3 floors of pumping beats and flamboyant disco. Essential and recommended.

Dog Days, 100/2-6 Phra Arthit Rd, Banglamphu, daily 1000-1500, 1700-2400. Art bar, serving a limited menu of decent food and drinks. A favourite for *tom-dees* (lesbians).

Kitchenette, Duchess Plaza, Sukhumvit Soi 55, Mon-Sat 1700-2400. Chilled bar, with an older *tom-dee* scene. Live folk music Fri and Sat.

🎭 Entertainment

Thai Boxing

Thai boxing is both a sport and a means of self-defence and was first developed during the Ayutthaya period, 1351-1767. It differs from western boxing in that contestants are allowed to use almost any part of their body. There are 2 main boxing stadiums in Bangkok: **Lumpini**, Rama IV Rd, near Lumpini Park, T02-2514303, and **Rachdamnern Stadium**, Rachdamnern Nok Av, T02-2814205. At Lumpini, boxing nights are Tue and Fri (1830-2300) and Sat (1700); tickets cost up to and over ฿1000 for a ringside seat (depending on the card); cheaper seats cost from about ฿150 (in reality, standing) with so-called second-class seats at ฿400. At Rachdamnern Stadium, boxing nights are Mon and Wed (1800-2200), Thu (1700 and 2100), Sun (1600 and 2000), seats ฿160-500.

🎉 Festivals and events

Mar-Apr International Kite Festival is held at Sanaam Luang when kite fighting and demonstrations by kite-flyers take place.

Apr Songkran. The beginning of the Buddhist New Year. Marked by excessive and exuberant water-throwing sessions in parts of Bangkok.

🛍 Shopping

From flowers and fruit sold at energetic all-night markets through to original and fake Louis Vuitton, Bangkok has the lot. Most street stalls will try and fleece you, so be prepared to shop around and bargain hard. Arcades target the wealthier shopper and are dominated by brand-name goods and designer wear, although branded, western goods are often cheaper back home. Department stores tend to be fixed price. Most shops do not open until 1000-1100.

Sukhumvit Rd and the sois to the north are lined with shops and stalls, especially around the Ambassador and Landmark hotels. Many tailors and made-to-measure shoe shops are to be found in this area. Higher up on Sukhumvit Rd particularly around Soi 49 are various antique and furnishing shops.

Antiques

Jim Thompson's, Surawong Rd, www.jimthomspon.com, for a range of antiques, wooden artefacts, furnishings and carpets.

L'Arcadia, 12/2 Sukhumvit Soi 23, Burmese antiques, beds, ceramics, doors, good quality and prices are fair.

River City, a shopping complex next to the Royal Orchid Sheraton Hotel houses a large number of the more expensive antique shops and is an excellent place to start. Reputable shops here include **Verandah** on the top floor, the **Tomlinson Collection Room**, nos 427-428, and **Acala Room**, 312, for Tibetan and Nepalese art.

Clothes and tailoring

Bangkok's tailors are skilled at copying anything, either from fashion magazines or from a piece of your own clothing. Always request a fitting, ask to see a finished garment, ask for a price in writing and pay as small a deposit as possible. Tailors are concentrated along Silom, Sukhumvit and Ploenchit rds and on Gaysorn Sq.

Cheap designer wear is available just about everywhere, and especially in tourist areas like Patpong and Sukhumvit. Note that the less you pay, generally, the more likely that the dyes will run, shirts will downsize after washing, and buttons will eject themselves at will.

Kai Boutique, 4th floor of Times Square. This building is worth visiting for those interested in what the best designers in Thailand are doing.

Vipavee, 1st floor of The Emporium at Sukhumvit Soi 24 (there are lots of other places here as well), for unique funky designer clothes of Indian inspiration.

Handicrafts

Cocoon, 3rd floor, Gaysorn Plaza. Here traditional Thai objects have been transformed by altering the design slightly and using bright colours. Great for unusual and fun gifts.

Jewellery

Thailand has become the world's largest gem-cutting centre and it is an excellent place to buy both gems and jewellery. The best buy of the native precious stones is the sapphire. Modern jewellery is well designed and of a high quality. Always insist on a certificate of authenticity and a receipt.

Ban Mo, on Pahurat Rd, north of Memorial Bridge, is the centre of the gem business although there are shops in all the tourist areas particularly on Silom Rd near the intersection with Surasak Rd, eg **Rama Gems** at no987. **Uthai Gems**, 28/7 Soi Ruam Rudi, off Ploenchit Rd, just east of Witthayu Rd, is recommended, as is **P Jewellery** (Chantaburi), 9/292 Ramindra Rd, Anusawaree Bangkhan, T02-5221857.

For western designs, **Living Extra** and **Yves Joaillier** are to be found on the 3rd floor of the Charn Issara Tower, 942 Rama IV Rd. **Jewellery Trade Centre** (aka Galleria Plaza), next door to the Holiday Inn Crowne Plaza on the corner of Silom Rd and Surasak Rd contains a number of gem dealers and jewellery shops on the ground floor. **Tabtim Dreams** at Unit 109 is a good place to buy loose gems.

Markets

The markets in Bangkok are an excellent place to browse, take photographs and pick up bargains.

Bangrak Market, south of the General Post Office, near the river and the Shangri-La Hotel, sells exotic fruit, clothing, seafood and flowers.

Khaosan Rd Market (if it can be called such), close to Banglamphu Market, is geared to the needs and desires of the foreign tourist: CDs and cassettes, batik shirts, leather goods and so on.

Nakhon Kasem, known as the Thieves' Market, in the heart of Chinatown, see p78, houses a number of 'antique' shops selling brassware, old electric fans and woodcarvings (tough bargaining recommended, and don't expect everything to be genuine).

Pahurat Indian Market, a small slice of India in Thailand, with mounds of sarongs, batiks, buttons and bows.

Pak Khlong Market is a wholesale market selling fresh produce, orchids and cut flowers and is situated near the Memorial Bridge on Tri Phet Rd. An exciting place to visit at night when the place is a hive of activity.

Patpong Market, arranged down the middle of Patpong Rd, linking Silom and Surawong rds, opens up about 1700 and is geared to tourists. Bargain hard.

Tewes Market, near the National Library, is a photographer's dream; a daily market, selling flowers and plants.

Weekend Market is the largest and is at Chatuchak Park (see p82).

Silk

Silk varies greatly in quality. Generally, the heavier the weight the more expensive the fabric. One-ply is the lightest and cheapest (about ฿200 per metre), 4-ply the heaviest and most expensive (about ฿300-400 per m). Silk also comes in 3 grades: Grade 1 is the finest and smoothest and comes from the inner part of the cocoon. There is also 'hard' and 'soft' silk, soft being rather more expensive. There are a number of specialist silk shops at the top of Surawong Rd (near Rama IV) and a number of shops along the bottom half of Silom Rd (towards Charoen Krung) and in the Siam Centre on Rama I Rd.

Anita Thai Silk, 294/4-5 Silom Rd, slightly more expensive than some, but the extensive range makes it worth a visit.

Cabbages and Condoms, Sukhumvit Soi 12 and Raja Siam, Sukhumvit Soi 23. Village-made silks.

Jagtar, 37 Sukhumvit Soi 11, has some lovely silk curtain fabrics as well as cushion covers in unusual shades and other accessories made from silk. Originality means prices are high.

Jim Thompson's, top of Surawong Rd, www.jimthompson.com, daily 0900-2100. Famous silk shop which is expensive, but has the best selection.

Shopping malls

The Emporium, on Sukhumvit Soi 24, daily 1000-2200, (directly accessible from BTS Phrom Phong Station) is an enormous place with many clothes outlets as well as CD and book shops, designer shops and more.

Mah Boonkhrong Centre (MBK) on the corner of Phayathai and Rama 1, is long-established and downmarket and packed full of bargains with countless small shops and stalls.

Panthip Plaza, Phetburi Rd, opposite Amari Watergate, daily 1000-2000. A large covered hi-tech market.

Peninsula Plaza, between the Hyatt Erawan and Regent hotels, is considered one of the smarter shopping plazas.

Siam Discovery Centre (Siam Tower), 6 storeys of fashion across the road from Siam Sq, is more sophisticated than MBK and you are unlikely to pick up many cut-price goods. All the top designers have a presence here.

Siam Square, at the intersection of Phayathai and Rama I rds. For teenage trendy western clothing, bags, belts, jewellery and some antique shops.

▲ Activities and tours

Boat tours

Either book a tour at your hotel or go to one of the piers and organize your own trip. The most frequented piers are located between the Oriental Hotel and the Grand Palace, or under Taksin Bridge (which marks the end of the Skytrain line). The pier just to the south of the Royal Orchid Sheraton Hotel is recommended. Organizing your own trip gives greater freedom to stop and start when the mood takes you. It is best to go in the morning (0700).

City tours

Bangkok has innumerable tour companies that can take visitors virtually anywhere. If there is not a tour to fit your bill – most run the same range of tours – many companies will produce a customized one for you, for a price. Most top hotels have their own tour desk and it is probably easiest to book there (arrange to be picked up from your hotel as part of the deal). Prices per person are about ฿400-800 for a half day, ฿1000-2000 for a full day (including lunch).

Tour operators

Asian Trails Ltd, 9th Floor, SG Tower, 161/1 Soi Mahadlek Luang 3, Rajdamri Rd, Lumpini, Pathumwan, T02-626 2000, www.asiantrails.com. Southeast Asia specialists.

Massage

Wat Pho. The centre is located at the back of the wat, on the opposite side from the entrance, T02-211-2974, www.watpho.com. The school offers body massage, body massage with herbs, and foot massage. The massage service is available 0800-1700 and the cost of a

30-min massage is ฿150 or ฿250 for an hour-long body massage. The herbal body massage costs ฿350. A foot massage is ฿250 for 45 mins. For westerners wishing to learn the art of traditional Thai massage, special 30-hr courses can be taken for ฿7,000, stretching over either 15 days (2 hrs per day) or 10 days (3 hrs per day). There is also a foot massage course at ฿3,600 which stretches over 15 hrs during 3 days.

⊖ Transport

Air

For airport information, see p70; for flight information, see Essentials p18.

Airline offices Air France, Vorawat Building, 20th Floor, 849 Silom Rd, T02-6351199. **Alitalia**, SSP Tower 3, 15th Floor, Unit 15A, 88 Silom Rd, T02-6341800. **American Airlines**, 518/5 Ploenchit Rd, T02-2511393. **Bangkok Airways**, Queen Sirikit National Convention Centre, New Rajdapisek Rd, Klongtoey, T02-2293456, www.bangkokair.com. **British Airways**, 14th Floor, Abdulrahim Place, 990 Rama 1V Rd, T02-6361747. **Canadian Airlines**, 6th Floor, Maneeya Building, 518/5 Ploenchit Rd, T02-2514521. **Cathay Pacific**, 11th Floor, Ploenchit Tower, 898 Ploenchit Rd, T02-2630606. **Continental Airlines**, CP Tower, 313 Silom Rd, T02-2310113. **Delta Airlines**, 7th Floor, Patpong Building, Surawong Rd, T02-2376838. **Eva Airways**, Green Tower, 2nd Floor, 425 Rama IV Rd, opposite Esso Head Office. **Finnair** 6th Floor, Vorawat Building, 849 Silom Rd, T02-6351234. **Gulf Air**, 12th Floor, Maneeya Building, 518 Ploenchit Rd, T02-2547931. **KLM**, 19th Floor, Thai Wah Tower 11, 21/133-134 South Sathorn Rd, T02-6791100. **Lufthansa**, 18th Floor, Q-House (Asoke), Sukhumvit Rd Soi 21, T02-2642400. **Qantas**, 14th Floor, Abdulrahim Place, 990 Rama IV Rd, T02-6361747. **SAS**, 8th Floor, Glas Haus I, Sukhumvit Rd Soi 25, T02-2600444. **Singapore Airlines**, 12th Floor, Silom Centre, 2 Silom Rd, T02-2365295/6. **Swiss**, 21st Floor Abdulrahim Place, 990 Rama 1V Rd, T02-6362160. **THAI**, 485 Silom Rd, T02-2343100. 89 Vibhavadi-Rangsit Rd, T02-5130121. **Vietnam Airlines**, 7th Floor, Ploenchit Centre, 2 Sukhumvit 2 Rd, T02-6569056.

Metro

The new **Metro**, www.bangkok metro.co.th, loops through 18 stations and also intersects with the Skytrain. The entire network is a/c, the comfortable trains run every 5-7 mins 0600-2400 and stations are well-lit and airy. There is a lack of integration with the Skytrain – seperate tickets are needed and interchanges are awkward and badly planned. At present, fares for the Metro are cheap, ฿14-฿36.

Motorcycle taxi

These are used to run up and down the long sois that extend out of the main thoroughfares. Riders wear numbered vests and tend to congregate at the end of the busiest sois. The short-hop fare is about ฿10 and there is usually a price list (in Thai) at the gathering point. Some riders will take you on longer journeys across town and fares will then need to be negotiated – expect to pay ฿25-฿100, dependent on your negotiating skills.

River transport

The cheapest way to travel on the river is by regular water taxi. There are three types. The **Chao Phraya Express River Taxi** (*rua duan*) runs between Nonthaburi in the north and Rajburana (Big C) in the south. Fares are calculated by zone and range from ฿4-10 for the daily **Standard Express Boat** and ฿10 for the **Special Express Boat**. At peak hours boats leave every 10 mins, off-peak about 15-25 mins. **Standard Express Boats** operate daily 0600-1840, and **Special Express Boats** 0600-0900 and 1200-1900, Mon-Fri (see p95). The journey from one end of the route to the other takes 75 mins.

Top tips

Chao Phraya River Express

Rua duan (boats) link almost 40 *tha* (piers) along the Chao Phraya River from Tha Rajburana (Big C) in the south to Tha Nonthaburi in the north. Selected piers and places of interest, travelling upstream are as follow:

Tha Sathorn Pier with the closest access to the Skytrain (Taksin Bridge, S6).

Tha Orienten By the Oriental Hotel; access to Silom Road.

Tha Harbour Department In the shadow of the Royal Orchid Hotel, on the south side and close to River City shopping centre.

Tha Ratchawong Access to Chinatown and Sampeng Lane.

Tha Saphan Phut Under the Memorial Bridge and close to Pahurat Indian Market.

Tha Rachini Pak Khlong Market; just upstream, the Catholic seminary surrounded by high walls.

Tha Tien Close to Wat Pho; Wat Arun on the opposite bank; and, just downstream from Wat Arun, the Vichaiprasit Fort (headquarters of the Thai navy), lurking behind crenellated ramparts.

Tha Chang Just downstream is the Grand Palace; Wat Rakhang with its white corn-cob prang lies opposite.

Tha Maharaj Access to Wat Mahathat and Sanaam Luang.

Tha Phra Arthit Access to Khaosan Road.

Tha Visutkasat Just upstream from the elegant central Bank of Thailand.

Tha Thewes Just upstream are boatsheds with royal barges.

Tha Wat Chan Just upstream is the Singha Beer Samoson brewery.

Tha Wat Khema Wat Khema in large, tree-filled compound.

Tha Wat Khian Wat Kien, semi-submerged.

Tha Nonthaburi Last stop on the express boat route.

Special Express Boats, flying either a red/orange or a yellow pennant, do not stop at all piers; boats without a flag are the **Standard Express Boats** and stop at all piers. Also, boats will only stop if passengers wish to board or alight, so make your destination known. Be warned that Thais trying to sell boat tours will tell you Express Boats are not running and will try to extort grossly inflated prices. Walk away and find the correct pier!

Ferries also ply back and forth across the river, between Bangkok and Thonburi.

Khlong or long-tailed boats (*hang yaaw*) can be rented for ฿200 per hr, or more (see p93), if you feel like splashing out in more ways than one. See the khlong trips outlined on p79 for information on what to see on the river. A good map, 'Rivers and Khlongs', is available from the TAT office.

Skytrain (BTS)

The **Skytrain**, T02-6177300, www.bts.co.th, runs on an elevated track through the most developed parts of the city - it is quite a ride, veering between the skyscrapers. Trains run 0600-2400, every 3-5 mins during peak periods and every 10-15 mins out of the rush hour. Fares are ฿10 for one stop, ฿40 for the whole route. Multi-trip tickets can also be purchased, which makes things cheaper.

Taxis are usually metered (they must have a/c to register) – look for the 'Taxi Meter' illuminated sign on the roof. Check that the meter is 'zeroed' before setting off. Flag fall is ฿35 for the first 2 km, ฿4.50 per km up to 12 km, and ฿5 per km thereafter. Most trips in the city should cost ฿40-100. If the travel speed is less than 6 kph – always a distinct possibility in the traffic choked capital – a surcharge of ฿1.25 per min is automatically added. Passengers also pay the tolls for using the expressway. Taxi drivers sometimes refuse to use the meter despite the fact that they are required to do so by law. Taxis should not be tipped, although it is usual to round fares up to the nearest ฿5. To call a taxi T1545 or T1661, they charge ฿20 plus the fare on the meter.

Tuk-tuk

Best for short journeys, they are uncomfortable and, being open to the elements, you are likely to be asphyxiated by car fumes. Bargaining is essential and the fare should be negotiated before boarding, though most tuk-tuk drivers

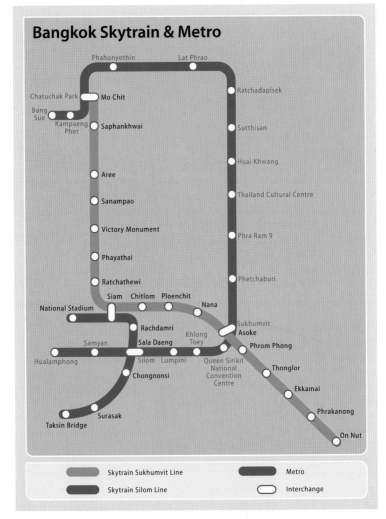

Bangkok Skytrain & Metro

Phahonyothin
Lat Phrao
Chatuchak Park
Mo Chit
Ratchadapisek
Bang Sue
Kampaeng Phet
Saphankhwai
Sutthisan
Huai Khwang
Aree
Sanampao
Thailand Cultural Centre
Victory Monument
Phra Ram 9
Phayathai
Ratchathewi
Phetchaburi
Siam Chitlom Ploenchit
Nana
National Stadium
Rachdamri
Sukhumvit
Asoke
Samyan
Sala Daeng
Khlong Toey
Phrom Phong
Hualamphong
Silom Lumpini
Queen Sirikit National Convention Centre
Thonglor
Chongnonsi
Ekkamai
Phrakanong
Surasak
On Nut
Taksin Bridge

| | Skytrain Sukhumvit Line | | Metro |
| | Skytrain Silom Line | | Interchange |

try to rip tourists off and taking a metered taxi will be less hassle and cheaper. Expect to pay anything from ฿30-100 for a short hop across town.

❶ Directory

Banks
There are countless exchange booths in all the tourist areas open 7 days a week, mostly 0800-1530, some 0800-2100. Rates vary only marginally between banks, although if changing a large sum, it is worth shopping around. ATMs abound in Bangkok and can be used with all recognized credit cards and bank cards. Open 24 hrs a day.

Embassies and consulates
Australia, 37 South Sathorn Rd, T02-2872680. **Cambodia**, 185 Rachdamri Rd, T02-2546630, same-day visas available, ฿1000. 1 photo and photocopy of your passport required. **Canada**, 15th Floor Abdulrahim Place, 990 Rama 1V Rd, T02-6360541. **Laos**, 502/1-3 Soi Ramkhamhaeng 39, T02-5396667. **New Zealand**, 93 Wireless Rd, T02-2542530. **South Africa**, 6th Floor, Park Place, 231 Soi Sarasin, Rachdamri Rd, T02-2538473. **UK**, 1031 Wireless Rd, T02-2530191/9. **USA**, 95 Wireless Rd, T02-2054000. **Vietnam**, 83/1 Wireless Rd, T02-2517202. 2 photos required, same-day visas available for ฿2700.

Internet
There are thousands of internet cafés. Most offer hi-speed access and away from the tourist areas will cost from ฿15 per hour while along Khaosan and Sukhumvit prices are ฿30-60 per hr.

Immigration
Sathorn Tai Soi Suanphlu, Silom district, T02-2873101.

Medical services
Bangkok Adventist Hospital, 430 Phitsanulok Rd, Dusit, T02-2811422/ 2821100. Efficient vaccination service and 24-hr emergency unit. **Bangkok General Hospital**, New Phetburi Soi 47, T02-3180066.

Post
Central GPO (Praysani Klang for taxi drivers): 1160 Charoen Krung, opposite the Ramada Hotel. Mon-Fri 0800-2000 and 0800-1300 weekend and holidays. 24-hr telephone service (phone rates are reduced 2100-0700) and a packing service. There is a small post office on the ground floor of the Siam Sq Car Park, behind Siam Sq.

Tourist police
Unico House, Ploenchit Soi Lang Suan, T1699 or T02-6521721. There are also dedicated tourist police offices in main tourist areas.

Bangkok Listings

Hanoi and around

Street scene, Hanoi

Don't miss...

★1 Old City and Hoan Kiem Lake ▶▶ p104.

★2 Ho Chi Minh's Mausoleum ▶▶ p109.

★3 Halong Bay ▶▶ p114.

★4 Eating cha ca Hanoi in a city restaurant ▶▶ p117.

★5 Old City shopping ▶▶ p121.

Cam Pha

Halong

Halong Bay

★3

Cat Ba Town

QUANG NINH

Uong Bi

Do Son

Haiphong

Gulf of Tonkin

N

10 km

Hai Duong

HAI DUONG

VIETNAM

THAI BINH

Bac Ninh

BAC NINH

HUNG YEN

Hung Yen

NAM DINH

Nam Dinh

5

HANOI

★1 ★2
★5
★4

1

Phu Ly

HA NAM

Hoa Lu

Ninh Binh

Tam Coc

NINH BINH

Ha Dong

HA TAY

Perfume Pagoda

Son Tay

6

HOA BINH

Hoa Binh

Muong Khen

Ma

Hanoi, with its superb colonial and communist legacy, lies nearly 100 km from the sea on a bend in the Red River. From this geographical feature the city derives its name – Hanoi – meaning 'within a river bend'. It is a city of broad, tree-lined boulevards, lakes, parks, weathered colonial buildings, elegant squares and some of the newest office blocks and hotels in Southeast Asia. It also has some of the finest restaurants to be found anywhere serving some of the most delicious cuisine in the world.

Hanoi is the capital of the world's 14th most populous country. Nevertheless, in an age of urban sprawl, the city remains small and compact, historic and charming. At the heart of the city is Hoan Kiem Lake and the famous Sunbeam Bridge. The Old City (36 Streets and Guilds) area, north of the lake, is densely packed and bustling with commerce, its ancient buildings crumbling from the weight of history and activity. The French Quarter, which still largely consists of French buildings, is south of the lake. Here are the Opera House and the grandest hotels, shops and offices.

Accessible on a tour from the city, the primates at Cuc Phuong National Park and the waters of Halong Bay make this area one of the most visited in Vietnam.

Hanoi & around

Ratings

Landscape
★★★★

Relaxation
★★★

Activities
★★★

Culture
★★★★

Wildlife
★

Costs
$$$-$

Hanoi and around

Much of the charm of Hanoi lies not so much in the official 'sights' but in the unofficial and informal: the traffic zooming around the broad streets or the cyclos taking a mellow pedal through the Old City, small shops packed with traders' goods or stacks of silk for visitors, skewered poultry on pavement stalls, mobile flower stalls piled on the backs of bikes, the bustle of pedestrians, the ubiquitous tinkle of the ice cream man's bicycle, an evening visit to Hoan Kiem Lake and the political posters, now raised to an art form, dotted around the city.

Like China, when it first began to 'open up' to western tourists in the late 1970s, the primary interest lies in the novelty of exploring a city which, until recently, opted for a firmly socialist road to development and was insulated from the West.

⊘ **Getting there** Plane, train or bus.

⊖ **Getting around** Walking, cyclo or *xe ôm*.

⊕ **Time required** 2-3 days.

⊛ **Weather** Hot and sticky in summer, chilly in winter.

⊜ **Sleeping** A small number of luxurious hotels and medium-priced guesthouses. Standard budget options.

⊙ **Eating** Superb range of food and outstanding cuisine.

▲ **Activities and tours** Shopping, eating, water puppetry.

★ **Don't miss...** The Old City ▸▸ *p 104.*

Ins and outs ⊖ ▸▸ *p124*

Getting there

Air Noi Bai Airport (HAN), T04-8866527, T04-5844427, is 35 km from Hanoi, a 45-minute to 1-hour drive, and is the hub for international and domestic flights. In the main terminal building there are two snack bars, the Aerocafé, toilets, a bank of telephones, post office, pharmacy and a first-aid unit, two bureaux de changes and a Vietcombank branch with an ATM (0730-1600 Mon-Fri). Incombank accepts Visa and MasterCard (0600-2400 daily). There is a tourist information desk with scant information (0700-1700 daily) and an airport information desk (0600-2300 daily).

The official **Airport Taxi**, T04-88 65615, charges a fixed price of US$10 (150,000d) to the city centre. The airport minibus service (every 30 mins, 0900-2000 daily, US$2), terminates opposite the **Vietnam Airlines** office, Quang Trung Street, T04-8250872. Return buses leave the Vietnam Airlines office at 0500, 0530, 0600, 0730, 0800, 0830, 0900, 0930, 1020, 1500, 1600, 1730, 1820.
▸▸ *For flight information, see Getting there and flying around, p18 and p20.*

Bus Open Tour Buses leave and depart from tour operator offices in the city (try **Sinh Café** or **Kim Café**, p122) for destinations in the south, including Hué, Hoi An, Dalat, Nha Trang, Mui Ne and Ho Chi Minh City.

Train The train station is a short taxi ride (40-65,000 d) from the Old City, north of Hoan Kiem Lake. There are regular trains to Ho Chi Minh City, and all points on the route south, as well as to Lao Cai (for Sapa) in the north.

At the heart of the city is Hoan Kiem Lake. The majority of visitors make straight for the Old City (36 Streets and Guilds) area north of the lake, which is densely packed and bustling with commerce. The French Quarter, which still largely consists of French buildings, is south of the lake. Here are the Opera House and the grandest hotels, shops and offices. To the north of the city, meanwhile, is the West Lake, Tay Ho District, fringed with the suburban homes of the new middle class.

Hanoi is getting more frenetic by the minute as wealth is invested in the internal combustion engine but, thanks to the city's elegant, tree-lined boulevards, walking and cycling can still be delightful. If you like the idea of being pedalled around town, then a cyclo is the answer but be prepared for some concentrated haggling. There are also motorbike taxis (*xe ôm*), self-drive motorbikes for hire as well as a fleet of metered taxis.

Best time to visit

For much of the year Hanoi's weather is decidedly untropical. It benefits from glorious Europe-like springs and autumns, when temperatures are warm but neither too hot, nor too cold. From May until early November Hanoi is fearfully hot and steamy and you won't be able to take a step without breaking into a sweat. The winter months from November to February can be chilly: Hanoins wrap themselves up well in coats, woolly hats, gloves and scarves.

Tourist information

Good tourist information is available from the multitude of tour operators in the city. ▲▲▶▶ *p122.*

Background

The origins of Hanoi as a great city lie with a temple orphan, Ly Cong Uan. Ly rose through the ranks of the palace guards to become their commander and in 1010, four years after the death of the previous King Le Hoan, was enthroned, marking the beginning of the 200-year Ly Dynasty. On becoming king, Ly Cong Uan moved his capital from Hoa Lu to Dai La, which he renamed **Thang Long** ('Soaring Dragon'). Thang Long is present-day **Hanoi**.

Join the locals and cycle your way around the city.

During the period of French expansion into Indochina, the Red River was proposed as an alternative trade route to that of the Mekong. The French attacked and captured the citadel of Hanoi under the dubious pretext that the Vietnamese were about to attack. Recognizing that if a small expeditionary force could be so successful, then there would be little chance against a full-strength army, Emperor Tu Duc acceded to French demands. At the time that the French took control of Annam, Hanoi could still be characterized more as a collection of villages than a city. From 1882 onwards, Hanoi, along with the port city of Haiphong, became the focus of French activity in the north. Hanoi was made the capital of the new colony of Annam and the French laid out a residential and business district, covering 2 sq km. They constructed mansions, villas and public buildings incorporating both French and Asian architectural styles. At the end of the Second World War, with the French battling to keep Ho Chi Minh and his forces at bay, Hanoi became little more than a service centre. After the French withdrew in 1954, Ho Chi Minh concentrated on building up Vietnam and in particular Hanoi's industrial base.

Although Ho Chi Minh City has attracted the lion's share of Vietnam's foreign inward investment, Hanoi, as the capital, also receives a large amount. But whereas Ho Chi Minh City's investment tends to be in industry, Hanoi has received a great deal of attention from property developers, notably in the hotel and office sectors.

Central Hanoi ⊜🚋🏍🎵🍽⬜🛖🍴🎫 ›› *pp115-125*

Hoan Kiem Lake

Hoan Kiem Lake, or Ho Guom (Lake of the Restored Sword) as it is more commonly referred to, is named after an incident that occurred during the 15th century. Emperor Le Loi (Le Thai To, 1428-1433), following a momentous victory against an army of invading Ming Chinese, was sailing on the Lake when a golden turtle appeared from the depths to take back the charmed sword which had secured the victory and restore it to the Lake from whence it came. Like the sword in the stone of British Arthurian legend, Le Thai To's sword assures the Vietnamese of divine intervention in time of national crisis and the story is graphically portrayed in water puppet theatres across the country. There is a modest and rather dilapidated tower, known as the **Tortoise Tower**, commemorating the event on an islet in the southern part of the lake. The Lake still contains large turtles, believed to be a variety of Asian softshell tortoise; one captured in 1968 was reputed to have weighed 250 kg.

Located on a small island on the lake, the **Ngoc Son Temple** ① *0730-1800, 3000d*, was constructed in the early 19th century on the foundations of the old Khanh Thuy Palace, which had been built in 1739. The temple is dedicated to Van Xuong, the God of Literature, although the 13th-century hero Tran Hung Dao, the martial arts genius Quan Vu and the physician La To are also worshipped here. The island is linked to the shore by a red, arched wooden bridge, the **The Huc (Sunbeam) Bridge**, constructed in 1875.

The park that surrounds the shore is used by the residents of the city every morning for jogging and t'ai chi (Chinese shadow boxing) and is regarded by locals as one of the city's beauty spots.

Old City and 36 Streets

Stretching north from the Lake is the Old City (36 Streets and Guilds or 36 Pho Phuong), the most beautiful area of the city. The narrow streets are each named after the products that are (or were) sold there (Basket Street, Paper Street, Silk Street, etc) and create an intricate web of activity and colour. By the 15th century there were 36 short lanes here, each specializing in a particular trade and representing one of the 36 guilds. Among them were the **Phuong Hang**

Old City

Dao (Dyers' Guild Street), and the **Phuong Hang Bac** (Silversmiths' Street). Some of the area's past is still in evidence: at the south end of **Hang Dau Street**, for example, is a mass of stalls selling nothing but shoes, while Tin Street is still home to a community of tinkers. Although, in many cases, the crafts and trades of the past have given way to new activities – karaoke bars, video rental and tourist shops – it is remarkable the extent to which the streets still specialize in the production and sale of a particular item.

The dwellings in this area are known as **nha ong** ('tube houses'); they have narrow shop fronts, sometimes only 3 m wide, but can stretch back from the road for up to 50 m. In the countryside the dimensions of houses were calculated on the basis of the owner's own physical dimensions; in urban areas the tube houses evolved so that each house could have an (albeit very small) area of shop frontage facing onto the main street, its width determined by the social class of the owner. The houses tend to be interspersed by courtyards or 'wells' to permit light into the house and allow some space for outside activities like washing and gardening. The structures were built of bricks 'cemented' together with sugar-cane juice. Older houses tend to be low rise, since commoners were not permitted to build higher than the Emperor's own residence. Other regulations prohibited attic windows on the street side of the building to prevent anyone from looking down on a passing king and to prevent assassination attempts. Colours purple and gold were strictly for royal use only, as was the decorative use of the dragon.

By the early 20th century, inhabitants were replacing their traditional tube houses with buildings inspired by French architecture. Many fine buildings from this era remain and are best appreciated by standing back and looking upwards. Shutters, cornices, columns and wrought-iron balconies and balustrades are common decorative features. An ornate façade sometimes conceals a pitched roof behind. There are some good examples on **Nguyen Sieu Street**. The house at **87 Ma May Street** ⓘ *0800-1700, 5000d*, is a wonderfully preserved example of an original Chinese shophouse.

Further north is the large and varied **Dong Xuan Market**, on Dong Xuan Street. This covered market was destroyed in a disastrous fire in 1994 but has since been rebuilt.

Hanoi Opera House

St Joseph's Cathedral

To the west of Hoan Kiem Lake, in a little square, stands the rather sombre, twin-towered neo-Gothic Saint Joseph's Cathedral. Built in 1886, the cathedral is important as one of the very first colonial-era buildings to be completed in Hanoi, just one year after the Treaty of Tientsin, which gave France control over the whole of Vietnam. Some fine stained-glass windows remain.

Opera House

ⓘ *Not open to the public except during public performances. See the billboards outside or visit the box office for details.*

South east of Hoan Kiem Lake is the proud-looking French-era Opera House. It was built in 1911 by François Lagisquet and is one of the finest French colonial buildings in Hanoi. Work began in 1901, when some 35,000 bamboo piles were sunk into the mud of the Red River to provide foundations for the lofty edifice. The exterior is a delightful mass of shutters, wrought-iron work, little balconies and a tiled frieze. The top balustrade is capped with griffins. Inside, there are dozens of little boxes and fine decoration evocative of the French era. Having suffered years of neglect, the Opera House was eventually lavishly restored, opening in time for the Francophone Summit held in 1997. The restoration cost US$14 million, a colossal sum to spend on the reappointment of a colonial edifice.

Vietnam History Museum

ⓘ *1 Trang Tien St, Tue-Sun 0800-1100, 1330-1630, 15,000d.*

The history museum (Bao Tang Lich Su) is housed in a splendid building, completed in 1931. It was built by Ernest Hébrard as the home of the École Française d'Extrême-Orient, a distinguished archaeological, historical and ethnological research institute. The collection spans Vietnamese history from the Neolithic period up to the 20th century of Ho Chi Minh.

Galleries on the first floor lead from the Neolithic (Bac Son) represented by stone tools and jewellery to the Bronze Age (Dong Son) with some finely engraved ceremonial bronze drums, symbolizing wealth and power. Wooden stakes that were used to impale invading Chinese forces in 1288 were found in 1976 at the cross of the Chanh River and Bach Dang River – a photo of some remaining in the river bed is interesting and a giant oil painting depicting the famous battle is hypnotically fascinating. The giant turtle, a symbol of longevity, supports a vast stela which praises the achievements of Le Loi (reigned 1428-1433), founder of the Le Dynasty who harnessed nationalist sentiment and succeeded in repelling the war-hungry Chinese. A replica of the oldest Buddha Amitabha statue dominates the far end of the first floor. Amitabha is the Buddha of Infinite Light and the original dates from 1057 and was from Phat Tich Pagoda in Bac Ninh Province. Opposite the statue the oldest minted coins in Vietnam are displayed. They date from AD 968 and were minted by the Dinh Dynasty. A collection of out-sized paper currency from the French colonial days is also interesting. These date from 1875 when the French established the Bank of Indochina. The second floor begins with the 15th century to the present day; Champa is represented by some remarkably well-preserved stone carvings of apsaras, mythical dancing girls and a head of Garuda, found at Quang Nam. There are relics such as 18th-century, unusually shaped, bronze pagoda gongs and urns of successive royal dynasties from Le to Nguyen. Unfortunately, some of the pieces are reproductions, including a number of the stelae.

Hoa Lo Prison

ⓘ *1 Hoa Lo, 0800-1130, 1330-1630, 5000d which includes a useful pamphlet.*

Hoa Lo Prison (Maison Centrale), better known as the **Hanoi Hilton**, is the prison where US POWs were incarcerated, some for six years, during the Vietnamese War. Up until 1969, prisoners were also tortured here. Two US Airforce officers, Charles Tanner and Ross Terry, rather than face torture, concocted a story about two other members of their squadron who had been court-martialled for refusing to fly missions against the north. Thrilled with this piece of propaganda, visiting Japanese communists were told the story and it filtered back to the US. Unfortunately for Tanner and Terry, they had called their imaginary pilots Clark Kent and Ben Casey (both TV heroes) and, when the Vietnamese realized they had been duped, the two prisoners were again tortured. The final prisoners of war were not released until 1973, some having been held in the north since 1964. At the end of 1992, a US mission was shown around the prison where 2000 inmates had been housed in cramped, squalid conditions.

Despite pleas from war veterans and party members, the site was sold to a Singapore-Vietnamese joint venture and is now a hotel and shopping complex, Hanoi Towers. As part of the deal the developers had to leave a portion of the prison for use as a museum. There are recreations of conditions under colonial rule when the French incarcerated patriotic Vietnamese: by 1953 they were holding 2000 prisoners in a space designed for 500. Less prominence is given to the role of the prison for holding American pilots, but Douglas 'Pete' Peterson, the first post-war American Ambassador to Vietnam (1997-2001), who was one such occupant, has his mug-shot on the wall. The conditions in which the Viet Cong held their captives were, however, recorded on film.

West of the Citadel ❼ ›› pp115-125

Vietnam Military History Museum

ⓘ *28 Dien Bien Phu St. Tue-Thu, Sat and Sun 0800-1130, 1300-1630. 5000d, camera 5000d.*

Tanks, planes and artillery fill the courtyard of the Army Museum (Bao Tang Quan Doi). Symbolically, an untouched Mig-21 stands at the museum entrance, while the wreckage of B-52s, F1-11s and Q2Cs is piled up at the back. The museum illustrates battles and episodes in Vietnam's fight for independence, from the struggles with China through to the anti-French resistance and the Battle of Dien Bien Phu (illustrated by a good model). Inevitably, of course, there are lots of photographs and exhibits of the American war but, although much is self-evident, unfortunately a lot of the explanations are in Vietnamese.

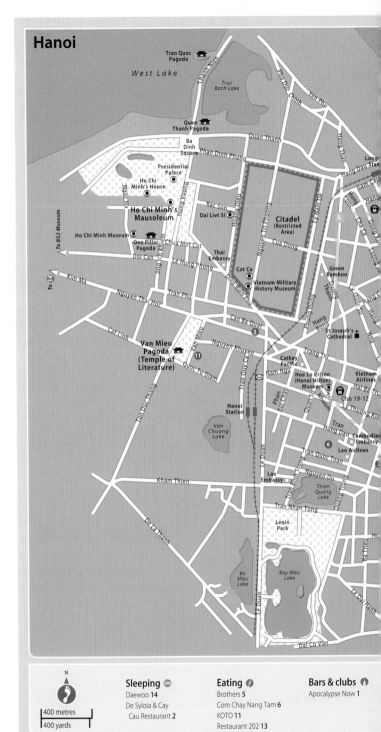

Hanoi

Tran Quoc Pagoda

West Lake

Truc Bach Lake

Thanh Nien

Pho Dui Chinh

Ten Phu

Quan Thanh Pagoda

Quan Thanh

Ba Dinh Square

Phan Dinh Phung

Hang Than

Long

Hang Dau Stat

Gam Cai

Presidential Palace

Ong Ich Khiem

Hoang Dieu

Bac Son

Nguyen Tri Phuong

Hane

Hang Cha

Dong A

Ho Chi Minh's House

Dai Liet Si

Cua Dong

Hang

Cha Ca

Huong

Ho Chi Minh's Mausoleum

Chua Mot Cot

Nam De

Citadel (Restricted Area)

To B52 Museum

Ho Chi Minh Museum

One Pillar Pagoda

Doi Can

Thai Embassy

Cot Co

Green Bamboo

Le Hong Phong

Dien Bien Phu

Vietnam Military History Museum

Hang Bong

Duong Thanh

Ly Quoc Su

To 14

Kim Ma

Nguyen Thai Hoc

Tran Phu

Cao Ba Quat

St Joseph's Cathedral

Cat Linh

Van Mieu Pagoda (Temple of Literature)

Nguyen Khuyen

Trang Thi

Cathay Pacific

Hoa Lo Prison (Hanoi Hilton) Museum

Vietnam Airlines

Quoc Tu Giam

Tran Quy Cap

Nam Ngu

Phan Boi Chau

Ly Thuong Kie

Cho 19-12

Ton Duc Thang

Tran Mieu

Hanoi Station

Tran Hung Dao

Cambodia Embassy

Lao Airlines

Van Chuong Lake

Tran Quoc Toan

Kham Thien

Lao Embassy

Nguyen Du

Thien Quang Lake

De La Thanh

Tran Nhan Tong

Lenin Park

Le Dai Hanh

Ba Mau Lake

Bay Mau Lake

Le Duan

Dai Co Viet

Sleeping 😴
Daewoo **14**
De Syloia & Cay
Cau Restaurant **2**

Eating 🍴
Brothers **5**
Com Chay Nang Tam **6**
KOTO **11**
Restaurant 202 **13**

Bars & clubs 🍸
Apocalypse Now **1**

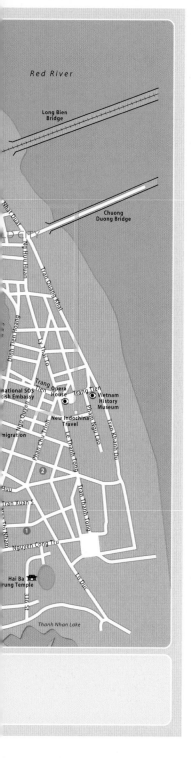

In the precincts of the museum is the **Cot Co**, a flag tower, raised up on three platforms. Built in 1812, it is the only substantial part of the original **citadel** still standing. There are good views over Hanoi from the top. The walls of the citadel were destroyed by the French between 1894 and 1897, presumably as they symbolized the power of the Vietnamese emperors. The French were highly conscious of the projection of might, power and authority through large structures, which helps explain their own remarkable architectural legacy. Other remaining parts of the citadel are in the hands of the Vietnamese army and out of bounds to visitors. Across the road from the museum's front entrance is a **statue of Lenin**.

Ho Chi Minh's Mausoleum and Ba Dinh Square

ⓘ *Tue-Thu, Sat and Sun 0730-1030 (1 Apr-31 Oct) and 0800-1100 (1 Nov-31 Mar), 4000d. Opening hours are extended by 30 mins on national holidays, Sat and Sun. Before entering the mausoleum, visitors must leave possessions at the office (Ban To Chuc) on Huong Vuong, just to the south; do not leave your camera here, instead, take it through to another drop off point and it will be returned to you at a kiosk at the exit. Visitors must be respectful: dress neatly, walk solemnly, and do not talk.*

The Vietnamese have made the mausoleum housing Ho Chi Minh's embalmed corpse (Lang Chu Tich Ho Chi Minh) a holy place of pilgrimage. The embalming and eternal display of Ho Chi Minh's body was contrary to Ho's own wishes: he wanted to be cremated and his ashes placed in three urns to be positioned atop three unmarked hills in the north, centre and south of the country. He once wrote that "cremation is not only good from the point of view of hygiene, but it also saves farmland". The embalming of Ho's body was undertaken by the chief Soviet embalmer, Dr Sergei Debrov, who also pickled such communist luminaries as President Klenient Gottwald of Czechoslovakia, Prime Minister Georgi

Dimitrov of Bulgaria and President Forbes Burnham of Guyana. Debrov was flown to Hanoi from Moscow as Ho lay dying, bringing with him two transport planes packed with air conditioners (to keep the corpse cool) and other equipment. To escape US bombing, the team moved Ho to a cave, taking a full year to complete the embalming process. Russian scientists still check-up on their handiwork, servicing Ho's body regularly. Their embalming methods and the fluids they use are still a closely guarded secret. In an interview, Debrov noted with pleasure the poor state of China's Chairman Mao's body, which was embalmed without Soviet help.

The mausoleum, built between 1973 and 1975, is a massive, square and forbidding structure and must be among the best constructed, maintained and air-conditioned buildings in Vietnam. Opened in 1975, it is a modelled closely on Lenin's Mausoleum in Moscow. Ho lies with a guard at each corner of his bier and visitors march past in file to see his body.

In front of Ho Chi Minh's Mausoleum is **Ba Dinh Square** where Ho read out the Vietnamese Declaration of Independence on 2 September 1945. Following Ho's declaration, 2 September became Vietnam's National Day. Coincidentally, 2 September was also the date on which Ho died in 1969, although his death was not officially announced until 3 September in order not to mar people's enjoyment of National Day in the beleaguered north of the country.

Ho Chi Minh's house and the Presidential Palace

ⓘ *Tue-Thu, Sat and Sun, 0730-1130, 5000d.* From the mausoleum, visitors are directed to Ho Chi Minh's house built in the compound of the former Presidential Palace. The palace, now a party guesthouse, was the residence of the Governors-General of French Indochina and was built between 1900 and 1908. In 1954, when North Vietnam's struggle for independence was finally achieved, Ho Chi Minh declined to live in the palace, saying that it belonged to the people. Instead, he stayed in what is said to have been an electrician's house in the same compound. Here he lived from 1954 to 1958, before moving to a new stilt house built on the other side of a small lake, swarming with massive and well-fed carp. The modest house was designed by Ho and an architect, Nguyen Van Ninh, and is made of rare hardwoods raised up on wooden pillars. It is airy, intimate and immaculately kept. Ho conducted meetings under the house and slept and worked above. Behind the house is Ho's bomb shelter and, behind that, the hut where he died in 1969.

One Pillar Pagoda and Ho Chi Minh Museum

Close by is the **One Pillar Pagoda** (Chua Mot Cot), one of the few structures remaining from the original foundation of the city. It was built in 1049 by Emperor Ly Thai Tong, although the shrine has since been rebuilt on several occasions, most recently in 1955 after the French destroyed it, before withdrawing from the country. The emperor built the pagoda in a fit of religious passion after he dreamt that he saw the goddess Quan Am (Vietnam's equivalent of the Chinese goddess Kuan-yin, see box, p113), sitting on a lotus and holding a young boy, whom she handed to the Emperor. On the advice of counsellors who interpreted the dream, the Emperor built a little lotus-shaped temple in the centre of a water-lily pond and shortly afterwards his queen gave birth to a son. As the name suggests, it is supported on a single (concrete) pillar with a brick and stone staircase running up one side. The pagoda symbolizes the 'pure' lotus sprouting from the sea of sorrow. Original in design, with dragons running along the apex of the elegantly-curved tiled roof, the temple is one of the most revered monuments in Vietnam.

Overshadowing the One Pillar Pagoda is the **Ho Chi Minh Museum**, ⓘ *Tue-Thu, Sat*
0800-1130, 1400-1600, 5000d, opened in 1990 in celebration of the centenary of Ho's birth.
Contained in a large and impressive modern building, it is the best arranged and most
innovative museum in Vietnam. The displays trace Ho's life and work from his early
wanderings around the world to his death and final victory over the south.

Temple of Literature

ⓘ *Entrance on Quoc Tu Giam St. Summer 0800-1700, winter 0730-1700. 5000d, 45-min tour in
French or English 50,000d, brochure 3000d.*

The Temple of Literature (Van Mieu Pagoda) is the largest and, probably, the most important,
temple complex in Hanoi. It was founded in 1070 by Emperor Ly Thanh Tong, dedicated to
Confucius who had a substantial following in Vietnam, and modelled, so it is said, on a temple
in Shantung, China, the birthplace of the sage. Some researchers, while acknowledging the
date of foundation, challenge the view that it was built as a Confucian institution pointing to
the ascendancy of Buddhism during the Ly Dynasty. Confucian principles and teaching
rapidly replaced Buddhism, however, and Van Mieu subsequently became the intellectual
and spiritual centre of the kingdom as a cult of literature and education spread amongst the
court, the mandarins and then among the common people. At one time there were said to
be 20,000 schools teaching the Confucian classics in northern Vietnam alone.

The temple and its compound are arranged north-south; visitors enter at the southern
end from Quoc Tu Giam Street. On the pavement two pavilions house stelae bearing the
inscription *ha ma* (climb down from your horse), a nice reminder that even the most elevated
dignitaries had to proceed on foot. The main **Van Mieu Gate** (Cong Van Mieu Mon) is
adorned with 15th-century dragons. Traditionally, the large central gate was opened only on
ceremonial occasions. The path leads through the Cong Dai Trung to a second courtyard and
the **Van Khue Gac Pavilion**, which was built in 1805 and dedicated to the Constellation of
Literature. The roof is tiled according to the yin-yang principle.

Beyond lies the **Courtyard of the Stelae** at the centre of which is the rectangular
pond or Cieng Thien Quang (**Well of Heavenly Clarity**). More important are the stelae
themselves, on which are recorded the names of 1306 successful examination scholars
(*tien si*). Of the 82 stelae that survive (30 are missing), the oldest dates back to 1442 and the
most recent to 1779. Each stela is carried on the back of a tortoise, symbol of strength and
longevity. The stelae are arranged in no order but three chronological categories can be
identified. Fourteen date from the 15th and 16th centuries; they are the smallest and
embellished with floral motifs and yin-yang symbols but not dragons (a royal emblem).
Twenty-five stelae are from the 17th century and ornamented with dragons (by now
permitted), pairs of phoenix and other creatures mythical or real. The remaining 43 stelae
are of 18th-century origin; they are the largest and decorated with two stylized dragons,
some merging with flame clouds.

Passing the examination was not easy: in 1733, out of some 3000 entrants only eight
passed the doctoral examination (*Thai Hoc Sinh*) and became Mandarins, a task that took 35
days. This tradition was begun in 1484, on the instruction of Emperor Le Thanh Tong, and
continued through to 1878, during which time 116 examinations were held. The Temple of
Literature was not used only for examinations, however: food was also distributed from here to
the poor and infirm, 500 g of rice at a time. In 1880, the French Consul Monsieur de Kergaradec
recorded that 22,000 impoverished people came to receive this meagre handout.

Continuing north, the **Great Success Gate** (Dai Thanh Mon) leads on to a courtyard
flanked by two buildings which date from 1954, the originals having been destroyed in 1947.
These buildings were reserved for 72 disciples of Confucius. Facing is the **Great House of
Ceremonies** (Dai Bai Duong) which was built in the 19th century but in the earlier style of the

B-52 Museum

Le Dynasty. The carved wooden friezes with their dragons, phoenix, lotus flowers, fruits, clouds and yin-yang discs are all symbolically charged, depicting the order of the universe and by implication reflecting the god-given hierarchical nature of human society, each in his place. It is not surprising that the Communist government has hitherto had reservations about preserving a temple extolling such heretical doctrine. Inside is an altar on which sit statues of Confucius and his closest disciples. Adjoining is the **Great Success Sanctuary** (Dai Thanh Sanctuary), which also contains a statue of Confucius.

B-52 Museum

ⓘ *157 Doi Can St, west of the centre, free.* The remains of downed B-52s have been hawked around Hanoi over many years but seem to have found a final resting place at the **Bao Tang Chien Tang B-52** (B-52 Museum). This curious place is not really a museum at all (the museum building is yet to open) but this doesn't matter because all anyone wants to do is to walk over the wings and tail of a shattered B-52 that lies in pieces around the yard. The size and strength of the B-52 is simply incredible and needs to be seen to be believed. As visitors to Vietnamese museums will come to expect, the enemy objects are heaped up as junk, while the Vietnamese pieces are painted, cared for and carefully signed with the names of the heroic unit that used them. There are examples of anti-aircraft guns, devastating SAMs (which wreaked so much havoc on the US Airforce) and a Mig-21. Curiously the signs omit to mention the fact that all this hardware was made in Russia.

Vietnam Museum of Ethnology

ⓘ *Nguyen Van Huyen Rd, some distance west of the city centre in Cau Giay District. Tue-Sun 0830-1730. 10,000d. Take a taxi or catch the No 14 minibus from Dinh Tien Hoang St, north of Hoan Kiem Lake, to the Nghia Tan stop; turn right and walk down Hoang Quoc Viet St for 1 block, before turning right at the Petrolimex station down Nguyen Van Huyen; the museum is on the left.* The excellent Ethnology Museum brings together a collection of some 25,000 artefacts, 15,000 photographs, plus documentaries of practices and rituals, all attractively and informatively presented, with labels in Vietnamese, English and French. It displays the material culture (textiles, musical instruments, jewellery, tools, baskets and the like) of the majority Kinh people and Vietnam's 53 other designated minority peoples. While the focus is

The story of Quan Am

Quan Am was turned onto the streets by her husband for some unspecified wrong-doing and, dressed as monk, took refuge in a monastery. There, a woman accused her of fathering, and then abandoning, her child. Accepting the blame (why, no one knows), she was again turned out onto the streets, only to return to the monastery much later when she was on the point of death – to confess her true identity. When the Emperor of China heard the tale, he made Quan Am the Guardian Spirit of Mother and Child, and couples without a son now pray to her.

Quan Am's husband is sometimes depicted as a parakeet, with the Goddess usually holding her adopted son in one arm and standing on a lotus leaf (the symbol of purity).

largely historical, the museum is also attempting to build up its contemporary collection. There is a shop attached to the museum and ethnic minorities' homes have been recreated in the grounds. There is also a Discovery Room for children, with plenty of activities (0830-1130, 1330-1630).

Around Hanoi ⊕▲ » pp115-125

There are a number of worthwhile day and overnight trips from Hanoi: the Perfume Pagoda lies to the southwest; Tam Coc and Cuc Phuong National Park are some three hours south, while Halong Bay, best visited on an overnight trip, is three hours to the east.

Perfume Pagoda
ⓘ *60 km southwest of Hanoi. A tour from Hanoi costs about US$30 and includes the return boat trip along the Yen River.*
The Perfume Pagoda (Chua Huong or Chua Huong Tich) is dedicated to Quan Am (see above). It is one of a number of shrines and towers built amongst limestone caves and is regarded as one of the most beautiful spots in Vietnam. Emperor Le Thanh Tong (1460-97) described it as '*Nam Thien de nhat dong*' or 'foremost cave under the Vietnamese sky'. It is a popular pilgrimage spot, particularly during the festival months of March and April. A sampan takes visitors along the Yen River, a diverting 4-km ride through a flooded landscape to the Mountain of the Perfume Traces. From here it is a 3-km hike up the mountain to the cool, dark cave where the Perfume Pagoda is located. The stone statue of Quan Am in the principal pagoda was carved in 1793 after Tay Son rebels had stolen and melted down its bronze predecessor to make cannon balls.

Tam Coc
ⓘ *The turning to Tam Coc is 4 km south of Ninh Binh on Highway 1. US$2 plus US$1.50 per person for the boat ride. Tam Coc can easily be reached from Hanoi on a day trip, either as part of an organized tour or by hiring a car and driver. Take plenty of suncream and a hat.*
An area of enchanting natural beauty, Tam Coc means literally 'three caves'. Those who have seen the film *Indochine*, some of which was shot here, will be familiar with the nature of the beehive-type scenery created by limestone towers, similar to those of Halong Bay. The highlight of this excursion is an enchanting boat ride up the little Ngo Dong River through the

eponymous three caves. The exact form varies from wet to dry season; when flooded, the channel disappears and one or two of the caves may be drowned; in the dry season, the shallow river meanders between fields of golden rice. Women punt pitch-and-resin tubs that look like elongated coracles through the tunnels. It is a leisurely experience and a chance to observe at close quarters the extraordinary method of rowing with the feet. The villagers have a rota to decide whose turn it is to row and, to supplement their fee, will try and sell visitors embroidered tablecloths. Enterprising photographers snap you setting off from the bank and will surprise you 1 km upstream with copies of your cheesy grin already printed. On a busy day the scene from above is like a two-way, nose-to-tail procession of waterboatmen, so to enjoy Tam Coc at its best, make it your first port of call in the morning.

Cuc Phuong National Park

ⓘ *Nho Quan district, 120 km south of Hanoi and 45 km west of Ninh Binh, T30-848006, dulichcucphuong@hn.vnn.vn. 40,000d. Cuc Phuong can be visited as a day trip from Hanoi (early start), either on an organized tour (a sensible option for lone travellers or pairs) or by hiring a car with driver or a motorbike.*

Located in an area of deeply-cut limestone and reaching elevations of up to 800 m, this park is covered by 22,000 ha of humid tropical montagne forest. It is home to an estimated 1880 species of flora, including the giant parashorea, cinamomum and sandoricum trees. Wildlife, however, has been much depleted by hunting, so that only 89 mammal, 320 bird species and 110 reptiles and amphibians are thought to remain. April and May sees fat grubs and pupae metamorphosing into swarms of beautiful butterflies that mantle the forest in fantastic shades of greens and yellows. The government has resettled a number of the park's 30,000 Muòng minority people but Muòng villages do still exist and can be visited. The **Endangered Primate Rescue Centre** ⓘ *www.primatecenter.org, 0900-1130, 1330-1600, 10,000d*, is a big draw in the park, with more than 30 cages, four houses and two semi-wild enclosures for the animals.

Halong Bay

ⓘ *Most boats depart from Halong City, 110 km east of Hanoi, http://halongbay.halong.net.vn/ has comprehensive information on the area, including transport details. US$1 admission for each cave and attraction. You need 4-5 hrs to see the bay properly but an overnight stay aboard a boat is enjoyable. The majority of people visit on an all-inclusive tour with tourist cafés or tour operators from Hanoi. It can be stormy in Jun, Jul and Aug; Jul and Aug are also the wettest months; winter is cool and dry; rain is possible at all times of year.* ▲▲▸▸ *p122.*

Halong means 'descending dragon'. An enormous beast is said to have careered into the sea at this point, cutting the fantastic bay from the rocks as it thrashed its way into the depths. Vietnamese poets, including the 'Poet King' Le Thanh Tong, have traditionally extolled the beauty of this romantic area, with its rugged islands that protrude from a sea dotted with sailing junks. Artists, too, have drawn inspiration from the crooked islands, seeing the forms of monks and gods in the rock faces, and dragons' lairs and fairy lakes in the depths of the caves. Another myth says that the islands are dragons sent by the gods to impede the progress of an invasion flotilla. The area was the location of two famous sea battles in the 10th and 13th centuries and is now a UNESCO World Heritage Site.

Geologically, the tower-karst scenery of Halong Bay is the product of millions of years of chemical action and river erosion working on the limestone to produce a pitted landscape. At the end of the last ice age, when the glaciers melted, the sea level rose and inundated the area turning hills into islands. The islands of the bay are divided by a broad channel: to the east are the smaller outcrops of Bai Tu Long, while to the west are the larger islands with caves and secluded beaches. Rocks can be treacherously slippery, so sensible footwear is

Halong Bay

advised. Many of the caves are a disappointment, with harrying vendors, mounds of litter and disfiguring graffiti. Among the more spectacular, however, are **Hang Hanh**, which extends for 2 km. Tour guides will point out fantastic stalagmites and stalactites which, with imagination, become heroes, demons and animals. **Hang Luon** is another flooded cave, which leads to the hollow core of a doughnut-shaped island. It can be swum or navigated by coracle. **Hang Dau Go** is the cave in which Tran Hung Dao stored his wooden stakes prior to studding them in the bed of the Bach Dang River in 1288 to destroy the boats of invading Mongol hordes. **Hang Thien Cung** is a hanging cave, a short 50-m haul above sea level, with dripping stalactites, stumpy stalagmites and solid rock pillars.

⊜ Sleeping

Old City buildings are tightly packed and have small rooms, sometimes without windows. Hotels in this area offer the best value for money.

Central Hanoi *p104, map p117*
A De Syloia, 17A Tran Hung Dao St, T04-8245346, www.desyloia.com. An attractive and friendly small boutique hotel south of the lake. The superior accommodation with nice bathrooms is furnished with bedside lamps, beds are decorated with welcome roses and guests receive complimentary fruit.
A-B Dan Chu, 29 Trang Tien St, T04-8254937, www.danchuhotel.com. Very pleasant, friendly, state-run hotel with clean and spacious rooms. Older rooms overlooking Trang Tien St are the cheapest; new rooms set back from the street cost more. Good restaurant.
B Eden, 78 Tho Nhuom St, T04-9423273, eden@hn.vnn.vn. Good location but small rooms so it's worth paying more for the suites. Popular and handy for **A Little Italian** restaurant.
B-C Ho Guom, 76 Hang Trong St, T04-8243565, hoguomtjc@hn.vnn.vn. Very near the lake but enjoying a peaceful location set back from the road. Some of the rooms have forest-green shuttered windows overlooking the courtyard. All rooms are furnished in Hué imperial style and are fully equipped. Staff are friendly and helpful. Rates include breakfast and taxes.
B-D Hoa Linh, 35 Hang Bo St, T04-8243887, hoalinhhotel@hn.vnn.vn. Right in the centre of the Old City, this hotel has lovely bedrooms decked out in

Budget busters

Hanoi

LL-L Sofitel Metropole, 15 Ngo Quyen St, T04-8266919, www.accorhotels.com/asia. The only hotel in its class in central Hanoi and often full. It boasts a diversity of bars and restaurants: the Met Pub is a popular live music bar; Le Beaulieu is one of the finest restaurants in Hanoi. There is also a business centre, useful bookshop and a small pool with attractive poolside Bamboo Bar. The hotel has retained most of its business despite competition from newer business hotels away from the city centre and remains a hub of activity. Graham Greene stayed here in the 1950s.

L Hilton Hanoi Opera, 1 Le Thanh Tong St, T04-9330500, www.hanoi.hilton.com. Built adjacent to and architecturally in keeping with the Opera House, this is a lofty edifice and provides the highest levels of service and hospitality. Its foyer is very art deco, with marbled flooring and enormous decorated columns. The stylishly furnished rooms enjoy separate bathtubs and showers and broadband internet access. There is a French restaurant, Chinese restaurant, bakery and sports bar.

the dark wood of Hué imperial style: bedsteads are ornately carved with dragons; screens and bedside tables are inlaid with mother of pearl. The larger, more expensive rooms have a double and a single bed and a balcony. It is worth paying extra for a view of the decoration on the crumbling buildings opposite. Bathrooms are basic with plastic showers and no curtains. Breakfast included but not taxes.

C Hong Ngoc, 34 Hang Manh St, T04-8285053, hongngochotel@hn.vnn.vn. This is a real find. Small, family-run hotel, with huge, comfortable rooms and bathrooms. Writing desk, bathtub. Spotlessly clean throughout, cheerful and helpful staff. Breakfast included.

There are 2 other Hong Ngoc's in the Old City: **Hong Ngoc 2**, 14 Luong Van Can St, T04-8267566, and **Hong Ngoc 3**, 39 Hang Bac St, T04-9260322.

C-D Anh Dao, 37 Ma May St, T04-8267151, anhdao@camellia-hotels.com. This hotel has 34 large, clean a/c rooms, with hot water and bathtubs as standard. Unflustered English-speaking staff make guests feel welcome. Buffet breakfast and use of internet included, excellent value, understandably popular.

C-E My Lan, 70 Hang Bo St (through the dentist's surgery), T04-8245510, hotelmylan@yahoo.com. Elderly French-speaking doctor has 10 rooms to rent, a/c in summer, rather tightly packed but light and breezy; also 1 nice roof-top apartment with kitchen and terrace.

D Hang Trong, 56 Hang Trong St, T04-8251346, thiencotravel@yahoo.com. A/c and hot water showers, a few unusual and quite decent rooms set back from the road, either on a corridor or in a courtyard. Very convenient position for every part of town.

E-F A-Z Queen Café and Guesthouse, 50 Hang Be St, T04-8267356, www.azqueencafe.com. 18 basic but adequate rooms, the more expensive are singles/doubles with a/c. Very cheap dormitories with clean shared bathrooms. The dorms are actually cleaner and brighter than the separate rooms. Downstairs is a popular travel café offering a good range of tours including trekking, mountain biking and kayaking. Free internet access.

Eating

Hanoi has western-style coffee bars, restaurants and watering holes that stand up well to comparison with their equivalents in Europe. It also has a good number of excellent Vietnamese restaurants.

A few words of caution: dog (*thit chó* or *thit cay*) is an esteemed delicacy in the

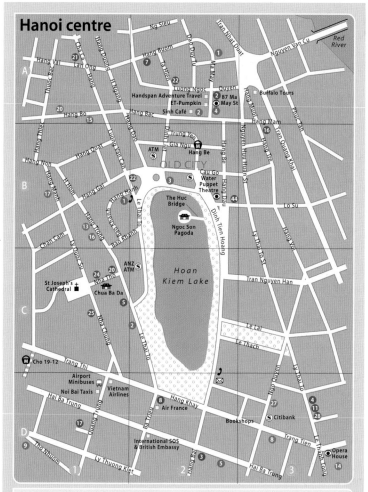

Hanoi centre

Red River

OLD CITY

Handspan Adventure Travel
ET-Pumpkin
Sinh Café

Buffalo Tours

87 Ma May St

Cau Go Water Puppet Theatre

The Huc Bridge

Ngoc Son Pagoda

Hoan Kiem Lake

St Joseph's Cathedral
Chua Ba Da

Cho 19-12

Airport Minibuses
Noi Bai Taxis
Vietnam Airlines

Air France

Bookshops

International SOS & British Embassy

Opera House

200 metres
200 yards

Sleeping
Anh Dao **1** *A2*
A-Z Queen Café & Guesthouse **2** *A2*
Dan Chu **8** *D3*

Eden & A Little Italian Restaurant **9** *D1*
Hang Trong **13** *B1*
Hilton Hanoi Opera **14** *D3*
Hoa Linh **15** *A1*
Ho Guom **16** *B1*
Hong Ngoc **17** *B1*
My Lan **20** *A1*
Sofitel Metropole & Le Beaulieu Restaurant **27** *D3*

Eating
69 Restaurant Bar **2** *A2*
Al Fresco's **3** *D2*
Au Lac **4** *D3*
Bit Tet **7** *A2*
Bobby Chinn **8** *D2*
Café Moca **24** *C1*
Café Thyme **44** *B2*
Club Opera **11** *D3*
Highway 4 **16** *B3*
Hoa Sua **17** *D1*
La Brique **20** *C1*

La Vong (Cha Ca) **21** *A1*
Little Hanoi **22** *B2, A2*
No Noodles **25** *C1*
Press Club **28** *D3*.
Rendez-Vous **5** *C1*

Bars & clubs
Funky Monkey **1** *B1*
Ho Guom Xanh **2** *C2*
Legends **3** *B2*
Red Beer **4** *A2*
Spotted Cow **5** *D2*

north but is mostly served in shacks on the edge of town – so you are unlikely to order it inadvertently.

Central Hanoi *p104, map p117*

Asian

Bobby Chinn, 1 Ba Trieu St, T04-9348577, daily 1100-2300. One of the most stylish restaurants in Vietnam with an award-winning wine list. Rose buds hang from the ceiling, gold drapes abound and a glass façade ensures views of Hoan Kiem Lake. The Asian fusion menu is excellent value, with set menus from US$20. Dine on rice paper-wrapped foie gras with ginger sauce, pan roasted salmon on wassabi mashed potatoes, grilled vegetables and ginger demi-glaze or filet mignon and mashed potato with mushroom ragout in a red wine sauce.

International

Al Fresco's, 23L Hai Ba Trung St, T04-8267782, daily 1100-2200. A popular Australian grill bar serving ribs, steak, pasta, pizza and fantastic salads. Giant portions, lively atmosphere, a memorable experience. There's a special 2-for-1 pizza offer on Tue. Recommended.

Le Beaulieu, 15 Ngo Quyen St (in the **Metropole Hotel**), T04-8266919, daily 0630-1030, 1130-1400 and 1830-2300. A good French and international restaurant. Its Sun brunch buffet is regarded as one of the best in Asia. A great selection of French seafood, oysters, prawns, cold and roast meats and cheese.

Press Club, 59A Ly Thai To St, T04-340888, www.hanoi-pressclub.com, Mon-Fri 1100-1500, 1800-2300, Sat and Sun dinner only. 3 good food outlets in this stylish complex directly behind the **Sofitel Metropole Hotel**: The Restaurant, The Deli and Les Comptoirs. **The Restaurant** is one of the most popular dining experiences in Hanoi. It is luxurious with polished, dark wood floors and print-lined walls. The expensive haute cuisine menu includes deconstructed Vietnamese pho with lobster, foie gras and truffle. Chef's chocolate pavlova with passion fruit ice cream is an essential dessert. Al fresco dining is possible.

Café Thyme, 18 Lo Su St, T04-8267929, daily 0900-2300. Small, cosy restaurant tucked into an Old City street run by a Canadian long-term resident. The menu keeps in step with the seasons. Tantalizing dishes include onion tart with red cabbage quenelle, roast clams with crispy shallots and crab cakes with orange and thyme mayonnaise. Round it off with fresh Dalat strawberries or frozen mango and Grand Marnier soufflé.

Hoa Sua, 28A Ha Hoi St (off Quang Trung), T04-9424448, www.hoasua school.com, daily 1100-2200. French training restaurant for disadvantaged youngsters, where visitors eat excellently prepared French and Vietnamese cuisine in an attractive and secluded courtyard setting. Reasonably cheap and popular.

La Brique, 6 Nha Tho St, T04-9285638, daily 1000-2230. Dinner by candlelight in a cool, bare, brickwork setting. La Brique serves up the most deliciously succulent *cha ca Hanoi* to the sounds of Manu Chau. The dish is cooked on charcoal at your table and served with herbs and white noodles. Seafood is a strong feature on the menu, including crab soup with corn, stuffed squid and squid sate.

Au Lac, 57 Ly Thai To St, T04-8257807, daily 0700-2300. A café-cum-bar serving light meals and good coffee in the patio garden of a French villa. Breakfasts, sandwiches, pizzas, soups and pastas are available. The green papaya salad with grilled beef and sesame seeds is recommended as are the sautéed oysters with turmeric and lemon grass.

Café Moca, 14-16 Nha Tho, T04-8256334, daily 0700-2400. This open space has big windows, wafting fans, marble-topped tables and modern urban touches, including exposed red-brick walls and a chrome flue. Cinnamon-flavoured cappuccino, smoked salmon and Bengali specials are all served on

Street smart in Vietnam

Odd numbers usually run consecutively on one side of the street, evens on the other; *bis* after a number, as in 16 bis Hai Ba Trung Street, means there are two houses with the same number and *ter* after the number means there are three houses with the same number. Large buildings with a single street number are usually subdivided 21A, 21B etc; some buildings may be further subdivided 21C1, 21C2, and so on. An oblique (/ – *sec* or *tren* in Vietnamese) in a number, as in 23/16 Dinh Tien Hoang Street, means the address is to be found in a small side street (*hem*) – in this case running off Dinh Tien Hoang by the side of no 23: the house in question will probably be signed 23/16 rather than just 16. Usually, but by no means always, a hem will be quieter than the main street. Q stands for *quân* (district); this points you in the right general direction and will be important in locating your destination as a long street may run through several quan.

pretty, brown floral crockery. Service can be slack at times.

Little Hanoi, 21 Hang Gai St, T04-8288333, daily 0730-2300. An all-day café. The sandwiches are particularly outstanding for US$2-3 but then so too are the cappuccinos, the home-made yoghurt with honey and the apple pie.

Rendez-Vous, 136 Hang Trong St, T04-8289705. This is a good café overlooking Hoan Kiem Lake. Ice creams, coffees and good value buffet lunches. For sheer spectacle, try an Irish coffee.

No Noodles, 20 Nha Chung St, T04-9285969, daily 0900-2100. Hanoi's original sandwich bar. Delicious and inexpensive sandwiches, so big you can't fit them in your mouth. Free delivery service in central Hanoi.

Vietnamese

Club Opera, 59 Ly Thai To St, T04-8246950, daily 1100-1400 and 1730-2230. A small, cosy restaurant with an extensive Vietnamese menu in the attractive setting of a restored French villa. Tables are beautifully laid and the food is appealingly presented with exquisitely carved vegetables. Try

seaweed salad with shrimps and dried shredded squid. Beef, chicken and fish are served as main courses but the dessert menu is uninspired. The back room bar is reminiscent of a quaint English pub.

69 Restaurant Bar, 69 Ma May St, T04-9261720, www.69vn.com, daily 0700-2300. The restaurant is up a steep flight of wooden stairs in a restored 19th-century house in the Old City, with 2 tables on the tiny shuttered balcony. Plenty of Vietnamese and seafood dishes, including Hong Kong duck (chargrilled and stuffed with five spices, ginger, onion and garlic) and sunburnt beef: beef strips deep fried in five spice butter. Special mulled wine is offered on cold nights.

Brothers, 26 Nguyen Thai Hoc St, T04-7333866, Mon-Sat 1100-1400, 1830-2200, Sun 1830-2200. Part of the pleasure of dining here is the sumptuous surroundings of a delightfully restored villa. The leafy patio has umbrella-shaded tables and stalls offering tempting dishes. The multi-course buffet lunch is one of the best value meals in the country. Dinners are bbq buffets.

Cay Cau, De Syloia Hotel, 17A Tran Hung Dao St, T04-8245346, daily

1100-1400, 1800-2200. Popular with well-to-do Vietnamese, this small restaurant offers excellent set menus from US$7.50 for 8 courses. Try the full crab menu – fried soft shell crab with butter – or simmered pigeon with garlic. Beancurd dishes feature strongly. Eat outdoors or inside under a wooden, decorated ceiling. Live music 1930-2130.

Highway 4, 5 Hang Tre St, T04-9260639, www.highway4.com, daily 0900-0200. Another branch at 54 Mai Hac De St, T04-9762647. Quite a remarkable experience. This restaurant specializes in ethnic minority dishes from the north of Vietnam and features bull penis and testicles on the menu! The highlight, though, is the selection of fruit and rice wines. Fairly conventional restaurant downstairs but on the upper 2 floors, guests sit cross-legged on cushions.

La Vong (also **Cha Ca**), 14 Cha Ca St, T04-8253929, daily 1100-1400 and 1700-2200. Serves one dish only, the eponymous *cha ca Hanoi*, fried fish fillets in mild spice and herbs served with noodles, popular with both visitors and locals.

Restaurant 202, 202A Hue St, T04-9760487, daily 1000-2200. Vietnamese and French menu, superb food, prices have edged up steadily but it still represents excellent value.

Bit Tet (Beefsteak), 51 Hang Buom St, T04-8251211, evenings only, last orders around 2100. Possibly the most authentic Vietnamese diner in town. It's rough and ready and you'll share your table but the soups and steak frites are simply superb. At around US$3 per head, it is understandably crowded.

Com Chay Nang Tam, 79A Tran Hung Dao St, T04-9424140, daily 1100-1400, 1700-2200. This popular little a/c vegetarian restaurant is down an alley off Tran Hung Dao St. Serves excellent and inexpensive 'Buddhist' dishes.

West of the Citadel *p107, map p108*

International

KOTO, 61 Van Mieu St, T04-7470337, www.streetvoice.com.au, daily 0630-1630, also Fri-Sun1800-2130. A training restaurant for underprivileged young people. Vegetarian dishes include tomato and courgette risotto and aubergine salad. Also lemongrass-skewered chicken kebabs, Bun Bo Nam Bo (southern-style marinaded beef) and even beer-battered fish and chips with tartare sauce.

Bars and clubs

Central Hanoi *p104, maps p108 and p117*
The Bao Khanh and Hang Hanh area is packed with bars. It's very lively all day and evening but, like most places in Hanoi, shuts down around midnight.

Apocalypse Now, 5C Hoa Ma St, T04-9712783, daily 2000-0200. A cavernous venue in a dusty pink warehouse with green shutters. Sand sacking, billiard tables and a very large oil painting of Marlon Brando as Colonel Kurtz on the wall. Filled with local and visiting revellers in search of a legend, it plays dance music 'til the early hours.

Funky Monkey, 15B Hang Hanh St, daily 1000-late. Stylish decor, good music and a good atmosphere. Darts, pool and bar football. Happy hour 1600-1900 for beer, 1900-2100 for cocktails.

Ho Guom Xanh, 32 Le Thai To St, T04-8288806, daily 1800-2400. From outside its impossible to imagine the colourful and operatic stageshows this nightclub puts on nightly at 2200. Drinkers hang out in the submarine-like entrance before moving to the main arena for lasers and live music. Always packed and popular with a mainly local crowd. Drinks are fairly expensive.

Legends, 1-5 Dinh Tien Hoang, T04-9360345, www.legendsbeer.com.vn, daily 0900-2300. One of Hanoi's popular micro-breweries, serving strong and tasty

German light and dark beers. Tremendous views over Hoan Kiem Lake and an extensive food menu, including good snacks and ice cream.

Red Beer, 97 Ma May St, T04-8260247, daily 1000-2300. This micro-brewery serves outstanding Belgian brews. The smell of hops hits you as you walk through the door. Copper vats and stainless steel vessels line the back wall.

Spotted Cow, 23C Hai Ba Trung St, T04-8241028, daily 1130-0300. Cheerful and lively pub decorated in Friesian cows. Happy hour until 1800, food until 2400.

Entertainment

Central Hanoi *p104, map p117*
Dance and theatre
Opera House, T04-9330113, nthavinh@hn.vn.vn, box office daily 0800-1700. Housed in an impressive French-era building at the east end of Trang Tien St (see p106). A variety of Vietnamese and western concerts, operas and plays are staged. Schedule in *Vietnam News* or from the box office.

Water puppet theatre
Water Puppetry House, 57 Dinh Tien Hoang St, T04-8249494, www.thanglong waterpuppet.org, box office daily 0830-1200, 1530-2000. Fabulous shows with exciting live music and beautiful comedy: the technical virtuosity of the puppeteers is astonishing. Performances Mon-Sat 1715, 1830 and 2000, plus an additional matinee on Sun 0930. Admission 40,000d (1st class), 20,000d (2nd class); children 10,000d and 5000d.

Festivals and events

Around Hanoi *p113*
Perfume Pagoda from 6th day of the 1st lunar month to end of 3rd lunar month (15th-20th day of 2nd lunar month is the main period) 12 Feb-27 Apr 2006, 4 Mar-16 May 2007, 21 Feb-4 May 2008, 9 Feb-24 Apr 2009. This festival focuses on the worship of the Goddess of Mercy (Quan Am), see p113. Thousands flock to this famous pilgrimage site during the festival period. Worshippers take part in dragon dances and a royal barge sails on the river.

Shopping

Central Hanoi *p101, map p117*
The city is a shopper's paradise with cheap silk and expert tailors, handicrafts and antiques and some good designer shops. Hang Gai St is well geared to the foreign souvenir hunter and stocks an excellent range of clothes, ethnographia, fabrics and lacquerware.

Antiques
Shops along Hang Khay and Trang Tien streets, on the south edge of Hoan Kiem Lake, sell silver ornaments, porcelain, jewellery and carvings. Not everything is either antique or silver; bargain hard.

Art
Art shops abound near Hoan Kiem Lake, especially on Trang Tien St and on Dinh Tien Hoang St at the northeast corner.
Ancient Gallery, 11 Trang Thi St, T04-9349410, www.apricot-art vietnam.com, daily 0800-2000. A well-known gallery. It exhibits an eclectic mixture of styles and mediums from thickly spread oil paintings to lacquer work using montage and from screens to small tiles. Also displays the populist images of conical-hatted workers in fields of young rice. Prices vary according to the artists on show.
Apricot Gallery, 40B Hang Bong St, T04-8288965. Another gallery with high prices and spectacular art. It belongs to the same owners as the Apricot Gallery but tends to feature different artists.
Hanoi Gallery, 110 Hang Bac St, T04-9261064. This is a great find: hundreds of propaganda posters for sale, US$7-US$200, covering various political, historical and socio-cultural themes.

Clothes, fashions, silk and accessories

The greatest concentration is in the Hoan Kiem Lake area particularly on Nha Tho, Nha Chung, Hang Trong and Hang Gai.
Co, 18 Nha Tho, T04-289925, conhatho@yahoo.com, daily 0830-1900. This tiny clothes shop has a very narrow entrance. It has some unusual prints and the craftsmanship is recommended.
Ipa Nima, 59G Hai Ba Trung, T04-9421872, www.ipa-nima.com, Mon-Sat 0900-1900, Sun 1000-1800. You're greeted by a Dali-esque lips sofa and a dazzling mosaic before entering the glittering and sparkling world of Ipa Nima. Shiny shoes, bags, clothes and jewellery boxes. Hong Kong designer Christina Yu is the creative force behind the label. Some shoe sizes are not available.
Song, 5 Nha Tho, T04-8286965, songshops@asiasongdesign.com, daily 0900-2000. The Song shop is run by friendly staff and has beautiful designer clothes and accessories but its floor space is much smaller than the Ho Chi Minh City store (see p231).
Tina Sparkle, 17 Nha Tho St, T04-9287616, tinasparkle@ipa-nima.com, daily 0900-2000. Funky boutique that sells mostly bags in a glittering array of designs, from tropical prints to big sequinned flowers (around US$35). Also, divine sequinned shoes by Christina Yu (around US$60). Occasional sales will save you 50%.

Handicrafts
Chi Vang, 17 Trang Tien, T04-9360027, chivang@fpt.vn, daily 0800-2000. A beautifully restored building selling exquisitely embroidered cloths, babies' bed linen and clothing, cushion covers, tablecloths and unusual-shaped cushions artfully arranged in the spacious interior.
Mosaique, 22 Nha Tho St, T04-9286181, daily 0830-2000. An Aladdin's cave of embroidered table runners, lamps and stands, beautiful silk flowers for accessorising, silk curtains, furry silk cushions, metal ball lamps, pillow cushions and lotus flower- shaped lamps.

▲ Activities and tours

Hanoi *maps p108 and p117*
Tour operators
The most popular option for travellers are the budget cafés, which offer reasonably priced tours and an opportunity to meet fellow travellers. Operators match their rivals' prices and itineraries closely and indeed many operate a clearing system to consolidate passenger numbers to more profitable levels. Many Hanoi tour operators run tours to **Halong Bay**, see p114. Some also offer kayaking trips.
Ann Tours, 18 Duong Thanh St, T8-9231366, www.anntours.com. Excellent company with knowledgeable guides. Local and general tours as well as veteran tours, golf and culinary tours.
A-Z Queen Travel, 50 Hang Be St, T04-8267356, www.azqueencafe.com.

A well-connected organization capable of handling tailor-made as well as standard tours for individuals as well as groups.

Buffalo Tours Vietnam, 9-13 Hang Muoi St, T04-8280702, www.buffalotours.com. Well-established and well-regarded organization. It offers tours to the north and day trips around Hanoi and also operates the *Jewel of the Bay* boat around Halong Bay. This comfortably furnished boat with capacity for 10 includes children's toys, a deck for sunbathing and star-watching, enormous amounts of food and welcoming staff. Kayaks are also available for exploration from the boat.

Discovery Indochina, 63A Cua Bac St, T04-7164132, www.discoveryindochina.com. Private and customized tours.

Ethnic Travel, 35 Hang Giay St, T04-9261951, www.ethnictravel.com. Little more than a one-man show but, to judge by the comments of satisfied customers, it is well worth investigating.

Individual non-gimmicky tours to Bai Tu Long Bay (next to Halong Bay) and Ninh Binh. Also homestays. Always tries to shows travellers the 'real' Vietnam.

ET-Pumpkin, 82 Ma May St, T04-9260739, www.et-pumpkin.com. Very professional in attitude, offering a good selection of travel services, particularly for visitors to the northwest. Good place for jeep hire.

Exotissimo, 26 Tran Nhat Duat St, T04-8282150, www.exotissimo.com. Specializes in more upmarket tours, good nationwide service.

Green Bamboo, 2A Duong Thanh St, T04-8286504, www.greenbamboo travel.com. Another well-established leader in the budget market.

Haivenu Tours, 12 Nguyen Trung Truc St, Ba Dinh, T04-9272917, www.haivenu-vietnam.com.

Handspan Adventure Travel, 80 Ma May St, T04-9260581, www.handspan.com.

Email: info@buffalotours.com
www.buffalotours.com

Your key to unlocking the treasures of Vietnam and Cambodia

Hanoi: 9-13 Hang Muoi Str - Tel: 84-4-828-0702
HCMC: Suite 302 Jardine House, 58 Dong Khoi Str - Tel: 84-8-827-9169

DISCOVERY INDOCHINA
63A Cua Bac Str. Hanoi, Vietnam
Tel:(+84-4) 7 164132,
Fax: (+84-4) 7 164133

Vietnam, Cambodia, Laos, Myanmar
Private and Customized tours

Discover the mystique and treasures of Indochina, mountain tribal markets, ancient temple ruins, deserted island beaches, intriguing local culture and friendly people.

www.discoveryindochina.com
info@discoveryindochina.com

Reputable and well-organized business. Specializes in adventure tours, trekking in the north and kayaking in Halong Bay, also has its own junk in Halong Bay.

Kim Café, 31 Ha Tien St, T04-8364212, www.kimcafetravel.com. Budget tours across the country, car rental, flight and Open Tour Bus tickets, restaurant and hotel reservations and visa arrangement.

New Indochina Travel, 4C Dang Thai Than, T04-9330599, rockydang@ yahoo.com. Specialists in youth travel. Cheapest student airfares out of Vietnam.

Queen Travel, 65 Hang Bac St, T04-8260860, www.queencafe.com.vn. A well-connected, large organization, capable of handling tailor-made as well as standard nationwide and local tours. Offers other tourist services.

Real Darling Café, 33 Hang Quat St, T04-8269386, darling_café@hotmail.com. Long-established and efficient. Concentrates on tours of the north, visas.

Sinh Café, 52 Hang Bac St, T04-4926585, sinhcafevn.com. One of the most successful operations in the country. Good for individual off-the-peg tours and, with their wide range of contacts, pretty well geared to offer more specialist travel.

Topas, 74A Nguyen Truong To St, Truch Bach Ward, Bah Dinh District, T04-7151005, www.topas-adventure-vietnam.com. Well-run and good tour operator.

⊖ Transport

Hanoi *maps p108 and p117*

Air

For airport information, see p70; for details of international and domestic flights, see p18. **Airline offices** Air France, 1 Ba Trieu St, T04-8253484. Cathay Pacific, 49 Hai Ba Trung St, T04-8267298 (Noi Bai, T04-8261113). **Lao Airlines**, Quang Trung St, T/F4-8229951. **Malaysian Airlines**, 15 Ngo Quyen St, T04-8268820. **Pacific Airlines**, 100 Le Duan, T04-8515356. **Singapore Airlines**, 17 Ngo Quyen St, T04-8268888. **Thai**, 44B Ly Thuong Kiet St, T04-8266893. **Vietnam Airlines**, 1 Quang Trung St, T04-8320320.

Bicycle

This is the most popular form of local mass transport and is an excellent way to get around the city. Bikes can be hired from the little shops at 29-33 Ta Hien St and from most tourist cafés and hotels; expect to pay about US$1-2 per day.

Bus

Tour operators such as **Sinh Café** run Open Tour buses from offices in the Old City to major tourist destinations in the south. See Getting around, p21.

Cyclo

Cyclos are ubiquitous especially in the Old City. A trip from the railway station to Hoan Kiem Lake should not cost more than 15,000d. The same trip on a *xe ôm* would be 10,000d.

Motorbike

Hiring a motorbike is a good way of getting to some of the more remote places. Tourist cafés and hotels rent a variety of machines for US$6-8 per day. Note that hire shops insist on keeping the renter's passport, so it can be hard to rent other than at your hotel. **Cuong's Motorbike Adventure**, 40 Luong Ngoc Quyen St, T04-8266586, buys, sells, rents and repairs Minsks only.

Taxi and private car

There are plenty of metered taxis in Hanoi: **Airport Taxi**, T04-8733333; **City Taxi**, T04-8222222; **Hanoi Taxi**, T04-8535252; **Mai Linh Taxi**, T04-8222666. Private cars with drivers can be chartered from most hotels and from many tour operators, see p122.

Train

The **central station** (*Ga Hanoi*) is at 126 Le Duan St (a 10-min taxi ride from the centre of town), T04-942 3697. For trains to **Ho**

Chi Minh City and the south, enter the station from Le Duan St. For trains to **Lao Cai** (for Sapa) enter the station from Tran Quy Cap St. It is possible to walk across the tracks if you go to the wrong part. There are daily connections with **Ho Chi Minh City**; advance booking required.

Overnight trains from Hanoi to **Lao Cai**, 8½-10 hrs, from where a fleet of minibuses ferries passengers on to **Sapa**. The train carriages are run by different companies, as follows. The very popular **Victoria Express**, with dining carriage, is for Victoria Hotel guests only, and departs Hanoi on Mon, Wed, Fri and Sat at 2200 (service LC5), arriving 0630 the following morning. The return trip departs from Lao Cai on Tue 1900 (LC2) arriving 1600, on Thu and Sat at 1020 (LC4) arriving 0810, and on Sun at 2115 (LC6) arriving 0600. Prices vary, US$90-US$220 return. **Royal Train**, T04-8245222, leaves Hanoi daily at 2130 (service SP1) arriving at 0600 and returns from Lao Cai at 2115 daily (LC6) arriving at 0600, tickets from 200,000d one way. **Tulico** carriages, T04-8287806, leave on the 2200 LC5 service, arriving at Lao Cai at 0630, 250,000d for a first class cabin, 200,000d for second class. This service returns on the LC6 at 2115 Sun arriving 0600. **Ratraco** (part of Vietnam Railways), 2F Vietnam Railtour Building, 95-97 Le Duan St, T04-9422889, ratraco@hn.vnn.vn, has berths on several trains from 210,000d.

⊙ Directory

Hanoi *maps p108 and p117*
Banks
Commission is charged on cashing TCs into US$ but not into dong. It is better to withdraw dong from the bank and pay for everything in dong. Most hotels will change dollars, often at quite fair rates. ATMs are now to be found in most large hotels and in some post offices. **ANZ Bank**, 14 Le Thai To St, T04-8258190, Mon-Fri 0830-1600. Provides full banking services including cash advances on credit cards, 2% commission on TCs,

24-hr ATMs. **Citibank**, 17 Ngo Quyen St, T04-8251950. Cashes TCs into dong. **Commercial & Industrial Bank**, 37 Hang Bo St, T04-8285359. Dollar TCs can be changed here, with 1.25% commission for converting dollars cash. **Vietcombank**, 198 Tran Quang Khai St, T04-8243108. 2% commission if converted to dollars cash.

Embassies and consulates
Australia, 8 Dao Tan St, T04-8317755. **Cambodia**, 71 Tran Hung Dao St, T04-9424789. **Canada**, 31 Hung Vuong St, T04-8235500. **Laos**, 22 Tran Binh Trong St, T04-9424576. **Thailand**, 63-65 Hoang Dieu St, T04-8235092. **UK**, Central Building, 31 Hai Ba Trung St, T04-8252510. **USA**, 7 Lang Ha St, T04-8431500.

Hospitals
Hanoi Family Medical Practice, 109-112 Van Phuc, T04-8430748, 24 hour emergency (T090401919). 24-hr medical service, also dental care. **Hospital Bach Mai**, Giai Phong St, T04-8693731. English-speaking doctors. Dental service. **International SOS**, Central Building, 31 Hai Ba Trung St, T04-9340666, http://www.internationalsos.com/countries/Vietnam/. 24-hr, emergencies and medical evacuation. Dental service too.

Immigration
Immigration Dept, 40A Hang Bai St, T04-8266200.

Internet
Internet access is cheap and easy. All the travel cafés now have services. The cheapest rates are about 3000d per hr, the most expensive are 200-300d/min.

Post office
GPO, 75 Dinh Tien Hoang St. International telephone service also available at the PO at 66-68 Trang Tien St and at 66 Luong Van Can St and at the PO on Le Duan next to the train station. **DHL**, in GPO.

Northwest Vietnam

Fields among the high mountains, Sapa

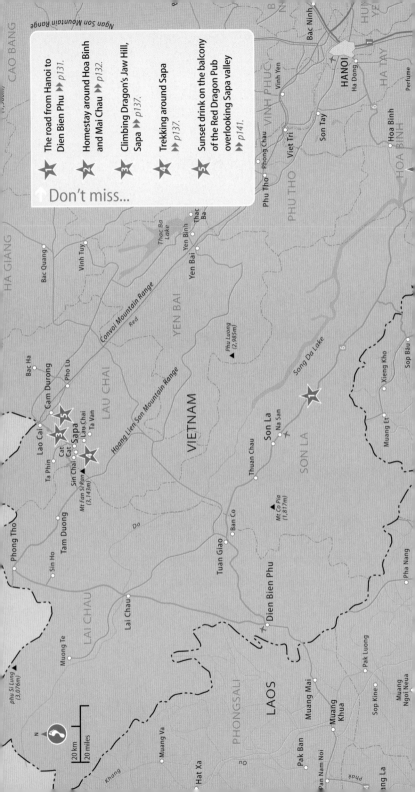

Ngan Son Mountain Range

↑ Don't miss...

★1 **The road from Hanoi to Dien Bien Phu** ▶▶ *p131.*

★2 **Homestay around Hoa Binh and Mai Chau** ▶▶ *p132.*

★3 **Climbing Dragon's Jaw Hill, Sapa** ▶▶ *p137.*

★4 **Trekking around Sapa** ▶▶ *p137.*

★5 **Sunset drink on the balcony of the Red Dragon Pub overlooking Sapa valley** ▶▶ *p141.*

The north is a mountainous region punctuated by limestone peaks and luscious valleys of terraced paddy fields, tea plantations, stilt houses and water hyacinth-quilted rivers. Sapa, in the far northwest, is a former French hill station, home of the Hmông and set in a stunning valley, carpeted with Alpinese flowers. It is a popular centre for trekking. Scattered around are market towns and villages populated by Vietnam's ethnic minorities such as the Black Hmông, Red Dao, Flower Hmông, Phu La, Dao Tuyen, La Chi and Tày – the latter being Vietnam's largest ethnic minority.

Nor is the region without wider significance; the course of world history was altered at Dien Bien Phu in May 1954 when the Vietnamese defeated the French. In 2004 a vast bronze statue commemorating the victory was erected; it towers over the town. Closer to Hanoi is Hoa Binh where villages of the Muòng and Dao can be seen and the beautiful Mai Chau Valley, home to the Black and White Thái whose attractive houses nestle amid the verdant paddies of the hills.

Ratings

Landscape
★★★★★

Relaxation
★★

Activities
★★

Culture
★★★

Wildlife
★

Costs
$$$-$$

Northwest Vietnam

The geology of much of northwest Vietnam is limestone; the humid tropical climate and the resulting streams and rivers have a remarkable effect on this soft rock. Large cones and towers, some with vertical walls and overhangs, rise dramatically from the flat alluvial plains. This landscape, dotted with bamboo thickets, is one of the most evocative in Vietnam; its hazy images seem to linger deep in the collective Vietnamese psyche and perhaps symbolize a sort of primaeval Garden of Eden, an irretrievable age when life was simpler and more innocent.

Incorporated into this landscape are the homes of the ethnic minorities, beautiful tiled houses in the main. Passing through, you will see people tending paddies in traditional clothing and boys on the backs of buffalos. In the

> ◯ **Getting there** Either take the train direct to Sapa or tackle the whole route by organized tour, hired jeep or motorbike.
> ◯ **Getting around** Organized transport or hired motorbike.
> ◯ **Time required** Minimum 4 days.
> ◯ **Weather** Wet May-Sep; cold in winter.
> ◯ **Sleeping** Good range of accommodation in Sapa, homestays around Hoa Binh, Mai Chau and Sapa.
> ◯ **Eating** Northern cuisine and international menus in Sapa.
> ▲ **Activities and tours** Horse riding, cycling, motorbiking and trekking.
> ★ **Don't miss...** Trekking around Sapa when the paddies are at their most verdant. ▸▸ *p137.*

far-flung northwest corner is Dien Bien Phu, the site of the overwhelming defeat of the French in Vietnam in 1954 and now home to the largest monument in the country, erected in 2004 to commemorate the 50th anniversary of the Vietnamese victory.

Ins and outs ◯ ▸▸ *p142*

Getting there and around

There are three points of entry for the northwest circuit: to the south **Hoa Binh** (reached by road); to the north **Lao Cai/Sapa** (reached by road or preferably by train) and, bang in the middle, **Dien Bien Phu** reached by road or by plane. Which option you pick will depend upon how much time you have available and how much flexibility you require.

Expect overland journeys to be slow and sometimes arduous in this mountainous region but the discomfort is more than compensated for by the sheer majesty of the landscapes. The road south of Dien Bien Phu has been significantly upgraded over recent years but the route north to Sapa is still poor and a 4WD is recommended. Jeeps with driver can be hired from some tour operators in Hanoi (see p122) for the five- or six-day round trip for US$330-370. A good and slightly cheaper option is to leave the jeep in Sapa (about US$275) and catch the overnight train back to Hanoi from Lao Cai. For those willing to pay more, Japanese land cruisers offer higher levels of comfort.

Another option is to do the whole thing by motorbike. The rugged terrain and relatively quiet roads make this quite a popular choice for many people. It has the particular advantage of allowing countless side trips and providing

Paddy fields around Sapa

access to really remote and untouched areas. It is not advised to attempt the whole circuit using public transport as this would involve fairly intolerable levels of discomfort and a frustrating lack of flexibility.

Best time to visit

The region is wet from May to September. This makes travel quite unpleasant. Owing to the altitude of much of the area winter can be quite cool, especially around Sapa, so make sure you go well prepared.

Towards Dien Bien Phu ⊜❼❻❶▲❸❻ » pp139-143

The road from Hanoi to Dien Bien Phu winds its way for 420 km into the Annamite Mountains that mark the frontier with Laos. The round trip from Hanoi and back via Dien Bien Phu and Sapa is about 1200 km and offers, perhaps, the most spectacular scenery anywhere in Vietnam. Opportunities to experience the lives, customs and costumes of some of Vietnam's ethnic minorities abound. The loop can be taken in a clockwise or anti-clockwise direction; the advantage of following the clock is the opportunity to recover from the rigours of the journey in the tranquil setting of Sapa.

Highway 6, which has been thoroughly rebuilt along almost the entire route from Hanoi to Son La, leads southwest out of Hanoi to Hoa Binh. Setting off in the early morning (this is a journey of dawn starts and early nights), the important arterial function of this road to Hanoi can be clearly seen: ducks, chickens, pigs, bamboo and charcoal all pour in – the energy and building materials of the capital – much of it transported by bicycle. Beyond the city limits, the fields are highly productive, with market gardens and intensive rice production.

Hoa Binh

Hoa Binh, on the banks of the Da (Black) River, marks the southern limit of the interior highlands. It is 75 km from Hanoi, a journey of about 2½ hours. Major excavation sites of the Hoabinhian prehistoric civilization (10,000 BC) were found in the province, which is its main claim to international fame.

Traditional Muòng house in the hills near Hoa Binh

Hoa Binh Province Museum (Bao Tang Tinh Hoa Binh) ⓘ *daily 0800-1030, 1400-1700, 5000d*, contains items of archaeological, historical and ethnographical importance. Relics of the First Indochina War, including a French amphibious landing craft, remain from the bitterly fought campaign of 1951-1952 which saw Viet Minh forces successfully dislodge the French.

Muòng and **Dao minority villages** are accessible from Hoa Binh. **Xom Mo** is 8 kmfrom Hoa Binh and is a village of the Muòng minority. There are around 10 stilt houses, where overnight stays are possible (contact **Hoa Binh Tourist**, T018-854370/372), and there are nearby caves to visit. **Duong** and **Phu** are villages of the Dao Tien (Money Dao), located 25 km up river. Boat hire (US$25) is available from **Hoa Binh Tourist**. A permit is required for an overnight stay.

Mai Chau and Lac

After leaving Hoa Binh, Highway 6 heads in a south-southwest direction as far as the Chu River. Thereafter it climbs through some spectacular mountain scenery before descending into the beautiful Mai Chau Valley. During the first half of this journey, the turtle-shaped roofs of the Muòng houses predominate but, after passing Man Duc, the road enters the territory of the Thái, northwest Vietnam's most prolific ethnic minority, heralding a subtle change in the style of stilted-house architecture. This region is dominated by Black Thái communities (a sub-ethnic group of the Thái) but White Thái also live in the area.

The growing number of foreign and domestic tourists visiting the area in recent years has had a significant impact on the economy of Mai Chau and the lifestyles of its inhabitants. Some foreign visitors complain that the valley offers a manicured hill-tribe village experience to the less adventurous tourist who wants to sample the quaint lifestyle of the ethnic people without too much discomfort. There may be some truth in this allegation, yet there is another side to the coin. Since the region first opened its doors to foreign tourists in 1993, the **Mai Chau People's Committee** has attempted to control the effect of tourism on the valley. **Lac** (WhiteThái village) is the official tourist village to which tour groups are led and, although it is possible to visit and even stay in the others, the committee hopes that by 'sacrificing' one village to tourism, the impact on other communities will be limited. Income generated from tourism by the villagers of Lac has

Rice farming in the Mai Chau valley

brought about a significant enhancement to the lifestyles of people throughout the entire valley, enabling many villagers to tile their roofs and purchase consumer products such as television sets, refrigerators and motorbikes.

Lac is easily accessible from the main road from the direction of Hoa Binh. Take the track to the right, immediately before the ostentatious, red-roofed **People's Committee Guesthouse**. This leads directly into the village. You can borrow or rent a bicycle from your hosts and wobble across narrow bunds to the neighbouring hamlets, enjoying the ducks, buffalos, children and lush rice fields as you go – a delightful of experience.

About 5 km south of Mai Chau on Route 15A is the Naon River on which, in the dry season, a boat can be taken to visit a number of large and impressive **grottoes**. Others can be reached on foot. If you wish to visit them, ask your hosts or at the **People's Committee Guesthouse** for details, see p139.

Dien Bien Phu
ⓘ *The airport is 2 km north of town. The battlefield sites, most of which lie to the west of the Nam Yum River, are a bit spread out and best visited by car or by motorbike. Since the majority of visitors arrive in Dien Bien Phu using their own transport, this is not normally a problem.*

Dien Bien Phu lies in the Mường Thanh valley, a region where, even today, ethnic Vietnamese still represent less than one-third of the total population. For such a remote and apparently insignificant little town to have earned itself such an important place in the history books is a considerable achievement. And yet, the Battle of Dien Bien Phu in 1954 was a turning point in colonial history. It was the last calamitous battle between the French and the forces of Ho Chi Minh's Viet Minh and was waged from March to May 1954. The French, who under Vichy rule had accepted the authority of the Japanese during the Second World War, attempted to regain control after the Japanese had surrendered. Ho, following his Declaration of Independence on 2 September 1945, thought otherwise, heralding nearly a decade of war before the French finally gave up the fight after their catastrophic defeat here. It marked the end of French involvement in Indochina and heralded the collapse of its colonial empire. Had the Americans, who shunned French appeals for help, taken more careful note of what happened at Dien Bien Phu they might have avoided their own calamitous involvement in Vietnamese affairs just a decade later.

Victory Monument, Dien Bien Phu

General de Castries' bunker ⓘ *daily 0700-1100, 1330-1700, 5000d*, has been rebuilt on the sight of the battlefield and eight of the 10 French tanks are scattered over the valley, along with US-made artillery pieces. East of the river, **Hill A1** ⓘ *daily 0700-1800*, known as Eliane 2 to the French, was the scene of the fiercest fighting. Remains of the conflict include a bunker, the 'bison' (tank) known as 'Gazelle', a war memorial dedicated to the Vietnamese who died on the hill and, around at the back, the entrance to a tunnel dug by coal miners from Hon Gai. Their tunnel ran for several hundred metres to beneath French positions and was filled with 1000 kg of high explosives. It was detonated at 2300 on 6 May as a signal for the final assault. The huge crater is still there. Opposite the hill, the renovated **Historic Victory Exhibition Museum** (Nha Trung Bay Thang Lich Su Dien Bien Phu) ⓘ *daily 0700-1100, 1330-1800, 5000d*, has a good collection of assorted Chinese, American and French weapons and artillery in its grounds. Inside are photographs and other memorabilia, together with a large illuminated model of the valley, illustrating the course of the campaign, and an accompanying video. While every last piece of Vietnamese junk is carefully catalogued, displayed and described, French relics are heaped into tangled piles. The **Revolutionary Heroes' Cemetery** ⓘ *opposite the Exhibition Museum next to Hill A1, daily 0700-1100, 1330-1800*, contains the graves of 15,000 Vietnamese soldiers killed during the course of the Dien Bien Phu campaign. At the north end of town, the **Victory monument** (Tuong Dai Chien Dien Bien Phu) ⓘ *entrance next to the TV station on 6 Pho Muong Thanh; look for the tower and large pond*, erected on D1 at a cost of US$2.27 mn, is the largest monument in Vietnam. The enormous, 120-tonne bronze sculpture was created by former army soldier Nguyen Hai and depicts three Vietnamese soldiers standing on top of de Castries' bunker. It was commissioned to mark the 50th anniversary of the Vietnamese victory.

Sapa and around ⊜❼⓭⊕⊘▲⊜⓲ ›› *pp139-143*

Despite the countless thousands of tourists who have poured in every year for the past decade, Sapa retains great charm. Its beauty derives from two things: the impressive natural setting high on a valley side, with Fan Si Pan, Vietnam's tallest mountain either clearly visible or brooding in the mist; and the clamour and colour of the ethnic minorities selling jewellery and clothes. Distinctly oriental but un-Vietnamese in manner and appearance are the Hmông, Dao and other groups who come to Sapa to trade. Interestingly, the Hmông (normally so reticent) have been the first to seize the commercial opportunities presented by tourism. Saturday night is always a big occasion for Black Hmông and Red Dao teenagers in the Sapa area, as youngsters from miles around come to the so-called 'Love Market' to find a partner. The market proved so popular with tourists that the teenagers now arrange their trysts and liaisons in private. Sapa's regular market is at its busiest and best on Sunday mornings, when most tourists scoot off to Bac Ha (see p138).

Ins and outs

Getting there and around Travel to Sapa is either by road on the northwest circuit or by overnight train from Hanoi, via Lao Cai. A fleet of minibuses ferries passengers from Lao Cai railway station to Sapa. Sapa is a charming town, small enough to walk around easily. From Sapa there are a great many walks and treks to outlying villages. 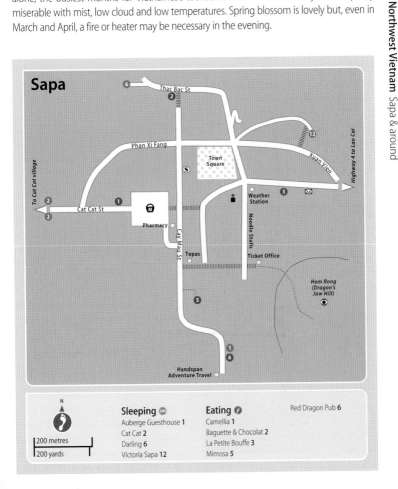 ▸▸ *p124 and p142.*

Best time to visit At 1650 m Sapa enjoys warm days and cool evenings in the summer but gets very cold in winter. Snow falls, on average, every couple of years and settles on the surrounding peaks of the Hoang Lien Son Mountains. Rain and cloud can occur at any time of year but the wettest months are May to September with nearly 1 m of rain in July and August alone, the busiest months for Vietnamese tourists. December and January can be pretty miserable with mist, low cloud and low temperatures. Spring blossom is lovely but, even in March and April, a fire or heater may be necessary in the evening.

Northwest Vietnam Sapa & around

Sapa

200 metres
200 yards

Sleeping
Auberge Guesthouse 1
Cat Cat 2
Darling 6
Victoria Sapa 12

Eating
Camellia 1
Baguette & Chocolat 2
La Petite Bouffe 3
Mimosa 5

Red Dragon Pub 6

Morning mist shrouds the peaks around Sapa

Background

Originally a Black Hmông settlement, Sapa was first discovered by Europeans when a Jesuit missionary visited the area in 1918. By 1932 news of the quasi-European climate and beautiful scenery of the Tonkinese Alps had spread throughout French Indochina. By the 1940s an estimated 300 French buildings – including a sizeable prison and the summer residence of the Governor of French Indochina – had sprung up. Until 1947 there were more French than Vietnamese in the town, which became renowned for its many parks and flower gardens. However, as the security situation began to worsen during the latter days of French rule, the expatriate community steadily dwindled and, by 1953, virtually all had gone. Immediately following the French defeat at Dien Bien Phu in 1954, victorious Vietnamese forces razed a large number of Sapa's French buildings to the ground.

Sapa church

Sights

Sapa is a pleasant place to relax in and unwind. Being comparatively new it has no important sights but several French buildings in and around are worth visiting. The huge scale of the Fan Si Pan range gives Sapa an Alpine feel and this impression is reinforced by *haut savoie* vernacular architecture, with steep pitched roofs, window shutters and chimneys. Each house has its own neat little garden of temperate flora – foxgloves, roses, apricot and plum trees – carefully nurtured by generations of gardeners. But in an alluring blend of European and Vietnamese vegetation, the gardens are cultivated alongside thickets of bamboo and delicate orchids, just yards above the paddy fields.

Trekking rules

Tourists wanting to trek around Sapa are no longer allowed to go it alone. Visitors must now have a touring card, sightseeing ticket and a licensed tour guide to trek six permitted routes in the area, although it is possible to trek to Cat Cat only without a ticket and a guide. Additional routes may be added in the future. Ticket checkpoints have been set up at starting points. Tour guides who violate these new rules will have their licences withdrawn and tourists who do so will be disciplined, according to the People's Committee of Sapa District. The following are permitted routes from Sapa:

- Round trip to Cat Cat and Sin Chai
- Round trip to Cat Cat, Y Linh Ho, Lao Chai and Ta Van
- Round trip to Lao Chai, Ta Van, Ban Ho, Thanh Phu and Nam Cang
- Round trip to Lao Chai, Ta Van, Su Pan and Thanh Kim
- Round trip to Ta Phin, Mong Sen and Takco
- Ascent of Mount Fan Si Pan

The **church** in the centre of Sapa was built in 1930. In the churchyard are the tombs of two former priests, including that of Father Thinh, who was brutally murdered. In the autumn of 1952, Father Thinh confronted a monk named Giao Linh who had been discovered having an affair with a nun at the Ta Phin seminary. Giao Linh obviously took great exception to the priest's interference, for shortly after this, when Father Thinh's congregation arrived at Sapa church for mass one foggy November morning, they discovered his decapitated body lying next to the altar.

Ham Rong (Dragon's Jaw Hill), ⓘ *daily 0600-1800, 15,000d, 5000d children*, offers excellent views of the town. The path winds its way through a number of interesting limestone outcrops and miniature grottoes as it nears the summit. Ethnic minority dance performances take place on the mountain. 🎵 ▸▸ *p141*.

Around Sapa

Trekking to the villages around Sapa is a highlight of this region. It is a chance to observe rural life led in reasonable prosperity. Wet rice forms the staple income, weaving for the tourist market puts a bit of meat on the table. Here, nature is kind: there is rich soil and no shortage of water. It's clear how the landscape has been engineered to suit man's needs: the terracing is on an awesome scale (in places more than 100 steps), the result of centuries of labour to convert steep slopes into level fields which can be flooded to grow rice. Technologically, and in no sense pejoratively, the villages might be described as belonging to a bamboo age: bamboo trunks carry water huge distances from spring to village; water flows across barriers and tracks in bamboo aqueducts; mechanical rice huskers made of bamboo are driven by water requiring no human effort; houses are held up with bamboo; bottoms are parked on bamboo chairs; and tobacco and other substances are inhaled through bamboo pipes. In late 2004, regulations were brought in, which mean that trekking without a licensed guide is no longer possible, see Trekking regulations, above.

Children gathering wood around Sapa (left) and a woman from the Flower Hmông tribe

The track heading west from Sapa through the market area offers either a short 5-km round-trip walk to the Black Hmông village of **Cat Cat** (accessible without a guide) or a longer 10-km round-trip walk (with a licensed guide only, see above) to **Sin Chai** (Black Hmông). Both options take in some beautiful scenery; foreigners must pay 5000d to use the track. The path to Cat Cat leads off to the left of the Sin Chai track after about 1 km, following the line of pylons down through the rice paddies to Cat Cat village; beyond the village over the river bridge you can visit the **cascade waterfall** (from which the village takes its name) and an old French hydro-electric power station that still produces electricity. Sin Chai village is 4 km northwest of here. Walking to **Lai Chai village** (Black Hmông) and **Ta Van village** (Zay or Giáy) with a licensed guide is a longer round trip of 20 km taking in minority villages and beautiful scenery. **Mount Fan Si Pan**, at a height of 3,143 m, is Vietnam's highest mountain and is a three-day trek from Sapa. It lies on a bearing of 240° from Sapa; 9 km as the crow flies but 14 km by track. The route involves dropping to 1200 m and crossing a rickety bamboo bridge before ascending.

North of Sapa is an abandoned **French seminary**, where the names of the bishop who consecrated it and the presiding Governor of Indochina can be seen engraved on stones at the west end. Built in 1942 and under the ecclesiastical jurisdiction of the Parish of Sapa, the building was destroyed 10 years later by militant Vietnamese hostile to the intentions of the order. Beyond the seminary, the path descends into a valley of beautifully sculpted rice terraces and past Black Hmông settlements, with their shy and retiring inhabitants, to **Ta Phin**, a Red Dao village.

Bac Ha, located to the northeast of Sapa, is really only notable for one thing and that is its Sunday morning market. That 'one thing', however, is very special. Hundreds of local minority people flock in from the surrounding districts to shop and socialize, while tourists from all corners of the earth pour in to watch them do it. The market draws in the Flower Hmông, Phu La, Dao Tuyen, La Chi and Tày, and is a riot of colour and fun. While the women trade and gossip, the men consume vast quantities of rice wine; by late morning they can no longer walk so are heaved onto donkeys by their wives and led home. If you have your own transport arrive early; if you haven't, nearly all the hotels and all the tour operators in Sapa organize trips. ▲▶▶ *p142.*

🛏 Sleeping

Hoa Binh *p131*

B Hoa Binh 1, 54 Phuong Lam, T018-852051, F854372. On Highway 6 out of Hoa Binh towards Mai Chau. Clean and acceptable standards, some rooms built in minority style, also an ethnic minority dining experience complete with rice drunk through bamboo straws. Gift shop sells ethnic produce, so for those venturing no further, stock up here.
B Hoa Binh 2, 160 An Duong Vuong, T018-852001. The same facilities as its sister hotel but no restaurant.

Mai Chau and Lac *p132*

Trips to homestays must be booked by tour operators, usually in Hanoi. For a 2-day trip visitors share communal sleeping areas on either wooden beds or, if it is a bamboo home, on the floor. Mattresses, pillows, sheets and mosquito nets are provided. Clean, cold water showers and clean outside natural toilets are available in all homestays. For 2-3 people, US$126 per person including transport, food, an English-speaking guide and transfers. In Mai Chau, visitors can spend the night in a White Thái ethnic house on stilts. Mat, hard pillow, mosquito net, basic washing facilities (cold tap or a well) and sometimes fan provided. This is particularly recommended as the hospitality and easy manner of the people is a highlight of many visitors' stay in Vietnam. Food and local rice wine provided. Avoid the large houses in the centre if possible.
D-E People's Committee Guesthouse, T018-867262. Fan rooms, basic, no restaurant. Competition from the ethnic houses means the guesthouse does not always operate.

Dien Bien Phu *p133*

C Muong Thanh Hotel, 25 Him Lam-TP, T023-810043, F810713. 62 standard rooms with TV, a/c, minibar and fan.

Breakfast included. Internet service. Swimming pool (10,000d for non-guests), karaoke, Thai massage and free airport transfer. Souvenir shop and bikes for rent, 30,000d.
D May Hong, T023-826300. Opposite Vietnam Airlines booking office. Standard rooms with a/c and hot water.
E Beer Hotel (Khach San Cong Ty Bia), Hoang Van Thai St, beyond Hill A1 at the east end of town (no phone), F023-825576. 10 rooms, basic and clean, with fan or a/c, no restaurant but, as the name suggests, beer is served and plenty of it. A little *bia hoi* next to the gate offers fresh cool beer at 7000d a bottle.

Sapa *p134, map p135*

A host of guesthouses has sprung up to cater for Sapa's rejuvenation and the appeal of the town has, perhaps, been a little compromised by the new structures. (Certainly none of them can compare with the style of the lovely old French buildings.) Prices tend to rise Jun-Oct to coincide with northern hemisphere university vacations and at weekends. Hoteliers are accustomed to bargaining; healthy competition ensures rates in Sapa are fair market prices.
B-D Auberge Guesthouse, T020-871243, auberge@sapadiscovery.com. Mr Dang Trung, the French-speaking owner, shows guests his wonderful informal garden with pride: sweet peas, honeysuckle, snap dragons, foxgloves, roses and irises – all familiar to visitors from temperate climes – grow alongside sub-Alpine flora and a fantastic collection of orchids. The rooms are simply furnished but clean and boast bathtubs and log fires in winter. There's a restaurant on the lovely terrace and internet terminals.
B-D Darling, T020-871349. It's a short walk from town to this secluded building but for those seeking peace, it's worth every step. Simple, clean and a warm welcome, stunning views and a colourful garden. A new wing has 12 rooms, rather more expensive but comfortable, and

Northwest Vietnam Listings

Budget busters

Highland retreats

L-A **Victoria Sapa**, T020-871522, www.victoriahotels-asia.com. Opened in 1998 with 76 rooms, a nice position above the town and a pleasant aspect: this hotel is easily the best in town. Comfortable, with well-appointed rooms, it is a lovely place in which to relax and enjoy the peace. In winter there are warming open fires in the bar and dining rooms. The food is very good and the set buffets are excellent value. The Health Centre offers everything from the traditional massage to reflexology. The centre, pool, tennis courts and sauna are open to non-guests. Packages are available.

L **Topas Eco Lodge**, Than Kimh, Lao Cai, 18 km from Sapa, T020-872404, www.topas-eco-lodge.com. Vietnam's virst eco-lodge is perched on a plateau overlooking the Hoang Vien Valley. Palm-thatched bungalows, each with its own bathroom and porch, run on solar power, enjoy fantastic views over the valley. Trekking, horse riding, mountainbiking and handicraft workshops are organized daily for guests and are included in the full-board price. Free transport from Sapa; discounts available.

again, all with fabulous views. The top terrace bedroom has the best view in all of Sapa.

C-D Cat Cat, on the Cat Cat side of town through the market, T020-871946, catcatht@hn.vnn.vn. The guesthouse has expanded up the hillside, with new terraces and small bungalows with balconies all with views down the valley. A friendly and popular place, its 28 rooms span the price range but all represent good value for money. Some of its rooms enjoy some of the the best views in Sapa. The hotel has a good restaurant and, like most others, arranges tours and provides useful information.

Around Sapa *p137*
It is possible to spend the night in one of the ethnic houses in the Sapa district. However, in line with the trekking rules (see p137), homestays must be organized through reputable tour operators and are only permitted in the following villages: **Ta Van Giay**, **Ban Den**, **Muong Bo**, **Ta Phin Commune Central Area**, **Sa Xeng Cultural Village** and **Sin Chai**, as well as at **Topas Eco Lodge** (see Budget buster, above). The Black Hmông villages are

probably the best bet, though facilities are considerably more basic than in the Muòng and Thái stilted houses of Hoa Binh and Mai Chau and travellers will need to bring their own bedding materials and mosquito net. A contribution of around 30,000d should be made (or more if dinner is included).

🍴 Eating

Hoa Binh *p131*
🍴 **Thanh Toi**, 22a Cu Chinh Lan, T018-853951. Local specialities, wild boar and stir-fried eggplant.

Mai Chau and Lac *p132*
Most people will eat with their hosts. Mai Chau town itself has a couple of simple *com pho* places near the market. The rice wine in Mai Chau is excellent, particularly when mixed with local honey.

Dien Bien Phu *p133*
🍴 **Lien Tuoi**, 27 Muong Thanh 8 St, next to the Vietnamese cemetery and Hill A1, T023-824919, daily 0700-2200. Delicious local fare including 14 fish dishes.

¶ **Muong Thanh Hotel** restaurant, 25 Him Lam-TP, T023-810043, daily 0600-2200. Breakfasts, plenty of Vietnamese dishes and a few pasta dishes. Also seafood.

Sapa *p134, map p135*

There are rice and noodle stalls in the market and along the path by the church.

¶¶¶ **Victoria Sapa**, T020-871522, daily 0630-2200. The food is very good, served in the large dining room with an open fire, and the set buffets are excellent value.

¶ **Camellia**, just through market on the right, T020-871455, daily 0600-2300. Long menu, delicious food, plus rice and fruit wine. They'll actually warm the rice bowls for you in winter. The beef steak is rather like dried buffalo but the grilled deer is good, the Camellia salad is spicy and the apple wine is warm and strong.

¶ **La Petite Bouffe**, in the Gecko hotel, T020-871504, daily 0730-2230. A restaurant with a small outdoor terrace almost exclusively devoted to French dining. For the main dishes try the *magret d'oie grille*, grilled goose breast served with rum and pepper sauce, or the *bouef bourguignon au vin rouge*. Lovely French crêpes are served for dessert. From the Vietnamese list, the vast portion of fried noodles is good and perfect before a trek. Vegetarian dishes also served.

¶ **Mimosa**, Cay Mau St, T020-871377, daily 0700-2300. A small, slightly chaotic, family-run restaurant. Sit cosy indoors or in the fresh air on a small terrace. A long menu of good western and Asian dishes. Very popular and service is incredibly slow when busy. Pizzas, pastas and burgers as well as boar, deer, pork and vegetarian dishes.

¶ **Red Dragon Pub**, 21 Muong Hoa St, T020-872085, reddragonpub@hn.vnn.vn, daily 0800-2300 (food until 2130). Done out like an English tearoom with faux Tudor beams and red and white checked tablecloths. Nosh to match: cornflakes, tea and a mean shepherd's pie. Pub upstairs. Fantastic views of the valley.

¶¶-¶ **Baguette & Chocolat**, T/F020-871766, hoasuaschoolsp @hn.vnn.vn, Mon-Sat 0700-2100, Sun 0700-1400. A stylish restaurant and café, with small boulangerie attached. Picnic kits from 32,000d are a useful and welcome service.

🎧 Bars and clubs

Sapa *p134, map p135*

Red Dragon Pub, see Eating. The balcony is perfect for a sunset drink.

Tau Bar, 42 Cau May St, beneath the Tau Hotel, T020-871322, daily 2000-late. It must have the longest bar made of a single tree trunk in the world and worth a beer just to see it. Minimalist, with white walls, stools, darts board and pool table. Range of beers and spirits.

🎵 Entertainment

Hoa Binh *p131*

Hoa Binh Ethnic Minority Culture Troupe, Hoa Binh 1 Hotel. 1-hr shows featuring dance and music of the Muòng, Thái, Hmông and Dao.

Mai Chau and Lac *p132*

Mai Chau Ethnic Minority Dance Troupe. Thái dancing culminating in the communal drinking of sweet, sticky rice wine through straws from a large pot. This troupe performs most nights in Lac in one of the large stilt houses. Admission is included for people on tours; otherwise give a small contribution.

Sapa *p134, map p135*

Ethnic minority dancing, Dragon's Jaw hill at 0915 and 1500 daily, 10,000d.

🛍 Shopping

Mai Chau and Lac *p132*

Villagers offer a range of woven goods and fabrics on which they are becoming dependent for a living. There are also local paintings and wicker baskets, pots,

5 best

Trekking areas

Sapa (Northwest Vietnam) Ethnic minority villages and the highest mountain in Vietnam are all within reach ▶▶ *p134.*
Yok Don National Park (Central Vietnam) Hike and camp among rare wild animals ▶▶ *p192.*
Muang Sing (Northern Laos) Home to the Akha whose rituals and architecture draw interested visitors ▶▶ *p344.*
Luang Namtha (Northern Laos) 30 ethnic minorities share this region with the Nam Ha National Protected Area ▶▶ *p344.*
Phongsali (Northern Laos) A remote, flower-crowned outpost in the far north ▶▶ *p348.*

traps and pouches all well made. Mai Chau is probably the best place for buying handicrafts in the northwest.

Sapa *p134, map p135*
Sapa is the place for buying ethnic clothes but it is not possible to buy walking shoes, rucksacks, coats, jackets or any mountaineering equipment here.
Wild Orchid, 3 shops on Cau May St, T020-871665. Really beautiful wall hangings for around US$15 and clothes.

▲ Activities and tours

Hoa Binh *p131*
Hoa Binh Tourist, Song Da, T018-854370/372. Can arrange boat hire as well as visits to minority villages.

Mai Chau and Lac *p132*
Hanoi tour operators run tours. The cost for a night and two days with transport should be no more than about US$60.

Sapa *p134, map p135*
Therapies
Victoria Sapa. Massage and other treatments are available in the hotel treatment centre. Swimming pool.

Tour operators
Handspan, 8 Cau May St, T020-872110, www.handspan.com. Offers a diverse range of tours in the vicinity of Sapa, including a range of

treks, mountain bike excursions, homestays and jeep expeditions.
Topas, T020-871331, www.topas-adventure-vietnam.com. A combined Danish and Vietnamese operator offering treks from fairly leisurely 1-day walks to an arduous 4-day assault on Mount Fan Si Pan. Also organizes bicycling tours, horse riding and family tours. Well-run operation, with an office in Hanoi.

⊖ Transport

For overland transport, see p130.

Dien Bien Phu *p133*
Air
The airport (T023-824416) is 2 km north of town, off Highway 12. Flights to and from **Hanoi** with **Vietnam Airlines**, office inside Airport Hotel, daily 0700-1100, 1330-1630.

Sapa *p134, map p135*
Train
For all train details, see Hanoi Transport, p124. Passengers alighting at Lao Cai will either be met by their hotel (eg Victoria Sapa) or there is a desk selling minibus tickets to Sapa. Tour operators in Hanoi can also book your ticket for you for a small fee from the top of the class – the Victoria Sapa carriage – downwards. It is often less hassle than organizing it yourself and, if you are in a hurry, it's a great time saver.

Travellers' tales

Vox pop

I met Han in a bar. After downing some seahorse-infused rice wine I felt emboldened enough to start a conversation about things that were not openly talked about in today's Vietnam. Han's father had fought with the North Vietnamese Army and was a staunch communist. Han, however, had studied in Paris, was fluent in French and English and was familiar with living in a democracy. He was at odds with his father over his political beliefs. Han believed in democratic change. He joked about the electoral system – did I know that in one year people were asked to vote for a candidate that had died?, he told me. He said he had agitated for change in France but here, in Vietnam, things were different. Han did have friends who wanted change but they lacked the drive to pursue it for two different reasons, he said. In Vietnam, there is a fear of prosecution. Censorship is all pervasive and those who speak out against the state are persecuted. But, also, a second phenomenon seems to be arresting any political change. Since *doi moi* (the liberalising of the economy) was launched, Han said, the Vietnamese have been able to have, hoard and trade in more money than they have ever known was possible. Han said that for many of his friends the chief topic of conversation was what kind of motorbike they could afford and what were the latest models they should aspire to buying or which ringtone they should acquire for their mobile phone. Han was not disparaging about his friends as he had felt the thrill himself of this new-found economic freedom. However, he feared that the lure of money will keep the Vietnamese diverted for a long time away from pushing for change to the country's political system. *Mary Townsend*

Directory

Dien Bien Phu *p133*
Banks Vietcombank and Nong Nghiep Bank. **Internet** Muong Thanh Hotel.

Sapa *p134, map p135*
Banks The bank will change US$ cash, as will most hotels but at poor rates. Convert before you travel. **Internet** Many of the better hotels have email and allow their customers to use it, normally for around 400-500d per min. **Post office** There are 2 in Sapa from where international phone calls can be made.

Central Vietnam

p148

N

40 km
40 miles

South China Sea

QUANG
BINH

Dong Hoi

▲ Da Mao
Mountain (665m)

▲ Len Mu
Mountain
(918m)

Tunnels of
Vinh Moc

17th Parallel

Muang Sen

Ko

Nabo

Xepon

Lao
Bao

Dong Ha

Quang Tri

Dan Bong

Khe Sanh
(Huong Hoa)

Hué

Muang
Phin

That Hai

LAOS

Tahoy

Tomb of Minh Mang

Tomb of
Gia Long

Lang Co

Danang Bay

Hai Van Pass

Danang

Nadou Gnai

SALAVAN

Bana

Salavan

Vinh Dien

Kiem Lam

My Son

Nam Phuoc

Hoi An

QUANG NAM

p166

Dak Klao

Tam Ky

Van Tat

Ngoc Linh
(2,598m)

Quang Ngai

QUANG
NGAI

VIETNAM

Tasseing

KONTUM

Kontum

Hoai Nhon

BINH
DINH

Ba Mountain
(892m)

Kontum
Plateau

Play Ku
(Pleiku)

GIA LAI

Quy Nhon

Virachey

ROTANOKIRI

Ban Lung

Bokeo

Song Cau

Voen
Kham

STUNG TRENG

Lumphat

Central
Highlands

Ba River

PHU YEN

Tuy Hoa

Stung Treng

Da Rang River

CAMBODIA

KRATIE

Kratie

Chhlong

Mekong

Sen Monorom

MONDOLKIRI

Yok Don
National Park

Dac Lac Plateau

14

Buon Ma Thuot

26

Ninh Hoa

Dray Sap

Lak Lake

Buon Juin

DAK LAK

Langbian
(2,400m)

KHANH
HOA

Nha Trang

Snuol

Ta Dung
(1,971m)

Truong Son
Mountain Range

Prenn Falls

Dalat

Ban Ngoi

Cam Ranh

BINH PHUOC

Dak Nong

14

NINH
THUAN

Dong Xoai

Bao Loc

LAM DONG

Duc Trong

20

Phan Rang

Khanh Hai

Tay
Ninh

TAY
NINH

Dau
Tieng
Lake

Cao Dai
Great Temple

Dong Phu

Tan Phu

Tri An
Lake

Dinh Quan

BINH
DUONG

BINH THUAN

Ham Thuan Bac

Phuoc Dan
Ca Na

Bac Binh

Svay
Rieng

Moc Bai

Bavet

Cu Chi

DONG NAI

Bien Hoa

Xuan Loc

Phan Thiet

Mui Ne

p185

Ho Chi Minh City
(Saigon)

LONG AN

Don't miss...

⭐ 1 Hué's imperial tombs
by boat ▶▶ *p153*.

⭐ 2 Húe to Danang by train
▶▶ *p162*.

⭐ 3 Hoi An's tailors ▶▶ *p183*.

⭐ 4 Kontum's unusual
architecture ▶▶ *p193*.

⭐ 5 Mui Ne ▶▶ *p197*.

The central region extends over 1000 km north to south. It includes the mountains of the Annamite chain, which form a natural frontier with Laos to the west and, in places, extend almost all the way to the sea in the east. This hinterland is the domain of numerous ethnic minorities and is peppered with former French hill stations. The narrow, coastal strip, sometimes only a few kilometres wide, supported the former artistically accomplished kingdom of Champa.

The middle part of the central region is home to World Heritage Sites: the gracious imperial city of Hué stands on the Perfume River, with the artistic tomb complexes of the emperors – built in accordance with the rules of geomancy – resting along the banks. Inland are the brick-carved towers of My Son, spiritual capital of the Cham Kingdom; and, close to the coast, Hoi An is an old mercantile port town that retains traditional architecture and overflows with great shops and restaurants. Its silk shops are famed and its food is fêted. Just 5 km away are the bright sands of Cua Dai Beach.

The southern part of this diverse region is garlanded with stunning coast and beaches: Nha Trang and Mui Ne are ideal spots for a few days by the sea.

Ratings

Landscape
★★★

Relaxation
★★

Activities
★★★

Wildlife
★

Culture
★★★

Costs
$$$-$

Hué, an imperial city that housed generations of the country's most powerful emperors, was built on the banks of the Huong Giang, (Perfume River), 100 km south of the 17th parallel. The river is named after a scented shrub which is supposed to grow at its source.

In many respects, Hué epitomizes the best of Vietnam and, in a country that is rapidly disappearing under concrete, it represents a link to a past where people live in old buildings and don't lock their doors. Whether it is because of the royal heritage or the city's Buddhist tradition, the people of Hué are the gentlest in the country. They speak good English and drive their motorbikes more carefully than anyone else.

⚡ **Getting there** Plane, train or Open Tour Bus.
⊖ **Getting around** Foot, cyclo, motorbike or organized tour.
⊕ **Time required** 1-3 days.
⬙ **Weather** Known for its rain.
⊖ **Sleeping** Good-value, quality accommodation is in short supply.
⚡ **Eating** Good restaurants. Royal court cuisine is a speciality.
▲▲ **Activities and tours** Boat trips on the Perfume River.
★ **Don't miss...** Visiting the Imperial Tombs by boat, along the Perfume River ⟩⟩ *p153*.

Just south of the city are the last resting places of many Vietnamese emperors (p153). A number of war relics in the Demilitarized Zone (DMZ) can be easily visited from Hué (p159).

Ins and outs

Getting there Hué's Phu Bai airport is a 15-20 min drive from the city. There are daily connections with Hanoi and Ho Chi Minh City. **Vietnam Airlines** runs a bus service in to town which costs 25,000d; a taxi costs 90,000d. The railway station is more central. The trains tend to fill up, so advance booking is recommended, especially for sleepers. ⊖ ⟩⟩ *p165*.

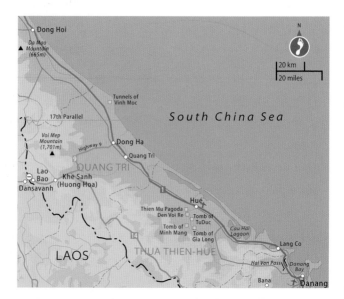

Dragon boats on the Perfume River at Hué

Getting around For the city itself, walking is an option, interspersed, perhaps, with the odd cyclo journey. However, most guesthouses hire out bicycles and this is a very pleasant and slightly more flexible way of exploring Hué and some of the surrounding countryside. A motorbike provides even more independence and makes it possible to visit many more sights in a day. There is also the usual array of *xe ôm* motorbike taxis. The many tour operators in the city will also provide plenty of information and advice.

Getting to and around the **Imperial Tombs** is easiest by motorbike or car as they are spread over a large area. Most hotels and cafés organize tours either by minibus or by boat. Sailing up the Perfume River is the most peaceful way to travel but only a few of the tombs can be reached by boat so *xe ôm* wait at the riverbank to take passengers on to the tombs. All the tombs are accessible by bicycle but you'll need to set out early. It is also possible to go on the back of a motorbike taxi. Further details are given for each individual tomb. ▲▲▶▶ *p164*.

Best time to visit Hué has a reputation for bad weather. Rainfall of 2770 mm has been recorded in a single month. The rainy season runs from September to January and rainfall is particularly heavy between September and November; the best time to visit is therefore between February and August. However, even in the 'dry' season an umbrella is handy. Temperatures in Hué can also be pretty cool in winter, compared with Danang, Nha Trang and other places to the south, as cold air tends to get bottled here, trapped by mountains to the south. For several months each year neither fans nor air-conditioning are required.

Background

Hué was the capital of Vietnam during the Nguyen Dynasty, which ruled Vietnam between 1802 and 1945. For the first time in Vietnamese history a single court controlled the land from Yunnan (southern China) southwards to the Gulf of Siam. To link the north and south (more than 1500 km), the Nguyen emperors built and maintained the Mandarin Road (Quan Lo), interspersed with relay stations. Even in 1802, when it was not yet complete, it took couriers just 13 days to travel between Hué and Ho Chi Minh City, and five days between Hué and Hanoi. If they arrived more than two days late, couriers were punished with a flogging. There cannot have been a better road in Southeast Asia nor a more effective incentive system.

Central Vietnam Hué & around

Although the Confucian bureaucracy and some of the dynasty's technical achievements may have been remarkable, there was continual discontent and uprisings against the Nguyen emperors. The court was packed with scheming mandarins, princesses, eunuchs and scholars writing wicked poetry.

In 1883 a French fleet assembled at the mouth of the Perfume River and opened fire. After taking heavy casualties, Emperor Hiep Hoa sued for peace and signed a treaty making Vietnam a protectorate of France. As French influence over Vietnam increased, the power and influence of the Nguyen waned. The undermining effect of the French presence was compounded by significant schisms in Vietnamese society. In particular, the spread of Christianity was undermining traditional hierarchies. Despite the impressive tombs and palace around Hué, many scholars maintain that the Nguyen Dynasty was simply too short-lived to have ever had a 'golden age'. Although the French and then the Japanese found it to their advantage to maintain the framework of Vietnamese imperial rule, the system became hollow and, eventually, irrelevant. The last Nguyen Emperor, Bao Dai, abdicated on 30 August 1945.

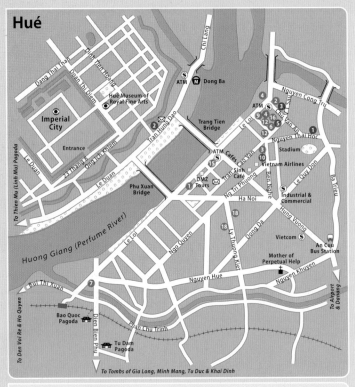

Hué

N

200 metres
200 yards

Sleeping
18 Le Loi **1**
A Dong 1 **2**
Ben Nghe Guesthouse **3**
Century Riverside **4**
Dong Loi & La Carambole
  Restaurant **6**
Hoang Huong **9**
Le Loi Hué **7**
Mimosa **12**
Saigon Morin **15**
Thanh Thuy **16**
No 5 & No 14 **18**

Eating
Am Phu **1**
Dong Tam **5**
Lac Thien & Lac Thanh **2**
Stop & Go **10**
Tropical Garden **3**

Bars & clubs
DMZ **4**
Why Not **12**

During the 1968 Tet offensive, Viet Cong soldiers holed up in Hué's Citadel for 25 days. The bombardment which ensued, as US troops attempted to root them out, caused extensive damage to the Thai Hoa Palace and other monuments. During their occupation of Hué, the NVA forces settled old scores, shooting, beheading and even burning alive 3000 people, including civil servants, police officers and anyone connected with, or suspected of being sympathetic to, the government in Ho Chi Minh City.

Central Hué ⬤🚻🛏🍴🛍⛰🚌🍷 ▸▸ pp162-165

Imperial City

ⓘ *Entrance through the Ngo Mon Gate, 23 Thang 8. Summer 0630-1730 daily, winter 0700-1700 daily. 55,000d; guided tour US$3 for 1½ hrs; English, French and Japanese spoken. Highly enjoyable performances of traditional Vietnamese court music are held in the Royal (East) Theatre, 15,000d.*

The Imperial City at Hué is built on the same principles as the Forbidden Palace in Beijing. It is enclosed by thick outer walls (**Kinh Thanh**), 7-10 m thick, along with moats, canals and towers. Emperor Gia Long commenced construction in 1804 after geomancers had decreed a suitable location and orientation for the palace. The site enclosed the land of eight villages (for which the inhabitants received compensation) and covered 6 sq km, sufficient area to house the emperor and all his family, courtiers, bodyguards and servants. It took 20,000 men to construct the walls alone. Not only has the city been damaged by war and incessant conflict, but also by natural disasters such as floods which, in the mid-19th century, inundated the city to a depth of several metres.

Chinese custom decreed that the 'front' of the palace should face south (like the Emperor) and this is the direction from which visitors approach the site. Over the outer moat, a pair of gates pierce the outer walls: the **Hien Nhon** and **Chuong Duc** gates. Just inside are two groups of massive cannon; four through the Hien Nhon Gate and five through the Chuong Duc Gate. These are the Nine Holy Cannon (**Cuu Vi Than Cong**), cast in bronze in 1803 on the orders of Gia Long. The cannon are named after the four seasons and the five elements, and on each is carved its name, rank, firing instructions and how the bronze of which they are made was acquired. They are 5 m in length but have never been fired. Like the giant urns outside the Hien Lam Cac (see p153), they are meant to symbolize the permanence of the empire. Between the two gates is a massive **flag tower**, from which the flag of the National Liberation Front flew for 24 days during the Tet Offensive in 1968.

Northwards from the cannon, and over one of three bridges which span a second moat, is the **Ngo Mon**, or Royal Gate (**1**), built in 1833 during the reign of Emperor Minh Mang. (The ticket office is just to the right.) The gate, remodelled on a number of occasions since its original construction, is surmounted by a pavilion from where the emperor would view palace ceremonies. Of the five entrances, the central Ngo Mon was only opened for the emperor to pass through. UNESCO has thrown itself into the restoration of Ngo Mon with vigour and the newly finished pavilion atop the gate now gleams and glints in the sun; those who consider it garish can console themselves with the thought that this is how it might have appeared in Minh Mang's time.

North from the Ngo Mon is the **Golden Water Bridge** (**2**) – again reserved solely for the emperor's use – between two tanks (**3**), lined with laterite blocks. This leads to the **Dai Trieu Nghi** (Great Rites Courtyard, **4**), on the north side of which is the **Thai Hoa Palace** (Palace of Supreme Harmony), constructed by Gia Long in 1805 and used for his coronation in 1806. From here, sitting on his golden throne raised up on a dais, the emperor would receive ministers, foreign emissaries, mandarins and military officers during formal ceremonial

---

occasions. In front of the palace are 18 stone stelae, which stipulate the arrangement of the nine mandarinate ranks on the Great Rites Courtyard: the upper level was for ministers, mandarins and officers of the upper grade; the lower for those of lower grades. Civil servants would stand on the left and the military on the right. Only royal princes were allowed to stand in the palace itself, which is perhaps the best-preserved building in the Imperial City complex. Its red and gold columns, tiled floor and fine ceiling have all been restored.

North of the Palace of Supreme Harmony is the **Tu Cam Thanh** (Purple Forbidden City), reserved for the use of the emperor and his family, and surrounded by walls, 1 m thick, to form a city within a city. Tragically, the Forbidden City was virtually destroyed during the 1968 Tet offensive. The two **Mandarin Palaces** and the **Royal Reading Pavilion (10)** are all that survive. The Royal Reading Pavilion has been rebuilt but, needless to say, has no books.

At the far side of Thai Hoa Palace are two enormous **bronze urns** (Vac Dong) decorated with birds, plants and wild animals, and weighing about 1500 kg each. On either side are the **Ta (6)** and **Huu Vu (7)** pavilions, one converted into a souvenir art shop, the other a mock throne room in which tourists can pay US$5 to dress up and play the part of king. On the far side of the palace are the outer northern walls of the citadel and the north gate.

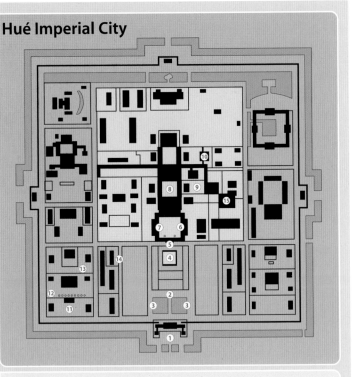

Hué Imperial City

100 metres
100 yards

1 Ngo Mon (Royal Gate)
2 Golden Water Bridge
3 Tanks
4 Dai Trieu Nghi (Great Rites Courtyard) & Thai Hoa Palace (Palace of Supreme Harmony)
5 Red Gate
6 Ta Pavilion
7 Huu Vu Pavilion
8 Central Pavilion, private apartments of the Emperor
9 Quang Minh Palace
10 Royal Reading Pavilion
11 Hien Lam Cac
12 9 Bronze urns
13 Thé Temple
14 Waiting Pavilion, (Huu Ta Dai Lam Vien)
15 Royal (East) Theatre

Tu Cam Thanh (Purple Forbidden City)

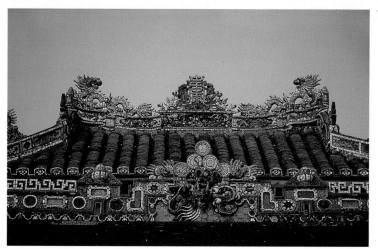

Royal Reading Pavilion, Purple Forbidden City

Most of the surviving buildings of interest are to be found on the west side of the palace, running between the outer walls and the walls of the Forbidden City. At the southwest corner is the well-preserved and beautiful **Hien Lam Cac** (**11**), a pavilion built in 1821, in front of which stand nine massive **bronze urns** (**12**) cast between 1835 and 1837 on the orders of Emperor Minh Mang. It is estimated that they weigh between 1500 kg and 2600 kg, and each has 17 decorative figures, animals, rivers, flowers and landscapes representing between them the wealth, beauty and unity of the country. The central, largest and most ornate urn is dedicated to the founder of the empire, Emperor Gia Long. Next to the urns walking northwards is **Thé Temple** (Temple of Generations, **13**). Built in 1821, it contains altars honouring 10 of the kings of the Nguyen Dynasty (Duc Duc and Hiep Hoa are missing) behind which are meant to be kept a selection of their personal belongings. It was only in 1954 that the stelae depicting the three Revolutionary emperors, Ham Nghi, Thanh Thai and Duy Tan, were brought into the temple. The French, perhaps fearing they would become a focus of discontent, prevented the Vietnamese from erecting altars in their memory. North of the Thé Temple is **Hung Temple**, built in 1804 for the worship of Gia Long's father, Nguyen Phuc Luan, the father of the founder of the Nguyen Dynasty.

Hué Museum of Royal Fine Arts

ⓘ *3 Le Truc St. Tue-Sun 0700-1700, until 1730 in summer (14 Apr-14 Oct). 22,000d. No cameras or video cameras; over shoes are provided; information in English.*

Housed in the Long An Palace, the museum contains a reasonable collection of ceramics, furniture, screens and bronzeware and some stunning, embroidered imperial clothes. The building itself is worthy of note for its elegant construction. Built by Emperor Thieu Tri in 1845, it was dismantled and erected on the present site in 1909.

The Perfume River and the imperial tombs

As the geographical and spiritual centre of the Nguyen Dynasty, Hué and the surrounding area is the site of numerous pagodas, seven imperial tombs and the tombs of numerous other royal personages, countless courtiers and successful mandarins. Many of these are located close to the Perfume River.

Each of the tombs follows the same stylistic formula, although they also reflect the individual tastes and predilections of the emperor in question. The tombs were built during the lifetime of each emperor, who took a great interest in their design and construction; they were, after all, meant to ensure his comfort in the next life. Each mausoleum, variously arranged, has five design elements: a courtyard with statues of elephants, horses and military and civil mandarins (usually approached through a park of rare trees); a stela pavilion (with an engraved eulogy composed by the king's son and heir); a Temple of the Soul's Tablets; a pleasure pavilion, and a grave. Geomancers decreed that they should also have a stream and a mountainous screen in front. The tombs faithfully copy Chinese prototypes, although most art historians claim that they fall short in terms of execution.

Thien Mu Pagoda
ⓘ *An easy 4-km bicycle (or cyclo) ride, following the north bank of the river upstream (west).*
Thien Mu Pagoda (the Elderly Goddess Pagoda), also known as the Thien Mau Tu Pagoda, and locally as the **Linh Mu Pagoda** (the name used on most local maps), is the finest in Hué and beautifully sited on the north bank of the Perfume River. It was built in 1601 by Nguyen Hoang, the governor of Hué, after an old woman appeared to him and said that the site had supernatural significance and should be marked by the construction of a pagoda. The monastery is the oldest in Hué, and the seven-storey **Phuoc Duyen** (Happiness and Grace Tower), built later by Emperor Thieu Tri in 1844, is 21 m high, with each storey containing an altar to a different Buddha. The summit of the tower is crowned with a water pitcher to catch the rain, water representing the source of happiness. Arranged around the tower are four smaller buildings one of which contains the **Great Bell**, cast in 1710 under the orders of the Nguyen Lord, Nguyen Phuc Chu, and weighing 2200 kg. Beneath another of the surrounding pavilions is a monstrous **marble turtle** on which is a stela, carved in 1715 and 2.6 m high, recounting the development of Buddhism in Hué. Beyond the tower, the entrance to the pagoda is through a triple gateway patrolled by six carved and vividly painted guardians, two on each gate. The roof of the sanctuary itself is decorated with jataka stories (birth stories of the Buddha). At the front of the sanctuary is a laughing Buddha in brass. Behind that are an assortment of gilded Buddhas and a crescent-shaped gong, cast in 1677 by Jean de la Croix. Thich Quang Duc, the first monk to commit suicide through self immolation, came from this pagoda (see p216); the grey Austin in which he made the journey to his death in Ho Chi Minh City is still kept here in a garage in the temple garden.

Tomb of Emperor Gia Long
ⓘ *South of town on a tributary of the Perfume River. Daily 0630-1800. 50,000d. Get there by bicycle or motorbike; for directions, see p155.*
The Tomb of Emperor Gia Long is the most distant from Hué and is rarely visited. Overgrown with venerable mango trees and devoid of tourists, touts and ticket sellers, it is the most atmospheric of all the tombs. And, given the historical changes that were to be wrought by the dynasty Gia Long founded, this is arguably the most significant tomb in Hué.

Nguyen Anh, or Gia Long as he was crowned in 1802, came to power with French support. His reign was despotic: when his European advisers suggested that encouragement of industry would lead to the betterment of his poorer subjects, Gia Long replied that he preferred them poor. In fact, the poor were virtual slaves during his reign: the price for one healthy young buffalo was one healthy young girl. It's not surprising, then, that a study by a Vietnamese scholar estimated that there were 105 peasant uprisings between 1802 and 1820 alone. The Vietnamese have never forgiven Gia Long for his despotism nor for the fact that he gave the French a foothold in Vietnam; they still say of him that "*cong ran can ga nha*" (he carried home the snake that killed the chicken).

Background

The death and burial of Emperor Gia Long (1820)

When the Emperor Gia Long died on 3 February 1820, the thread on the ancestors' altar (representing his soul) was tied. The following day the corpse was bathed and clothed in rich garments, and precious stones and pearls were placed in his mouth. Then a ritual offering of food, drink and incense was made, before the body was placed in a coffin made of catalpa wood (*bignonia catalpa*) – a wood impervious to insect attack. At this point, the crown prince announced the period of mourning that was to be observed, a minimum of three years. Relatives of the dead emperor, mandarins and their wives each had different forms and periods of mourning to observe, depending upon their position.

Three days after Gia Long's death, a messenger was sent to the Hoang Nhon Pagoda to inform the dead empress of the demise of her husband. Meanwhile, the new Emperor Minh Mang had the former ruler's deeds recorded and engraved on golden sheets which were bound together as a book. Then astrologers selected an auspicious date for the funeral. After some argument they chose 27 May, although 11 May also had its supporters. On 17 May, court officials told the heaven, the earth and the dynastic ancestors of the details for the funeral and at the same time opened the imperial tomb. On 20 May, the corpse was informed of the ceremony. Four days later the coffin left the palace for the three-day journey to its final resting place. Then, at the appointed time, the coffin was lowered into the sepulchre – its orientation correct – shrouded in silk cloth, protected by a second outer coffin, covered in resin and, finally, bricked in. Next to Gia Long, a second grave was dug into which were placed an assortment of objects useful in his next life. The following morning, Emperor Minh Mang, in full mourning robes, stood outside the tomb facing east, while a mandarin facing in the opposite direction inscribed ritual titles on the tomb. The silk thread on the ancestors' altar, the symbol of the soul, was untied, animals slaughtered and the thread was then buried in the vicinity of the tomb.

(This account is adapted from James Dumarçay's *The palaces of South-East Asia*, 1991.)

To reach Gia Long's tomb, take Dien Bien Phu Street out of town. After a couple of kilometres turn right at the T-junction facing pine-shrouded Dan Nam Giao Temple and take the first left onto Minh Mang. Continue past the sign marking your departure from Hué and take the right-hand branch of the fork in the road. After a short distance the road joins the river bank and heads for some 2 km towards the new Hué bypass (Highway 1) across the river. Follow the riverbank directly underneath this bridge and continue straight on as the road begins to deteriorate. A few metres beyond the Ben Do 1 km milestone is a red sign to 'Gia Long Tomb'. Down a steep path a sampan waits to ferry passengers across this tributary of the Perfume River (bargain but expect to pay US$2-3 return); on the far side, follow the track upstream for about 1 km. Turn right by a café with two billiard tables and then, almost immediately, turn left. Keep on this path. Ask for directions along the way!

Gia Long's geomancers did a great job finding this site: with the mountainous screen in front it is a textbook example of a final resting place. Interestingly, although they had first choice of all the possible sites, this is the furthest tomb from the palace: clearly they took their task seriously. Gia Long's mausoleum was built between 1814 and 1820 (see p155, for an account of the emperor's burial) and, as the first of the dynasty, set the formula for the later tombs. There is a surrounding lotus pond and steps lead up to a courtyard, where the Minh Thanh ancestral temple stands resplendent in red and gold. To the right is a double burial chamber, walled and locked, where Gia Long and his wife are interred (the emperor's tomb is fractionally the taller). The chamber is perfectly lined up with the two huge obelisks on the far side of the lake. Beyond this is a courtyard with five, now headless, mandarins, horses and elephants on each side; steps lead up to the stela eulogizing the emperor's reign, composed, presumably, by his eldest son, Minh Mang, as was the custom. This grey monolith, engraved in Chinese characters, remained miraculously undisturbed during two turbulent centuries.

Tomb of Emperor Minh Mang

ⓘ *12 km south of Hué. Daily 0630-1800. 55,000d. To get there by bicycle or motorbike follow the directions for Gia Long's tomb (p155) but cross the Perfume River using the new road bridge; on the far side of the bridge turn left.*

The Tomb of Emperor Minh Mang is possibly the finest of all the imperial tombs. Built between 1841 and 1843, it is sited among peaceful ponds south of the city. In terms of architectural poise and balance, and richness of decoration, it has no peer in the area. The tomb's layout, along a single central and sacred axis (*Shendao*), is unusual in its symmetry; no other tomb, with the possible exception of Khai Dinh (p157), achieves the same unity of constituent parts, nor draws the eye onwards so easily and pleasantly from one visual element to the next. The tomb was traditionally approached through the **Dai Hong Mon**; today, visitors pass through a side gate into the ceremonial courtyard, which contains an array of statuary. Next is the stela pavilion in which there is a carved eulogy to the dead emperor composed by his son, Thieu Tri. Continuing downwards through a series of courtyards visitors see, in turn, the **Sung An Temple** dedicated to Minh Mang and his

Tomb of Emperor Minh Mang

Tomb of Khai Dinh (left) and Temple of the Elephant Trumpet (right)

empress; a small garden with flower beds that once formed the Chinese character for 'longevity', and two sets of stone bridges. The first consists of three spans, the central one of which (**Trung Dao Bridge**) was for the sole use of the emperor. The second, single bridge, leads to a short flight of stairs with naga balustrades at the end of which is a locked bronze door (no access). The door leads to the tomb itself which is surrounded by a circular wall.

Tomb of Tu Duc

ⓘ *7 km south Hué. Daily 0630-1800. 55,000d. If you're travelling by boat, a return xe ôm trip from the riverbank is 20,000d.*

The Tomb of Tu Duc was built between 1864 and 1867 in a pine wood. The complex is enclosed by a wall and encompasses a lake, with lotus and water hyacinth. An island on the Lake has a number of replicas of famous temples, built by the king, which are now rather difficult to discern. Tu Doc often came here to relax and, from the pavilions that reach out over the lake, composed poetry and listened to music. The **Xung Khiem Pavilion**, built in 1865, has recently been restored with UNESCO's help and is the most attractive building here.

West of the lake, the tomb complex follows the formula described above: ceremonial square, mourning yard with pavilion and then the tomb itself. To the left of Tu Duc's tomb are the tombs of his Empress, Le Thien Anh, and adopted son, Kien Phuc. Many of the pavilions are crumbling and ramshackle, lending the complex a rather tragic air. This is appropriate since, though he had 104 wives, Tu Duc fathered no sons and was therefore forced to write his own eulogy, a fact which he took as a bad omen. The eulogy itself recounts the sadness in Tu Duc's life. It was shortly after Tu Duc's reign that France gained full control of Vietnam.

Tomb of Khai Dinh

ⓘ *10 km south of Hué. Daily 0630-1800. 55,000d. To get there by motorbike or bicycle follow the directions for Gia Long's tomb (p155) but turn immediately left past small shops after the new river crossing (Highway 1) and head straight on, over a small crossroads, parallel to the main road. If you're travelling by boat, a return xe ôm trip from the riverbank is 25,000d.*

The Tomb of Khai Dinh was built between 1920 and 1932 and is the last mausoleum of the Nguyen Dynasty. By the time Khai Dinh was contemplating the afterlife, brick had given way in popularity to concrete, so the structure is now beginning to deteriorate. Nevertheless, it occupies a fine position on the Chau Mountain facing southwest towards a large white statue of Quan Am (see p113), also built by Khai Dinh. The valley, used for the cultivation of cassava and sugar cane, and the pine-covered mountains, make this one of the most beautifully sited and peaceful of the tombs. Indeed, before construction could begin, Khai Dinh had to remove the tombs of Chinese nobles who had already selected the site for its beauty and auspicious orientation. A total of 127 steep steps lead up to the Honour Courtyard with statuary of mandarins, elephants and horses. An octagonal stela pavilion in the centre of the mourning yard contains a stone stela engraved with a eulogy to the emperor. At the top of some more stairs, are the tomb and shrine of Khai Dinh, containing a bronze statue of the emperor sitting on his throne and holding a jade sceptre. The body is interred 9 m below ground level. The interior is richly decorated with ornate and colourful murals (the artist incurred the wrath of the emperor and only just escaped execution), floor tiles, and decorations built up with fragments of porcelain. It is the most elaborate of all the tombs and took 11 years to build. Such was the cost of construction that Khai Dinh had to levy additional taxes to fund the project. The tomb shows distinct European stylistic influences.

Amphitheatre and Elephant Temple

ⓘ *South bank of the river, about 3 km west of Hué railway station. Free. To get there by bicycle or motorbike turn left up a paved track opposite 203 Bui Thi Xuan St; the track for the Elephant Temple runs in front of the amphitheatre (off to the right).*

The Ho Quyen (Amphitheatre) was built in 1830 by Emperor Minh Mang as a venue for the popular duels between elephants and tigers. This royal sport was in earlier centuries staged on an island in the Perfume River or on the river banks themselves but, by 1830, it was considered desirable for the royal party to be able to observe the duels without placing themselves at risk from escaping tigers. The amphitheatre is said to have been last used in 1904 when, as was usual, the elephant emerged victorious. The walls of the amphitheatre are 5 m high and the arena is 44 m in diameter. On the south side, beneath the royal box, is one large gateway (for the elephant) and, to the north, five smaller entrances for the tigers.

Den Voi Re, the Temple of the Elephant Trumpet, dedicated to the call of the fighting elephant, is a few hundred metres away. It is a modest little place and fairly run down, with a

Thanh Toan Covered Bridge

large pond in front and two small elephant statues. Presumably this is where elephants were blessed before battle or perhaps where the unsuccessful ones were mourned.

Thanh Toan Covered Bridge

ⓘ *8 km west of Hué.* The bridge was built in the reign of King Le Hien Tong (1740-1786) by Tran Thi Dao, a childless woman, as an act of charity, hoping that God would bless her with a baby. The structure, with its shelter for the tired and homeless, attracted the interest of several kings who granted the village immunity from a number of taxes. Unfortunately, the original yin-yang tiles have been replaced with ugly green enamelled tube tiles but the bridge is still in good condition. The route to the bridge passes through beautiful countryside where ducks waddle along roads and paddy fields line the route. Travel there by bicycle or motorbike in the glow of the late afternoon sun.

Around Hué

The Demilitarized Zone (DMZ)

ⓘ *Most visitors see the sights of the DMZ, including Khe Sanh and the Ho Chi Minh Trail, on a tour. A 1-day tour of all the DMZ sights can be booked from any of Hué's tour operators for around US$10; depart 0600, return 1900.* ▲▲ ▶▶ *p164.*

The incongruously named Demilitarized Zone (DMZ), scene of some of the fiercest fighting of the Vietnam War, lies along the **Ben Hai River** and the better-known **17th Parallel**. The **Hien Luong Bridge** on the 17th parallel is included in most tours. The DMZ was the creation of the 1954 Geneva Peace Accord, which divided the country into two spheres of influence prior to elections that were never held. Like its counterpart in Germany, the boundary evolved into a

---

ZOLL
DOUANE

Border with Laos

The Vietnamese border post is 3 km beyond Lao Bao village at the western end of Highway 9; Lao immigration is 500 m west at Dansavanh. Once in Laos, Route 9 heads west over the Annamite Mountains to Xepon (45 km) and on to Savannakhet (236 km from the border). We have received reports of long delays at this border crossing, particularly entering Vietnam, as paperwork is scrutinized and bags are checked and double checked. Don't be surprised if formalities take 1 hr – and keep smiling! The problem seems to be at Vietnamese immigration but those with a Vietnam visa should be OK. Expect to pay 'over-time fees' on the Lao side if you come through on a Saturday or Sunday. Lao immigration can issue 15-day tourist visas for US$30. You can also get a Lao visa in advance from the Lao consulate in Danang (12 Tran Qui Cap St, T511-821208, 0800-1100, 1400-1600); it takes 24 hrs to process. The closest Vietnamese consulate is in Savannakhet; see p379 for visa application details and opening hours.

◉ E **Mountain**, Lao Bao village. A simple, clean and friendly guesthouse.

◉ There are buses from Hué to Khe Sanh, for connections to Lao Bao. There are also buses direct to the border from Le Duan St in Dong Ha, 1-1.5 hrs. *Xe ôm* from Khe Sanh to the border costs US$3, or from Lao Bao village to the border, US$1. There are daily departures for the Lao town of Savannakhet from Dansavanh. Buses also depart from Xepon (45 km west of the border) to Savannakhet 0800 daily, 30,000 kip. Those crossing into Vietnam from Laos may be able to get a ride with the DMZ tour bus from Khe Sanh back to Hué (see p159) in the late afternoon. Otherwise, there are Vietnam-bound buses from Savannakhet (see p378) and numerous songthaews to the border from the market in Xepon, 45 km, 1 hr, 20,000 kip but you'll need to get there by 0700 to ensure a space.

national border, separating communist from capitalist but, unlike its European equivalent, it was the triumph of communism that saw its demise.

At **Dong Ha**, to the north of Hué, Highway 9 branches off the main coastal Highway 1 and heads 80 km west to the border with Laos (see below). Along this route is **Khe Sanh** (now called Huong Hoa), the site of one of the most famous battles of the war (see p161). The battleground is 3 km from the village. There's also a small **museum** (25,000d) at the former Tacon military base, surrounded by military hardware.

A section of the **Ho Chi Minh Trail** runs close to Khe Sanh. This is another popular but inevitably disappointing sight, given that its whole purpose was to be as inconspicuous as possible and anything you see was designed to be invisible, from the air at least. However, it's worthy of a pilgrimage considering the sacrifice of millions of Vietnamese porters and the role it played in the American defeat (see p222).

17th Parallel, DMZ

Tours to the DMZ usually also include the tunnels of **Vinh Moc** ⓘ *13 km off Highway 1 and 6 km north of Ben Hai River, 25,000d*, which served a similar function to the better known Cu Chi tunnels in the south. They evolved as families in the heavily bombed village dug themselves shelters beneath their houses and then joined up with their neighbours. Later the tunnels developed a more offensive role when Viet Cong soldiers fought from them. Some visitors regard these tunnels as more 'authentic' than the 'touristy' tunnels of Cu Chi.

The **Rock Pile** is a 230-m-high limestone outcrop just south of the DMZ. It served as a US observation post, with troops, ammunition, Budweiser and prostitutes all being helicoptered in. Jon Swain, the war correspondent, describes in his memoirs, *River of Time*, how his helicopter got lost around the Rock Pile and nearly came to disaster in this severely contested zone. Although it was chosen as an apparently unassailable position, the sheer walls of the Rock Pile were eventually scaled by the Viet Cong.

Hai Van Pass and Lang Co

Between Hué and Danang a finger of the Truong Son Mountains juts eastwards, extending all the way to the sea: almost as though God were somewhat roguishly trying to divide the country into two equal halves. The mountains act as an important climatic barrier, trapping the cooler, damper air masses to the north and bottling them up over Hué, which accounts for Hué's shocking weather. They also mark an abrupt linguistic divide: the Hué dialect (the language of the royal court) to the north is still the source of bemusement to many southerners. The physical barrier to north-south communication has resulted in some spectacular engineering solutions: the single track and narrow gauge **railway line** closely follows the coastline, sometimes almost hanging over the sea (see p162), while Highway 1 winds its way equally precariously over the Lang Co lagoon and Hai Van Pass.

The road passes through many pretty, red-tiled villages, compact and surrounded by clumps of bamboo and fruit trees, which provide shade, shelter and sustenance. And, for

Background

The battle at Khe Sanh (1968)

In early 1968, the North Vietnamese Army (NVA) tried to inflict a humiliating defeat on American forces at Khe Sanh (already the site of a bloody confrontation in April and May 1967). Their apparent aim was to replicate their victory over the French at Dien Bien Phu (see p133); one of the NVA divisions, the 304th, even had Dien Bien Phu emblazoned on its battle streamers.

The US Commander, General Westmoreland, in turn, hoped to bury Ho Chi Minh's troops under tonnes of high explosive and achieve a Dien Bien Phu in reverse. Unlike the French in the previous decade, however, the American high command had some warning of the attack: a North Vietnamese regimental commander was killed while surveying the base on 2 January and that was interpreted as a sign that the NVA were planning a major assault. Special US forces long-range patrols were dropped into the area around the base and photo reconnaissance increased. It became clear that 20,000-40,000 NVA troops were converging on Khe Sanh.

By January 1968 the US Marines were effectively surrounded in a place which the assistant commander of the 3rd Marine Division referred to as "not really anywhere". There was a heavy exchange of fire, with the Marine artillery firing 159,000 shells and B-52s carpet-bombing the surrounding area, obliterating each 'box' with 162 tonnes of bombs. However, the commanders of the NVA knew there was no chance of repeating their success at Dien Bien Phu against the US military; instead the attack on Khe Sanh was designed to distract US attention away from urban centres in preparation for the Tet offensive (see p56).

The 77-day seige of Khe Sanh cost many thousands of NVA lives (one estimate is 10,000-15,000 as against only 248 Americans) but the Tet offensive proved to be a remarkable psychological victory for the NVA. Again, a problem for the US military was one of presentation. Even Walter Cronkite, the doyen of TV reporters, informed his audience that the parallels between Khe Sanh and Dien Bien Phu were "there for all to see".

colour, there's the bougainvillea, which, through grafting, produces pink and white leaves on the same branch. Windowless jalopies from the French era trundle along picking up passengers and their bundles, while station wagons from the American era provide an inter-village shared taxi service. The idyllic fishing village of **Lang Co** is just off Highway 1, about 65 km south of Hué, and has a number of cheap and good seafood restaurants.

Shortly after crossing the Lang Co lagoon, dotted with coracles and fish traps, the road begins the long haul up to **Hai Van Pass**, (Deo Hai Van or 'Pass of the Ocean Clouds'), known to the French as 'Col des Nuages'. The pass is 497 m above the dancing white waves that can be seen at its foot and once marked the border between the kingdoms of Vietnam and Champa. The pass is peppered with abandoned pillboxes and crowned with an old fort, originally built by the Nguyen Dynasty from Hué and used as a relay station for the pony express on the old Mandarin Road. Subsequently used by the French, it is a pretty shabby

Travellers' tales

By train from Hué to Danang

The train journey from Hué to Danang is regarded as not just one of the most scenic in Vietnam, but in the world.

Paul Theroux in his book *The Great Railway Bazaar* recounts his impressions as the train reached the narrow coastal strip, south of Hué and approaching Danang.

"The drizzle, so interminable in the former Royal Capital, gave way to bright sunshine and warmth; 'I had no idea,' I said. Of all the places the railway had taken me since London, this was the loveliest. We were at the fringes of a bay that was green and sparkling in bright sunlight. Beyond the leaping jade plates of the sea was an overhang of cliffs and the sight of a valley so large it contained sun, smoke, rain, and cloud – all at once – independent quantities of colour. I had been unprepared for this beauty; it surprised and humbled me …

Who has mentioned the simple fact that the heights of Vietnam are places of unimaginable grandeur? Though we can hardly blame a frightened draftee for not noticing this magnificence, we should have known all along that the French would not have colonized it, nor would the Americans have fought so long, if such ripeness did not invite the eye to take it."

(Penguin, London, 1977)

affair today, collecting wind-blown litter and sometimes used by the People's Army for a quiet brew-up and a smoke. Looking back to the north, stretching into the haze is the littoral and lagoon of Lang Co; to the south is Danang Bay and Monkey Mountain, and at your feet lies a patch of green paddies which belong to the leper colony, accessible only by boat.

🛏 Sleeping

Hué *p148, map p150*

Considering the town's tourist appeal, some accommodation in Hué is generally below par. Most hotels lie to the south of the Perfume River, although there are a couple to the north in the old Vietnamese part of town.

LL-A Saigon Morin, 30 Le Loi St, T054-823526, www.morinhotel.com.vn. The best hotel in Hué, this is still recognizable as the fine hotel built by the Morin brothers in the 1880s. Arranged around a courtyard with a small pool, the rooms are large and comfortable. All have a/c, satellite TV and hot water. The courtyard, lit with candles, is a delightful place to sit in the evening and enjoy a quiet drink.

A-B Century Riverside, 49 Le Loi St, T054-823390, www.centuryhotels.com. This is a rather imposing hotel. It does, however, have fabulous river views and the more expensive rooms are larger and better decorated than the cheaper ones. All have en suite bathrooms and come with complimentary fruit and water.

B-D Dong Loi, 19 Pham Ngu Lao St, T054-822296, www.hotelguide.com. Well situated and surrounded by internet cafés, shops and restaurants, this is a bright, breezy, airy and comfortable hotel. All rooms have a/c and hot water and all except the cheapest have a bathtub. Family-run, friendly and helpful service.

5 best

Ruins

Imperial city, Hué ▸▸ *p151.*
Angkor Wat, Cambodia ▸▸ *p286.*
The Bayon, Cambodia ▸▸ *p289.*
Ta Prohm, Cambodia ▸▸ *p291.*
Banteay Srei, Cambodia ▸▸ *p293.*

The excellent **La Carambole Restaurant** adjoins the hotel.

C **No 5**, 5 Ly Thuong Kiet St. Nice colonial façade, 1 room has a lovely balcony.

C **No 14**, 14 Ly Thuong Kiet St, T054-825461. Four spacious rooms, lovely garden, good breakfast.

C-D **A Dong 1**, 1 bis Chu Van An St, T054-824148, adongcoltd@dng.vnn.vn. Seven rooms in this friendly hotel, with a/c, fridge and bathtub; also has an attractive upstairs terrace.

C-D **Le Loi Hué**, 2 Le Loi St, T054-822153, leloihotel@ dng.vnn.vn. Not far from the station, consists of 6 blocks of differing comfort, some a/c, clean, hot-water showers, good value.

D **18 Le Loi**, 18 Le Loi St, T054-823720, F825814, huetc@dng.vnn.vn. Nice position not far from the river, 10 rooms, avoid downstairs and try the larger airy 1st floor rooms, all a/c, hot water. Bikes available for rent.

E **Ben Nghe Guesthouse**, 10 Ben Nghe St, T054-889106. Some quite comfortable rooms, 14 in all, with fan and a/c, offering good value for budget travellers. The **Stop and Go Café** is attached.

The little *hem* (alley) opposite the **Century Riverside** (see above) has some really nice rooms in comfortable and cheerful guesthouses – easily the best-value accommodation in Hué. Particularly recommended are:

E **Hoang Huong**, 66/2 (2 Kiet 66) Le Loi St, T054-828509. Some a/c or cheaper rooms with fan, friendly and helpful family guesthouse. Cheap dormitories.

E **Mimosa**, 66/10 (10 Kiet 66) Le Loi St, T054-828068. Eight rooms, with a/c, hot water, bathtub, quiet, simple and clean, French spoken.

E **Thanh Thuy**, 66/4 (4 Kiet 66) Le Loi St, T054-824585, thanhthuy66@dng.vnn.vn. Small, peaceful, clean and friendly family-run guesthouse. 4 rooms, with a/c and hot water. Car hire at good rates.

🍴 Eating

Hué cuisine is excellent. The influence of the royal court is evident in the large number of dishes served, each dish being relatively light. Hué food is also delicately flavoured and requires painstaking preparation in the kitchen: in short, it is a veritable culinary harem in which even the most pampered and surfeited king could find something to tickle his palate. Apart from this 'nibble' food, other Hué dishes are more robust, notably the famed *bun bo Hué* – round white noodles in soup, with slices of beef, laced with chilli oil of exquisite piquancy.

Hué *p148, map p150*

🍴 **La Carambole**,19 Pham Ngu Lao, T054-810 491, la_carambole @hotmail.com, daily 0700-2300. One of the most popular restaurants in town and deservedly so. The ceiling is decorated with beautiful kites, shot through with sticks capped by feathers. It is incredibly busy especially for dinner when the imperial-style dinner is recommended.

🍴 **Saigon Morin**, see Sleeping. Dining on the nightly buffet (1930-2130), accompanied by traditional music in the candle-lit courtyard is a pleasurable experience. The vast spread consists of

Central Vietnam Hué & around Listings

beef, squid, fish, pork, shrimp pancakes, rice cakes and apple fritters.

¶¶-¶ **Tropical Garden Restaurant**, 27 Chu Van An St, T054-8471431, daily 0830-2200. Dine alfresco in a leafy garden, just a short walk from the Perfume River. Beef soup with starfruit and mackerel baked in pineapple are among the flavoursome choices.

¶ **Am Phu** (Hell), 35 Nguyen Thai Hoc St. Do not confuse with An Phu; spell it for your cyclo driver rather than relying on your Vietnamese pronunciation. Excellent Vietnamese dishes in a spit-and-sawdust type eatery. Popular with locals.

¶ **Dong Tam**, 66/7 (7 Kiet 66) Le Loi St, T054-828403. Tucked away in the little *hem* opposite **Century Riverside**, this is Hué's vegetarian restaurant. Sit in a pleasant and quiet yard surrounded by plants and topiary, while choosing from the very reasonably priced menu. Its credentials are reflected in its popularity with the city's monkish population.

¶ **Lac Thien** and **Lac Thanh**, 6 Dinh Tien Hoang St. Arguably Hué's most famous restaurants, run by schismatic branches of the same deaf-mute family in adjacent buildings. You go to one or the other: under no circumstances should clients patronize both establishments. **Lac Thien** (frequented by Footprint) serves excellent dishes from a diverse and inexpensive menu, its Huda beers are long and cold and the family is riotous and entertaining, but service has been known to be slack.

¶ **Stop and Go**, 10 Ben Nghe St, T054-827051. Next door to **Ben Nghe Guesthouse**. Travel café run by the silver-haired Mr Do. Specialities include rice pancakes and the Hué version of spring rolls, excellent and cheap.

🎵 Bars and clubs

Hué *p148, map p150*
DMZ Bar, 44 Le Loi St, T054-823414. Hué's first bar, with pool table, cold beer and spirits at affordable prices.

Why Not?, 21 Vo Thi Sau St. Slightly arty café bar, with a decent selection of food and drink.

🎵 Entertainment

Hué *p148, maps p150*
Rent a **dragon boat** and sail up the Perfume River with your own private singers and musicians; tour offices and major hotels will arrange groups; **Sinh Café** charges just 50,000d per person.

Traditional and colourful court performances are given at the **Royal Theatre** in the Imperial City, every 30 mins 0900-1030 and 1430-1600; tickets 20,000d.

🛍 Shopping

Hué *p148, maps p150*
There is a much wider range of goods on sale in Hué now than was the case in the past. Shops around the **Century Riverside Hotel**, for example Le Loi and Pham Ngu Lao streets, sell ceramics, silk and clothes. The *non bai tho* or 'poem hats' are also available. These are a unique Hué form of the standard conical hat (*non lá*), made from bamboo and palm leaves, with love poetry, songs, proverbs or simply a design stencilled on to them. The decoration is only visible if the hat is held up to the light and viewed from the inside.

No Vietnamese visitor would shake the dust of Hué off his feet without having previously stocked up on *me xung*, a sugary, peanut and toffee confection coated in sesame seeds; it's quite a pleasant energy booster to carry while cycling around the tombs.

🏔 Activities and tours

Hué *p148, maps p150*
Tour operators
Almost every travellers' café acts as an agent for a tour operator and will take bookings. Bus and boat tours to the

Imperial Tombs are organized by tour operators and hotels. **Sinh Café** charges as little as 50,000d per person excluding tomb fees. The **Saigon Morin** (see Sleeping) organizes nighttime boat trips 2000-2200 for US$10; a performance of folk songs on the boat is US$40.

There are also day tours to some of the sights of the Vietnam War, US$10 for about 9 sights, including **Vinh Moc** tunnels and museum, the **Ho Chi Minh Trail** and **Khe Sanh**, depart 0600, return 2000. Those wishing to travel overland to Laos can arrange to be dropped off in Khe Sanh and pay less.

Adventure Centre, 15 Ly Thuong Kiet St, T054-823071, www.buffalotours.com. Cycling around Hué, Lang Co and Hoi An using German (Merida) multi-purpose road bikes. Treks also arranged.

DMZ Tours, 26 Le Loi St, T054-825242, vanthy2002vn@yahoo.com. This operator knows the area well and runs tours of the DMZ (all-day tour, around US$10), organizes boat trips on the river to see the tombs and temples, and sell tickets to onward destinations like Danang, Hoi An, Ho Chi Minh City, etc. Opening hours are erratic so phone ahead.

Sinh Café, 7 Nguyen Tri Phuong St, T054-845022, sinh5hue@dng.vnn.vn. A number of competitively priced tours and money changing facilities.

⊖ Transport

Hué *p148, maps p150*
Air
There are flights to and from Hanoi and Ho Chi Minh City. **Airline offices Vietnam Airlines** (in Thuan Hoa Hotel), 7 Nguyen Tri Phuong St, T054-824709.

Bicycle and motorbike
Bikes and motorbikes (US$6 per day) can be hired from most hotels, guesthouses and cafés.

Boat
It is possible to charter boats to the Imperial Tombs (the most romantic way to visit them) from the river bank between the **Huong Giang Hotel** and the Trang Tien Bridge and also from the dock behind the Dong Ba Market.

Bus
Open Tour buses can be booked from hotels or tour agencies.

Cyclo and xe ôm
Cyclos and *xe ôm* are available everywhere. Cyclos are pleasant for visiting the more central attractions. *Xe ôm* are a speedier way to see the temples, as the terrain south of town is quite hilly.

Taxi
Hué Taxi, T054-833333; **Mai Linh Taxi**, T054-898989.

Train
Hué Railway Station, 2 Bui Thi Xuan, west end of Le Loi St, T054-822175, booking office daily 0700-1100, 1330-1800 and 1900-2200. It serves all stations south to **Ho Chi Minh City** and north to **Hanoi**. Advance booking, especially for sleepers, is essential. The journey to **Danang** is recommended (p162).

❶ Directory

Hué *p148, maps p150*
Banks Industrial & Commercial Bank, 2A Le Quy Don St, 0700-1130 and 1330-1700, closed Thu pm. **Vietcom Bank**, 78 Hung Vuong St, 0700-2200. **Internet** Several establishments, charging as little as 50d per min, can be found on Ben Nghe. Pham Ngu Lao and Doi Cung streets each have several internet cafés. **Hospitals** Hué General Hospital, 16 Le Loi St, T054-822325. **Post office and telephone** 8 Hoang Hoa Tham St and 91 Tran Hung Dao, daily 0630-2130.

Hoi An, Danang and around

The city of Danang has no real charm and no sense of permanence but few cities in the world have such spectacular beaches on their doorstep, let alone three UNESCO World Heritage sites – Hué, Hoi An and My Son – within a short drive. The ancient town of Hoi An (formerly Faifo) lies on the banks of the Thu Bon River. During its heyday 200 years ago, when trade with China and Japan flourished, it was a prosperous little port. Much of the merchants' wealth was spent on family chapels and Chinese clan houses which remain little altered today. The city of Hoi An is currently experiencing a revival: the river may be too shallow for shipping but it is perfect for tourist boats; the silk merchants may not export any produce but that's because everything they make leaves town on the backs of satisfied customers.

⚫ **Getting there** Open Tour Bus direct to Hoi An; train or plane to Danang.
⚫ **Getting around** Walk around Hoi An; cyclo or *xe ôm* in Danang; tours to My Son.
⚫ **Time required** 1-3 days
⚫ **Weather** Hot but can be wet May-Sep.
⚫ **Sleeping** Good range of quality accommodation in Hoi An.
⚫ **Eating** Varied, good value, exciting cuisine.
▲ **Activities and tours** Cookery classes, cycling, tours to My Son.
★ **Don't miss...** Hoi An's tailors
▶▶ *p182.*

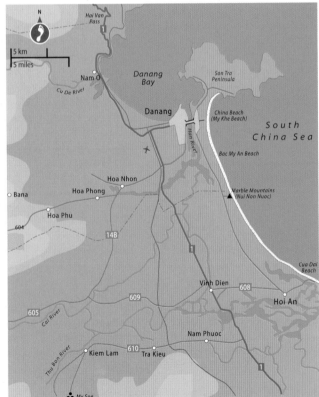

Japanese Covered Bridge, Hoi An

Hoi An ⚫🕐👤🎡⬜🔺⬛🄲 ›› p178-184.

Hoi An's tranquil riverside setting, its diminutive scale, friendly people and its shops and galleries have made it one of the most popular destinations in Vietnam for foreign travellers. There is much of historical interest in the town, plus a nearby beach and plenty of superb, inexpensive restaurants. That said, Hoi An's historic character is being slowly submerged by the rising tide of tourism. Although physically intact, virtually every one of its fine historic buildings either markets some aspect of its own heritage or touts in some other way for the tourist dollar; increasingly it is coming to resemble the 'Vietnam' pavilion in a Disney theme park. Nevertheless, visitors to Hoi An are charmed by the gentleness of the people and the sedate pace of life.

Most of Hoi An's more attractive buildings and assembly halls (*hoi quan*) are found either on, or just off, Tran Phu Street, which stretches west to east from the Japanese Covered Bridge to the market, running parallel to the river.

Ins and outs

Getting there and around There are direct Open Tour Bus connections to Hoi An from Ho Chi Minh City, Hanoi, Hué and Nha Trang. The quickest way of getting from Hanoi or Ho Chi Minh City, however, is by flying to Danang airport (see p172) and then getting a taxi direct to Hoi An (40 mins, US$9). The town itself is compact, quite busy and best explored on foot, although guesthouses also hire out bicycles. ⚫ ›› p184.

Best time to visit On the 14th day of the lunar month the town converts itself into a Chinese lantern fest and locals dress in traditional costume. The old town is pedestrianised for the night and poetry and music are performed in the streets.

Tourist information Hoi An Tourist Office ⓘ *12 Phan Chu Trinh St, T510-861276, www.hoianworldheritage.org; also at 1 Nguyen Truong To St, T510-861327, daily 0600-1900,* has English-speaking staff and can arrange car and minibus hire as well as sightseeing guides. It also sells the tickets required for entrance to most historic buildings in the town,

50,000d. The ticket is valid for three days and allows visitors free admission to one of each of the following sights: museum, old house, assembly hall, concert and handicraft workshop, plus either the Japanese Bridge or Quan Cong's Temple. Tokens for each additional sight cost 10,000d. At least a full day is needed to see the town properly.

Background

Hoi An is divided into five quarters, or 'bangs', each of which would traditionally have had its own pagoda and supported one Chinese clan group. The Chinese, along with some Japanese, settled here in the 16th century and controlled trade between the islands of Southeast Asia, East Asia (China and Japan) and India. Portuguese and Dutch vessels also docked at the port. Chinese vessels tended to visit Hoi An during the spring, returning to China in the summer. By the end of the 19th century the Thu Bon River had started to silt up and Hoi An was gradually eclipsed by Danang as the most important port of the area.

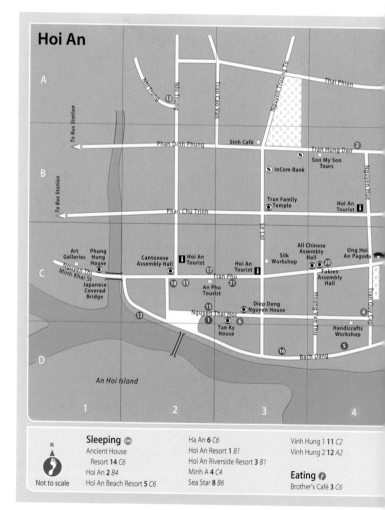

Hoi An

Not to scale

Sleeping
Ancient House Resort **14** C6
Hoi An **2** B4
Hoi An Beach Resort **5** C6
Ha An **6** C6
Hoi An Resort **1** B1
Hoi An Riverside Resort **3** B1
Minh A **4** C4
Sea Star **8** B6
Vinh Hung 1 **11** C2
Vinh Hung 2 **12** A2

Eating
Brother's Café **3** C6

Japanese Covered Bridge (Cau Nhat Ban)

ⓘ *Tran Phu St, 1 token; keep your ticket to get back across the bridge.*

The Japanese Covered Bridge – also known as the Pagoda Bridge and the Faraway People's Bridge – is Hoi An's most famous landmark and was built in the 16th century. Its popular name reflects a long-standing belief that it was built by the Japanese, although no documentary evidence exists to support this. One of its other names, the Faraway People's Bridge, is said to have been coined because vessels from far away would moor close to the bridge. On its north side there is a pagoda, Japanese in style, for the protection of sailors, while at each end of the bridge are statues of two dogs (at the west end) and two monkeys (at the east end). It is said that the bridge was begun in the year of the monkey and finished in the year of the dog, although some scholars have pointed out that this would mean a two-year period of construction, an inordinately long time for such a small bridge. They maintain, instead, that the two animals represent points of the compass, WSW (monkey) and NW (dog). Father Benigne Vachet, a missionary who lived in Hoi An between 1673 and 1683, notes in his memoirs that the bridge was the haunt of beggars and fortune tellers hoping to benefit from the stream of people crossing over it.

Central Vietnam Hoi An, Danang & around

Bach Dang Street and the French quarter

Just south of the Covered Bridge is Bach Dang Street, which runs along the bank of the Thu Bon River, where there are boats, activity and often a cooling breeze, before looping round to the Hoi An Market. Further on, the small but interesting French quarter around Phan Boi Chau Street is worth taking time over; it's not on the regular 'tourist circuit' and requires no entry fee but the colonnaded fronts here are particularly attractive. As in all historical quarters of Vietnamese towns, visitors should raise their gaze above street level to appreciate the architectural detail of upper floors, which is more likely to have survived, and less likely to be covered up.

Assembly Halls (Hoi Quan)

Chinese traders in Hoi An (like elsewhere in Southeast Asia) established self-governing dialect associations or clan houses which owned their own schools, cemeteries, hospitals and temples. The clan houses (*hoi quan*) may be dedicated to a god or an illustrious individual and may contain a temple, although they are not themselves temples. There are five *hoi quan* in Hoi An, four for use by people of specific ethnicities – Fukien, Cantonese, Hainan, Chaozhou – and the fifth for use by any visiting Chinese sailors or merchants.

Café III 21 *C3*
Café des Amis 5 *D4*
Cargo Club 1 *C2*
Han Huyen 12 *D2*
Nhu Y 14 *C5*
Tam Tam Café 15 *C2*
Thanh 16 *D3*
Vinh Hung 18 *C2*
Yellow River 20 *C4*

Cantonese Assembly Hall, Hoi An

Strolling east from the Covered Bridge down Tran Phu Street all the assembly halls can be seen. Merchants from Guangdong would meet at the **Cantonese Assembly Hall** (Quang Dong Hoi Quan) ⓘ *176 Tran Phu St, 1 'assembly hall' token*. This assembly hall is dedicated to Quan Cong, a Han Chinese general and dates from 1786. The hall, with its fine embroidered hangings, is in a cool, tree-filled compound and is a good place to rest.

Next is the **All Chinese Assembly Hall** (Ngu Bang Hoi Quan) ⓘ *64 Tran Phu St, free*, sometimes referred to as **Chua Ba** (Goddess Temple). Unusually for an assembly hall, it was a mutual aid society open to any Chinese trader or seaman, regardless of dialect or region of origin. The assembly hall would help shipwrecked or ill sailors and also performed the burial rites of merchants with no relatives in Hoi An. Built in 1773 as a meeting place for all five groups (the four listed above plus Hakka) and also for those with no clan house of their own, today it accommodates a Chinese School, Truong Le Nghia, where children of the diaspora learn the language of their forebears.

The **Fukien Assembly Hall** (Phuc Kien Hoi Quan) ⓘ *46 Tran Phu St, 1 'assembly hall' token*, was founded around 1690 and served Hoi An's largest Chinese ethnic group, those from Fukien. It is an intimate building within a large compound and is dedicated to Thien Hau, goddess of the sea and protector of sailors. She is the central figure on the main altar, clothed in gilded robes, who, together with her assistants, can hear the cries of distress of drowning sailors. Immediately on the right on entering the temple is a mural depicting Thien Hau rescuing a sinking vessel. Behind the main altar is a second sanctuary which houses the image of Van Thien whose blessings pregnant women invoke on the lives of their unborn children.

Further east, the **Hainan Assembly Hall** (Hai Nam Hoi Quan) ⓘ *10 Tran Phu St, free*, has a rather more colourful history. It was founded in 1883 in memory of more than 100 sailors and passengers who were killed when three ships were plundered by an admiral in Emperor Tu Duc's navy. In his defence the admiral claimed that the victims were pirates; some sources maintain he even had the plundered ships painted black to strengthen his case.

Exquisite wood carving is the highlight of the **Chaozhou (Trieu Chau) Assembly Hall** ⓘ *157 Nguyen Duy Hieu St, 1 'assembly hall' token*. The altar and its panels depict images from the sea and women from the Beijing court, which were presumably intended to console homesick traders.

Ong Hoi An Pagoda, Hoi An

Merchants' houses and temples

Tan Ky House ⓘ *101 Nguyen Thai Hoc St, 1 'old house' token*, dates from the late 18th century. The Tan Ky family had originally arrived in Hoi An from China 200 years earlier and the house reflects not only the prosperity the family had acquired in the intervening years but also the architecture of their Japanese and Vietnamese neighbours, whose styles had presumably influenced the aesthetic taste and appreciation of the younger family members.

Tran Family Temple ⓘ *junction of Le Loi and Phan Chu Trinh sts, daily 0730-1745, 1 'old house' token*, has survived for 15 generations but the current generation has no son, which means the lineage has been broken. The building exemplifies well Hoi An's construction methods and the harmonious fusion of Chinese and Japanese styles. It is roofed with heavy yin and yang tiling, which requires strong roof beams; these are held up by a triple-beamed support in the Japanese style (also seen on the roof of the covered bridge). Some beams have Chinese-inspired ornately carved dragons. The outer doors are Japanese, the inner are Chinese. On a central altar rest small wooden boxes which contain the photograph or likeness of the deceased together with biographical details. Beyond, at the back of the house, is a small, raised Chinese herb, spice and flower garden with a row of bonsai trees. As at all Hoi An's family houses, guests are received warmly and courteously and served lotus tea and dried coconut.

Diep Dong Nguyen House ⓘ *80 Nguyen Thai Hoc St*, with two Chinese lanterns hanging outside, was once a Chinese dispensary. The owner is friendly, hospitable and not commercially minded. He takes visitors into his house and shows them everything with pride and smiles.

Just east of the Japanese Bridge is **Phung Hung House** ⓘ *4 Nguyen Thi Minh Khai St, 1 'old house' token*. Built over 200 years ago it has been in the same family for eight generations. The house, which can be visited, is constructed of 80 columns of ironwood on marble pedestals. During the floods of 1964, Phung Hung House became home to 160 locals who camped upstairs for three days as the water rose to a height of 2.5 m.

Ong Hoi An Pagoda and around

At the east end of Tran Phu Street, at No 24, close to the intersection with Nguyen Hue Street, is the **Ong Hoi An Pagoda**. This temple is in fact two interlinked pagodas built back-to-back: Chua

Quan Cong, and behind that Chua Quan Am. Their date of construction is not known, although both certainly existed in 1653. In 1824 Emperor Minh Mang made a donation of 300 luong (1 luong being equivalent to 1.5 oz of silver) for the support of the pagodas. They are dedicated to Quan Cong and Quan Am (see p113) respectively.

Virtually opposite the Ong Hoi An Pagoda is **Hoi An Market** (Cho Hoi An). The market extends down to the river and then along the river road (Bach Dang Street, see above). At the Tran Phu Street end it is a covered market selling mostly dry goods. Numerous cloth merchants and seamstresses will produce made-to-measure shirts in a few hours but not all to the same standard. On the riverside is the local **fish market**, which comes alive at 0500-0600 as boats arrive with the night's catch.

Cua Dai Beach
ⓘ *5 km east of Hoi An. You must leave your bicycle (5000d) or moto (1000d) just before Cua Dai beach in a car park.*
A very white sand beach with a few areas of shelter, Cua Dai Beach is a pleasant 20-minute bicycle ride or one-hour walk from Hoi An. Head east down Tran Hung Dao Street or, for a quieter route, set off down Nguyen Duy Hieu Street, which peters out into a walking and cycling path. This is a lovely route past paddy fields and ponds; nothing is signed but those with a good sense of direction will make their way back to the main road a kilometre or so before Cua Dai and those with a poor sense of direction can come to no harm. Behind the beach are a handful of hotels where food and refreshments can be bought.

Danang ⊜❼▲⊟❻ ⇢ *pp178-184*

Danang, Vietnam's third-largest port and a trading centre of growing importance, is situated on a peninsula of land at the point where the Han River flows into the South China Sea. It was first known as Cua Han ('Mouth of the Han River') and renamed Tourane (a rough transliteration of Cua Han) by the French. It later acquired the title, Thai Phien, and finally Danang. An important port from French times, Danang gained world-wide renown when two US Marine battalions landed here in March 1965 to secure the airfield. They were the first of a great many more US military personnel who would land on the beaches and airfields of South Vietnam.

Ins and outs
Getting there Flights from Bangkok, Hanoi, Ho Chi Minh City, Buon Ma Thuot, Dalat, Pleiku and Nha Trang arrive at Danang airport on the edge of the city; a taxi into town costs US$2 and takes five to 10 minutes. Danang is on the north-south railway line linking Hanoi and Ho Chi Minh City. Regular Open Tour Bus connections link Danang with all major cities in the south as far as Ho Chi Minh City, and in the north as far as Hanoi. There are also daily buses from Danang to the Lao town of Savannakhet on the Mekong via the border at Lao Bao (see p159.) ⊟ ⇢ *p184*.

Getting around Danang is a sizeable town, rather too large to explore on foot, but there is abundant public transport, including cyclos, taxis and *xe ôm*. Bicycles and motorbikes are available for hire from most hotels and guesthouses.

Tourist information Danang Tourist Office ⓘ *76 Hung Vuong St, T0511-821423, also at 92A Phan Chu Trinh St*, arranges cars and guides.

Museum of Champa Sculpture

ⓘ *Intersection of Trung Nu Vuong and Bach Dang sts. Daily 0700-1700. 20,000d. The museum booklet (10,000d) has been written as an art history, not as a guide to the collection, and is of little help but there are now books on Champa art, which extensively catalogue the exhibits, US$10. Labels are in French and English.*

The museum (Bao Tang Dieu Khac Champa Da Nang) contains the largest display of Cham art anywhere in the world and testifies to a lively, creative and long-lasting civilization. Each room is dedicated to work from a different part of the Champa kingdom and, since different parts of Champa flowered artistically at different times from the fourth to the 14th centuries, the rooms reveal the evolution of Cham art and the prevailing outside influences, from Cambodia to Java.

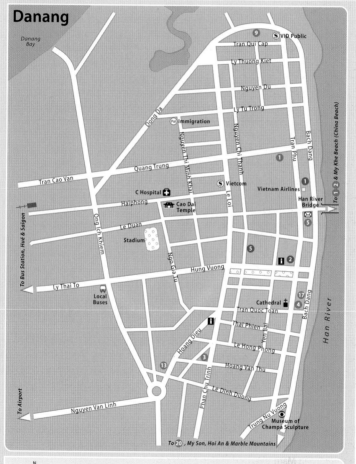

Danang

Danang Bay

Tran Qui Cap
ⓢ VID Public
Ly Thuong Kiet
Nguyen Du
Ly Tu Trong
ⓟ Immigration
Dong Da
Quang Trung
Tran Cao Van
ⓢ Vietcom
Vietnam Airlines
C Hospital ✚
Haiphong
Cao Dai Temple
Le Duan
Stadium
Le Loi
Han River Bridge
✉
Ly Thai To
Local Buses
Hung Vuong
Cathedral ✝
Tran Quoc Toan
Thai Phien
Hoang Dieu
Le Hong Phong
Hoang Van Thu
Phan Chu Trinh
Le Dinh Duong
Nguyen Van Linh
Museum of Champa Sculpture
Trung Nu Vuong

To Bus Station, Hué & Saigon
To Airport
Han River
To ① ② & My Khe Beach (China Beach)
Bach Dang
Tran Phu
Nguyen Chi Thanh
Nguyen Thi Minh Khai
Ngo Gia Tu
To ⑳ , My Son, Hoi An & Marble Mountains

N
500 metres
500 yards

Sleeping 🛌
Bamboo Green Central **3**
Bamboo Green Harbourside **4**
Bamboo Green Riverside **5**
Danang **9**

Furama Resort **20**
My Khe Beach **1**
Phuong Lan **13**
Tan Minh **17**
Tourane **2**

Eating 🍴
Bach Dang Hotel **1**
Christie's & Cool Spot **2**
Hoang Ngoc **5**

→ **Background**

Kingdom of Champa

The powerful kingdom of Champa was one of the most glorious in ancient Southeast Asia. Chinese texts suggest that in AD 192 a group of tribes, probably of Indonesian descent, formed a union known as Lin-Yi, later to become Champa. The first Champa capital, Tra Kieu (fourth to 10th centuries), was about 30 km from Danang, but the kingdom's territories extended far afield and other major sites included Dong Duong (eighth to 10th centuries), Po Nagar, Thap Mam and Cha Ban. Tra Kieu, My Son (p177) and Dong Duong were the three most important centres of the kingdom.

The polytheistic religion of Champa was a fusion of Buddhism, Sivaism, local elements and, later, Islam, and was expressed in an abundance of religious (and secular) sculptures and monuments. The kingdom reached its apogee in the 10th and 11th centuries but, unlike the Khmers, Champa never had the opportunity to create a capital city matching the magnificence of Angkor. For long periods the Cham were compelled to pay tribute to the Chinese and, after that, they were dominated in turn by the Javanese, Annamese (the Vietnamese) and then the Khmers. The Cham kingdom was finally eradicated in 1471, although there are still an estimated 90,000 Cham living in central Vietnam (mostly Brahmanists and Muslims). Given this turbulent history, it is perhaps surprising that the Cham found any opportunity for artistic endeavours. It should perhaps be added that since the demise of the kingdom, the number of Cham sculptures has increased enormously as forgers have carved more of these beautiful images.

Many pieces from **My Son** (p177) illustrate the Hindu trinity: Brahma the Creator, Vishnu the Preserver and Siva the Destroyer. An altar is inscribed with scenes from the wedding story of Sita and Rama, taken from the *Ramayana*, the Hindu epic. Ganesh, the elephant-headed son of Siva, was a much-loved god and is also well represented here.

At the end of the ninth century **Dong Duong** replaced My Son as the centre of Cham art. At this time Buddhism became the dominant religion of court, although it never fully replaced Hinduism. The Dong Duong room is illustrated with scenes from the life of Buddha. Faces from this period become less stylistic and more human and the bodies of the figures are more graceful and flowing.

The subsequent period of Cham art is known as the late **Tra Kieu** style. In this section there are *apsaras* (celestial dancing maidens), whose fluid and animated forms are exquisitely captured in stone. Thereafter Cham sculpture went into artistic decline.

The **Thap Mam** style (late 11th to early 14th century) sees a range of mythical beasts whose range and style is unknown elsewhere in Southeast Asia. Also in this room is a pedestal surrounded by 28 breast motifs. It is believed they represent Uroha, the mythical mother of the Indrapura nation (incorporating My Son, Tra Kieu, Dong Duong), but the meaning of the pedestal and others like it is unknown.

Apsara at the Museum of Champa Sculpture, Danang

China Beach (My Khe)

ⓘ *A short ride from the centre of Danang by bicycle or motorbike (15-20 mins) via the new River Han Bridge. Turn right just after the bridge, then take the first big turning on the left into Nguyen Cong Tru St; the beach is right at the end.*

Despite being only 20 minutes from the centre of Danang, **China Beach** (My Khe Beach) is an 'undiscovered' and undeveloped asset, with the potential to transform Danang into the Río de Janeiro of Asia. It has miles and miles of fine white sand, clean water and a glorious setting: the hills of Monkey Mountain to the north and the Marble Mountains clearly visible to the south. There is a merciful absence of vendors, no litter, only a few hotels and a number of excellent seafood restaurants. At times, though, there is a strong and dangerous cross-current and undertow.

As an R&R retreat during the Vietnam War, the white sand and surf made My Khe popular with American soldiers, who named it China Beach. It became a fabled resort celebrated in rock songs. Since 1975, however, it has been called T20 Beach, after the military code used by the North Vietnamese Army. Today the whole area including the hotels still belongs to the Vietnamese Army.

China (My Khe) Beach, Danang

Two kilometres south of China Beach and 8 km from the centre of Danang is **Bac My An Beach**, next to the **Furama Resort**. This is a clean and attractive beach with some seafood stalls. Most visitors here go direct to the resort from the airport.

Around Danang

Marble Mountains (Nui Non Nuoc)

ⓘ *12 km from Danang, 20 km from Hoi An. Daily 0600-1700. 10,000d. Many visitors stop off at Marble Mountain en route to Hoi An; catch the red-and-white bus towards Hoi An from Danang's local bus station (opposite 350 Hung Vuong St), 25 mins, or take a xe ôm.*

The Marble Mountains overlook the city of Danang and its airfield, about 12 km to the west of town. The views from the mountain sides, overlooking Danang Bay, are impressive.

The name was given to these five peaks by the Nguyen Emperor Minh Mang on his visit in 1825, although they are in fact limestone crags with marble outcrops. The mountains' numerous caves and grottos are formed by chemical action on the limestone rock. They are also known as the mountains of the five elements (fire, water, soil, wood and metal). An important religious spot for the Cham, the peaks became havens for communist guerrillas during the war, owing to their commanding view over Danang airbase. From here, a force with sufficient firepower could control much of what went on below, and the guerrillas harried the Americans incessantly.

Of the mountains, the most visited is **Thuy Son**. There are several grottos and cave pagodas in the mountain, which are marked by steps cut into the rock. The **Tam Thai Pagoda**, reached by a staircase cut into the mountain, is on the site of a much older Cham place of worship. Constructed in 1825 by Minh Mang, and subsequently rebuilt, the central statue is of the Buddha Sakyamuni (the historic Buddha) flanked by the Bodhisattva Quan Am (a future Buddha and the Goddess of Mercy, see p113) and a statue of Van Thu (symbolizing wisdom). At the rear of the grotto is another cave, the **Huyen Khong Cave**. Originally a place of animist worship, it later became a site for Buddhist pilgrimage. The entrance is protected by four door guardians. The high ceiling of the cave is pierced by five holes through which the sun filters and, in the hour before midday, illuminates the central statue of the Buddha

Sakyamuni. In the cave are various natural rock formations which, according to the young cave guides look like storks, elephants, an arm, a fish and a face.

A few hundred metres to the south on the right is a track leading to **Chua Quan The Am**, which has its own grotto, complete with stalactites, stalagmites and pillars.

My Son

ⓘ *60 km south of Danang via Tra Kieu or 45 km west of Hoi An via Nam Phuoc. The ticket office is 6 km beyond the village of Kiem Lam; from the ticket office it's a 2 km jeep ride (included in the ticket price) and a short walk to My Son. Daily 0800-1800. 50,000d. Tour operators in Hoi An and Danang offer tours: half-day coach tour, US$1.50-3; full-day boat trip, US$4. 1½ hrs each way from Hoi An by xe ôm (US$7). It is not clear how thoroughly the area has been de-mined so do not stray too far from the road and path. Take a hat, sun cream and water.*

My Son, with its detailed carved masonry, was the spiritual centre of the Cham empire (see p174). Declared a World Heritage site by UNESCO in 1999, it is one of Vietnam's most ancient monuments. Weather, jungle and years of strife have wrought their worst on My Son. But, arguably, the jungle under which My Son remained hidden to the outside world provided it with its best protection, for more has been destroyed in the past 40 years than the previous 400. Today, far from anywhere, My Son is a tranquil archaeological treasure. Not many visitors have time to make an excursion to see it which makes it all the more appealing to those that do. The thin red bricks of the towers and temples have been beautifully carved and the craftsmanship of many centuries still remains abundantly visible today. The trees and creepers have been pushed back but My Son remains cloaked in green; shoots and saplings sprout up everywhere and one senses that were its custodians to turn their backs for even a short time My Son would be quickly reclaimed by nature.

My Son consists of more than 70 monuments spread over a large area. It was rediscovered and investigated by French archaeologists of the École française d'Extrême-Orient in 1898. Their excavations revealed a site that had been settled from the early eighth to the 15th centuries, the longest uninterrupted period of development of any monument in Southeast Asia. Its maximum population is unknown but it seems to have had a

My Son

Central Vietnam Hoi An, Danang & around

holy or spiritual function rather than being the seat of power and was, very probably, a burial place of its god kings. Unfortunately, My Son was a Viet Cong field headquarters, located within one of the US 'free fire' zones during the Vietnam War. The finest sanctuary in the complex was demolished by US sappers and temple groups A, E and H were badly damaged. Groups B and C have largely retained their temples but many statues, altars and linga have been removed to the Museum of Champa Sculpture in Danang (p173).

It is important to see My Son in the broader context of Indian influence on Southeast Asia, not just in terms of architecture but also in terms of spiritual and political development around the region. Falling as it did so strongly under Chinese influence, it is all the more remarkable to find such compelling evidence of Indian culture and iconography in Vietnam. Indeed this was one of the criteria cited by UNESCO as justification for My Son's World Heritage listing.

Angkor in Cambodia, with which My Son is broadly contemporaneous, is the most famous example of a temple complex founded by a Hindu or Sivaist god king (*deva-raja*). The Hindu cult of *deva-raja* was developed by the kings of Angkor and later employed by Cham kings to bolster their authority but, because Cham kings were far less wealthy and powerful than the god kings of Angkor, the monuments are correspondingly smaller and more personal. One of the great joys of Cham sculpture and building is its unique feel, its graceful lines and unmistakable form.

The characteristic Cham architectural structure is the tower, built to reflect the divinity of the king: tall and rectangular, with four porticoes, each of which is 'blind' except for that on the west face. Orginally built of wood (not surprisingly, none remains), they were later made of brick, of which the earliest (seventh century) are located at My Son. The bricks are exactly laid and held together with a form of vegetable cement, probably the resin of the day tree. Sandstone is sometimes used for plinths and lintels but, overwhelmingly, brick is the medium of construction. It is thought that on completion, each tower was surrounded by wood and fired over several days in what amounted to a vast outdoor kiln. The red bricks at My Son have worn amazingly well and are intricately carved with Hindu, Sivaist and Buddhist images and ornaments. Sivaist influence at My Son is unmissable, with Siva often represented, as in other Cham relics thoughout Vietnam, by the linga or phallus.

Sleeping

Hoi An *p166, map p168*

A Ancient House Resort, 61 Cua Dai St, T0510-923377, www.ancienthouse resort.com. This is a beautiful, small hotel set around a small garden with a series of landscaped ponds and potted frangipani. All the 42 rooms are decorated in virginal white. There is a pool, shop, billiards, free shuttle to town and beach, free bicycle service and a restaurant. Behind the hotel is a traditional Ancient House. Below ground art work and an unusual linga sculpture are displayed.

A-B Hoi An, 10 Tran Hung Dao St, T0510-861445, www.hoiantourist.com. An attractive colonial building, well back from the road in spacious grounds. The comfortable rooms are set around a beautiful pool. Some rooms are fairly small and some are more stylish than others; but all are good value. The complex, popular with European tour groups, has a pool table, tennis court, badminton court, children's playground, beauty salon and souvenir shop. Staff are welcoming and offer a host of activities, see p183.

B-C Vinh Hung 1, 143 Tran Phu St, T0510-861621, quanghuy.ha @dng.vnn.vn. An attractive old building with a splendid ornate reception room, decorated with dark wood in Chinese style. 12 rooms at a range of prices, some large and traditionally furnished, others rather small and lacking a window. A popular choice.

B-C **Vinh Hung 2**, Nhi Trung St,
T0510-863717, uanghuy.ha@dng.vnn.vn.
A new sister hotel with 40 rooms, a short
walk away, built in traditional style, with a
pool and all mod cons but lacking the
atmosphere of the original.

C **Ha An Hotel**, 6-8 Phan Boi Chau St,
T0510-863125. In the heart of the French
quarter, with a white, balustraded
balcony, this pleasant hotel has very
attractive rooms decorated in scarlet
and white, with ethnic drapes adorning
the walls. Rooms are fairly small, but
adequate. Those around the front garden,
opposite an open-air café, are a little
larger. Communal seating area with TV
and a restaurant.

C-D **Minh A**, 2 Nguyen Thai Hoc St,
T0510-861368. This is a very special little
place. An old family house with just 4
guestrooms, all different and all different
prices. Guests are made to feel part of the
family. All rooms have hot water and fan.
Right next to the market in a busy part of
town. Very welcoming.

D-E **Sea Star (Sao Bien)**, 15 Cua Dai St,
on the road to the beach, T0510-861589,
F861382. A newish, privately run hotel.
Rooms with a/c and hot water. Travel
services, bicycle, motorbike and car hire
on offer. Efficient and popular but
possibly a little complacent.

Danang *p172, map p173*

A-B **Bamboo Green Central**,
158 Phan Chu Trinh St, T0511-822996,
bamboogreen@dng.vnn.vn.
Adequately furnished large rooms in the
heart of town. The hotel facilities include
two restaurants, a tour service, massage
and sauna.

B **Bamboo Green Riverside**,
68 Bach Dang St, T0511-83259,
www.vietnamtourism-vitours.com.vn.
Close to the Han River bridge, which leads
to My Khe beach, is this well-run hotel
with twin-bedded en suite rooms. River
views, efficient staff, excellent value for
money. 24-hr ATM outside the main door.
Another hotel in this group is the
Bamboo Green Harbourside, 177 Tran
Phu Street, T0511-822722.

B-C **Danang**, 1-3 Dong Da St,
T0511-821986, dananghotel@dng.vnn.vn.
Large hotel now merged with the old
Marble Mountain hotel next door. 160
rooms, some around a courtyard at the
back with balconies. Restaurant and tours.

C **Phuong Lan**, 142 Hoang Dieu St,
T0511-820373, F820382. A/c, satellite TV,
hot water, good value (after some
bargaining), free airport pick-up,
motorbikes for rent.

C-D **Tan Minh**, 142 Bach Dang St,
T0511-827456, F830172. On the
riverfront, a well-kept small hotel, friendly
and intelligent staff speak good English.

Central Vietnam Hoi An, Danang & around Listings

Beachside luxury

LL-L Furama Resort, 68 Ho Xuan Huong St, Bac My An, 8 km from Danang, T0511-847888, www.furamavietnam.com. One of the most attractive aspects of Furama is its fabulously opulent foyer with smart seating and warm lighting. It has two pools, one of which is an infinity pool overlooking the private beach. All its facilities, including three restaurants, are first class. The Indochine restaurant and health centre with therapies galore is particularly memorable. Watersports, mountain biking, tennis, archery and beach volleyball available. The resort operates a free shuttle to Danang, Marble Mountains and Hoi An.

LL-L Hoi An Resort, Cua Dai Beach, T0510-927040, www.victoriahotels-asia.com. A charming and attractive resort right on the beach. All rooms, some with balconies, face the sea. The superior room is quite plain with shower only whereas the deluxe boasts a four-poster bed, wooden floors and a bathtub. There is a large, but slightly exposed, pool, restaurants and charming service. Do not be surprised to see a long line of craters running down the beach, they belong to the hotel's pet elephant, Darling, who ambles up and down the beach giving rides. A free shuttle bus runs between the hotel and the town; there are children's activities and tennis.

L Hoi An Riverside Resort, Cua Dai Rd, T0510-864800, www.hoianriverresort.com A short, 5 min cycle ride from Cua Dai beach, this Khai Silk hotel faces the Thu Bon River with lovely views. There is a dark, slate-lined pool surrounded by white umbrellas and white seats, set in landscaped gardens with hammocks. Standard rooms have balconies with beautifully made beds, decorated in tiny red and pink flowers and plenty of cushions in wine, white and beige. All rooms, with gorgeous ethnic drapes on the walls, have showers. The Song Do restaurant is the best place to be at sunset as it has uninterrupted views of the river.

L-A Hoi An Beach Resort, 1 Cua Dai St, T0510-927011, www.hoiantourist.com. A quiet, attractively designed resort with its own stretch of private beach just across the road. Its rooms are simply designed and spacious with large bathrooms; some enjoy little terraces or balconies overlooking the river. The large restaurant also overlooks the river, and the pool, which is close to the restaurant, is particularly inviting. A good choice for some peace and quiet but with a free shuttle service to town.

China Beach (My Khe) *p175*

B Tourane, My Khe Beach, T0511-932666, touranehotel@dng.vnn.vn. A 'resort' type hotel with accommodation in decent villa-type blocks. 30 rooms all with a/c and hot water.

C My Khe Beach, 241 Nguyen Van Thoai St, My Kh Beach, T0511-836125, F836123. Facing the beach and set back from the quiet beach road. Rooms are in blocks amongst the sea pines. Deluxe rooms enjoy sea views, a sitting room and a double and single bed with firm mattresses. **Conroy's Bar**, 1 of 3 eating outlets here, caters to western tastes with sandwiches, hamburgers and cold beer as well as seafood and is on the ground floor of the block nearest the sea.

● Eating

Hoi An *p166, map p168*

A Hoi An speciality is *cao lau*, a special noodle soup with slices of pork and croutons and traditionally made with water from one particular well. The quality of food in Hoi An, especially the fish, is outstanding and the value for money is not matched by any other town in Vietnam. Bach Dang St is particularly pleasant in the evening, when tables and chairs are set up almost the whole way along the river.

♥♥ **Brother's Café**, 27 Phan Boi Chau St, T0510-914150. It is excellent news that these little cloistered French houses should have been put to such good use and renovated in such exquisite taste. The house and garden leading down to the river are beautifully restored. The menu is strong on Vietnamese specialities, especially seafood, and at US$12 the daily set menu still offers good value in such charming surroundings.

♥♥ **Café des Amis**, 52 Bach Dang St, near the river. The set menu of fish/seafood or vegetarian dishes changes daily and is widely acclaimed. At about US$5 for 5 dishes and 2 local beers, it is also excellent value. The owner, Mr Nguyen Manh Kim, spends several months a year cooking in Europe.

♥♥ **Han Huyen** (Floating Restaurant), Bach Dang St, T0510-861462. Just east of the footbridge to An Hoi island. Serves excellent seafood.

♥♥ **Nhu Y** (aka Mermaid), 2 Tran Phu St, T0510-861527. This sweet, little, candy pink-walled restaurant is framed by the beautiful, purple creeper flower *hoa cat dang*. Miss Vy turns out all the local specialities, as well as some of her own, and there's a streetside cake cabinet for

passing visitors. The 5-course set dinner is particularly recommended.

♥♥ **Tam Tam Café**, 110 Nguyen Thai Hoc St, T0510-862212. This is a great little café in a renovated tea house. Cocktails, draft beer, music, book exchange, plus attached restaurant serving French and Italian cuisine. A relaxing place for a drink, expresso or meal.

♥♥ **Thanh**, 76 Bach Dang St, T0510-861366. A charming old house overlooking the river, recognizable by its Chinese style and flowering *hoa cat dang* creepers; the shrimp is excellent. Friendly service.

♥♥ **Vinh Hung**, 147B Tran Phu St, T0510-862203. Belongs to the hotel of the same name (see Sleeping). Another attractive building finely decked with Chinese lanterns and traditional furniture. An excellent range of seafood dishes and Vietnamese specials at fair prices.

♥♥-♥ **Cargo Club Restaurant and Hoi An Patisserie**, 107-109 Nguyen Thai Hoc St, T0510-910489. Decorated with ethnic cushions and drapes. Riverside and streetside vantage points. Breakfasts, sandwiches, homemade ice cream, cakes and desserts. International menu features goat's cheese and spinach lasagne and passion mousse with chocolate.

♥ **Café 111/Hai's Scout Café**, 111 Tan Phu St/98 Nguyen Thai Hoc St, T0510-863210. The central area of these back-to-back cafés has a photographic exhibition of the WWF's invaluable work in the threatened environment around Hoi An. Between them they offer good food in a relaxing courtyard or attractive café setting. Cookery courses can be arranged.

♥ **Yellow River**, 38 Tran Phu St, T0510-861053. Good Hoi An family eatery, fried wanton is recommended. French spoken.

Danang *p172, map p173*

Seafood is good here and Danang has its own beers, Da Nang 'Export' and Song Han. There are a number of cafés and restaurants along Bach Dang St, overlooking the river.

¶¶ **Bach Dang Hotel**, 50 Bach Dang St. Informal restaurant, with glimpses of river and decent food.

¶¶ **Christie's** and **Cool Spot**, 112 Tran Phu St, T0511-824040, ccdng@dng.vnn.vn. Frequented by expats from Danang and outlying provinces, it has a small bar downstairs with a restaurant above serving cold beer and western and Japanese food, plus a mean all-day breakfast. Tasty homemade pizzas and lemon pie. Happy hour 1600-2000.

¶ **Hoang Ngoc**, 106 Nguyen Chi Thanh St, T0511-821214. Extensive menu, good food and welcoming atmosphere make this place popular.

China Beach (My Khe) *p175*
The many restaurants here are virtually indistinguishable and it is impossible to single any one out for special mention. They all have excellent fish, prawn, crab, clams and cuttlefish, grilled, fried or steamed. Two people can eat well for US$7-10 including local beers.

🌙 Bars and clubs

Hoi An *p166, map p168*
Champa, 75 Nguyen Thai Hoc St, T0510-862974. This is a rambling place with pool tables and an upstairs cultural show in the evenings. Downstairs hits from the 1960s and '70s predominate.

Lounge Bar, 102 Nguyen Thai Hoc St, T0510-910480. A new bar playing reggae sounds. Its red theme incorporates big red Chinese lanterns, hanging incense cones, bar stools and comfy sofas. Happy hour 1600-2100.

Tam Tam Café, 110 Nguyen Thai Hoc St. Mainly a café/restaurant but also has a good bar. An attractive place to sit.

Treats, 158 Tran Phu St, T0510-861125, 1200-2400. One of Hoi An's few bars and a very well run one. 2 pool tables, airy, attractive style: popular happy hour and balcony. Also at 31 and 13 Phan Dinh Phung, very popular at night.

🎭 Entertainment

Hoi An *p166, map p168*
Hoi An Handicraft Workshop, 9 Nguyen Thai Hoc St, T0510-910216, www.hoianhandicraft.com. Traditional music performances at 1015 and 1515 Tue-Sun, with the Vietnamese monochord and dancers. At the back there is a potters' wheel and craftspeople making straw mats, embroidery, conical hats, wood carvings and iron ornaments.

🛍 Shopping

Hoi An *p166, map p168*
Hoi An is a shopper's paradise. Tran Phu and Le Loi are the main shopping streets. Two items stand out, paintings and clothes.

Accessories and handicrafts
Hoi An is the place to buy handbags and purses and attractive Chinese silk lanterns, indeed anything that can be made from silk, including scarves and shoes. The shop at 41 Le Loi Street is a silk workshop where the whole process from silkworm to woven fabric can be seen and fabrics purchased, daily 0745-2200. There is also a lot of chinaware available, mostly modern, some reproduction and a few antiques.

53a Le Loi, 53a Le Loi, T091-4097344 (mob). A handbag and shoe shop unit with a large variety of choices. Have your bag made here but definitely not your shoes.

Darling Deco, 16-17 Nhi Trung, T0510-910717, ligiphi@dng.vnn.vn, daily 0900-2130. Specialising in interior furnitures, artistic handicrafts and hand embroidery, this 2-storey shop has some great beds and chairs, beautiful keepsake boxes and unusual ethnic wall hangings as well as the usual crafts.

Reaching Out, Hoa-nhap Handicrafts, 103 Nguyen Thai Hoc, T0510-910168, www.hoanhap.panya.de, Tue-Sun

0730-1730. Fair trade shop selling arts and crafts, cards and notebooks, textiles and silk sleeping bags all made by disabled artisans living in Hoi An. Profits support the disabled community. There is usually someone at work in the shop so you can see what they are getting up to.

Art

Vietnamese artists have been inspired by Hoi An's old buildings and a Hoi An school of art has developed. Countless galleries sell original works of art but the more serious galleries are to be found in a cluster on Nguyen Thi Minh Khai St, west of the Japanese Bridge.

Tailors

Hoi An is famed for its tailors – there are now reckoned to be more than 140 in town – who will knock up silk or cotton clothing in 24 hrs. The quality of the stitching varies from shop to shop, so see some samples first, and the range of fabrics is limited, so many people bring their own. A suit can cost US$30-100, depending on fabric and quality of workmanship. Note that Thai silk costs more than Vietnamese silk and Hoi An silk is quite coarse.

Visitors talk of the rapid speed at which shops can produce the goods but bear in mind that, if every visitor to Hoi An wants something made in 12-24 hrs, this puts enormous strain on staff. Quite apart from the workers having to stay up all night, the quality of the finished garment could suffer. So, if you are in Hoi An for a few days, do your clothes shopping on the first day to give you time to accommodate 2nd or 3rd fittings which may be necessary.

Thanh Ha, 1A Nhi Trung St, T0510-864533, leco50@hotmail.com, daily 0900-2200. This shop unit is recommended because of the speed of service, the quality of the goods, the excellent prices and the fact that, unlike many other tailors in town, 2nd, 3rd or even 4th fittings are usually not required.

Yaly, 47 Nguyen Thai Hoc, T0510-910474, yalyshop@dng.vnn.vn, daily 0700-2030. Professional staff, very good, quality results across a range of clothing, including shoes, in a lovely old building.

▲▲ Activities and tours

Hoi An *p166, map p168*
Boat rides

Boat rides are available on the Thu Bon River. Local boatwomen charge US$1 or so an hour – a tranquil and relaxed way of spending the early evening.

Cookery classes
Red Bridge Cooking School, Thon 4, Cam Thanh, T0510-933222, www.visithoian.com. It is run by the **Hai Scout Café**, 98 Nguyen Thai Hoc St, T0510-863210. Day-long cookery courses (US$12) are held all year. Visit the market to be shown local produce, then take a 20-min boat ride to the school where you're shown the herb garden. Watch a demonstration by chefs on how to make dishes such as warm squid salad served in half a pineapple and grilled eggplant stuffed with veg. Move inside and you get to make your own fresh spring rolls and learn Vietnamese food carving, which is a lot harder than it looks. The restaurant is open to the public.

Tour operators
An Phu Tourist, 141 Tran Phu St, T0510-861447, www.anphutouristhoian.com. Several offices in town, offering a wide range of tour services.
Hoi An Tourist Company, at Hotel Hoi An, 6 Tran Hung Dao St, and at Hoi An Beach Resort, T0510-862224, www.hoiantravel.com. Local and nationwide tours, plus visits to carpentry and pottery villages, with the added interest of learning some local activities such as fishing, farming and making Chinese lanterns.
Mr Tung, 21 Cua Dai St, T0510-914218, tungtravel@hotmail.com. A small,

one-man operation but does a good job booking bus tickets and arranging tours to My Son, US$1 by bus or US$2.50 by bus and boat, entrance fee extra. Among the cheapest rates for taxis to Danang airport. **Sinh Café**, 2 Phan Dinh Phung St, T0510-863948, www.sinhcafevn.com, daily 0630-2200. Branch of the ubiquitous chain, offering tours, transport, reservations and internet.

Son My Son Tours, 17/2 Tran Hung Dao St, T0510-861121, mysontour@dng.vnn.vn. Cheap minibus tickets to Hué (US$3), Nha Trang (US$5) and Ho Chi Minh City (US$15) plus car and motorbike hire and useful advice.

Danang *p172, map p173*
Therapies
Furama Resort, 68 Ho Xuan Huong St, Bac My An Beach, T0511-847333, www.furamavietnam.com. A full range of treatments available in its health centre.

⊖ Transport

Hoi An *p166, map p168*
Bicycle and motorbike
Hotels have 2- and 4-wheel vehicles for hire. Bicycle hire, 5000d per day, motorbike US$4 per day.

Bus
Open Tour Buses cost around US$10 to **Hanoi** and US$12 to **Ho Chi Minh City**. Book through local tour operators (see above).

Danang *p172, map p173*
Air
The airport is 2½ km southwest of the city. Connections with **Ho Chi Minh City**, **Hanoi**, **Buon Ma Thuot**, **Dalat** and **Nha Trang**. Also direct flights to **Bangkok** several times a week.

    Airline offices Thai International, in the airport, T0511-656060. **Vietnam Airlines**, 35 Tran Phu St, T0511-821130.

Bicycle
Bicycles available from many hotels from around US$1 per day. Some cafés and hotels also rent motorbikes for US$5-7 per day. Otherwise the usual cyclo or *xe ôm* are ubiquitous.

Taxi
Airport Taxi, T0511-825555. **Dana Taxi**, T0511-815815.

Train
Danang Railway Station, 122 Haiphong St, 2 km west of town, T0511-823810. There are express trains to and from **Hanoi**, **Ho Chi Minh City** and **Hué** (see p162).

❶ Directory

Hoi An *p166, map p168*
Banks **Hoi An Bank**, 4 Hoang Dieu. Accepts most major currencies, US$ withdrawal from credit/debit card, no commission for cashing AmEx traveller's cheques, daily 0730-1900. **Hoi An Incombank**, Le Loi St, offers identical services. ATM on Tran Hung Dao St.
Hospitals 4 Tran Hung Dao St, T0510-863166, daily 0700-2200.
Internet Widely available in cafés and hotels, often 100d per min. **Post office** 5 Tran Hung Dao St. International telephone available.

Danang *p172, map p173*
Banks VID Public Bank, 2 Tran Phu St. Vietcombank, 104 Le Loi St, will change most major currencies, cash and traveller's cheques. **Hospitals** C Hospital, 74 Haiphong St, T0511-821480.
Immigration Police Nguyen Thi Minh Khai St, opposite Hai Van Hotel. **Internet** There are numerous internet cafés all over town. **Post office** 60 Bach Dang St, corner of Bach Dang and Le Duan sts, telex, fax and telephone facilities.

Central Highlands and the coast

The Central Highlands consist of the Truong Son Mountain Range and its immediate environs. The mountain range is commonly referred to as the backbone of Vietnam and borders Laos and Cambodia to the west. The highlands provide flowers and vegetables to the southern lowlands and have several tea and coffee plantations that supply the whole of Vietnam. Tourism is an additional source of revenue. Most highlanders belong to one of 26 indigenous groups and, beyond the main towns of Dalat, Buon Ma Thuot, Play Ku (Pleiku) and Kontum, their way of life remains unchanged.

East of the highlands, on the coast, Nha Trang is a seaside resort with diving, boat tours and spas to entice foreign visitors. Further south, Mui Ne has golden sands and the best kitesurfing in Vietnam.

⊘ **Getting there** Plane to Dalat, Buon My Thuot, Play Ku or Nha Trang. Open Tour Buses to Dalat, Nha Trang and Mui Ne.

⊖ **Getting around** Organized tour or hired motorbike.

⊖ **Time required** Minimum 1 day for Nha Trang; 5 days for the Central Highlands.

⊚ **Weather** Tropical storms are a possibility May-Nov.

⊜ **Sleeping** Town hotels, villas and beachfront properties.

⊘ **Eating** Varied cuisine from highland dishes to seafood.

▲▲ **Activities and tours** Kayaking and mountain biking in the highlands; boat tours, diving and spas in Nha Trang; kitesurfing in Mui Ne.

★ **Don't miss...** the painted fishing boats at Nha Trang ›› p193.

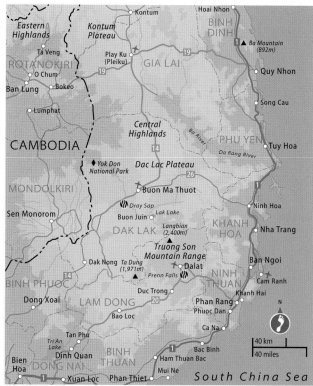

Best time to visit In terms of climate, the best time to visit this region is from December to April. However, as there are many different indigenous groups within its borders, there are festivals in the region all year round.

Background

The Central Highlands have long been associated with Vietnam's hill tribes. Under the French, the colonial administration deterred ethnic Vietnamese from settling here but missionaries were active among the minorities of the region, although with uneven success. Bishop Cuenot (p193) dispatched two missionaries to Buon Ma Thuot, where they received a hostile reception from the M'nong, however in Kontum, among the Bahnar, they found more receptive souls for their evangelizing. Today many of the ethnic minorities in the Central Highlands are Roman Catholic, although some (such as the Ede) are Protestant.

At the same time French businesses were hard at work establishing plantations to supply the home market. Rubber and coffee were the staple crops. The greatest difficulty they faced was recruiting sufficient labour. Men and women of the ethnic minorities were

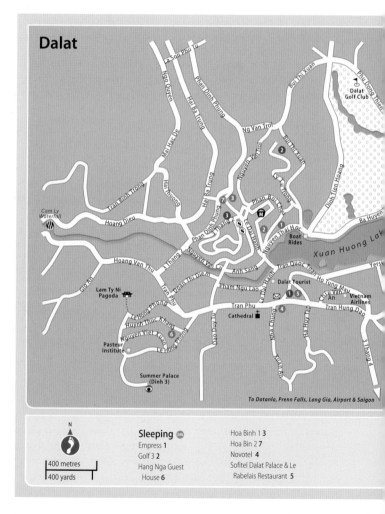

Dalat

To Datanla, Prenn Falls, Lang Gia, Airport & Saigon

N

400 metres
400 yards

Sleeping
Empress 1
Golf 3 2
Hang Nga Guest
  House 6

Hoa Binh 1 3
Hoa Bin 2 7
Novotel 4
Sofitel Dalat Palace & Le
  Rabelais Restaurant 5

happy in their villages drinking rice wine and cultivating their own small plots. They were poor but content and saw no reason to accept the hard labour and slave wages of the plantation owners. Norman Lewis travelled in the Central Highlands and describes the situation well in his book, *A Dragon Apparent*.

Since 1984 there has been a bit of a free-for-all and a scramble for land in the highlands. Ethnic Vietnamese have encroached on minority land and planted it with coffee, pepper and fruit trees. As an indicator of progress, Vietnam is now the second-largest producer of coffee in the world, although it produces cheaper robusta rather than arabica coffee. The way of life of the minorities is disappearing with the forests: there are no trees from which to build traditional stilt houses nor shady forests in which to live and hunt.

Dalat 🖾🖈🖸🅾️⛰🚌🅲 ▸▸ pp198-205

Dalat is situated on a plateau in the Central Highlands, at an altitude of almost 1500m. The town itself, a former French hill station, is centred on a Lake – Xuan Huong – amidst rolling countryside. To the north are the five volcanic peaks of **Langbian Mountain**, rising to 2400 m.

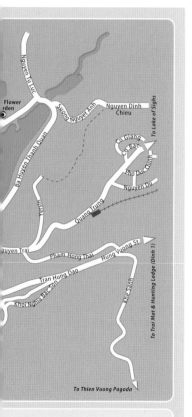

The ascent is recommended for stunning views and abundant birdlife. In the vicinity of Dalat are lakes, forests, waterfalls, and an abundance of orchids, roses and other temperate flora. Newly-weds should note that Dalat is the honeymoon capital of southern Vietnam and there is a quaint belief that unless you go on honeymoon to Dalat you are not really married at all.

Ins and outs

Getting there and around There are daily direct flights to Dalat from Ho Chi Minh City. Open Tour Buses pass through Dalat heading to Nha Trang and Ho Chi Minh City and innumerable local buses plough the inter-provincial routes between Dalat, Play Ku, Kontum, Ho Chi Minh City, Nha Trang, Buon Ma Thuot, Phan Thiet and Phan Rang. Alternatively it is possible to hire a car and driver. Taxis and *xe ôm* are available around town and the cool climate means that it is very pleasant to reach outlying attractions by bicycle. In fact a day spent travelling can be more enjoyable than the sights themselves. 🚍 ▸▸ *p204*.

Tourist information Dalat Tourist ⓘ *35 Tran Huong Dao St, T063-822317, www.dalattourist.com*, is the state-run travel company for Lam Dong Province. There are also a number of tour operators in town ▲▲ ▸▸ *p203*.

Eating 🍴
Le Café de la Poste **1**
Long Hoa **3**
Stop & Go Café **2**

Central Vietnam Central Highlands & the coast

Washing carrots, Dalat

Background

Dr Alexandre Yersin, a protégé of Luis Pasteur, founded Dalat in 1893. He stumbled across Dalat as he was trying to find somewhere cool to escape from the sweltering summer heat of the coast and lowlands. The lush alpine scenery of Dalat impressed the French and it soon became the second city in the south after Saigon. In the summer months the government and bureaucrats moved lock, stock and barrel to Dalat where it was cooler. There are still plenty of original French-style villas in the town, many of which have been converted into hotels. The last Emperor of Vietnam Bao Dai also lived here.

Dalat soon took on the appearance of Paris in the mountains. A golf course was made and a luxurious hotel was built. In both the Second World War and the American War, high-ranking officials of the opposing armies would while away a pleasant couple of days playing golf against each other before having to return to the battlefields. Of all the highland cities, Dalat was the least affected by the American War. The main reason being that, at the time, the only way to Dalat was via the Prenn pass. There was a small heliport at Cam Ly and also a radio-listening station on Langbian Mountain but nothing else of note.

Xuan Huong Lake and the centre

Xuan Huong Lake was created as the Grand Lake in 1919, after a small dam was constructed on the Cam Ly River, and renamed in 1954. It is a popular exercise area for the local inhabitants, many of whom walk around the Lake first thing in the morning, stopping every so often to perform t'ai chi exercises. Pedalloes are available from **Than Thuy restaurant**, for 30,000d per hour. At the northeast end of the Lake is the **Dalat Flower Garden** ① *0730-1600, 10,000d*. Established in 1966, it supports a modest range of temperate and tropical plants including orchids (of which Dalat is justly renowned throughout Vietnam), roses, camellias, lilies and hydrangeas.

Dalat Cathedral ① *mass 0515 and 1715 Mon-Sat, 0515, 0700, 0830, 1430 and 1600 Sun*, is a single-tiered cathedral, visible from the lake. It is referred to locally as the 'Chicken Cathedral' because of the chicken-shaped wind dial at the top of the turret. Construction began in 1931, although the building was not completed until the Japanese 'occupation' in the 1940s. The stained-glass windows, with their vivid colours and use of pure, clean lines, were crafted in France by Louis Balmet, the same man who made the windows in Nha Trang and Danang Cathedrals, between 1934 and 1940. Sadly, most have not survived the ravages of time. The cathedral has a good choir and attracts a large and enthusiastic congregation for mass.

At the end of Nguyen Thi Minh Khai Street, **Dalat Market (Cho Dalat)** sells an array of tempereate fruits and vegetables: plums, strawberries, carrots, potatoes, loganberries, cherries, apples, onions and avocados. The forbidding appearance of the market is masked by the riot of colourful flowers also on sale, including gladioli, irises, roses, chrysanthemums and marigolds.

Tran Hung Dao Street

Many of the large **colonial villas**, almost universally washed in pastel yellow, are 1930s and 1940s vintage. Some have curved walls, railings and are almost nautical in inspiration; others are reminiscent of houses in Provence. Many of the larger villas can be found along **Tran Hung Dao Street,** although many have fallen into a very sorry state of repair. Perhaps the largest and most impressive house on Tran Hung Dao is the former residence of the Governor General at No.12. It occupies a magnificent position set among mountain pines, overlooking the town. The villa, now the **Hotel Dinh 2**, is 1930s in style, with large airy rooms and uncomfortable furniture.

Bao Dai's Summer Palace (Dinh 3)

ⓘ *Le Hong Phong St, about 2 km from the town centre, daily 0700-2000, 5000d; visitors have to wear covers on their shoes to protect the wooden floors.*

Vietnam's last emperor, Bao Dai, chose Dalat for his Summer Palace, built between 1933 and 1938 on a hill with views on every side, it is art deco in style, both inside and out, and rather modest for a palace. The stark interior contains little to indicate that this was the home of an emperor, especially since almost all of Bao Dai's personal belongings have been removed. The impressive dining room contains an etched-glass map of Vietnam, while the study has Bao Dai's desk, books, a few personal ornaments and, notably, photographs of the royal family, who were exiled permanently to France in 1954. One of the photos shows Bao Dai's son, the prince Bao Long, in full military dress uniform. He was a distinguished and gallant soldier who died during the war. Of all the members of the royal family, he is the only one regarded with respect by the government, as a good, patriotic Vietnamese who fought for his country. The emperor's bedroom, balcony and bathroom are also open to the public, as is the family drawing room. The gardens are colourful and well maintained.

Lam Ty Ni Pagoda and around

Lam Ty Ni Pagoda, off Le Hong Phong St, is unremarkable save for the charming monk, Vien Thuc, who has lived here since 1968. He has created a garden, almost Japanese in inspiration, around the pagoda, known as the Divine Calmness Bamboo Garden. Vien Thuc is a scholar, poet, artist, philosopher, mystic, divine and entrepreneur but is best known for his paintings of which, by his own reckoning, there are more than 100,000. Wandering through the maze of rustic huts and shacks tacked on to the back of the temple you will see countless hanging sheets bearing his simple but distinctive calligraphy and philosophy: "Living in the present how beautiful this very moment is", "Zen painting destroys millennium sorrows", and so on. Vien Thuc's work is widely known and has been exhibited in Paris, New York and the Netherlands, as well as on the internet.

The slightly wacky theme is maintained at the nearby **Hang Nga Guest House and Art Gallery (Crazy House)** ⓘ *3 Huynh Thuc Khang, T063-22070; art gallery 0700-1900, 5000d,* where Doctor Hang Viet Nga has, over a period of many years, built up a hotel in organic fashion. Rooms and gardens resemble scenes from the pages of a fairy storybook; guests sleep inside mushrooms, trees and giraffes, and sip tea under giant cobwebs. It is not a particularly comfortable place to stay and the number of visitors limits privacy but it is well worth visiting. ● ⤬ *p198.*

The numerous waterfalls near Dalat are a popular excursion from town

Bao Dai's hunting lodge (Dinh 1)

ⓘ *Huong Vuong St, east of town, daily 0700-1130, 1300-1630, 10,000d.*

The emperor's hunting lodge was recently restored as a museum and opened to the public by the Sofitel hotel. The lodge sports 1930s furniture, antique telephone switchboards and, although it is not sumptuous, has a feel of authenticity. The gardens are green but lacking in intimacy, although, as very few tourists visit, you can often have the place to yourself.

Railway to Trai Mat Village

Dalat Railway Station, off Quang Trung Street to the east of the centre, was opened in 1938 and is the last station in Vietnam to retain its original French art deco architecture and coloured-glass windows. In 1991, a 7-km stretch of railway to the village of **Trai Mat** was reopened and every day a small Russian-built diesel car makes the journey ⓘ *daily when full, 78,000d.* The journey to Trai Mat takes you near the **Lake of Sighs**, 5 km northeast of Dalat. The Lake is said by some to be named after the sighs of the girls being courted by handsome young men from the military academy in Dalat. Another theory is that the name was coined after a young Vietnamese maiden, Mai Nuong, drowned herself in the Lake in the 18th century, believing that her lover, Hoang Tung, had rejected her. Not long ago the Lake was surrounded by thick forest but today it is a thin wood. The track also passes immaculately tended vegetable gardens; no space on the valley floors or sides is wasted and the high intensity agriculture is a marvellous sight. Trai Mat itself is a prosperous K'Ho village with a market selling piles of produce from the surrounding area. Walk 300 m up the road and take a narrow lane to the left to reach Chua Linh Phuoc, an attractive Buddhist temple, notable for its huge Buddha and mosaic-adorned pillars, made from broken rice bowls and fragments of beer bottle.

Waterfalls around Dalat

Cam Ly Waterfall ⓘ *2 km from the centre of town, daily 0700-1700, 10,000d,* is the closest waterfall to Dalat town centre. It is pleasant enough but should be avoided during the dry season, as it is the overflow for the sewerage system in Dalat. The falls are not particularly noteworthy but the gardens are peaceful and serene.

More cascades can be found south of town off Highway 20 towards Ho Chi Minh City. The first of these is **Datanla Falls**, 5 km out of town. A path leads steeply downwards into a forested ravine; it is an easy hike to get there, but tiring on the return journey. The falls are hardly spectacular but few people come here, except at weekends, so they are usually peaceful. Not far from the falls is the terminus of the **Dalat cable car** ⓘ *daily 0800-1600 but may be closed May-Nov if the wind is too strong, 20,000d one way*, which starts from the top of Prenn Pass, about 100 m from the bus station. The journey from top to bottom takes about 15 minutes and gives a different perspective of the Dalat area.

Prenn Falls, next to Highway 20, 12 km south of Dalat, were dedicated to Queen Sirikit of Thailand when she visited in 1959. The falls are not that good but there is a rope bridge that can be crossed and pleasant views of the surrounding area. About 20 km north of Bao Loc on the Bao Loc Plateau are the **Dambri Falls** ⓘ *Highway 20, 120 km from Dalat, Jul-Nov only; get a xe ôm from Bao Loc or take a tour.* These are considered the most impressive falls in southern Vietnam and are worth an excursion for those who have time.

Central provinces 🚌🚌 ▸▸ *pp198-205*

Ins and outs

Getting there and around There are direct flights from Ho Chi Minh City and Danang to Buon Ma Thuot and Play Ku. Innumerable local buses plough the inter-provincial routes between Dalat, Play Ku, Kontum, Ho Chi Minh City, Nha Trang, Buon Ma Thuot, Phan Thiet and Phan Rang. Alternatively it is possible to hire a car and driver. 🚌 ▸▸ *p204*.

Buon Ma Thuot

Buon Ma Thuot, the provincial capital of Daklak Province, is located at the junction of Highway 14 and Highway 26. Until the 1950s big game hunting was Buon Ma Thuot's main claim to fame but now the town has surpassed its illustrious and renowned neighbour of Dalat to be the main centre for tea and coffee production. With the rise of the Trung Nguyen coffee empire, Buon Ma Thuot has changed from a sleepy backwater to a thriving modern city. The government also instigated a resettlement programme here, taking land from the hill tribes to give to Vietnamese settlers. The Ede did not take kindly to having their land encroached upon by outsiders; tensions reached their peak in late 2001 and early 2002, when there was widespread rioting in Buon Ma Thuot. Today, the best Ede village to visit is **Buon Tur**, southwest of Buon Ma Thuot, off Highway 14. Apart from the odd TV aerial, life has changed little in this community of 20 stilt houses and, despite the efforts of the government to stop it, Ede is still taught in school. **Daklak Tourist Office** ⓘ *3 Phan Chu Trinh St (within Thang Loi Hotel), T050-852108, www.daklaktourist.com*, provides useful information about the province and has knowledgeable, English-speaking staff.

Dray Sap waterfalls
ⓘ *2 km off Highway 14 towards Ho Chi Minh City, 20 km from Buon Ma Thuot, daily 0700-1700, 5000d.* The waterfalls consist of several different cascades all next to each other. The 100-m wide torrent is particularly stunning in the wet season when the spray justifies the name 'waterfall of smoke'. There are two paths to choose from: one down by the river and the other on the high ground. Note, though, that access may occasionally be limited in the wet season, if the paths are too treacherous to use.

Lak Lake
The serene **Lak Lake** is about 50 km southeast of Buon Ma Thuot and can be explored by dugout (US$10 per hour through **Daklak Tourist**, or for less than one third if arranged independently). It is an attraction in its own right but is all the more compelling on account of the surrounding **M'nong villages**. Early morning mists hang above the calm waters and mingle with the columns of woodsmoke rising from the longhouses. The M'nong number about 50,000 and are matriarchal. They have been famed as elephant catchers for hundreds of years, although the elephants are now used for tourist rides rather than in their traditional role for dragging logs from the forest. In order to watch the elephants taking their evening wallow in the cool waters and to appreciate the tranquility of sunrise over the lake, stay overnight at a M'nong village, **Buon Juin**. An evening supping with your hosts, sharing rice wine and sleeping in the simplicity of a M'nong longhouse is an ideal introduction to these genial people. ●▶▶ *p198.*

Yok Don National Park
ⓘ *40 km northwest of Buon Ma Thuot, T050-783056, parcyd@dng.vnn.vn. Daily 0730-1700. Entrance US$3; guided hiking US$10-30 plus entrance fee; elephant rides for 2 people, US$17 per hour or US$45 per day. A park guesthouse and camping is available.*
This 115,000 ha wildlife reserve is home to 200 species of birds and at least 63 species of mammals, 17 of which are on the worldwide endangered list. It is believed that several rare white elephants survive here. The best chance of spotting wildlife is on an overnight guided hike or elephant safari. Within the park boundaries are also 17 different ethnic tribes.

Play Ku (Pleiku) and around
Nearly 200 km north of Buon Ma Thuot, Play Ku is located in a valley at the bottom of a local mountain and is visible from 12 kilometres away. It is a modern, thriving, bustling town, surrounded by rubber, pepper, coffee and tea plantations. There was fierce fighting here during the American War and, as a result, the town itself has little to offer the tourist but nearby are several Jarai villages that are worth a visit. Contact **Gia Lia Tourist Service Co** ⓘ *215 Hung Vuong St (in Hung Vuong Hotel), T059-8574571, gialiatourist@fptnet.com.vn*, for information and, for the sake of preserving the traditional way of life, only visit those villages where foreigners no longer need a licence.

Plei Fun is about 20 km north of Play Ku and is the village **Gia Lai Tourist** will take you to if you book a tour through them. The local villagers have wised up to tourism and may try and charge you 30,000d to see their graveyard, in which tiled or wooden roofs shelter the worldly possessions of the deceased: bottles, bowls and even the odd bicycles. Traditional Jarai carved hardwood statues guard the graves. Push on to **Plei Mun**, another 5 km down the road and left 2 km down a dirt road, for some even finer examples. There is also a traditional wooden *rong* house here but it has a corrugated iron roof.

Kontum

Kontum is a small, sleepy market town, 44 km north of Play Ku on Highway 14. There are a couple of notable sights that make a sidetrip to Kontum worthwhile, plus scores of Bahnar villages in the vicinity that can be reached by motorbike and on foot. Contact **Kontum Tourist Office** ⓘ *2 Phan Dinh Phung St (on the ground floor of the Dakbla Hotel), T060-862703, ktourist@dng.vnn.vn*, for further information.

The French Bishop and missionary Stephano Theodore Cuenot founded Kontum in the mid 1800s and succeeded in converting many of the local tribespeople to Christianity. He was arrested on Emperor Tu Duc's orders but died in Binh Dinh prison on 14 November 1861, a day before the beheading instructions arrived. He was beatified in 1909. Cuenot and other French priests and missionaries slain by Emperor Tu Duc are commemorated by a plaque set into the altar of **Tan Huong Church** ⓘ *85 Nguyen Hue St*. The whitewashed façade has an interesting depiction of St George and the dragon. It is not immediately evident that the church is built on stilts, but crouch down and look under one of the little arches that run along the side and the stilts, joists and floorboards are clear. Many of the windows are original but, unfortunately, the roof is a modern replacement, although the original style of fishscale tiling can still be seen in the tower. The interior of the church is exquisite, with dark wooden columns and a fine vaulted ceiling made of wattle and daub.

Further east (1 km) on the same street is the superb **Wooden Church**. Built by the French with Bahnar labour in 1913, it remains largely unaltered, with the original wooden frame and wooden doors. Inside, the blue walls combine with the dark-brown polished wood to produce a very serene effect. Unfortunately the windows are modern tinted glass and rather crude. In the grounds to the right stands a *rong* house and a statue of Cuenot, the first Catholic bishop of East Cochin China diocese.

Nha Trang ⊜❷❻❶▲⊜❻ » *pp198-205*

Nha Trang is Vietnam's only real seaside town, with a long, golden beach. The centuries-old fishing settlement nestles in the protective embrace of the surrounding hills and islands at the mouth of the Cai Estuary. The light here has a beautifully radiant quality and the air is clear: colours are vivid, particularly the blues of the sea, sky and fishing boats moored on the river. The name Nha Trang is thought to be derived from the Cham word *yakram*, meaning bamboo river. Certainly, the surrounding area was a focal point of the Cham Kingdom (see p174), with some of the country's best-preserved Cham towers located near by.

Nha Trang's clear waters and offshore islands won wide acclaim in the 1960s and its current prosperity is based firmly on tourism. Word has spread and Nha Trang's days as an undiscovered treasure are over. The town is now a firmly established favourite of Vietnamese as well as foreign visitors. There is a permanent relaxed holiday atmosphere, the streets are not crowded and the motorbikes cruise at a leisurely pace. There are, in reality, two Nha Trangs: popular Nha Trang, which is a sleepy, sedate seaside town consisting of a long, palm and casuarina-fringed beach and one or two streets running parallel to it, and commercial Nha Trang to the north of Yersin Street, which is a bustling city with an attractive array of Chinese shophouses.

Getting there The airport is 34 km from Nha Trang at Cam Ranh. There are daily flights to Hanoi and Ho Chi Minh City and regular flights to Danang. The town is on the main north-south railway line, with trains to Ho Chi Minh City, Hanoi and stops between. Open Tour Buses also link the town with other centres on the north-south route. 🚌 ⟩⟩ *p198.*

Getting around Nha Trang is just about negotiable on foot but there are also bicycles and motorbikes for hire everywhere and the usual cyclos and motorbikes.

Central Vietnam Central Highlands & the coast

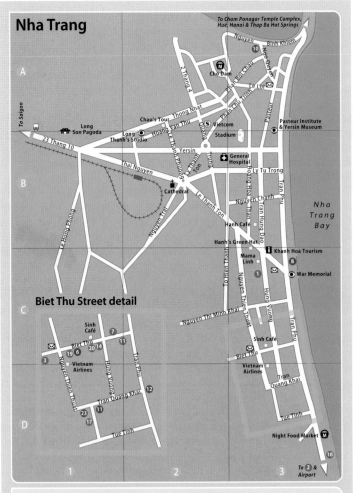

Nha Trang

Biet Thu Street detail

N

300 metres
300 yards

Sleeping
Ana Mandara **18** *D3*
Bao Dai's Villas **2** *D3*
Blue House **1** *C3*
Hanoi **3** *C1*
La Suisse **17** *D1*
Perfume Grass Inn **7** *C1*
Sao Xanh **11** *C1*

Truc Linh
& Restaurant **14** *C1*

Eating
Cyclo **23** *D1*
Good Morning
Vietnam **6** *C1*
La Bella Napoli **8** *C3*

Lac Canh **10** *A3*
Mai Anh **11** *D1*
Nha Trang Sailing
Club **12** *D2*

Bars & clubs
Crazy Kim **19** *C1*
Guava **20** *C1*

Tourist office Khanh Hoa Tourism ⓘ *1 Tran Hung Dao St, T058-822753, www.nha trangtourist.com.vn*, is the official tour office and can arrange visa extensions, car and boat hire and tours of the area.

Sights

Known as Thap Ba, the temple complex of **Cham Ponagar** ⓘ *follow 2 Thang 4 St north out of town; Cham Ponagar is just over Xom Bong bridge, daily 0600-1800, 4000d*, is on a hill just outside the city. Originally the complex consisted of eight towers, four of which remain. Their stylistic differences indicate they were built at different times between the seventh and 12th centuries. The largest (23 m high) was built in AD 817 and contains a statue of Lady Thien Y-ana, also known as Ponagar (the beautiful wife of Prince Bac Hai), as well as a fine and very large linga. She taught the people of the area weaving and new agricultural techniques, and they built

Cham Ponagar, Nha Trang

the tower in her honour. The other towers are dedicated to gods: the central tower to Cri Cambhu (which has become a fertility temple for childless couples); the northwest tower to Sandhaka (wood cutter and foster-father to Lady Thien Y-ana); and the south tower to Ganeca (Lady Thien Y-ana's daughter). The best time to visit the towers is in the afternoon, after 1600.

En route to the towers, the road crosses the **Cai River estuary**, where you'll see Nha Trang's elegant fleet of blue fishing boats, decorated with red trim and painted eyes for spotting the fish. The boats have coracles (*cái thúng*) for getting to and from the shore and mechanical fish traps, which take the form of nets supported by long arms; the arms are hinged to a platform on stilts and are raised and lowered by wires connected to a capstan which is turned, sometimes by hand but more commonly by foot.

The best known pagoda in Nha Trang is the **Long Son Pagoda**, built in 1963, which can be found at 23 Thang 10 Street. Inside the sanctuary is an unusual image of the Buddha, backlit with natural light. Murals depicting the jataka stories (birth stories of the Buddha) decorate the upper walls. To the right of the sanctuary, stairs lead up to a 9-m-high white Buddha, perched on a hill top, from where there are fine views. The pagoda commemorates those monks and nuns who died demonstrating against the Diem government, in particular those who, through their self-immolation, brought the despotic nature of the Diem regime and its human rights abuses to the attention of the American public. Before reaching the white pagoda, take a left on the stairs. Through an arch behind the pagoda you'll see a 14-m long reclining Buddha. Commissioned in 2003, it is an impressive sight.

The **Yersin Museum** ⓘ *8 Tran Phu St, Mon-Fri 0800-1100 and 1400-1630, Sat 0800-1100, 26,000d*, is contained within the colonnaded **Pasteur Institute** founded by the great scientist's protégé, Dr Alexandre Yersin. Swiss-born Yersin first arrived in Vietnam in 1891 and spent much of the rest of his life in Nha Trang. He was responsible for identifying the bacillus which causes the plague. The museum contains the lab equipment used by Yersin, his library and stereoscope through which visitors can see in 3-D the black-and-white slides, including shots taken by Yersin on his visits to the highlands. The museum's curator is helpful and friendly, and fluent in French and English.

Evening in Nha Trang harbour

The **Cho Dam** (central market) close to Nguyen Hong Son Street is a good place to wander and browse and is quite well-stocked with useful items. In the vicinity of the market, along **Phan Boi Chau Street** for example, are some bustling streets with old colonial-style shuttered houses.

Long Thanh is one of Vietnam's most distinguished photographers and has a **gallery** ⓘ *126 Hoang Van Thu St, near the railway station, T058-824875, lvntrang50@hotmail.com*, in his native Nha Trang. Long Thanh works only in black and white and has won a series of international awards and recognition for his depictions of Cham children and of wistful old men and women, who have witnessed generations of change in a single lifetime. Many of his famous pictures were taken in and around Nha Trang. Long Thanh speaks English and welcomes visitors to his gallery; he is also willing, by pre-arrangement, to meet photographers and organize photographic expeditions

Thap Ba Hot Springs

ⓘ *2 km beyond Cham Ponagar, not far from the Cai River, T058-835335, www.thapbahotspring.com. Mineral mud tub 250,000d for 2 people or 50,000d per person, 25,000d per child; mineral water bath 50,000d for 2 or 35,000d per person, 15,000 per child. Tour operators run trips.*

A soak in mineral water or a mud bath is a relaxing and refreshing experience. Baths and pools of differing sizes are available for individuals, couples and groups. The water is 40° Celsius and is rich in sodium silicate chloride. The mineral mud stimulates the nerves under the skin. Steam baths and massages are also available.

Islands around Nha Trang

ⓘ *The islands are reached on boat trips from Cau Da pier. Departures 0900. Around US$7 including a seafood lunch, snorkelling equipment and pick up; cold beers and a bamboo basket cost extra. Boat charters also available; fees payable to dock at some islands.*

The **islands** off Nha Trang are sometimes known as the **Salangane** islands after the sea swallows that nest here in such profusion. The sea swallow (*yen* in Vietnamese) produces the highly prized bird's nest from which the famous soup is made.

There's an uninspiring aquarium on **Mieu Island** but no other sights, as such. In fact, the islands (including **Hon Mun**, **Hon Tam** and **Hon Mot**) are usually a bit of an anticlimax for, as

Nha Trang beach

so often in Vietnam, to travel is better than to arrive: it's often a case of lovely boat trip, disappointing beach. The best part is anchoring offshore and jumping into the exquisitely cool water while your skipper prepares a sumptuous seafood feast and the beers chill in the ice bucket. The best known boat trips to the islands are run by **Hanh's Green Hat** and **Mama Linh** ▲ ⇒ *p203.*

Mui Ne ⊜❼❶▲⊜⓿ ⇒ *pp198-205*

Further down the coast and east of the small fishing town of **Phan Thiet** is Mui Ne, a 20-km sweep of golden sand where Vietnam's finest coastal resorts can be found. Watersports are available here as well as one of the country's most attractive golf courses . ▲⇒ *p204.*

Ins and outs
Getting there Open Tour Buses nearly all divert to Mui Ne and drop off/pick up from just about every hotel along the beach. It is also possible and quicker to hire a car; from Ho Chi Minh City to Mui Ne will cost approximately US$40-50. ⊜ ⇒ *p205.*

Best time to visit The weather is best in the dry season, November to May. Mui Ne is most popular with overseas visitors in the Christmas to Easter period when prices at the some of the better hotels rise by 20% or more.

Sights
Mui Ne (Cape Ne) is the name of the famous sandy cape and the small fishing village that lies at its end. Mui Ne's two claims to fame are its *nuoc mam* (fish sauce) and its **beaches**, where it's possible to play a host of watersports. The cape is dominated by some impressive **sand dunes**, which are quite red in parts due to the underlying geology.

Around the village, visitors may notice a strong smell of rotting fish. This is the unfortunate but inevitable by-product of fish sauce fermenting in wooden barrels. The process takes a year but to Vietnamese palates it is worth every day. The *nuoc mam* of Phan Thiet is made from anchovies and is highly regarded but not as reverentially as that from the southern island of Phu Quoc.

Central Vietnam Central Highlands & the coast

● Sleeping

Dalat *p187, map p186*

A Empress Hotel, 5 Nguyen Thai Hoc St, T063-833888, empressdl@hcm.vnn.vn. This is a particularly attractive hotel in a lovely position overlooking the lake. All rooms are arranged around a small courtyard which traps the sun and is a great place for breakfast or to pen a postcard. The rooms are large with very comfortable beds and the more expensive ones have luxurious bathrooms so try to get a room upgrade. Attentive and courteous staff. Arguably the best value hotel in Dalat and with the best view of Xuan Huong Lake.

B Golf 3 Hotel, 4 Nguyen Thi Minh Khai St, T063-826042, golf3hot@hcm.vnn.vn. Smart, new, centrally located hotel, with comfortable rooms. Cheaper rooms have showers only. It has a good range of facilities, including bar, restaurant, massage, nightclub and karaoke. The location by Dalat market is excellent. One drawback though is that because it is so near to the market the rooms facing the street are noisy.

B Hang Nga (Tree House), 3 Huynh Thuc Khang St, T063-822070, F831480. If you fancy a fantasy night in a mushroom, a tree or a giraffe then this is the place for you. It is an architectural meander through curves, twists and bizarre rooms and ornamentation. The guesthouse was designed by Hang Nga, whose father, Truong Chinh, formed the triumvirate of power following the death of Ho Chi Minh. Prices are reasonable but the rooms tend to be visited by curious tourists and the furniture is sturdily made and not too comfortable.

B Novotel 7, Tran Phu St, T063-825777, novotel@bdvn.vnd.net. Formerly the Dalat Hotel, it is opposite the post office and near the **Sofitel**, with which it shares its management and many facilities. Rooms nicely restored and comfortably furnished, although the standard rooms are small. There is no restaurant but breakfast is served here and **Café de la Poste** is just over the road.

E Hoa Binh 1, 64 Truong Cong Dinh St, T063-822787. One of the better low-cost places with 15 rooms in a good location, including 5 at the back around a small yard, quiet but not much view. Rooms at the front have a view but can be a bit noisy. Furniture is a bit battered but it's a friendly place and has an all-day café.

E Hoa Binh 2, 67 Truong Cong Dinh St, T063-822982. Almost opposite its sister hotel, this is rather a clean and attractive 1930s building. Some rooms have small balconies.

Buon Ma Thuot *p191*

B Thang Loi, 1 Phan Chu Trinh St, T050-857615, www.daklaktourist.com. A modern hotel in a central location. The rooms are all large and come with en suite facilities. The staff speak good English. Food in the restaurant is fresh, well presented, good value and plentiful.

C White Horse Hotel, White Horse Hotel, 50-54 Hai Ba Trung St, T050-850379. A slightly cheaper alternative.

Lak Lake *p192*

It costs US$3-5 to stay in a Mnong longhouse at **Buon Juin**; contact **Daklak Tourist** for arrangements.

Play Ku *p192*

C Ialy Hotel, 89 Hung Vuong St, T059-824843, ialyhotel@dng.vnn.vn. Reasonable sized, good value rooms with en suite facilities, a/c and satellite TV. Staff are friendly enough. The restaurant on the first floor is only open for breakfast. ATM in the lobby.

Kontum *p193*

C Dakbla 1 Hotel, 2 Phan Dinh Phung St, T060-863333, F863336. Set in attractive grounds, this hotel has a small restaurant and jetty on the riverbank. Staff are friendly and helpful and have a basic understanding of English and French.

Budget busters

Highland luxury

LL-L Ana Mandara Villas Dalat & Spa, Le Lai St, Dalat, T063-520819, www.sixsenses.com. Restored French villas are perched on a hillside, surrounded by fruit farms. Each villa (3-5 bedrooms) has its own small garden, a sitting room, conservatory and a terrace for private dining. A number of pools are scattered about the hotel complex. There is also a central villa that houses a French bistro and wine bar. The Six Senses Spa experience has been created in one of the villas with river and mountain views, outdoor pools and hot tubs.

L Sofitel Dalat Palace, 12 Tran Phu St, Dalat, T063-825444, www.sofitel.com. This rambling old building was built in 1922 and restored to its former glory in 1995. Those that knew it before the renovation will be amazed: curtains, furniture, statues, gilt mirrors and chandeliers adorn the rooms which are tastefully arranged as the French do best. The view over Xuan Huong Lake to the hills beyond is lovely and the extensive grounds of the hotel are beautifully laid out. Hotel restaurant, ▥▥▥ **Le Rabelais**, has a superb dining room with views down to the Lake and offers French specialities and an excellent wine list. Hotel guests get special green fees on the nearby golf course. Staff are friendly if somewhat haughty. Wonderful but overpriced.

Rooms are large, if a little drab, and come with en suite bathrooms. The restaurant provides good Vietnamese and international food at a reasonable price.

Nha Trang *p193, map p194*

A-C Bao Dai's Villas, Tran Phu St (just before Cau Da village), T058-590147, www.vngold.com/nt/baodai. Several villas of former Emperor Bao Dai, with magnificent views over the harbour, are sited on a small promontory full of frangipani. The large rooms are essentially open-plan studios and look very dated, while more modern rooms have little space, but the winning views more than make up for it. There are 2 restaurants, motorbike and bicycle hire, internet, tennis court and fishing tours.

B-D La Suisse Hotel, 34 Tran Quang Khai St, T058-524353, lasuissehotelnt @dng.vnn.vn. Excellent new hotel with 24 rooms on 5 floors, nicely built, and offering excellent value for money. The best rooms (VIP) are large and have attractive balconies with sea view. All

rooms have bathtubs. Breakfast included.

D Perfume Grass Inn (Que Thao), 4A Biet Thu St, T058-826345, www.perfume-grass.com. Well-run and friendly family hotel with 21 rooms. Restaurant and internet service. Good value for money. Book in advance.

D-E Blue House, 12/8 Hung Vuong St, T058-824505. Down a little alley in a quiet setting. 14 a/c and fan rooms in a small, neat blue building. Friendly and excellent value for money.

D-E Hanoi, 31C Biet Thu St, T058-813629. Set in a quiet cul-de-sac at the end of the road, this small 12-room hotel has a/c and fan rooms. Includes breakfast, helpful.

D-E Sao Xanh (Blue Star), 1B Biet Thu St, T058-826447, quangc@dng.vnn.vn. Another popular, clean and friendly family-run hotel. 23 rooms, free coffee and bananas, more expensive rooms have breakfast included. Near the beach and in a popular area.

D-E Truc Linh, 11 Biet Thu St, T058-825742, internet_bt@yahoo.com. Best known for its restaurant, this guesthouse is popular with budget travellers. Some rooms have a/c; all have hot water.

Mui Ne *p197, map p200*
L Victoria Phan Thiet, Km 9, Phu Hai, Phan Thiet, T062-847171, www.victoriahotels-asia.com. Part of the French-run Victoria Group, the resort has 50 thatch-roof bungalows of different sizes in an attractive landscaped setting. It is well equipped with restaurants, several bars, an attractive pool and health club.

L-A Coco Beach (Hai Duong), T062-847111-3, www.cocobeach.net. Coco Beach was the first resort on Mui Ne and remains among the best. Wooden bungalows and 2-bedroom 'villas' facing the beach in a beautiful setting with a lovely pool. Not luxurious and rooms can be dark but bathrooms do have an enclosed shower. There are 2 restaurants: **Champa** (French; Tue-Sun 1500-2300) and **Paradise Beach Club** (all day). Also library, table tennis and table football.

A Bamboo Village Beach Resort, T062-847007, www.bamboovillage resort.com. Attractive, simple, hexagonal bamboo huts peppered around a lovely shady spot at the top of the beach. 'Deluxe' bungalows with 2 beds, a small bathroom and private balconies that look over the beach. The 'lodges' are not recommended. Excellent restaurant, attractive swimming pool with jacuzzi, table tennis, pool table, internet, library, windsurf facilities and massage service.

A-B Sailing Club, T062-847440, www.sailingclubvietnam.com. This is a stunning resort, designed in the most charming style with bungalows and rooms that are simple and cool and surrounded by dense vegetation. It has a small pool and a good restaurant and bar. Remarkably good value but the cocktails are a little pricey. A popular place and sun loungers get snapped up fast so don't dally in the mornings.

B Sinh Café, T062-847542, muine@ sinhcafevn.com. Large and new hotel that has cleverly packed the narrow site with 48 rooms and brick-built bungalows. It has a nice pool, bar and restaurant.

B-C Full Moon Beach, T062-847008, www.windsurf-vietnam.com. A variety of brick and bamboo rooms with the most attractive rooms having a seaview. The

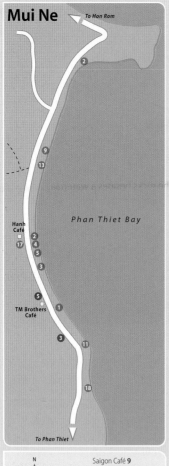

Mui Ne

To Hon Rom

Phan Thiet Bay

Hanh Café

TM Brothers Café

To Phan Thiet

N

1 km
1 mile

Sleeping
Bamboo Village **1**
Canary **2**
Coco Beach
  (Hai Duong) **3**
Full Moon Beach **4**
Hiep Hoa **5**

Saigon Café **9**
Sailing Club **11**
Sinh Café **13**
Thuy Thuy **17**
Victoria Phan Thiet **18**

Eating
Luna D'autonno **3**
Sunset **5**

Bars & clubs
Jibe's Beach Club **2**

Central Vietnam Central Highlands & the coast Listings

Budget busters

Luxury on the South China Sea

LL-L Ana Mandara, Tran Phu St, Nha Trang, T058-524705, www.six-senses.com/ana-mandara. Nha Trang's finest beach resort is where those who can afford it relax in unashamed and exquisitive luxury. Simple but elegant designs are set against cool woods, wafting fans and icy a/c, all in pitched battle against the scorching sun that blazes down on the beach outside. 78 rooms, 2 pools, tennis court, and every conceivable facility in this enchanting retreat. Two restaurants serving exquisite food (♦♦♦): the Ana Pavilion, which is open air and open 24 hours, and the Beach Restaurant for buffet and à la carte options. For those wishing further pampering there is the Six Senses Spa.

LL Ana Mandara Evason Resort, Ninh Vinh Bay, off Nha Trang, T058-829829, www.sixsenses.com. The über-cool island resort of Ana Mandara is the ultimate pleasurable experience. Scattered villas at the all-white hideway boast large, stand-alone wooden bathtubs, a wine cellar, outdoor plunge pool and CD and inhouse video with movies on request. Some come with a spa suite. The restaurant serves fusion meals and opens out to the open air. The Six Senses spa blends into the rocks besides a waterfall.

L Whale Island Resort, off Nha Trang, T058-840501, www.whale islandresort.com. This is a great place in which to relax amid the aquamarine waters of the South China Sea. Bamboo bungalows are scattered around the resort, which offers watersports including diving, catamarans, windsurfs and canoes. Between April and July you maybe lucky enough to see whale sharks. Rates include three meals, transfer from Nha Trang and boat transfer to Whale Island.

brick rooms are more comfortable with low slung, Japanese-style beds and low-ceilinged rooms. Only the villas for 4 have a/c.

B-C Thuy Thuy, T062-847357. Currently 4 pleasant a/c bungalows set on the 'wrong' side of the road (ie away from the beach). Charming and nicely run little place, highly praised by guests. Attractive pool.

C Hiep Hoa, T062-847262. Attractive and simple little place. Only 7 rooms, fan and cold water only, but quiet, clean and with its own stretch of beach. Small restaurant. Popular so book in advance.

C-D Canary, T062-847258, www.canary resort.com. Named for its colour, this pleasant-enough place lies quite far along Mui Ne. 23 satisfactory a/c and fan rooms plus 17 bamboo bungalows.

E Saigon Café, T062-847091. With just 10 simple huts and a nice shady garden, this is a most relaxing and inexpensive place to stay. Friendly reception with English spoken. Good café and travel services.

Eating

Dalat p187, map p186
In the evening, streetstalls line Nguyen Thi Minh Khai St, leading to Dalat market, which is itself the ideal place to buy picnic provisions. Lakeside cafés and restaurants may look attractive but they are badly staffed and serve indifferent food. See also Budget busters, p199.

♦♦♦ **Empress Restaurant**, Empress hotel. Open all day and specializing in Chinese fare but with a good selection of

Vietnamese and western dishes. Ideal breakfast setting, al fresco around the fountain in the courtyard of the hotel.

🍴 **Hoa Binh 1**, 67 Truong Cong Dinh St. An all-day eatery serving standard backpacker fare: fried noodles, vegetarian dishes and pancakes at low prices.

🍴 **Le Café de la Poste**, 12 Tran Phu St. Adjacent to the Sofitel and under the same management, international food and a not very well-stocked deli but spot-on if you are craving cheese. Bar and nightclub upstairs.

🍴 **Long Hoa**, 6 3 Thang 2, T063-822934. In the best traditions of French family restaurants. Delicious food, super breakfasts, popular with Dalat's expats and visitors. Fairly priced. Chicken soup and beefsteak, just over US$2, are particularly recommended. Also sample Madam's homemade strawberry wine, US$6 per bottle. Service is highly erratic. Get there well before 2200.

🍴 **Stop and Go Café**, 2A Ly Tu Trong St, T063-828458. A café and art gallery run by the local poet, Mr Duy Viet. Sit inside or on the terrace as he bustles around rustling up breakfast, pulling out volumes of his own collected works. The garden is an overrun wilderness where tall fir trees sigh in the breeze.

Nha Trang *p193, map p194*

A local speciality is *nem nuong*, grilled pork wrapped in rice paper with salad leaves and bun, fresh rice noodles. The French bread in Nha Trang is also excellent. On the beach near **Nha Trang Waterpark** is a night market, where stalls serve freshly cooked fish and barbecued meat. See also Budget busters, p201.

🍴 **Sailing Club**, 72-74 Tran Phu St, T058-826528, daily 0700-2300. Although best known as a bar, this busy and attractive beachfront area also includes several restaurants: Japanese, Italian and Indian. None is cheap but all serve good food and represent decent value.

🍴 **Truc Linh**, 21 Biet Thu St, T058-821259. The fresh seafood displayed on large platters on the pavement will entice you in to this lovely, thatched-roof restaurant. Barbecued fish is deliciously tender.

🍴 **Cyclo**, 5A Tran Quang Khai St, T058-524208. A really outstanding little family-run restaurant. Italian and Vietnamese dishes. Real attention to detail in the bamboo decor and cooking.

🍴 **Good Morning Vietnam**, 19B Biet Thu St, T058-815071, daily 1000-2300. Popular Italian restaurant, part of a small chain to be found in major tourist centres.

🍴 **Lac Canh**, 44 Nguyen Binh Khiem St, T058-821391, daily 0900-2130 sharp. Specializes in beef, squid and prawns, which you barbecue at your table. Also excellent fish and a special dish of eel mixed with vermicilli. Smoky atmosphere and can be hard to get a table.

Mui Ne *p197, map p200*

Of the hotel restaurants the Sailing Club, Bamboo Village and Coco Beach stand out, see Sleeping, p200.

🍴 **Luna D'autonno**, T062-847591. One of the best Italian restaurants in the country is set under a large, bamboo roof in a rustic-style building, surrounded by plants. Inspired menu, huge portions and good wine list. Daily fish specials, full pasta range as well as veal, squid, beef and wood-fired pizzas. Barbecues on Fri and Sat nights.

🍴 **Sunset**, T062-847605. Good Vietnamese food, especially fish, efficient service and excellent value.

🎵 Bars and clubs

Nha Trang *p193, map p194*

Crazy Kim, 19 Biet Thu St, T058-816072, open until late. A busy, lively bar in the heart of a popular part of town. Pool, table tennis, food.

Guava, 17 Biet Thu St, T058-524140, www.clubnhatrang.com, daily 1100-2400. Striking orange front. Stylish café and cocktail bar. Relaxing place with garden and lounge bar areas. Good music. Bar games and burgers.

Sailing Club, 74-76 Tran Phu St, T058-826528, open until late. Lively bar, especially on Sat nights when locals and visitors congregate to enjoy pool, cold beer, dancing and music.

Mui Ne *p197, map p200*

Jibe's Beach Club, Full Moon Beach Resort, T062-847405, daily 0730-0300. Jibe's has the only separate bar on the beach and drinks are cheaper than in the resorts. There's a barbecue party every Sat night with happy hour.

O Shopping

Dalat *p187, map p186*

Dalat has a well-deserved reputation for producing not only beautiful flowers but also some of the best handmade silk paintings in Vietnam.

▲ Activities and tours

Dalat *p187, map p186*

Golf

Dalat Palace Golf Course, 1 Phu Dong Thien Vuong St, T063-823507, dpgc@hcm.vnn.vn. A US-owned and IMG-managed 18-hole golf course originally developed by Emperor Bao Dai in 1922 and rebuilt in 1994. Rated by some as the finest in Vietnam and one of the best in the region. Beautiful setting with fairways, bent grass tees and greens overlooking Xuan Huong Lake.

Tour operators

Action Dalat, 114 3 Thang 2 St, T063-829422. Trekking, boat rides, camping, climbing and abseiling on Langbian Mountain and excursions to minority villages. Around US$20 per day.
Dalat Toserco, 7, 3 Thang 2 St, T063-822125, F828330. Budget transport and a good selection of tours. Slightly more expensive then Sinh Café.
Dalat Tourist, 35 Tran Huong Dao St, T063-822317, www.dalattourist.com. The state-run travel company for Lam Dong

Province. Good but expensive.
Phat Tire Adventures, 73 Truong Cong Dinh St, T063-829422, www.phattire adventures.com. A US operator offering trekking, mountain biking, canyoning and kayaking tours with qualified instructors.
Sinh Café, 4a Bui Thi Xuan, T063-822663, www.sinhcafevn.com. Part of the nationwide Sinh Café chain. Primarily provides cheap travel to Ho Chi Minh City and Nha Trang. Also arranges local tours.

Nha Trang *p193, map p194*

Diving

Dry season only (Jan-May).
Rainbow Divers, operates from the Sailing Club, T058-829946, T091-3408146 (mob), www.divevietnam.com. A full range of courses. Good reports regarding equipment and focus on safety. Qualified instructors speak a variety of European languages. Also at the Whale Island Resort, www.whaleislandresort.com.
   The **Ana Mandara Resort** also offers diving packages.

Fishing

Boats and equipment can be hired from Cau Da Pier; contact **Khanh Hoa Tourism**, 1 Tran Hung Dao St, T058-822753, www.nhatrangtourist.com.vn, for details.

Therapies

Six Senses Spa, Ana Mandara Resort, www.sixsenses.com. Exotic treatments: Japanese and Vichy showers, hot tubs and massages (US$45 for 50 mins and upwards), in beautiful surroundings.

Watersports

The **Ana Mandara Resort** offers wind-surfing, parasailing, hobiecats and fishing.

Tour operators

The following tour operators also arrange trips to **Buon Ma Thuot** and the **Central Highlands**.
Chau's Tour, 22 Le Thanh Phuong St, T090-3598159 (mob), havanchau @hotmail.com. Boat tours run by the

engaging Chau (Captain Cook) who is highly entertaining, knowledgable, speaks excellent English and runs a good ship. Tours cost slightly more than the standard (US$8-10 per day) but are worth the extra. Chau now also organizes and leads tours around Vietnam. Interesting and lively.

Hanh's Green Hat, 44 Le Thanh Ton St and 2A Biet Thu St, T058-821309. Boat trips (US$7 including lunch and pick-up from hotel). Also other local tours, car, motorbike and bicycle hire.

Mama Linh, 2A Hung Vuong St, T058-826693. Standard boat trips for US$7 and minibus tickets to Hoi An, Phan Thiet, Ho Chi Minh City and Dalat.

Sinh Café, 10 Biet Thu St, T058-811981, www.sinhcafevn.com. Offers tours and Open Bus Tour tickets.

Mui Ne *p197, map p200*

Diving
Scuba diving trips organized by the **Hotel Victoria Phan Thiet**, see Sleeping.

Golf
Ocean Dunes Golf Club, T062-823366. Phan Thiet's 18-hole golf course, designed by Nick Faldo, is regarded by golfers as one of the best in Vietnam. Fully equipped club house with bar and restaurant. Green fee US$80, caddy US$15.

Therapies
Sailing Club, T062-847440, www.sailingclubvietnam.com. Massage treatments are available in special cabins in the grounds.

Tour operators
Sinh Café, Mui Ne Resort, T062-847542, www.sinhcafevn.com. Good for Open Tour and local tours.
TM Brother's, T062-847359. Local tours and Open Tour Bus service.

Watersports
Wind surfing, kite surfing and other watersports are popular in Mui Ne. The wind is normally brisk and the sight of the kite surfers zooming around on the waves is great for those of us too cowardly to try. Equipment and training is offered by a couple of resorts.

Airwaves, Sailing Club, www.airwaves kitesurfing.com. Airwaves can organize kitesurfing, windsurfing, sailing, surfskiing and surfing and hires out all equipment. Also has hobie cats. Kitesurfing is taught by internationally qualified instructors. Prices vary according to lessons and equipment needed. Windsurfing, half day US$25, lessons US$30 an hour. Catamaran sailing, half day US$60. Surfing, half day US$1, 1 hr lesson, US$20. Boogie boards, US$3. Surfskis, half day US$15-21.

Jibe's Beach Club, T062-847405, www.windsurf-vietnam.com, part of and close to Full Moon Beach Resort. The main centre for kite surfing in the area, Jibe's offers a range of watersports, with instruction in 9 languages. Kite surfing: 2-hr private lesson with equipment US$85; 2-hr group lesson US$75. Kite and board rental: half day US$55, week US$375; board only US$15, kite only US$40. Gear insurance varies. Also windsurfers, surfboards, sea kayaks and boogie boards for hire, US$5-30 half day or US$60-210 per week, plus insurance.

⊖ Transport

Dalat *p187, map p186*

Air
See p187. **Vietnam Airlines**, 40 Ho Tuong Mau St, T/F063-833499.

Bus
Open Tour Bus companies operate daily trips to **Ho Chi Minh City** and **Nha Trang**.

Car
It is possible to hire cars and taxis. Many tour operators have cars for hire and there are numerous taxis to choose from. One way by car/van to Ho Chi Minh City is US$60.

Central provinces *p191*

Air

Vietnam Airlines has offices at Buon Ma Thuot (T050-954442) and Play Ku (T059-823058) airports and at 129, Ba Trieu St in Kontum, T060-862282.

Bus

Regular local buses link provincial centres throughout the region.

Car

Cars with drivers are available for hire; contact the provincial tourist offices or your hotel. Play Ku to **Buon Ma Thuot**, 3½ hrs, US$50.

Nha Trang *p193, map p194*

Air

See p194. Some hotels offer complimentary bus rides to town. The airport bus costs 20,000d each way, 34 km. **Vietnam Airlines**, 91 Nguyen Thien Thuat St, T058-826768.

Bicycles and motorbikes

Bicycles can be hired from almost every hotel and every café for around 10,000d per day for a bicycle. Motorbikes can be hired from hotels and cafés for around 60,000d per day.

Bus

Open Tour Buses arrive at and depart from their relevant operator's café (see Tour operators above).

Taxi

Khanh Hoa Taxi, T058-810810.

Train

There are regular train connections with stops to and from **Hanoi** and **Ho Chi Minh City**. The station is at 17 Thai Nguyen St, T058-822113.

Mui Ne *p197, map p200*

Bus

A local bus plies the route from Phan Thiet bus station to **Mui Ne**, 8000d, as do taxis. **Sinh Café** and **TM Brother's** Open Tour Buses drop off and pick up from all resorts on **Mui Ne**, US$6. Avoid catching the **Saigontourist** Open Tour Bus as this refuses to stop where guests wish and heads directly for the **Saigontourist** hotel.

ⓘ Directory

Dalat *p187, map p186*

Banks BIDV, 42 Hoa Binh Square, closes at 1630 Sat. **Incombank**, 46-48 Hoa Binh Square. It has a bureau de change and also cashes Tcs, closes at 1100 Sat. **Hospitals** 4 Pham Ngoc Thach St, T063-822154. Well-equipped hospital. The doctors speak English and French. **Internet** There are internet cafes galore along Nguyen Chi Thanh St, heading from Hoa Binh Square to Xuan Huong Lake. **Post office** 14 Tran Phu St, opposite Novotel Hotel. Offers internet and IDD.

Nha Trang *p193, map p194*

Banks **Vietcombank**, 17 Quang Trung. Will change most major currencies, cash, TCs (2% commission), and arrange cash advances on some credit cards. There's a **Vietcombank** exchange bureau at 8A Biet Thu St. **Hospitals** General Hospital, 19 Yersin St, T58-822168. **Internet** There are email cafés all over town, particularly in Biet Thu St. Around 100d per min. **Post office** GPO, 2 Le Loi St. Also in Biet Thu St, near Nguyen Thien Thuat St.

Mui Ne *p197, map p200*

Banks There are two banks in Mui Ne. BIDV, on the right hand side of Swiss Village, Mon-Fri 0730-1200, 1300-1630. Charges 2% commission on traveller's cheques and 3% on cash advances. **Internet** Some tour cafes, offer free service to customers and almost all hotels offer internet access to their guests.

Ho Chi Minh City and the south

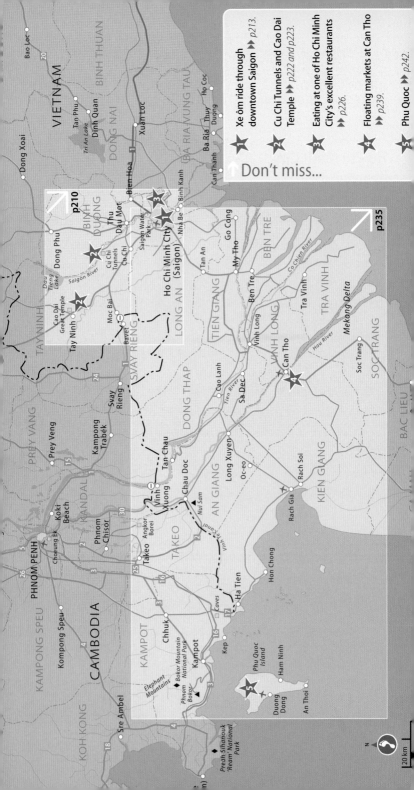

p210

p235

Don't miss...

1 Xe ôm ride through downtown Saigon ►► p213.

2 Cu Chi Tunnels and Cao Dai Temple ►► p222 and p223.

3 Eating at one of Ho Chi Minh City's excellent restaurants ►► p226.

4 Floating markets at Can Tho ►► p239.

5 Phu Quoc ►► p242.

Ho Chi Minh City is a manic, capitalistic hothouse, clogged with traffic, bursting with energy and enlivened by top restaurants, shops and bars. Its streets are evidence of a vibrant historical past with pagodas and temples and a bustling Chinatown. In more recent times it was the seat of the South Vietnam government until events in 1975 led to the country's reunification. Today, it is a burgeoning city, dedicated to commerce and hedonistic pleasures.

Ho Chi Minh City is surrounded by fascinating historical sights to the north and by the liquid fingers of the river delta to its south. The Mekong region is a veritable Garden of Eden, stuffed full of bountiful fruit trees, decorated in pink bougainvillea and carpeted with brilliant green rice paddies. Waterways are as busy as highways, with fishing boats chug chug chugging their way along the brown river. Elsewhere in the south, historical, cultural, religious and pleasurable treasures abound: the Viet Cong tunnels at Cu Chi, the fantastical Cao Dai temple at Tay Ninh and dazzling white, remote beaches at Phu Quoc.

Ratings

Landscape
★★★

Relaxation
★★

Activities
★★

Culture
★★★

Wildlife
★

Costs
$$$-$

Ho Chi Minh City and around

Officially renamed in 1975, Ho Chi Minh City remains to most the bi-syllabic, familiar 'Saigon'. During the 1960s and early 1970s, Saigon, the Pearl of the Orient, boomed and flourished under the American occupation. Today, it is the largest city in Vietnam and still growing at a prodigious rate. It is a place of remorseless, relentless activity and expanding urban sprawl. It is also the nation's foremost commercial and industrial centre. For the visitor, Ho Chi Minh City is a fantastic place to shop, eat and drink, while admiring its historical past and enjoying its energetic present.

☑ **Getting there** Plane, train or Open Tour Bus.
⊖ **Getting around** Foot, cyclo, taxi or *xe ôm*.
⊖ **Time required** 1-4 days.
🌢 **Weather** Hot, with heavy rain May-Oct.
☐ **Sleeping** 5-star hotels and good-value budget choices.
⊘ **Eating** World-class restaurants serving outstanding cuisine.
▲▲ **Activities and tours** Visit Cu Chi Tunnels and Cao Dai Temple.
★ **Don't miss...** A ride on a *xe ôm* through the streets of downtown Saigon ▸▸ *p213 and p232.*

Ins and outs

Getting there Tan Son Nhat international airport (SGN), T08-848 5383/832 0320, is 30 minutes from the centre. An airport bus, no 152, travels from here to Pham Ngu Lao backpacker area, Ben Thanh Market and on to Dong Khoi Street, every 15 minutes 0520-2055, 2000d. Otherwise take an **Airport Taxi**, T08-844 6666, around 50,000-70,000d on the meter. (Note that when travelling from the city to the airport, it costs an additonal 5000d to enter the airport area, on top of your taxi fare.) Facilities in arrivals include tourist information, two banks and a post office; in departures, there is a **Vietindebank**, post office, first-aid office and telephone service. There are also small duty-free shops and poor but expensive

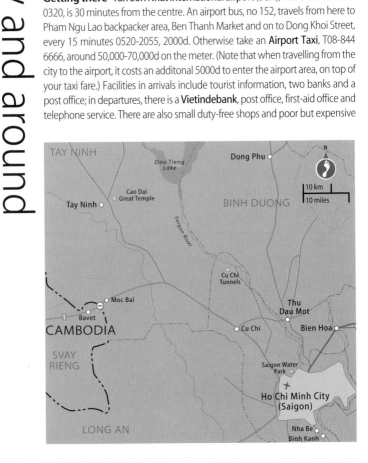

Central Ho Chi Minh City and the Saigon River

cafés and bars. On the right of the international terminal is the **domestic terminal**. It has toilets, a shop, telephones and a reasonable restaurant.

Open Tour Buses generally depart and leave from offices in the Pham Ngu Lao district. There is also a daily bus service from Ho Chi Minh City to Phnom Penh (Cambodia). The **railway station** is northwest of the city centre. There are regular daily connections to/from Hanoi and all stops on the line north. see p232.

Getting around   Ho Chi Minh City has abundant transport. Metered taxis, motorcycle taxis and cyclos vie for business. Buses have now become more reliable and frequent and are a safer and cheaper alternative to other modes of urban transport. Those who prefer some level of independence opt to hire (or even buy) a bicycle or motorbike. There are now so many motorbikes on the streets of Ho Chi Minh City that intersections seem lethally confused. Miraculously, the riders miss each other (most of the time), while pedestrians safely make their way through waves of machines (see Crossing the road, p214). Take an organized tour to reach sights outside the city.

Orientation   Virtually all of Ho Chi Minh City lies to the west of the Saigon River. Most visitors to Ho Chi Minh City head straight for hotels in Districts 1 or 3. Many will arrive on buses in De Tham or Pham Ngu Lao streets, the backpacker area, in District 1, not far from the city centre. Many of the sights are also in District 1 (also still known as Saigon). Cholon or Chinatown (District 5) is a mile west of the centre. All the sights of Central Ho Chi Minh City can be reached on foot or cyclo in no more than 30 minutes from the major hotels on Nguyen Hue, Dong Khoi and Ton Duc Thang streets.

Background

Before the 15th century, Ho Chi Minh City was a small village surrounded by a wilderness of forest and swamp. Through the years it was ostensibly incorporated into the Funan and then the Khmer empires but it's unlikely that these kingdoms had any lasting influence on the community. In fact, the Khmers, who called the region *Prei Nokor*, used it for hunting. By 1623 the town had become an important commercial centre and, in the mid-17th century, it became the residence of the so-called Vice-King of Cambodia. In 1698, the Viets managed to

212 extend their control to the far south and Saigon was finally brought under Vietnamese control. By 1790, the city had a population of 50,000 and Emperor Gia Long made it his place of residence until Hué was selected as the capital of the Nguyen Dynasty.

In the middle of the 19th century, the French began to challenge Vietnamese authority in the south. Between 1859 and 1862, in response to Nguyen persecution of the Catholics in Vietnam, the French attacked and captured Saigon. The Treaty of Saigon in 1862 ratified the conquest and created the new French colony of Cochin China. Saigon was developed in French style, with wide, tree-lined boulevards, street-side cafés, elegant French architecture, boutiques and the smell of baking baguettes.

During the course of the Vietnam War, as refugees spilled in from a devastated countryside, the population of Saigon almost doubled from 2.4 million in 1965 to around 4.5 million by 1975. With reunification in 1976, the new communist authorities pursued a policy of depopulation, believing that the city had become too large and parasitic, preying on the surrounding countryside.

The population of Ho Chi Minh City today is officially six million and rising fast as the rural poor are lured by tales of streets paved with gold. Vietnam's economic reforms are most in evidence in Ho Chi Minh City, where average annual incomes, at US$480, are more than double the national average. It is also here that the country's largest population (around

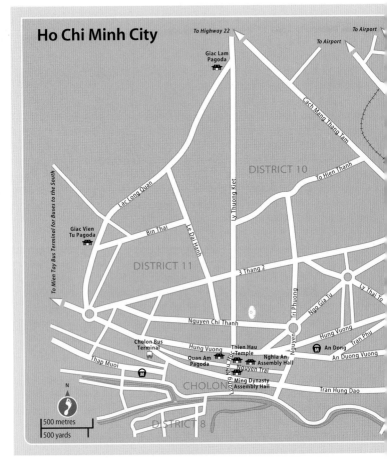

380,000) of Hoa (ethnic Chinese) is to be found. Once persecuted for their economic success, they still have the greatest economic influence and acumen. Under the current regime, best described as crony capitalist, the city is once more being rebuilt.

City centre 🚇🛈🏨🏪🏛️⛰️✉️🎭 ⏩ pp224-234

The centre of Ho Chi Minh City is, in many respects, the most interesting. A saunter down Dong Khoi Street, the old rue Catinat, can still give an impression of life in a more elegant and less frenzied era. Much remains on a small and personal scale and within a 100 yard radius of Dong Khoi or Thai Van Lung streets there are dozens of cafés, restaurants and boutiques.

Around Lam Son Square

Lam Son Square is the centre of Ho Chi Minh City. The **Rex Hotel**, a pre-Liberation favourite with US officers, stands at the intersection of Le Loi and Nguyen Hue boulevards. This was the scene of the daily 'Five o'clock follies' where the military briefed an increasingly sceptical press corps during the Vietnam War. A short distance northeast of the **Rex**, is the once impressive, French-era **Opera House**, once home to the National Assembly. When it is functioning, it provides a varied programme of events.

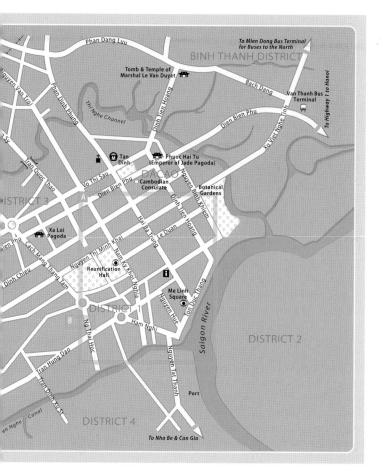

Ho Chi Minh City & the south City centre

Top tips

Crossing the road

Ho Chi Minh City's streets may look anarchic but they are not. A strict code of conduct applies: the main difference between Vietnam's roads and those of the west is that, in Vietnam, the individual abdicates responsibility for his personal safety and assumes an obligation on the part of everyone else; it is the closest Vietnam has ever come to true communism!

Watch Vietnamese cross a busy street: unlike westerners they do not wait for a lull in the traffic but launch themselves straight into the flow, chatting and laughing with their friends, eyes ahead so as to avoid walking into a passing bicycle (their sole duty), no looking left and right, no ducking and weaving – responsibility for their safety rests entirely with the oncoming cyclists. In order to make it easier for cyclists not to hit them they walk at a steady, even pace with no deviation from a clearly signalled route, as any slight change in trajectory or velocity would spell certain disaster.

At the northwest end of Nguyen Hue Boulevard is the yellow and white **City Hall**, now home to Ho Chi Minh City People's Committee, which overlooks a **statue of Bac Ho** (Uncle Ho) offering comfort, or perhaps advice, to a child. On weekend evenings literally thousands of young city men, women and families cruise up and down Nguyen Hue and Le Loi boulevards and Dong Khoi street on bicycles and motorbikes; this whirl of people and machines is known as *chay long rong*, 'cruising', or *song voi*, 'living fast'.

To the left of the Opera House is the **Continental Hotel**, built in 1880 and an integral part of the city's history. Graham Greene stayed here and the hotel features in the book version of *The Quiet American*. The old journalists' haunt, the 'Continental Shelf', was described as "a famous verandah where correspondents, spies, speculators, traffickers, intellectuals and soldiers used to meet during the war to glean information and pick up secret reports, half false, half true or half disclosed. All of this is more than enough for it to be known as Radio Catinat".

Notre Dame Cathedral

Cong Xa Pari (Paris Square)

In the middle of Cong Xa Pari is the imposing and austere **Notre Dame Cathedral** ⓘ *open to visitors 0800-1030 and 1500-1600 Mon-Sat; communion several times daily,* built between 1877 and 1880, allegedly on the site of an ancient pagoda. The red-brick, twin-spired cathedral overlooks a grassy square with a statue of the Virgin Mary holding an orb.

Facing onto Paris Square is the **General Post Office**, built in the 1880s, a particularly distinguished building despite the veneer of junk that has been slapped onto it. The front façade has attractive cornices with French and Khmer motifs and the names of distinguished French men of letters and science. Inside, the high, vaulted ceiling and fans create a deliciously cool atmosphere in which to scribble a postcard. Note the old wall-map of Cochin-China, which has miraculously survived.

Reunification Hall

ⓘ *Nam Ky Khoi Nghia St, T08-8223652. Daily 0730-1100 and 1300-1600; sometimes closed for state occasion. 15,000d, children 2000d, brochure 5000d. Tours every 10 mins; the guides are friendly but their English is not always very good.*

The residence of the French governor was built on this site in 1868 and later became Ngo Dinh Diem's **Presidential Palace**. In February 1962, a pair of planes took off to attack Viet Cong emplacements but turned back to bomb the Presidential Palace in a futile attempt to assassinate President Diem who had been living there since 1954. The president escaped with his family to the cellar but the palace had to be demolished and replaced with a new building, now renamed Reunification Hall, or the **Thong Nhat Conference Hall**. One of the two pilots, Nguyen Thanh Trung, is now Vice President of Vietnam Airlines and still flies government officials around to keep his pilot's licence current.

One of the most memorable photographs taken during the war was of a North Vietnamese Army (NVA) tank crashing through the gates of the Palace on 30 April 1975, symbolizing the end of South Vietnam and its government. A similar tank is now displayed in the forecourt. The President of South Vietnam, General Duong Van Minh, along with his entire cabinet, was arrested in the palace shortly afterwards but the hall has been preserved as it was found in 1975. In the Vice President's Guest Room is a lacquered painting of the

War Remnants Museum

Temple of Literature in Hanoi, while the Presenting of Credentials Room contains a fine 40-piece lacquer work showing diplomats presenting their credentials during the Le Dynasty (15th century). In the basement, there are operations rooms, military maps, radios and other official paraphernalia.

War Remnants Museum

ⓘ *28 Vo Van Tan St, District 3, T08-9306325. Mon-Fri and public holidays 0730-1145 and 1330-1715. 10,000d.*

All the horrors of the Vietnam War from the Vietnamese perspective are piled from floor to ceiling in this museum. The courtyard is stacked with tanks, bombs, planes and helicopters, while the museum, arranged in rooms around the courtyard, record man's inhumanity to man, with displays of deformed feotuses alongside photographs of atrocities and of military action. The exhibits cover the Son My (My Lai) massacre on 16 March 1968, the effects of napalm and phosphorous, and the after-effects of Agent Orange defoliation. Many of the pictures are horrific.

One of the most interesting rooms is dedicated to war photographers and their pictures. It is a requiem to those who died pursuing their craft and, unusually, depicts the military struggle from both sides. The war, as captured through the lens, is an Heironymous Bosch-like hell of mangled metal, suffocating mud and injured limbs. The wall-to-wall images include shots from Robert Capa's last roll of film (before the famous photographer stood on a land mine on 25 May 1954 and died); *Life* magazine's first colour coverage of the conflict, and quotes from those that perished, including a memorable one from Georgette Louise Meyer, aka Dickey Chapelle, who described the thrill of being on the "bayonet border" of the world. Understandably, there is no record of North Vietnamese atrocities carried out on US and South Vietnamese troops.

Xa Loi Pagoda

ⓘ *89 Ba Huyen Thanh Quan St. Daily 0630-1100 and 1430-1700.*

The Xa Loi Pagoda is not far from the War Remnants Museum and is surrounded by foodstalls. Built in 1956, the pagoda contains a multi-storeyed tower, which is particularly revered, as it houses a relic of the Buddha. The main sanctuary contains a large, bronze-gilded

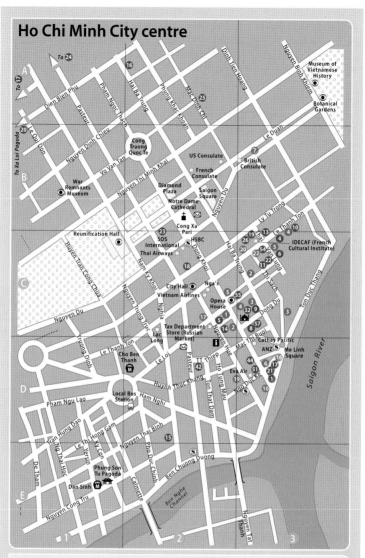

Ho Chi Minh City centre

Ho Chi Minh City & the south City centre

N

400 metres
400 yards

Sleeping

Bong Sen **2** *C2*
Bong Sen 2 **3** *C3*
Caravelle & Port Orient **4** *C3*
Continental **5** *C2*
Duxton **19** *D3*
Grand **6** *D3*
Majestic **10** *D3*
Mogambo **22** *C3*

Renaissance Riverside
& Kabin Restaurant **16** *D3*
Rex **17** *C2*
Sofitel Plaza Saigon **7** *B3*
Spring **20** *C3*

Eating

An Vien **16** *A2*
Al Fresco **57** *C3*
Au Manoir De Khai **20** *B1*
Au Parc **23** *B2*
Ashoka **4** *C3*
Augustin **5** *C2*
Bi Bi **6** *C3*
Blue Ginger **15** *D2*

Bombay **8** *C3*
Camargue & Vasco Bar **11** *C3*
Chao Thai **13** *C3*
Ciao Café **14** *C2*
Com Nieu Saigon **17** *A1*
Hoa Vien **25** *A2*
Hoang Yen **17** *D3*
Huong Lai **18** *C2*
Java **9** *C3*
La Casa Latina **22** *C3*
La Fourchette **21** *D3*
Le Jardin **19** *C3*
Luong Son **26** *C3*
Ma Mo BBQ **54** *C3*
Mosque **32** *C3*

Pacific **10** *B3*
Pho **51** *D3*
Pho Hoa Pasteur **24** *A1*
Qucina & Q Bar **55** *C3*
Restaurant 13 **1** *D3*
Temple Club **42** *D2*
Underground **44** *D3*

Bars & clubs

Alibi **1** *C2*
Apocalypse Now **3** *C3*
Blue Gecko **2** *C3*
Heart of Darkness **4** *B3*
Wild Horse Saloon
& Bop **5** *C3*

Buddha in an attitude of meditation. Around the walls are a series of silk paintings depicting the previous lives of the Buddha (with an explanation of each life to the right of the entrance into the sanctuary). The pagoda is historically, rather than artistically, important as it became a focus of dissent against the Diem regime in 1963 when several monks committed suicide through self-immolation.

Le Duan Street

Le Duan Street was the former corridor of power with Ngo Dinh Diem's Palace at one end, the zoo at the other and the former embassies of the three major powers, France, the US and the UK, in between. Nearest the Reunification Hall is the compound of the **French Consulate**. A block away is the **US Consulate General**. After diplomatic ties were resumed in 1995, the Americans lost little time in demolishing the 1960s embassy, which held so many bad memories, and constructing a new building. A **memorial** outside, on the corner of Mac Dinh Chi Street, records the attack by Viet Cong special forces during the Tet Offensive of 1968 and the final victory in 1975. On the other side of the road, a little further northeast at 25 Le Duan, is the **former British Embassy**, erected in the late 1950s, which now serves as the British Consulate General and British Council.

Museum of Vietnamese History

ⓘ *2 Nguyen Binh Khiem St, T08-8298146. Mon-Sat 0800-1100 and 1330-1600, Sun 0830-1600. 10,000d. No photograpy allowed. Water puppet shows 0900, 1000, 1400, 1500 and 1600 with an extra 1300 performance on Sun, 15 mins, 15,000d.*

The history museum (Bao Tang Lich Su Viet Nam) occupies an elegant 1928 building with a pagoda-based design. The collection spans a wide range of artefacts from the prehistoric (300,000 years ago) and the Dong Son periods (3,500BC-AD100), right through to the birth of the Vietnamese Communist Party in 1930. Particularly impressive are the Cham sculptures, of which the standing bronze Buddha, showing Indian stylistic influence, is probably the finest. There is also a delicately carved Devi (goddess) dating from the 10th century, as well as the head of Siva (Hindu destroyer and creator) and Ganesh (elephant-headed son of Siva and Parvati) both dating from the eighth to the ninth century.

Representative pieces from the Chen-la, Funan, Khmer, Oc-eo and Han Chinese periods are also on display, along with items from the various Vietnamese dynasties and some hill-tribe artefacts. Other highlights include the wooden stakes planted in the Bach Dang riverbed to repel the war ships of the Mongol Yuan in the 13th century; a beautiful Phoenix head from the Tran Dynasty (13th to 14th century) and a Hgor (big drum) of the Jorai people, made from the skin of two elephants.

Ben Thanh Market (Cho Ben Thanh)

A large, covered central market, Ben Thanh Market faces a statue of Tran Nguyen Han at a large and chaotic roundabout, known as the Ben Thanh gyratory system. Ben Thanh is well stocked with clothes, household goods, a good choice of souvenirs, lacquerware, embroidery and so on, as well as some terrific lines in food, including cold meats, fresh and dried fruits. It is not cheap (most local people window-shop here and purchase elsewhere) but the quality is high and the selection probably without equal. Outside the north gate (*cua Bac*) on Le Thanh Ton Street are some particularly tempting displays of fresh fruit (the oranges and apples are imported) and beautiful cut flowers. The **Ben Thanh Night Market** has flourished since 2003; starting at dusk and continuing until after midnight, it offers clothes and cheap jewellery and an abundance of food stalls.

❝❞ the gold of the rice-fields under a flat late sun: the fishers' fragile cranes hovering over the fields like mosquitoes: the cups of tea on an old abbot's platform...

Graham Greene, The Quiet American (Heinemann, London 1954)

Phung Son Tu Pagoda and Dan Sinh market

On Nguyen Cong Tru Street is **Phung Son Tu Pagoda**, a small temple built just after the Second World War by Fukien Chinese; its most notable features are the wonderful painted entrance doors with their fearsome armed warriors. Incense spirals hang in the open well of the pagoda, which is dedicated to Ong Bon, the Guardian of Happiness and Virtue.

Close to the pagoda, on the same street, is the **War Surplus (Dan Sinh) market**. Merchandise on sale includes dog tags and military clothing and equipment (not all of it authentic). The market is popular with western visitors looking for mementoes of their visit, so bargain particularly hard.

Pham Ngu Lao

Most backpackers arriving overland in Ho Chi Minh City are dropped off in this bustling district, a 10- to 15-minute walk from downtown. There are countless hotels, guesthouses and rooms to rent and the area is peppered with restaurants, cafés, bars, email services, tour agencies and money changers, all fiercely competitive.

Cholon (Chinatown)

Cholon (*Cho lon* or 'big market' or Chinatown), which encompasses District 5 to the southwest of the city centre, is inhabited predominantly by Vietnamese of Chinese origin. Since 1975, the authorities have alienated many Chinese, causing hundreds of thousands to leave the country. (Between 1977 and 1982, 709,570 refugees were recorded by the UNHCR as having fled Vietnam.) In making their escape many have died, either through drowning – as their perilously small and overladen craft foundered – or at the hands of pirates in the South China Sea. By the late 1980s, the flow of boat people was being driven by economic rather than by political forces: there was little chance of making good in a country as poor, and in an economy as moribund, as that of Vietnam. Even with this exodus of Chinese out of the country, there is still a large population of Chinese Vietnamese living in Cholon, an area which, to the casual visitor, appears to be the most populated, noisiest and, in general, the most vigorous part of Ho Chi Minh City, if not of Vietnam. It is here that entrepreneurial talent and private funds are concentrated; both resources that the government are keen to mobilize in their attempts to reinvigorate the economy.

Cholon is worth visiting not only for the bustle and activity, but also because the temples and assembly halls found here are the finest in Ho Chi Minh City. As with any town in Southeast Asia boasting a sizeable Chinese population, the early settlers established meeting rooms which offered social, cultural and spiritual support to members of a dialect group. These assembly halls (*hoi quan*) are most common in Hoi An and Cholon. Temples within the buildings attract Vietnamese as well as Chinese worshippers and, today, the halls serve little of their former purpose.

Nghia An Assembly Hall ⓘ *678 Nguyen Trai St*, has a magnificent, carved, gold-painted wooden boat hanging over the entrance. To the left, on entering the temple, is a larger than life representation of Quan Cong's horse and groom. At the main altar are three figures in glass cases: the central red-faced figure with a green cloak is Quan Cong himself; to the left and right are his trusty companions, General Chau Xuong (very fierce) and the mandarin Quan Binh respectively. On leaving the temple, note the fine gold figures of guardians on the inside of the door panels.

Thien Hau Temple ⓘ *710 Nguyen Trai St*, is one of the largest in the city. Constructed in the early 19th century, it is Chinese in inspiration and is dedicated to the worship of both the Buddha and the Goddess Thien Hau (goddess of the sea and

Incense spirals in Thien Hau Temple

the protector of sailors). Thien Hau was born in China and, as a girl, saved her father from drowning but not her brother. Thien Hau's festival is marked here on the 23rd day of the third lunar month. Inside, the principal altar supports the gilded form of Thien Hau, with a boat to one side. Silk paintings depicting religious scenes decorate the walls. By far the most interesting part of the pagoda is the roof, which can be best seen from the small open courtyard. It is one of the finest and most richly ornamented in Vietnam, with a high-relief frieze depicting episodes from the Legends of the Three Kingdoms. In the post-1975 era, many would-be refugees prayed here for safe deliverance before casting themselves adrift on the South China Sea. A number of those who survived the perilous voyage sent offerings to the merciful goddess and the temple has been well maintained since. Look up on leaving

Monks in Cholon

Ho Chi Minh City & the south Cholon

to see, over the front door, a picture of a boiling sea peppered with sinking boats. A benign Thien An looks down mercifully from a cloud.

Ming Dynasty Assembly Hall (Dinh Minh Huong Gia Thanh) ⓘ *380 Tran Hung Dao St,* was built by the Cantonese community, which arrived in Ho Chi Minh City via Hoi An in the 18th century. The assembly hall was built in 1789 to the dedication and worship of the Ming Dynasty, although the building today dates largely from an extensive renovation carried out in 1960s. In the main hall there are three altars, which following imperial tradition: the central altar is dedicated to the royal family (Ming Dynasty in this case); the right-hand altar to two mandarin officers (military), and the left-hand altar to two mandarin officers (civil).

Quan Am Pagoda ⓘ *12 Lao Tu St (just off Luong Nhu Hoc St),* is thought to be one of the oldest in the city. Its roof supports four sets of impressive mosaic-encrusted figures, while inside, the main building is fronted with gold and lacquer panels of guardian spirits. The altar supports a seated statue of A-Pho, the Holy Mother. In front of the main altar is a white ceramic statue of Quan Am, the Goddess of Purity and Motherhood (Goddess of Mercy), see p113.

Outer districts

The outlying areas of Ho Chi Minh City include a clutch of scattered pagodas in districts 3, 10, 11 and Binh Thanh. All are accessible by cyclo, moto or taxi.

Pagodas

Giac Vien Pagoda (Buddha's Complete Enlightenment) ⓘ *at the end of a narrow, rather seedy 400-m-long alley running off Lac Long Quan Street, District 11,* was built in 1771 and dedicated to the worship of the Emperor Gia Long. Although restored, Giac Vien remains one of the best preserved temples in Vietnam. It is lavishly decorated, with more than 100 carvings of various divinities and spirits, dominated by a large gilded image of the Buddha of the Past (Amitabha or *A Di Da Phat* in Vietnamese).

In District 10, the **Giac Lam Pagoda** (Forest of Enlightenment) ⓘ *118 Lac Long Quan St, through an arch and down a short track about 300 m from the intersection with Le Dai Hanh St,* was built in 1744 and is the oldest pagoda in Ho Chi Minh City. There is a sacred Bodhi tree in the temple courtyard and the pagoda is set among fruit trees and vegetable plots. The interior of Giac Lam feels, initially, like a rather cluttered private house. In one section, there are rows of funerary tablets with pictures of the deceased. The main altar is particularly impressive, with layers of Buddhas, dominated by the gilded form of the Buddha of the Past. Note the 49-Buddha oil lamp with little scraps of paper tucked in to it. On these scraps are the names of the mourned. Behind the main temple in the section with the funerary tablets is a bust of Ho Chi Minh. At the very back of the pagoda is a hall with murals showing scenes of torture from hell. Each sin is punished in a very specific and appropriate way. An unusual feature is the use of blue and white porcelain plates to decorate the roof and some of the small towers in the garden facing the pagoda. These towers are the burial places of former head monks.

Phuoc Hai Tu (Emperor of Jade Pagoda) ⓘ *73 Mai Thi Luu St, off Dien Bien Phu St,* can be found, nestling behind low pink walls, just before the Thi Nghe Channel. The Emperor of Jade is the supreme god of the Taoists, although this temple, built in 1900, contains a wide range of other deities. These include the archangel Michael of the Buddhists, a Sakyamuni (historic) Buddha, statues of the two generals who tamed the Green Dragon (representing the east) and the White Dragon (representing the west) to the left and right of the first altar respectively and Quan Am (see p113). The Hall of Ten Hells in the left-hand sanctuary has reliefs depicting the 1000 tortures of hell.

Background

Ho Chi Minh Trail

The Ho Chi Minh Trail was used by the North Vietnamese Army to ferry equipment from the North to the South via Laos. The road, or more accurately roads (there were between eight and 10 routes to reduce "choke points") were camouflaged in places, allowing the NVA to get supplies to their comrades in the South through the heaviest bombing by US planes. Even the USA's use of defoliants such as Agent Orange only marginally stemmed the flow. Neil Sheehan, in his book *A Bright Shining Lie*, estimates that at no time were more than one third of the supply trucks destroyed and, by marching through the most dangerous sections, the forces themselves suffered a loss rate of only 10-20%.

The Ho Chi Minh Trail was built and kept operational by 300,000 full-time workers and by another 200,000 part-time North Vietnamese peasants. Initially, supplies were carried along the trail on bicycles; later, as supplies of trucks from China and the Soviet Union became more plentiful, they were carried by motorized transport. By the end of the conflict the Trail comprised 15,360 km of all-weather and secondary roads. It One Hero of the People's Army is said, during the course of the war, to have carried and pushed 55 tonnes of supplies a distance of 41,025 km – roughly the circumference of the world.

The Ho Chi Minh Trail represents perhaps the best example of how, through revolutionary fervour, ingenuity and weight of people (not of arms), the Viet Cong were able to vanquish the might of the US. But American pilots did exact a terrible toll through the years. Again, Sheehan writes: "Driving a truck year in, year out with 20-25% to perhaps 30% odds of mortality was not a military occupation conducive to retirement on pension."

The cemetery for those who died on the trail covers 16 ha and contains 10,306 named headstones; many more died unnamed and unrecovered.

Around Ho Chi Minh City ▲ » *p231*

The Cu Chi Tunnels and Cao Dai temple at Tay Ninh are the most popular day trips, followed closely by an excursion to the Mekong Delta, especially My Tho (see p237).

Cu Chi Tunnels

ⓘ *About 40 km northwest of Ho Chi Minh City, T08-794 6442. Daily 0700-1700. 65,000d for Ben Dinh (Cu Chi 1) and 65,000d for Ben Duoc (Cu Chi 2). Most visitors reach Cu Chi on a tour or charter a car (about US$20-30 per day, including a visit to Tay Ninh).*

Begun by the Viet Minh in 1948, these tunnels were later expanded by the Viet Cong and used for storage and refuge. Between 1960-1970, 200 km of tunnels were built, containing sleeping quarters, hospitals and schools. The original tunnels were only 80 cm high and the width of the tunnel entry at ground level was 22 cm by 30 cm. The tunnels have now been enlarged to 1.20 m to cater for larger western visitors.

Cu Chi was one of the most fervently communist districts around Ho Chi Minh City and the tunnels were used as the base from which the VC mounted the operations of the Tet Offensive in 1968. When the Americans first discovered this underground network on their doorstep (Dong Du GI base was nearby) they would simply pump CS gas down the tunnel openings and then set explosives. They also pumped river water in and used German Shepherd dogs to smell out air holes., although the VC smothered the holes in garlic to deter the dogs. Around 40,000 VC were killed in the tunnels in 10 years but, later, realizing the tunnels might also yield valuable intelligence, the Americans sent volunteer 'tunnel rats' into the earth to capture prisoners.

Cu Chi district initially was a free-fire zone and was assaulted using the full battery of ecological warfare. Defoliants were sprayed and 20-tonne Rome Ploughs carved up the area in the search for tunnels. It was said that even a crow flying over Cu Chi district had to carry its own lunch. Later it was carpet bombed: 50,000 tonnes were dropped on the area in 10 years evidenced by the B-52 bomb craters.

In **Cu Chi 1**, visitors are shown a somewhat antique but interesting film of the tunnels during the war before being taken into the tunnels themselves and seeing some of the rooms and the booby traps the GIs encountered. In **Cu Chi 2**, visitors are invited to a firing range to try their hand with ancient AK47s or a revolver for 15,000d a round.

In the grounds of Cu Chi 2 is a pagoda, built in 1993, devoted to the memory of the dead and visited by those whose relatives are still "missing". The sculpture behind the temple is of a massive tear cradled in the hands of a mother.

Cao Dai Great Temple

ⓘ *Tay Ninh, 64 km beyond Cu Chi town (96 km northwest of Ho Chi Minh City). It can be visited on a day trip from the city and can easily be combined with a visit to the Cu Chi tunnels. Ceremonies 1 hr daily 0600, 1200, 1800 and 2400; visitors should not wander in and out during services but can watch from the cathedral's balcony. At other times keep to the side aisles and do not enter the central portion of the nave. Photography is allowed. Shoes must be removed.*

The Cao Dai religion was founded on Phu Quoc Island (p242) in 1920, when civil servant Ngo Van Chieu communed with the spirit world and made contact with the Supreme Being. The idiosyncratic, twin-towered Cao Dai Great Temple, the 'cathedral' of the religion, was built

Cao Dai Great Temple

Worshippers inside Cao Dai Great Temple

from 1933 to 1955 and is European in inspiration but with distinct Oriental features. On the façade are figures of Cao Dai saints in high relief and, at the entrance to the cathedral, there is a painting depicting writer Victor Hugo flanked by the Vietnamese poet Nguyen Binh Khiem and the Chinese nationalist Sun Yat Sen.

The temple provokes strong reactions: Novelist Graham Greene in *The Quiet American* called it "The Walt Disney Fantasia of the East". Monsieur Ferry, an acquaintance of travel writer Norman Lewis, described the cathedral in even more outlandish terms, saying it "looked like a fantasy from the brain of Disney, and all the faiths of the Orient had been ransacked to create the pompous ritual...". Lewis himself was clearly unimpressed with the structure and the religion, writing in *A Dragon Apparent* that this "cathedral must be the most outrageously vulgar building ever to have been erected with serious intent".

After removing shoes and hats, women enter the cathedral through a door to the left, men to the right, and they then proceed down their respective aisles towards the altar, usually accompanied by a Cao Dai priest dressed in white with a black turban. During services they don red, blue and yellow robes signifying Confucianism, Taoism and Buddhism respectively. Two rows of pink pillars entwined with green, horned dragons line the nave, leading up to the main altar which supports a large globe on which is painted a single staring eye: the divine, all-seeing eye. Above the altar is the Cao Dai pantheon: at the top in the centre is Sakyamuni Buddha; next to him, on the left, is Lao Tzu, master of Taosim; left of Lao Tzu is Quan Am, Goddess of Mercy, sitting on a lotus blossom; on the other side of the Buddha statue is Confucius; right of the sage is the red-faced Chinese God of War, Quan Cong; below Sakyamuni Buddha is the poet and leader of the Chinese saints, Li Ti Pei; below him is Jesus, and, below Christ, is Jiang Zhia, master of Geniism.

● Sleeping

City centre *p213, map p217*

L **Majestic**, 1 Dong Khoi St, T08-829 5517, www.majesticsaigon.com. Built in 1925, this riverside hotel has character and charm and has been tastefully restored

and recently expanded. Its bar, the Bellevue (1600-2400), is on the 8th floor and enjoys magnificent views of the river. Perfect for a sunset drink.

A **Continental**, 132-134, Dong Khoi St, T08-829 9252, www.continental vietnam.com. Built in1880 and renovated in 1989, this is an integral part of the city's history (see p214). It has an air of faded colonial splendour and its large but dated rooms need upgrading. The hotel boasts a couple of restaurants, a business centre, fitness room and a pool.

A **Grand**, 8 Dong Khoi St, T08-823 0163, www.grandsaigon.com. A 1930s building, extensively renovated but, happily, the stained glass and marble staircase have largely survived the process. The pool is surrounded by a tiled and potted plant-filled patio. Good value hotel with a very reasonably priced restaurant, coffee shop, sauna, steambath, jacuzzi and massage service.

A **Rex**, 141 Nguyen Hue Blvd, T08-829 2185, www.rexhotelvietnam.com. A historically important hotel with unusual interior decor. The large lobby is decorated entirely in wood. Superior rooms have small bath and are interior facing. Deluxe rooms are double the size but those on the main road are noisy. The Mimosa Club has a pool, rooftop tennis court, fitness centre and beauty salon.

A-B **Bong Sen**, 117-123 Dong Khoi St, T08-829 1516, www.hotelbongsen.com. Operated by **Saigontourist**. Well-run and upgraded. Good value for the location but standard rooms are very small. Larger superior rooms are only slightly more expensive and have baths. Also, **Bong Sen Hotel Annex**, 61-63 Hai Ba Trung St, T08-823 5818.

A-B **Spring**, 44-46 Le Thanh Ton St, T08-829 7362, springhotel@hcm.vnn.vn. Central, comfortable with charming and helpful staff. Well-run family hotel that is excellent value. Hotel guests have access to free internet and local phone calls.

C **Mogambo**, 20Bis Thi Sach St, T08-825 1311, mogambo@saigonnet.vn. A small hotel above a bar-diner. Perfect for the budget conscious. Large rooms, 5 with a double bed and 5 with twin beds, all have en suite bathrooms.

Pham Ngu Lao *p219*

Shared rooms can be had for as little as US$4-5 per night and dormitory rooms for less but facilities and comfort levels at the bottom end are very basic.

C-D **Hong Hoa**, 185/28 Pham Ngu Lao St, T08-836 1915, honghoavn.com. A well-run family hotel. Good value, bright and airy with 3 types of room. Conveniently, the downstairs has banks of email terminals and a supermarket.

D-E **Linh**, 40/10 Bui Vien St, T/F08-836 9641, linh.hb@hcm.vnn.vn. Well-priced, small, very friendly, family-run hotel. All rooms are twin-bedded with small bathrooms. Free internet for guests and, amazingly at this price, cable TV, a/c, hot water and a fridge.

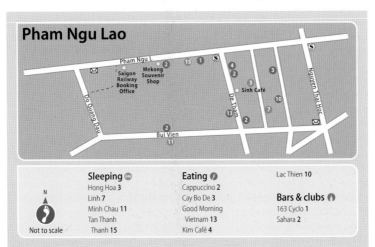

Pham Ngu Lao

N
Not to scale

Sleeping	Eating	Lac Thien 10
Hong Hoa 3	Cappuccino 2	
Linh 7	Cay Bo De 3	**Bars & clubs**
Minh Chau 11	Good Morning	163 Cyclo 1
Tan Thanh	Vietnam 13	Sahara 2
Thanh 15	Kim Café 4	

Budget busters

Pearls of the Orient

LL-L Caravelle, 19-23 Lam Son Square, T08-823 4999, www.caravellehotel.com. Central and one of Ho Chi Minh City's top hotels. Comfortable with well-trained and friendly staff. **Port Orient** serves a fantastic buffet lunch and dinner with free flow of fine French wine included (see Eating), and **Saigon Saigon**, the roof-top bar, draws the crowds until the early hours of the morning (see Bars and clubs). Also has a suite of boutique shops and ATM.

LL-L Duxton, 63 Nguyen Hue Blvd, T08-822 2999, www.duxton.com. The Duxton Hotel is a very attractively appointed and well finished hotel. It has a health club (but no pool) and several restaurants including a Japanese one.

LL-L Renaissance Riverside, 8-15 Ton Duc Thang St, T08-822 0033, www.renaissancehotels.com/sgnbr. Despite its 21 floors and 349 rooms and suites this is, in style and feel, almost a boutique hotel. Very well run, comfortable and popular with its customers. It also boasts Vietnam's highest atrium. It has several excellent restaurants, including **Kabin** Chinese restaurant, and an attractive pool.

LL-L Sofitel Plaza Saigon, 17 Le Duan St, T08-824 1555, www.sofitel.com. Many regard this as Ho Chi Minh City's top hotel, smart, fashionable and comfortable, with 300 rooms, roof-top pool and gym, Provençal restaurant and coffee shop.

D-E Minh Chau, 75 Bui Vien St, T08-836 7588. Price includes breakfast, some a/c, hot water. Spotlessly clean, with private bathrooms, run by 2 sisters. It has been recommended by lone women travellers.

D-E Tan Thanh Thanh, 205 Pham Ngu Lao St, T08-836 7027. A/c and fan rooms, some dorm accommodation, roof-top bar and 'grill'; better stick to the beer and enjoy the breeze.

Eating

Ho Chi Minh City has a rich culinary tradition and, as home to people from most of the world's imagined corners, its cooking is diverse. Do not overlook street-side stalls whose staples consist of *pho* (noodle soup), *bánh xeo* (savoury pancakes), *cha giò* (spring rolls) and *banh mi pate* (baguettes stuffed with pâté and salad, all usually fresh and very cheap).

City centre *p213, map p217*
Asian

The area between Le Thanh Ton and Hai Ba Trung sts has become a 'Little Tokyo' and 'Little Seoul' because of the number of Japanese and Korean restaurants.

¶¶¶ **Kabin**, Renaissance Riverside Hotel (see Budget busters, above), T08-822 0033, daily for lunch and dinner. One of the city's best Chinese restaurants. Features visiting chefs from China.

¶¶ **Ashoka**, 17A/10 Le Thanh Ton St, T08-823 1372, daily 1100-1400 and 1700-2230. Delicious food from an extensive menu. Very good value set lunch menus, too.

¶¶ **Chao Thai**, 16 Thai Van Lung St, T08-8241457, daily 1100-2200. Regarded as the best Thai restaurant in town. Attractive setting and attentive service.

¶¶ **Ma Mo BBQ**, 19 Le Thanh Ton St, T090-395 5889 (Mob), daily 0700-2200. A Korean pork barbecue restaurant, very informal, all-expense-spared decor, open to the street. At night, flourescent tubes light it up like a Vietnamese fishing boat. Excellent kim chi and Korean rice wine.

† Mosque, 66 Dong Du St. Walk around to the back of the mosque (infidels, women and shoes permitted), superb vegetarian and meat curries as well as stuffed bread.

† Bombay, 49 Dong Du St, T08-829 8354, daily for lunch and later until 2200. Almost opposite the mosque; a long-established and informal restaurant whose halal status munificently stretches to alcohol. Excellent curries. Very good paratha, always served hot.

International

††† Au Manoir de Khai, 251 Dien Bien Phu St, District 3, T08-930 3394, daily 1100-1330, 1800-2130. Au Manoir is Khai's (of **Khaisilk** fame) French restaurant. As one would expect, it scores well in the design and style departments. The villa is nicely restored and the garden is beautiful. Food is lavishly presented.

††† Bi Bi, 8A/8D2 Thai Van Lung St, T08-829 5783, Mon-Sat 1000-2300, Sun 1700-2300. Ideal for long lunches. Popular with the French. Informal atmosphere and excellent food. Most highly recommended is the superb Chateaubriand (for 2), served with a range of sauces and delicious frîtes.

††† Camargue, 16 Cao Ba Quat St, T08-824 3148, daily 0900-1600, 1800-2300. Camargue is one of Ho Chi Minh City's longest standing restaurants and bars and remains one of the most successful and popular places in town. Large French villa with a lovely upstairs open-air terrace restaurant. Consistently excellent food from an international menu with a strong French bias. Downstairs is a relaxing garden area and the ever popular **Vasco** nightclub (see Bars and clubs).

††† Port Orient, Caravelle Hotel (see Budget busters, p226), Lam Son Sq, T08-8234999, daily 1145-1430, 1745-2200. Japanese sushi, Chinese dim

sum, seafood, cheeses and puddings galore. The food is stacked up so luxuriously and abundantly, it is like a gastro-cinematic experience. Weekends are especially extravagant with tender roast beef. The free wine makes it tremendous value for money.

††† Qucina, 7 Lam Son Sq, T08-824 6325, Mon-Sat 1800-2300, closed Sun. Smart and chic Italian restaurant in the basement of the Opera House. The sophisticated menu includes grilled tuna in black butter and rolled chocolate cake with vanilla cream – enough to satisfy any gourmet.

†††-†† La Fourchette, 9 Ngo Duc Ke St, T08-829 8143, daily 1130-1430, 1830-2130. Truly excellent and authentic French bistro offering a warm welcome, well-prepared dishes and generous portions of tender local steak.

†† Al Fresco, 27 Dong Du St, T08-822 7318, daily 0900-2230. A huge success from its first day. Australian run. Specializes in ribs, steak, pizzas, hamburgers and Mexican dishes which are all excellent and highly popular.

†† Augustin, 10 Nguyen Thiep St, T08-829 2941, Mon-Sat 1100-1400, 1800-2230, closed Sun. Some of the best, unstuffy French cooking in Ho Chi Minh City; tables pretty closely packed, congenial atmosphere. Excellent onion soup, baked clams and rack of lamb. Very good value.

†† Hoa Vien, 28 bis Mac Dinh Chi St, T08-829 0585, daily 0900-2300. A vast beer cellar boasting Ho Chi Minh City's first microbrewery. Freshly brewed dark and light beer available by the litre or in smaller measures. Grilled mackerel, pork, sausages and the like are very useful for soaking up the alcohol.

†† Le Jardin, 31 Thai Van Lung St, T08-8258465, daily 1100-1400, 1700-2130. Excellent French café. Eat inside or in the shady garden, good food, fairly priced.

†† Underground, 69 Dong Khoi St, T08-829 9079, daily 0900-24000. Instantly recognisable by its London Underground symbol, this bar in its stygian gloom is an unlikely place to find some of Ho Chi Minh City's best food. The menu spans the Mediterranean and Mexico. Portions are gigantic and prices are reasonable. Lunchtime specials are excellent value.

††-† Au Parc, 23 Han Thuyen St, T08-829 2772, Mon-Sat 0700-2130, Sun 0800-1530. Attractive café serving snacks, light meals, sandwiches, salads, juices and drinks. Also does a good Sun brunch.

††-† Ciao Café, 72 Nguyen Hue Blvd, T08-825 1203, daily 0700-2330. Ice cream, pasta, fruit juice, coffee, popular rendezvous spot.

† Java, 38-42 Dong Du St, T08-823 0187, daily 0730-2330. Rich smoothies, muffins and bagels with cream cheese and smoked salmon are served in this glass-fronted café. Rattan furniture, sofas and camouflage- print lamps make this a popular hang out for expats. Good for breakfast or a mid-morning break.

Vietnamese

††† An Vien, 178A Hai Ba Trung St, T08-824 3877, daily 1000-2300. Excellent and intimate restaurant that serves the most fragrant rice in Vietnam. Attentive service and rich decor: carpets, tasseled lampshades and silk-embroidered cushions. The *banh xeo* and crispy fried squid are recommended.

†† Blue Ginger, at the Saigon Times Club, 37 Nam Ky Khoi Nghia St, T08-829 8676, daily 0700-1400, 1700-2200. A gorgeous restaurant that offers a feast for diners with more than 100 dishes on the menu. Dine indoors in the cellar-like restaurant or outdoors in a small courtyard. Charming staff offer courteous and discrete service.

†† Com Nieu Saigon, 6C Tu Xuong St, District 3, T08-932 6388, daily 1000-2200. Best known for the theatrics which accompany the serving of the speciality baked rice: one waiter smashes the earthenware pot before tossing the contents across the room to his nimble-fingered colleague standing by

your table. Deserves attention for its excellent food and selection of soups.

†† Hoang Yen, 5-7 Ngo Duc Ke St, T08-823 1101. Utterly plain setting and decor but absolutely fabulous Vietnamese dishes, as the throngs of local lunchtime customers testify; soups and chicken dishes are ravishing.

†††-†† Temple Club, 29 Ton That Thiep St, T08-829 9244, daily 1100-1400, 1730-2230. Beautifully furnished club and restaurant open to non-members. French-colonial style and tasty Vietnamese dishes. Excellent value.

†† Restaurant 13, 15 Ngo Duc Ke St, T08-823 9314, daily 0600-2300. Fresh, well cooked, honest Vietnamese fare. Chicken in lemon grass (no skin, no bone) is a great favourite and *bo luc lac* melts in the mouth. Popular with locals, expats and travellers.

††-† Huong Lai, 38 Ly Tu Trong St, T08-822 6814, daily 1150-1410, 1800-2115. Right behind the town hall. An interesting little 1st-floor place operated rather successfully by former street children. Try sautéed shrimp with coconut sauce.

† Luong Son (aka Bo Tuong Xeo), 31 Ly Tu Trong St, T08-825 1330, daily 0900-2200. Noisy, smoky, chaotic and usually packed. Specializes in *bo tung xeo* (sliced beef barbecued at the table served with mustard sauce). Also the place to sample unusual dishes such as scorpion and cockerel's testicles.

† Pacific, 15A Le Thanh Ton St. Central and excellent *bia hoi*. Packed every night. The beer is served in a pint glass as soon as you arrive and is ridiculously cheap. Also a decent range of simple dishes: deer, beef, squid and chips.

† Pho, 37 Dong Khoi St, T08-829 6415, daily 0700-2400. Japanese-run *pho* shop. A bowl of *pho* is cheap but drinks are (by comparison) a bit expensive. Eccentrically furnished with heavy wooden tables and chairs and an interesting collection of pictures and ornaments.

Pho Hoa Pasteur, 260C Pasteur St, daily 0600-2400. Probably the best known *pho* restaurants. Costs more than average but serves good *pho* and is usually packed.

Foodstalls
Just north of the centre on the south side of Tan Dinh market **Anh Thu**, 49 Dinh Cong Trang St (and numerous other stalls nearby) serve excellent *cha gio*, *banh xeo*, *bi cuon* and other Vietnamese street food.

Also head north of the market to the foodstalls on Hia Ba Trung St. Everyone has their favourite but nos **362-376** and no **381** (Hong Phat) are particularly good. All charge just over US$2 for steamed chicken and rice (*com gà hap*) with soup.

Pham Ngu Lao *p219, map p225*
Pham Ngu Lao, the backpacker area, is chock-a-block with low-cost restaurants many of which are just as good as the more expensive places elsewhere. All restaurants here are geared to the habits and tastes of westerners.

International
Good Morning Vietnam, 197 De Tham St, T08-837 1894, daily 0900-2400. Italian owned and serving authentic Italian flavours. Good but not cheap. The pizzas are delicious and salads are good.

Cappuccino, 258 and 222 De Tham St, T08-8371467, daily 0800-2300. A good range of well-prepared Italian food at sensible prices. Very good lasagne and zabaglione. Also at 86 Bui Vien St, T08-898 9706.

Cay Bo De (Original Bodhi Tree), 175/4 Pham Ngu Lao St, T08-837 1910, daily 0800-2200. Ho Chi Minh City's most popular vegetarian eatery. Excellent food at amazing prices. Mexican pancake, vegetable curry, rice in coconut and braised mushrooms are classics.

Kim Café, 268 De Tham St, T08-836 8122, open all day. Wide range of food, popular with travellers and expats. The breakfast must rate among the best value in the country.

Vietnamese
Lac Thien, 175/12 Pham Ngu Lao St, T08-836 0799, daily 0800-2300. Outpost of the well-known Lac Thien in Hué and run by the same family. *Banh xeo* (savoury pancake) is a major feature on the menu.

Bars and clubs

Some of these bars sometimes succeed in staying open until 0200 or 0300 but at other times the police shut them down at 2400. Those in the Pham Ngu Lao area tend to be busy later at night and tend to stay open longer than those in the centre. Many also have pool tables.

City centre *p213, map p217*
Alibi Club, 6 Nguyen Thiep St, www.alibiclub.com, Mon-Sat 1100-2400, Sun 1600-2400. Café, lounge and restaurant with a narrow entrance. A relaxing place with a comfy, laid-back seating area behind the bar, playing lounge music .

Apocalypse Now, 2C Thi Sach St. This legendary venue remains one of the most popular and successful bars and clubs in Ho Chi Minh City. Draws a very wide cross section of punters of all ages and nationalities. Quite a large outside area at the back where conversation is possible.

Blue Gecko 31 Ly Tu Trong St, T08-824 3483, daily 1700-late. This bar has been adopted by Ho Chi Minh City's Australian community so expect cold beer and Australian flags above the pool table.

Bop, 8a1/d1 Thai Van Lung, T08-825 1901, daily 1630-2400. Ho Chi Minh City's first jazz club. All-white, sleek musical venue, with photographic images of skyscrapers lining the walls. Top cocktails and good live tunes daily.

Heart of Darkness, 17B Le Thanh Ton St, T08-823 1080, daily 1700-2400. Off-shoot of the famous Phnom Penh bar. Khmer in style with Cambodian-style carvings and decor. Ladies get free gin 1900-2100.

Q Bar, 7 Lam Son Square, T08-823 3479, daily 1800-late. Haunt of a wide cross-section of Saigon society: the sophisticated, intelligent, witty, rich, handsome, cute, curvaceous, camp, glittering and famous are all to be found here. Striking decor and design, with Caravaggio-esque murals.

Rex Hotel, 14 Nguyen Hue Blvd. The open-air rooftop bar that is the height of bad taste, with giant animal statues, strange fish tanks, song birds and topiary. Come for the good views, cooling breeze, snacks – and for a link with history (p213).

Saigon Saigon, 10th floor, Caravelle Hotel, 19 Lam Son Sq, T08-824 3999. Breezy and cool, with large comfortable chairs and superb views by day and night. Excellent cocktails but not cheap.

Underground, 69 Dong Khoi St, T08-829 9079. Screens football, rugby, F1 racing and other sporting events. As the evening wears on, tables are packed away and the space fills with drinkers and dancers.

Vasco, Camargue restaurant (see Eating), 16 Cao Ba Quat St, T08-824 3148. A great spot any evening but only gets busy after 2200 Fri and Sat when a live band plays. The small dance floor generates a lot of energy. Also has a garden. Very popular with younger expats.

Pham Ngu Lao *p219, map p225*
163 Cyclo Bar, 163 Pham Ngu Lao St, T08-920 1567, daily 0700-2400. A clean, civilised and very welcome addition to this neighbourhood. There's an open bar downstairs; upstairs has a/c and live music from 2000 nightly. Inexpensive drinks and light meals. Charming and capable staff.

Sahara, 277 Pham Ngu Lao, T08-837 8084, daily until 0500/0600. Happy hour 1000-2200 says it all. Popular late-night bar with dancing at the back.

Evening cafés

Vietnamese tend to prefer non-alcoholic drinks. Young romantic couples sit in virtual darkness listening to Vietnamese love songs, all too often played at a deafening volume, while sipping coffee.

The furniture tends to be rather small for the western frame but these cafés are an agreeable way of relaxing after dinner in a more typically Vietnamese setting.
Thien Ha Café at 25A Tu Xuong, District 3, which features piano and violin duets, is a prime and popular example.

Entertainment

City centre *p213, map p217*
Cinemas
French Cultural Institute (Idecaf), 31 Thai Van Lung, T08-829 5451. French films are screened here.
Diamond Plaza, 34 Le Duan St. The cinema on the 13th floor of this centre screens English-language films.

Shopping

City centre *p213, map p217*
Antiques
Most antique shops are on Dong Khoi, Mac Thi Buoi and Ngo Duc Ke sts but for less touristy stuff visitors would be advised to spend an hour or so browsing the shops along Le Cong Trieu St. It runs between Nam Ky Khoi Nghia and Pho Duc Chinh sts just south of Ben Thanh market. Among the bric-a-brac are some interesting items of furniture, statuary and ceramics. Bargaining essential.
Lac Long, 143 Le Thanh Ton St, daily 0800-1900. Mr Long sometimes has some unusual items for sale even if there is nothing of interest on display.

Art, crafts and home accessories
Ancient/Apricot, 50-52 Mac Thi Buoi St, T08-822 7962. Specializes in famous artists and commands high prices.
Art Arcade, 151 Dong Khoi St. An informal arcade where local artists sell their paintings and lacquerware.
Celadon Green, 51 Ton That Thiep St, T08-914 4697, daily 0900-2000. Beautifully designed and presented ceramics mostly in cream and green,

including complete Vietnamese tea sets, bowls, pots and dishes.

Gaya, 39 Ton That Thiep, daily 0900-2100. A 3-storey shop with heavenly items. The 1st floor has embroidered tablecloths, bamboo bowls, ceramics and screens. The 2nd floor is stuffed with silk designer clothes by Romyda Keth.

Mosaique, 98 Mac Thi Buoi, T/F08-823 4634, daily 0900-2100. Like its sister store in Hanoi, this boutique is a home accessories parlour.

Nga's Shop, 61 Le Thanh Ton St, T08-825 6289, Mon-Sat 0800-2000, Sun 0900-1800. One of the best known lacquer stores as a result of the high quality products. Beautiful dishes coloured in silver and gold, plus small pieces of wooden furniture, top quality rosewood and ceramic handicrafts.

Red Door Deco, 20A Thi Sach St, T08-825 8672, daily 0800-1900. Stylish, innovative and well made furniture, fabrics and ornaments.

Saigon Kitsch, Ton That Thiep St, daily 0900-2000. Communist kitsch ranging from big propaganda art posters to place mats and mugs. Also retro bags and funky jewellery on sale.

Clothing and silk

Many female visitors head straight for Dong Khoi St for Vietnamese silk and traditional dresses (*ao dai*). Also check out Ben Thanh market in Binh Thanh District.

Khai Silk, 107 Dong Khoi, T08-829 1146, daily 0800-2000. Part of Mr Khai's growing empire. Beautifully made, quality silks in a range of products from dresses to scarves to ties.

Song, 76D Le Thanh Ton, T08-824 6986, daily 0900-2000. A beautiful clothes emporium. Lovely, flowing summer dresses from designer Valerie Gregori McKenzie plus other stylish and unique pieces and accessories.

Department stores

Tax Department Store (Russian market), corner of Le Loi and Nguyen Hue sts. The widest range of shopping under one roof

in Ho Chi Minh City: CDs, DVDs (all pirate, of course) and a good selection of footwear, coats and shirts.

▲ Activities and tours

Around Ho Chi Minh City *p222*
Swimming

Saigon Water Park, Go Dua Bridge, Kha Van Can St, Thu Duc District, T08-897 0456, Mon-Fri 0900-1700, Sat 0900-1800, Sun 0800-2000, 70,000d for adults, 30,000d for children. A western-style water park, 10 km outside Ho Chi Minh City. It has a variety of water slides of varying degrees of excitement and a child's pool on a 5-ha site. To get there jump in a taxi, 70,000d, or catch a bus from Ben Thanh market
Some hotels may also allow non-residents to use their pool for a fee.

City centre *p213, map p217*
Tour operators

Asian Trails Ltd, Unit 712 7/F, Saigon Trade Center, 37 Ton Duc Thang St, District 1, T08-910 2871/3, www.asian trails.com. Southeast Asia specialists.

Buffalo Tours Vietnam, Suite 302, Jardine House, 58 Dong Khoi St, District 1, T08-827 9169, www.buffalotours.com. Organizes general tours, a Cu Chi cycling trip with good bikes, overland trips to Dalat and trips to Can Tho.

Cuu Long Tourist, 97A Nguyen Cu Trinh St, District 1, T08-920 0339, cuulongtourist@hcm.vnn.vn. Branch of Vinh Long provincial tourist authority. For tours to the Mekong Delta.

Exotissimo, Saigon Trade Center, 37 Ton Duc Thang St, District 1, T08-8251723, www.exotissimo.com. An efficient agency that can handle all the travel needs of visitors to Vietnam.

Kim Café, 270 De Tham St, District 1, T08-8368122, cafekim@hcm.vnn.vn. Organizes minibuses to Nha Trang, Dalat etc and tours of the Mekong. A good source of information.

Saigontourist, 49 Le Thanh Ton St, District 1, T08-8295834, www.saigontourist.net. Traditionally tended to concentrate on the more expensive tours but has diversified into the growing budget tour market with subsidiaries like **Delta Adventure Tours**, 187A Pham Ngu Lao St, District 1, T08-836 8542, www.delta adventuretours.com.

Sinh Café, 248 De Tham St, District 1, T08-836 9420, www.sinhcafevn.com. Tours are generally good value and the open ticket is excellent value. For many people, especially budget travellers, Sinh Café is the first port of call. Tours to the Mekong Delta arranged.

Vidotour, 145 Nam Ky Khoi Nghia St, District 1, T08-933 0457, www.vidotour travel.com. One of the most efficient organizers of group travel in the country.

⊖ Transport

Ho Chi Minh City *p210, maps p212, p217 and p225*

Air

See p210. **Airline offices** Air France, 130 Dong Khoi St, T08-829 0981. **British Airways**, 114A Nguyen Hue St, T08-930 2937. **Cathay Pacific**, 58 Dong Khoi St, T08-822 3203. **Emirates Airlines**, 114A Nguyen Hue St, T08-930 2936. **Eva Air**, 32-34 Ngo Duc Ke St, T08-822 4488. **KLM**, 2A-4A Ton Duc Thang St, T08-823 1990. **Lufthansa**, Continental Hotel, 132 Dong Khoi St, T08-829 8549. **Pacific Airlines**, 177 Vo Thi Sau St, District 3, T08-932 5979. **Qantas**, 114A Nguyen Hue St, T08-930 2939. **Siem Reap Airways International**, 132-134 Dong Khoi St, T08-823 9288. **Thai Airways**, 65 Nguyen Du St, T08-822 3365. **United Airlines**, 58 Dong Khoi St, T08-823 4755. **Vietnam Airlines**, 116 Nguyen Hue Blvd, T08-832 0320.

Bicycle

Bikes and motorbikes can be hired from some of the cheaper hotels and cafés, especially in Pham Ngu Lao St. They should always be parked in the roped-off compounds (*gui xe*), found all over town; they will be looked after for a small fee (500d by day, 1000d after dark, 2000d for motorbikes; always get a ticket).

Boat

Victoria Hotels & Resorts, 2nd Floor, 101 Tran Hung Dao St, District 1, T08-837 3031, www.victoriahotels-asia.com, runs boats by request from Ho Chi Minh City to **Can Tho**, 0800, 5 hrs, US$55 per person, min 5 people; also to **Chau Doc**, 0800, 8 hrs, US$80 per person, min 5 people. A chartered boat to Chau Doc costs a prohibitive US$800.

Bus

Local All city buses start from or stop by the **Travel Information Centre** opposite Ben Thanh Market, District 1, T08-8214444. A free map of all bus routes can also be obtained here. The buses are green or yellow and run at intervals of 10-20 mins depending on the time of day; during rush hours they are jammed with passengers and can run late. There are bus stops every 500 m. Tickets for all routes are 2000d per person.

Open Tour Buses The buses leave from company offices in the centre, including **Sinh Café** in Pham Ngu Lao.

Cyclo

Cyclos are a peaceful way to get around the city. They can be hired for approximately US$2 per hr or to reach a specific destination. Some drivers speak English. Some visitors complain that cyclo drivers in Ho Chi Minh City have an annoying habit of forgetting the agreed price, however, the drivers themselves will argue that cyclos are being banned from more and more streets in the centre of Ho Chi Minh City, which means that journeys are often longer and more expensive then expected.

Motorcycle taxi

Honda om or *xe ôm* are the quickest way to get around town and are cheaper than

Trails of Asia

Journey through lost kingdoms and
hidden history of Southeast Asia
and let Asian Trails be your guide!

Blazing new paths in travel

Choose Asian Trails, the specialists in Southeast Asia.
We will organise your holiday, hotels, flights and tours to the region's
most fascinating and undiscovered tourist destinations.
Contact us for our brochure or log into
www.asiantrails.net or www.asiantrails.com

CAMBODIA
No. 33, Street 240, P.O. Box 621, Phnom Penh
Tel: (855 23) 216 555, Fax: (855 23) 216 591, E-mail: res@asiantrails.com.kh

INDONESIA
JL. By Pass Ngurah Rai No. 260, Sanur, Denpasar 80228, Bali
Tel: (62 361) 285 771, Fax: (62 361) 281 515, E-mail: renato@asiantrailsbali.com

LAO P.D.R.
Unit 1,Ban Hai Sok, P.O.Box 815, Chanthabouly Dis., Vientiane,
Lao P.D.R.Tel: (856 21) 263 936 Mobile: (856 205) 211 950
Fax: (856 21) 262 956, E-mail: vte@asiantrails.laopdr.com

MALAYSIA
11-2-B Jalan Manau off Jalan Kg. Attap 50460 Kuala Lumpur, Malaysia
Tel: (60 3) 2274 9488, Fax: (60 3) 2274 9588, E-mail: res@asiantrails.com.my

MYANMAR
73 Pyay Road, Dagon Township, Yangon, Myanmar
Tel: (95 1) 211 212,223 262, Fax: (95 1) 211670, E-mail: res@asiantrails.com.mm

THAILAND
9th floor SG Tower, 161/1 Soi Mahadlek Luang 3, Rajdamri Road,
Lumpini, Pathumwan, Bangkok 10330, Thailand
Tel: (66 2) 626 2000, Fax: (66 2) 651 8111, E-mail: res@asiantrails.org

VIETNAM
Unit 712 7/F Saigon Trade Center
37 Ton Duc Thang St., D. 1, Ho Chi Minh City
Tel: (84 8) 9 10 28 71-3 Fax: (84 8) 9 10 28 74, E-mail: asiantrails@hcm.vnn.vn

cyclos; just agree a price and hop on the back. *Xe ôm* drivers can be recognized by their baseball caps and their tendency to chain smoke; they hang around on most street corners.

Taxi

All taxis are metered. **Airport** (white or blue), T08-844 6666. **Festival** (grey), T08-845 4545. **Mai Linh Deluxe** (white), T08-826 2626. **Mai Linh Taxi** (green and white), T08-822 2666. **Saigon Tourist** (red), T08-822 2206. **Vinasun** (white), T08-827 2727. **Vinataxi** (yellow), T08-811 1111.

Train

Thong Nhat Railway Station, 1 Nguyen Thong St, Ward 9, District 3, T08-843 6528, is 2 km from the centre of the city; ticket office daily 0700-1900, T08-931 0666, T08-931 8952. There is now also a **Train Booking Agency**, 275c Pham Ngu Lao St, T08-836 7640, daily 0730-1130, 1330-1630, which saves a journey out to the station. Much improved facilities include a/c waiting room, post office and bank (no travellers' cheques). Daily connections with **Hanoi** and all points north.

● Directory

Ho Chi Minh City *p210, maps p212, p217 and p225*

Banks

There are now dozens of ATMs in shops, hotels and banks. **ANZ Bank**, 11 Me Linh Sq, T08-823 2218, 2% commission charged on cashing TCs into US$ or VND, ATM cashpoint. **HSBC**, 235 Dong Khoi St, T08-829 2288, provides all financial services, 2% commission on TCs, ATM cashpoint. **Vietcombank**, 8 Nguyen Hue Blvd (opposite the Rex Hotel), 1.1% commission on cashing TCs in US$, 0.6% into VND.

Embassies and consulates

Australia, Landmark Building, 5B Ton Duc Thang St, T08-829 6035. **Cambodia**, 41 Phung Khac Khoan St, T08-829 2751. **Canada**, The Metropolitan, 235 Dong Khoi St, T08-824 5025. **Laos**, 93 Pasteur St, T08-829 7667. **New Zealand**, 41 Nguyen Thi Minh Khai St, District 3, T08-822 6907. **Thailand**, 77 Tran Quoc Thao St, District 3, T08-932 7637. **United Kingdom**, 25 Le Duan St, T08-829 8433. **USA**, 4 Le Duan St, T08-822 9433.

Immigration

Immigration Office, 254 Nguyen Trai St, T08-832 2300. For visa extensions and to change visas to specify overland travel to Cambodia via Moc Bai (see p241) or for overland travel to Laos.

Internet

There are numerous internet cafes in all parts of town, charging 4000d per hr.

Laundry

There are several places that will do your laundry around Pham Ngu Lao St.

Medical services

Columbia Asia (Saigon International Clinic), 8 Alexander de Rhodes St, T08-823 8455, T08-823 8888 (24-hr emergency service), www.columbiaasia.com, international doctors offering a full range of services. **Ho Chi Minh City Family Medical Practice**, Diamond Plaza, 34 Le Duan St, T08-822 7848, T091-323 4911 (24-hr emergency service), well-equipped practice, emergency and evacuation service with Australian and European doctors. Tropical disease specialists and dental services offered as well as a full range of other services. **International SOS**, 65 Nguyen Du St, T08-829 8424, T08-829 8520 (24 hrs), www.international sos.com/countries/Vietnam/, offers comprehensive 24-hr medical and dental service and medical evacuation.

Post office and telephone

The **GPO** is at 2 Cong Xa Paris (facing the cathedral), daily 0630-2100.

Far south

At its verdant best the Mekong Delta is a riot of greens: pale rice seedlings deepen in shade as they sprout ever taller; palm trees and orchards make up an unbroken horizon of foliage. But at its muddy worst the paddy fields ooze with slime and sticky clay; grey skies, hostile clouds and incessant rain make daily life a misery and the murky rising waters, the source of all the natural wealth of the delta, also cause hundreds of fatalities.

Boat trips along canals, down rivers and around islands are the highlights of this region. And, on dry land, driving past paddy fields or cycling through orchards is often more enchanting than the official tourist stops.

235

Getting there Boat, plane, tour or hire a driver and car.

Getting around Boat, tour or hire a driver and car.

Time required 2-4 days.

Weather Hot and humid; flooding liable Sep-Nov.

Sleeping Homestays, basic guesthouses and a handful of luxury hotels in the delta. Beach resorts on Phu Quoc.

Eating Lots of fish. A small number of good restuarants.

Activities and tours Boating along the Mekong, homestays in local villages.

★ **Don't miss...** The floating markets around Can Tho ▸ p239.

Ho Chi Minh City & the south Far south

Phung Hiep floating market, near Can Tho

Getting there and around There are several highways throughout the Mekong Delta linking the major towns. Highway 1 from Saigon goes to My Tho, Vinh Long and Can Tho and Highway 91 links Can Tho, Long Xuyen and Chau Doc. Beyond these towns, however, roads are narrow and pot-holed and travel is generally slow. Ferry crossings make travel more laborious still. The easiest way to explore the region is to take a tour from Ho Chi Minh City to Can Tho, My Tho or Chau Doc. There are also flights to Can Tho and, if money is no object, the **Victoria** hotel group runs boats from Ho Chi Minh City to Can Tho and Chau Doc. For transport to Phu Quoc Island, see p242. ● ▶▶ *p248.*

Best time to visit December to May is when the Mekong Delta is at its best. During the monsoon, from June to November, the weather is poor, with constant background drizzle, interrupted by bursts of torrential rain.

Background

The Mekong River enters Vietnam in two branches known traditionally as the Mekong (to the north) and the Bassac but now called the Tien and the Hau respectively. Over the 200 km journey to the sea they divide to form nine mouths, the so-called 'Nine Dragons' or Cuu Long of the delta. In response to the rains of the southwest monsoon, river levels in the delta begin to rise in June, usually reaching a peak in October and falling to normal in December. This seasonal pattern is ideal for growing rice, around which the whole way of life of the delta has evolved. Even prior to the creation of French Cochin China in the 19th century, rice was being transported from here to Hué, the imperial capital.

The region has had a restless history. Conflict between Cambodians and Vietnamese for ownership of the wide plains resulted in ultimate Viet supremacy (although important Khmer relics remain). From 1705 onwards Vietnamese emperors began building canals to improve navigation in the delta. This task was taken up enthusiastically by the French in order

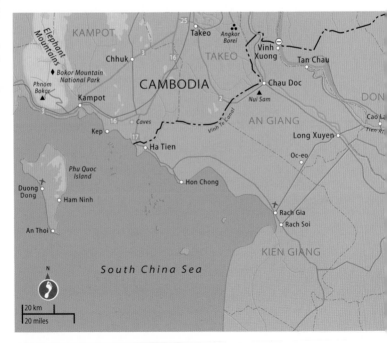

to open up new areas to rice cultivation and export. By the 1930s the population of the delta had reached 4.5 million with 2,200,000 ha of land under rice cultivation. The Mekong Delta, along with the Irrawaddy (Burma) and Chao Phraya (Thailand) became one of the great rice-exporting areas of Southeast Asia, shipping over 1.2 million tonnes annually. During the French and American wars, the Mekong Delta produced many of the most fervent fighters for independence.

Today, the Mekong Delta remains Vietnam's rice bowl. The delta covers 67,000 sq km, of which about half is cultivated. Rice yields are in fact generally lower than in the north but the huge area under cultivation and the larger size of farms means that both individual households and the region produce a surplus for export. In the Mekong Delta there is nearly three times as much rice land per person as there is in the north. It is this that accounts for the relative wealth of the region.

My Tho ⊖🖈🛈🔺⊖🛈 ➤➤ pp244-249

My Tho is an important riverside market town on the banks of the Tien River, a tributary of the Mekong. The town has had a turbulent history: it was Khmer until the 17th century, when the advancing Vietnamese took control of the surrounding area. In the 18th century Thai forces annexed the territory, before being driven out in 1784. Finally, the French gained control in 1862. This historical melting pot is reflected in **Vinh Trang Pagoda** 🛈 *60 Nguyen Trung Truc St, daily 0900-1200 and 1400-1700*, which was built in 1849 and displays a mixture of architectural styles – Chinese, Vietnamese and colonial. The façade is almost fairytale in inspiration and the entrance to the temple is through an ornate porcelain-encrusted gate.

Ins and outs
From Ho Chi Minh City to My Tho the main route is Highway 1. The majority of travellers join an inclusive tour or catch an Open Tour Bus, which allows greater flexibility. ⊖ ➤➤ *p248*.

Tien River islands
🛈 *Take a tour with the many operators along 30 Thang 4 St. Prices vary according to the number of people but expect to pay around US$20-25 to charter a boat for a few hours; you can also travel by ferry from the terminal in Le Thi Hong Gam St* ▲▲ ➤➤ *p247*.

There are four islands in the Tien River between My Tho and Ben Tre: Dragon, Tortoise, Phoenix and Unicorn. Immediately opposite My Tho is **Tan Long** (Dragon Island), noted for its longan cultivation. Honey tea is made on the islands from the longan flower, with a splash of kumquat juice to balance the flavour. There are many other fruits to sample here, as well as rice whisky. It is also pleasant to wander along the island's narrow paths.

The Island of the Coconut Monk, also known as **Con Phung** (Phoenix Island), is about 3 km from My Tho. The 'Coconut Monk' established a retreat on this island

Ho Chi Minh City & the south Far south

Vinh Trang Pagoda, My Tho (left) and a trip to the Tien River islands (right)

shortly after the end of the Second World War where he developed a new 'religion', a fusion of Buddhism and Christianity. He is said to have meditated for three years on a stone slab, eating nothing but coconuts. Persecuted by both the South Vietnamese government and by the communists, the monastery on the island has since fallen into disuse.

On **Con Qui** (Tortoise Island) there is an abundance of dragon fruit, longan, banana and papaya. Here visitors are treated to singing accompanied by a guitar and Vietnamese monochord.

Vinh Long and around ⊕❷▲ℂ ➤ pp244-249

Vinh Long is a rather ramshackle riverside town on the banks of the Co Chien River. It was one of the focal points in the spread of Christianity in the Mekong Delta and there is a cathedral and Roman Catholic seminary in town as well as a Cao Dai church. The main reason for visiting Vinh Long is to spend a night at a homestay on the lovely and tranquil island of An Binh.

Ins and outs
Tourist information Cuu Long Tourist ① *1 1 Thang 5 St, T070-823616, cuulongtourist1@ hcm.vnn.vn*, is one of the friendlier and more helpful of the state-run companies. Ask for Mr. Phu; he is helpful and has a good understanding of English and French.

Around Vinh Long
The river trips taking in the islands and orchards around Vinh Long are as charming as any in the delta but can be expensive. Officially, **Cuu Long Tourist** has a monopoly on excursions by foreigners and charges US$30 for two for a four-hour trip, although there have been reports of bargaining them down. Local boatmen are prepared to risk a fine and take tourists for one-tenth of that amount. **Binh Hoa Phuoc Island** makes a pleasant side trip (see also Sleeping, p244) or you could spend a morning visiting the floating market at **Cai Be**, about 10 km from Vinh Long. It's not quite as spectacular as the floating markets around Can Tho (see p239) but nevertheless makes for a diverting trip.

An **Binh Island** is just a 10-minute ferry ride from Phan Boi Chau Street and represents a great example of a delta landscape, stuffed with fruit-bearing trees and flowers. It is a large island that is further sliced into smaller islands by ribbons of small canals. Sights include the ancient **Tien Chau Pagoda** and a *nuoc mam* (fish sauce factory). Travel is by sampan or walking down the winding paths that link the communities. If you choose to stay on the island, you will be given tea and fruit at a traditional house, see ricecakes and popcorn being made, and visit a brick factory, where terracotta pots are made and then fired in pyramid-shaped kilns. A dawn paddle in the Mekong, surrounded by floating water hyacinth and watching the sun rise, is the reward for early risers.

Can Tho and around ⊜🅕🔺🅑🅒 » pp244-249

Can Tho is a large and rapidly growing commercial town situated in the heart of the Mekong Delta. Lying chiefly on the west bank of the Can Tho River, it is the largest city in the delta and also the most welcoming and agreeable. It is the launch pad for trips to some of the region's floating markets. A small settlement was established at Can Tho at the end of the 18th century, although the town did not prosper until the French took control of the delta a century later and rice production for export began to take off. Despite the city's rapid recent growth there are still strong vestiges of French influence apparent in the broad boulevards flanked by flame trees, as well as many elegant buildings. Can Tho was also an important US base.

Ins and outs

Getting there and around   Vasco Airlines fly to Can Tho but most visitors still arrive by road. There is also a fast boat connection from Ho Chi Minh City, operated by the **Victoria Can Tho Hotel** (see p245) for its hotel guests only; the service continues to Chau Doc. Most of Can Tho can be explored on foot but the floating markets are best visited by boat. ⊜ » p248.

Sights

Hai Ba Trung Street, alongside the river, is the heart of the town, where, at dusk, families stroll in the park in their Sunday best. There is also a bustling **market** here, along the bank of the river. Opposite the park, at number 34, is **Chua Ong Pagoda**, dating from 1894 and built by Chinese from Guangzhou. Unusually for a Chinese temple it is not free standing but part of a terrace of buildings. The right-hand side of the pagoda is dedicated to the Goddess of Fortune, while the left-hand side belongs to General Ma Tien, who, to judge from his unsmiling statue, is fierce and warlike and not to be trifled with.

Floating markets

ⓘ *Sampans are available to rent in Hai Ba Trung St. The best time to go is 0600-0900, the earlier the better, before the flotilla of tour boats arrive. To Phung Hiep (33 km), 9 hr round trip, 20,000d per hr for two people. To Phong Dien (15 km), 20,000d per hr for 2 people. To Cai Rang (7 km), 150,000d per boat for up to 3 people.*

The river markets near Can Tho are colourful and bustling confusions of boats, goods, vendors, customers, and tourists. From their boats the market traders attach samples of their wares to bamboo poles, which they hold out to attract customers. Up to seven vegetables can be seen dangling from the staffs – wintermelon, pumpkin, spring onions, giant parsnips, grapefruit, garlic, mango, onions and Vietnamese plums – and the boats are usually piled high with more produce. Housewives paddle their sampans from boat to boat and barter, haggle, and gossip; small sampans are the best means of transport here as they can negotiate the narrowest canals to take the shopper (or the visitor) into the heart of the area. It is recommended to take at least a five-hour round trip in order to see the landscape at a leisurely pace.

Ho Chi Minh City & the south Far south

Floating market near Can Tho

Chau Doc and around ⬛🍴ℹ️🛏️ ›› pp244-249.

Chau Doc was once an attractive, bustling riverside town on the west bank of the Hau or Bassac River, bordering Cambodia. It is still a bustling market town but no longer so appealing, since it has become an important trading and marketing centre for the surrounding agricultural communities. One of its biggest attractions, however, is the nearby **Nui Sam** (Sam Mountain), which is dotted with pagodas and tombs, and from whose summit superb views of the plains below can be enjoyed.

Tay An Pagoda, Nui Sam

Ins and outs

Getting there and around Chau Doc is an increasingly important border crossing into Cambodia. There are connections by boat with Phnom Penh as well as by road. There are tours to Chau Doc from Ho Chi Minh City. It is also possible (but expensive) to arrive by boat from Can Tho or Ho Chi Minh City (private charter only or with the **Victoria Hotel**). Chau Doc itself is easily small enough to explore on foot and Nui Sam, the nearby sacred mountain, can be reached by motorbike. ⬛›› p244 .

Best time to visit Nui Sam is one of the holiest sites in southern Vietnam and, as such, has vast numbers of pilgrims visiting it on auspicious days. From a climatic viewpoint, the best time to visit is between December and April.

Background

Until the mid-18th century Chau Doc was part of Cambodia: it was given to the Nguyen lord, Nguyen Phuc Khoat, after he had helped to put down an insurrection in the area. The area still supports a large Khmer population, as well as the largest Cham settlement in the delta. Cambodia's influence can be seen in the tendency for women to wear the *kramar*, Cambodia's characteristic chequered scarf, instead of the *non lá* conical hat, and in the people's darker skin, indicating Khmer blood.

Nui Sam (Sam Mountain)

ⓘ *5 km southwest of Chau Doc. 2000d.*

Nui Sam is one of the holiest sites in southern Vietnam. Rising from the flood plain, it is a favourite spot for Vietnamese tourists who throng here, especially at festival time. The mountain, really a barren, rock-strewn hill, can be seen at the end of the continuation of Nguyen Van Thoai Street. It is literally honeycombed with tombs, sanctuaries and temples. It is possible to walk or drive right up the hill for good views of the surrounding countryside and from the summit it is easy to appreciate that this is some of the most fertile land in Vietnam.

The **Tay An Pagoda**, at the foot of the hill, facing the road, represents an eclectic mixture of styles – Chinese, Islamic, perhaps even Italian – and contains a bewildering display of more

---

Border with Cambodia

There are two Vietnam/Cambodia border crossings. The river crossing is on the Mekong at **Chau Doc** and the land crossing is at **Moc Bai**, close to Tay Ninh in Vietnam and Bavet in Cambodia. If you intend to enter Cambodia from Vietnam you will need to obtain a visa in advance (available from the Immigration Office in Ho Chi Minh City, p234). If you are travelling into Vietnam you must also have purchased a visa in advance as they are not issued at the border crossing.

Towards Cambodia Daily morning boat departures from Chau Doc through the crossing at Vinh Xuong can be arranged through tour operators in Chau Doc, 9 hrs, US$6-15. A quicker option is the fast boat offered by **Victoria Hotels & Resorts**, www.victoriahotels-asia.com, but it is open to hotel guests only, leaving Chau Doc at 0700, 5 hrs, US$50, minimum 2 people. The return leaves at 1330. There is also an uncomfortable 10-hour public bus ride from Chau Doc to Phnom Penh via Moc Bai. **Sinh Café**, 248 De Tham St, Ho Chi Minh City, T08-8369420, www.sinhcafevn.com, runs a 2-day tour through the Mekong Delta from Ho Chi Minh City to Phnom Penh by land, US$21. To travel direct from Ho Chi Minh City to Moc Bai takes about 3 hrs, and from Moc Bai to Phnom Penh a further 6 hrs, with one ferry crossing. A share taxi from the border at Bavet to Phnom Penh along National Route 1 (an attractive route) should cost around US$10.

Towards Vietnam There is a bus connection from Phnom Penh to Ho Chi Minh City via Bavet and Moc Bai, 0630 Tue, Thu and Sat but it is desperately slow, 8 hrs, US$14. The service is run by **Ho Wah Genting**, T023-210359 (departing from Charles de Gaulle Blvd, near the Central Market) and **Capitol Tour**, T023-217627, capitol@online.com.kh, (from its terminal at No 14, St 182). Overland travellers are better advised to travel on a minibus organized by tour operators and change at the border to a share taxi. It is also possible to get to Vietnam by bus and boat, crossing at Chau Doc, depart 0800, arrive Chau Doc 1400, US$12. **Capitol Tour** (as above) and **Narin Guesthouse**, No 20, St 111, off Sihanouk Blvd, T023-986131, touchnarin@hotmail.com, organize buses to the Neak Luong ferry crossing on the Mekong, from where a fast boat transports passengers to the Vietnamese border. After the border crossing there is a boat to Chau Doc. Travel agents can organize a seat on these boats. A more luxurious and much pricier alternative is **Pandaw**, www.pandaw.com.

than 200 statues. A short distance on from the pagoda, to the right, past shops and stalls, is the **Chua Xu**. It is rather a featureless building, though highly revered by the Vietnamese and honours the holy Lady Xu, whose statue is enshrined in the new multi-roofed pagoda. From the 23rd to the 25th of the fourth lunar month the holy lady is commemorated, during which time, hundreds of Vietnamese flock to see her being washed and reclothed. Lady Xu is a major pilgrimage for traders and business from Ho Chi Minh City and the south, all hoping that sales will soar and profits leap during this auspicious time.

On the other side of the road is the tomb of **Thoai Ngoc Hau** (1761-1829); an enormous head of the man graces the entranceway. Thoai is a local hero having played a role in the resistance against the French but is known more for his engineering feats in canal building and draining swamps.

Hang Pagoda is a 200-year-old temple situated half way up Nui Sam and is worth visiting for several reasons. In the first level of the temple are some vivid cartoon drawings of the tortures of hell. The second level is built at the mouth of a cave, which, last century, was home to a woman named Thich Gieu Thien. Her likeness and tomb can be seen in the first pagoda. Fed up with her lazy and abusive husband she left her home in Cholon and came to live in this cave, as an ascetic supposedly waited on by two snakes.

Phu Quoc Island ⊜⊘▲⊖⊙ ⟫ pp244-249

Lying off the southwest coast of the country, Phu Quoc is Vietnam's largest island. It remains largely undeveloped, with beautiful sandy beaches along much of its coastline and forested hills inland. Most of the beaches benefit from crystal clear waters, making them perfect for swimming. The island's remoteness and lack of infrastructure means that tourism here is still in its infancy, and, although new resorts are planned, the pace of development is slow. After the rigours of sightseeing, Phu Quoc is well worth a visit for a few days' relaxation in southern Vietnam.

Ins and outs

Getting there and around You can get to Phu Quoc by plane from Ho Chi Minh City and most hotels will provide a free pick-up service from the airport if accommodation is booked in advance. There is also a high-speed boat service to the island from Rach Gia. There are only two asphalt roads on the island from Duong Dong to An Thoi and from Duong Dong to Ham Ninh. Hiring a motorbike is cheap and convenient but makes for dusty and very hot travelling; limited signposting can make some places pretty hard to find without local assistance. There are also plenty of motorbike taxis available, as well as cars with drivers at fairly reasonable prices; ask at hotels. ⊜ ⟫ p248.

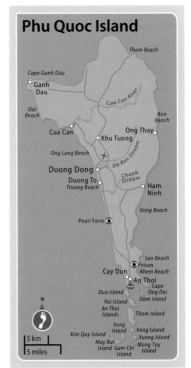

Phu Quoc Island

Thom Beach
Cape Ganh Dau
Ganh Dau
Dai Beach
Cua Can River
Bon Beach
Cua Can
Ong Thay
Khu Tuong
Ong Lang Beach
Da Ban Stream
Duong Dong
Duong To
Chanh Stream
Truong Beach
Ham Ninh
Vong Beach
Pearl Farm
Sao Beach
Prison
Cay Dun
Khem Beach
An Thoi
Cape Ong Doi
Dua Island
Dam Island
Roi Island
An Thoi Islands
Thom Island
Vong Island
Vang Island
Kim Quy Island
May Rut Island
Gam Chi Island
Mong Tay Island
Xuong Island
N
5 km
5 miles

The brilliant blue seas and lush vegetation of Phu Quoc Island

Around the island

Vietnamese fish sauce (*nuoc mam*) is produced on Phu Quoc. You'll see dozens of fish laid out to dry on land and on trestle tables, destined for the fish sauce factory at **Duong Dong**, the main town on the island. Here, 95 massive wooden barrels act as vats, each containing fish and salt weighing in at 14 tonnes and ringing in the till at US$5000 a barrel. If the sauce is made in concrete vats, the taste is lost and so the sauce is cheaper.

The island is also a centre for South Sea pearls, with 10,000 collected offshore each year. At the **Phu Quoc Pearl Gallery** ⓘ *10 km south of Duong Dong, daily 0800-1800, café*, a video and gallery exhibits demonstrate the farming operation, the tasting of pearl meat and the pearl-making process. South of the pearl farm, on the coast road, are two **whale dedication temples**. Whales have long been worshipped in Vietnam. Ever since the days of the Champa, the whale has been credited with saving the lives of drowning fishermen. The Cham believed that Cha-Aih-Va, a powerful god, could assume the form of a whale in order to rescue those in need. Emperor Gia Long is said to have been rescued by a whale when his boat sank. After he ascended the throne, Gia Long awarded the whale the title 'Nam Hai Cu Toc Ngoc Lam Thuong Dang Than' – Superior God of the Southern Sea. Coastal inhabitants always try to help whales in difficulty and cut them free of their nets. If a whale should die, a full funeral is arranged.

Inland, the **Da Ban** and **Chanh** streams and waterfalls are not very dramatic in the dry season but still provide a relaxing place to swim and walk in the forests.

The stunning, dazzling-white sands of **Sao Beach**, on the southeast coast, are worth visiting by motorbike but finding the beach can be difficult, as it is not well signposted, so you made need your resort or a tour operator to help you. There's a restaurant, firmly entrenched at the back of the beach (see Eating, p247). One of the biggest draws are the boat trips around the **An Thoi islands**, which are scattered off the southern coast and offer opportunities for swimming, snorkelling and fishing.

● Sleeping

My Tho p237

B-C Chuong Duong, 10 30 Thang 4 St, T073-870875. This large, new hotel occupies a prime riverside location. It is by far the best hotel in town and is very good value. All the rooms overlook the river and have en suite facilities, satellite TV and minibar. The in-house restaurant provides good food and some tables enjoy river views.
E Cong Doan, on the corner of Le Loi and 30 Thang 4 sts. Clean hotel with fan rooms, good views.

Vinh Long and around p238

A Mekong Homestays, An Binh Island, Vinh Long. Organized by Cuu Long Tourist, p238. Accommodation is basic, with camp beds, shared bathrooms and mosquito nets, and a home-cooked dinner of the fruits of the delta. Evening entertainment consists of sunset drinks, chatting with the owner. The price includes a boat trip around the island, transfers from Vinh Long, local guide, 1 dinner and 1 breakfast.
B Cuu Long (B), 1 1 Thang 5 St (ie No 1 1st May St), T070-823656, cuulonghotelvl@hcm.vnn.vn. Set back from the river and conveniently opposite the quay where boats leave for An Binh Island. Comfortable rooms are en suite and there is a restaurant, internet and travel service (**Cuu Long Tourist**).
D-E Nam Phuong, 11 Le Loi St, T070-822226. Better rooms have a/c and hot water, cheaper rooms have fan and cold water only, clean and cheap.

Can Tho p239

L-A Golf Can Tho Hotel, 2 Hai Ba Trung St, T071-812210, http://golfhotel.vnn.vn. Newest and tallest hotel in town. The staff are friendly, knowledgeable and multi lingual. The rooms are well equipped with a/c, satellite TV, en suite facilities, decent-sized bathtub, well stocked minibar, electronic safe in the room. The restaurants provide fine dining and the views from the **Windy Restaurant** (8th floor) are superb.
A-B Saigon Can Tho, 55 Phan Dinh Phung St, T071-825831, www.saigon-cantho.com. A/c, comfortable, good value central business hotel in the competent hands of **Saigontourist**. The staff are friendly and helpful. Rooms are well-equipped with a/c, satellite TV, en suite facilities, minibar.
B-C Hoa Binh Hotel, 5 Hoa Binh Av, T071-820536, www.hoabinnct.com. This is a perfectly comfortable, quiet, budget hotel just 10 mins' walk from the riverside promenade, next to a bank with an ATM and around the corner from an excellent bakery. Rooms are spartan, fairly basic and could do with some updating but are still good value. A/c and stand alone fan, spacious bathrooms with piping hot water and limited satellite TV.
D-E Hau Giang B, 27 Chau Van Liem St, T071-821950. A/c, fan rooms all with hot water, used by backpacker tour groups from Ho Chi Minh City, good value but a little cramped. The staff are friendly and have a good understanding of English, French and German.

Budget busters

Delta dreams

L-A **Victoria Can Tho**, Cai Khe Ward, T071-810111, www.victoriahotelsasia.com. This is one of the most beautiful hotels in Vietnam. With its riverside garden location, combined with an harmonious interior, breezy, open reception area and emphasis on comfort and plenty of genuine period features, it inspires relaxation. The centerpiece is the gorgeous, flood-lit pool, flanked by the lobby bar and restaurant. Rooms are elegantly decorated. Other facilities include a tennis court and therapies in divine massage cabins. A complimentary shuttle runs from the Ninh Kieu jetty on Hai Ba Trung St in town to the little peninsula on the banks of the Hau River but is often suspended due to technical problems.

L **Victoria Chau Doc**, 32 Le Loi St, T076-865010, victoriachaudoc @hcm.vnn.vn. This old, cream building with its riverfront pool is the perfect location in which to relax and lookout on the busy, three-way Mekong T-junction on which the hotel sits. All rooms are attractively decorated.

LL-A **Saigon Phu Quoc Resort**, 1 Trang Hung Dao St, Duong Dong, T077-846999, www.vietnamphuquoc.com. This resort, overlooking the sea, has a very attractive swimming pool surrounded by bungalows of varying prices and is set on a hillside garden. An enviable list of facilities includes a reasonably priced restaurant, internet, play equipment, motorbikes for rent, fishing, tennis, massage, snorkelling, horse riding and bicycling. Airport transfer, free. 200,000d to ferry port.

Chau Doc p240

C-D **Ben Da Sam Mountain Resort**, Highway 91, T/F076-862151. This resort consists of 4 hotels, a restaurant and bar. The staff speak good English. If you want a little bit of luxury then this would be the place to stay. Sam Mountain is 5 mins' walk away.

C-D **My Loc**, 51 Nguyen Van Thoai St, T076-866455. Some a/c, more expensive rooms get breakfast included, friendly, quiet area.

D-E **Thuan Loi**, 18 Tran Hung Dao St, T076-866134, F865380. A/c and good river views, clean and friendly, restaurant.

E-F **Mekong Guesthouse**, Duong Len Tao Ngo, Nui Sam, T076-861870, mekongguesthouse@yahoo.com. A blue-painted guesthouse on the lower slopes of the mountain. A good base for walking in the area. All rooms have fan, mosquito nets, blankets and cold water shower, except the dormitory which has shared bathroom. Food is served all day. Hammocks, DVDs, book exchange, internet access and bicycle hire. Free transport from the **Mekong Café**, 5-6 Nguyen Huu Canh St (8000d on *xe ôm*).

Phu Quoc p242

During peak periods, such as Christmas and Tet, it is advisable to book accommodation well in advance, otherwise accommodation is easily obtained on arrival at the airport. Representatives from different resorts meet most flights, providing free transfers and touting for business. Most of the resorts lie along the west coast to the south of Duong Dong and are within a few kilometres of the airport. Others are on On Lang Beach and in An Thoi.

A-C **Tropicana Resort**, Duong Dong, T077-847127, tropicana_vn@yahoo.com.

High-quality wooden bungalows and rooms set in a tropical garden next to the beach with a lovely pool and a good restaurant. Bungalows have wooden terraces with seating, large glass doors, mosquito nets and good showers. Motorbike hire is 100,000d, or 400,000d for 4WD with driver. Free return transfer to airport. Transfer from port, 200,000d.

B-C Kim Hoa Resort, Duong Dong, T077-848969, kskimhoa@saigonnet.vn. This small resort offers typical wooden bungalows on a clean strip of sand in front of the resort. Bungalows have 1 double and 1 single bed. Other rooms have small bathrooms and are basic. The resort has a restaurant and rents cars and motorbikes. Free pick up from the airport.

B-E Mango Bay Resort, T091-3917369 (mob), mangobay@hcm.vnn.vn. This is a lovely and welcoming resort. It has 3 bungalows, rooms and bunks, a beach-front restaurant and a bar. The bungalows come with fans and coconut door knobs and are kitted out with bamboo furniture and tiled floors. The 5 rooms share a wonderful, large communal verandah but have cold water only. Some have outdoor bathrooms. The resort has information on birds and fish, a swimming pool and the restaurant provides a mixture of Vietnamese and western food at very reasonable prices. The resort will pay 50% of the cab fare from the airport or the full fare by moto.

C-D Thang Loi, Ong Lang Beach, T091-8073494 (mob), www.phu-quoc.de. A rustic hotel with wooden bungalows set in a remote coconut plantation on Ong Lang beach for those who want complete peace and quiet. Good bar and restaurant with friendly German owners. Bungalows are basically furnished with bamboo, fans and mosquito nets; some have hot water. There is a library, music CDs and a good restaurant. A newly built jetty juts out into the sea, a short walk from the bungalows. Taxi from the airport costs 80,000d, moto taxi, 20,000d; from the ferry, 50,000d moto, 280,000d taxi.

⊘ Eating

My Tho *p237*

A speciality of the area is *hu tieu my tho* – a spicy soup of vermicelli, sliced pork, dried shrimps and fresh herbs. At night, noodle stalls spring up on the pavement on Le Loi St at the junction with Le Dai Han St.

¶ **Cay Bo De**, 32 Nam Ky Khoi Nghia St. Good, cheap vegetarian dishes including a delicious veggie *hu tieu*.

¶ **Quan Thu 46**, 15 Trung Trac St, T073-874696, daily 0600-2100. This small, local restaurant, on the main riverfront street, around the corner from the Chuong Duong hotel, specializes in *bánh xèo*, savoury pancakes filled with bean sprouts, mushrooms and prawns. It also does nippers of crabs fried with rice flour.

Vinh Long and around *p238*

There are a few restaurants along 1 Thang 5 St, just beyond Cuu Long (A) Hotel.

¶ **Lan Que**, 2 2 Thang 9 St, T070-823262. Away from the hotels but worth finding, friendly, good food, open till 2200.

Can Tho *p239*

Hai Ba Trung St by the river offers a good range of excellent and very well-priced little restaurants; the riverside setting is an attractive one.

¶¶¶ **Victoria Can Tho restaurant**, see Budget buster, p245. Excellent location on the river bank where it's possible to dine al fresco or inside the elegant restaurant. The food is delicious and the service is excellent.

¶¶ **Nam Bo**, 50 Hai Ba Trung St, T071-823908, daily 0900-1400, 1700-2200. This is a delightful French house with custard yellow and brown awnings on the corner of a street. Its balcony seating area overlooks the market clutter and riverside promenade. Vietnamese and French dishes. Try Can Tho fried spring rolls. Snake meat, western dishes for kids and vegetarian options available.

❦ **Mekong**, 38 Hai Ba Trung St. Perfectly good little place near the river in this popular restaurant strip. Serves decent Vietnamese fare at reasonable prices.

❦ **Phuong Nam**, 48 Hai Ba Trung St, T071-812077. Similar to the next door Nam Bo, good food, less stylish, a popular travellers' haunt and reasonable prices.

Chau Doc *p240*

❦❦❦ **Victoria Chau Doc Hotel restaurant**, see Budget buster, p245. The extravagant French and Vietnamese menus at this riverside restaurant include rack of lamb coated in Mekong herbs, sweet potato puree and pork wine reduction or spaghetti with flambéed shrimps in vodka paprika sauce.

❦❦ **Bay Bong**, 22 Thung Dang Le St, T076-867271. Specializes in hot pots and soups and also offers a good choice of fresh fish. The staff are friendly.

❦❦ **Lam Hung Ky**, 71 Chi Lang St. Excellent freshly prepared and cooked food.

Phu Quoc *p242*

❦❦ **Tropicana Resort Restaurant**, Duong Dong, T077-847127. This is one of the best restaurants on the island where a sun-drenched terrace and well-stocked bar allows luxuriant alfresco dining overlooking the sea. Enjoy succulent squid stir-fried with lemon grass, braised shrimps in coconut juice, Italian spaghettis or a range from the set menus.

❦ **My Lan**, Sao Beach, T077-844447, dungmyt@yahoo.com, daily 0600-2100. A gorgeous setting on a gorgeous beach. Tables are under little thatched roofs. Sit back and enjoy a beer with the fresh seafood dishes.

▲ Activities and tours

My Tho *p237*

You can hire boats to take you to visit the islands. Once there, walk or cycle.

Tour operators

Mekotours (Cong Doan Tourist), Hotel Cong Doan, 61 30 Thang 4 St, T073-874324, congdoantourist @hcm.vnn.vn. Trips to My Tho and Thoi Son Island with visits to orchards, a bee farm, fish market and coconut candy workshop etc. Homestays at Than Phu or Thoi Son Island, plus night tours (1900–1300) which include a traditional meal and folk music.

Song Tien Tourist Company, 11 Trung Trac St, T073-883133.

Tien Giang Tourist, 8 30 Thang 4 St (on the dock), T073-873184, www.tiengiangtourist.com. Trips are made to Unicorn Island, with visits to orchards, coconut candy workshops and traditional houses. Longer tours take in a coconut plantation, handicraft village, bee farm and tea- and wine-tasting.

Vinh Long and around *p238*

Tour operators

Cuu Long Tourist, 1 1 Thang 5 St, T070-823616, cuulongtourist1 @hcm.vnn.vn. Offers 1-, 2- and 3-day tours and homestays.

Can Tho *p239*

Boat trips

Trans Mekong, 97/10 Ngo Quyen, P An Cu, T071-829540, www.transmekong.com. Operates the *Bassac*, a converted 24-m wooden rice barge which can sleep 12 passengers in 6, air-conditioned cabins with private bathrooms.

Swimming

The **Victoria Can Tho**, has a pool open to the public for a fee.

Therapies

The **Victoria Can Tho**, see p245, has several beautiful massage cabins right on the riverfront in which it is possible to get a host of treatments. Open to non-guests and recommended.

Tour operators

Can Tho Tourist, 20 Hai Ba Trung St, T071-821852, www.canthotourist.com.vn. Ecology and culture tours encompassing visits to creeks, orchards, noodle mills, rice mills, rice wine mills, boat workshops, ironsmith's, a stork sanctuary, a fish sanctuary and village school. Learn to be a Mekong delta farmer for the day: fishing, harvesting, ploughing, folk music and an overnight stay at a farmer's house. Cycle tours also possible.

Phu Quoc Island *p242*
Diving

Rainbow Divers, T091-3400964 (mob), www.divevietnam.com, operates out of the Rainbow Bar between the Saigon Phu Quoc resort and the Kim Hoa resort.

Tour operators

Discovery Tour, Tran Hung Dao St, Duong Dong, T077-846587, daily 0700-1800. Run by the friendly Mr Loi. **Tony's Tour**, T091-3197334, T077-847127 or in Ho Chi Minh City contact T08-820 6481, galaxy-pms@hcm.vnn.vn. Tony knows Phu Quoc extremely well and speaks fluent English. He would be able to organize almost anything: island tours, snorkelling and deep-sea fishing excursions, car and motorbike rental and hotel and transport reservations.

⊖ Transport

My Tho *p237*
As in all Mekong Delta towns local travel to visit the orchards, islands and remoter places is often by boat. On land there are *xe ôms* and the *xe lôi*, the local equivalent of the cyclo, consisting of a trailer towed by a bicycle or a motorbike.

Can Tho *p239*
Air

Vasco Airlines, B114, Bach Dang St, Ward 2, Tan Binh District, Ho Chi Minh City, T08-8489134, flies to Can Tho.

The airport is about 3 km from the centre of Can Tho.

Boat
Victoria Hotels & Resorts, 2nd Floor, 101 Tran Hung Dao St, District 1, Ho Chi Minh City, T08-8373031, www.victoriahotels-asia.com, runs boats from Can Tho to **Chau Doc** 1330, 3 hrs, US$35 per person, minimum two people. The same journey by chartered boat, US$300. Also by request to **Ho Chi Minh City**,1100, 5 hrs, US$55 per person, minimum 5 people; chartered boat, US$550.

Car
Cars with drivers can be hired from the larger hotels.

Taxi
Mai Linh Taxi, T071-822266.

Chau Doc *p240*
Boat

Victoria Hotels & Resorts, 2nd Floor, 101 Tran Hung Dao St, District 1, Ho Chi Minh City, T08-837 3031, www.victoriahotels-asia.com, runs daily boats to **Can Tho**, 0730, 3 hrs, US$35 per person, minimum 2 people. A chartered boat costs US$300. To **Ho Chi Minh City**, 0800, 8 hrs, US$80 per person, minimum 5 people. Chartered boat, US$800. Hotels and guesthouses also organise boats to **Phnom Penh**, see also p241 for further information.

Phu Quoc Island *p242*
Air

Vietnam Airlines fly from Ho Chi Minh City.

Boat
There are 3 express boat services from **Rach Gia** on the mainland to Phu Quoc: **Haiau**, 16 Trang Hung Dao, Duong Dong, T088-981000, taucaotochaiau @hcm.vnn.vn, leaves Rach Gia daily 0830, returns from Phu Quoc, 1330, 2 hrs 15 mins, 160,000d adults on the top floor,

130,000d ground floor, children half price. **Superdong**, Duong Dong, T077-846180 (and in An Thoi, T077-990368, superdongexpressship@yahoo.com) departs Rach Gia 0800, arrives An Thoi 1035; from An Thoi departs 1300, arriving 1535, 130,000d adult, 70,000d child. **Tramexco**, Khu Pho 1, Duong Dong, T077-980666, departs Rach Gia 1330, 2 hrs 10 mins; departs from Phu Quoc 0830, 130,000d adult, 70,000d child.

Car and bicycle
Cars and bicycles can be rented from resorts such as the **Tropicana** and **Saigon Phu Quoc**.

Motorbike
Motorbikes can be rented from most resorts for about US$5-6 per day.

ⓘ Directory

My Tho _p237_
Bank BIDV, 5 Le Van Duyet St. Offers a bureau de change service. **Internet** The post office and **Choung Dong** hotel are the best places. **Post office** 59 30/4 St, T108, daily 0600-2100. Also has facilities for international telephone calls.

Vinh Long and around _p238_
Banks Nong Nghiep Bank (Agricultural Bank), 28 Hung Dao Vuong St. **Internet** La Huy, 37 Trung Nu St. **Post office** 144 Nguyen Hue St, T070-830801, daily 0600-2100. It also has internet access.

Can Tho _p239_

Banks Nong Nghiep Bank, 3 Phan Dinh Phung St. **Vietcombank**, 7 Hoa Binh Blvd, T071-820445. **Internet** Sseveral to be found on Vo Van Tan St. **Post office** 2 Hoa Binh Bld, T071-827280. It offers internet access, 171 calling (cheap long distance and international calls).

Chau Doc _p240, map p_
Banks Nong Nghiep Bank, 51B Ton Duc Thang St. **Vietcombank**, 1 Hung Vuong St. **Internet** Available in the post office and also in Victoria Chau Doc Hotel. **Medical services** Located opposite the Victoria Chau Doc Hotel, 5 Le Loi St, T076-560851. **Post office** 73 Le Loi St, T866191, , daily 0600-2200, internet access (0600-2100 only), 171 service and fax service.

Phu Quoc Island _p242_
Banks It is best to bring enough money with you to Phu Quoc. Some resorts will exchange traveller's cheques as will the banks in Duong Dong but rates are worse than on the mainland. **Phu Quoc Bank**, Duong Dong, cashes TCs. **Vietcom Bank**, daily 0700-1100, 1300-1700, has Visa and Mastercard ATM. **Medical services** The hospital is in Khu Pho, 1 Duong Dong, T077-848075. **Post office** Phu Quoc Post Office, Khu Pho 2, Duong Dong, T077-846079, daily 0645-2030, fax and internet access.

Cambodia

Bakong, Angkor Wat

Don't miss...

1 Royal Palace and Silver Pagoda, Phnom Penh ▶▶ p258.

2 Sihanoukville's beaches and islands ▶▶ p262.

3 Kampot ▶▶ p264.

4 Angkor Wat ▶▶ p286.

5 The Bayon ▶▶ p289.

Southeast Asia's best-kept secret has been catapulted onto the world stage, its well-deserved recognition largely spurred on by the popularity of the magnificent Angkor complex. Aside from Cambodia's spectacular monuments, the country is home to beautiful beaches, great lakes, misty national parks and bustling metropolitan life.

In the northwest is the country's heart and soul – Angkor, headquarters of the ancient Khmer empire. Further south, Cambodia's capital, Phnom Penh, exudes a faded charm, with wide, tree-lined boulevards that are punctuated by a smattering of colonial buildings, communist-style constructions and modern architectural feats. The splendid Royal Palace is the gem of the city, while Tuol Sleng and Cheoung Ek are poignant reminders of the country's terrible past.

For those interested in beaches or a change of pace look no further than the coastal areas and Kampot. Sihanoukville has numerous postcard-perfect beaches and islands, Kampot retains a misty olde-worlde charisma, and Kep, set amid lush gardens and crumbling colonial villas, is simply beautiful.

Ratings

Landscape
★★★★

Relaxation
★★★

Activities
★★

Wildlife
★★

Culture
★★★★★

Costs
$$$-$

Phnom Penh and the south

It is not hard to imagine Phnom Penh in its heyday, with wide, shady boulevards, beautiful French buildings and exquisite pagodas. They're still all here but are in a derelict, dust-blown, decaying state surrounded by growing volumes of cars, pick-up trucks and motorcyclists. It all leaves you wondering how a city like this works. But it does, somehow.

Phnom Penh is a city of contrasts: East and West, poor and rich, serenity and chaos. Although the city has a reputation as a frontier town, due to drugs, gun ownership and prostitution, a more cosmopolitan character is being forged out of the muck. Monks' saffron robes are once again lending a splash of colour to the capital's streets, following the reinstatement of Buddhism as the national religion in 1989, and stylish restaurants and bars line the riverside. However, the amputees on street corners are a constant reminder of Cambodia's tragic story. Perhaps the one constant in all the turmoil of the past century has been the monarchy – shifting, whimsical, pliant and, indeed, temporarily absent as it may have been. The splendid royal palace, visible to all, was a daily reminder of this ultimate authority whom even the Khmer Rouge had to treat with caution. The royal palace area, with its glittering spires, wats, stupas, national museum and broad green spaces, is perfectly sited alongside the river and is as pivotal to the city as the city is to the country.

> ◑ **Getting there** Plane, bus, boat, shared taxi.
> ◐ **Getting around** Taxi, motodop, bicycle, walking, cyclo.
> ◔ **Time required** 1-3 days.
> ◍ **Weather** Hot and sticky in summer, very wet in the rainy season (May-Jun).
> ◐ **Sleeping** A handful of luxurious hotels, plenty of mid-range accommodation and lots of backpacker options.
> ◑ **Eating** Excellent range of international restaurants and bars, serving global cuisine.
> ★ **Don't miss...** The Royal Palace and Silver Pagoda ▸▸ *p258*.

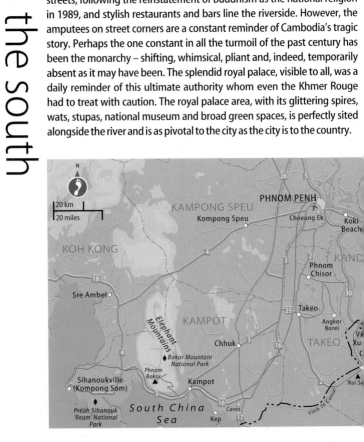

66 99 Phnom Penh in early 1970 was ravishing. Buddhist monks in saffron robes walking down avenues of blossom-scented trees... a curious sensation that time stood still.

Jon Swain, River of Time (Minerva, London 1995).

Ins and outs

Getting there

Air Phnom Penh International airport lies approximately 10 km west of the city on Road No 4. There are flights to Phnom Penh from Bangkok, Ho Chi Minh City, Vientiane and Siem Reap. The airport has a taxi service, a couple of cafés and a phone box. A taxi from the airport to town costs US$7 and a moto about US$3. The journey takes between 40 minutes and one hour although at peak times the roads are often gridlocked so be prepared for delays in the morning and late afternoon.

Boat and bus There is a river crossing with Laos at Voen Kham with the first town of note being Stung Treng, see p274. It is also possible to get to Phnom Penh by boat and bus from Chau Doc in Vietnam and by road crossing at Moc Bai, see p241. ◐ ⇥ p273.

Getting around

Taxis are rare on the streets of Phnom Penh, particularly after dark. A fleet of tuk-tuks (*lomphata*) have sprung up that provide a good, cheaper alternative to cars. Nevertheless, hotels can arrange car hire around town and surrounding areas. Most visitors use the local motodops (motorbike taxis). There are cyclos too. Horizontal steets are evenly numbered and odd numbers are used for the vertical ones.

The royal quarter lies to the east of the town; north of here is what might be regarded as a colonial quarter with government ministries, banks, hotels and museums, many housed in French era buildings. Chinatown, the commercial quarter, surrounds the central covered market, Psah Thmey. Sisowath Quay is where many visitors head as it has the highest concentration of restaurants and bars.

Tourist information

Ministry of Tourism, 3 Monivong Boulevard, T023-427130.

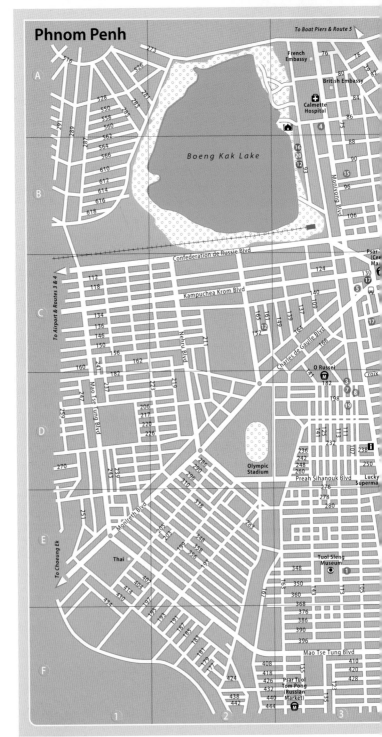

Phnom Penh

To Boat Piers & Route 5

French Embassy

British Embassy

Calmette Hospital

Boeng Kak Lake

Montvong Blvd

Psar (Cen Ma

Confederation de Russie Blvd

To Airport & Routes 3 & 4

Kampuchea Krom Blvd

Nehru Blvd

Charles de Gaulle Blvd

O Russei

Croix

Mao Tse Tung Blvd

Olympic Stadium

Preah Sihanouk Blvd

Lucky Superma

Monireth Blvd

To Choeung Ek

Thai

Tuol Sleng Museum

Mao Tse Tung Blvd

Psar Tuol Tom Pong (Russian Market)

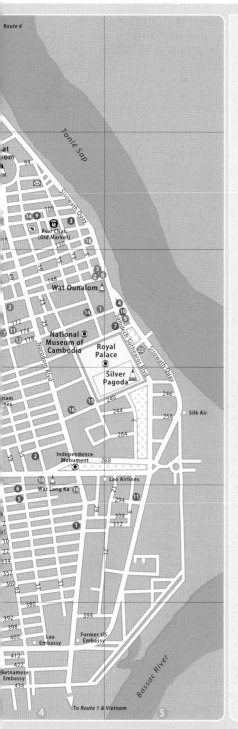

Route 6

Tonlé Sap

Sisowath Quay

Psar Chah
(Old Market)

Wat Ounalom

National
Museum of
Cambodia

Royal
Palace

Silver
Pagoda

Samdech Sothearos Blvd

Sisowath Quay

Silk Air

Independence
Monument

Lao Airlines

Wat Lang Ka

Bassac River

Lao
Embassy

Former US
Embassy

Vietnamese
Embassy

To Route 1 & Vietnam

N

200 metres
200 yards

Sleeping 😊

Amanjaya & K West **2** *C4*
Billabong **17** *C3*
Boddhi Tree **1** *E3*
Bougainvillier & XXL Auberge **6** *C4*
Café Freedom, Grandview
  Guesthouse & Happy
  Guesthouse **20** *B3*
Capitol **3** *D3*
Diamond **5** *C3*
FCCC **9** *C5*
Flamingo **11** *C4*
Golden Gate **10** *D4*
Happy **7** *D3*
Hello **8** *D3*
Juliana **12** *C2*
KIDS Guesthouse **13** *C4*
Last Home **14** *B4*
Le Royal **15** *B3*
Mikey's Guesthouse **18** *B4*
Phnom Penh **4** *A3*
Renakse **22** *C5*
Scandic **16** *E4*
Spring Guesthouse **19** *D3*
Walkabout **27** *C4*

Eating 🍴

Baan Thai **1** *E4*
Cantina & Happy
  Herb Pizza **4** *C5*
Comme à la Maison **5** *E4*
Elsewhere **2** *D4*
Friends **14** *C4*
Khmer Borane **7** *C5*
Khmer Surin **6** *E4*
Lazy Gecko &
  The Flying Elephant **16** *B3*
Peking Canteen **17** *C3*
Pyong Yang **8** *E3*
Rendezvous **9** *B4*
Rising Sun **10** *C5*
Riverhouse **3** *B4*
Talkin to a Stranger **11** *E5*
Tamarind **15** *D4*
The Family Restaurant **12** *B3*
The Shop **18** *D4*

Bars & clubs 🍸

Ginger Monkey **1** *C4*
Heart of Darkness **2** *C4*
Riverside Tom's Irish Bar **3** *C4*

Cambodia Phnom Penh & the south

Background

Phnom Penh lies at the confluence of the Sap, Mekong and Bassac rivers and quickly grew into an important commercial centre. Years of war have taken a heavy toll on the city's infrastructure and economy, as well as its inhabitants. Refugees first began to flood in from the countryside in the early 1950s during the First Indochina War and the population grew from 100,000 to 600,000 by the late 1960s. In the early 1970s there was another surge as people streamed in from the countryside again, this time to escape US bombing and guerrilla warfare. On the eve of the Khmer Rouge takeover in 1975, the capital had a population of two million, but soon became a ghost town. On Pol Pot's orders it was forcibly emptied and the townspeople frog-marched into the countryside to work as labourers. Only 45,000 inhabitants were left in the city in 1975 and a large number were soldiers. In 1979, after four years of virtual abandonment, Phnom Penh had a population of a few thousand. People began to drift back following the Vietnamese invasion (1978-1979) and as hopes for peace rose in 1991, the floodgates opened yet again: today the population is approaching one million.

Phnom Penh has undergone an economic revival since the Paris Peace Accord of 1991. Following the 1998 coup, however, there was an exodus of businesses and investors for whom this bloody and futile atrocity was the final straw. The relative stability since the coup has seen a partial revival of confidence but few are willing to risk their capital in long-term investments.

Sights ⬤🎭🎵🎢🛏️⛰️🏪🎯 ▸▸ *pp265-276*

Royal Palace and Silver Pagoda
ⓘ *Entrance on Samdech Sothearos Blvd. Daily 0730-1100, 1430-1700. US$3, plus US$2 for camera or US$5 for video camera.*

The Royal Palace and Silver Pagoda were built mainly by the French in 1866, on the site of the old town. The **Throne Hall**, the main building facing the Victory Gate, was built in 1917 in Khmer style; it has a tiered roof and a 59-m tower, influenced by Angkor's Bayon Temple. The steps leading up to it are protected by multi-headed nagas. It is used for coronations and other official occasions: scenes from the *Ramayana* adorn the ceiling. Inside stand the sacred gong and French-style thrones only used by the sovereign. Above the thrones hangs Preah Maha Svetrachatr, a nine-tiered parasol, which symbolizes heaven. There are two chambers for the king and queen at the back of the hall, which are used only in the week before a coronation when the royal couple were barred from sleeping together. The other adjoining room is used to house the ashes of dead monarchs before they are placed in a royal stupa.

The **Royal Treasury** and the **Napoleon III Pavilion** (summer house), built in 1866, are to the south of the Throne Room. The latter was presented by Napoleon III to his Empress Eugenie as accommodation for the princess during the Suez Canal opening celebrations. She later had it dismantled and dispatched it to Phnom Penh as a gift to the king.

The **Silver Pagoda** is often called the Pagoda of the Emerald Buddha or Wat Preah Keo Morokat after the statue housed here. The wooden temple was originally built by King Norodom in 1892 to enshrine royal ashes and then rebuilt by Sihanouk in 1962. The pagoda's steps are Italian marble, and inside, its floor comprises of more than 5000 silver blocks which together weigh nearly six tonnes. All around are cabinets filled with presents from foreign dignitaries. The pagoda is remarkably intact, having been granted special dispensation by the Khmer Rouge, although 60 per cent of the Khmer treasures were stolen from here. In the centre of the pagoda is a magnificent 17th-century emerald Buddha statue made of Baccarat crystal. In front is a 90-kg golden Buddha studded with 9584 diamonds, dating from 1906. It

Throne Hall, Royal Palace (left) and a wedding party at Wat Phnom (right)

was made from the jewellery of King Norodom and its vital statistics conform exactly to his – a tradition that can be traced back to the god-kings of Angkor.

National Museum of Cambodia
ⓘ *Entrance is on the corner of streets 13 and 178. Daily 0700-1130, 1400-1700. US$2, camera US$3, video US$3; photographs only permitted in the garden; French- and English-speaking guides are available, mostly excellent.*

The National Museum of Cambodia was built in 1920 and contains a collection of Khmer art – notably sculpture – throughout the ages (although some periods are not represented). Galleries are arranged chronologically in a clockwise direction. Most of the exhibits date from the Angkor period but there are several examples from the pre-Angkor era (that is from the kingdoms of Funan, Chenla and Cham). The collection of Buddhas from the sixth and seventh centuries includes a statue of Krishna Bovardhana found at Angkor Borei showing the freedom and grace of early Khmer sculpture. The chief attraction is probably the pre-Angkorian statue of Harihara, found at Prasat Andat near Kompong Thom. There is a fragment from a beautiful bronze statue of Vishnu found in the West Baray at Angkor, as well as frescoes and engraved doors.

The riverside and Wat Ounalom
Sisowath Quay is Phnom Penh's Left Bank. A broad pavement runs along the side of the river and on the opposite side of the road a rather splendid assemblage of colonial buildings looks out over the broad expanse of waters. The erstwhile administrative buildings and merchants' houses today form an unbroken chain – almost a mile long – of bars and restaurants, with the odd guesthouse thrown in. While foreign tourist commerce fills the street, the quayside itself is dominated by local Khmer families who stroll and sit in the cool of the evening, served by an army of hawkers.

Phnom Penh's most important wat, **Wat Ounalom**, is north of the national museum, at the junction of Street 154 and Samdech Sothearos Boulevard, facing the Tonlé Sap. The first building on this site was a monastery, built in 1443 to house a hair of the Buddha. Before

The riverside promenade, Phnom Penh

1975, more than 500 monks lived at the wat but the Khmer Rouge murdered the Patriarch and did their best to demolish the capital's principal temple. Nonetheless it remains Cambodian Buddhism's headquarters. The complex has been restored since 1979 although its famous library was completely destroyed. The stupa behind the main sanctuary is the oldest part of the wat.

Central Market, Wat Phnom and Boeng Kak Lake

The stunning Central Market (Phsar Thmei) is a perfect example of art-deco styling and one of Phnom Penh's most beautiful buildings. Inside a labyrinth of stalls and hawkers sell everything from jewellery through to curios. Those after a real bargain are better off heading to the Russian Market where items are much cheaper.

Wat Phnom stands on a small hill and is the temple from which the city takes its name. It was built by a wealthy Khmer lady called Penh in 1372. The sanctuary was rebuilt in 1434, 1890, 1894 and 1926. The main entrance is to the east; the steps are guarded by nagas and lions. The principal sanctuary is decorated inside with frescoes depicting scenes from Buddha's life and the *Ramayana*. At the front, on a pedestal, is a statue of the Buddha. There is a statue of Penh inside a small pavilion between the vihara and the stupa, with the latter containing the ashes of King Ponhea Yat (1405-1467). The surrounding park is tranquil and a nice escape from the madness of the city. Monkeys with attitude are in abundance but they tend to fight between themselves.

Boeng Kak Lake is the main area budget travellers stay in. The lakeside setting with the all important westerly aspect – ie sunsets – appeals strongly to the nocturnal instincts of guests. Some bars and restaurants open 24 hours a day. The Lake is quite beautiful, but close to the guesthouses it becomes more like a floating rubbish tip.

Around Independence Monument

South of the Royal Palace, between Street 268 and Preah Sihanouk Boulevard, is the **Independence Monument**. It was built in 1958 to commemorate independence but has now assumed the role of a cenotaph. **Wat Lang Ka**, on the corner of Sihanouk and Norodom boulevards, was another beautiful pagoda that fell victim to Pol Pot's architectural holocaust. Like Wat Ounalom, it was restored in Khmer style on the direction of the Hanoi-backed government in the 1980s. It is a really soothing getaway from city madness and the monks here are particularly friendly. They hold a free meditation session every Monday and Thursday night at 1800; anyone is welcome to join in.

Tuol Sleng Museum ('Museum of Genocide')

ⓘ *Street 113. Tue-Sat 0800-1100, 1400-1730; public holidays 0800-1800. US$2; free film show at 1000 and 1500.*

After 17 April 1975 the classrooms of Tuol Svay Prey High School became the Khmer Rouge main torture and interrogation centre, known as Security Prison 21 or S-21. More than 20,000 people were taken from S-21 to their executions at Choeung Ek extermination camp, see below. Countless

Choeung Ek

others died under torture and were thrown into mass graves in the school grounds. Only seven prisoners survived because they were sculptors and could turn out countless busts of Pol Pot. One block of classrooms is given over to photographs of the victims. All the Khmer Rouge victims were methodically numbered and photographed.

Former US Embassy

The former US Embassy, now home to the Ministry of Fisheries, is at the intersection of Norodom and Mao Tse Tung boulevards. As the Khmer Rouge closed on the city from the north and the south in April 1975, US Ambassador John Gunther Dean pleaded with Secretary of State Henry Kissinger for an urgent airlift of embassy staff. But it was not until the very last minute (just after 1000 on 12 April 1975, with the Khmer Rouge firing mortars from across the Bassac River onto the football pitch near the compound that served as a landing zone) that the last US Marine helicopter left the city. Flight 462, a convoy of military transport helicopters, evacuated the 82 remaining Americans, 159 Cambodians and 35 other foreigners to a US aircraft carrier in the Gulf of Thailand. Their departure was overseen by 360 heavily armed marines. Despite letters to all senior government figures from the ambassador, offering them places on the helicopters, only one, Acting President Saukham Khoy, fled the country. The American airlift was a deathblow to Cambodian morale. Within five days, the Khmer Rouge had taken the city and within hours all senior officials of the former Lon Nol government were executed on the tennis courts of the embassy.

Choeung Ek

ⓘ *Southwest on Monireth Blvd, about 15 km from town. US$2. Return trip by moto US$2-5, however, a shared car (US$10) is far more comfortable because of the dust on the mainly unsurfaced road.*

In a peaceful setting, surrounded by orchards and rice fields, Choeung Ek was the execution ground for the torture victims of Tuol Sleng, the Khmer Rouge extermination centre, S-21 (see above). It is referred to by some as 'The killing fields'. Today a huge glass tower stands on the site, filled with the cracked skulls of men, women and children exhumed from 129 mass graves in the area (which were not discovered until 1980). To date 8985 corpses have been exhumed from the site. Rather disturbingly, rags and crumbling bones still protrude from the mud.

Southern Cambodia ⬛🚻👣▲🚌☕ ⤷ *pp265-276*

Cambodia's coast may be fringed by mile after mile of fabulously soft white sand but it is not the place for a seaside holiday – not yet, anyway. There is currently not a single beach resort, though the main town, Sihanoukville, will, in a few years, sport resort hotels comparable with any in Southeast Asia. In the meantime, it has to make do with a small number of fairly basic guesthouses. The beautiful coastal scenery between Sihanoukville and Kep should not be missed, however, particularly the stretch around Kampot.

Ins and outs

From Phnom Penh there are regular departures in comfortable, well-maintained, a/c coaches to Sihanoukville, costing US$3-4. Buses generally leave every half hour from 0700 until 1330. Taxis cost US$20-30. Departing from Sihanoukville there are taxis to Kampot and Phnom Penh around 0700-0800, US$5-6. 🚌 ⤷ *p275*.

Sihanoukville

Sihanoukville, or Kompong Som as it is called during the periods the king is in exile or otherwise 'out of office', was founded in 1964 by Prince Sihanouk to be the nation's sole deep-water port. It is also the country's prime seaside resort. In its short history it has crammed in as much excitement as most seaside towns see in a century – but not of the sort that resorts tend to encourage. Sihanoukville was used as a strategic transit point for weapons used in fighting the USA, during the Vietnam War. In 1975, the US bombed the town when the Khmer Rouge seized the container ship *SS Mayaguez*. Sihanoukville has turned a corner and with rapid development has firmly secured its place in Cambodia's 'tourism triangle', alongside Phnom Penh and Angkor Wat.

Sihanoukville occupies a lovely site on a small peninsula, its nobbly head jutting out into the Gulf of Thailand. There are first-rate beaches, clean water, trees and invigorating breezes. Cambodia's beaches are comparable to those in Thailand but are yet to yield the tourism masses, so make the most of it while you can as there are big plans for this area. Most people head for one of the three beaches which, from the north, are: Victory, Independence and Ochheauteal. This is where the best hotels are.

Victory Beach is a thin, 2-km-long beach, just down from the port, and offers reasonably secluded beaches. The original backpackers' beach, it's now somewhat deserted, usurped by the popularity of Ochheauteal Beach. The area does afford a good sunset view. **Independence Beach** does not currently have anywhere to stay other than the once bombed and charred Independence Hotel. The location of the hotel is magnificent and the grounds, even in their currently neglected state, are a reminder of the former grandeur. With restoration of this marvellous hotel near completion, its opening would do a lot to revive Independence Beach's fortunes. **Sokha Beach** is arguably Sihanoukville's most beautiful beach. The shore laps around a kilometre arc and even though the large Sokha Beach Resort has taken up residence it is very rare to see more than a handful of people along the beach. This beach is stunning and relatively hassle-free. **Ochheauteal Beach** lies furthest to the south and is the all-round favourite. Like most of Sihanoukville's beaches, the sand is dazzling in its fine whiteness and copious deckchairs sporting large beach umbrellas shade the lovely beach. The beach commonly referred to as **Serendipity Beach** is at the very north end of Ochheauteal. This little strand has gained flavour with travellers, due in part to being the first beach in Sihanoukville to offer a wide range of accommodation on the beach. This is definitely the most aesthetic piece of Ochheauteal, with large ashen rocky outcrops, smaller rock pools, jungled hills and a much cleaner shoreline.

Fishing at Sihanoukville

Preah Sihanouk 'Ream' National Park
ⓘ *T012-875096. Daily 0700-1700. Boat trip (half or 1 day), US$30 for 4 people. Nature trek with a guide (3- to 5-hrs) ,US$2 per person.*

This beautiful park is a short 30-minute drive from Sihanoukville, hugging the coastline of the Gulf of Thailand. It includes two islands and covers 21,000 ha of beach, mangrove swamp, offshore coral reef and the Prek Tuk Sap Estuary. Samba deer, endangered civet species, porcupines and pangolin are said to inhabit the park, as well as dolphins. To arrange a guided tour visit the park office or arrange one through a guesthouse in Sihanoukville.

Kampot and around

Kampot is a charming riverside town that was established in the early 1900s by the French. The town lies at the base of the Elephant Mountain Range, 5 km inland on the River Prek Thom and was for a long time the gateway to the beach resort at Kep, see below. On one side of the river are tree-lined streets, crumbling mustard yellow French shop fronts and a sleepy atmosphere whilst on the other side you will find locals working in the surrounding salt pans. The town the feel of another era – with a dabbling of Chinese architecture and overall French colonial influence – which, with a bit of restoration work, could easily be compared to UNESCO World Heritage sites such as Hoi An, Vietnam and Luang Prabang in Laos. Life is very laid-back in Kampot and the town has become a regular expat retreat with Phnom Penh-ites ducking down here for a breath of fresh air and a cooler climate.

Bokor Mountain National Park

ⓘ 42 km (90 mins) from Kampot. US$5. Park rangers can speak some English and have a small display board on the flora and fauna in the park at their office. There are dorms (US$5) and double rooms (US$20) and a few basic dishes available. A moto and driver for the day will cost around US$15 or a car for around US$30.

Bokor Mountain National Park's plateau, at 1040 m, peers out from the southernmost end of the Elephant Mountains with a commanding view over the Gulf of Thailand and east to Vietnam. Bokor Hill (Phnom Bokor) is densely forested and in the remote and largely untouched woods scientists have discovered 30 species of plants unique to the area. Not for nothing are these called the Elephant Mountains and besides the Asian elephant there are tigers, leopards, wild cows, civets, pigs, gibbons and numerous bird species. At the peak of the mountain is Bokor Hill Station, where eerie, abandoned, moss-covered buildings sit in dense fog. The buildings were built by the French, who attracted by Bokor's relative coolness, established a 'station climatique' on the mountain in the 1920s. In 1970 Lon Nol shut it down and Bokor was quickly taken over by communist guerrillas; it later became a strategic military base for the Khmer Rouge. In more recent years there was a lot of guerrilla activity in the hills, but the area is now safe, with the exception of the danger, ever-present in Cambodia, of landmines. The ruins are surprisingly well preserved but bear evidence of their tormented past. There is a double waterfall called **Popokvil Falls**, a 2-km walk from the station, which involves wading through a stream, though in the wet season this is nigh on impossible.

Kbal Romeas caves and temple

ⓘ 10 km from Kampot, on the road towards Kep. Many motos and cars now do trips.

Outside Kampot, on the roads to both Phnom Penh and to Kep, limestone peaks harbour interesting caves with stalactites and pools. It is here that you can find one of Cambodia's hidden treasures – an 11th-century temple slowly being enveloped by stalactites and hidden away in a cave in Phnom Chhnok, next to the village of Kbal Romeas. The temple, which is protected by three friendly monks, was discovered by Adhemer Leclere in 1866.

Kep

ⓘ Jul-Oct Kep is subject to the southeast monsoon, occasionally rendering the beach unswimmable because of the debris brought in.

Tucked in on the edge of the South China Sea, Kep was established in 1908 by the French as a health station for their government officials and families. The ruins of their holiday villas stand along the beachfront and in the surrounding hills. They were largely destroyed during the civil war under Lon Nol and by the Khmer Rouge. They were then further ransacked during the famine of the early 1980s when starving Cambodians raided the villas for valuables to exchange for food.

Kep is very popular on weekends with holidaying Cambodians who have managed to keep this idyllic town one of the country's best kept secrets. Beautiful gardens and lush green landscape juxtaposed against the blue waters make it one of the most wonderfully relaxing places in the country. The town itself only has one major beach, a pebbly murky water pool which doesn't really compare with Sihanoukville beaches but they can be found at almost all of the thirteen outlying islands where you can snorkel and dive although this is better around the islands off Sihanoukville; Kep is considerably more beautiful than Sihanoukville and much more relaxing. It is famous for the freshly caught crab which is best eaten on the beach ($1.50 per kilo) and the *tik tanaout jiu,* palm wine. From Kep it is possible to hire a boat to **Rabbit Island** (Koh Toensay). ⓘ *Expect to pay about US$10 to hire a boat for the day.* There are four half-moon beaches on this island which have finer, whiter sand than Kep beach.

🛏 Sleeping

Phnom Penh *p254, map p256*
Boeung Kak Lake has become somewhat of a Khaosan Rd, with most backpackers opting to stay there. Street 182 also offers a selection of cheaper alternatives. The majority of hotels organize airport pick-up and most of them for free.

L-AL Amanjaya, corner of St 1 and Sisowath Quay, T023-214747, amanjaya@ online.com.kh. Absolutely stunning rooms with full amenities, beautiful furniture and sitting area, creative finishing touches. **K-West** restaurant downstairs.

L-A Phnom Penh Hotel, 54 Monivong Blvd, T023-724851, www.phnom penhhotel.com. This hotel comes most recommended from almost everyone in Cambodia's tourism industry. 407 well-appointed rooms with TV, a/c, internet. Health club, spa and an outdoor swimming pool. Exceptional value.

A Bougainvillier Hotel, 277G Sisowath Quay, T023-220528, www.bougain villierhotel.com. Lovely riverside boutique hotel, rooms decorated in a very edgy, modern Asian theme, with a/c, safe, cable TV and minibar. Good French restaurant.

A Foreign Correspondents Club of Cambodia (FCCC), 363 Sisowath Quay, T023-210142, www.fcccambodia.com. Known locally as the FCC. 3 decent sized rooms are available in this well-known Phnom Penh landmark.

A Juliana, No 16, St 152, T023-366070, www.julianacambodia.com.kh. A very attractive resort-style hotel with 91 rooms, and decent sized pool in a secluded garden which provides plenty of shade; several excellent restaurants.

A-B Diamond, 172-184 Monivong Blvd, T023-217221/2, diamondhotels@ online.com.kh. Hotel in a good central location. A little overshadowed by some of the newer and better hotels but the staff are exceptionally helpful and friendly. Rooms are clean with TV and bath.

B Flamingo Hotel, No 30, St 172, T023-221640, reservation@flamingo.com.kh. Reasonably new hotel, bit garish from the outside but good facilities. Well-fitted rooms with all the amenities, including a bath. Free internet, gym and restaurant.

B Renakse, 40 Samdech Sothearos Blvd, T023-215701, renakse-htl@camnet. com.kh. Splendid yellow French colonial building in large grounds immediately opposite the Royal Palace. This hotel has the feel of a bygone era. Rooms are decorated in a tasteful, modern Asian style, with Thai-style cushion seats and adjoining mosaic-tiled bathroom.

B Scandic Hotel (also known as the Scandanavian) No 4, St 282, T023-214498, nisse@online.com.kh. Well-appointed, clean rooms with a/c and TV. Very clean. Rooftop restaurant/bar. Pool and Finnish sauna.

B XXL Auberge, No 277 Sisowath Quay, T023-990691, xxlbouffe@hotmail.com. Riverfront guesthouse with great balcony views (especially at sunset). Good but a tad pricey in the restaurant.

B-C Golden Gate Hotel, No 9, St 278 (just off St 51), T023-721161, goldengatehtls

Budget busters

Cambodia

LL Le Royal, St 92, Phnom Penh, T023-981888, www.raffles-hotelleroyal.com. A wonderful colonial era hotel built in 1929 which has been superbly renovated by the Raffles Group. The renovation was done tastefully, incorporating many of the original features and something of the old atmosphere. The hotel has excellent bars, restaurants and a delightful tree-lined pool. 2 for 1 cocktails 1600 to 2000 daily at the Elephant Bar is a must.

L-A Sokha Beach Resort and Spa, Street 2 Thnou, Sangkat 4, Sokha Beach, T034-935999, www.sokhahotels.com. Sihanoukville's only luxury hotel. A deluxe, 180-room beachfront resort and spa, set amid an expansive 15 ha of beachfront gardens and fronting pristine white sandy beach. Guests have a choice between hotel suites or private bungalows dotted in the tropical gardens. Rooms are quite impressive, with beautiful Italian linen and lovely bathtubs. The hotel has fantastic facilities including a large, landscaped pool, tennis court and archery range. The hotel has very low occupancy, so it is worthwhile to check out if they can offer you a discount as they are always running special deals.

@hotmail.com. Very popular and comparatively good value for the facilities offered. Clean rooms with TV, fridge, hot water and a/c.

C Billabong, No 5, St 158, T023-223703, www.billabongcambodia.com. Reasonably new hotel with well-appointed and well-decorated rooms. Breakfast included. Swimming pool, poolside bar and deluxe rooms with balconies overlooking the pool. Internet.

C-D Boddhi Tree, No 50, St 113, T016-865445, www.boddhitree.com. A tranquil setting. Lovely old wooden building with guest rooms offering simple amenities, fan only, some rooms have private bathroom. Great gardens and fantastic food at very reasonable prices.

C-D KIDS Guesthouse, No 17A, St 178, T012-410406, ryan@ryanhem.com. A rather a good find. Guesthouse of the Khmer Internet Development Service (KIDS) set in a small tropical garden, spotted with a couple of cabana-style internet kiosks. A couple of rooms are a decent size, quite clean and equipped with a huge fridge. Discount on internet use for guests. Welcoming, safe and free coffee.

C-E Walkabout Hotel, corner of St 51 and St 174, T023-211715, www.walkabout hotel.com. A popular Australian-run bar, café and guesthouse. 23 rooms ranging from small with no windows and shared facilities to large rooms with own bathroom and a/c. Rooms and bathrooms are okay but lower-end rooms are a little gloomy and cell-like. 24-hr bar.

D Mikey's Guesthouse, 213 Sisowath Quay, T023-991190, reservations@ mikeysguesthouse.com. Riverside guesthouse with well-appointed rooms – TV, minibar, a/c and some with bathtub. Large open bar and restaurant downstairs.

D Spring Guesthouse, No 34, St 111 (next to the German Embassy), T015-888777, spring_guesthouse@yahoo.com. Newly established guesthouse in good location. Fan, cable, a/c, hot shower.

D-F Capitol, No 14, St 182, T023-364104, capitol@online.com.kh. As they say, 'A Phnom Penh institution'. What, in 1991, was a single guesthouse has expanded to 5 guesthouses all within a stone's throw. All aim at the budget traveller and offer travel services as well as a popular café and internet access. There are a number of other cheap guesthouses in close proximity, such as **Happy Guesthouse** (next door to Capitol Guesthouse) and **Hello Guesthouse** (No 24, 2 St 107) – all about the same ilk.

E Last Home, No 47, St 108, T023-724917, sakith@forum.org.kh. A popular guesthouse, especially with journos. 25 average rooms with basic facilities, cheaper rooms fan and shared toilet. The pricier rooms have a/c and shower. Dark, dilapidated hallways. Amicable staff, large selection of books, and good, cheap home-cooked food.

F Café Freedom, lakeside, T012-807345, www.cafefreedom.org.uk. There are only 7 rooms so more often than not this place is booked out. Nice, relaxing atmosphere, except for fierce guard dogs.

F Grandview Guesthouse, just off the lake, T023-430766. This place is streets ahead of local competition. Clean, basic rooms. A few extra bucks gets you a/c. Nice rooftop restaurant affording good sunset views, with large breakfast menu, pizza, Indian and Khmer food. Travel services and internet.

F Happy Guesthouse and Restaurant, No 11, St 93 (on the lake), T023-877232. If you're idea of good accommodation is staying in a cupboard, then this is the place for you. 40 basic rooms, most with shared facilities but a few with private bathroom. Restaurant, free pool and lovely veranda area.

Sihanoukville *p262*

B Chez Claude, between Sokha Beach and Independence Beach, T012-824870. 9 bungalows occupy a beautiful hillside spot. The accommodation represents a cross-section of indigenous housing. The restaurant has fantastic views.

C-D Chez Mari-yan, Sankat 3, Khan Mittapheap, T034-916468. Currently the best bungalow-style place to stay in this end of town. Offers a block of hotel rooms and simple wooden and concrete bungalows perched on stilts at the top of a hill affording nice sea views. Restaurant sports a short menu which features fish, squid and crab.

C-D Orchidée Guesthouse, Tola St, T034-933639, www.orchideeguest house.com. Does not belie its name and the courtyard full of beautiful orchids provides an auspicious welcome, well run, properly maintained, clean and well-aired rooms, a/c and hot water. Restaurant with Khmer and western seafood. Nice pool area, a 5-min walk to the Ochheauteal Beach.

D-F Mealy Chenda, on the crest of Weather Station Hill, T034-670818. Very popular hotel offering accommodation to suit a wide range of budgets from dorm rooms through to a/c double rooms. Sparkly clean with fantastic views from the restaurant.

E-F Sakal Bungalows, near the end of Weather Station Hill, T012-806155, 012806155@mobitel.com.kh. 10 simple but cheap bungalows in a garden setting. Restaurant and bar, cheap internet. Closest bungalows to Victory Beach.

Kampot and around *p264*

C Little Garden Bar, T033-256901, www.littlegardenbar.com. Basic, clean rooms, fan and bathroom. Restaurant offering panoramic views of Mount Bokor.

D-E Molieden, a block away from the main bridge, T033-932798, chuy_seth@ yahoo.com. A surprisingly good find, its hideous façade gives way to a very pleasant interior. Large, tastefully decorated modern art deco rooms with TV and fan. The rooftop restaurant also serves some of the best western food in town.

E-F Blissful Guesthouse, next to **Acleda Bank**. Converted colonial building with lovely surrounding gardens. Rooms are simple with mosquito net, fan and attached bath. High on atmosphere and very popular with locals and expats alike. Affable Khmer manager, Elvis and owner, Angela make this a very pleasant place to stay. Recommended.

Kep *p264*

B Champey Inn, on ocean road, before you reach Kep beach, T012-501742, champeyinn@mobitel.com.kh. A notch above the rest. Elegant bungalows, 4-poster beds, open-air showers and large terrace all set in wonderful, manicured gardens, pool. Popular with the elite expat crowd. Travel services. Good French restaurant.

D Verandah Resort and Bungalows, next door to N4, further up Kep Mountain, T012-888619. Superb accommodation. Large wooden bungalows set in a large, enchanting garden of ripe fruits, vines and tropical flowers which weave around the stairways criss-crossing the hillside. Each bungalow includes a good-sized balcony, fan, mosquito net and nicely decorated mosaic bathroom. The restaurant offers the perfect vista of the ocean and surrounding countryside. Epicureans will love the variety of international cuisines including: poutine of Quebec, smoked ham linguini, fish fillet with olive sauce.

Eating

Phnom Penh *p254, map p256*

Most places are relatively inexpensive – US$3-6 per head. There are several cheaper cafés along Monivong Blvd, around the lake, Kampuchea Krom Blvd (St 128) in the city centre and along the river. Generally the food in Phnom Penh is good and the restaurants surprisingly refined. One of the most remarkable assemblages of restaurants is to be found on Highway 6, several kilometres beyond the Japanese Friendship (or Chruoy Changvar) Bridge. Also around here is an area that the expats refer to as the 'hammock bar stretch'. A strip of restaurants and beer parlours with a multitude of hammocks which boast great sunset views. Excellent, cheap Khmer food and loads of cold beer, a must. To get there just look for the anchor beer signs on the side of the road.

₸₸₸-₸₸ Comme à la Maison, No 13, St 57, T023-360801. Great French delicatessen-type restaurant-cum-café. Good pizzas and breakfast is exceptional.

₸₸₸-₸₸ Elsewhere, No 175, St 51, T023-211348. An oasis in the middle of the city offering delectable modern western cuisine. Seats are speckled across wonderful tropical gardens, all topped off by a well-lit pool. This place has everything right – the food, the setting, the music.

₸₸₸-₸₸ Foreign Correspondents Club of Cambodia (FCCC), No 363 Sisowath Quay, T023-210142. A Phnom Penh institution that can't be missed. Superb colonial building, 2nd-floor bar and restaurant overlooks the Tonlé Sap. Extensive menu with an international flavour, fantastic pizzas and creative salads.

₸₸₸-₸₸ K-West, corner of St 154 and Sisowath Quay, T023-214747. Beautiful spacious restaurant that offers respite from the outside world. Khmer and European food. Extensive cocktail list. Surprisingly, the prices aren't that expensive considering how upmarket it is.

₸₸₸-₸₸ Riverhouse, corner of St 110 and Sisowath Quay, T023-220180. Mediterranean/Thai restaurant in a lovely restored building overlooking the river. Brilliant food, particularly the steak, which is cooked to perfection. Upstairs is a comfortable lounge bar which also serves light meals.

₸₸-₸ Baan Thai, No 2, St 306, T023-362991. 1130-1400, 1730-2200. Thai, excellent food and attentive service. Popular restaurant. Garden and old wooden Thai house setting with sit down cushions.

₸₸-₸ Boddhi Tree, No 50, St 113, T016-865445, www.boddhitree.com. A delightful garden setting and perfect for lunch, a snack or a drink. Delicious salads, sandwiches, barbecue chicken and cheddar is exquisite. Very, very good Khmer food.

Travellers' tales

Pyong Yang palate

I was told I should check out the North Korean Pyong Yang Restaurant ...when I got there the restaurant was sterile with a blindingly clean tiled floor, plastic plants and synthetic wooden vines. The ostentatious wooden furnishings were framed by rouched, velveteen-style drapes. It was like a movie set restaurant. Once I was seated, the waitresses descended on the table like android clones all wearing exactly the same chequered drop waist dress, duplicate white patent shoes, the trinkets were on the same wrists and every strand of hair had been combed back identically. If it hadn't been for the name tags, which were almost like bar codes, I could have easily believed it was the same girl in duplicate, seven times. I was starting to feel that I had stepped into some kind of Communist Star Trek fantasy, then dinner was served.

The food was nothing short of exceptional. Mid meal there was a waitress vacuum, five minutes later they returned in a whirl and music piped up from nowhere as they broke into a cabaret show. They started with the can-can, moved on to Frank Sinatra, next they were strumming away to a violin and finally the performance moved from techno to karaoke. It was truly an entertainment extravaganza, all very entertaining but very bizarre.

Aleta Moriarty

♥♥-♥ Cantina, No 347 Sisowath Quay. Great Mexican restaurant and bar opened by long-time local identity, Hurley Scroggins III. Fantastic food made with the freshest of ingredients. The restaurant attracts an eclectic crowd and can be a source of great company.

♥♥-♥ Khmer Borane, No 389 Sisowath Quay, T012-290092. Open till 2300. Excellent Khmer restaurant just down from the FCC. Wide selection of very well prepared Khmer and Thai food. Try the Amok.

♥♥-♥ Pyong Yang Restaurant, 400 Monivong Blvd, T023-993765. This North Korean restaurant is an all-round experience not to be missed. The food is exceptional but you need to get there before 1900 to get a seat before their nightly show starts. All very bizarre: uniformed, clone-like waitresses double as singers in the nightly show, which later turns into open-mic karaoke, see above.

♥♥-♥ Rendezvous, No 239, T023-736622. Large comfortable chairs, great place for breakfast or a leisurely lunch and very popular for its 2 for 1 happy hour everyday from 1600-1800. Khmer owned.

♥♥-♥ Rising Sun, No 20, St 178 (just round the corner from the FCC). English restaurant with possibly the best breakfast in town. Ginormous roast and excellent iced coffee.

♥♥-♥ Talkin to a Stranger, No 21, St 294, T012-798530. Wed-Sun. Fantastic bar and restaurant with beer garden. Run by a friendly Australian couple, Derek and Wendy. High on atmosphere, brilliant photographic display, wide selection of innovative meals.

♥♥-♥ Tamarind, No 31, St 240, T012-830139. Stylish place specializing in French and Mediterranean, great kebabs and couscous. Bar and tapas. Atmospheric.

♥ The Family Restaurant, St 93, lakeside. A small, unassuming family-run,

Vietnamese restaurant serving brilliant (and quite adventurous) food at ridiculously low prices. Great service, lovely owners.

¶ **The Flying Elephant**, No 3A, St 93, just off the lake, T012-263332. Good cross-section of western foods and drinks. Good salads, burgers and cheap breakfast.

¶ **Friends**, No 215, St 13, T023-426748. Non profit restaurant run by street kids being trained in the hospitality industry. The food is delicious and cheap.

¶ **Happy Herb Pizza**, No 345 Sisowath Quay, T023-332349. A Phnom Penh institution. Watch out for the 'happy' pizza full of hash – it has a nasty kick. Free pizza delivery.

¶ **Khmer Surin**, No 9, St 57, T023-363050. Closes at 2230. Set in an attractive building with some traditional Thai style seating on cushions, this restaurant is a little way south of Sihanouk Blvd. Quiet.

¶ **Lazy Gecko**, St 93, lakeside. Popular, chilled out restaurant/café/bar offering a good selection of sandwiches, burgers and salads in large portions. Good home-cooked Sunday roast. Affable owner, Juan, is a good source of information. Selection of new and used books for sale. Good trivia night on Thu.

¶ **Peking Canteen**, No 393, St 136, T011-909548. Open till 2200. Hole in the wall Chinese restaurant famous for its cheap dumplings (which come either steamed or fried). Very busy at lunch time.

¶ **The Shop**, No 39, St 240, T012-901964, 0900-1800. Deli and bakery, sandwiches, juices, fruit teas, salads and light lunches.

Cafés and bakeries

Asia Europe Bakery, No 95 Sihanouk Blvd, T012-893177. One of the few western-style bakery/cafés in the city. Delicious pastries, cakes and excellent breakfast and lunch menu.

Garden Centre Café, No 23, St 57, T023-363002. Popular place to go for lunch and breakfast, perhaps not surprisingly, the garden is nice too.

Java, No 56 Sihanouk Blvd. Contenders for best coffee in town. Nice use of space – open-air balcony and pleasant surroundings. Delightful food. Features art and photography exhibitions on a regular basis.

Sihanoukville *p262*

¶¶¶-¶¶ **Chez Mari-yan**, Victory Beach area, has a good seafood restaurant with probably the nicest setting in Sihanoukville.

¶¶¶-¶¶ **La Paillote**, top of Weather Station Hill. This is the finest dining establishment in town and one of the best in the country. It has everything right: the service can't be surpassed; high on atmosphere – cocooned from the noisy street and lit by soft glowing candles; the chef from Madagascar greets the customers (often to explain that he uses ganja as a flavour and not as a happy herb style ingredient) and the food, is superb.

¶¶-¶ **Holy Cow**, Ekareach St, on the way out of town. Ambient restaurant offering a selection of healthy, western meals: pasta, salads, baked potatoes. The English owner is a long-term resident and very good source of local information. To his credit he has created a lovely atmosphere and provides impeccable working conditions for his staff.

¶¶-¶ **Mick and Craig's**, Ochheauteal Beach. Thankfully, the menu here is a lot more creative than the venue's name. Sufficiently large meals with a bit of pizzazz: pizzas, burgers, houmus, etc. The restaurant also offers 'themed food nights' Sun roast, BBQ and 'all you can eat' nights.

¶¶-¶ **Starfish Cafe**, behind **Samudera Supermarket**. Small café-cum-bakery in a very peaceful garden setting. Here you can eat great food, while knowing that you are supporting a good cause. The organization was originally established to help rehabilitate people with disabilities and has extended its services to cover a whole range of poverty reducing schemes. A very positive place that oozes goodness in its food, environment and service – good western breakfasts, cakes, sandwiches, salads and coffees. A non-profit massage business has also opened on premises.

Kampot and around p264

¶¶¶-¶ Molieden Restaurant, on the roof of the guesthouse of the same name. Extensive selection of pastas, soup and Italian seafood dishes. Fantastic food.

¶¶-¶ Bamboo Light, on the river road, near the Old Market, T012-602661. Great little Sri Lankan restaurant with a large selection of tasty dishes. Large choice for vegetarians. Outdoor and indoor seating. Elegantly decorated restaurant and intimate bar area.

¶¶-¶ The Little Garden Bar, T012-994161. Also on the riverfront, this is an attractive and relaxed bar and restaurant offering delicious Khmer and western food for reasonable prices. The rooftop bar is the place to be for the spectacular sunset descending over the Elephant Mountains.

¶¶-¶ Rusty Key Hole Bar and Restaurant, on the river road, past Bamboo Light. Western food; the BBQ seafood and ribs come highly recommended.

🎧 Bars and clubs

Phnom Penh p254, map p256

The vast majority of bars in Phnom Penh attract prostitutes.

Elsewhere, No 175, St 51. Highly atmospheric, upmarket bar set in garden with illuminated pool and spot seating, lit by candle. Great cocktails and wine. Very popular with the expats, who have been known to strip off for a dip. Livens up on the last Sat of every month for parties.

Elephant Bar, Le Royal Hotel. Open until 2400. Stylish and elegant bar in Phnom Penh's top hotel, perfect for an evening gin. 2 for 1 happy hour everyday with unending supply of nachos, which makes for a cheap night out in sophisticated surroundings. Probably the best drinks in town.

Foreign Correspondents Club of Cambodia (FCCC), 363 Sisowath Quay. Satellite TV, pool, *Bangkok Post* and *The Nation* both available for reading here, happy hour 1700-1900. Perfect location overlooking the river.

Ginger Monkey, No 29, St 178. Stylish, well decorated bar with faux Angkorian reliefs. Chilled out atmosphere. Quite popular with the younger expat crowd.

Heart of Darkness, No 26, St 51. Heaving. Reasonable prices, friendly staff and open late. Has been Phnom Penh's most popular hangout for a number of years. Absolutely full of prostitutes, but your best bet for a night of dancing.

The Rising Sun, No 20, St 178, T023-970719. Closes at 2400. Just around the corner from the FCCC. An English pub whose emphasis is just as much on food as beer.

Riverhouse Lounge, No 6, St 110 (Sisowath Quay). 1600-0200. Upmarket, cocktail bar and club. Nice views of the river and airy open balcony space. Live music (Sun) and DJs (Sat).

Tom's Irish Bar, No 63 St 170, T023-363161. Comfortable, homely feeling. A popular drinking hole with some of the older expats.

Sihanoukville p262

Papagayo, Weather Station Hill, offers pool tables, cheap cocktails, email on premises, comfy cane lounges. The tapas is exceptionally good value.

🎭 Entertainment

Phnom Penh p254, map p256

Pick up a copy of the *Cambodia Daily* and check out the back page which details up-and-coming events.

Dance

National Museum of Cambodia, St 70. Folk and national dances are performed by the National Dance group as well as shadow puppets and circus. Every Fri and Sat 1930, US$4.

Memphis Pub, St 118 (off Sisowath Quay). Open till 0200. Small bar off the river, very loyal following from the NGO crowd. Live rock and blues music from Tue-Sat.

Riverhouse Lounge, No 6, St 110 (Sisowath Quay). Usually has a guest DJ on the weekends and live jazz on Tue and Sun.

○ Shopping

Phnom Penh *p254, map p256*
Art galleries
Reyum Institute of Arts and Culture, No 4, St 178, T023-217149, www.reyum.org. This is a great place to start for those interested in Cambodian modern art. Some absolutely world-class artists have been mentored and exhibit here.

Handicrafts
Many non-profit organizations have opened stores to help train or rehabilitate some of the country's underprivileged. **Disabled Handicrafts Promotion Association**, No 317, St 63. Handicrafts and jewellery made by people with disabilities and widows.
Le Rit's Nyemo, 131 Sisowath Quay. Non-profit shop with a wide range of silk products.
The National Centre for Disabled People, 3 Norodom, T023-210140. Great store with handicrafts such as pillow cases, tapestries and bags made by people with disabilities.
Orange River, 361 Sisowath Quay (under FCCC), T023-214594, has a selection of beautifully designed decorative items and a very good stock of fabrics and silks which will leave many wishing for more luggage allowance. Pricier than most other stores.
Rajana, No 170, St 450, next to the Russian Market. Traditional crafts, silk paintings, silver and jewellery.

Markets
Tuol Tom Pong, between St 155 and St 163 to east and west, and St 440 and St 450 to north and south. Known to many as the Russian Market. Sells antiques (genuine articles and fakes) and jewellery as well as clothing, pirate CDs and computer software, videos, sarongs, fabrics and an immense variety of tobacco – an excellent place for buying souvenirs, especially silk. Most things at this market are about half the price of the Central Market.
Central Covered Market (Psar Thmei), just off Monivong Blvd, distinguished by its central art deco dome (built 1937), is mostly full of stalls selling silver and gold jewellery.

Shopping centres
Sorya Shopping Centre, St 63, besides the Central Market. The only 'mall' in the whole country, a modern, 7-floor, a/c shopping centre.

Silverware and jewellery
Old silver boxes, belts, antique jewellery along Monivong Blvd (the main thoroughfare), Samdech Sothearos Blvd just north of St 184, has a good cluster of silver shops.

Supermarkets
Sharky Mart, No 124, St 130 (below Sharkys Bar), T023-990303. 24-hr convenience store.

▲ Activities and tours

Phnom Penh *p254, map p256*
Cookery courses
Cambodia Cooking Class, No 14, St285, T023-882314, www.cambodia-cooking-class.com.

Language classes
The Khmer School of Language, 529 St 454, Tuol Tumpung 2, Chamcar Morn, T023-213047, www.camb comm.org.uk/ksl.

Tour operators

Asian Trails Ltd, No 33, St 240, PO Box 621, T023-216555, www.asiantrails.com. Offers a broad selection of tours: Angkor, river cruises, remote tours, biking trips.

Capitol Tours, No 14AE0, St 182 (see Capitol Guesthouse), T023-217627, www.bigpond.com.kh/users/capitol. Cheap tours around Phnom Penh's main sites. Also organizes tours around the country. Targeted at budget travellers.

Exotissimo Travel, 46 Norodom Blvd, T023-218948, www.exotissimo.com. Wide range of day trips and classic tours covering mainstream destinations: Angkor, Sihanoukville etc. Also offers tailor-made trips.

PTM Tours, No 333B Monivong Blvd, T023-986363, www.ptm-travel.com. Reasonably priced package tours to Angkor and around Phnom Penh. Also offers cheap hotel reservations.

RTR Tours, No 54E Charles de Gaulle Blvd, T023-210468, www.rtrtours.com.kh. Organizes tours plus other travel services, including ticketing. Friendly and helpful.

Sihanoukville *p262*
Diving

Scuba Nation Diving Centre, Weather Station Hill, T012-604680, www.dive cambodia.com. This company has the best reputation in the country and is the longest-established PADI dive centre. Open Water Course, US$350; dive trips, US$70.

Fishing

The Fishermen's Den, 1 block back from Ekareach St, next to the **Small Hotel**. Runs daily fishing trips for US$25 per person. If you have caught something worth eating, the proprietor, Brian, will organize the restaurant to prepare a lovely meal from the catch (if not, there is plenty of backup seafood on hand). The boat is fully equipped with showers, toilets, life jackets, etc.

🚍 Transport

Phnom Penh *p254, map p256*
Air

Royal Phnom Penh Airways has connections with **Siem Reap** and **Stung Treng**. Bangkok/Siem Reap Airways has connections with **Siem Reap**.

Airline offices Most airline offices are open 0800-1700, Sat 0800-1200. **Air France**, Samdeck Sothearos Blvd (Hong Kong Centre), T023-2192200. **Bangkok/Siem Reap Airways**, No 61A, St 214, T023- 426624, www.bangkokair.com. **Lao Airlines**, 58C Sihanouk Blvd, T023-216563. **President Airlines**, 13-14, 296 Mao Tse Toung Blvd, T023-993088/89. **Silk Air**, Himawari Hotel, 313 Sisowath Quay, T023-426808, www.silkair.com. **Thai**, 294 Mao Tse Tung Blvd, T023-890292. **Vietnam Airlines**, No 41, St 214, T023-363396/7, www.vietnamairlines.com.

Bicycle

Hire from guesthouses for around US$1 per day. Bicycling is probably the best way to explore the city. It is mostly flat, so not too exhausting.

Boat

Ferries leave from wharves on the river north of the Japanese Friendship Bridge and from Sisowath Quay daily. There are supposed to be connections to **Siem Reap** (Angkor), **Kratie** and **Stung Treng**. In recent times the Mekong service (Kratie, Stung Treng) hasn't been running as they can't get enough customers now the roads have been improved. Fast boat connections (5 hrs) with **Siem Reap**, US$25 1-way, **Kratie**, US$7.85, and **Stung Treng** US$15.70. In the low season the trip to Siem Reap can take up to 6-7 hrs. Boats do sometimes break down and promised express boats often turn out to be old chuggers but it costs less than flying. All boats leave early, 0700 or earlier. Most hotels will supply ferry tickets (happy to collect the commission).

Most buses leave southwest of Psar Thmei (Central Market) by the Shell petrol station. **Capitol Tours**, T023-217627, departs from its terminal, No 14, St 182. **GST**, T012-838910, departs from the southwest corner of the Central Market (corner of St 142). **Phnom Penh Public Transport Co** (formerly Ho Wah Genting Bus Company), T023-210359, departs from Charles de

---

Border with Laos

The border crossing between Voen Kham, Laos and Koh Chheuteal or Don Kralor, Cambodia. The border is open daily from 0700-1700. You should aim to cross early in the day to avoid hassles and travelling at night. In 2005 it still wasn't recognized as a proper international crossing but nonetheless hundreds of tourists have poured across here. You will need to arrange visas beforehand in either Phnom Penh or Vientiane. Many tourists have encountered problems including inflated transportation costs and having to pay bribes, so try and be patient and keep smiling. A boat from Stung Treng to the Laos border (Koh Chheuteal) costs US$7 (per person or US$35 for the whole boat) and takes roughly one hour 10 minutes. Boats depart quite regularly (depending on passengers), approximately every two hours between 0700 and 1600. A departure tax of US$1-3 (depending on how hungry the customs officials are) will need to be paid at each side. Most hotels (Sekong, Riverside in Stung Treng can organize tickets.

Daily buses leave from Phnom Penh to Stung Treng but you wouldn't be able to make the trip from Phnom Penh across the border in a day. Phnom Penh Public Transport Co buses leave from Psar Thmei, Phnom Penh at 0700 and the journey takes nine-10 hours, 40,000 riel. Buses from Stung Treng to Phnom Penh leave from the bus stand near the park but this office was declared 'temporary' at the time of writing at 0700, 40,000 riel. The same bus will stop at Kratie, US$5. Share taxis to Phnom Penh leave at 0600 from the taxi rank near the river, seven hours, US$15.

Few people choose to stay in Stung Treng, as the town is short on charm. However, there is plenty of accommodation should you get stranded. Most tourists head to Kratie three to four hours south of Stung Treng. Taxis leave regularly for Kratie and cost around US$4 per person. To get to Kratie from Phnom Penh takes six-seven hours and both the Hour Lean Bus Company, T012-535387, and Phnom Penh Transport Company, T012-523400, both run buses to Kratie for US$4.50 at 0730, departing from Psar Thmei, Phnom Penh. Pick-ups and share taxis also regularly connect Phnom Penh with Kratie.

On the Lao side

The Lao border town is Voen Kham, which is 35 km, 45 minutes from Ban Nakasong, see p388, by minivan/tuk-tuk and costs between US$5-15 (price contingent on the number of passengers going) and can be organized by most other guesthouses/hotels in the Siphandon area (for example Mr Pon at Pon's Travel). For those heading to Don Khone it is best to go to Ban Hat Xai Koune, about 20 minutes longer and a few extra dollars. Once you have crossed the border it is a one-hour journey by boat to Stung Treng, Cambodia (US$30-70 for the whole boat divided by the number of passengers). The Don Kralor border crossing (8 km from Voen Kham) can be undertaken by vehicle and includes a 60 km drive from the border to Stung Treng. It is reported that Cambodian visas are available at this crossing for US$30 but it is still not set in concrete, so best to organize one in advance in your home country or in Vientiane. The exit fee charged on departure from Laos is set at the steep US$2. There have been countless reports of dodgy Lao border officials hiking the rate up exponentially to account for overtime (Saturday and Sunday), with some people even asked as much as US$10.

Gaulle Blvd, near the Central Market. To **Kratie**, 1 bus per day (US$4); **Capitol Tours** runs a bus to **Kampot**, 0800, US$2.50. There are also frequent departures from the Central Market (Psar Thmei) bus terminal. Around Khmer New Year and during the peak season you will need to book tickets the day before travel. **Phnom Penh Bus Co** to **Sihanoukville**, 0700, 0730, 0830, 1230 and 1330. **GST** buses leave at 0715, 0815, 1230 and 1330, 4 hrs. To Siem Reap, see p299.

Car
Chauffeur-driven cars are available at most hotels from US$25 per day upwards. Several travel agents will also hire cars. Prices increase if you're venturing out of town. **Car Rental**, T012-950950.

Cyclo
Plentiful but slow. Fares can be bargained down but are not that cheap – a short journey should be no more than 1000 riel. A few cyclo drivers speak English or French. They are most likely to be found loitering around the big hotels and can also be hired for the day (around US$5).

Moto
'Motodops' are 50-100cc motorbike taxis and the fastest way to get around Phnom Penh. Standard cost per journey is around US$0.50 for a short hop but expect to pay double after dark. If you find a good, English-speaking moto driver, hang on to him and he can be yours for US$8-10 per day.

Shared taxi
These are either Toyota pick-ups or saloons. For the pick-ups the fare depends upon whether you wish to sit inside or in the open; vehicles depart when the driver has enough fares. **Psar Chbam Pao**, just over Monivong Bridge on Route 1, for **Vietnam**. For **Sihanoukville** and **Siem Riep**, take a shared taxi from the Central Market (Psar Thmei). Leave early 0500-0600. Shared

taxi to **Kampot** takes 2-3 hrs, US$4, leaving from Doeum Kor Market on Mao Tse Tung Blvd.

Taxi
There are only a few taxis in Phnom Penh as the risk of being held up at gunpoint is too high. It is possible to get a taxi into town from the airport and one or two taxi companies can be reached by telephone but expect to see no cabs cruising and no meter taxis. **Taxi Vantha**, T012-855000/ 023-982542, 24 hrs.

Phnom Penh hotels will organize private taxis to **Sihanoukville** for around US$25.

Sihanoukville *p262*
Motos cost 2000 riel around town or 3000 from the centre to a beach. Taxis charge US$5 to a beach.

Bus to **Phnom Penh** from the station on the corner of Ekareach and Sopheakmongkol Streets; **Phnom Penh Public Transport Co**, 0710, 0800, 1215, 1310, 1400 and **GST** 0715, 0815, 1230, 1315. There are no longer any security risks on this route. To **Kampot** shared taxi, around 10,000 riel per person, 4 hrs.

Kampot and around *p264*
Vehicles leave from the truck station next to the Total gas station for **Phnom Penh** at 0700 until 1400 for US$3.50 and private US$20. Most guesthouses can arrange transport and tickets. To **Sihanoukville**, shared taxi, US$3, private US$18. **Kep**, taxi, US$8, return US$14-15.

Kep *p264*
Kep is 25 km from **Kampot**, 30-45 mins. There are a few early-morning pick-ups from Kampot's market, US$3, or else you can hire a moto (US$2-3 1-way, US$5-6 return) or car (US$14 return).

❶ Directory

Phnom Penh *p254, map p256*
Banks ANZ Royal Bank, Russian Bvd, 20 Kramuon Sar (corner of street 67), has recently opened a number of ATMs throughout Phnom Penh: also near the Independence Monument and at 265 Sisowath Quay. **Canadia Bank**, No 126 Charles de Gaulle Blvd, T023-214668; 265-269 Ang Duong St, T023-215286. Cash advances on credit cards. **Cambodia Commercial Bank** (CCB), No130 Monivong Blvd (close to the Central Market), T023-426208. Cash advance on credit cards, TCs and currency exchange. **Union Commercial Bank** (UCB), No 61, St 130, T023-724931. Most banking services, charges no commission on credit card cash advances. **Embassies and consulates** Australia, No 11, St 254, T023-213470, australia.embassy. cambodia@dfat.gov.au. **Canada**, No 11, St 254, T023-213470, pnmpn@dfait-maeci.gc.ca. **France**, 1 Monivong Blvd, T023-430020, sctipcambodge@ online.com.kh. **Laos**, 15-17 Mao Tse Tung Blvd, T023-983632. **Thailand**, 196 Norodom Blvd, T023-726306-10, thaipnp@mfa.go.th. **United Kingdom**, No 29, St 75, T023-427124, britemb@ online.com.kh. **USA**, No16, St 228, T023-216436, usembassy@ camnet.com.kh (A new US Embassy was under construction near Wat Phnom at the time of publication). **Vietnam**, 436 Monivong Blvd, T023-362531, embvnpp@camnet.com.kh.
Immigration Opposite the international airport. Visa extensions, photograph required, 1-month US$30.

Internet Cheap and ubiquitous. Rates can be as low as US$0.50 per hr although in many places they are higher. **Medical services** It is highly advisable to try and get to Bangkok if you are seriously ill or have injured yourself as Cambodia's medical services are not up to scratch. **Calmette Hospital**, 3 Monivong Blvd, T023-426948, is generally considered the best, 24-hr emergency. **Surya Medical Services**, No 39, St 294, T016-8450000. After hours emergency care available 24-hrs. General medicine, tropical medicine. Mon-Fri 0700-2000, Sat-Sun 0700-1800. **Pharmacy de la Gare**, 81 Monivong Blvd, T023-526855. **Post office** Main post office, St 13, possible to make international telephone calls from here.

Sihanoukville *p262*
Banks There are 4 banks in town (often shut): **Acleda, UCB, Canadia** and the **Mekong Bank,** all on Ekareach St. UCB and Canadia do Visa/MasterCard cash advances. Cash advances are also available at **Samudera Supermarket**, in town, 5% commission, and **Lucky Web**, on Weather Station Hill, charges 4% commission. **Internet** All tourist areas in Sihanoukville have internet within 1-2 mins walking distance. Prices vary from 300-8000 riel per hr.

Kampot and around *p264*
Banks Canadia Bank, close to the Borey Bokor 1 Hotel. Cash advances on Visa and MasterCard (with no commission). **Internet** There is a cluster of cafés on the road between the river and the central roundabout – US$1 per hr. International calls can be made and vary between 600-900 riel per min.

Angkor

The huge temple complex of Angkor, the ancient capital of the powerful Khmer Empire, is one of the archaeological treasures of Asia and the spiritual and cultural heart of Cambodia. The empire reached its peak between the ninth and 15th centuries, when most of the legendary temples, sanctuaries, barays and roads were built. Henri Mouhot, the Frenchman who rediscovered it, wrote "it is grander than anything of Greece or Rome". Angkor Wat is arguably the greatest temple within the complex, both in terms of grandeur and sheer magnitude. After all, it is the biggest religious monument in the world, its outer walls clad with one of the longest continuous bas-relief ever created. The diverse architectural prowess and dexterity of thousands of artisans is testified by around 100 brilliant monuments in the area. Of these the Bayon, with its beaming smiles; Banteay Srei, which features the finest most intricate carvings; and the jungle temple of Ta Prohm are unmissable. Others prefer the more understated but equally brilliant temples of Neak Pean, Preah Khan and Pre Rup. The petite town of Siem Reap sits nearby the Angkor complex, and is home to a gamut of world-class hotels, restaurants and bars. A hop, skip and a jump from the town is Southeast Asia's largest lake, the Tonlé Sap, with floating villages, teeming with riverine life.

◪ **Getting there** Plane, bus, boat, shared taxi.
◔ **Getting around** Elephant, tuk-tuk, moto, car, bicycle.
◔ **Time required** 2 days - 1 week.
◍ **Weather** Hot and sticky in summer, very wet in the rainy season (May-Jun).
◓ **Sleeping** Several luxurious hotels, and plenty of mainstream guesthouses and standard budget options.
◉ **Eating** Superb range of international food and outstanding cuisine to suit every kind of budget.
▲▲ **Activities and tours** Boat trips to the floating villages on Tonlé Sap, traditional dance and puppetry shows, Beatocello.
★ **Don't miss...** Sunrise at Angkor ►► p286.

Cambodia Angkor

Ins and outs

Getting there
Air The airport (REP), T063-963148, is 7 km from Siem Reap, the town closest to the Angkor ruins (see p299), with flights from Phnom Penh, Ho Chi Minh City, Bangkok and Vientiane. The airport has a taxi service, café, internet access, phone service and gift shop. A moto into town is US$1, by taxi US$7. Guesthouse owners often meet flights and offer free rides. At the airport there is a post office, a small and expensive duty free, internet and café. Visas can be issued upon arrival US$20 (฿1000), photo required.

Boat A boat from Phnom Penh costs US$25, five to six hours. The trip is fantastically atmospheric and a good way to kill two birds with one stone and see the mighty Tonlé Sap Lake. The boat is a less appealing option in the dry season when low water levels necessitate transfers to small, shallow draft vessels. In case of extremely low water levels a bus or pick-up will need to be taken for part of the trip. The mudbank causeway between the Lake and the outskirts of Siem Reap is hard to negotiate and may necessitate some walking (it is 12 km from Bindonville harbour to Siem Reap). Boats depart from the Phnom Penh Port on Sisowath Quay (end of 106 Street) 0700, departing Siem Reap 0700 from Chong Khneas on the Tonlé Sap Lake.

Bus The air-conditioned buses are one of the most convenient and comfortable ways to go between Phnom Penh and Siem Reap, US$3.50-4, six hours. Almost every guesthouse or hotel sells the tickets although it is easy enough to pick-up from the bus stations/terminal. In peak periods, particularly Khmer New Year, it is important to purchase tickets a day or two prior to travel. A shared taxi from Phnom Penh will cost you US$10. ❿ ↦ *p299.*

Getting around
Most of the temples within the Angkor complex (except the Roluos Group) are located in an area 8 km north of Siem Reap, with the area extending across a 25 km radius. The Roluos Group are 13 km east of Siem Reap and further away is Banteay Srei (32 km).

    Cars with drivers and guides are available from larger hotels from around US$20 per day plus US$20 for a guide. The **Angkor Tour Guide Association** and most other travel agencies can also organize this. Expect to pay around US$7-8 per day for a **moto** unless the driver speaks good English in which case the price will be higher. This price will cover trips to the Roluos Group of temples but not to Banteay Srei. No need to add more than a dollar or two to the price for getting to Banteay Srei unless the driver is also a guide and can demonstrate to you that he is genuinely going to show you around. **Tuk-tuks** and their ilk have appeared on the scene in recent years and a trip to the temples on a motorbike drawn cart is quite a popular option for 2 people, U$10 a day (maximum of two people).

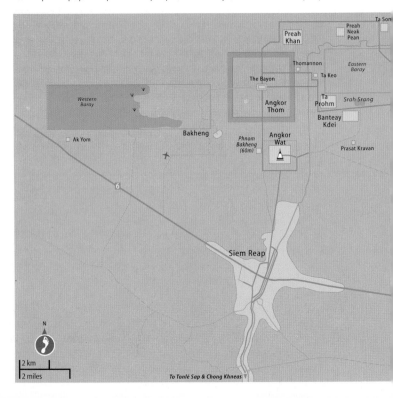

Bicycle hire, US$2-3 per day from most guesthouses, represents a nice option for those who feel reasonably familiar with the area. However, if you are on a limited schedule and only have a day or two at the temples you won't be able to cover an awful lot of the temples on a pedal bike as the searing temperatures and sprawling layout can take even the most advanced cyclists a considerable amount of time. Angkor Wat and Banteay Srei have official parking sites, 1000 riel (US$0.25) and at the other temples you can quite safely park and lock your bikes in front of a drink stall. For those wishing to see Angkor from a different perspective it is possible to charter a **helicopter**. **Elephants** are stationed near the Bayon or at the South Gate of Angkor Thom during the day. In the evenings, they are located at the bottom of Phnom Bakheng, taking tourists up to the summit for sunset. ▲▲▶▶ *p298*.

Best time to visit
Angkor's peak season coincides with the dry season, November-February. Not only is this the driest time of year it is also the coolest (which can still be unbearably hot). The monsoon lasts from June to October/November. At this time it can get very muddy.

Tourist information
Guides can be invaluable when navigating the temples, with the majority being able to answer most questions about Angkor as well as providing additional information about Cambodian culture and history. Most hotels and travel agents will be able to point you in the direction of a good guide. The **Khmer Angkor Tour Guide Association** ① *on the road to Angkor, T063-964347*, has pretty well-trained guides. Most of the guides here are very well-briefed and some speak English better than others. The going rate is US$20-25 per day. If you do wish to buy an additional guidebook Dawn Rooney's *Angkor: An Introduction to the Temples* and *Ancient Angkor* by Michael Freeman and Claude Jacques are recommended.

Temple fees and hours One-day pass US$23, two- or three-day pass US$43, four- to seven-day pass US$63. Most people will be able to cover the majority of the temples within three days. If you buy your ticket after 1715 the day beforehand, you get a free sunset thrown in. For any ticket other than the one-day ticket you will need a passport photograph. The complex is open daily 0530-1830.

Safety Landmines were planted on some outlying paths to prevent Khmer Rouge guerrillas from infiltrating the temples; they have pretty much all been cleared by now, but it is safer to stick to well-used paths. Wandering anywhere in the main temple complexes is perfectly safe. Be especially wary of **snakes** in the dry season. The very poisonous Hanuman snake (lurid green) is fairly common in the area.

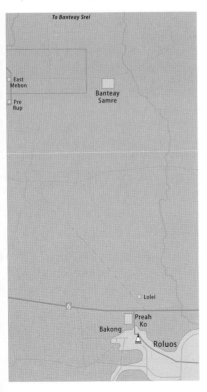

Cambodia Angkor

Beating the crowds

✅ These days avoiding traffic within the Angkor complex is difficult but still moderately achievable. As it stands there is a pretty standard one-day tour itinerary that includes: Angkor Wat (sunrise), Angkor Thom, the Bayon etc (morning), break for lunch, Ta Prohm (afternoon), Preah Khan (afternoon) and Phnom Bakheng (sunset). If you reverse the order, peak hour traffic at major temples is dramatically reduced. As many tour groups trip into Siem Reap for lunch this is an opportune time to catch a peaceful moment in the complex, just bring a packed lunch or eat at 1100 or 1400.

✅ To avoid the masses at the draw-card attraction, Angkor Wat, try to walk around the temple, as opposed to through it. Sunset at Phnom Bakheng has turned into a circus fiasco, so aim for Angkor or the Bayon at this time as they are both relatively peaceful. Sunrise is still relatively peaceful at Angkor, grab yourself the prime position behind the left-hand pond (you need to depart Siem Reap no later than 0530), though there are other stunning early morning options, such as Srah Srang or Bakong. Bakheng gives a beautiful vista of Angkor in the early-mid morning.

Photography A generalization, but somewhat true, is that black and white film tends to produce better-looking tourist pictures than those in colour. Plenty of hawkers have clicked onto this and sell Fuji SS fine-grain black and white film (US$2-3 a roll). The best colour shots usually include some kind of contrast against the temples, a saffron-clad monk or a child. Don't forget to ask if you want to include people in your shots. In general, the best time to photograph the great majority of temples is before 0900 and after 1630.

Itineraries

The temples are scattered over an area in excess of 160 sq km. There are three so-called 'circuits'. The **Petit Circuit** takes in the main central temples including Angkor Wat, Bayon, Baphuon and the Terrace of the Elephants. The **Grand Circuit** takes a wider route, including smaller temples like Ta Prohm, East Mebon and Neak Pean. The **Roluos Group Circuit** ventures further afield still, taking in the temples near Roluos – Lolei, Preah Ko and Bakong. The order of visiting Angkor's temples is very much a matter of opinion and available time; here are some options:

Half day South Gate of Angkor Thom, Bayon, Angkor Wat.

One day Angkor Wat (sunrise or sunset), South Gate of Angkor Thom, Angkor Thom Complex (Bayon, Elephant Terrace, Royal Palace) and Ta Prohm. This is a hefty schedule for one day; you'll need to arrive after 1615 and finish just after 1700 the following day.

Two days The same as above but with the inclusion of the rest of the Angkor Thom, Preah Khan, Srah Srang (sunrise) and at a push, Banteay Srei.

Three days Day 1 Sunrise at Angkor Wat; morning South Gate of Angkor Thom, Angkor Thom complex (aside from Bayon); Ta Prohm; late afternoon-sunset at the Bayon. **Day 2** Sunrise Srah Srang; morning Banteay Kdei and Banteay Srei; late afternoon Preah Khan; sunset at Angkor Wat. **Day 3** Sunrise and morning Roluos; afternoon Ta Keo and sunset either at Bakheng or Angkor Wat.

The five towers of Angkor Wat

Those choosing to stay one or two days longer should try to work Banteay Samre, East Mebon, Neak Pean and Thomannon into their itinerary. A further two to three days warrants a trip to Prasat Kravan, Ta Som, Beng Melea and Kbal Spean.

Background

Khmer Empire

Under **Jayavarman VII (1181-1218)** the Angkor complex stretched more than 25 km east to west and nearly 10 km north to south, approximately the same size as Manhattan. For five centuries (ninth-13th), the court of Angkor held sway over a vast territory. At its height Khmer influence spanned half of Southeast Asia, from Burma to the southernmost tip of Indochina and from the borders of Yunnan to the Malay Peninsula. The only threat to this great empire was a riverborne invasion in 1177, when the Cham used a Chinese navigator to pilot their war canoes up the Mekong. Scenes are depicted in bas-reliefs of the Bayon temple.

Jayavarman II (802-835) founded the Angkor Kingdom, then coined Hariharalaya to the north of the Tonlé Sap, in the Roluos region (Angkor), in 802. Later he moved the capital to Phnom Kulen, 40 km northeast of Angkor, where he built a Mountain Temple and Rong Shen shrine. After several years he moved the capital back to the Roluos region. **Jayavarman III** (835-877) continued his father's legacy and built a number of shrines at Hariharalaya. Many historians believe he was responsible for the initial construction of the impressive laterite pyramid, Bakong, considered the great precursor to Angkor Wat. Bakong, built to symbolize Mount Meru, was later embellished and developed by Indravarman. **Indravarman** (877-889) overthrew his predecessor violently and undertook a major renovation campaign in the capital Hariharalaya. The majority of what stands in the Roluos Group today is the work of Indravarman. A battle between Indravarman's sons destroyed the palace and the victor and new king **Yasovarman I** (889-900) moved the capital from Roluos and laid the foundations of Angkor itself. He dedicated the temple to his ancestors. His new capital at Angkor was called Yasodharapura, meaning 'glory-bearing city', and here he built 100 wooden ashramas, retreats (all of which have disintegrated today). Yasovarman selected Bakheng as the location for his temple-mountain and after flattening the mountain top, set about creating another

→ **Motifs in Khmer sculpture**

Apsaras These are regarded as one of the greatest invention of the Khmers. The gorgeous temptresses – born, according to legend, 'during the churning of the Sea of Milk' – were Angkor's equivalent of pin-up girls and represented the ultimate ideal of feminine beauty. They lived in heaven where their sole raison d'être was to have eternal sex with Khmer heroes and holy men. The apsaras are carved in seductive poses with splendidly ornate jewellery and clothed in the latest Angkor fashion. Different facial features suggest the existence of several races at Angkor. Together with the five towers of Angkor Wat they have become the symbol of Khmer culture. The god-king himself possessed an apsara-like retinue of court dancers – impressive enough for Chinese envoy Chou Ta-kuan to write home about it in 1296.

Garuda Mythical creature – half-man, half-bird – was the vehicle of the Hindu god, Vishnu, and the sworn enemy of the nagas. It appeared relatively late in Khmer architecture.

Kala Jawless monster commanded by the gods to devour his own body – made its first appearance in lintels at Roluos. The monster represented devouring time and was an early import from Java.

Makara Mythical water-monster with a scaly body, eagles' talons and an elephantine trunk.

Naga Sacred snake. These play an important part in Hindu mythology and the Khmers drew on them for architectural inspiration. Possibly more than any other single symbol or motif, the naga is characteristic of Southeast Asia and decorates objects throughout the region. The naga is an aquatic serpent and is intimately associated with water (a key component of Khmer prosperity). In Hindu mythology, the naga coils beneath and supports Vishnu on the cosmic ocean. The snake also swallows the waters of life, these only being set free to reinvigorate the world after Indra ruptures the serpent with a bolt of lightning. Another version has Vishnu's servants pulling at the serpent to squeeze the waters of life from it (the so-called churning of the sea, see p284).

Singha Lion in stylized form; often the guardians to temples.

Mount Meru. The temple he constructed was considered more complex than anything built beforehand, a five-storey pyramid with 108 shrines. A road was then built to link the former and present capitals of Roluos and Bakheng. Like the Kings before him, Yasovarman was obliged to construct a major waterworks and the construction of the reservoir – the East Baray (now completely dry) – was considered an incredible feat. After Yasovarman's death in 900 his son **Harshavarman** (900-923) assumed power for the next 23 years. During his brief reign, Harshavarman is believed to have built Baksei Chamkrong (northeast of Phnom Bakheng) and Prasat Kravan (the 'Cardamom Sanctuary'). His brother, **Ishanarvarman II** (923-928), resumed power upon his death but no great architectural feats were recorded in this time. In 928, **Jayavarman IV** moved the capital 65 km away to Koh Ker. Here he built the grand state temple Prasat Thom, an impressive seven-storey, sandstone pyramid. Following

Monks at the baray, Angkor Wat

the death of Jayavarman things took a turn for the worst. Chaos ensued under **Harshavarman's II** weak leadership and over the next four years, no monuments were known to be erected. Jayavarman's IV nephew, **Rajendravarman** (944-968), took control of the situation and it's assumed he forcefully relocated the capital back to Angkor. Rather than moving back into the old capital Phnom Bakheng, he marked his own new territory, selecting an area south of the East Baray as his administrative centre. Here, in 961 he constructed the state temple, Pre Rup, and constructed the temple, East Mebon (953), in the middle of the baray. Srah Srang, Kutisvara and Bat Chum were also constructed, with the help of his chief architect, Kavindrarimathana. It was towards the end of his reign that he started construction on Banteay Srei, considered one of the finest examples of Angkorian craftsmanship in the country. Rajendravarman's son **Jayavarman V** (968-1001) became the new king in 968. The

Background

→ The Churning of the Sea

The Hindu legend, the Churning of the Sea, relates how the gods and demons resolved matters in the turbulent days when the world was being created. The elixir of immortality was one of 13 precious things lost in the churning of the cosmic sea. It took 1000 years before the gods and demons, in a joint dredging operation – aided by Sesha, the sea snake, and Vishnu – recovered them all.

The design of the temples of Angkor was based on this ancient legend. The moat represents the ocean and the gods use the top of Mount Meru – represented by the tower – as their churning stick. The cosmic serpent offered himself as a rope to enable the gods and demons to twirl the stick.

Paul Mus, a French archaeologist, suggests that the bridge with the naga balustrades which went over the moat from the world of men to the royal city was an image of the rainbow. Throughout Southeast Asia and India, the rainbow is alluded to as a multi-coloured serpent rearing its head in the sky.

administrative centre was renamed Jayendranagari and yet again, relocated. More than compensating for the unfinished Ta Keo was Jayavarman's V continued work on Banteay Srei. Under his supervision the splendid temple was completed and dedicated to his father.

Aside from successfully extending the Khmer Empire's territory **King Suryavarman I** (1002-1049), made a significant contribution to Khmer architectural heritage. He presided over the creation of a new administrative centre – the Royal Palace (in Angkor Thom) – and the huge walls that surround it. The next in line was **Udayadityavarman II** (1050-1066), the son of Suryavarman I. The Baphuon temple-mountain was built during his relatively short appointment. After overthrowing his Great-Uncle Dharanindravarman, **Suryavarman II** (1112-1150), the greatest of Angkor's god-kings, came to power. His rule marked the highest point in Angkorian architecture and civilization. Not only was he victorious in conflict, having beaten the Cham whom couldn't be defeated by China, he was responsible for extending the borders of the Khmer Empire into Myanmar, Malaya and Siam. This aside, he was also considered one of the era's most brilliant creators. Suryavarman II was responsible for the construction of Angkor Wat, the current day symbol of Cambodia. Beng Melea, Banteay Samre and Thommanon are also thought to be the works of this genius. He has been immortalized in his own creation – in a bas-relief in the South Gallery of Angkor Wat the glorious King Suryavarman II sitting on top of an elephant. After a period of political turmoil, which included the sacking of Angkor, **Jayavarman VII** seized the throne in 1181 and set about rebuilding his fiefdom. He created a new administrative centre – the great city of Angkor Thom. The mid-point of Angkor Thom is marked by his brilliant Mahayana Buddhist state temple, the Bayon. It is said that the Bayon was completed in 21 years. Jayavarman took thousands of peasants from the rice fields to build it, which proved a fatal error, for rice yields decreased and the empire began its decline as resources were drained. The temple, which consists of sculptured faces of Avolokiteshvara (the Buddha of compassion and mercy) are often said to also encompass the face of their great creator, Jayavarman VIII. He was also responsible for restoring the Royal Palace, renovating Srah Srang and constructing the Elephant Terrace, the Terrace of the Leper King and the nearby baray (northeast of Angkor Thom), Jayatataka reservoir. At the centre of his reservoir he built Neak Pean. Jayavarman VII adopted Mahayana Buddhism; Buddhist principles replaced the Hindu pantheon, and were invoked as the basis of royal authority. This spread of Buddhism is thought to have caused some of the earlier Hindu temples to be neglected. The king paid tribute to his Buddhist roots through his monastic temples – Ta Prohm and Preah Khan.

The French at Angkor

Thai ascendency and eventual occupation of Angkor in 1431, led to the city's abandonment and the subsequent invasion of the jungle. Four centuries later, in 1860, Henri Mouhot – a French naturalist – stumbled across the forgotten city, its temple towers enmeshed in the forest canopy. Locals told him they were the work of a race of giant gods. Only the stone temples remained; all the wooden secular buildings had decomposed in the intervening centuries. In 1873 French archaeologist Louis Delaporte removed many of Angkor's finest statues for 'the cultural enrichment of France'. In 1898, the École Française d'Extrême Orient started clearing the jungle, restoring the temples, mapping the complex and making an inventory of the site. Delaporte was later to write the two-volume *Les Monuments du Cambodge*, the most comprehensive Angkorian inventory of its time, and his earlier sketches, plans and reconstructions, published in *Voyage au Cambodge* in 1880 are without parallel.

Angkor temples

The temples at Angkor were modelled on those of the kingdom of Chenla (a mountain kingdom centred on northern Cambodia and southern Laos), which in turn were modelled on Indian temples. They represent Mount Meru – the home of the gods of Indian cosmology. The central towers symbolize the peaks of Mount Meru, surrounded by a wall representing the earth and moats and basins representing the oceans. The devaraja, or god-king, was enshrined in the centre of the religious complex, which acted as the spiritual axis of the kingdom. The people believed their apotheosized king communicated directly with the gods.

The central tower sanctuaries housed the images of the Hindu gods to whom the temples were dedicated. Dead members of the royal and priestly families were accorded a status on a par with these gods. Libraries to store the sacred scriptures were also built within the ceremonial centre. The temples were mainly built to shelter the images of the gods – unlike Christian churches, Moslem mosques and some Buddhist pagodas, they were not intended to accommodate worshippers. Only priests, the servants of the god, were allowed into the interiors. The 'congregation' would mill around in open courtyards or wooden pavilions.

The first temples were of a very simple design, but with time they became more grandiose and doors and galleries were added. Most of Angkor's buildings are made from a soft sandstone which is easy to work. It was transported to the site from Phnom Kulen, about 30 km to the northeast. Laterite was used for foundations, core material, and enclosure walls, as it was widely available and could be easily cut into blocks. A common feature of Khmer temples was false doors and windows on the sides and backs of sanctuaries and other buildings. In most cases there was no need for well-lit rooms and corridors as hardly anyone ever went into them. That said, the galleries round the central towers in later temples, such as Angkor Wat, indicate that worshippers did use the temples for ceremonial circumambulation when they would contemplate the inspiring bas-reliefs from the important Hindu epic, *Ramayana* (see p73) and *Mahabharata* (written between 400 BC and AD 200).

Despite the court's conversion to Mahayana Buddhism in the 12th century, the architectural ground-plans of temples did not alter much – even though they were based on Hindu cosmology. The idea of the god-king was simply grafted onto the new state religion and statues of the Buddha rather than the gods of the Hindu pantheon were used to represent the god-king (see Bayon, p289). One particular image of the Buddha predominated at Angkor in which he wears an Angkor-style crown, with a conical top which is encrusted with jewellery.

Angkor Wat

The awe-inspiring sight of Angkor Wat, first thing in the morning, is something you're not likely to forget. Angkor literally means 'city' or 'capital' and it is is the biggest religious monument ever built and certainly one of the most spectacular. The temple complex covers 81 ha. Its five towers are emblazoned on the Cambodian flag and the 12th-century masterpiece is considered by art historians to be the prime example of classical Khmer art and architecture. It took more than 30 years to build and is dedicated to the Hindu god Vishnu, personified in earthly form by its builder, the god-king Suryavarman II, and is aligned east to west.

Angkor Wat differs from other temples, primarily because it is facing westward, symbolically the direction of death, leading many to originally believe it was a tomb. However, as Vishnu is associated with the west, it is now generally accepted that it served both as a temple and a mausoleum for the king. Like other Khmer temple-mountains, Angkor Wat is an architectural allegory, depicting in stone the epic tales of Hindu mythology. The central sanctuary of the temple complex represents the sacred Mount Meru, the centre of the Hindu universe, on whose summit the gods reside. Angkor Wat's five towers symbolize Meru's five peaks; the enclosing wall represents the mountains at the edge of the world and the surrounding moat, the ocean beyond.

The temple complex is enclosed by a square moat – more than 5 km in length and 190 m wide – and a high, galleried wall, which is covered in epic bas-reliefs and has four ceremonial tower gateways. The main gateway faces west and the temple is approached by a 475-m-long road, built along a causeway, which is lined with naga balustrades. At the far end of the causeway stands a **cruciform platform**, guarded by stone lions, from which the

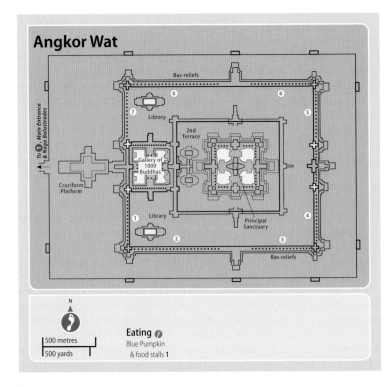

Angkor Wat

Bas-reliefs

To ① Main Entrance & Naga Balustrades

Library

7

6

6

5

2nd Terrace

Gallery of 1000 Buddhas

Cruciform Platform

Library

1

2

Principal Sanctuary

3

4

Bas-reliefs

500 metres
500 yards

N

Eating ●
Blue Pumpkin
& food stalls 1

Top tips

Anti-clockwise round Angkor Wat's bas-reliefs

1. Western gallery The southern half represents a scene from the Mahabharata of a battle between the Pandavas (with pointed headdresses, attacking from the right) and the Kauravas. The two armies come from the two ends of the panel and meet in the middle. The southwest corner has been badly damaged – some say by the Khmer Rouge – but shows scenes from Vishnu's life.

2. Southern gallery The western half depicts Suryavarman II (builder of Angkor Wat) leading a procession. He is riding a royal elephant, giving orders to his army before leading them into battle against the Cham. The rank of the army officers is indicated by the number of umbrellas. The undisciplined, outlandishly dressed figures are the Thais.

3. Southern gallery The eastern half was restored in 1946 and depicts the punishments and rewards one can expect in the after life. The damned are depicted in the bottom row, while the blessed, depicted in the upper two rows, are borne along in palanquins surrounded by large numbers of bare breasted apsaras.

4. Eastern gallery The southern half is the best-known part of the bas-relief – the churning of the sea of milk by gods and demons to make ambrosia (the nectar of the gods which gives immortality). In the centre, Vishnu commands the operation. Below are sea animals and above, apsaras.

5. Eastern gallery The northern half is an unfinished representation of a war between the gods for the possession of the ambrosia. The gate in the centre was used by Khmer royalty and dignitaries for mounting and dismounting elephants.

6. Northern gallery Represents a war between gods and demons. Siva is shown in meditation with Ganesh, Brahma and Krishna. Most of the other scenes are from the *Ramayana*, notably the visit of Hanuman (the monkey god) to Sita.

7. Western gallery The northern half has another scene from the *Ramayana* depicting a battle between Rama and Ravana who rides a chariot pulled by monsters and commands an army of giants.

devaraja may have held audiences; his backdrop being the three-tiered central sanctuary. Commonly referred to as the Terrace of Honour, it is entered through the colonnaded processional gateway of the outer gallery. The transitional enclosure beyond it is again cruciform in shape. Its four quadrants formed galleries, once stocked full of statues of the Buddha. Only a handful of the original 1000-odd images remain.

The cluster of **central towers**, 12 m above the second terrace, is reached by 12 steep stairways, which represent the precipitous slopes of Mount Meru. Many historians believe that the upwards hike to this terrace was reserved for the high priests and king himself. Today, anyone is welcome but the difficult climb is best handled slowly by stepping sideways up the steep incline. The five lotus flower-shaped sandstone towers – the first appearance of these features in Khmer architecture – are believed to have once been covered in gold. The eight-storey towers are square, although they appear octagonal, and give the impression of a sprouting bud. The central tower is dominant, as is the Siva shrine and principal sanctuary, whose pinnacle rises more than 30 m above the third level and, 55m above ground level. This sanctuary would have contained an image of Siva in the likeness of King Suryavarman II, as it was his temple-mountain. But it is now a Buddhist shrine and contains statues of the Buddha.

More than 1000 sq m of bas-relief decorate the temple. Its greatest sculptural treasure is the 2-m-high **bas-reliefs**, around the walls of the outer gallery. It is the longest continuous bas-relief in the world. In some areas traces of the paint and gilt that once covered the carvings can still be seen. Most famous are the hundreds of figures of deities and apsaras in niches along the walls.

The royal city of Angkor Thom

Construction of Jayavarman VII's spacious walled capital, Angkor Thom (which means 'great city'), began at the end of the 12th century: he rebuilt the capital after it had been captured and destroyed by the Cham. Angkor Thom was colossal: the 100-m-wide moat surrounding the city, which was probably stocked with crocodiles as a protection against the enemy, extended more than 12 km. Inside the moat was an 8-m-high stone wall, buttressed on the inner side by a high mound of earth along the top of which ran a terrace for troops to man the ramparts.

Four great gateways in the city wall face north, south, east and west and lead to the city's geometric centre, the Bayon. The fifth, Victory Gate, leads from the royal palace (within the

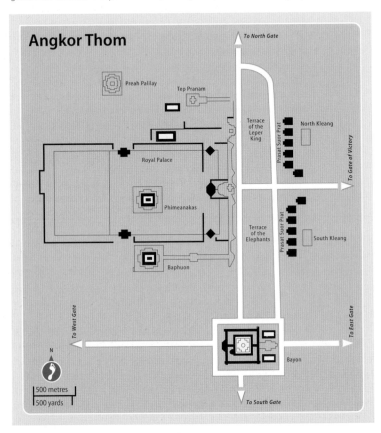

Angkor Thom

Bas-relief of a victory procession at the Bayon, Angkor Thom

Royal Palace) to the East Baray. The height of the gates was determined by the headroom needed to accommodate an elephant and howdah, complete with parasols. The flanks of each gateway are decorated by three-headed stone elephants, and each gateway tower has four giant faces, which keep an eye on all four cardinal points. Five causeways traverse the moat, each bordered by sculptured balustrades of nagas gripped, on one side, by 54 stern-looking giant gods and on the other by 54 fierce-faced demons. The balustrade depicts the Hindu legend of the churning of the sea (see p284).

The **South Gate** provides the most common access route to Angkor Thom, predominantly because it sits on the path between the two great Angkor complexes. The gate is a wonderful introduction to Angkor Thom, with well-restored statues of asuras (demons) and gods lining the bridge. The figures on the left, exhibiting serene expression, are the gods, while those on the right, with grimaced, fierce-looking heads, are the asuras.

The **Bayon** was Jayavarman VII's own temple-mountain, built right in the middle of Angkor Thom; its large faces have now become synonymous with the Angkor complex. It is believed to have been built between the late 12th century to early 13th century, around 100 years after Angkor Wat. The Bayon is a three-tiered, pyramid-temple with a 45-m-high tower, topped by four gigantic carved heads. These faces are believed to be the images of Jayavarman VII as a Bodhisattra, and face the four compass points. They are crowned with lotus flowers, symbol of enlightenment, and are surrounded by 51 smaller towers each with heads facing north, south, east and west. There are more than 2000 large faces carved throughout the structure. The first two of the three levels feature galleries of bas-relief (which should be viewed clockwise); a circular central sanctuary dominates the third level. The **bas-reliefs** which decorate the walls of the Bayon are much less imposing than those at Angkor Wat. The sculpture is carved deeper but is more naive and less sophisticated than the bas-reliefs at Angkor Wat. The relief on the outside depicts historical events; those on the inside are drawn from the epic world of gods and legends, representing the creatures who were supposed to haunt the subterranean depths of Mount Meru. In fact the reliefs on the outer wall illustrating historical scenes and derring-do with marauding Cham were carved in the early 13th century during the reign of Jayavarman; those on the inside which illuminate the Hindu cosmology were carved after the king's death when his successors turned from Mahayana Buddhism back to Hinduism. Two recurring themes in the bas-reliefs are the powerful king and the Hindu epics. Jayavarman is depicted in the throes of battle with the Cham – who are recognizable thanks to their unusual and distinctive headdress, which looks like an inverted lotus flower. The other bas-reliefs give a good insight into Khmer life at the time – the warrior elephants, ox carts, fishing with nets, cockfights and skewered fish drying on racks. Other vignettes show musicians, jugglers, hunters, chess players, people nit-picking hair, palm-readers and reassuringly down-to-earth scenes of Angkor citizens enjoying drinking sessions. In the naval battle scenes, the water around the war-canoes is depicted by the presence of fish, crocodiles and floating corpses.

The **Royal Palace**, to the north of the Bayon, had already been laid out by Suryavarman I: the official palace was in the front with the domestic quarters behind, its gardens surrounded by a laterite wall and moat. Suryavarman I also beautified the royal city with ornamental pools. Jayavarman VII simply improved his designs. In front of the Royal Palace, at the centre of Angkor Thom, Suryavarman I laid out the first Grand Plaza with the **Terrace of the Elephants** (also called the Royal Terrace). The 300-m-long wall derives its name from the large, life-like carvings of elephants in a hunting scene, adorning its walls. The 2½-m wall also features elephants flanking the southern stairway. It is believed it was the foundations of the royal reception hall. Royalty once sat in gold-topped pavilions at the centre of the pavilion, and here there are rows of garudas (bird-men), their wings lifted as if in flight. They were intended to give the impression that the god-king's palace was floating in the heavens, like the imagined flying celestial palaces of the gods. At the northeast corner of the 'central square' is the 12th-century **Terrace of the Leper King**, which may have been a cremation platform for the aristocracy of Angkor. The 7-m-high double terrace has bands of bas-reliefs, one on top of the other, with intricately sculptured scenes of royal pageantry and seated apsaras as well as nagas and garudas which frequented the slopes of Mount Meru. Above is a strange statue of an earlier date, which probably depicts the god of death, Yama, and once held a staff in its right hand. The statue's naked, lichen-covered body gives the terrace its name – the lichen gives the uncanny impression of leprosy. The **Phimeanakas** (meaning Celestial or Flying Palace in Sanskrit) inside the Royal Palace was started by Rajendravarman and used by all the later kings. Lions guard all four stairways to the central tower. It is now ruined but was originally covered in gold.

South of the Royal Palace is the **Baphuon**, built by Udayadityavarman II. The temple was approached by a 200-m-long sandstone causeway, raised on pillars, which was probably constructed after the temple was built. **Preah Palilay**, just outside the north wall of the Royal Palace, was also built by Jayavarman VII.

Around Angkor Thom

Phnom Bakheng

ⓘ *Either climb the steep hill (slippery when wet), ride an elephant to the top of the hill (US$15) or walk up the gentle zig-zag path the elephants take.*

Yasovarman's temple-mountain stands at the top of a natural hill, Phnom Bakheng, 60 m high, affording good views of the plains of Angkor. A pyramid-temple dedicated to Siva, Bakheng was the home of the royal linga and Yasovarman's mausoleum after his death. It is composed of five towers built on a sandstone platform. There are 108 smaller towers scattered around the terraces. The main tower has been partially demolished and the others have completely disappeared. It was entered via a steep flight of steps which were guarded by squatting lions. The steps have deteriorated with the towers. Foliate scroll relief carving covers much of the main shrine – the first time this style was used. This strategically placed hill served as a camp for various combatants, including the Vietnamese, and suffered accordingly.

Gigantic carved head at the Bayon, Angkor Thom (left); Prasat Kravan (right)

Ta Prohm

For all would-be Mouhots and closet Indiana Joneses, the temple of Ta Prohm, is the perfect lost-in-the-jungle experience. Unlike most of the other monuments at Angkor, it has been only minimally cleared of its undergrowth, fig trees and creepers. It is widely regarded as one of Angkor's most enchanting temples.

Ta Prohm was consecrated in 1186 – five years after Jayavarman VII seized power. It was built to house the divine image of the Queen Mother. The outer enclosures of Ta Prohm are somewhat obscured by dense foliage but reach well-beyond the temple's heart (1 km by 650 m). The temple proper consists of a number of concentric galleries, featuring corner towers and the standard gopuras. Other buildings and enclosures were built on a more ad hoc basis.

Within the complex walls lived 12,640 citizens. It contained 39 sanctuaries or prasats, 566 stone dwellings and 288 brick dwellings. Ta Prohm literally translates to the 'Royal Monastery' and that is what it functioned as, home to 18 abbots and 2740 monks. By the 12th century, temples were no longer exclusively places of worship – they also had to accommodate monks, so roofed halls were increasingly built within the complexes.

The trees burgeoning their way through the complex are predominantly the silk-cotton tree and the aptly named strangler fig. Naturally, the roots of the trees have descended towards the soil, prying their way through the temples foundations in the process. As the vegetation has matured, growing stronger, it has forced its way further into the temples structure, damaging the man-built base and causing untold destruction.

Banteay Kdei, Srah Srang, Prasat Kravan and Pre Rup

The massive complex of **Banteay Kdei**, otherwise known as 'the citadel of cells', is 3 km east of Angkor Thom. Some archaeologists think it may be dedicated to Jayavarman VII's religious teacher. The temple has remained in much the same state it was discovered in – a crowded collection of ruined laterite towers and connecting galleries lying on a flat plan, surrounded by a galleried enclosure. It is presumed that the temple was a Buddhist monastery and in recent years hundreds of buried Buddha statues were excavated from the site. Like Ta Prohm it contains a Hall of Dancers (east side), an open roof building with four separate quarters. The second enclosure runs around the perimeters of the inner enclosure. The third inner enclosure contains a north and south library and central sanctuary. The central tower was never finished. And the square pillars in the middle of the courtyard still can not be explained by scholars. There are few inscriptions here to indicate either its name or purpose, but it is almost certainly a Buddhist temple built in the 12th century, about the same time as Ta Prohm. The Lake (baray) next to Banteay Kdei is called **Srah Srang** – 'Royal Bath' – which was used for ritual bathing. The steps down to the water face the rising sun and are flanked with lions and nagas. This sandstone landing stage dates from the reign of Jayavarman VII but the Lake itself is thought to date back two centuries earlier. A 10th-century inscription reads 'this water is stored for the use of all creatures except dyke breakers', ie elephants. The baray (700 m by 300 m), has been filled with turquoise-blue waters for more than 1300 years. With a good view of Pre Rup across the lake, some archaeologists believe that this spot affords the best vista in the whole Angkor complex.

Prasat Kravan, built in 921, means 'Cardamom Sanctuary' and is unusual in that it is built of brick. By that time brick had been replaced by laterite and sandstone. It consists of five brick towers arranged in a line. The Hindu temple, surrounded by a moat, consists of five elevated brick towers, positioned in a North-South direction. Two of the five decorated brick towers contain bas-reliefs (the north and central towers). The central tower is probably the most impressive and contains a linga on a pedestal. The sanctuary's three walls all contain pictures of Vishnu.

Northeast of Srah Srang is **Pre Rup**, the State Temple of King Rajendravarman's capital. Built in 961, the temple-mountain representing Mount Meru is larger, higher and artistically superior than its predecessor, the East Mebon, which it closely resembles. Keeping with tradition of state capitals, Pre Rup marked the centre of the city, much of which doesn't exist today. The pyramid-structure, which is constructed of laterite with brick prasats, sits at the apex of an artificial, purpose-built mountain. The central pyramid-level consists of a three-tiered, sandstone platform, with five central towers sitting above. Its modern name, 'turning the body', derives from local legend and is named after a cremation ritual in which the outline of a body was traced in the cinders one way and then the other. The upper levels of the pyramid offer a brilliant, panoramic view of the countryside.

Preah Khan

The 12th-century complex of Preah Khan, one of the largest complexes within the Angkor area, was Jayavarman VII's first capital before Angkor Thom was completed. Preah Khan means 'sacred sword' and is believed to have derived from a decisive battle against the Cham, which created a 'lake of blood', but was invariably won by Jayavarman VII. It is similar in ground-plan to Ta Prohm (see p291) but attention was paid to the approaches: its east and west entrance avenues leading to ornamental causeways are lined with carved-stone boundary posts. Evidence of 1000 teachers suggests that it was more than a mere Buddhist monastery but most likely a Buddhist university. Nonetheless an abundance of Brahmanic iconography is still present on site. Around the rectangular complex, is a large laterite wall, surrounded by large garudas wielding the naga (each more than 5 m in height), the theme continues across the length of the whole 3-km external enclosure, with the motif dotted every 50 m. Within these walls lies the surrounding moat.

Preah Neak Pean

To the east of Preah Khan is the Buddhist temple Preah Neak Pean built by Jayavarman VII. The exquisite temple of Neak Pean is also a fountain, built in the middle of a pool and representing the paradisiacal Himalayan mountain-lake, Anaavatapta, from Hindu mythology. It is a small sanctuary on an island in the baray of Preah Khan. Two nagas form the edge of the island, and their tails join at the back. The temple pools were an important part of the aesthetic experience of Preah Khan and Neak Pean – the ornate stone carving of both doubly visible by reflection.

Outlying temples

The Roluos Group
The Roluos Group receives few visitors but is worth visiting if time permits. Jayavarman II built several capitals including one at Roluos, at that time called Hariharalaya. This was the site of his last city and remained the capital during the reigns of his three successors. The three remaining Hindu sanctuaries at Roluos are **Preah Ko**, **Bakong** and **Lolei**. They were finished in 879, 881 and 893 respectively by Indravarman I and his son Yashovarman I and are the best-preserved of the early temples. All three temples are built of brick, with sandstone doorways and niches. Sculptured figures which appear in the Roluos group are the crouching lion, the reclining bull (Nandi – Siva's mount) and the naga (snake).

Preah Ko, meaning 'sacred ox', was named after the three statues of Nandi (the mount of the Hindu god, Siva) which stand in front of the temple. Orientated east-west, there is a cluster of six brick towers arranged in two rows on a low brick platform, the steps up to which are guarded by crouching lions while Nandi, looking back, blocks the way. The front row of towers was devoted to Indravarman's male ancestors and the second row to the female. Indravarman's temple-mountain, **Bakong**, is a royal five-stepped pyramid-temple with a sandstone central tower built on a series of successively receding terraces with surrounding brick towers. Indravarman himself was buried in the temple. Bakong is the largest and most impressive temple in the Roluos Group by a long way. A bridge flanked by a naga balustrade leads over a dry moat to the temple. The central tower was built to replace the original one when the monument was restored in the 12th century and is probably larger than the original. The Bakong denotes the true beginning of classical Khmer architecture and contained the god-king's Siva linga. **Lolei** was built by Yashovarman I in the middle of Indravarman's baray. The brick towers were dedicated to the king's ancestors, but over the centuries they have largely disintegrated; of the four towers two have partly collapsed.

Banteay Srei
Banteay Srei, 25 km from Ta Prohm along a decent road, was built by the Brahmin tutor to King Rajendravarman, Yajnavaraha, grandson of Harshavarman, and founded in 967. Banteay Srei translates to 'Citadel of Women', a title bestowed upon it in relatively recent years due to the intricate apsara carvings that adorn the interior. The temple is considered by many historians to be the highest achievement of art from the Angkor period. The explicit preservation of this temple reveals covered terraces, of which only the columns remain, which once lined both sides of the

Garuda, Banteay Srei

Cambodia Angkor

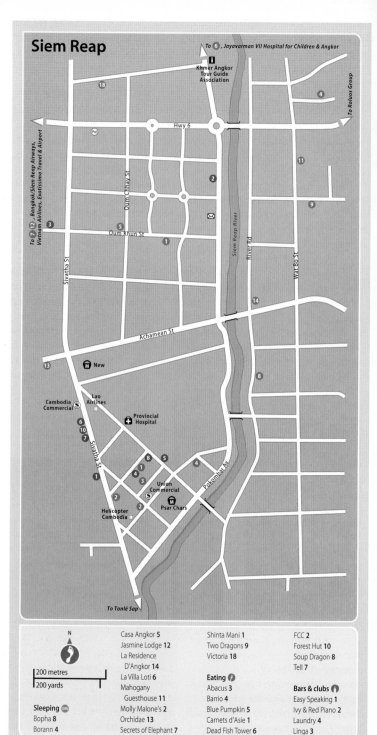

Siem Reap

To **6** , Jayavarman VII Hospital for Children & Angkor

Khmer Angkor
Tour Guide
Association

To Roluos Group

Hwy 6

Oum Chhay St

Oum Khun St

Sivatha St

Siem Reap River

River Rd

Wat Bo St

Achamean St

New

Cambodia
Commercial

Lao
Airlines

Provincial
Hospital

Sivatha St

Union
Commercial

Psar Chars

Helicopter
Cambodia

Pokombar Av

To **7** **12** , Bangkok/Siem Reap Airways,
Vietnam Airlines, Exotissimo Travel & Airport

To Tonlé Sap

N

200 metres
200 yards

Sleeping 🛏
Bopha **8**
Borann **4**

Casa Angkor **5**
Jasmine Lodge **12**
La Residence
  D'Angkor **14**
La Villa Loti **6**
Mahogany
  Guesthouse **11**
Molly Malone's **2**
Orchidae **13**
Secrets of Elephant **7**

Shinta Mani **1**
Two Dragons **9**
Victoria **18**

Eating 🍴
Abacus **3**
Barrio **4**
Blue Pumpkin **5**
Carnets d'Asie **1**
Dead Fish Tower **6**

FCC **2**
Forest Hut **10**
Soup Dragon **8**
Tell **7**

Bars & clubs 🍸
Easy Speaking **1**
Ivy & Red Piano **2**
Laundry **4**
Linga **3**

primary entrance. In keeping with tradition, a long causeway leads into the temple, across a moat, on the eastern side. The main walls, entry pavilions and libraries have been constructed from laterite and the carvings from pink sandstone. The layout was inspired by Prasat Thom at Koh Ker. Three beautifully carved tower-shrines stand side by side on a low terrace in the middle of a quadrangle, with a pair of libraries on either side enclosed by a wall. Two of the shrines, the southern one and the central one, were dedicated to Siva and the northern one to Vishnu; both had libraries close by, with carvings depicting appropriate legends. The whole temple is dedicated to Brahma. Having been built by a Brahmin priest, the temple was never intended for use by a king, which goes some way towards explaining its small size – you have to duck to get through the doorways to the sanctuary towers. Perhaps because of its modest scale Banteay Srei contains some of the finest examples of Khmer sculpture. Finely carved and rare pink sandstone replaces the plaster-coated carved-brick decoration, typical of earlier temples. All the buildings are covered in carvings: the jambs, the lintels, the balustered windows. Banteay Srei's ornamentation is exceptional – its roofs, pediments and lintels are magnificently carved with tongues of flame, serpents' tails, gods, demons and floral garlands.

Siem Reap ⬤🚲🛏🏊⬤⛰⬤⬤ ›› pp295-299

›› pp295-299

The nearest town to Angkor, Siem Reap is seldom considered as anything other than a service centre and it is true that without the temples, few people would ever find themselves here. The town has smartened itself up quite substantially in the past couple of years and, with the blossoming of hotels, restaurants and bars, it is now a pleasant place in its own right.

The Old Market area is the most touristed part of the town. Staying around here is recommended for independent travellers and those staying more than two or three days. A sprinkling of guesthouses are here but a much greater selection is offered just across the river, in the Wat Bo area.

Cambodia Angkor Listings

⬤ Sleeping

Siem Reap *p295*

A-B Casa Angkor, corner of Chhay St and Oum Khun St, T063-963658, www.casaangkorhotel.com. This is a good-looking, pleasant and well-managed 21-room hotel. Three classes of room, all decent size, well appointed and with cool wooden floors. Friendly reception and efficient staff. Restaurant, beer garden and reading room.

A-B Molly Malone's, Old Market area, T063-963533. Fantastic rooms with 4-poster beds and good clean bathrooms. Irish pub downstairs. Lovely owners. Recommended.

B Borann, T063-964740, www.borann.com. This is an attractive hotel in a delightful garden with a swimming pool. It is secluded and private. 5 small buildings each contain 4 comfortable rooms with terracotta floors

and a lot of wood. Some rooms have a/c, some fan only: price varies accordingly.

B La Villa Loti ('Coconut House'), 105 River Rd, T012-888403, resinf@lavillaloti.com. Fantastic guesthouse, with 8 rooms in a big, wooden house. Good for laying back in a deckchair, amongst the tropical gardens, after a tiring day at the temples. Internet, massage, bicycles. French run.

B Secrets of Elephants Guesthouse, Highway 6, T016-901901, info@angkortravel.com. Traditional wooden Khmer house, with just 8 rooms. French-run but English spoken. The garden is a mini jungle. The house is beautifully furnished with antiques, silks, ornaments and hangings. All rooms have their own private bathroom but not necessarily en suite. Breakfast included and other meals prepared to order. Some rooms a/c, some fan only.

Budget busters

Angkor sleeping and tours

LL **Victoria Angkor Hotel**, Route 6, Siem Reap, T063-760428, www.victoriahotels-asia.com. Perfection. A beautiful hotel, with that 1930s east-meets-west style that exemplifies the French tradition of 'art de vivre'. The superb decor make you feel like you are staying in another era. Each room is beautifully decorated with local fabrics and fantastic furniture. Swimming pool, open-air salas, jacuzzi and spa. It's the small touches and attention to detail that stands this hotel apart from the rest.

L-A **La Residence D'Angkor Hotel**, River Rd, T063-963390, angkor@pansea.com. This is a hotel to aspire to. With its beautifully laid out rooms all lavishly furnished with marble and hardwoods, it is reassuringly expensive. Each room has a huge, free-form bathtub – which is the perfect end to a day's touring. The pool is lined with handmade tiles in a variety of green hues in true Angkor style, like the rest of the hotel.

L-A **Shinta Mani**, junction of Oum Khum and 14th St, T063-761998, www.shintamani.com. This 18-room boutique, luxury hotel is wonderful in everyway: the design, the amenities, the food and the service. The hotel also offers a beautiful pool, library and has mountain bikes available. Provides vocational training to underprivileged youth.

Helicopters Cambodia, Old Market area, Siem Reap, T012-814500, helicopter.cam.s@online.com.kh, run 8-min charter flights to Angkor Wat for US$204 per person (1-2 people) or US$68 (3-5 people) – great for gaining a perspective on the sheer scale of the complex. It also provides a longer 14-min tour to some of the outlying temples, US$360 per person (1-2 people) or US$120 per person (3-5 people). For charter flights further afield, the company charges a whopping US$1400 per hr. Credit cards accepted (3% surcharge).

B-C **Bopha**, T063-964928, bopharesa@everyday.com.kh. Stunning hotel. Good rooms with all the amenities, decorated with local furniture and fabrics. Brilliant Thai-Khmer restaurant.

C-D **Two Dragons Guesthouse**, Wat Bo Village, T012-868551. Really nice, clean rooms with beautiful photographs decorating them. Good little Thai restaurant. Gordon, the owner of this place, is one of the well-briefed guys in Siem Reap and runs www.talesofasia.com website. He can organize a whole range of unique and exciting tours in the area.

D-F **Jasmine Lodge**, Highway 6, T012-784980, jasminelodge@ camnet.com.kh. Good budget accommodation, clean rooms (the outside ones are better). Lots of travel services. Often gets booked out in advance so contact them first.

D-F **Orchidae Guesthouse**, T012-939964, 012939965@mobitel.com.kh. Hammocks, restaurant and decent sized, clean rooms with shower or shared facilities.

E **Mahogany Guesthouse**, Wat Bo St, T063-963417, proeun@bigpond.com.kh. Fan and now some a/c. An attractive and popular guesthouse, lovely wooden floor upstairs (try to avoid staying downstairs), coffee-making facilities and a friendly crowd of guests.

🍴 Eating

Angkor *p277*

Near the moat there are a number of cheap food and drink stalls, bookshops and posse of hawkers selling film, souvenirs etc. Outside the entrance to Angkor Wat is a larger selection of cafés and restaurants including the sister restaurant to **Blue Pumpkin**, serving good sandwiches and breakfasts, ideal for takeaway.

Siem Reap *p295, map p294*

Abacus, Oum Khun St, off Sivatha, T012-644286. Considered one of the best restaurants in town – offering French and Cambodian food. A little further out from the main Old Market area. Everything is fantastic here, the fish is superb, the steak is to die for.

Barrio, Sivatha St, away from the central area. Fantastic French and Khmer food. A favourite of the expats. Recommended.

Carnets d'Asie, 333 Sivatha St, T016-746701. Primarily a French restaurant, also offering some Khmer and Thai dishes. Outdoor and indoor seating, amongst a garden, dotted with traditional Khmer parasols and a lovely water feature. Can't beat this one for atmosphere.

FCC, Pokamber Av, T063-760280. Sister to the Phnom Penh restaurant, this one is a bit more schmick. Good range of world-class food and drinks, nice surroundings. Great armchairs. Very sophisticated.

Blue Pumpkin, T063-963574. Western and Asian food and drinks. Sandwiches, ice cream, pitta, salads and pasta. White minimalist decor. Good breakfasts and cheap cocktails. Eat on the 2nd level. Branches at both the international and domestic airport terminals and across from Angkor Wat.

Bopha, east side of the river, slightly up from Passagio, T012-964928. Fantastic Thai-Khmer restaurant in a lovely, tranquil garden setting. One of the absolute best in town.

Dead Fish Tower, Sivatha St, T063-963060. Thai and Khmer restaurant in a fantastically eclectic modern Thai setting. Multiple platforms, quirky decorations, sculptures and Apsara dance shows, small putting range and a crocodile farm all add to the fantastic atmosphere of this popular restaurant.

Molly Malone's, T063-963533. Lovely Irish bar and restaurant offering classic dishes like Irish stew, shepherd's pie, roasts and fish and chips.

Soup Dragon, near the hospital, T063-964933. Serves a variety of Khmer and Vietnamese dishes but its speciality is soups in earthenware pots cooked at the table. Breezy and clean, a light and colourful location sitting on a corner terrace surrounded by plants. Upstairs bar, happy hour 1600-1930.

Tell, 374 Sivatha St, T063-963289. Swiss, German, Austrian restaurant and bar. Branch of the long-established Phnom Penh restaurant. Serves excellent fondue and raclette, imported beer and sausages. Reasonable prices and generous portions.

Forest Hut Restaurant, 21 Sivatha St. Large portions of well-cooked western and Asian dishes.

Orchidae Guesthouse, fantastic Asian meals and omelettes.

🍸 Bars and clubs

Siem Reap *p295, map p294*

Dead Fish, bar and informal diner serving Thai food.

Easy Speaking, T012-865332. Good little bar with inside and outside seating.

Ivy, popular bar and restaurant opposite Old Market. 0700 until late. Pool table, all-day breakfast for US$4.

Laundry, near the Old Market, turn right off Bar St, T016-962026. Funky little bar open till late.

Linga, Laneway behind Bar St, T012-246912. Gay-friendly bar offering a wide selection of cocktails. Great whisky sour.

Red Piano, Bar St, Old Market Area, T012-854150. A comfortable bar/diner furnished with large wicker armchairs.

Temple Bar, Bar St. Popular drinking hole, dimly lit, good music.

Entertainment

Siem Reap *p295, map p294*

Shadow puppetry is one of the finest performing arts of the region. The **Bayon Restaurant**, Wat Bo road, has regular shadow puppet shows in the evening. Local NGO, Krousar Thmey, often tour its shadow puppet show to Siem Reap. The show is performed by underprivileged children (who have also made the puppets) at **La Noria Restaurant** (Wed, 1930 but check as they can be a tad irregular). Donations accepted.

A popular Sat evening attraction is the one-man concert put on by **Dr Beat Richner** (Beatocello), founder of the Jayavarman VII hospital for children. Run entirely on voluntary donations the 3 hospitals in the foundation need US$9 million per year in order to treat Cambodian children free of charge. He performs at the hospital, on the road to Angkor, at 1915, 1 hr, free admission but donations gratefully accepted. An interesting and worthwhile experience.

Shopping

Siem Reap *p295, map p294*

Outside Phnom Penh Siem Reap is about the only place whose markets are worth browsing in for genuinely interesting souvenirs. **Old Market (Psar Chars)** is not a large market but stallholders and keepers of the surrounding shops have developed quite a good understanding of what tickles the appetite of foreigners: Buddhist statues and icons, reproductions of Angkor figures, silks, cottons, kramas,

sarongs, silverware, leather puppets and rice paper rubbings of Angkor bas-reliefs are unusual mementos.

Chantiers Écoles, down a short lane off Sivatha St, T/F063-964097. School for orphaned children which trains them in carving, sewing and weaving. Products are on sale under the name Les Artisans d'Angkor and raise 30% of the school's running costs.

Senteurs d'Angkor, opposite Old Market, T063-964801. Sells a good selection of handicrafts, carvings, silverware, silks, handmade paper, cards, scented oils, incense, pepper and spices.

Activities and tours

Siem Reap *p295, map p294*

Therapies

Khmer, Thai, reflexology and Japanese massage are readily available. Many masseuses will come to your hotel.

Franginpani, near old market, down the side street opposite Kokoon, T063-757120. Professional masseuse, offering aromatherapy, reflexology and other treatments.

Seeing Hands massage, T063-836487, by seeing impaired individuals, US$3 an hr. Highly recommended.

Tour operators

Asian Trails, No. 273,1 Group, Kruos Village, T063-964595, www.asiantrails.com. Offers a broad selection of tours to Angkor and beyond. Also cruises and biking trips.

ATS, Sivatha St, T063-760041. All manner of local arrangements, boat tickets, minibus tickets, car hire. Visa service. Internet service.

Data Sight Travel, 430 Sivatha St, T063-963081, info@datasighttravel.com. Very, very helpful travel agent. Organizes tours, ticketing and a whole range of tourist services. Ask for Lim.

Exotissimo Travel, No 300, Highway 6 , T063-964323, www.exotissimo.com. Tours of Angkor and sites beyond.

Hidden Cambodia Adventure

Tours, T012-934412, www.hidden cambodia.com. Specializing in dirt bike tours to some of Cambodia's remote areas and off-the-track temple locations. Recommended for the adventurers.

Journeys Within, on the outskirts of Siem Reap towards the temples, T063-964748, www.journeys-within.com. Specializes in private, customized tours, visiting temples and experiencing the everyday lives of Cambodians.

RTR Tours, No 331, Group 7, Modul 1 (in the Old Market Area) T063-964646, www.rtrtours.com.kh. Organizes tours plus other travel services, including ticketing. Friendly and helpful.

Terre Cambodge, on Frangipani premises, Old Market area, T012-843401, www.terrecambodge.com. Tours with a twist, including cruises on an old sampan. Particularly good option for tours of the floating villages of the Tonlé Sap. Not cheap but worth it for the experience.

⊖ Transport

Siem Reap *p295, map p294*
Air
Airline availability and flight schedules are particularly prone to sudden change, so ensure you check /book well in advance.
Airline offices   Bangkok Airways/Siem Reap Airways, Highway 6, T063-380191. 6 flights a day from Bangkok. **Helicopters Cambodia**, near Old Market, T012-814500. A New Zealand company offers chartered flights around the temples. **Lao Airlines**, opposite provincial hospital, T/F063-963283, 3 flights a week to Vientiane via Pakse. **President Airlines**, Sivatha St, T063-964338. **Vietnam Airlines**, Highway 6, T063-964488, www.vietnamairlines.com. Also general sales agent in town opposite provincial hospital, T063-964929.

Bicycle
Khemara, opposite the Old Market, T063-964512, rents bicycles for US$2 per day.

Bus
Neak Krorhorm Travel, GST, Mekong Express and **Capitol** go to and from Siem Reap. Most buses depart Phnom Penh bus station between 0630 and 0800 and the same from Siem Reap (departing near the Old Market). The best bus service to Phnom Penh is the Mekong Express, US$6 if you buy (just down from the DHL office. It has the quickest service (about 5 hrs).

Helicopter and balloon
For helicopter flights, see Budget busters, p296. A cheaper (but not nearly as fun) alternative for a good aerial view is to organize a balloon ride above the temples. The tethered balloons float 200 m above Angkor Wat for about 10 mins, US$10 per trip. The balloon company is based about 1 km from the main gates from Angkor Wat, on the road from the airport to the temples.

❶ Directory

Siem Reap *p295*
Banks   Cambodia Commercial Bank, 130 Sivatha St. Currency and TC exchange. Advance on Visa, MasterCard, JCB, AMEX. **Mekong Bank**, 43 Sivatha, Mon-Fri, Sat am, US dollar TCs cashed, 2% commission, cash advance on Visa and JCB cards only. **Union Commercial Bank**, north of Old Market, Mon-Fri and Sat am. Cash advance on MasterCard and Visa (no commission). Cash TCs. **Internet**   Rates vary but should be around 3000 riel per hr. Most internet cafés now offer internet calls. **Medical services**   The medical facilities are okay here but by now means of an international standard. In most cases it is probably best to fly to Bangkok. **Naga International Clinic**, Highway 6 (airport road), T063-965988. International medical services. 24-hr emergency care. **Post office**   Pokamber Av, on the west side of Siem Reap River but can take up to a month for mail to be delivered, 0700-1700.

Vientiane and northern Laos

Wat Mai, Luang Prabang

80977

Job Assignments

CAL STEAM ™ WHOLESALE PLUMBING DISTRIBUTOR

■ 777 Mariposa Street, San Francisco, CA 94107 ■ (415) 861-3071 ■ 1-800-334-PIPE

Molly's mother
— 971-5639 —
Jessica's friend
Mary.

ask@mary.com
(handwritten)

$$21 \times 15$$
$$105$$
$$21$$
$$315$$

Vientiane, Laos' capital city, has a small-town atmosphere, fusing rural life with a sprinkling of metropolitan bustle; merging east and west, communist and capitalist into a colourful amalgam. A short trip north of Vientiane is Vang Vieng, a favourite of adventure enthusiasts, with caving, kayaking, tubing, trekking and more on offer.

North again is Luang Prabang, the enchanting former royal capital. A spellbinding plethora of gilded temples, shrines, stupas and French colonial buildings decorate the magical town, which is surrounded by mountains and anchored at the crossways of the Nam Khan and Mekong rivers. Nearby are the Kwang Si Falls, where billowing cascades create natural, turquoise pools. The areas further north are home to a rich tapestry of wilderness, with vast tracts of jungle and jagged mountains inhabited by many ethnic minority groups. The areas around Muang Sing, Luang Namtha, Phongsali and Nong Khiaw are perfect for trekking or just kicking back.

For something different, the northeast encompasses the mysterious Plain of Jars and Vieng Xai's Pathet Lao caves, both testament to the country's enigmatic and, at times, horrific, history.

Introduction

Northern Laos

Ratings

Landscape
★★★★

Relaxation
★★

Activities
★★★

Wildlife
★★

Culture
★★★

Costs
$$-$

In 1563, King Setthathirat made the riverine city of Vientiane the capital of Laos. Or, to be more historically accurate, Wiang Chan, the 'City of the Moon', became the capital of Lane Xang.

Snuggled in a curve of the Mekong, Vientiane is the most modest capital city in the region. Colourless concrete communist edifices sit alongside chicken farmers; outdoor aerobics fanatics are juxtaposed with locals making merit at the city's wats; and a couple of traffic lights command a dribble of chaotic cars, bikes, tuk-tuks and buses. Vientiane's appeal lies in its largely preserved fusion of Southeast Asian and French colonial culture, expressed especially in its food and buildings.

⚋ **Getting there** Plane, bus, car, songthaew.
⚊ **Getting around** Taxi, tuk-tuk, cycling, walking, motorbike
⊖ **Time required** Up to 4 days
⚌ **Weather** Hot and sticky in summer, very wet in the rainy season (Jun-Jul)
⚊ **Sleeping** A variety of hotels and guesthouses but limited at the upper end.
⚋ **Eating** Range of international restaurants and bars.
▲▲ **Activities and tours** Tubing, caving, kayaking and elephant trekking.
★ **Don't miss...** Tubing on the Nam Xong River ▸▸ p323.

Close to the city is Xieng Khuan, popularly known as the Buddha Park, a bizarre collection of statues and monuments, while, to the north, Vang Vieng, the adventure capital of Laos, attracts backpackers with a multitude of outdoor activities.

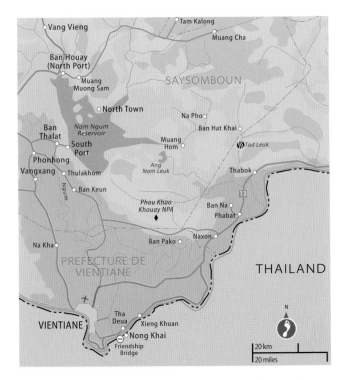

Ins and outs ◉ ▸ *p323*

Getting there

Air Most visitors arrive in Vientiane by air, the great bulk on one of the daily connections from Bangkok, with **Thai Air** or **Lao Airlines**. **Lao Airlines** (www.laoairlines.com) also runs international flights to and from Hanoi, Ho Chi Minh City, Phnom Penh and Siem Reap. **Wattay International Airport** lies 6 km west of the town centre, T021-212066. The international terminal is the bigger building on the west side. Vientiane is the hub of Laos' domestic airline system and to travel from the north to the south or vice versa it is necessary to change planes here. Both terminals have restaurants, telephones, taxis and information booths. Only taxis are allowed to pick up passengers at the airport (US$5 to the centre of town, 20 minutes) although tuk-tuks can drop off here. Tuk-tuks can be taken from the main road and sometimes lurk at the far side of the airport, near the exit (40,000 kip to the centre).

A cheaper alternative from Thailand is to fly from Bangkok to **Udon Thani** on a budget airline (www.nokair.co.th, www.airasia.com) and then continue by road to Vientiane via the Friendship Bridge (see below), which lies just 25 km downstream from the capital (allow three hours). Shuttle buses from Udon Thani airport usually run to the border after every flight. There are several flights a day between Udon Thani and Bangkok. ▸▸ *For further flight information, see Essentials p18.*

Bus There are three public bus terminals in Vientiane. The **Southern bus station** is 9 km south of the city centre on Route 13. Most international buses bound for Vietnam depart from here as well as buses to southern and eastern Laos. The station has a VIP room, restaurants, a few shops, mini-mart and a guesthouse nearby.

⊘ ZOLL DOUANE Border with Thailand: Friendship Bridge

The bridge is 25 km southeast of Vientiane; catch bus No 14 from the Talaat Sao terminal (1000 kip) or hire a tuk-tuk US$5 (see p325). The border is open 0600-2200 daily. Shuttle minibuses take punters across the bridge every 20 minutes for 2500 kip or ฿20, stopping at the Thai and Lao immigration posts where an overtime fee is charged after 1630 and at weekends.

There are good facilities at the Lao border, including a telephone box, a couple of duty free shops, some drinks and snack stalls and a post office. Allow up to one hour 30 minutes to get to the bridge and through formalities on the Lao side. The paperwork is pretty swift, unless you are arriving in Lao and require a visa or are leaving the country and have over-stayed your visa.

The Thai side is über-efficient but not nearly as friendly. Tuk-tuks wait to take punters to Nong Khai (10 minutes); Udon Thani is another hour further on; taxis from the Thai side of the border charge about ฿500 to get you there; add another ฿300 from the Lao side. If you get stuck in Nong Khai, **Mut Mee Guesthouse** is recommended. From Udon Thani you can get to Bangkok easily by budget airline. Discount airlines (Air Asia, Nok Air) fly several times daily. From Udon Thani, you can catch a minibus or taxi to the Lao border or a bus directly to the Talaat Sao bus terminal in Vientiane for ฿80 . Taking the Udon/Friendship Bridge option between Bangkok and Vientiane will probably only add one hour to your journey, since immigration at Wattay Airport tends to be slow. Another option is to catch the overnight train from Nong Khai to Bangkok's Hualamphong Station (11 hrs, ฿800 for a sleeper). Buses also run from both Udon Thani and Nong Khai to Bangkok.

306	The **Northern bus station** is on Route T2, about 3 km north of the centre before the airport, T021-260255, and serves destinations in northern Laos. Most tuk-tuks will take you there from the city for 10,000-15,000 kip; ask for "*Bai thay song*". There are English-speaking staff at the help desk.

The **Talaat Sao bus station** is across the road from the Morning Market, in front of Talaat Kudin, on the eastern edge of the city centre. This station serves destinations within Vientiane Province, buses to and from the Thai border and international buses to Nong Khai and Udon Thani in Thailand. It is also a good place to pick up a tuk-tuk.

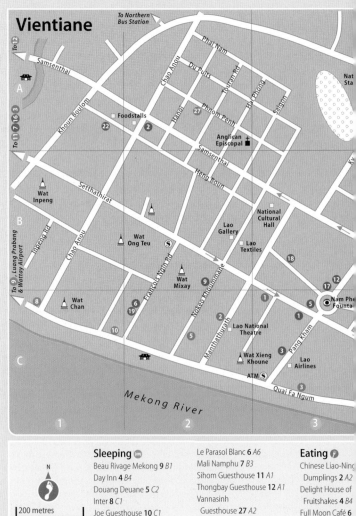

Sleeping
Beau Rivage Mekong **9** *B1*
Day Inn **4** *B4*
Douang Deuane **5** *C2*
Inter **8** *C1*
Joe Guesthouse **10** *C1*
Lane Xang **3** *C3*
Le Parasol Blanc **6** *A6*
Mali Namphu **7** *B3*
Sihom Guesthouse **11** *A1*
Thongbay Guesthouse **12** *A1*
Vannasinh
  Guesthouse **27** *A2*

Eating
Chinese Liao-Ning
  Dumplings **2** *A2*
Delight House of
  Fruitshakes **4** *B4*
Full Moon Café **6**
Joma **1** *C3*

Vientiane is small and manageable and is one of the most laid-back capital cities in the world. The local catch phrase 'bopenyang' (no worries) has permeated through every sector of the city, so much so that even the mangy street dogs look completely chilled out. The core of the city is negotiable on foot and even outlying hotels and places of interest are accessible by bicycle. Cycling remains the most flexible way to negotiate the city. It can be debilitatingly hot at certain times of year but there are no great hills to struggle up. If cycling doesn't appeal, a combination of foot and tuk-tuk or small 110-125cc scooters take the effort out of sightseeing.

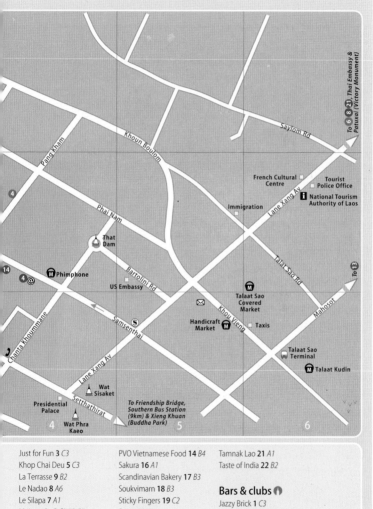

Just for Fun **3** C3
Khop Chai Deu **5** C3
La Terrasse **9** B2
Le Nadao **8** A6
Le Silapa **7** A1
Maison du Café **12** B3
Nong Vong **13** B6

PVO Vietnamese Food **14** B4
Sakura **16** A1
Scandinavian Bakery **17** B3
Soukvimarn **18** B3
Sticky Fingers **19** C2
Sweet Home
 & Bakery **20** B1

Tamnak Lao **21** A1
Taste of India **22** B2

Bars & clubs

Jazzy Brick **1** C3
Muzaic **2** C2
Wind West **3** A1

Vientiane can be rather confusing for the first-time visitor as there are few street signs and most streets have two names, pre- and post-revolutionary but, because Vientiane is so small and compact, it doesn't take long to get to grips with the layout. The names of major streets (*thanon*) usually correspond to the nearest wat, while traffic lights, wats, monuments and large hotels serve as directional landmarks.

Tourist information

Tourist office Lao National Tourism Authority ⓘ *Lane Xang (towards Patuxai), T021-212769, T021-212248 for information,* can provide information regarding ecotour operators and trekking opportunities. The Tourist Police are next door.

Background

Vientiane is an ancient city. There was probably a settlement here, on a bend on the left bank of the Mekong, in the 10th century but knowledge of the city before the 16th century is sketchy. From the chronicles, scholars do know that King Setthathirat decided to relocate his capital here in the early 1560s. It seems that it took him four years to build the city, constructing a defensive wall (hence 'Wiang', meaning a walled or fortified city), along with Wat Phra Kaeo and a much enlarged That Luang. Vieng Chan remained intact until 1827 when it was ransacked by the Siamese; this is why many of its wats are of recent construction.

The city was abandoned for decades and erased from the maps of the region. It was only conjured back into existence by the French, who commenced reconstruction at the end of the 19th century. They built rambling colonial villas and wide tree-lined boulevards, befitting their new administrative capital, Vientiane. At the height of American influence in the 1960s, it was renowned for its opium dens and sex shows.

For the moment, the city retains its unique innocence: DJs are officially outlawed (although this is not enforced); there is a 2330 curfew; a certain percentage of music played at restaurants and bars every day is supposed to be Lao (overcome by banging out the Lao tune quota at 0800) and women are urged to wear the national dress, the *sinh*. However, to describe the Lao government as autocratic is unfairly negative. Vientiane's citizens are proud of their cultural heritage and are usually very supportive of the government's attempts to promote it. The government is trying, by and large, to maintain the national identity and protect its citizens from harmful outside influences, which becomes more understandable when you consider that every country bordering Laos is facing an AIDS epidemic.

Sights ⊟🏛🎭🎵❄️⭕🔺📷☕ » *pp315-327*

Most of the interesting buildings in Vientiane are of religious significance. All tour companies and many hotels and guesthouses will arrange city tours and excursions to surrounding sights but it is just as easy to arrange a tour independently with a local tuk-tuk driver; the best English speakers (and thus the most expensive) can be found in the car park beside Nam Phou. Those at the Morning Market (Talaat Sao) are cheaper.

That Luang

ⓘ *That Luang Rd, 3.5 km northeast of the city centre. Daily 0800-1200, 1300-1600 (except 'special' holidays). 2000 kip; a booklet about the wat is on sale at the entrance.*

That Luang is Vientiane's most important site and the holiest Buddhist monument in the country. The golden spire looks impressive at the top of the hill, overlooking the city. According to legend, a stupa was first built here in the third century AD by emissaries of the Moghul Emperor Asoka. Excavations on the site, however, have only located the remains of

That Luang

an 11th- to 13th-century Khmer temple, making the earlier provenance doubtful in the extreme. The present monument, encompassing the previous buildings, was built in 1566 by King Setthathirat, whose statue stands outside. Plundered by the Thais and the Chinese Haw in the 18th century, it was restored by King (Chao) Anou at the beginning of the 19th century.

The reliquary is surrounded by a square cloister, with an entrance on each side, the most famous on the east. There is a small collection of statues in the cloisters, including one of the Khmer King Jayavarman VII. The cloisters are used as lodgings by monks who travel to Vientiane for religious reasons and especially for the annual **That Luang Festival** (see p320). The base of the stupa is a mixture of styles – Khmer, Indian and Lao – and each side has a *hor*

Patuxai

vay or small offering temple. This lowest level represents the material world, while the second tier is surrounded by a lotus wall and 30 smaller stupas, representing the 30 Buddhist perfections. Each of these originally contained smaller golden stupas but they were stolen by Chinese raiders in the 19th century. The 30 m-high spire dominates the skyline and resembles an elongated lotus bud, crowned by a stylized banana flower and parasol. It was designed so that pilgrims could climb up to the stupa via the walkways around each level.

Patuxai (Victory Monument)
ⓘ *Junction of That Luang Rd and Lane Xang Av. Mon-Fri 0800-1100, 1400-1630, but these hours seem to be posted only for fun, 1000 kip.*
At the end of That Luang is the oriental answer to Paris' Arc de Triomphe and Vientiane's best known landmark, the Patuxai (Victory Monument). It was built by the former regime in memory of those who died in the wars before the Communist takeover, but the cement ran out before its completion. Refusing to be beaten, the regime diverted hundreds of tonnes of cement, part of a US aid package to help with the construction of runways at Wattay Airport, to finish off the monument in 1969.

Wat Sisaket
ⓘ *Junction of Lane Xang Av and Setthathirat Rd. Daily 0800-1200, 1400-1600. 2000 kip. No photographs in the sim.*
Further down Lane Xang is the **Morning Market** or **Talaat Sao** (see p321) and beyond, is one of Vientiane's two national museums, **Wat Sisaket**. Home of the head of the Buddhist community in Laos, Phra Sangka Nagnok, it is one of the most important buildings in the capital and houses more than 7000 Buddha images. Wat Sisaket was built in 1818 during the reign of King Anou. A traditional Lao monastery, it was the only temple that survived the Thai sacking of the town in 1827-1828, making it the oldest building in Vientiane.

The main sanctuary, or **sim**, with its sweeping roof, shares many stylistic similarities with Wat Phra Kaeo (see below): window surrounds, lotus-shaped pillars and carvings of deities held up by giants on the rear door. The sim contains 2052 Buddha statues (mainly terracotta, bronze and wood) in small niches in the top half of the wall. There is little left of the Thai-style *jataka* murals on the lower walls but the depth and colour of the originals can be seen from the few remaining pieces.

The **cloisters** were built during the 1800s and were the first of their kind in Vientiane. They shelter 120 large Buddhas in the attitude of subduing Mara, plus a number of other images in assorted mudras, and thousands of small figures in niches, although many of the most interesting Buddha figures are now in Wat Phra Kaeo.

The whole ensemble is washed in a rather attractive shade of caramel and, combined with the terracotta floor tiles and weathered roof, is an attractive sight.

Phou Khao Khouay National Park

Phou Khao Khouay (pronounced *poo cow kway*) is one of Laos' premier national parks. The park extends across 2000 sq km and incorporates an attractive sandstone mountain range. It is crossed by three large rivers, smaller tributaries and two stunning waterfalls at Tad Leuk and Tad Sae, which weave and weft their way into the Ang Nam Leuk reservoir, a stunning man-made dam and Lake that sits on the outskirts of the park. Within the protected area is a diverse array of wildlife, including wild elephants, gibbons, tigers, clouded leopards and Asiatic black bears.

Elephant treks within the park can be arranged at **Ban Na** (T020-220 8286) where there is also an elephant observation tower. The village's sugar cane plantations attract a herd of wild elephants, which have, in the past, destroyed the villagers' homes and even killed a resident but now the village, in conjunction with the **National Tourism Authority** (T021-212248), has started running trekking tours to see these massive creatures in their natural habitat. One- to three-day treks through the national park cross waterfalls, pass through pristine jungle and, with luck, offer the opportunity to spot the odd wild elephant. This is the only ecotour of its kind in Laos. Advance notice is required so it's advisable to book with a tour operator in Vientiane. Visit www.trekkingcentrallaos.com and contact the National Tourism Authority in Vientiane or **Green Discovery Tours** (see p322).

Ban Hat Khai is home to 90 families from the Lao Loum and Lao Soung ethnic groups. It is also a starting point for organized treks through mountain landscapes, crossing the Nam Mang River and the Phay Xay cliffs. Tad Sae Falls can be reached on a boat trip from the village.

⊖ The park is northeast of Vientiane along Route 13 South. To get to Ban Na you need to stop at Tha Pabat Phonsanh, 80 km northeast of Vientiane; the village is a further 2 km from here. For Ban Hat Khai continue on Route 13 to Thabok, where a songthaew or boat can take you the extra 7 km to the village. Buses to Paksan from the Talaat Sao bus station and That Luang market in Vientiane stop at Thabok.

Going further

Wat Phra Kaeo

ⓘ *Setthathirat Rd. Daily 0800-1200, 1300-1600, closed public holidays. 5000 kip. No photographs in the sim.*

Opposite Wat Sisaket is **Wat Phra Kaeo**. It was originally built by King Setthathirat in 1565 to house the Emerald Buddha (or Phra Kaeo), now in Bangkok, which he had brought from his royal residence in Chiang Mai. It was never a monastery but was kept instead for royal worship. The Emerald Buddha was removed by the Thais in 1779 and Wat Phra Kaeo was destroyed by them in the sacking of Vientiane in 1827. The whole building was in a bad state of repair after the sackings, the only thing remaining fully intact was the floor.

The building was expertly reconstructed in the 1940s and 1950s and is now surrounded by a garden. During renovations, the interior walls of the wat were restored using a plaster made of sugar, sand, buffalo skin and tree oil.

The **sim** stands on three tiers of galleries, the top one surrounded by majestic, lotus-shaped columns. The tiers are joined by several flights of steps and guarded by *nagas*. The main, central (southern) door is an exquisite example of Lao wood sculpture with carved angels surrounded by flowers and birds; it is the only notable remnant of the original wat. (The central door at the northern end, with the larger carved angels supported by ogres, is new.) The sim now houses a superb assortment of Lao and Khmer art and some pieces of Burmese and Khmer influence, mostly collected from other wats in Vientiane. Although people regularly come and pray here the wat's main purpose is as a quasi-museum.

Xieng Khuan

ⓘ *Route 2 (25 km east of Vientiane). Daily 0800-1700. 5000 kip, plus 5000 kip for cameras; food vendors sell drinks and snacks. Bus No 14 (1 hr), tuk-tuk (100,000 kip), private vehicle hire (US$15), or cycle because the road follows the river and is reasonably level the whole way.*

Otherwise known as the **Garden of the Buddhas** or **Buddha Park**, Xieng Khuan is close to the frontier with Thailand. It has been described as a Lao Tiger Balm Gardens and has reinforced concrete Buddhist and Hindu sculptures of Vishnu, Buddha, Siva and various other assorted deities and near-deities. There's also a bulbous-style building with three levels containing smaller sculptures of the same gods.

The garden was built in the late 1950s by a priest-monk-guru-sage-artist called Luang Pu Bunleua Sulihat, who studied under a Hindu *rishi* in Vietnam and then combined the Buddhist and Hindu philosophies according to his own very peculiar view of the world. He left Laos because his anti-communist views were incompatible with the ideology of the Pathet Lao (or perhaps because he was just too weird) and settled across the Mekong near the Thai town of Nong Khai, where he proceeded to build an equally revolting and bizarre concrete theme park for religious schizophrenics, called Wat Khaek. With Luang Pu's forced departure from Laos his religious garden came under state control and it is now a public park.

Vang Vieng ⬤⬤⬤⬤⬤⬤ ▶▶*p315-327.*

The drive from Vientiane to Vang Vieng, on the much improved Route 13, follows the valley of the Nam Ngum north and then climbs steeply onto the plateau where Vang Vieng is located, 160 km north of Vientiane. The surrounding area is inhabited by the Hmong and Yao hill peoples and is particularly picturesque: craggy karst limestone scenery, riddled with caves, crystal-clear pools and waterfalls. As many visitors have remarked, in the early morning the views are reminiscent of a Chinese Sung Dynasty painting.

The town itself is also attractive, nestled in a valley on the bank of the Nam Xong River, amid a misty jungle. It enjoys cooler weather and offers breathtaking views of the imposing mountains of Pha Tang and Phatto Nokham.

The town's laid-back feel has made it a popular haunt for the backpacker crowd, while the surrounding landscape has helped to establish Vang Vieng as Laos' premier outdoor activity destination, especially for rock climbing, caving and kayaking. Elephant trekking is also possible. Its popularity in many ways has also become its downfall: neon lights, pancake stands, 'happy' this, 'happy' that and an oversupply of pirated *Friends* videos now pollute this former oasis. Nevertheless, the town and surrounding area is still full of wonderful things to do and see.

Safety Although Laos is a very safe country for tourists, a disproportionate number of accidents and crimes seem to happen in Vang Vieng. Theft is routinely reported, ranging from robberies by packs of kids targeting tubers on the river to the opportunist theft of items from guests' rooms. Most guesthouses won't take responsibility for valuables left in rooms, instead it is usually advisable to hand in valuables to the management. Otherwise, you will need to padlock your bag. Another major problem is the sale of illegal drugs. Police often go on sting operations and charge fines of up to US$600 for possession. Legal issues aside, numerous travellers have become seriously ill from indulging in the 'happy' supplements supplied by the restaurants. There are also, of course, significant safety risks involved in adventure activities ▲▲▶▶ *p322*.

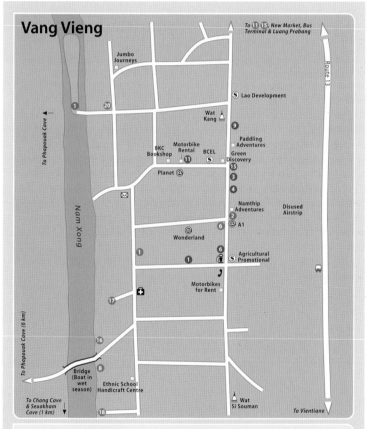

Vang Vieng

To 11 15, New Market, Bus Terminal & Luang Prabang

Route 13

Jumbo Journeys

Nam Xong

To Phapouak Cave

S Lao Development

Wat Kang

9

Paddling Adventures

BKC Bookshop — Motorbike Rental 11 — BCEL S — Green Discovery 15

Planet @

3

4

Namthip Adventures

2

@ A1

6

Wonderland

Disused Airstrip

To Phapouak Cave (6 km)

1

1

6

Agricultural Promotional

♪

Motorbikes for Rent

17

16

8

Bridge (Boat in wet season)

Ethnic School Handicraft Centre

To Chang Cave & Seuakham Cave (1 km)

18

Wat Si Souman

To Vientiane

N
Not to scale

Sleeping 🛏
Amphone **1**
Ban Sabai
Bungalows **17**
Erawan **6**
Le Jardine
Bungalows **18**
Nam Song **8**
Organic Mulberry
Farm **11**

Thavonsouk Resort **16**
Vang Vieng Eco
Lodge **15**
Vang Vieng Orchid **20**

Eating 🍴
Ahea **1**
Give Pizza a Chance **9**
Luang Prabang Bakery **11**
Nangbot **3**

Nazim's **4**
Organic Farm Café **6**
Vieng Champa **15**

Bars & clubs 🍸
Island Bar **1**
Jay Dees **2**

Karst scenery around Vang Vieng

Caves

ⓘ *Each cave has an entrance fee of 3000 -10,000 kip and many have stalls where you can buy drinks and snacks. You can buy hand-drawn maps from the town but all the caves are clearly signposted in English from the main road so these are not really necessary.*

Vang Vieng is best known for its limestone caves, sheltered in the mountains flanking the town. Pretty much every guesthouse and tour operator offers tours to the caves (the best of these is **Green Discovery**) and, although some caves can be accessed independently, it is advisable to take a guide to a few as they are dark and difficult to navigate. Often children from surrounding villages will take tourists through the caves for a small fee. Don't forget to bring a torch, or even better a headlamp, which can be picked up cheaply at the markets both in Vang Vieng and Vientiane.

Of Vang Vieng's myriad caves, **Tham Chang** is the most renowned of all. Tham Chang penetrates right under a mountain and is fed by a natural spring, perfect for an early morning dip. From the spring it is possible to swim into the cave for quite a distance (bring a waterproof torch, if possible). The cave is said to have been used as a refuge during the 19th century from marauding Chinese Haw bandits and this explains its name: *chang* meaning 'loyal' or 'steadfast'. To reach the cave, cross the rickety bamboo bridge in rainy season or wade across during the dry season. For your US$1 or 10,000 kip entrance fee you not only get into the caves but the lighting system will also be turned on. Although the cave is not the most magnificent, it serves as a superb lookout point.

Another popular cavern is **Tham Poukham** ⓘ *7 km from Vang Vieng, 5000 kip*. The cave is often referred to as the cave of the Golden Crab and is highly auspicious. It's believed that if you catch a golden crab you will have a lifetime of fortune. To get there you need to cross the foot-bridge near the **Nam Song Hotel**, and then follow the road for a further 6 km until you reach the village of Ban Nathong. From the village the cave is 1 km walk and a short climb up quite a steep hill. Mossy rocks lead the way into the main cavern area where a large bronze reclining Buddha is housed. Here there is an idyllic lagoon, with glassy green-blue waters, that's great for a swim.

Tham None ⓘ *4 km north of Vang Vieng, 5000 kip*, is known locally as the 'Sleeping Cave' because 2000 villagers took refuge in it during the war. The large cave is dotted with stalagmites and stalactites, including the 'magic stone of Vang Vieng', which reflects light. Lots of bats reside in the grotto. In the wet season it is possible to swim here.

Tham Xang ① *14 km north of Vang Vieng on the banks of the Nam Xong, 2000 kip,* also known as the 'Elephant Cave', is named after the stalagmites and stalactites that have created an elephant formation (you may need to squint to see it). The cave also contains some Buddha images, including the Footprint of Buddha. From this cave there is a signposted path that leads to **Tham Hoi** ① *15 km from town, 5000 kip,* a long spindly cave that is believed to stretch for at least 7 km. It takes about two hours to explore the cavern and at the end of one of the off-shoots is a crystal-clear pool, perfect for a dip. The cave is guarded by a large Buddha figure and is home to loads of bats, which the locals capture by splashing water on them. Do not visit Tham Hoi without a guide as there have been a couple of fatalities here.

● Sleeping

Vientiane *p304, map p306*
Hotels priced over US$30 accept major credit cards.

A-B Beau Rivage Mekong, Fa Ngum Rd, T021-243350, www.hbrm.com. One of the first western-style boutique hotels in Vientiane. Beautifully furnished, with superb Mekong River views. Its location, just out of the centre of town, ensures peace and quiet but it's still only a 5-min walk to the hustle and bustle.

A-B Lane Xang Hotel, Fa Ngum Rd, T021-214100/7, CLHotel@yahoo.com. This was the original 'luxury' hotel in Vientiane, built by the French in the 1960s. It has an undefinable charm, despite the fact that some of its retro-hip Soviet fittings and furniture have been ripped out to make way for a more contemporary look. The a/c rooms are now well equipped, with excellent bathrooms, making the hotel the best value in town, with a great central position on the river. Go for a deluxe room, with its own bar and velour bed fittings, to indulge in a 1970s, porn-flick nostalgia trip. The service here is unmatched. The international restaurant has traditional Lao dancing shows every night and a cabaret on Wed, with a bird impressionist and contortionist. Other facilities include a pool, nightclub, bar, snooker hall, sauna and fitness centre.

A-C Hotel Day Inn, Pang Kham Rd, T021-214792, dayinn@laotel.com. Run by a friendly Cambodian, this renovated villa is in a good position in quiet part of town, just to the north of the main concentration of bars and restaurants. Attractive, airy, clean, large rooms, with a/c, and excellent bathrooms. Restaurant serves tasty food. Also bike hire.

A-C Inter Hotel, 24-25 Fa Ngum Rd, T021-242842, www.laointerhotel.com. This Thai-owned hotel is one of the oldest in Vientiane, now operating for over 30 years. Recent renovations have made it sparkle: mosaics, relief sculptures and murals adorn the walls, and traditional shutters, silk hangings and furniture feature in every room. The a/c rooms are light and spacious with slick bathrooms and fantastic balconies overlooking the Mekong. Lovely atrium, a good restaurant (excellent steak) and a gift shop with beautiful antique costumes.

B-C Douang Deuane, Nokeo Khoummane Rd, T021-222301/3. From the exterior, this looks like a classic communist edifice, but the rooms are fantastic: parquet wood floors, art deco furniture, excellent bathrooms, satellite TV and a decent size. Try and get a balcony room for lovely patchwork views of the roofs of the city. Also has restaurant, free airport transfer, DHL service and cars for rent. The room rates have remained competitive and include breakfast.

B-C Le Parasol Blanc, behind National Assembly, close to Victory Gate (not very well marked), T021-216091. A very attractive leafy haven. Spacious a/c rooms, with wooden floors and sizeable bathrooms. Some look onto the garden, with sitting area in front, the most expensive are alongside the pool. Charming place, well run, many French visitors. Restaurant (see Eating, below).

B-C Mali Namphu Guesthouse, 114 Pang Kham Rd, T021-215093, www.mali.com. It looks like a small shopfront but the façade is deceiving, as the foyer opens onto a beautifully manicured courtyard surrounded by quaint, terraced rooms. Clean, bright rooms are traditionally decorated with a modern twist and come with a/c, hot water, cable TV and a fantastic breakfast. Friendly staff.

B-D Vannasinh Guesthouse, 51 Phnom Penh Rd, T021-218707. Huge warren-like house, well managed, with friendly staff (good English and French spoken). Clean, large rooms, some with a/c. Bicycles for hire. Well priced and very popular.

D Thongbay Guesthouse, off Luang Prabang Rd, turn right before the Novotel, Ban Non Douang, T/F021-242292, thongbay@laotel.com. Lovely traditional Lao house set in a lush tropical garden. Rooms have traditional-style fittings, mosquito nets and fan or a/c. The guesthouse also runs cooking classes on request (US$10), including purchasing ingredients at the local market. The only drawback of this place is its distance from the city centre. Perfect if you wish to relax.

E Joe Guesthouse, 112 Fa Ngum Rd, T021-241936, joe_guesthouse@yahoo.com. Wonderful family-run guesthouse on the riverfront. Light, clean and airy. Good coffee shop downstairs. Fantastic service.

E Sihom Guesthouse, 27 Sihom Rd, T021-214562. Mixture of rooms, some with TV, some with a/c. All with rattan furniture and huge en suite bathrooms with hote water. The rooms are kept in excellent condition and a café out front serves snacks. Good value for fan rooms.

Vang Vieng *p312, map p313*

The town's popularity has ensured a uniformity among almost all places catering to tourists: most restaurants feature the same menu and there isn't much individuality in guesthouses either. Most are geared to the needs of travellers and offer a laundry service, guides, bicycles, inner tubes (for the river) and maps of the area. They are good sources of information regarding the caves and other sights in the vicinity of town.

A-C Thavonsouk Resort, T021-511096, thavonsouk@hotmail.com. This lovely place offers several different styles of accommodation. There is a traditional Lao house, decorated with Lao furnishings, suitable for a family or big group, plus suites (TV, fridge, bath, a/c) and standard accommodation. Fantastic restaurant. Keep your eye out for local home-grown pop star, Aluna, who runs the place.

B-C Ban Sabai Bungalows, T021-511088. A stunning complex of individual bungalows in a spectacular location, with all the modern fittings. Hot water, a/c, breakfast included.

B-C Nam Song Hotel, T021-213506, milestone at the gate. This hotel sits in a beautiful location overlooking the Nam Xong within its own spacious grounds, but has a bit of a communist institution feel. However, the renovations underway at the time of publication looked pretty promising and, when the final product is finally unveiled, expect large rooms with bath, TV and a/c.

D Vang Vieng Orchid, T021-511172. Comfortable fan or a/c rooms. Hot water in the bathrooms, clean tiled floors, very comfortable rooms. Friendly owners. The rooms with the private balconies are well worth the few extra dollars because you will have your own personal piece of the phenomenal view.

E-F Erawan, T021-511093. This place is a hotbed of tourists and is a font of useful information on things to do in the area. Rooms are similar to others in town, but this place also boasts a TV, bar and restaurant, and is always buzzing.

F Amphone T021-511180. Nicer than many alternatives, although nothing particularly out of the ordinary. Spotless rooms with hot water en suite bathrooms and a friendly proprietor, who also just happens to be a dab hand at knocking up beautifully tailored trousers, shorts and skirts in his shop opposite.

F Le Jardine Bungalows, about 900 m from the centre of town along the river, T021-5111340. There are 3 sets of bungalows here: the best are superb; the worst, falling down. It is far enough from town for the surrounding beauty to remain undisturbed but close enough for convenience (a tuk-tuk runs into town until 2000). The views are remarkable and the restaurant is quite good too.

Out of town
Places on the outskirts are great for those who wish to escape into a more natural landscape. The lack of facilities and transport in the area ensures tranquillity but also makes it difficult to get to town.
B-C Vang Vieng Eco-Lodge, 7 km north of town, T021-5513785, tatluang@laotel.com. Although this isn't an eco-lodge it is still an exceptionally beautiful place to stay. Set on the banks of the river with stunning gardens and beautiful rock formations, it is a perfect place to get away from it all. The 10 chalet-style bungalows have been nicely decorated, with beautiful balconies, comfortable furnishings and big hot water bath. Management assures a tuk-tuk is just a phone call away. Good Lao restaurant. Also arranges activities. Low season discount.
E-F Organic Mulberry Farm, 3 km north of town, T021-511220, www.laofarm.org. This mulberry farm is a very popular drop-off spot for tubers. Basic rooms with mosquito net, dorm accommodation, full board. Cheaper rates in the low season. Hugely popular restaurant, serving great starfruit wine and famous mulberry pancakes.

🅾 Eating

Vientiane *p304, map p306*
Chinese
The Chinese quarter is around Chao Anou, Heng Boun and Khoun Boulom and is a lively spot in the evenings. There are a number of noodle shops here, all of which serve a palatable array of vermicelli, *muu daeng* (red pork), duck and chicken. **Chinese Liao-ning Dumpling Restaurant**, Chao Anou Rd, is a firm favourite with expats.

European
₸₸₸-₸₸ Le Nadao, Ban Donmieng (on the right-hand side of the Patuxai roundabout), 1100-1400, 1700-2230 daily. This place is difficult to find but definitely worth every second spent searching the back streets of Vientiane in the dark. Sayavouth, who trained in Paris and New York, produces simply delectable French cuisine: soups, venison, lamb, puddings. Fantastic. The US$5 set lunch menu is one of the best lunches you will get in town.
₸₸₸-₸₸ Le Silapa, Sihom Rd, opposite Shell petrol station, T021-219689, 1130-1400, 1800-2200 daily. Anthony and Fred provide a fantastic menu and atmosphere for fine dining without blowing the budget. Great set lunch menu. Part of the profits are donated to disadvantaged families, usually for expensive but life-saving surgical procedures. Closes annually for a month during Jul.
₸₸-₸ La Terrasse, 55/4 Nokeo Koummane Rd, T021-218550, Mon-Sat 1100-1400, 1800-2200. This is the best European restaurant in terms of variety and price. Large fail-safe menu offering French, European, Lao and Mexican food. Good desserts, especially the rich chocolate mousse, and a good selection of French wine. Fantastic service. Reasonable prices with an excellent 'plat du jour' each day.

Indian
₸₸₸-₸₸ Taste of India, Lao Hotel, 53/9 Hengboun Rd, T030-5255403, 1200-1400 and 1700-2230 daily. By far the best Indian in Vientiane. A delicious lunch buffet is available. A bit pricier than other Indian restaurants but worth it.

International

Quite a few places listed here under 'international' also serve good Lao/Thai food and a handful also experiment with fusion cuisine.

¶¶-¶ **Full Moon Café**, François Ngin Rd, T021-243373, 1000-2200 daily. Delectable Asian fusion cuisine and western favourites. Huge pillows, good lighting and great music make this place very relaxing. Fantastic chicken wrap and some pretty good Asian tapas. Also a book exchange.

¶¶-¶ **Sticky Fingers**, François Ngin Rd, T021-215972, Tue-Sun 1000-2300. Very popular small restaurant and bar serving Lao and international dishes including fantastic salads, pasta, burgers and such like. Fantastic comfort food and the best breakfast in town. Great cocktails, lively atmosphere, nice setting. The staff, particularly Mr Nam, are as sharp as a tack. Deliveries available. Stickies should be the first pit-stop for every visitor needing to get grounded quickly, as food aside, the expats who frequent the joint are full to the brim with local knowledge.

Japanese

¶¶¶-¶ **Sakura**, Luang Prabang Rd, Km 2/ Soi 3 (the soi runs along the side of the Novotel), T021-212274, Mon 1730-2200, Tue-Sun 1030-1400 and 1730-2200. Regarded as the best Japanese food in town. Expensive for Vientiane but good value by international standards. The restaurant is in a converted private house.

Korean sindat

The Korean-style barbeque, *sindat*, is extremely popular, especially among the younger Lao, as it is a very social event and very cheap. It involves cooking finely sliced meat on a hot plate in the middle of the table, whilst forming a broth with vegetables around the sides of the tray. Reminiscent of a '70s fondue evening. **Seendat**, Sihom Rd, 1730-2200 daily, is a favourite amongst the older Lao for its clean food and good atmosphere.

Lao

The absolutely best place to get Lao food is from the open-air stalls that line the banks of the Mekong along Fa Ngum. The restaurants are ridiculously low on price and high on atmosphere, particularly at night with their flickering candles. From time to time the government kicks all the eateries off the patch but they usually return with a vengeance. The **Dong Palane Night Market**, on Dong Palane, and the night markets near the corner of Chao Anou and Khoun Boulom Rd are also good places to go for Lao stall food. There are various other congregations of stalls and vendors around town, most of which set up shop around 1730 and close down by 2100. Be sure to sample Lao ice cream with coconut sticky rice.

¶¶¶-¶¶ **Soukvimarn**, T021-214441, 1100-1400, 1800-2100. Heavily influenced by traditional southern Lao flavours. Well worth the experience as it offers the opportunity to tempt the tastebuds with a wider variety of Lao cuisine than most other eateries offer.

¶¶¶-¶¶ **Tamnak Lao Restaurant**, That Luang Rd, T021-413562, 1200-2200. It's well worth deviating from the main Nam Phou area for a bite to eat here. This restaurant and its sister branch in Luang Prabang have a reputation for delivering outstanding Lao and Thai food, usually prepared with a modern twist.

¶¶-¶ **Just for Fun**, 57/2 Pang Kham Rd, opposite Lao Airlines. Good Lao food with vegetarian dishes, coffees, soft drinks and the largest selection of teas in Laos, if not Southeast Asia. The atmosphere is relaxed with a/c, newspapers and comfy chairs (also sells textiles and other handicrafts).

¶¶-¶ **Khop Chai Deu**, Setthathirat Rd, on the corner of Nam Phou Rd, 0800-2330 daily. This recently renovated place is one of the city's most popular venues with both locals and travellers. Garden seating, good atmosphere at night with soft lantern lighting, and an eclectic menu of Indian, Italian, Korean and international dishes (many of which come from nearby restaurants). The best value are the local Lao dishes, though, which are made on site and toned down for the falang palate. Also serves draft or bottled beer at a pleasant a/c bar. Excellent lunch buffet.

Vietnamese

♦ **Nong Vong Restaurant**, on the road between Sisavong Rd and That Luang, T021-415818. This little, tucked away eatery is an all-time favourite with long-term expats who refer to it as 'Vongs'. Impeccable service and a huge selection of superb Lao, Thai and Vietnamese-inspired dishes. You can take 4 people to dinner and still come back with change from US$10. Open for dinner, but lunch seems to be its forte.

♦ **PVO Vietnamese Food**, 344 Samsenthai Rd, T021-215265, 0700-2100/2200. A firm favourite. Full menu of freshly prepared Vietnamese food but best known for baguettes, stuffed with your choice of paté, salad, cheese, coleslaw, vegetables and ham. Bikes and motorbikes for rent too. Keep an eye out for the miniature dog wearing the Hannibal Lector style dog-mask – a very popular doggy accessory with those Vientiane citizens paranoid about rabies. Brilliant cheap food and a joyfully raucous atmosphere makes this a fantastic choice.

Cafés, cakeshops and juice bars

Pavement cafés are ten a penny in Vientiane. You need not walk more than half a block for some hot coffee or a cold fruit shake. On Chao Anon you'll find **Liang Xiang Bakery**, **Sweet Home** and **Nai Xiang Chai** (good juices and shakes). **Joma** is on Setthathirat Rd, **Maison du Café**, 70 Pang Kham Rd, the **Scandinavian Bakery**, Nam Phou Circle, and **Delight House of Fruit Shakes**, Samsenthai Rd.

Vang Vieng *p312, map p313*

There is a string of eating places on the main road through town. Generally, the cuisine available includes hamburgers, pasta, sandwiches, basic Asian dishes and

what seems to have become the local speciality, the 'Israeli Salad'. Most of the restaurants offer 'happy' upgrades – marijuana or mushrooms in your pizza, cake or lassi. Although many people choose the 'happy' offerings some of these wind up very ill.

♦♦-♦ **Ahea**, T021-511141. Sweet little place, set away from the main strip and offering a good line in decent, cheap Lao food. The milkshakes are to die for and the breakfast comes highly recommended. A welcome break for anyone looking to escape the crowds.

♦♦-♦ **Give Pizza a Chance**. This little place offers a broad sample of western fillers, including pesto spaghetti, salads, burgers and baked potatoes. Lao food is referred to as 'ethnic food' on the menu.

♦♦-♦ **Luang Prabang Bakery Restaurant**, just off the main road, near BCEL. Excellent pastries, cakes and shakes and pretty delicious breakfasts.

♦♦-♦ **Nangbot**, T021-511018. This proper sit-down restaurant is one of the oldest tourist diners in town and serves a few traditional dishes, such as bamboo shoot soup and *laap* with sticky rice, alongside the usual western fare.

♦♦-♦ **Nazim's**, T021-511214. Largest and most popular Indian in town. Good range of South Indian and buriyani specialities, plus selection of vegetarian meals.

♦♦-♦ **Organic Farm Cafe**, further down the main road. Small café offering over 15 different tropical fruit shakes and a fantastic variety of food. Mulberry shakes and pancakes are a must and the harvest curry stew is absolutely delicious. The sister branch is at the **Organic Mulberry Farm** (see Sleeping).

♦♦-♦ **Vieng Champa Restaurant**, T021-511037. Refreshingly this family-run restaurant seems to have a greater selection of Lao food than most other places on the street. Most meals between 15,000 and 20,000 kip. The only drawback is the highly unflattering green fluorescent lighting.

🎵 Bars and clubs

Vientiane *p304, map p306*
Bars
There are a number of bar stalls, which set up in the evening along Quai Fa Ngum (the river road); a good place for a cold beer as the sun sets. Most bars will close at 2300 in accordance with the local curfew laws; some places seem to be able to stay open past this time although that varies on a day-to-day basis. Government officials go through phases of shutting down places and restricting curfews.
Jazzy Brick, Setthathirat Rd, near Phimphone Market, is a very sophisticated small modern den; **Khop Chai Deu**, Setthathirat Rd, is probably the most popular bar for tourists in a casual setting with nightly band. **Muzaik**, Nokeo Khoummane Rd, is a funky little bar that is a popular haunt with locals as the last stop on Fri and Sat nights; **Sticky Fingers**, François Ngin Rd, is a small and intimate bar and restaurant run by two Australian ladies; **Wind West**, opposite Russian Cultural Centre by traffic lights, Luang Prabang Rd, is very popular with expats and tourists, as it usually stays open after 2300. Many wild nights happen here.

Vang Vieng *p312, map p313*
Island Bar, across the footbridge on the river. Crowds tend to gather here in the dry season.
Jay Dees, main street. Very popular, if pokey. The punters jam pack the place, giving it a very cosy feel.

🎵 Entertainment

Vientiane *p304, map p306*
Traditional dance
Lane Xang Hotel puts on an excellent traditional dance show every night, 1900-2145, in its restaurant, accompanied by Lao musicians, while you eat.
Lao National Theatre, Manthaturath Rd, T021-242978. Daily shows of Lao dancing,

2030. Performances represent traditional dance of lowland Lao as well as some minority groups. Tickets cost US$7.

✴ Festivals and events

Vientiane *p304, map p306*
1st weekend in Apr Pi Mai (Lao New Year) is celebrated with a 3-day festival and a huge water fight.
12 Oct Freedom of the French Day
Oct Boun Souang Heua (Water Festival) is a beautiful event on the night of the full moon at the end of Buddhist Lent. Candles are lit in all the homes and a candle-lit procession takes place around the city's wats and through the streets. Then, thousands of banana-leaf boats holding flowers, tapers and candles are floated out onto the river. The boats signify your bad luck floating away. On the second day, boat races take place, with 50 or so men in each boat; they power up the river in perfect unison. Usually, a bunch of foolhardy expats also tries to compete, much to the amusement of the locals.
Nov (moveable) Boun That Luang is celebrated in all of Vientiane's *thats* but most notably at That Luang (the national shrine). Originally a ceremony in which nobles swore allegiance to the king and constitution, it amazingly survived the communist era. On the festival's most important day, **Thak Baat**, thousands of Lao people pour into the temple at 0600 and again at 1700 to pay homage. Monks travel from across the country to collect alms from the pilgrims. It is a really beautiful ceremony, with monks chanting and thousands of people praying. Women who attend should invest in a traditional *sin*. A week-long carnival surrounds the festival with fireworks, music and dancing.

Shopping

Vientiane *p304, map p306*

Clothing and textiles

Coleur d'Asie, Nam Phou Circle. Modern-style Asian clothing. A bit expensive but quality high-end fusion fashion.

Ekhor Boutique, Pang Kham Rd, T021-517247/668. A small shop boasting a high quality selection of clothes and handicrafts, with prices to match.

Lao Textiles by Carol Cassidy, Nokeo Koummane Rd, T021-212123, Mon-Fri 0800-1200, 1400-1700, Sat 0800-1200. Exquisite silk fabrics, including *ikat* and traditional Lao designs, made by an American in a beautifully renovated colonial property. Dyeing, spinning, designing and weaving all done on premises (and can be viewed). Pricey, but many of the weavings are real works of art; custom-made pieces available on request.

Mandarina, Samsenthai Rd, T021-223857. Beautiful contemporary fashions in Lao silk, great colours, designed by stylish half-French Isabelle Souvanlasy.

Yani, Mixay Arcade, Setthathirat Rd. French-designed fashion using local fabrics, good quality and good value (by European standards), also a small selection of handicrafts.

Handicrafts and antiques

The main shops are along Setthathirat, Samsenthai and Pang Kham. The **Talaat Sao** (Morning Market) is also worth a browse, with artefacts, such as appliquéd panels, decorated hats and sashes, basketwork both old and new, small and large wooden tobacco boxes, sticky-rice lidded baskets, axe pillows, embroidered cushions and a wide range of silver work.

Oot-Ni Art Gallery, 306 Samsenthai Rd, with another door on Heng Boun Rd, T021-215911, T020-51453. A real Aladdin's cave of handicrafts and artefacts on the 1st floor including cottons and silks. Quite pricey but worth a look. Also has a branch in the morning market.

T'Shop Lai Gallery, Wat Inpeng Soi. Funky studio exhibiting local sculptures and art. Artists can be seen at work every day except Sun. Media include coconut shells, wood and metal, proceeds from sales are donated to Lao Youth projects.

Markets

Vientiane has several excellent markets. **Talaat Sao** (Morning Market), off Lane Xang Av, is currently undergoing major renovations that are expected to be finished sometime in 2007 but it's still the biggest and the best. It's busiest in the mornings (from around 1000), but operates all day. There are money exchanges here (quite a good rate), and a good selection of foodstalls selling western food, soft drinks and ice cream sundaes. It sells imported Thai goods, electrical appliances, watches, DVDs and CDs, stationery, cosmetics, a selection of handicrafts, an enormous choice of Lao fabrics, and upstairs there is a large clothing section, silverware, some gems and gold and a few handicraft stalls.

Supermarket

Phimphone Market, Setthathirath Rd, opposite Khop Chai Deu Restaurant. Known for its red chicken logo, this supermarket has everything a foreigner could ask for in terms of imported food, drink, magazines, translated books, personal hygiene products, household items and much more. Friendly efficient service and Phimphone herself is a source of information on Vientiane and Laos.

Activities and tours

Vientiane *p304, map p306*

Cooking

Thongbay Guesthouse (see Sleeping), T021-242292. Cooking classes. All aspects covered, from purchasing the ingredients – to eating the meal.

Cycling

Bicycles are available for hire from several places in town, see Transport, p94. A good outing is to cycle downstream along the banks of the Mekong. Cycle south on Tha Deua Rd until km 5 and then turn right down one of the tracks (there are a number) towards the riverbank. A path, suitable for bicycles, follows the river beginning at about km 4.5. There are monasteries and drinks sellers en route to maintain interest and energy.

Massage, saunas and spas

The best massage in town is given by the blind masseuses in a little street off Samsenthai Rd, 2 blocks down from Simuang Minimart (across from Wat Simuang). There are 2 blind masseuse businesses side by side and either one is fantastic: **Traditional Clinic**, T020-5659177, and **Porm Clinic**, T020-627633 (no English spoken). They are marked by blue signs off both Khou Vieng and Samsenthai rds.

LV Spa, Samsenthai Rd, T030-5256699, daily 0900-2000. The first large-scale spa in town and has certainly raised the bar in terms of service. Featuring all the usual forms of treatment at a fraction of the prices you'd expect to pay in the west.

Papaya Spa, opposite Wat Xieng Veh, T021-216550, daily 0900-2000. Surrounded by beautiful gardens. Massage, sauna, facials.

Tour operators

To organize any kind of ecotour , visit the **National Tourism Authority**. Most agents will use 'eco' somewhere in their title but this doesn't necessarily mean anything.

Asian Trails, Unit 1, Ban Hai Sok, Chanthabouly, T021-263936, www.asiantrails.com. Southeast Asia specialists.

Diethelm Travel, Nam Phou Circle, T021-213833, www.diethelm-travel.com.

Exotissimo, 6/44 Pang Kham Rd, T021-241861, www.exotissimo.com. Tours and travel services. Excellent service.

Green Discovery Laos, Setthathirat Rd, next to Xayoh Café, T021-251564, www.greendiscoverylaos.com. Specializes in ecotours and adventure travel.

Lao Travel-Eco Tourism Co, 248 Khou Vieng Rd, T021-263063, www.laoecotour.com. Quite upmarket tour company providing an interesting variety of travel experiences.

Weaving and dyeing courses

Houey Hong Vocational Training Centre, Ban Houey Hong, 20 mins north of Vientiane, T021-560006, hhwt@laotel.com. This small NGO runs training courses for underprivileged ethnic minorities. Tourists are welcome to join in the course for US$15 per day. Ask a songthaew to drop you off at Talaat Houey Hong, and follow the track 200 m west. Call the centre in advance.

Vang Vieng *p312, map p313*

Tour guides are available for hiking in the hills, rafting, visiting the caves and minority villages from most travel agents and guesthouses. Safety issues need to be considered when taking part in any adventure activity. There have been fatalities in Vang Vieng from boating, trekking and caving accidents. The Nam Xong River can flow very, very quickly during the wet season (Jul and Aug) and tourists have drowned here. Make sure you wear a life jacket during all water-borne activities and time your trip so you aren't travelling on the river after dark. A price war between tour operators has led to cost cutting, resulting in equipment that is not well maintained or does not exist at all. With all tour operators it is imperative you are given life jackets and helmets where necessary and that canoes, ropes, torches and other equipment is in a good state of repair. The more expensive, reputable companies are often the best option (see also Vientiane Tour operators, above). Reliable tour operators include:

Green Discovery, attached to Xayoh

Café. Probably the best operator in town. Very professional and helpful.

Namthip Adventures, main road. For adventure tourism it's better to go with either **Paddling Adventures**.

Paddling Adventures, Keomani Restaurant, T020-5624783.

Elephant trekking

Jumbo Journey, close to the **Vang Vieng Orchid Hotel**, T020-5624923. This outfit offers great half-day treks through and along the river. These trips are combined with visiting a cave. US$20.

Kayaking and rafting

Kayaking is a very popular activity around Vang Vieng and competition between operators is fierce. There are a wide variety of trips available, ranging from day trips (incorporating a visit to the caves and surrounding villages), to kayaking all the way to Vientiane, US$15-25. This adventure usually takes about 6 hrs, including a 30-min drive at the start and finish. All valuables are kept in a car which meets kayakers at the end of their paddle.

A few companies also offer 2-day rafting trips down the Nam Ngum River. The trip includes several grades 4 and 5 rapids and usually an overnight camp. US$100 per person but prices tend to be reduced for groups of more than 3.

Both **Green Discovery** and **Paddle Asia** are recommended for kayaking and rafting trips. Be wary of anyone operating intensive rafting or kayaking trips through risky areas during the wet season as it can be very dangerous.

Rock climbing

Vang Vieng is the only really established rock climbing area in the country, with over 50 sites recognized in the locality, ranging from grade 5 to 8A+. By 2005 almost all of these climbs had been 'bolted'. **Green Discovery** runs climbing courses almost every day in high season (US$20-45 per day, including equipment rental). The best climbing sites include:

Sleeping Cave, **Sleeping Wall** and **Tham Nam Them**.

Trekking

Almost all guesthouses and agents offer hiking trips, usually incorporating a visit to caves and minority villages and, possibly, some kayaking or tubing. Tour operators provide an English-speaking guide, all transport and lunch for US$10-15 per day.

Tubing

No trip to Vang Vieng is complete without tubing down the Nam Xong. Floating slowly along the river is an ideal way to take in the stunning surroundings of limestone karsts, jungle and rice paddies. The drop-off point is 3 km from town near the organic farm, where several bars and restaurants have been set up along the river. Try and start early in the day as it's dangerous to tube after dark and the temperature of the water drops dramatically. Tour operators and guesthouses in town offer tube rental, life jackets and drop-off for US$3-4. It is essential you wear a life jacket as people have drowned on the river, particularly in the wet season (Jul and Aug) when the river swells and flows very, very quickly.

⊖ Transport

Vientiane p304, map p306
Air

Lao Airlines, 2 Pang Kham Rd (near Fa Ngum), T021-212054, www.laoairlines.com, also at Wattay Airport; T021-212057 for international flights (0800-1700 daily), T021-512000 for domestic flights (Mon-Fri 0800-1200, 1300-1600, Sat 0800-1200). **Thai Airways**, Head Office, Luang Prabang Rd not far past the Novotel, T021-222527/9, www.thaiairways.com, Mon-Fri 0830-1200, 1300-1500, Sat 0830-1200; also on Pang Kham Rd, next to the bookshop and at Wattay Airport, 1st floor, Room 106, T021-512024, 0700-1200 and

1300-1600 daily. **Vietnam Airlines** Lao Plaza Hotel, T021-252618, www.vietnamairlines.com.vn, Mon-Fri 0800-1200, 1330-1630, Sat 0800-1200.

Lao Airlines to **Bangkok** (80 mins) daily; to **Luang Prabang** (40 mins) up to 3 flights daily; to **Pakse** (70 mins), 4 flights a week. To **Siem Reap** twice a week via Pakse and once direct. **Thai Airways** to **Bangkok** (70 mins), daily. **Vietnam Airlines**, to **Hanoi** (60 mins), daily. To **Saigon** (3 hrs), daily.

Bicycle and motorbike

For those energetic enough in the hot season, bikes are the best way to get around town. Many hotels and guesthouses have bikes available for their guests. Expect to pay about 5000-10,000 kip per day depending on the state of the machine. There are also many bike hire shops around town. Markets, post offices and government offices usually have 'bike parks' where it is advisable to leave your bike. A small minding fee is charged.

Motorbikes are for hire from many guesthouses and shops. Expect to pay US$5 per day and leave your passport as security. Insurance is seldom available anywhere on motorbikes but most places will also hire out helmets, a necessity.

PVO, Samsenthai Rd, has the most reliable selection of bicycles, motorbikes and trail bikes.

Bus

Vientiane has three main public bus terminals: **Northern**, **Southern** and **Talaat Sao** (Morning Market). There is currently confusion surrounding services from these terminals, as the government restructured the schedules and stations in late 2005, so always check before you set off. Many of the buses that traditionally departed from the Talaat Sao bus station have now been divided between the Southern and Northern terminals. Local taxis and tuk-tuks are still unfamiliar with the schedule changes, so leave enough time to get to another bus station, if necessary. The most comfortable buses are run by private companies, but these offer only a limited service.

Southern bus station Route 13, 9 km south of the city centre. Public buses depart daily for destinations in southern Laos. To **Thakhek**, 0400, 0500, 0600, 1200 daily, 6 hrs, 40,000 kip. To **Savannakhet**, 0530, 0630, 0700, 0730, 0800, 0830, 0900 daily, 8 hrs, 55,000 kip. To **Pakse**, 1000, 1230, 1300, 1330, 1400, 1430, 1500, 1530 daily, 15 hrs, 85,000 kip; there are also overnight a/c express buses to Pakse at 1800, 1830, 1900, 1930, 2000 daily, 11 hrs, 110,000 kip, and a VIP service at 2030 daily, which takes about the same time but has water, snacks etc, 130,000 kip. To **Sekong**, 1630 daily, 20 hrs, 100,000 kip. To **Voen Kham** (Cambodian border, see p274), 1100 daily, 18 hrs, 110,000 kip. To **Muang Khong** on Don Khong, 1030 daily, 18 hrs, 110,000 kip.

SDT Transport, T021-740521, runs a bus at 1900 daily to **Hanoi** (23 hrs, US$20). Another bus departs at 1900 daily with stops in **Hué** (21 hrs, US$20); **Danang** (23 hrs, US$20) and **Ho Chi Minh City** (48 hrs, US$45). VIP buses that are very comfortable night buses, usually allowing a good sleep during the trip – but watch out that they don't swap the normal VIP bus for a karaoke one! They provide snacks and have waitresses. Robberies have been reported on the night buses so keep your valuables somewhere secure.

KVT Buses, T021-242101, and **Laody**, T021-242102, run daily services down south. This is probably the best bet for travel to Thakhek or Pakse, as it's quick and easy. To **Pakse**, 2030 daily, 110,000 kip with a/c, also stop in **Thakhek**, 80,000 kip; schedule says it also stops in Savannakhet but it doesn't, it dumps you in a town called **Xeno**, 30 km from Savannakhet very early in the morning (80,000 kip). A/c buses also depart for Pakse at 0515, 1800, 1900, 2000 (110,000 kip).

Northern bus station Route T2, before the airport, 3½ km from the centre of town, T021-260255. Some southbound buses still depart from here (no logic to it but *bopenyang*): to **Thakhek**, 0400, 0500, 0600, 1200 daily, 40,000 kip; to **Savannakhet**, 0530, 0630, 0700, 0730, 0800, 0830, 0900 daily, 55,000 kip; to **Pakse**, 1000, 1200, 1300, 1400, 1500, 1600 daily, 85,000 kip; to **Don Khong**, 1030 daily, 100,000 kip); to **Voen Kham**, 1100 daily, 100,000 kip.

Northbound buses are regular and have a/c. For the more popular routes, there are also VIP buses which will usually offer snacks and service. To **Luang Prabang** (384 km), regular buses at 0730, 1100, 1330, 1600, 1800 daily, 11 hrs, 70,000 kip; a/c buses at 0630, 0900, 1930 daily, 10-11 hrs, 80,000kip; VIP buses at 0800 daily, 9 hrs, 100,000 kip. To **Udom Xai** (578 km), regular buses at 0645, 1400 daily, 14-15 hrs, 100,000 kip; a/c buses at 1630 daily, 110,000 kip. To **Luang Namtha** (676 km), 0830 daily, 19 hrs, 120,000 kip. To **Phongsali**, 0715 daily, 26 hrs, 135,000 kip. To **Houei Xai**, 1730 Mon, Wed and Fri, 25-30 hrs, 170,000 kip. To **Xam Neua**, 0700, 1000, 1230 daily, 14-23 hrs (depending on whether it goes via Phonsavanh), 130,000 kip. To **Phonsavanh**, regular at 0630, 0930, 1600 daily, 10 hrs, 75,000 kip; a/c at 0730 daily, 85,000 kip; VIP at 0800 daily, 95,000 kip.

Talaat Sao bus station Across the road from Talaat Sao, in front of Talaat Kudin, on the eastern edge of the city centre. Destinations, distances and fares are listed on a board in English and Lao. Most departures are in the morning and can leave as early as 0400, so many travellers on a tight schedule have regretted not checking departure times the night before. There is a useful map at the station, and bus times and fares are listed clearly in Lao and English. However, it's more than likely you will need a bit of direction at this bus station: staff at the ticket office only speak a little English so a better option is to chat to the friendly

chaps in the planning office, who love a visit, T021-216506. The times listed below vary depending on the weather and the number of stops en route.

To the **Southern bus station**, every 30 mins, 0600-1800, 2000 kip. To get to the **Northern bus station**, catch the Nongping bus (0630, 0810, 0940, 1110, 1230, 1430, 1600 and 1720 daily) and ask to get off at "*Thay song*" (1500 kip). To **Wattay Airport**, every 30 mins, 0640-1800, 3000 kip.

There are numerous buses criss-crossing the province; most aren't very useful for tourists. To the **Friendship Bridge** (Lao side), every 30 mins, 0650-1710, 3000 kip. To **Nong Khai** (Thai side of the Friendship Bridge), 0730, 1030, 1530 and 1800 daily, 1 hr including immigration, 8000 kip. To **Udon Thani** (Thailand), 0700, 0930, 1500, 1700 daily, allow 3 hrs (times vary depending on immigration procedures), 22,000 kip – a very cheap way to get to Udon Thani.

Other private bus services To **Vang Vieng**, **Green Discovery**, from its office on Setthathirat, 0100 and 1400 daily, 45,000 kip; also **Sabaidee Bus** for the same price and at the same time. Both services will pick you up from your guesthouse if you arrange in advance. **Sabaidee Bus** to **Luang Prabang**, Tue and Thu, 130,000 kip with a stopover in Vang Vieng on the way.

Taxi

These are mostly found at the Talaat Sao (Morning Market) or around the main hotels. Newer vehicles have meters but there are still some ageing jalopies. Flag fall is 8000 kip. A taxi from the Morning Market to the **airport**, US$5; to **Tha Deua** (for the Friendship Bridge and Thailand), 30,000 kip or US$9, though you can usually get the trip much cheaper but the taxis are so decrepit that you may as well take a tuk-tuk, US$5 (see below). To hire a taxi for trips outside the city costs around US$20 per day.

Lavi Taxi, T021-350000. The only reliable call-up service in town but after 2000 you may not get an answer.

Tuk-tuks

Tuk-tuks usually congregate around Nam Phou, Talaat Sao and Talaat Kudin. Tuk-tuks can be chartered for longer out-of-town trips (maximum 25 km, US$10-15) or for short journeys of 2-3 km within the city (5000 kip per person). There are also shared tuk-tuks, which run on regular routes along the cities main streets. Tuk-tuks are available around Nam Phou until 2330 but are quite difficult to hire after dark in other areas of town. To stop a vehicle, simply flag it down. A good, reliable driver is Mr Souk, T020-7712220, who speaks good English and goes beyond the call of duty.

Vang Vieng p312, map p313
Bicycle and motorbike

There are many bicycles for rent along the road east up from the old market (10,000 kip per day). There are also a few motorbike rental places (US$5 per day).

Bus

Buses leave from the makeshift bus terminal on the east side of the airstrip, T021-511341. There are plans to relocate all buses to the terminal at the New Market, 2 km north of town. Check before departing to either station. Public buses leave for **Vientiane** at 0530, 0600, 0620, 0700, 1230 and 1330 daily, 20,000 kip; songthaews depart every hour. To **Luang Prabang** at 0900, 7 hrs, 40,000 kip, or else catch a Vientiane-Luang Prabang bus as it passes through town. Although safe at the time of publication, check conditions on the Vang Vieng-Luang Prabang route before travelling as, in the past, buses on this leg of the route north have been periodically ambushed by bandits. Songthaews also regularly ply this route.

VIP buses (minivans) make trips to **Vientiane**, 0900, 1000, 1330 daily, 40,000 kip; to **Luang Prabang**, 0900 and 1000, 7 hrs, 75,000 kip. Every guesthouse and travel agent can book the VIP/minivans and they will pick-up from your guesthouse. Seats get booked up really quickly and buses take at least half an hour to make all their pick-ups, so expect long delays.

Tuk-tuk

Tuk-tuks will do a trip to the caves for US$7-10 for the whole day. There have been reports that some are offering trips to the caves for 10,000 kip per passenger and then demanding an outrageous fee for the return leg. Make sure all prices are set in stone before departing town.

⊙ Directory

Vientiane p304, map p306
Banks

See Money, p38, for details on changing money in Laos. At the time of writing there was only one ATM in the city, at the BCEL Bank on the corner of Fa Ngum and Pang Kham roads, which takes all the usual credit cards (maximum withdrawal 500,000 kip; much less on Sun). There are plans for many more but don't count on this coming to fruition. Banque Pour le Commerce Exterieur (BCEL), 1 Pang Kham Rd, traditionally offers the lowest commission (1½%) on changing US$ TCs into US$ cash; there is no commission on changing US$ into kip; also has an international ATM. Vientiane Commercial Bank, 33 Lane Xang Av (opposite Morning Market), T021-222700/5, cash advance on Visa at 3% commission.

Embassies and consulates

Australia, Nehru, Ban Phonxay Rd, T021-413602. Britain, contact the Australian Embassy. Cambodia, Tha Deua Rd, km 2, T021-314952, visas 0730-1030 daily; wait 3 days for US$20, same day $30. France, Setthathirat Rd, T021-215253(-9). Germany, 26 Sok Paluang Rd, T021-312110/1. Thailand, Phon Kheng Rd, T021-214581/2, (consular section on That Luang), Mon-Fri 0830-1200, 2-month visa costs ฿300 (payable in baht only) and takes 3 days to process. **USA**, That Dam Rd (off Samsenthai Rd), T021-212580. **Vietnam**, That Luang Rd, T021-413400, visas 0800-1045 and 1415-1615, 1-month visa costs US$50 and you must wait 3 days.

Immigration
Immigration office, Phai Nam Rd (near Morning Market), Mon-Fri 0730-1200, 1400-1700. For visa information, see Essentials p48.

Internet
Internet cafés have opened up all over the city, many on Setthathirat Rd. You shouldn't have to pay more than 200 kip per min. Internet phones are now very popular, with most cafés providing this service for under US$1 per min. **PlaNet Computers**, 205 Setthathirat Rd, Mon-Fri 0830-2300, Sat and Sun 0900-2300. **Star-net**, Mixay Rd, T021-504550, whose owner, Somphane Sihavong, is very helpful and speaks good English.

Medical services
There are 2 pretty good pharmacies close to the Talaat Sao Bus Station. **Australian Clinic**, Australian Embassy, T021-413603, Mon, Tue, Thu, Fri 0800-1200 and 1400-1700, Wed 0830-1200, for Commonwealth patients only (except in emergencies), US$50 to see the doctor.
   If you need a decent hospital, the closest are in Thailand, see p36. In cases of extreme emergency where a medical evacuation is required, contact **Lao Westcoast Helicopters**, Hangar 703, Wattay Airport, T021-512023, which will charter helicopters to Udon Thani for US$1500-2000, subject to availability and government approval.

Tourist Police Office, Lang Xang Av (next to the National Tourism Authority of Laos), T021-251128.

Post
Post Office, Khou Vieng Rd/Lane Xang Av (opposite market), T021-216425, offers local and international telephone calls. Also a good packing service and a philately counter. To send packages, use **DHL**, Nong No Rd, near the airport, T021-214868, or **TNT Express**, Thai Airways Building, Luang Prabang Rd, T021-261918.

Telephone
The international telephone office is on Setthathirat Rd, near Nam Phou Rd, 24 hrs.

Vang Vieng and around *p312, map p313*
Banks Agricultural Promotion Bank and the **Lao Development Bank**, on the main road, both exchange cash, 0830-1530. **BCEL**, T021-511480, exchanges cash, TC and will also do cash advances on Visa and MasterCard, 0830-1530. **Internet** There are a number of internet cafés along the main drag, all 200 kip per min; most offer international net calls from 3000 kip per min. **Wonderland Internet**, and **A1net**. **Medical services** Vang Vieng Hospital is located on the road that runs parallel to the river; it's terribly underequipped. In most cases it is better to go to Vientiane. **Post office** The post office is next to the former site of the old market, 0830-1600.

Luang Prabang and around

Anchored at the junction of the Mekong and Nam Khan rivers, the former royal capital of Lane Xang is now a UNESCO World Heritage site. It is home to a spellbinding array of gilded temples, weathered French colonial façades and art deco shophouses. In the 18th century there were more than 65 wats in the city. Yet for all its magnificent temples, this royal 'city' feels more like an easy-going provincial town: at daybreak, scores of monks in saffron robes amble silently out of the monasteries bearing gold-topped wooden boxes in which to collect offerings from the town's residents; in the early evening women cook, old men lounge in wicker chairs and young boys play takro in the streets.

The famous Pak Ou Caves and the Kwang Si Falls are located near the town.

Getting there Plane, bus, car (private vehicle with driver)
Getting around Songthaew, tuk-tuk, bicycle, walking
Time required 2-3 days
Weather Generally cooler than the rest of the country especially Nov-Dec but hot and sticky in summer. Wet and humid Jun-Jul.
Sleeping A handful of luxurious hotels plus mid-range accommodation and a large number of backpacker options.
Eating A reasonable selection of international restaurants catering for all budgets.
Activities and tours Trekking and boat trips.
★ **Don't miss...** Wat Xieng Thong ▶▶ p333.

Wat Phra That Chedi peeks above the trees on a bend in the Nam Khan River, near Luang Prabang

Getting there Flying is still the easiest option with daily connections from Vientiane, plus flights from Bangkok and Chiang Mai to **Luang Prabang International Airport** (LPQ) ① *4 km northeast of town, T071-212172/3*. The airport has a phone box, restaurants and handicraft shops. There is a standard US$2 charge for a tuk-tuk ride from the airport to the centre.

Route 13 is now safe, with no recent bandit attacks reported, and the road has been upgraded, shortening the journey from Vientiane to eight or nine hours. There are also overland connections with other destinations in northern Laos. Luang Prabang has two main bus stations: **Kiew Lot Sai Nuan** (northern bus station), located on the northeast side of Sisavangvong Bridge, for traffic to and from the north; and **Naluang** (southern bus station) for traffic to and from the south. Occasionally buses will pass through the opposite station to what you would expect, so be sure to double check. The standard tuk-tuk fare to and from either bus station is 5000-10,000 kip. If there are only a few passengers, it's late at night or you are travelling to or from an out-of-town hotel, expect to pay 15,000-20,000 kip. These prices tend to fluctuate with the international cost of petroleum. Another option is to travel by river: a firm favourite is the two-day trip between Luang Prabang and Houei Xai (close to the Thai border), via Pak Beng (see p346). Less frequent are the boats to Muang Ngoi and Nong Khiaw, via Muang Khua. ➲ ▸▸ *p341*.

Getting around Luang Prabang is a small town and the best way to explore is either on foot or by bicycle. Bicycles can be hired from most guesthouses for US$1 per day. Strolling about this beautiful town is a real pleasure but there are also tuk-tuks and saamlors for hire.

Best time to visit Luang Prabang lies 300 m above sea level on the upper Mekong, at its confluence with the Nam Khan. The most popular time to visit the town is during the comparatively cool months of November and December but the best time to visit is from December to February. After this the weather is hotting up and the views are often shrouded in a haze, produced by shifting cultivators using fire to clear the forest for agriculture. This does not really clear until May or, sometimes, June. During the months of March and April, when visibility is at its worst, the smoke can cause soreness of the eyes, as well as preventing aeroplanes from landing.

Tourist information Luang Prabang Tourism Office ① *near Wat Visoun, on Visunnarat St, T071-212487*, provides provincial information and offers a couple of good ecotourism treks (which support local communities), including one to Kwang Si and one in Chompet District. Ask for Vongdavone.

Background

According to legend, the site of Luang Prabang was chosen by two resident hermits and was originally known as Xieng Thong – 'Copper Tree City'. Details are sketchy regarding the earliest inhabitants of Luang Prabang but historians imply the ethnic Khmu and Lao Theung groups were the initial settlers. They named Luang Prabang, Muang Sawa, which literally translates as Java, hinting at some kind of cross-border support. By the end of the 13th century, Muang Sawa had developed into a regional hub.

A major turning point in the city's history came about in 1353, when the mighty Fa Ngum barrelled down the Nam Ou River, backed by a feisty Khmer army, and captured Muang Sawa. Here, the warrior king founded Lane Xang Hom Khao (Kingdom of a Million Elephants, White Parasol) and established a new Lao royal lineage, which was to last another 600 years. The name of the city refers to the holy Pra Bang, Laos' most sacred image of the Buddha, which was given to Fa Ngum by his father-in-law, the King of Cambodia.

The city had been significantly built up by the time King Visounarat came to power in 1512 and remained the capital until King Setthathirat, fearing a Burmese invasion, moved the capital to Vieng Chan (Vientiane) in 1563.

Luang Prabang didn't suffer as greatly as other provincial capitals during the Indochina wars, narrowly escaping a Viet Minh capture in 1953. During the Second Indochina War, however, the Pathet Lao cut short the royal lineage, forcing King Sisavang Vatthana to abdicate and sending him to a re-education camp in northeastern Laos where he, his wife and his son died from starvation. Despite the demise of the monarchy and years of revolutionary rhetoric on the city's tannoy system, Luang Prabang's dreamy streets have somehow retained the aura of old Lane Xang.

Sights ⊜🏛🎭🎨❋🏢⛰🚌🎵 ➤ pp337-342

The sights are conveniently close together but, to begin with, it is worth climbing Phousi or taking a stroll along the river roads to get a better idea of the layout of the town. Most of Luang Prabang's important wats are dotted along the main road, Phothisarath.

Luang Prabang

100 metres
100 yards

Sleeping ⊜
Apsara 9 *B5*
Jaliya Guesthouse 3 *C3*
Le Calao Inn 1 *A5*
Maison
  Souvannaphoum 18 *B2*
Mouang Luang 10 *C2*

Pack Luck 2 *A5*
Phou Vao 15 *D2*
Sala Luang Prabang 4 *A4*
Sayo 5 *A4*
Silichit Guesthouse 6 *A4*
Three Nagas 11 *B5*
Vanvisa Villa 23 *B2*

Villa Santi 13 *B5*
Viradesa 26 *B2*

Eating 🍴
Bougnisouk 4 *A4*
Café Ban Vat Sene 6 *B5*
Coleur Café 2 *A4*

Mount Phousi

ⓘ *The western steps lead up from Sisavangvong Rd. Daily 0800-1800. Admission at western steps 10,000 kip. If you want to watch the sun go down, get there early and jostle for position – don't expect to be the only person there.*

Directly opposite the Royal Palace is the start of the steep climb up Mount Phousi, the spiritual and geographical heart of the city and a popular place to come to watch the sunset over the Mekong, illuminating the hills to the east. Phousi is a gigantic rock with sheer forested sides, surmounted by a 25 m-tall *chedi*, **That Chomsi**. The *chedi* was constructed in 1804, restored in 1914 and is the designated starting point for the colourful Pi Mai (New Year) celebrations in April. Its shimmering gold-spired stupa rests on a rectangular base, ornamented by small metal bodhi trees. Next to the stupa is a little sanctuary, from which the candlelit procession descends at New Year, accompanied by effigies of Nang Sang Kham, the guardian of the New Year, and Naga, protector of the city.

Royal Palace

ⓘ *Sisavangvong Rd. Daily 0800-1100, 1330-1600. 20,000 kip. No shorts, short-sleeved shirts or strappy dresses; no photography.*

Also called the **National Museum**, the Royal Palace is right in the centre of the city on the main road and close enough to the Mekong to allow royal guests ready access by river. Unlike its former occupants, the palace survived the 1975 revolution and was converted into a museum the following year.

It was built by the French for the Lao King Sisavang Vong in 1904 in an attempt to bind him and his family more tightly into the colonial system of government. Later work saw the planting of the avenue of palms and the filling in of one of two fish ponds. Local residents regarded the ponds as the 'eyes' of the capital, so the blinding of one eye was taken as inviting bad fortune by leaving the city unprotected. The subsequent civil war seemed to vindicate these fears. The palace is Khmer in style, cruciform in plan and mounted on a small platform of four tiers. The only indication of French involvement can be seen in the two French lilies represented in stucco on the entrance, beneath the symbols of Lao royalty. There are a few Lao motifs but, in many respects, the palace is more foreign than Lao: it was designed by a French architect, with steps made from Italian marble; built by masons from Vietnam; embellished by carpenters from Bangkok, and funded by the largesse of the colonial authorities.

The small ornate pavilion of **Wat Ho Prabang** is located in the northeast corner of the palace compound, to the right of the

Vientiane & northern Laos Luang Prabang & around

Royal Palace

entrance to the Royal Palace. The chapel contains four Khmer Buddhas, ivories mounted in gold, bronze drums used in religious ceremonies and about 30 smaller Buddha images from temples all over the city. The Pra Bang, see below, is due to be moved here.

The main **entrance hall** of the palace was used for royal religious ceremonies, when the Supreme Patriarch of Lao Buddhism would oversee proceedings from his gold-painted lotus throne. It now contains a collection of 15th- to 17th-century Buddha statues. The room to the immediate right of the entrance was the King's reception room, also called the **Ambassadors' Room**. It contains French-made busts of the last three Lao monarchs, a model of the royal hearse (which is kept in Wat Xieng Thong) and a mural by French artist Alex de Fontereau, depicting a day in the life of Luang Prabang in the 1930s.

In comparison to the state rooms, the royal family's **private apartments** are modestly decorated. They have been left virtually untouched since the day the family left for exile in Xam Neua Province. To the rear of the entrance hall, the **Coronation Room** was decorated was interrupted because of the war. The walls are a brilliant red with Japanese glass mosaics embedded in a red lacquer base with gilded woodwork and depict scenes from Lao festivals.

To the left of the entrance hall is the reception room of the **King's Secretary**, and beyond it, the **Queen's reception room**, which together house an eccentric miscellany of state gifts from just about every country except the UK.

To the far right of the entrance to the palace is a room (viewed from the outside) in which sits the Pra Bang, or **Golden Buddha**, from which the city derived its name. The Buddha is in the attitude of Abhayamudra or 'dispelling fear'. Some believe that the original image is kept in a bank vault, though most dispel this as rumour. It is 90% solid gold. Reputed to have originally come from Ceylon, and said to date from any time between the first and ninth centuries, the statue was moved to Cambodia in the 11th century, given to King Phaya Sirichanta, and was then taken to Lane Xang by King Fa Ngum, who had spent some time in the courts of Angkor and married into Khmer royalty. An alternative story has the Pra Bang following Fa Ngum to the city: it is said he asked his father-in-law, the King of Angkor, to send a delegation of holy men to assist him in spreading the Theravada Buddhist faith in Lane Xang. The delegation arrived bringing with them the Pra Bang as a gift from the Cambodian King. The Pra Bang's arrival heralded the capital's change of name, from Xieng Thong to Nakhon Luang Prabang, 'The great city of the big Buddha'. In 1563 King Setthathirat took the statue to Lane Xang's new capital at Vientiane. Two centuries later in 1779 the Thais captured it but it was returned to Laos in 1839 and rediscovered in the palace chapel in 1975. The Pra Bang is revered in Laos as its arrival marked the beginnings of Buddhism in Lane Xang.

Wat Mai
ⓘ *Sisavangvong Rd. Daily 0800-1700. 5000 kip.*
Next to the Royal Palace is Wat Mai. This royal temple, inaugurated in 1788, has a five-tiered roof and is one of the jewels of Luang Prabang. It took more than 70 years to complete. It was the home of the Buddhist leader in Laos, Phra Sangkharath, until he moved to That Luang in Vientiane. During Pi Mai (New Year), the Pra Bang is taken from the Royal Palace and installed at Wat Mai for its annual ritual cleansing, before being returned to the palace on the third day.

The façade is particularly interesting: a large golden bas-relief tells the story of Phravet (one of the last reincarnations of the Gautama or historic Buddha), with several village scenes, including depictions of wild animals, women pounding rice and people at play. Inside, the interior is an exquisite amalgam of red and gold, with supporting pillars similar to those in Wat Xieng Thong.

Wat Sene (Wat Saen)
Further up the promontory, Wat Sene was built in 1718 and was the first sim in Luang Prabang to be constructed in Thai style, with a yellow and red roof. The exterior may lack subtlety, but the interior is delicate and rather refined, painted red, with gold patterning on every conceivable surface. Sen means 100,000 and the wat was built with a local donation of 100,000 kip from someone who discovered 'treasure' in the Khan River.

Wat Xieng Thong
ⓘ *Xiengthong Rd. Daily 0800-1700. 10,000 kip.*
Wat Xieng Thong Ratsavoraviharn, usually known as just Wat Xieng Thong, is set back from the road, at the top of a flight of steps leading down to the Mekong. It is arguably the finest example of a Lao monastery, with graceful, low-sweeping eaves, beautiful stone mosaics and intricate carvings. The wat has several striking chapels, including one that houses a rare bronze reclining Buddha and another sheltering a gilded wooden funeral chariot. Inside,

(Clockwise from top left): gilded door of the Chapel of the Funeral Chariot; the sim at Wat Xieng Thong, showing the thong tree of life; mosaics on a *hor song phra* at Wat Xieng Thong

resplendent gold-stencilled pillars support a ceiling with *dharma* wheels. The striking buildings in the tranquil compound are decorated in gold and post-box red, with imposing tiled roofs and mosaics, making this the most important and finest royal wat in Luang Prabang. It was built by King Setthathirat in 1559, and is one of the few buildings to have survived the successive Chinese raids that marked the end of the 19th century.

The **sim** is a perfect example of the Luang Prabang style. Locals believe the roof has been styled to resemble a bird, with wings stretched out to protect her young. The eight central wooden pillars have stencilled motifs in gold and the façade is finely decorated. The beautiful gold-leaf inlay is predominantly floral in design but a few images illustrate *Ramayana*-type themes and the interior frescoes depict *dharma* wheels and the enigmatic King Chantaphanit. At the rear of the sim is a mosaic representation of the thong copper 'Tree of Life' in glass inlay.

Behind the sim are two red *hor song phra* (**side chapels**): the one on the left is referred to as '**La Chapelle Rouge**' (the Red Chapel) and houses a rare Lao reclining Buddha in bronze, dating from the 16th century. The exterior mosaics which relate local tales, were added in 1957 to honour the 2500th anniversary of the Buddha's birth, death and enlightenment. The other *hor song phra*, to the right of the sim, houses a standing image of the Buddha which is paraded through the streets of the city each New Year and doused in water.

The **Chapel of the Funeral Chariot** is diagonally across from the sim and was built in 1962. The centrepiece is the grand 12 m-high gilded wooden hearse, with its seven-headed serpent, which was built for King Sisavang Vong, father of the last sovereign, and used to carry his urn to the stadium next to Wat That Luang where he was cremated in 1959. It was built on the chassis of a six-wheel truck by the sculptor, Thid Tan. On top of the carriage sit several sandalwood urns, none of which contain royal ashes. Originally the urns would have held the bodies of the deceased in a foetal position until cremation. The mosaics inside the chapel were never finished but the exterior is decorated with some almost erotic scenes from the *Ramakien* (the local version of the *Ramayana*), sculpted in enormous panels of teak wood and covered with gold leaf.

Wat Visunnarat (Wat Wisunarat) and That Makmo
ⓘ *0800-1700, 10,000 kip.*
This is better known as Wat Visoun and is on the south side of Mount Phousi. It is a replica of the original wooden building, constructed in 1513, which had been the oldest building in Luang Prabang, until it was destroyed by marauding Chinese tribes. The sim is virtually a museum of religious art, with numerous 'Calling to the Rain' Buddha statues: most are more than 400 years old and have been donated over the years by locals. Wat Visoun also contains the largest Buddha in the city and old stelae engraved with Pali scriptures (called *hiu chaluk*). The big stupa, commonly known as That Makmo ('melon stupa'), was built by Queen Visounalat in 1504. It is of Sinhalese influence with a smaller stupa at each corner, representing the four elements.

Wat Phra Maha That
Close to the **Hotel Phousi** on Phothisarath, this is a typical Luang Prabang wat, built in the 1500s and restored at the beginning of this century. The ornamentation of the doors and windows of the sim merit attention, with their graceful, golden figures from the Phra lak phra lam (the *Ramayana*). The pillars, ornamented with massive *nagas*, are also in traditional Luang Prabang style and reminiscent of certain styles adopted in Thailand.

Wat Manolom
South of Wat That Luang, Wat Manolom was built by the nobles of Luang Prabang to entomb the ashes of King Samsenthai (1373-1416) and is notable for its large armless bronze Buddha statue, one of the oldest Lao images of the Buddha, which dates back to 1372 and weighs two tonnes. Locals maintain that the arm was removed during a skirmish between Siamese and French forces during the latter part of the 19th century. While it is not artistically significant, the temple – or at least the site – is thought to be the oldest in the city, dating back, so it is said, to 1375 and the reign of Fa Ngum.

Wat Pa Phon Phao and Wat Phra That Chedi
ⓘ *3 km northeast of town, near Ban Phanom. Daily 0800-1000 and 1300-1630. Donation expected.*
Outside town, Wat Pa Phon Phao is a forest meditation centre renowned for the teachings of its famous abbot, Ajahm Saisamut, one of the most popular monks in Lao history. More famous to tourists, though, is **Wat Phra That Chedi**, known as the Peace Pagoda. It looks as

though it is made of pure gold from a distance but is rather disappointing close up. The wat was started in 1959 but was only completed in 1988; the names of donors are inscribed on pillars inside. It is modelled on the octagonal Shwedagon Pagoda in Yangon (Rangoon) and its inner walls are festooned with gaily painted frescoes of macabre allegories. Less grotesque paintings, extending right up to the fifth floor, document the life of the Buddha. On the second level, it is possible to duck through a tiny opening to admire the Blue Indra statues and the view of Luang Prabang.

Around Luang Prabang

Pak Ou caves

ⓘ *US$1, free for children. Torches are available but candles make it possible to see reasonably well after your eyes have become accustomed to the dark. A tour from Luang Prabang is probably the best way to reach the caves. Rest houses, tables and a basic toilet are available.*

The Pak Ou Caves are perhaps the most popular excursion from Luang Prabang and are located 25 km upstream from the city, set in the side of a limestone cliff opposite the mouth of the Mekong's Nam Ou tributary (Pak Ou means 'Mouth of the Ou'). The two caves are studded with thousands of wood and gold Buddha images – 2500 in the lower cave and 1500 in the upper – and are one of the main venues for Pi Mai in April, when hundreds make the pilgrimage upriver from Luang Prabang.

The two sacred caves were supposedly discovered by King Setthathirat in the 16th century but it is likely that the caverns were associated with spirit (*phi*) worship before the arrival of Buddhism in Laos. For years the caves, which locals still believe to be the home of guardian spirits, were inhabited by monks.

Kwang Si Falls

ⓘ *30 km south Luang Prabang, US$1.50, parking 2500 kip. There are public toilets and changing rooms. Travel agents run tours or charter a tuk-tuk for about US$15 return. Slow boats take 1 hr down and 2 hrs back upriver, via Ban Muang Khai (a pretty little village), where it is necessary to take a tuk-tuk for the last 6 km or so to the falls.*

Ban Pak Ou

These waterfalls are on a tributary of the Mekong. The trip to the falls is almost as scenic as the cascades themselves, passing through small Hmong and Khmu villages and vivid, green, terraced rice paddies. The falls are stunningly beautiful, misty cascades flowing over limestone formations, which eventually collect in several tiered, turquoise pools. Best of all, and despite appearances, it's still possible to take the left-hand path half way up the falls and strike out through the pouring torrents and dripping caves to the heart of the waterfall. Note that swimming is only permitted in designated pools and, as the Lao swim fully clothed, you should wear modest swimwear and bring a sarong.

● Sleeping

Luang Prabang *p328, map p330*
A Le Calao Inn, river road, T071-212100, www.calaoinn.laopdr.com. Enclosed by yellow walls, this recently renovated French colonial (1902) building boasts beautiful rooms in an incomparable position overlooking the Mekong. The balcony view is a real plus, so ensure you ask for a room with water views.
A Maison Souvannaphoum, Phothisarath, T071-212200, www.coloursofangsana.com /souvannaphoum/ Formally Prince Souvanna's residence, this place really is fit for royalty. There are 4 spacious suites and 18 rooms, with a/c, aromatherapy burners and special treats left in the rooms. The service is top-notch.
A Phou Vao, Phou Vao, T071-212194. This hotel is set on a hill slightly out of town. The 58 rooms are beautifully decorated and there are good views from the bedroom balconies. Very comfortable accommodation, with a/c, restaurant and pool. Credit cards accepted.
A Three Nagas Boutique Hotel, Sakkaline Rd, T071-253888, www.3nagas.com. Housed in a beautifully restored building, with an annex across the road, this boutique hotel is a running contender for best room in town. Attention to detail is what sets this hotel apart: from the four-poster bed covered with local fabrics through to the large deep-set bathtub with natural handmade beauty products. There's a lovely sitting area in each room, plus traditional *torchis* walls and teak floors. Breakfast (included) is served in the fantastic café downstairs.

A Villa Santi Hotel, Sisavangvong, T071-252158, www.villasantihotel.com. Almost an institution in Luang Prabang, this is a restored house from the early 20th century that served as the private residence of the first King Sisavong's wife and then Princess Manilai. It's a charming place, full of character and efficiently run. There are 11 traditional rooms in the old building, each of a different size, and 14 newer rooms, with baths and showers, in a stylishly-built annexe. The daughter of the official royal cook rustles up mouthwatering French cuisine in the **Princess Restaurant** and there are attractive seating areas in the garden, lobby or on the balcony.
A-B Pack Luck, opposite Le Elephant, T071-253373, packluck@hotmail.com. This boutique hotel is a relative newcomer. The 5 rooms are on the smallish side but are tastefully decorated with beautiful fabrics and have bathrooms with deep slate bathtubs.
A-B Sala Luang Prabang, 102/6 Ounkham Rd, T071-252460, salabang@laotel.com. Very chic, renovated 100-year old building overlooking the Mekong. Nice use of exposed beams and stone inlay in communal areas. Rooms have a minimalist, up-to-date edge with a/c and modern bathrooms, and doors either opening onto a small courtyard or river balcony (more expensive). Bus, car, bicycle hire available.
A-C The Apsara, Kingkitsarath, T071-212420, www.theapsara.com. Ivan Scholte, wine connoisseur and antique collector has done a perfect job on this establishment. Stunningly beautiful

rooms themed by colour, with 4-poster beds, changing screen, big bathtub and lovely balcony. Very romantic with a modern twist and recommended by a gamut of notable publications. The foyer and lovely restaurant (see Eating) are decorated with Vietnamese lanterns, Burmese offering boxes and modern art.

A-C Sayo Guesthouse, Sotikoumman Rd, T071-252614, sayo@laotel.com. Seriously lovely. The front rooms are beautifully and tastefully decorated with local fabrics and woodwork, polished wooden floors and furniture, and they boast a fantastic view over Wat Xieng Muang – you can watch the monks carving and painting and woodworking. The back ones aren't as good value but still recommended.

B-D Silichit Guesthouse, just off Ounkham Rd, T071-212758. New, sparkly clean guesthouse. Comfortable rooms with fan, en suite bathroom and hot water. Very friendly owners can speak English and French, and often invite guests to sit down for a family dinner. As with most budget places, it drops its prices dramatically in the low season. A guide runs popular tours to the Crystal Cave; he will probably show you the rave reviews he's received from past clients.

E Vanvisa Villa, T071-212925, vandara1@hotmail.com. Brightly coloured guesthouse down a quaint street. This is a little gem, with teak floors, large, characterful and immaculate rooms and friendly owners. The downstairs has beautiful handicrafts and antiques.

E Viradesa, off the river road, T071-252026. An old house with an extension. Good source of local knowledge for travellers. Some rooms have their own good-sized hot water bathrooms and others have shared facilities, all have portable fans.

E-F Jaliya, Phamahapasaman Rd, near Mano Guesthouse, T071-252154. Bungalow-type rooms, with varied facilities, from shared bathrooms and fan through to a/c and TV. Relaxing garden area with friendly pet deer. Bicycle rental.

🍴 Eating

Luang Prabang *p328, map p330*
The most famous local delicacy is *khai pehn*, dried 'seaweed', mainly from the Nam Khan, which is mixed with sesame and eaten nationwide. *Chao bong*, a mildly hot pimento purée, is also popular throughout the country. Other delicacies include: *phak nam,* a watercress that grows around waterfalls and is commonly used in soups and salads; *mak kham kuan* (tamarind jam) and *mak nat kuan* (pineapple jam). Note that, as Luang Prabang has a curfew, most places won't stay open past 2200.

♥♥♥-♥♥ Le Elephant, Ban Vat Nong, T071-252482. About as fine as dining gets in Luang Prabang. Very upmarket and utterly delectable cuisine. Pan-fried fillet of snapper, with capers and basil-flavoured mash is delicious, as are the simmered scallops. Also a number of Lao dishes. There are three set menus and an extensive wine list.

♥♥♥-♥♥ Phou Vao, Phou Vao Rd. This restaurant is attached to the Phou Vao Pansea hotel and is set on a hill outside town with great views over the city. Good Lao and continental à la carte menu. Locals worship the buffet.

♥♥-♥ The Apsara, see Sleeping. Lao/Thai restaurant offering cuisine, such as braised pork belly and pumpkin, great fish cakes. Good value.

♥♥-♥ Coleur Café/Restaurant, Ban Vat Nong, T020-5621064. The French expats in town have nothing but praise for this place with its reasonably priced French and Lao meals and ambient setting. The Lao casseroles are fantastic. At the time of publication a new menu was being created set to include salads, pizzas, quiches, steaks and a few Lao dishes. Friday's are ear-marked as a US$5 steak-and-wine special.

♥♥-♥ Dao Fa, Sisavangvong Rd, T071-215651, www.daofa-bistro.com. Crêperie with good savoury and sweet crepes, great selection of teas and coffees, fab ice creams and tasty homemade pasta. The latter is the real draw-card and is recommended. Brightly decorated space with pavement seating.

ŤŤ-Ť Park Houay Mixay, Sisavang Vatthana Rd, Ban Xing Mouang, T071-212260. This is a firm favourite with westerners and Lao alike. Lao food with a western twist: anise-flavoured stew, delicious fish and *laap*. At times the chef can go a bit ballistic with the oil.

ŤŤ-Ť Tamnak Lao, Sisavangvong Rd, opposite Villa Santi, T071-252525. Brilliant restaurant, serving modern Lao cuisine, with a strong Thai influence. The freshest ingredients are used: try fish and coconut wrapped in banana leaf or pork-stuffed celery soup. Atmospheric surroundings, particularly upstairs, and exceptional service. Best for dinner. Unmissable.

ŤŤ-Ť View Khaem Khong, Ounkham Rd, T071-212726. The most popular of the dining establishments along the river. Good for a beer at sunset. Tasty Luang Prabang sausage and *laap*.

Ť Bougnisouk, attached to the riverside guesthouse of the same name. Daily 0700-1000 for the best value Asian breakfast in town: noodle soup, fruit salad, juice, coffee or tea and fruit salad for under US$2.

Ť Maly Restaurant, Phou Vao Rd, T071-252013. It's a bit off the beaten track but most tuk-tuks know it as it's the most famous Lao restaurant in town. The building is nothing to look at but the food is brilliant. The specialty is the *sindad*, or Lao barbeque, where a hole in the centre of the table filled with burning coals serves as a barbeque. Anything you get here will be good, including fantastic fried chicken and fish in coconut milk. Serves lunch and dinner. Packed at night.

Cafés and bakeries
Great French food at **Café Ban Vat Sene**. **Joma**, Sisavangvong serves an utterly delicious array of comfort foods; **L'Etranger**, Kingkitsarath Rd, is a great little bookshop-cum-café. A movie is shown daily at 1600.

🎵 Bars and clubs

Luang Prabang *p328, map p330*
Le Elephant and **Apsara** provide attractive settings for a drink. **Hive Bar**, Kingkitsarath Rd, next to L'Etranger. Luang Prabang's most happening bar-club is good for a dance. **Khob Jai**, opposite Hive Bar) is a dedicated gay bar. **Lemongrass**, Ounkham Rd, is a very slick, upmarket wine bar, with green theme.

🎭 Entertainment

Luang Prabang *p328, map p330*
Theatre and dance
Traditional dance performances are held Mon, Wed, Sat, 1700, at the **Royal Palace**, US$15.

✳ Festivals and events

Luang Prabang *p328, map p330*
Apr Pi Mai (Lao New Year; movable) is the time when the tutelary spirits of the old year are replaced by those of the new. It has special significance in Luang Prabang, with certain traditions celebrated in the city that are no longer observed in Vientiane. It lasts 11 days.
May Vien Thiene (movable). Candlelit festival.
Aug Boat races (movable) are celebrated in Aug in Luang Prabang, unlike other parts of the country, where they take place in Sep.

🛍 Shopping

Luang Prabang *p328, map p330*
Ban Khilly Café and Paper Gallery, Sakkaline St, T071-212611. A *sa* crafts centre (*sa* is a rough, leaf-effect paper). The 1st floor sells scrolls, temple stencils, paper lanterns and cards. On the 2nd floor is a small gallery and a comfortable

balcony café that sells drinks.

Caruso Gallery, Sisavangvong Rd (towards the 3 Nagas Hotel) has some lovely but very expensive pieces.

Luang Prabang Handicraft Shop, Ounkham Rd, offers a good range of silks and cottons and handicrafts. The owner gets his products from local villages.

Naga Creations, Sisavangvong Rd, T071-212775. A large collection of jewellery and trinkets, combining Lao silver with quality semi-precious stones. Both contemporary and classic pieces.

OckPopTok, T071-253219. OckPopTok, which literally translates to 'east meets west', truly incorporates the best of both worlds in beautiful designs and fabrics. It specializes in naturally dyed silk, which is of a much better quality than synthetically dyed silk, as it doesn't run. Clothes, household items, hangings and custom-made orders.

Patthana Boupha Antique Gallery, Ban Visoun, T071-212262. This little gem can be found in a partitioned off area in a fantastic colonial building. Antique silverware and jewellery, Buddhas, old photos and fine textiles. Less common are furniture and household items. The owner is of aristocratic lineage. Reasonable prices. Often closed, so ring beforehand.

Satri Lao Silk, Sisavangvong, T071-219295. Truly beautiful silks and handicrafts for sale. Overpriced, but definitely worth a look.

Markets

Central market, housed in a concrete market building in the middle of town on the corner of Setthathirat and Chao Sisophon rds. It sells mostly imported goods – food-stuffs through to hardware – but there are a few stalls selling silver boxes and belts and a handful with textiles. The busiest time of day is 0900-1100, but it remains open until 1700 or 1800, depending on the stallholders.

The **night market**, daily 1700-2230, sprawls down several blocks of Sisavangvong Rd. Hundreds of villagers flock to the market to sell their handicrafts, ranging from silk scarves through to embroidered quilt covers and paper albums. The market is a 'must see' and most visitors won't leave without a great souvenir or two.

Phousy market, 1.5 km from the centre of town. This market is a real gem: aside from the usual fruit and vegetables, it is a fantastic place to pick up quality silk garments. Pre-made silk clothes are sold here for a fraction of the price of the shops in town. The clothes just need the odd button sewn on here or the hem taken in there. Make sure that you are very detailed with instructions though and ensure the same colour thread is used in any alterations.

Silver

There are several Lao silversmiths around the Nam Phou area (fountain), where you can watch the artisans ply their trade. **Thit Peng**, signposted almost opposite Wat That, is a workshop and small shop with jewellery and pots.

▲ Activities and tours

Luang Prabang *p328, map p330*
Courses
Tum Tum Cheng, Sakkaline, opposite Wat Siboun Heung, T071-252019. Lao cooking courses for 1 day (5 hrs; US$25) or 2 days (US$45), starting at 0900 Mon-Sat. Book in advance.

Sauna and massage
For sheer indulgence, the **Maison Souvannaphoum** (see Sleeping) has a spa with a range of luxurious and expensive treatments. There are also numerous massage places along Sisavangvong Rd.

Red Cross Sauna, opposite Wat Visunnarat, reservations T071-212303. Daily 0900-2100 (1700-2100 for sauna). Massage 30,000 kip per hr, traditional Lao herbal sauna 10,000 kip. Bring your own towel or sarong.

Spa Garden, Ban Phonheauang, T071-212325, spagardenlpb@ hotmail.com. More upmarket. Offers a wide selection of massage and beauty treatments. Aromatherapy massage US$12 per hr, skin detox US$25 per hr.

Tour operators
Action Max, Ban Xieng Muan, T071-252417, www.actionmaxasia.com. Trekking and adventure-based tours.
All Laos Service, Sisavangvong Rd. Large successful travel agency organizing ticketing and travel services.
Green Discovery, T071-212093, www.greendiscovery.com. Kayaking trips on the Nam Ou and treks around Tad Kwang Si waterfall. Home stays, rafting, kayaking, trips to Pak Ou caves etc.
Tiger Trails, Chau Fa Ngum, T071-252655, www.tigertrail-laos.com. Adventure specialists: elephant treks, trekking, mountain biking tours, rafting, rock climbing etc.

⊖ Transport

Luang Prabang *p328, map p330*
Air
Luang Prabang International Airport (LPQ) about 4 km from town, T071-212172-3. **Lao Airlines**, Phamahapasaman Rd, T071-212172, has 2 daily connections with **Vientiane**, 40 mins, and a service to **Chiang Mai**. **Bangkok Airways** runs daily flights to **Bangkok**, daily. **Siem Reap Airways** flies to **Siem Reap**.

Early morning departures are often delayed during the rainy season, as dense cloud can sometimes make Luang Prabang airport inoperable until about 1100. Airline tickets are more often than not substantially cheaper from travel agents (see Tour operators, above) than from the actual airline. Confirm bookings a day in advance and arrive at the airport early as flights have been known to depart as soon as they're full.

Bicycle
Bikes can be rented for US$1 per day from most guesthouses, depending on the state of the machine.

Boat
Tha Heua Mea Pier is the most popular departure point and has a blackboard listing all the destinations and prices available (open 0730-1130 and 1300-1600). Prices are largely dependent on the price of gasoline. There is also a dock at **Ban Don** (15 mins north of town by tuk-tuk, US$1-2).

Speedboats depart from Ban Don to **Houei Xai** (on the Thai border; see p346), US$30, in around 6 hrs, with a short break in **Pak Beng**, US$20. Tickets are available from most travel agents. The boats are horribly noisy and dangerous (numerous fatalities have been reported from boats jack-knifing when hitting waves). Ear plugs are recommended and ensure boatmen provide a helmet and life jacket. Far more enjoyable is the slow boat to Houei Xai, which leaves from the boat pier behind the Royal Palace, 2 days, with a break in Pak Beng after 6-7 hrs on the 1st day. It's often packed to the brim so wear something comfortable and bring some padding to sit on. (If the boat to Pak Beng is full, you can charter your own for about US$200-300.) Most travel agents in Luang Prabang sell tickets to Pak Beng for US$9; tickets for the onward trip to Houei Xai, can be purchased in Pak Beng.

A few boats travel up the Nam Ou to **Nong Khiaw**. However, these are infrequent, especially when the river is low. The journey usually takes 6 hrs to Nong Khiaw, 65,000 kip. The Nam Ou joins the Mekong near the Pak Ou Caves, so it is possible to combine a journey with a visit to the caves en route. Most of the travel agents on Sisavangvong organize small slow boats to make this journey and advertize individual seats depending on how many place they have booked, usually around US$10 per person. Or charter a slow boat for 1-6 people for

Vientiane & northern Laos Luang Prabang & around Listings

US$100. Speedboats to Nong Khiaw leave from Ban Don, expect to pay 150,000 kip. These boats are hazardous, uncomfortable and not environmentally friendly but the journey is exhilarating.

Bus/truck

The northern bus terminal is for northbound traffic and the southern for traffic to/from the south. Always double-check which terminal your bus is using, as unscheduled changes are possible.

From the northern terminal
To **Luang Namtha**, 1500 and 1730 daily, 8 hrs, usually via **Udom Xai**, 50,000kip. The 1730 bus has usually come from Vientiane and is often full. An alternative option is to break the journey by catching the bus to **Udom Xai**, 0800 and 1100 daily, 5 hrs, 30,000 kip, and then continuing on to Luang Namtha in the afternoon. There are also daily departures (usually in the morning) to **Houei Xai** on the Thai/Lao border, US$7, a pretty uncomfortably, bumpy trip. Upgrades in 2005 should make the road more bearable.

From the southern terminal
There are up to 10 buses to **Vientiane** daily, though scheduled departures tend to decline in the low season. The ordinary service departs at 0730, 0830, 1030, 1230, 1530, 1630 and 1800 daily, 10-11 hrs, 60,000 kip; the 1530 service stops in **Vang Vieng**, 6 hrs, 45,000 kip. VIP buses to Vientiane depart 0630, 0830, 0900, 1930, 9 hrs, 80,000kip; the 0900 service stops in Vang Vieng, 55,000 kip. There is also an additional so-called VIP service to Vang Vieng at 1000, 5 hrs, 65,000 kip.

To **Phonsavanh**, 1750 daily, 8-9 hrs, 70,000 kip. To **Xam Neua**, twice a week, 10-13 hrs depending on road conditions, 80,000 kip. To **Nong Khiaw** via Pakmong, 1330, 1 hr, 20,000 kip; there are also several daily songthaews/trucks to Nong Khiaw, 4 hrs, 18,000 kip.

Minibus

Check out the notice boards for services to **Vang Vieng**, 5 hrs, 85,000 kip, and **Vientiane**, 7 hrs, 180,000 kip; also to **Luang Namtha**.

Saamlor and tuk-tuk

Lots around town which can be hired to see the sights or to go to nearby villages. Barter hard! A short stint across town should cost about 5000 kip per person, but expect to pay 10,000 kip for anything more than 1 km. Most of the nearby excursions will cost US$5-10.

ⓘ Directory

Luang Prabang *p328, map p330*
Banks Lao Development Bank, 65 Sisavangvong Rd, Mon-Sat 0830-1200, 1330-1530, changes US$/β/TCs into dollars or kip, doesn't accept Visa. Banque pour le Commerce Exterieur Lao (BCEL), Mahapatsaman Rd, Mon-Sat 0830-1200, 1330-1530; all transactions in kip, will exchange β, US$, AU$, UK£, Euro and TCs, also cash advances on Visa cards. Many of the jewellery stalls in the old market, plus restaurant and tourist shop owners, will change US$ and Thai baht. **Internet** A concentration of places on Sisavangvong Rd. **Medical services** The main hospital is on Setthathirat, T071-252049. There are a few quite well-equipped pharmacies towards Villa Santi on Sisavangvong. **Post and telephone office** Corner of Chau Fa Ngum and Setthathirat, Mon-Fri 0830-1730, Sat 0830-1200, express mail service and international telephone facilities, philately section. There are IDD call boxes around the post office and on Sisavangvong. Hotels and some guesthouses also allow international calls from their reception phones (about US$5 a min). You are better off making international calls from one of the many internet cafés, which are dramatically cheaper.

Far north

The misty, mountain scenery of the far north conjures up classic Indochina imagery of striking rice terraces, golden, thatched huts and dense, tropical forests, all dissected by a cross-hatching of waterways. Here life is beautifully interwoven with the ebb and flow of the rivers. The mighty Mekong forges its way through picturesque towns, such as Pak Beng and Houei Xai, affording visitors a wonderful glimpse of riverine life, while, to the east, the Nam Ou attracts visitors to Nong Khiaw and, the latest traveller hot-spot, Muang Ngoi Neua.

The wonderful upland areas are home to around 40 different ethnic groups, including the Akha, Hmong, Khmu and Yao, and it's not surprising that the country's best trekking is also found here.

---

⑦ **Getting there** Plane, bus, car (private vehicle)

⊜ **Getting around** Songthaew, tuk-tuk, bicycle, walking.

⊕ **Time required** 4-5 days

⋙ **Weather** Hot in summer, very wet in the wet season (Jun-Jul), quite cold Nov-Jan. Chilly nights

⊜ **Sleeping** Limited mid-range hotels, some eco-resorts, a large number of backpacker options.

⑦ **Eating** Basic Lao and Thai/pan-Asian food at very cheap prices.

▲ **Activities and tours** Trekking and river trips.

★ **Don't miss...** Trekking in the Nam Ha National Protected Area, near Luang Namtha ›› *p344*.

Luang Namtha and around ⊜⑦▲⊜⑦ ›› *pp350-357*

This area has firmly established itself as a major player in Laos' ecotourism industry, primarily due to the **Nam Ha Ecotourism Project** (see p344), which was established in 1993 by NTA Lao and UNESCO to help preserve Luang Namtha's cultural and environmental heritage.

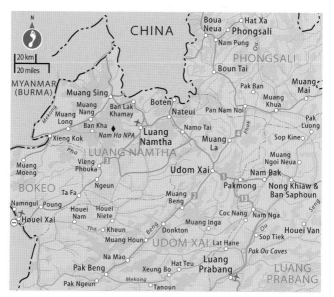

Heading northwest from Luang Prabang, travellers will reach **Udom Xai**, the capital of Udom Xai province. It's a hot and dusty town, with a truck-stop atmosphere that doesn't enamour it to tourists. Unfortunately, the other bad elements that come with major transport thoroughfares seem to be raising their heads here, too. However, the town does make a decent stop off point at a convenient junction; it's one of the biggest settlements in northern Laos and has excellent facilities.

Luang Namtha and around

Luang Namtha province has witnessed the rise and decline of various Tai Kingdoms and now more than 35 ethnic groups reside in the province, making it the most ethnically diverse in the country. Principal minorities include Tai Lu, Tai Dam, Lang Ten, Hmong and Khmu. The provincial capital was obliterated during the war and the concrete structures erected since 1975 have little charm but there are a number of friendly villages in the area. As with all other minority areas it is advised to visit villages with a local guide or endorsed tourism organization.

Ban Nam Chang is a Lanten village, 3 km along a footpath outside town; **Ban Lak Khamay** is quite a large Akha village 27 km from Luang Namtha on the road to Muang Sing. The settlement features a traditional Akha entrance; if you pass through this entrance you must visit a house in the village, or you are considered an enemy. Otherwise you can simply pass to one side of the gate but don't touch it. Other features of interest in Akha villages are the swing, located at the highest point in the village and used in the annual swing festival, and the meeting house, where unmarried couples go to court and where newly married couples live until they have their own house. You must not touch the swing. **Ban Nam Dee** is a small bamboo papermaking Lanten village about 6 km northeast of town. The small Tai Lue village of **Ban Khone Kam** is also worth a visit. The friendly villagers offer **homestays** here (30,000 kip/night, includes meals), for one or two nights. For information, contact the **Luang Namtha Boat Station**, T086-211305; **BAP Guesthouse** in Houei Xai, T084-211083, or the environmentally friendly **Boat Landing Guesthouse** in Luang Namtha.

Nam Ha National Protected Area

Vieng Phouka is a great base from which to venture into the Nam Ha National Protected Area, one of a few remaining places on earth where the rare black-cheeked gibbon can be found. If you're lucky you can hear the wonderful singing of the gibbons in the morning. The 222,400 sq km conservation area encompasses more than 30 ethnic groups and 37 threatened mammal species. Organizations currently lead two- and three-day treks in the area for small groups of four to eight culturally sensitive travellers. Treks leave three to four times a week; check with the **Luang Namtha Guide Service Unit** or **Green Discovery** for departure days; an information session about the trek is given at the Guide's Office. The price will cover the cost of food, water, transportation, guides, lodging and the trekking permit. All the treks utilize local guides who have been trained to help generate income for their villages. Income for conservation purposes is also garnered from the fees for trekking permits into the area. ▲▲▶▶ *p354*.

Muang Sing and around

Many visitors consider this peaceful valley to be one of the highlights of the north. The only way to get to Muang Sing is by truck or pickup from Luang Namtha. The road is asphalt but is sometimes broken and the terrain on this route is mountainous with dense forest. Muang Sing itself is situated on an upland plateau among misty, blue-green peaks. The town features some interesting old wooden and brick buildings and, unlike nearby Luang Namtha

Young Akha men and women in Muang Sing

and several other towns in the north, it wasn't bombed close to oblivion during the struggle for Laos. Numerous hill peoples come to the market trade, including Akha and Hmong tribespeople, along with Yunnanese, Tai Dam and Tai Lu.

Muang Sing Exhibition ⓘ *in the centre of town, Mon-Fri 0900-1200 and 1300-1600, 5000 kip,* is a beautiful building housing a range of traditional tools, ethnic clothes, jewellery, instruments, religious artefacts and household items, like the loom. The building was once the royal residence of the Jao Fa (Prince), Phanya Sekong.

The population of the district is said to have trebled between 1992 and 1996, due to the resettlement of many minorities, either from refugee camps in Thailand or from highland areas of Laos and, as a result, it is one of the better places in northern Laos to visit ethnic villages. The town is predominantly Tai Lu but the district is 50% Akha, with a further 10% Tai Nua. The main activity for visitors is to hire bicycles and visit the villages that surround the town in all directions; several guesthouses have maps of the surrounding area and trekking is becoming increasingly popular. However, please do not undertake treks independently as it undermines the government's attempts to make tourism sustainable and minimize the impact on the culture of local villages. ▲▲▸▸ *p354.*

Travellers' tales

> **Hiking with the Akha**
>
> I went out on the Akha Experience trek, with a group of Akha people, in the hills around Muang Sing. It was the first time they had officially run the trek and they were eager to impress. It was also the first time I had ever gone on a trek so I was hoping that my unfit body could endure the hike. The group was really fantastic and the Akha women, who are built like Olympians, almost carried me up the hills at some points. We learnt all about the jungle from our wonderful guides and helped collect bamboo shoots to make soup. I was the last to arrive at the waterfall for lunch and I noticed one of the women had her leg up in the air. Someone told me she had been bitten by a snake! To everyone's amusement our guide got a wild boar's tongue, which he had kept in his pocket for months in case of an emergency snake bite situation, and rubbed it on the bite. It did the trick: not only did she start walking again but she trekked another 7 km with 15 kg of wood in a basket on her back. Towards the end of the trip, when I was really starting to feel bad about all my gasping and tripping earlier on, the same woman turned to me and asked if she could carry my backpack! Of course, I didn't take her up on the offer. The trek and guides were brilliant and far exceeded any of my expectations.   *Joe Aston*

Along the Mekong ▸▸ pp350-357

The slow boat along the Mekong between Houei Xai and Luang Prabang is a favourite option for visitors travelling to and from the Thai border (see below). It's a charming trip through lovely scenery.

Houei Xai

Located southwest of Luang Namtha on the banks of the Mekong, Houei Xai is a popular crossing point to and from Thailand (see below), although few people spend more than one night in the town. Boats run between here and Luang Prabang, 2 days' journey downstream, via Pak Beng. Most passengers arrive close to the centre at the passenger ferry pier. The

----

Border with Thailand

Small boats ferry passengers across the Mekong between Houei Xai and Chiang Khong (Thailand) every 10-20 mins throughout the day, ฿20. Thai immigration is open 0800-1800 daily. A 2-week Thai visa is available at the border. Buses and taxis travel from Chiang Kong to Chiang Rai Airport where there are connections to Bangkok.

Crossing into Laos, immigration is open 0800-1800 daily, but expect to pay a ฿15 over-time fee at the weekend or after 1600. A 15-day tourist visa is available at the border for US$30. There is also a bank at the Lao border (daily 0830-1600).

vehicle ferry pier is 750 m further north (upstream). Although the petite, picturesque town is growing rapidly as links with Thailand intensify, it is still small and easy enough to get around on foot.

Wat Chom Kha Out Manirath, in the centre of town, is worth a visit for its views. The monastery was built at the end of the 19th century but, because it is comparatively well endowed, there has been a fair amount of re-building and renovation since then. There is also a large former French fort here called **Fort Carnot**, now used by the Lao army (and consequently out of bounds). The **Morning Market** can be entertaining, particularly for first-time visitors who have entered from Thailand, as this will be their first experience of a Lao market. There is little notable about the products on display but local tribespeople come from their villages to sell things here.

Pak Beng

This long thin strip of a village is perched half way up a hill, with fine views over the Mekong. Its importance lies in its location at the confluence of the Mekong and the Nam Beng. There is not much to do here but its a good place to stop en route between Houei Xai and Luang Prabang (or vice versa). The village is worth a visit for its traditional atmosphere and the friendliness of the locals, including various minorities. Just downstream from the port is a good spot for swimming in the dry season, but be careful as the current is strong. There are also a couple of monasteries in town. The locals are now organizing guided treks to nearby villages; check with the guesthouses.

Northeast of Luang Prabang ⬤⬤▲⬤⬤ ▸▸ *pp350-357*

In recent years the settlements of Nong Khiaw and Muang Ngoi Neua in the north of Luang Prabang province have become firm favourites with the backpacker set. In fact, idyllic Muang Ngoi Neua is often heralded as the new Vang Vieng, surrounded by stunning scenery and the fantastic ebb of life on the river. It is far more pleasant to travel between Luang Prabang and Nong Khiaw/Ban Saphoun, just south of Muang Ngoi Neua, by long boat, than by bus. The Nam Ou passes mountains, teak plantations, dry rice fields and a movable waterwheel mounted on a boat, which moves from village to village and is used for milling. But with the improvements that have been made to Route 13, road travel has now become the preferred option for many – partly because it is cheaper, and partly because it is quicker. Route 13 north runs parallel with the river for most of the journey to Nam Bak. There is trekking around Muang Khua further north upriver.

Nong Khiaw and Ban Saphoun

Nong Khiaw lies 22 km northeast of Nam Bak and is a delightful little village on the banks of the Nam Ou, surrounded by limestone peaks. There are, in fact, two settlements here: Ban Saphoun on the east bank of the Nam Ou and Nong Khiaw on the west. Confusingly, the combined town is sometimes called one name, sometimes the other and sometimes, Muang Ngoi, which is actually a town some way to the northeast (see below) and the name of the district. One reason why the area has become a popular stopping place for travellers is because of its pivotal position on the Nam Ou. It also makes for a more scenic alternate route to Phonsavanh. But most importantly, it is also a beautiful spot, the sort of place where time stands still, journals are written, books read and stress is a deeply foreign concept. It is possible to swim in the river (women should wear sarongs) or walk around the town or up the cliffs. The bridge across the Nam Ou offers fine views and photo opportunities. There are caves in the area and the Than Mok waterfall.

Going further

Phongsali

High up in the mountains at an altitude of about 1628 m, this northern provincial capital provides beautiful views and an invigorating climate. It is especially stunning from January to March, when wildflowers bloom in the surrounding hills. The town can be cold at any time of the year, so take some warm clothes. Mornings tend to be foggy and it can also be very wet.

Phongsali was one of the first areas to be liberated by the Pathet Lao in the late 1940s. The old post office (just in front of the new one), is the sole physical reminder of French rule. The town's architecture is a strange mix of Chinese post-revolutionary concrete blocks, Lao wood-and-brick houses, with tin roofs, and bamboo or mud huts, with straw roofs. The town itself is home to about 20,000 people, mostly Lao, Phou Noi and Chinese, while the wider district is a pot pourri of ethnicities, with around 28 minorities inhabiting the area.

It is not possible to hire bikes, tuk-tuks or even ponies here so walking is the only way to explore the fantastic landscapes of this region. Many paths lead out of town over the hills; the walking is easy and the panoramas are spectacular. Climb the 413 steps to the top of Mount Phouf for humbling views of the surrounding hills. The **tourism office** ① *on the way to Phou Fa Hotel, T088-210098, Mon-Fri 0730-1130, 1330-1630*, can arrange guided treks for up to 7 nights. **Chantha Sone**, T020-5688315, offers one- or two-day treks over the weekend; he has a number of different routes, visiting some of the ethnic villages in the area. **Mr Phonsai**, T020-5688357, is another local guide who comes recommended. Tourist agencies in Luang Prabang and Luang Namtha also organize group treks around Phongsali (see p340 and p354). Some people trek north from Phongsali to **Uthai**, staying in Akha villages en route. Uthai is probably as remote and unspoilt as it gets.

Muang Ngoi Neua

The town of Muang Ngoi Neua lies 40 km and one hour north of Nong Khiaw, along the Nam Ou. This small town surrounded by ethnic villages has become very popular with the backpacker set over the last few years. The town is a small slice of utopia, set on a peninsula at the foot of Mount Phaboom, shaded by coconut trees, with the languid river breeze wafting through the town's small paths. Most commonly known as Muang Ngoi, the settlement has had to embellish its name to distinguish it from Nong Khiaw, which is also often referred to as Muang Ngoi (see above). It's the perfect place to go for a trek to surrounding villages, or bask the day away swinging in your hammock. A market is held every 10 days to which the villagers come to sell produce and handicrafts. There are also caves and waterfalls in the area.

C **Phou Fa Hotel**, up the hill just past the Phongsaly Hotel. This hotel has good views over the town but feels a bit like an army barracks. Clean double rooms with en suite bathrooms and hot water. D **Viphahone Hotel**, next to the post office. Three-storey building with restaurant and 24 very clean, large and airy twin and double rooms, with excellent hot water bathrooms, some with western flush toilets. E **Sensaly Guesthouse**, up the hill and around the bend from the market, T088-210165. Worn but comfortable rooms in a concrete building, with squat toilets and scoop showers.

The few restaurants along the only road sell chips but there's a small Chinese restaurant near the Phongsaly hotel. **Yu Houa Guesthouse**, across the road from the market, has a short Lao section on an English menu; cheap and good.

You can travel from Muang Khua to Phongsali either by truck or by boat. Trucks depart from Pak Nam Noi (near Muang Khua); buy lunch from the market there before departure. The ride is long and difficult when the pick-up is full, but it's a great experience: the hilltribes along the way are very interesting and the scenery toward the Phongsali end of the trip is utterly breathtaking. Alternatively, catch a boat from Muang Khua to Hat Xa, 20 km or so to the northeast of Phongsali, 4-5 hrs, 60,000 kip. It's a beautiful trip, especially for birdwatching. The river is quite shallow in places, with a fair amount of white water. It can be cold and wet so wear waterproofs and take a blanket. Note that you may find yourselves stuck in Hat Xa, as there are no onward buses to Phongsali after mid-afternoon. Alternative routes to Phongsali are by bus to or from Udom Xai, 237 km, 9-10 hrs, 50,000 kip, or by plane to/from Vientiane, twice a week with **Lao Airlines**, T020-980180, although flights can be cancelled at short notice.

Muang Khua

Muang Khua is cuddled into the banks of the Nam Ou, close to the mouth of the Nam Phak, in the south of Phongsali province. Hardly a destination in itself, it's usually just a stop-over between Nong Khiaw and Phongsali. It only has electricity from 1900 to 2200 nightly. The Akha, Khmu and Tai Dam are the main hilltribes in the area. The nearest villages are 20 km out of town and you will need a guide if you want to visit them. Trekking around Muang Khua is fantastic and still a very authentic experience, as this region remains largely unexplored by backpackers. The friendly villages are very welcoming to foreigners, as they don't see as many here as in somewhere like Muang Sing. For these very reasons, it is very important to tread lightly and adopt the most culturally sensitive principles: don't hand out sweets and always ask before taking a photograph. Treks usually run for one to three days and involve a homestay at a villager's house (usually the Village Chief). ▲▲ ▸▸ *p354*.

● Sleeping

Udom Xai *p344*

D Hotel Fu Shan, opposite the market on the main street, T081-312198. A Chinese establishment, offering bare doubles with en suite hot shower and western toilet, TV and fan. Restaurant downstairs.

D-E Litthavixay Guesthouse, about 100 m before the turning onto the airport road, T081-212175. This place has the best rooms in town, large single, double and triple rooms, carpeted and all very clean. Rooms with lots of facilities. Hot water shower attached. Car rental service and free pickup from the airport. Best value internet in town.

Luang Namtha *p343, map p350*

A-C Boat Landing Guesthouse & Restaurant, T086-312398. Further out of town than most other guesthouses, this place is located right on the river. It's an eco-resort that has got everything just right: pristine surroundings, environmentally friendly rooms, helpful service and a brilliant restaurant serving traditional northern Lao cuisine. The rooms are very homely, combining modern design with traditional materials and decoration. Bill is a fantastic source of local information and speaks English.

E Guesthouse Restaurant. Clean and bright twin and double rooms, with en suite squat bathrooms. The twin rooms have large, comfy beds. There's satellite TV in most rooms and a/c in the most expensive rooms. Restaurant offers many Chinese delicacies – not suitable for vegetarians.

E Vila Guesthouse, further on from the Lao Mai on the right, T086-312425. A new 2-storey building with 11 of the cleanest rooms in town, lounge and sparkling en suite bathrooms, with hot water.

E-F Lao Mai Guesthouse and Restaurant, T086-312232. Lovely rooms with wooden floors, bamboo walls and hard but comfortable beds. Communal toilets are clean and well-maintained. Double rooms downstairs have en suite bathroom. Beautiful verandah with some spectacular views. Restaurant food is utterly scrumptious. Trekking and rafting.

F Bus Station Guesthouse, T086-211090. Sweet little rooms, clean and airy but with hard beds. Some have hot water. Friendly staff. Ideal for an early morning start.

F Luang Namtha Guesthouse, T086-312087. Run by 2 friendly Hmong brothers, one of whom speaks English. The house is an impressive building for Luang Namtha, with a grand staircase. All rooms are beautifully clean and furnished, with en suite hot water bathrooms and balconies. Satellite TV in the more pricey rooms. Free pickup from the bus station if you telephone ahead. Great setting.

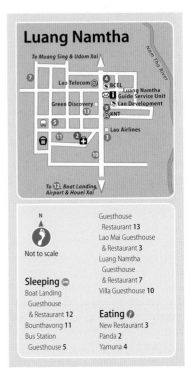

Luang Namtha

To Muang Sing & Udom Xai

Nam Tha River

Lao Telecom @

BCEL
Luang Namtha
Guide Service Unit

Green Discovery

Lao Development

@ KNT

Lao Airlines

To ⑫, Boat Landing,
Airport & Houei Xai

N
Not to scale

Sleeping ●
Boat Landing
 Guesthouse
 & Restaurant **12**
Bounthavong **11**
Bus Station
 Guesthouse **5**

Guesthouse
 Restaurant **13**
Lao Mai Guesthouse
 & Restaurant **3**
Luang Namtha
 Guesthouse
 & Restaurant **7**
Villa Guesthouse **10**

Eating ●
New Restaurant **3**
Panda **2**
Yamuna **4**

Muang Sing p344

D Pholou Guesthouse and **Phoulou 2**, T086-212348 at the southern end of town. Phoulou has large, clean double rooms, with en suite hot water bathrooms. From the balcony there is a superb view out over the town. Phoulou 2 has double bungalows of the same high quality and provides towels and bottled water. The lack of scenery at the latter is its only downfall.

D-E Adima Guesthouse, near Ban Oudomsin, north of Muang Sing towards the Chinese border, T020-2249008. A little hard to get to, but in a fantastic location. Peaceful bungalows constructed in traditional Yao and Akha style, plus a lovely open-air restaurant. There are only 10 rooms (more on the way) and they fill up quickly, so get there early. A calm retreat surrounded by rice fields. Minority villages are literally on the doorstep. Footprint does not endorse DIY treks using the guesthouse map, which are having a negative effect on local villages. If you wish to trek please visit the local tourism office or **Exotissimo**, see p354, to organize a bonafide eco trek. To get there, take a tuk-tuk (20,000 kip) or hire a bike. Alternatively, the owner runs in and out of town about 3 times a day (depending on bus arrival times) and will pick you up from the bus station for a small fee.

D-E Phoutat Guesthouse/Black Stupa, 6 km out of Muang Sing on the main road towards Luang Namtha. 10 wooden bungalows perched on the side of a hill, looking over the small town, mountains and rice paddies. Hot water, fan, western toilet and fantastic balcony. Stunningly beautiful. There is also quite a good restaurant on site.

E-F Inthanon Guesthouse, about 1 km north of the bus station. Run by the Lu tribe. Traditionally styled thatched huts, with en suite clean toilet and shower. Also 4 brand-spanking-new doubles, very clean, big rooms with hot shower. Friendly owners and a peaceful setting.

Houei Xai p346

D Thaveesinh, main street, north of the immigration intersection, T084-312039. Good rooms and location.

D-E Arimid Guesthouse, northwest end of the town, T084-9804693. The owners M and Mme Chitaly speak excellent French and a little English. Comfortable individual rattan-style bungalows, bathroom attached, hot water, nice garden area and great balconies. Some with a/c. Mme Chitaly will cook tasty food and serve it to you at your bungalow.

F Keo Champa, Sekhong St, 200m south of the immigration intersection. Rooms are basic with attached bathroom and fan. Very clean and quite nice view of the river. Possibly the best value for money.

F Thanormsub Guesthouse, Sekhong St. Double rooms, clean, hot water, fan and satin curtains to boot. Nice, helpful staff.

Pak Beng p347

During peak season, when the slow boat arrives from Luang Prabang, about 60 people descend on Pak Beng at the same time. As the town doesn't have an endless supply of great guesthouses, it is advisable to get someone you trust to mind your bags, while you make a mad dash to get the best room in town.

A-B Pakbeng Lodge. A wooden and concrete construction, built in Lao style, this stunning guesthouse sits perched on a hillside above the Mekong and includes 20 rooms with fan, toilet and hot water. Good restaurant and wonderful views.

D-E Sarika, T081-212 306. This is an elegant structure on the steep cliff overlooking the river. Big, clean rooms with toilet and shower en suite, tiled floors. There is a great restaurant, serving reasonably priced meals (see Eating).

E-F Donevilisack Guesthouse, T081-212 315. The popular Donevilasack offers a pretty reasonable choice of rooms. In the older building are basic budget rooms, with fan, mosquito net and shared hot water showers. More expensive rooms are

352 in the newer concrete building and have private cold water bathrooms.

Nong Khiaw and Ban Saphoun *p348*
E Phayboun Guesthouse, 1st guesthouse on the right as you enter Nong Khiaw from the west, T071-253928. Solid building with reasonable and clean doubles and twins. Balcony, toilet and en suite shower. Restaurant attached. Quiet location. Friendly owner.

F Sunset Guesthouse, down a lane about 100 m past the bridge, Ban Saphoun, T071-253933. Slap bang on the bank of the river – you couldn't ask for a more picturesque setting from which to watch the sunset. The charming, sprawling bamboo structure looks out onto tables and sun umbrellas liberally arranged over the various levels of decking that serve as a popular restaurant in the evenings. Western toilet and hot water shower outside. Eight rooms with hard mattresses on the floor but definitely worth it. A great favourite with travellers. Trekking can be arranged here, too.

F Manipoon Guesthouse, near the post office, Nong Khiaw, T071-253908. Slightly grander rooms than the other guesthouses, separated by wooden walls rather than just bamboo. Verandas offer unspectacular views of nearby rooftops.

Muang Ngoi Neua *p348*
All the accommodation in town is dirt cheap and of the same standard: bungalows with extremely welcoming hammocks on their balconies. Most offer a laundry service for around 10,000 kip per kilo and all have electricity 1800-2200 only. Rats are a problem here but, luckily, mosquito nets tend to keep them at bay. Options include: **Banana Café and Guesthouse**, in the centre overlooking the Nam Ou, with a restaurant; trekking, hiking and fishing can be arranged here, and movies are shown; **KaiKeo Bungalows**, just beyond the south end of the main road, beside the Nam Ou; **Ning Ning Guesthouse**, beside the boat

landing, with a great restaurant; **Phet Davanh Guesthouse**, concrete rooms, restaurant; **Riverview Bungalows**, centre of town, with restaurant, trips arranged; **Vita Guesthouse**, on the river down a path on the north of the road, good food.

Muang Khua *p349, map p*
D Sernnali Hotel, in the middle of town, near the top of the hill, T081-212445. The newest and by far the most luxurious lodging in town. 18 rooms with large double and twin beds, hot water scoop showers and western-style toilets, immaculately clean. Balconies overlook the Nam Ou.

F Nam Ou Guesthouse & Restaurant, follow the signs at the top of the hill, T081-210844. Looking out across the river where the boats land, this guesthouse is the pick of the budget bunch in Muang Khua. Singles, twins and doubles, some with hot water en suites, and 3 new rooms with river views. Great food (see Eating below). A popular spot.

Eating

Udom Xai *p344*
¶¶-¶ **Suphalin**, up the hill in a small alley near the post office. One of the better choices. A tad more expensive but worth it as the meals are larger. Great fruit shakes and spring rolls, though you will have to order the latter in advance.

¶ **Sinphet Guesthouse & Restaurant**, opposite Linda Guesthouse. One of the best options in town. English menu, delicious iced coffee with ovaltine, great Chinese and Lao food. Try curry chicken, *kua-mii* or yellow noodles with chicken.

Luang Namtha *p343, map p350*
¶¶-¶ **Boat Landing Guesthouse & Restaurant**, see Sleeping, T086-312398. Best place to eat in town, with a beautiful dining area and exceptionally, innovative cuisine: a range of local northern Lao dishes made from local produce that supports local villages.

¶¶-¶ **New Restaurant**, on the main road, towards the internet shop, T020-5718026. This restaurant is gaining favour with the locals and tourists for its good fruit shakes and Lao food. A few western dishes, too.

¶¶-¶ **Lao Mai** (see Sleeping). A large selection of Lao and Thai food, all of which is seriously good.

¶¶-¶ **Yamuna Restaurant**, on the main road, T020-5405698. A delicious Indian restaurant with veg and non-veg dishes and halal cuisine. Extensive, predominantly south Indian menu.

¶ **Panda Restaurant**, T086-211304. A goodie – very clean and small, with coloured lanterns strung throughout. Cheap and tasty food. The curries are outstanding. Friendly owner with English.

Muang Sing *p344*

¶¶-¶ **Taileu Guesthouse & Restaurant**. The most popular place to eat due to its indigenous Tai Leu menu. Well worth the trip with some unique and tasty meals including baked eggplant, with pork, soy mash and fish soup.

¶ **Music Oasis Bar**, just over the bridge, sells the heavenly combination of ice cream and beer and, as the name suggests, plays the music of your choice.

¶ **Sengdeuane Guesthouse & Restaurant**. A quieter option with an English menu, nice garden setting and a pair of green parakeets. Popular with the locals.

¶ **Viengphone Guesthouse & Restaurant**, next door to the Viengxai Guesthouse. This place has an English menu offering the usual fare. Excellent fried mushrooms.

¶ **Viengxai Guesthouse & Restaurant**, see Sleeping. Very good food, with some of the best chips in Laos, English menu, friendly service, reasonable prices.

Houei Xai *p346*

¶¶-¶ **Khemkhong Restaurant**, across from the immigration stand. Good option for those who want a drink after the cross-border journey. Lao and Thai food.

¶¶-¶ **Riverside**, just off the main road, near the Houay Xai Guesthouse, T084-211064. Huge waterfront restaurant on large platform. Mixture of Lao and Thai food.

¶ **Lao Chinese Restaurant**, on Sekhong, down from Houay Xai Guesthouse. No prizes for guessing what cuisine this restaurant specializes in. Reasonably priced food.

¶ **Mouang Neua**, main road opposite Thaveesinh guesthouse. Very good Lao and Thai food, cooked to perfection and ridiculously cheap.

¶ **Nutpop**, on the main road, down from Thanormsub guesthouse, T084-211037. The fluoro lights and garish beer signs don't give a good impression. However, this is quite a pleasant little garden restaurant, set in an atmospheric little lamp-lit building. Good Lao food – fried mushrooms and nice curry.

¶ **Sousada**, just down from Keo Champa guesthouse on the main road. Loads of dishes – pork, duck, fish, chicken – in a variety of Lao and Thai styles. Good fruit shakes made from local pasteurized milk. Good chicken curry (8000 kip).

Pak Beng *p347*

¶ **Khok Khor Bookstore & Café**. Stands out for its great coffee.

¶ **Sarika**, see Sleeping. An atmospheric restaurant downstairs with wonderful river views, fresh flowers, amazing variety on the menu, including cheese omelette, but interminably slow service.

Nong Khiaw and Ban Saphoun *p348*

Most of the guesthouses have cafés attached. A better option are the noodle shops alongside Sendoro selling very tasty fried rice, sticky rice, and vegetables – ask to see the English menu.

Muang Ngoi Neua *p348*

Sainamgoi Restaurant & Bar, in the centre of town, serves tasty Lao food in a pleasant atmosphere, with good background music. The bar, the only one in town, is in the next room. Further along

Vientiane & northern Laos Far north Listings

the main road, with a bomb casing out front, is **Sengdala Restaurant & Bakery**, which serves very good, cheap Lao food, terrific pancakes and freshly baked baguettes. Next to Banana Guesthouse, **Nang Phone Keo Restaurant**, serves all the usual Lao food plus some extras: try the 'Falang Roll' for breakfast (a combination of peanut butter, sticky rice and vegetables).

Muang Khua *p349*

The **Nam Ou Guesthouse & Restaurant** (see Sleeping) is up the mud slope from the beach, an incomparable location for a morning coffee overlooking the river; it has an English menu and friendly staff. The restaurant opposite the **Singsavanh** guesthouse has tasty fried noodles and rice dishes and an English menu.

▲ Activities and tours

Luang Namtha *p343, map p350*
Tour operators
Green Discovery, T086-211484, offers 1- to 7-day kayaking/rafting and trekking excursions into the Nam Ha NPA.
Luang Namtha Guide Service Unit, T086-211534. Information on treks into the Nam Ha NPA; ask to speak to Mr Bountha or Ms La Ong Kham.

Muang Sing *p344*
Trekking
Trekking has become a delicate issue around Muang Sing as uncontrolled tourism was beginning to have a detrimental effect on some of the surrounding minority villages. Luckily some sensible procedures and protocols have been put in place to ensure low impact tourism which still benefits the villages concerned.

Exotissimo (www.exotissimo.com) in cahoots with GTZ, a German aid agency, is launching some recommended treks, which will include tasty meals prepared by local Akha people.

The **tourist office**, in the centre of town, can organize pretty good treks for 1, 2 or 3 days including accommodation and food. The guides are supposedly from local villages and can speak the native tongue, Akha or Tai Leu.

Muang Ngoi Neua *p348*
Trekking, hiking, fishing, trips to the waterfalls and boat trips can be organized through most of the guesthouses. **Kongkeo**, who lives in the centre of town, is a former English teacher, who has been running treks since 1998. He does an overnight trek to the top of Mount Phaboom. It is also possible to canoe to nearby villages. A lovely 1-day hike into the rainforest can be arranged. **Lao Youth Travel**, www.laoyouth travel.com, 0730-1800. Half-day, day, overnight or 2-night treks. Also kayaking.

Muang Khua *p349*
Singsavanh Guesthouse can arrange tours to the surrounding hill villages for around US$30 per person for 2 days and 1 night, or about half that per day for trekking. The guides speak good English. **Mr Khammane**, khammaane @hotmail.com, is a former monk and chemistry teacher who guides treks to surrounding villages Jun-Aug and at weekends. **Mr Kak**, of the **Nam Ou Guesthouse**, guides 2- and 3-day treks.

⊖ Transport

Udom Xai *p344*
Air
There are flights to **Vientiane**, Tue, Thu and Sat from Udom Xai. **Lao Airlines** has an office at the airport, T081-312156.

Boat
There are boat connections on to Houei Xai west or Luang Prabang east (8 hrs).

Bus, truck or songthaew
The bus station is 1 km east of the town centre. Departures east to **Nong Khiaw**,

3 hrs, are fairly frequent. To **Luang Prabang**, direct, 0800, 1130 and 1400, 5 hrs, 38,000 kip. Direct bus to **Vientiane**, 1530 and 1800, 15 hrs, 100,000 kip.

Pickups to **Luang Namtha**, 0800, 1130 and 1530, 4 hrs, 26,000 kip.

There are services north on Route 4 to **Phongsali**, 0800, 9 hrs, 50,000 kip; this trip is long so bring something soft to sit on and try to get a seat with a view.

Luang Namtha *p343, map p350*
Air
The airport is 7 km south of town – 15,000 kip by tuk-tuk. Small planes fly to **Vientiane** 4 times per week, 55 mins. **Lao Airlines**, T086-312180, has an office at the airport and another south of town on the main road. Book flights well in advance.

Bicycle
Bicycles for hire from next door to the Manychan Guesthouse, opposite post office, for 15,000 kip a day.

Boat
Call T020-5686051 for information. Slow boats are the best and most scenic travel option but their reliability will depend on the tide and, in the dry season (Mar-May) they often won't run at all as the water level is too low. There isn't really a regular boat service from Luang Namtha, so you will have to either charter a whole boat and split the cost amongst the passengers or hitch a ride on a boat making the trip already; around US$100 to **Houei Xai**. The Boat Landing Guesthouse is a good source of information about boats; if arrangements are made for you, a courtesy tip is appreciated.

Bus, truck or songthaew
The bus station and its ticket office, T086-312164, daily 0700-1600, are about 100 m north of the Morning Market. If you want to get somewhere quickly and there's no bus, speak to the women in the nearby restaurants, who might be able to arrange transport, although it will come

at a price. Otherwise hop on a bus to Udom Xai for more frequent connections.

To **Muang Sing**, 0800, 0930 and 1100 daily, 2 hrs, 15,000 kip, additional pickups may depart throughout the rest of the day, depending on demand. To **Udom Xai**, 0830, 1200 and 1430 daily, 100 km, 4-6 hrs, 26,000 kip, additional services will leave in the early afternoon if there is demand.

To **Luang Prabang**, 0830 daily, 10 hrs, 55,000 kip, continuing to **Vientiane**, 20 hrs, 120,000 kip. To **Nong Khiaw**, 42,000 kip. To **Houei Xai**, 0800-0830 daily, 9-10 hrs by pickup in the dry season and almost impossible during rainy season, 60,000 kip; the road is largely unpaved and potholed but at the time of publication was receiving an overhaul.

Muang Sing *p344*
Bicycle
Available for rent from some of the guesthouses and bicycle hire shops on the main street. 10,000 kip per day.

Boat
It is sometimes possible to charter boats from Xieng Kok downstream on the Mekong to **Houei Xai**, 3-4 hrs. This is expensive – around US$150; contact Mr Chom. If you can't find a boat to Houei Xai, aim for Muang Mom, which will be cheaper and is a more common route for the speedboats.

Bus or truck
To **Luang Namtha**, by bus or pick-up, daily 0800, 0900, 1100, 1300 and 1500, 2 hrs, 15,000 kip. To charter a songthaew or tuk-tuk to Luang Namtha costs upwards of 150,000 kip.

Houei Xai *p346*
Lao National Tourism State Bokeo, near immigration, T084-211555, organizes the sale of boat, bus, pickup and other tickets and will deliver tickets to most hotels.

Air

Houei Xai airport is located 5 km south of town and has flights to **Vientiane**, Tue, Sat, Sun. Book in advance as it is a small plane and tends to fill up quickly.

Boat

The BAP Guesthouse in Houei Xai is a good place to find out about boat services. For services across the Mekong to Thailand, see p346. The slow boat to **Pak Beng** is raved about by many travellers. It leaves from a jetty 1½ km north of town, 0930-1000 daily, 6-7 hrs, 75,000 kip or 160,000 kip to **Luang Prabang**; another 7 hrs (2-day journey); it's worth getting a seat on the roof. Speedboats are a noisy, unrelaxing alternative; they leave from the jetty south of town, to Pak Beng, 3 hrs, 130,000 kip and to Luang Prabang, 270,000 kip. There have been reports of unscrupulous boatmen claiming there are no slow boats in the dry season to encourage travellers to take their fast boats. This is usually untrue.

Bus, truck or songthaew

The bus station is located at the Morning Market, 2 km out of Houei Xai, a tuk-tuk to the centre costs 5000-10,000 kip. Trucks, buses and minivans run to **Luang Namtha**, 0930-1130, 170 km, 8 hrs, 60,000 kip; to **Udom Xai**, 0900, 95,000 kip; to **Luang Prabang**, 0930, 6 hrs, 120,000 kip; to **Vientiane**, 0900, 20 hrs, 160,000 kip.

Pak Beng *p347*
Boat

The times and prices for boats are always changing in Pak Beng so it's best to check beforehand. The slow boat to **Houei Xai** leaves at around 0800 from the port and takes all day. The slow boat to **Luang Prabang** leaves around the same time. Speedboats to Luang Prabang (2-3 hrs) and Houei Xai leave throughout the day, when full, until early afternoon.

Bus, truck, songthaew

Buses leave from the Pak Beng jetty in the morning for the route north to **Udom Xai**, 6-7 hrs, 30,000 kip. Direct songthaews to Udom Xai are few, so an alternative is to take one to Muang Houn and catch a rather more frequent service from there. The road to Udom Xai passes through spectacular scenery and is currently being upgraded.

Nong Khiaw and Ban Saphoun *p348*
Boat

Boat services have become irregular following road improvements, although you may find a service to **Muang Noi Neua**, 1 hr, 13,000 kip, from the boat landing. Some vessels also head upriver to **Muang Khua**, 5 hrs, 60,000 kip.

Songthaew/truck

Regular connections to **Luang Prabang**, 3 hrs, 18,000 kip. Also several departures daily to **Nam Bak**, 30 mins, 7000 kip and on to **Udom Xai**. Alternatively, take one of the more regular songthaews to **Pak Mong**, 1 hr, 10,000 kip, where there is a small noodle shop, and then catch a vehicle on to Udom Xai.

Travelling east on Route 1, there are buses to **Vieng Thong**, 2 hrs, 15,000 kip, and **Nam Nouan**, and from here south on Route 6 to **Phonsavanh** and the **Plain of Jars**, 75,000 kip, or north to **Xam Neua**. The bus to Nam Nouan can be caught from the toll gate on the Ban Saphoun side of the river when it comes through from Vientiane at around 0730, 60,000 kip; it's usually quite crowded and you will probably have to stay overnight in Vieng Thong en route.

Muang Ngoi Neua *p348*
Boat

From the landing at the northern end of town, slow boats travel north to **Muang Khua**, 5 hrs, US$6), or charter your own for US$50 per boat. Slow boats go south to **Nong Khiaw**, 1 hr, 13,000 kip, and **Luang Prabang**, 8 hrs, US$100 per boat.

Speedboats to Nong Khiaw, 30 mins, 20,000 kip per person. Departure times vary; for more information and tickets, consult the booth at the landing.

Muang Khua *p349*
Boat
Road travel is now more popular but irregular boats still travel south on the Nam Ou to **Muang Ngoi/Nong Khiaw**, 4-5 hrs, 60,000 kip, if there is enough demand. Also north to **Phongsali** via Hat Xa. A jeep or truck transports travellers on from Hat Xa to Phongsali, 20 km, 2 hrs along a very bad road, 20,000 kip. Alternatively, charter a jeep, 100,000 kip.

Songthaew or truck
To **Phongsali**, take a songthaew to **Pak Nam Noi**, 0800, 1 hr 10,000 kip, then take the truck that passes through from Udom Xai around 1030, 7½ hrs, 40,000 kip.

To **Udom Xai**, pick-ups leave 0700-0800 from outside the Singsavanh Guesthouse and later in the day if you're prepared to wait around, about 4 hrs, 15,000 kip, and, again, a beautiful ride.

ⓘ Directory

Udom Xai *p344*
Banks Lao Development Bank, Udom Xai, just off the road on the way to Phongsali, changes US$ and Thai baht, cash and TCs. The BCEL Bank, on the main road, offers the same services. No credit card advances. **Internet** Available on Udom Xai main street opposite the petrol station for around 500-600 kip min; also internet calls overseas, with pretty bad connection but at a cheaper rate than the Lao Telecom Office. The most reliable internet is at Litthavixay Guesthouse.

Luang Namtha *p343, map p350*
Banks Lao Development Bank, changes US$ and Thai baht to kip, also

exchanges TCs but charges a sizeable commission. The BCEL changes US$ and baht and does cash advances on Visa. **Internet** KNT Computers, 500 kip per min. **Telephone** You can make international calls from Lao Telecom.

Muang Sing *p344*
Banks There is a small branch of the Lao Development Bank opposite the market which will exchange Thai baht and US$.

Houei Xai *p346*
Banks Lao Development Bank, next to the immigration office, changes TCs, US$ cash and baht. **Immigration** At the boat terminal and the airport, daily 0800-1800, ฿15 fee is charged Sat and Sun (see also p346).

Pak Beng *p347*
There is no bank in Pak Beng, but most of the guesthouses and restaurants will exchange cash Thai baht and US$ at a hefty commission.

Nong Khiaw and Ban Saphoun *p348*
Internet The only connection is at Sunset Guesthouse, 600 kip per min.

Muang Ngoi Neua *p348*
Bank Lattanavongsa Money Exchange on the main road.

Muang Khua *p349*
Bank Lao Development Bank, near the truck stop, Mon-Fri 0800-1130, 1300-1630, can change US$, baht and euro at quite bad rates. It won't change TCs or do cash advances on credit cards, so make sure you have plenty of cash before you come here. **Telephone** International calls can be made from the Telecom office, a small unmarked hut with a huge satellite, halfway up the winding road, behind the bank, domestic calls 1000 kip per min; international calls, 14,000-23,000 kip per min.

Plain of Jars and the northeast

Apart from the historic Plain of Jars, Xieng Khouang Province is best known for the pounding it took during the war. Many of the sights are battered monuments to the plateau's violent recent history. Given the cost of the return trip and the fact that the jars themselves aren't that spectacular, some consider the destination oversold. However, for those interested in modern history, it's the most fascinating area of Laos and helps one to gain an insight into the resilient nature of the Lao people. The countryside, particularly towards the Vietnam frontier, is beautiful – among the country's best – and the jars, too, are interesting by dint of their very oddness: as if a band of carousing giants had been suddenly interrupted, casting the jars across the plain in their hurry to leave. Bear in mind that the plateau can be cold from December to March.

⏺ **Getting there** Plane, bus, car (private vehicle)
⏺ **Getting around** Songthaew, walking, hired car with driver
⏺ **Time required**: 3 days
⏺ **Weather** Generally cooler than the rest of the country especially at higher altitudes at night but very hot and sticky in summer. Wet and humid Jun-Jul. Cold Nov-Feb.
⏺ **Sleeping** Accommodation tends to be mid-range and below.
⏺ **Eating** Cheap Lao food and generic Asian meals
⏺ **Activities** Walking around the Plain of Jars, caving
★ **Don't miss** The Plain of Jars
▸▸ p360.

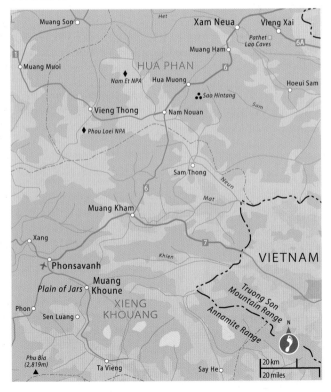

Plain of Jars

Background

Xieng Khouang Province has had a murky, blood-tinted, war-ravaged history. The town of Phonsavanh has long been an important transit point between China to the north, Vietnam to the east and Thailand to the south and this status made the town a target for neighbouring countries. What's more, the plateau of the Plain of Jars is one of the flatter areas in northern Laos, rendering it a natural battleground for the numerous conflicts that ensued from the 19th century to 1975.

Once the French departed from Laos, massive conflicts were waged in 1945 and 1946 between the Free Lao Movement and the Viet Minh. The Pathet Lao and Viet Minh joined forces and, by 1964, had a number of bases dotted around the Plain of Jars. From then on, chaos ensued, as Xieng Khouang got caught in the middle of the war between the Royalist-American and Pathet Lao-Vietnamese.

During the 'Secret War' (1964-1974) against the North Vietnamese Army and the Pathet Lao, tens of thousands of cluster bomb units (CBUs) were dumped by the US military on Xieng Khouang province. Each unit was armed with 150 anti-personnel plastic 'pineapple' bomblets, which still regularly kill children and cripple adults. The Plain of Jars was also hit by B-52s returning from abortive bombing runs to Hanoi, who jettisoned their bomb loads before heading back to the US air base at Udon Thani in northeast Thailand. Suffice it to say that, with over 580,944 sorties flown (one-and-a-half times the number flow in Vietnam), whole towns were obliterated and the area's geography was permanently altered. Today, as the **Lao Airlines** Y-12 turbo-prop begins its descent towards the plateau, the meaning of the term 'carpet bombing' becomes clear. On the final approach to the town of Phonsavanh, the plane banks low over the cratered paddy fields, affording a T-28 fighter-bomber pilot's view of his target, which in places has been pummelled into little more than a moonscape. Some of the craters are 15 m across and 7 m deep. Because the war was 'secret', there are few records of what was dropped and where and, even when the mines have been uncovered, their workings are often a mystery – the Americans used Laos as a testing ground for new ordnance so blueprints are unavailable. The UK-based **Mines Advisory Group** (MAG) is currently engaged in clearing the land of Unexploded Ordnance (UXO).

Xieng Khouang remains one of the poorest provinces in an already wretchedly poor country. The whole province has a population of only around 250,000, a mix of different ethnic groups, predominantly Hmong, Lao and a handful of Khmu.

Plain of Jars 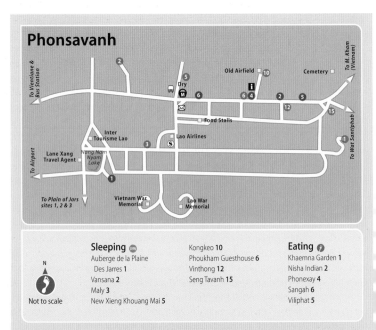 »» pp362-365

The undulating plateau of the Plain of Jars (also known as Plaine de Jarres or Thong Hai Hin) stretches for about 50 km east to west, at an altitude of 1000 m. In total there are 136 archaeological sites in this area, containing thousands of jars, discs and deliberately placed stones, but only three are open to tourists. **Phonsavanh** is the main town of the province today – old Xieng Khouang having been flattened – and its small airstrip is a crucial transport link in this mountainous region. It's the only base from which to explore the Plain of Jars, so it has a fair number of hotels and guesthouses. Note that travel agents and airlines tend to refer to Phonsavannh as Xieng Khouang, while the nearby town of 'old' Xieng Khouang is usually referred to as Muang Khoune.

Ins and outs

Getting there Phonsavanh Airport (aka Xieng Khouang airport) is 4 km west of Phonsavanh. A tuk-tuk to town costs 10,000 kip per person. The most direct route by road from Luang Prabang to Xieng Khouang is to take Route 13 south to Muang Phou Khoun and then Route 7 east; note that this road is periodically attacked by anti-government bandits, so check the security situation before travelling. An alternative, scenic, albeit convoluted, route is via Nong Khiaw (see p347), from where there are pick-ups to Pak Xeng and Phonsavanh via Vieng Thong on Route 1. Some visitors have said that this loop is impassable during the wet season due to the state of the road at Vieng Thong so check before you depart. The bus station is 3 km west of Phonsavanh on Route 7; a tuk-tuk to/from the centre costs 5000 kip.

Getting around and tourist information Public transport is limited and sporadic. At the time of publication, it was illegal to rent your own vehicle and tuk-tuks were barred from ferrying customers around the area so the only real way to get to outlying sites is by rented 4WD, with driver. It should be possible to drive from Phonsavanh to the Plain of Jars, see Site

Phonsavanh

To Vientiane & Bus Station
To Airport
Old Airfield 10
Cemetery
Dry
Inter Tourisme Lao
Nang Nam Nyam Lake
Lane Xang Travel Agent
Lao Airlines
Food Stalls
To M. Kham (Vietnam)
To Wat Santiphab
Vietnam War Memorial
Lao War Memorial
To Plain of Jars sites 1, 2 & 3

N
Not to scale

Sleeping
Auberge de la Plaine
Des Jarres 1
Vansana 2
Maly 3
New Xieng Khouang Mai 5

Kongkeo 10
Phoukham Guesthouse 6
Vinthong 12
Seng Tavanh 15

Eating
Khaemna Garden 1
Nisha Indian 2
Phonexay 4
Sangah 6
Viliphat 5

one and return to town in two hours. Expect to pay in the region of US$25 for an English-speaking guide and vehicle for 4 people, or US$60 for 7 people and a mini-van. Alternatively, hotels, guesthouses and tour companies in Phonsavanh run tours to the Plain of Jars, Muang Khoune (Xieng Khouang) and Hmong villages northeast of Phonsavanh. If you arrive by air, the chances are you'll be inundated with official and unofficial would-be guides as soon as you step off the plane. Note that it is not possible to walk from the airport to Site one, as there is a military base in between. It is recommended that you hire a guide, for at least a day, to get an insight into the history of the area. The cost of admission to each site is 7000 kip. ▲▲◉ ▸▸ *p364*.

Background

Most of the jars are generally between 1 m to 2½ m high, around 1 m in diameter and weigh about the same as three small cars. The largest are about 3 m tall. The jars have long presented an archaeological conundrum, leaving generations of theorists non-plussed by how they got there and what they were used for. Local legend relates that King Khoon Chuong and his troops from Southern China threw a stupendous party after their victory over the wicked Chao Angka and had the jars made to brew outrageous quantities of *lao-lao*. However, attractive as this alcoholic thesis is, it is more likely that the jars are in fact 2000-year-old stone funeral urns. The larger jars are believed to have been for the local aristocracy and the smaller jars for their minions. Tools, bronze ornaments, ceramics and other objects have been found in the jars, indicating that a civilized society was responsible for making them but no one has a clue which one, as the artefacts seem to bear no relation to those left behind by other ancient Indochinese civilizations. Some of the jars were once covered with round lids and there is one jar, in the group facing the entrance to the cave, that is decorated with a rough carving of a dancing figure .

The sites

More than 300 jars survive, mainly scattered on one slope at so-called 'Site one' or **Thong Hai Hin**, 10 km southwest of Phonsavanh. This site is closest to Phonsavanh and has the largest jar – along with a small restaurant. A small path, cleared by the MAG, winds through the site, with a warning not to walk away from delineated areas as UXO are still around. There are 250 jars at the site, each of which weighs about a tonne, although the biggest, called **Hai Cheaum**, is over 2 m tall and weighs over 6 tonnes.

True jar lovers should visit Site two, known as **Hai Hin Phu Salatao** (literally 'Salato Hill Stone Jar Site') and Site three called **Hai Hin Laat Khai**. Site two is 25 km south of Phonsavanh and features 90 jars spread across two hills. The jars are set in a rather beautiful location, affording scenic views. A further 10 km south of Site two, Site three is the most atmospheric of all the sites, set in verdant green rolling hills, swiss-cheesed with bomb craters. To get there you have to walk through some rice paddies and cross the small bamboo bridge. There are more than 130 jars at this site, which are generally smaller and more damaged than at the other sites. There's also a very small, basic restaurant, serving *feu*.

Sao Hintang

Sao Hintang, about 130 km north of Phonsavanh on Route 6, features hundreds of ancient upright stone pillars, menhirs and discs, gathered in Stonehenge-type patterns over a 10 km area, surrounded by jungle. This enigmatic site is as mysterious as the Plain of Jars: noone is quite sure who, or even which ethnic group, is responsible for erecting the stones and they have become steeped in legend. It is believed that the two sites are somehow linked, as they are fashioned from the same stone and share some archaeological similarities. Tours can be organized from Phonsavanh through Mr Sousath of **Maly Hotel** ▲▲ ▸▸ *p364*.

Going further

Vieng Xai (Viengsay) and the Pathet Lao caves

Tourists are often put off visiting Hua Phan Province by the long bus haul to get here but, considering the road passes through gorgeous mountain scenery, the trip is well worth the endeavour. The main roads in are the paved Route 6, from Phonsavanh and the south, and Route 1, from Vieng Thong and the west. **Xam Neua** (Sam Neua) is the main provincial town and the tourist office here can organize a car with driver to Vieng Xai caves. Summer is pleasant but temperatures plummet at night so you should bring a pullover. Mosquitoes are monstrous here; precautions against malaria are advised.

The village of **Vieng Xai** lies 31 km east of Xam Neua and the trip is possibly one of the country's most picturesque journeys, passing terraces of rice, pagodas, copper- and charcoal-coloured karst formations, dense jungle with misty peaks and friendly villages dotted among the mountains' curves. The limestone landscape is riddled with natural caves that proved crucial in the success of the left-wing insurgency in the 1960s and 1970s. From 1964 onwards, Pathet Lao operations were directed from cave systems at Vieng Xai, which provided an effective refuge from furious bombing attacks. The Pathet Lao leadership renamed the area Vieng Xai, meaning 'City of Victory' and it became the administrative and military hub of the revolutionary struggle. The village itself was built in 1973, when the bombing finally stopped and the short-lived Provisional Government of National Union was negotiated. Today the former capital of the liberated zone is an unlikely sight: surrounded by rice fields at the dead end of a potholed road, it features street lighting, power lines, sealed and kerbed streets and substantial public buildings – all in varying stages of decay.

Five caves, formerly occupied by senior Pathet Lao leaders (Prince Souphanouvong, Kaysone Phomvihan, Nouhak Phounsavanh,

◉ Sleeping

Phonsavanh *p360, map p360*
None of the streets in Phonsavanh are named.

A-B Auberge de la Plaine des Jarres
(aka Phu Pha Daeng Hotel), 1 km from the centreh, T/F021-312044. In a spectacular position on a hill overlooking the town are 16 attractive stone- and wood-built chalets, with living room, fireplace and shower room (occasional hot water). Clean and comfortable, flowers planted around the chalets. Restaurant serves good food. More expensive Oct-May. The friendly owner speaks French.

A-B Vansana, on a hill about 1 km out of town, T061-213170. One of the newest in town, opened in Nov 2004. Big, modern rooms with telephone, TV, mini bar, polished floorboards and tea/coffee-making facilities. Phenomenal views of the countryside. Opt for the rooms upstairs, with free-form bath tub and picturesque balcony views. Restaurant offers Lao and foreign cuisine. Airport pickup (look for Vong) and tour services available.

B-D Maly Hotel, down the road from local government offices, T061-312031. All rooms have hot water and are beautifully furnished with lovely local artefacts,

Khamtai Siphandon and Phoumi Vongvichit) are currently accessible to tourists although more should open in 2006. All the caves are within walking distance of the village; tickets, 10,000 kip, are sold at the **Kaysone Memorial Cave Tour Office** ⓘ *left-hand side of the government building, T020-765194, daily 0900-1630; contact Mr Siphon*. Expect to pay around US$5 for a guide (depending on the number of people). The caves have a secretive atmosphere, with fruit trees and frangipani decorating the exteriors. Each one burrows deep into the mountainside and features 60 cm-thick concrete walls, encompassing living quarters, meeting rooms, offices, dining and storage areas. The caves have been fitted with electric bulbs but you may find a torch useful.

😊🏨 Most visitors to Vieng Xai and the caves stay in Xam Neua and make a day trip out here but there is accommodation if required: **F Naxay Guesthouse**, T064-314336, is the best option. In Xam Neua choose from **D Boun Home**, T064-312 223, **Outhaithany**, T064-312 121, opposite the airport, a few km out of town, and **Shuliyo**, about 100 m from the bus station. ▼ **Mitsamphan**, opposite Boun Home Guesthouse in Xam Neua, T064-312151, is pretty accustomed to tourists and has an English menu.

⊖ There are regular trucks from Xam Neua to Vieng Xai, 60-90 mins, 10,000 kip, although there are virtually no services after 1500 so it's a better option to charter a vehicle for a whole day trip; songthaews will make the trip for US$15-20. Songthaews to **Nam Nouan** for connections to Phonsavanh, 0600 daily, 3-4 hrs on an excellent road, or through-services to **Phonsavanh**, 0900 and 1200 daily, up to 10 hrs, 60,000 kip. To **Luang Prabang**, usually around 0800 daily, 60,000 kip.

including a small (defused!) cluster bomb on the table. More expensive rooms on the upper floors have satellite TV, sitting area and other luxuries. Restaurant. Transport services available. The owner, Mr Sousath Phetrasy, runs exceptional tours (see p364).
B-D New Xieng Khouang Mai, behind the dry market, T061-312049. This hotel has been recently renovated and offers huge triples, with en suite hot water showers. More expensive rooms have baths and TV. Rates include breakfast.
E Phoukham Guesthouse, on the main road through town. A Hmong-owned hotel. Large rooms with hot water

bathroom but beds are a bit like sleeping on a rockface. The tours, which use local Hmong guides, are recommended.
F Seng Tavanh, T061-211131. Smallish rooms with hot water in the bathroom, some with shared squat toilet. Nice, helpful owners who can help manage tours and logistics around the area. Russian jeep for rent, with driver, US$35-40 per day. Restaurant attached. Some gems from the menu include: baked eel; swallow; frogs; hedgehog; intestine or beef placenta salad.
F Kongkeo. Nice new house with large, clean rooms, some with en suites. Also several wooden huts out the back. The

restaurant serves cheap and spicy food.
F Vinhthong, T061-312047. Very basic guesthouse. Mosquito net, bed, toilet, hot shower. The US$3 rooms are cell-like but others are clean and serviceable and some have enormous bathrooms. Friendly Vietnamese owner. The lobby is a taxidermy centre cum war museum with a display of shell casings, weapons and ammunition and interesting display of pictures, circa 1953, prior to the bombing of Old Xieng Khouang town. Tours of the Plain of Jars organized. Excellent value.

Eating

Phonsavanh *p360, map p360*

♥♥♥-♥♥ Maly Hotel, see Sleeping. A great little restaurant serving fantastic food from a very extensive menu: everything from duck curry through to beef steak. The best deal in town.

♥♥-♥ Khaemna Garden Restaurant. A fabulous setting by a Lake overlooking a long stretch of rice paddies (don't forget your mozzie repellent!). Super food (from the usual menu) and friendly service.

♥♥-♥ Sangah. Thai, Lao and Vietnamese (good noodle soup) dishes all available, as well as some western fare including steak and chips. Enormous portions.

♥ Nisha Indian, on the main road. The most unexpected find in Phonsavanh: north and south Indian food.

♥ Phonexay, on the main road, towards the Tourism Office. Excellent fruit shakes and good Asian dishes – fried noodles, sweet and sour. Exceptionally friendly.

♥ Viliphat, on the main road, T061-211422. Small hole-in-the-wall Vietnamese restaurant, serving great *feu* and coffee.

Festivals and events

Phonsavanh *p360, map p360*

Dec **National Day** on the 2nd is celebrated with horse-drawn drag-cart racing. Also **Hmong New Year** (movable), celebrated in a big way in this area.

▲ Activities and tours

Phonsavanh *p360, map p360*
Tour operators
There are no shortage of tour operators in Phonsavanh and most guesthouses can now arrange tours and transport. A full day tour for 4 people, travelling about 30 km into the countryside, should cost up to US$50-60, although you may have to bargain for it.

Indochina Travel, based at **Phoukham Guesthouse** (see Sleeping). Tour services throughout the area.

Inter-Lao Tourisme, slightly out of town, opposite the government office. Ask for Phet, a long-time guide, who has had rave reviews and knows the history of the area inside out.

Lane Xang, on the road to the market, T/F061-312171. Tours to Plain of Jars, plus trekking, cave trips, hot springs and more. Ask for Vong (the only English speaker), who comes highly recommended and will chatter away about local legends and history.

The most knowledgeable tour guide, however, is the owner of the Maly Hotel (see Sleeping). **Sousath Phetrasy** spent his teenage years in a cave at Xam Neua (see p362) during the war.

Transport

Phonsavanh *p360, map p360*
Air
To **Vientiane**, 30 mins.

Bus
To **Luang Prabang**, 0830 daily, 265 km on a sealed road, 0830, 7-8 hrs, 60,000 kip. To **Vientiane**, 0700, 0900, 1500 daily, 9-10 hrs, 75,000 kip, also a VIP bus at 0730 daily, 85,000 kip. To **Vang Vieng**, 0715 daily, 65,000 kip, and a VIP bus at 0730, 70,000 kip. To **Muang Kham**, 3 hrs, 20,000 kip. Also north to **Nam Nouan**, 4-5 hrs, 30,000 kip (change here for transport west to **Nong Khiaw**), and to

Sharing a joke in Xam Neua

Xam Neua, 0800 daily, 60,000 kip, a 10-hr haul through some of the country's most beautiful scenery.

Car

A full car with driver to the **Plain of Jars** will cost US$20 (US$5 each) to Site one, or US$30-40 to all 3 sites. Jeeps are available from **Seng Tavanh** (see Sleeping) for US$35-40 per day.

Directory

Phonsavanh *p360, map p360*
Banks Lao Development Bank, near Lao Airlines, 2 blocks back from the dry market, changes cash and TCs, Mon-Fri 0800-1200 and 1330-1600. **Internet** At the photo shop and next door, 500 kip per min. **Medical services** Pharmacies are ubiquitous in town. **Post office and telephone** Opposite the dry market with IDD telephone boxes outside.

Southern Laos

Don Khone, Siphandon

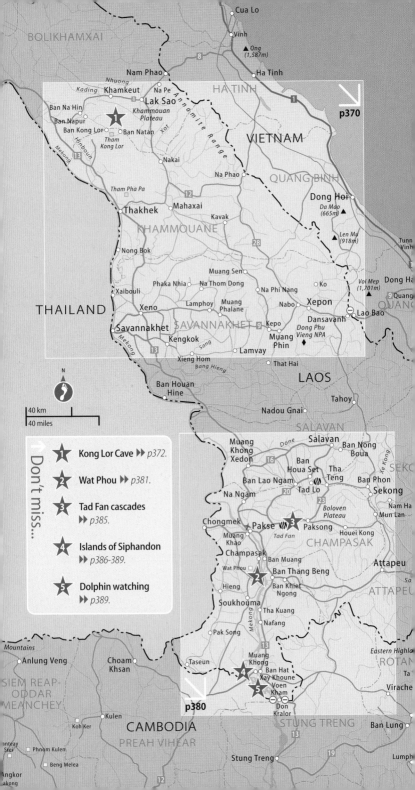

p370

p380

Don't miss...

⭐1 Kong Lor Cave ▸▸ *p372.*

⭐2 Wat Phou ▸▸ *p381.*

⭐3 Tad Fan cascades ▸▸ *p385.*

⭐4 Islands of Siphandon ▸▸ *p386-389.*

⭐5 Dolphin watching ▸▸ *p389.*

40 km
40 miles

Introduction

Southern Laos affords a somewhat different character to the northern regions, mostly driven by the many different minorities occupying the area, such as the Alak and Tahoy, and the influence of neighbouring countries.

Thakhek, Savannakhet and Pakse are picturesque reminders of the past, decked out with French colonial architecture, yet they exude a modern influence, deriving from trade with Thailand and Vietnam.

The overwhelming beautiful Khammouane Province with its gothic maze of limestone karst peaks, punctuated by caverns, rivers and clad in jungle, should not be missed. The giant Kong Lor Cave surrounded by imposing rock formations is the region's draw-card. Exploring this river cave is akin to a fantasy set from *Lord of the Rings*.

Base yourself out of Pakse to explore the many attractions of the far south including the romantic ruins of Wat Phou and the fertile Bolaven Plateau. The rivers running off the plateau have created a series of spectacular falls.

A highlight is Siphandon, the 'Four Thousand Islands' of the Mekong. The idyllic palm-fringed Don Khone, Don Deth and Don Khong provide perfect places to relax and absorb riverine life.

Ratings

Landscape
★★★★

Relaxation
★★

Activities
★★

Wildlife
★★★

Culture
★

Costs
$$-$

Central provinces

The central provinces of Laos, sandwiched between the Mekong (and Thailand) to the west and the Annamite Mountains (and Vietnam) to the east, are the least visited in the country which is a shame as the scenery here is stunning, with dramatic limestone karsts, enormous caves, beautiful rivers and forests. In particular, the upland areas to the east, off Route 8 and Route 12, in Khammoune and Bolikhamxai Province, are a veritable treasure trove of attractions, mottled with scores of caves, lagoons, rivers and rock formations. Visitors will require some determination in these parts, as the infrastructure around here is still being developed but a lot of new roads are planned to coincide with the construction of the Nam Theun II Dam. The Mekong towns of Thakhek and Savannakhet are elegant and relaxed and are the main transport hubs in the region.

⏣ **Getting there** Plane, bus
⏣ **Getting around** Songthaew, tuk-tuk, motorbike
⏱ **Time required** 2-3 days
☀ **Weather** Hot and sticky in summer, very wet and muddy in Jun-Jul.
⏣ **Sleeping** Reasonable choice in Thakhek and Savannakhet; limited elsewhere. Some homestays in remote areas.
⏣ **Eating** Try Mekong fish in Savannakhet. Less choice elsewhere.
▲▲ **Activities and tours** Cave swimming and ecotours
★ **Don't miss...** The boat trip to Tham Kong Lor ⏵ *p372*

Thakhek and around ⏣🌐⏣ ⏵ *pp375-379*

Located on the Mekong, at the junction of Routes 13 and 12, Thakhek is a quiet town, surrounded by beautiful countryside. It is the capital of Khammouane province and was founded in 1911-12, under the French. Apart from Luang

Prabang, Thakhek is probably the most outwardly French-looking town in Laos, with fading pastel villas clustered around a simple fountain area. It has a fine collection of colonial-era shophouses, a breezy riverside position and a relaxed ambience. One of Laos' holiest sites, That Sikhot, the stunning caves of the region and beautiful Mahaxai can all be visited from here.

Ins and outs

Getting there and around The bus terminal is 4 km from town. Services run to Savannakhet, Pakse and Vientiane. Tuk-tuks ferry people in from bus terminals and are available to hire for trips. Thakhek is small enough to negotiate on foot or by bicycle. 🌐 » p378.

Tourist information The tourism office is on Vientiane Road, T052-212512. The staff are particularly helpful and are champing at the bit to take tourists out on their new eco-tours to Buddha Cave and Phou Hin Protected Area. In addition to taking tourists off the beaten path, proceeds from the tours are given to poor, local communities.

That Sikhot

ⓘ *6 km south of Thakhek. Daily 0800-1800. 2000 kip. Private tuk-tuk 100,000 kip return or public tuk-tuk from the intersection of Ounkham and Kouvoravong rds.*

That Sikhot or **Sikhotaboun** is one of Laos' holiest sites. It overlooks the Mekong and the journey downstream from Thakhek, along a quiet country road, reveals bucolic Laos at its best. That Sikhot consists of a large gold stupa raised 29 m on a plinth, with a viharn upstream built in 1970 by the last king of Laos. A major annual festival is held here in July and during February. It is thought to have been built by Chao Anou at the beginning of the 15th century and houses the relics of Chao Sikhot, a local hero, who founded the old town of Thakhek. According to legend, Sikhot was bestowed with Herculean strength, after eating some rice he had stirred with dirty – but as it turned out magic – sticks. He conquered most of the surrounding area as well as Vientiane, whereupon he married the king of Vientiane's daughter. Sikhot foolishly revealed to his new wife that he could only be killed through his anus, so the King of Vientiane placed an archer at the bottom of Sikhot's pit latrine (a messy business that does not bear contemplating) and when the unfortunate Oriental Hercules came to relieve himself, he was killed by an arrow.

Tham Pha Pa (Buddha Cave)

ⓘ *Ban Na Khangxang, 22 km from Thakhek, off Route 12. 2000 kip for admission plus 2000 kip for a motorbike.*

A farmer hunting for bats accidently stumbled across the Buddha Cave in April 2004. On climbing up to the cave's mouth, he found 229 bronze Buddha statues, believed to be more than 450 years old, and ancient palm leaf scripts. Since its discovery, the cave has become widely celebrated, attracting pilgrims from as far away as Thailand, particularly around Pi Mai (Lao New Year). A new wooden ladder has now been built to access the cave but it is quite difficult to get to, as the road from Thakhek is poor, so organize a guide through the **Thakhek Tourism Office** to escort you. In the wet season, it is necessary to catch a boat.

Route 12 and the 'Loop'

The impressive karst landscape of the Mahaxai area is visible to the northeast of town and can be explored on a popular motorbike tour from Thakhek, known as the '**Loop**', which runs from Thakhek along Route 12 to Mahaxai then north to Lak Sao, west along Route 8 to Ban Na Hin and then south back to Thakhek on Route 13, taking in caves and other beautiful scenery along the way. The circuit should take approximately three days but allow four – particularly if you want to sidetrack to Tham Kong Lor (see p372).

Going further

Tham Kong Lor (Kong Lor cave)

ⓘ *entrance fee 3000 kip.*

This cave can only be described as sensational. The Nam Hinboun River has tunnelled through the mountain, creating a giant rocky cavern, 6 km long, 90 m wide and 100 m high, which opens out into the blinding bright light at Ban Natan on the other side. The cave is apparently named after the drum makers who were believed to make their instruments here.

It is almost impossible to do the nine- to 10-hour return trip from Ban Na Hin to Kong Lor in a day, as boat drivers won't travel in the dark. The first stage of the journey is by songthaew or tractor from Ban Na Hin to Ban Napur. From Ban Napur catch a boat along the Nam Hinboun to either Ban Phonyang, where eco-lodge **Sala Hin Boun** is located (see below), or to Ban Kong Lor, the closest village to the caves, where you can find a homestay for 50,000 kip, including food. Beyond Ban Phonyang the river route to Tham Kong Lor is gorgeous, with small fish skipping out of the water, languid buffalo bathing, kids taking a dip and ducks floating by – all surrounded by breathtaking cliffs and rocky outcrops. At the start of the cave, you will have to scramble over some boulders while the boatmen carry the canoe over the rapids, so wear comfortable shoes with a good grip. A torch or, better a headlamp (2000 kip at Thakhek market), is also recommended. About two-thirds of the way through the cave is an impressive collection of stalagmites and stalactites. It is possible to continue from Ban Natan, on the other side of Kong Lor, into the awesome Hinboun gorge. This is roughly 14 km long and, for much of the distance, vertical cliffs over 300 m high rise directly from the water on both sides

Contact **Thakhek Travel Lodge** (see Sleeping) for details of the route and for motorbike hire. Note that this whole region is very susceptible to change over the next few years due to the construction of the Nam Theun II dam, a US$1.45 billion hydropower project. The area between Mahaxai and Lak Sao will probably be flooded in parts and new roads will undoubtedly be built over the coming years, so it is imperative that you check for up-to-date information before travelling.

The caves along Route 12 can also be visited on day trips from Thakhek, although some are difficult to find without a guide and access may be limited in the wet season. Turn south off Route 12 at Km 7 to reach **Tham Xang** (Tham Pha Ban Tham), an important Buddhist shrine that contains some statues and a box of religious scripts. At Km 13, turn north on a track for 2 km to **Tha Falang** (Wang Santiphap), a lovely emerald billabong on the Nam Don River, surrounded by pristine wilderness and breathtaking cliffs. It's a nice place to spend the afternoon or break your journey. In the wet season it may be necessary to catch a boat (pirogue or canoe) from the Xieng Liab Bridge to get here. Turn south off Route 12 at Km 14 and follow the track south to reach **Tham Xiang Liab**, a reasonably large cave at the foot of a 300 m-high limestone cliff, with a small swimming hole (in the dry season) at the far end. It is not easy to access the interior of the cavern on your own and, in the wet season, it can only be navigated by boat, as it usually floods.

🛏 There are 2 guesthouses on Route 13 in Ban Lao, just past the Route 8 intersection, which are better than those in Ban Na Hin, which are very rustic. Homestays are available in Ban Kong Lor and Ban Natan and there's also **E Sala Kong Lor Lodge**, 1.5 km from Kong Lor cave, T051-214315. Four small huts with twin beds and a couple of rooms. Also a campsite for US$2 per night. The best option, however, is **B-C Sala Hin Boun**, Ban Phonyang, T051-214315, 8 km from Kong Lor Cave. It enjoys a scenic location on the riverbank amongst karst rock formations and has 10 well equipped and very pleasant rooms in 2 bungalows. Mr Kham, the manager, will arrange for a boat to pick you up in Napua for US$25, with advance notice. A tour to Kong Lor for 2-3 people is US$30 with picnic lunch. Discounts in low season.

🚌 There is a small transport terminus at the Route 13/Route 8 intersection in Ban Lao for north–south buses between Vientiane and Thakhek, Savannakhet or Pakse. Songthaews generally scurry through here from early in the morning to well into the afternoon to Ban Na Hin, 15,000 kip. Generally, a pick-up waits in Ban Na Hin to take passengers to Ban Kong Lor, 3 hrs, where you can pick up a cheap boat trip into the cave for US$10-15. Alternatively, pick up a songthaew, tuk-tuk or tractor from the centre of Ban Na Hin (opposite the market) for the 10 km journey to Ban Napur, 30 mins, and then catch a boat to Ban Phonyang, 2-3 hrs, and onto the cave, a further 1 hr, US$20.

At Km 17, beyond the narrow pass, turn to the north and follow the path for 400 m to reach **Tham Sa Pha In**, a cave containing a small Lake and a couple of interesting Buddhist shrines. Swimming in the Lake is strictly prohibited as the auspicious waters are believed to have magical powers. South of Route 12 a path leads 700 m to the entrance of **Tham Nan Aen** (admission 5000 kip). This is the giant of the local caverns at 1.5 km long and over 100 m high, with multiple chambers and entrances illuminated by fluorescent lighting; it also contains a small underground freshwater pool.

More difficult to find without a local guide is **Nam Don Resurgence**, close to Ban Na, 25 km northeast of Thakhek. This beautiful lagoon within a cave is shaded by a sheer 300 m cliff and filters off into an underground waterway network, believed to extend for 3 km. The **Provincial Tourism Office** tours include this sight.

Mahaxai

Mahaxai is a beautiful small town 50 km east of Thakhek off Route 12. The sunset here is quite extraordinary but even more beautiful is the surrounding scenery of exquisite valleys and imposing limestone bluffs. A visit to Mahaxai should be combined with a visit to one or more of the spectacular caves along Route 12 and some river excursions to see the Se Bangfai gorges or run the rapids further downstream.

Nam Hinboun River, near Kong Lor Cave

Savannakhet 🚌🚕⛺🏨🍴 ⏩ pp375-379

Situated on the banks of the Mekong at the start of Route 9 to Danang in Vietnam, Savannakhet – or Savan as it is usually known – is an important river port and gateway to the south. The city has a sizeable Chinese population and attracts merchants from both Vietnam and Thailand, while the ubiquitous colonial houses and fading shopfronts are an ever-present reminder of earlier French influence. Savannakhet Province has a multitude of natural attractions, although the majority are a fair hike from the provincial capital.

Ins and outs

Getting there and around It is possible to cross into Vietnam by taking Route 9 east over the Annamite Mountains via Xepon. The border is at Lao Bao (see p159), 236 km east of Savannakhet, with bus connections direct from Savan to Danang, Dong Ha and Hué. Domestic links aren't so good and are limited to buses and local transport. A new private bus station offers connections with Pakse and Vientiane. The government bus terminal is on the northern edge of town, near the market; a tuk-tuk to the centre should cost about 5000 kip. Just west of the bus station is the songthaew terminal, where vehicles depart to provincial destinations. Tuk-tuks, locally known as 'Sakaylab', criss-cross town. 🚌 ▸▸ *p378.*

Tourist information The Provincial Tourism Office ⓘ *T052-214203, savannakhet guides2@yahoo.com (ask for Mr Kaisee),* is one of the best in the country and runs a number of excellent eco-tours in the surrounding area, which should be organized in advance. The office can also arrange guides and drivers for other trips. ▲▲ ▸▸ *p378.*

Sights

Savan's **colonial heritage** can be seen throughout the town centre. Perhaps the most attractive area is the square east of the Immigration office between Khanthabouli and Phetsalath roads. **Wat Sounantha** has a three-dimensional raised relief on the front of the *sim*, showing the Buddha in the mudra of bestowing peace, separating two warring armies. **Wat Sayaphum**, on the Mekong, is rather more attractive and has several early 20th-century monastery buildings. It is both the largest and oldest monastery in town, although it was only built at the end of the 19th century. Evidence of Savan's diverse population is reflected in the **Chua Dieu Giac**, a Mahayana Buddhist pagoda that serves the town's Vietnamese population. The **Dinosaur Museum** ⓘ *Khantabouli Rd, Mon-Fri 0800-1200, 1400-1600, 5000 kip,* houses a collection of four different dinosaur and early mammalian remains, and even some fragments of a meteorite that fell to earth over 100 million years ago.

Dong Phu Vieng National Protected Area

The provincial tourism office (see Ins and outs) runs excellent treks through the Dong Phu Vieng National Protected Area, home to wildlife such as Siamese crocodiles, Asian elephants, the endangered Eld's deer, langurs and wild bison (most of which you would be incredibly lucky to see). Located within the NPA is a **Song Sa Kae** (Sacred Forest and Cemetery), revered by the local Katang ethnic group, who are known for their buffalo sacrifices. The well-trained, local guides show how traditional natural produce is gathered for medicinal, fuel or other purposes. The tours are exceptionally good value; most only run during the dry season.

● Sleeping

Thakhek *p370*

D Mekong Hotel, Setthathirat Rd (or Mekong Rd), T052-250777. Prime location overlooking the Mekong but a hideous building, painted in putrid baby blue. Exterior aside, the large 1950s hotel has 60 or so a/c rooms, whose wide balconies are perfect for the sunset vista. Large, plain but clean, with TV, telephone, fridge and bathtub. It is one of the best deals in town. Brilliant restaurant attached.

D-E Sooksomboon Guesthouse (formerly the Sikhot Hotel), Setthathirat Rd, T052-212225. An immensely attractive building facing the Mekong that was once the provincial police station. The interior has been decorated with art deco-inspired charm. The a/c rooms in the main house are best, with en suite bathrooms, fluffy chairs, some padded walls, fridge and TV. Also cheaper rooms in the motel-esque annexe. Restaurant. Helpful staff.

E **Thakhek Travel Lodge**, T020-5754009, 2 km from the centre of town. Popular guesthouse set in a beautifully restored and decorated house. Fantastic outdoor seating area and the furniture and embellishments are outstanding. However, the rooms are pretty average for the price and the service is a bit on the *bopenyang* side. Hotel restaurant is only passable but does have an espresso machine. Danish owners provide travel advice, when they're around, and there's an excellent logbook for those intending to travel independently around the 'Loop'. Motorcycle hire US$15 per day. Recommended for those planning adventure travel around the area.

F **Khammuan International** (formerly the Chaleunxay Hotel), Kouvoravong Rd, T052-212171. An oldish villa with rooms that are small without windows but some have a/c and the en suite bathrooms are good with hot water showers. Cheaper single rooms with super-powerful ceiling fans are also available. A/c restaurant.

Because of the irregular bus hours there is a small 'guesthouse' at the bus station, where you can rent a bed for 25,000 kip.

Mahaxai *p373*

F **Mahaxai Guesthouse**. 10 large clean airy rooms, with en suite showers, upstairs rooms are brighter. There is an attractive balcony overlooking the river, ideal for watching the world go by.

Savannakhet *p374, map p377*

B-C **Nanhai**, Santisouk Rd, T041-212371. This 7-storey hotel is considered one of the better places in town. The 42 rooms, karaoke bars and dining hall are a prime example of a mainland Chinese hotel except that the staff here are quite polite. Rooms have a/c, TV, fridge, IDD telephones and en suite bathroom but they smell musty and the single rooms are minuscule. The pool has no water.

D-F **Savanbanhao**, Senna Rd, T041-212202. 4 colonial-styles houses set around a quiet courtyard with a range of

rooms. Most expensive have en suite hot water showers. Beware of the lethal Soviet water boiler. Some a/c. Large balcony. **Savanbanhao Tourism Co** is attached (see Activities and tours) and private buses (US$12 to Vietnam) depart from here. Motorbike hire US$10 per day. Good for those who want to be in and out of Savannakhet, quickly.

E **Nongsoda**, Tha He Rd, T041-212522. Oodles of white lace draped all over the house. Clean rooms with a/c and en suite bathrooms with wonderfully hot water. During the low season the hotel drops its room rates to US$8, which is exceptionally good value.

E **Saisouk**, Makhavenha Rd, T041-212207. This breezy guesthouse has good sized twin and double rooms, immaculately furnished and spotlessly clean, some a/c, communal bathrooms. Beautifully decorated with interesting *objets d'art* (including 3 telephones) and what looks like dinosaur bones. Plenty of chairs and tables on the large verandahs. Very friendly staff, reasonable English. Laundry service.

F **Xayamoungkhun** (English sign just reads 'Guest House'), 85 Ratsavong Seuk Rd, T041-212426. An excellent little hotel with 16 rooms in an airy colonial-era villa. Centrally positioned with a largish compound. Range of very clean rooms available, more expensive have hot water, a/c and fridge. Very friendly owners. Second-hand books and magazines are available. Recommended.

🍴 Eating

Thakhek *p370*

There is the usual array of noodle stalls – try the one in the town 'square' with good fruit shakes. Warmed baguettes are also sold at the square in the morning. The best place to eat is definitely at one of the riverside restaurants on either side of fountain square, where you can watch the sunset, while knocking back a beer Lao and tasty BBQ foods. Otherwise, most restaurants are attached to hotels, the **Mekong Hotel** is the best of these, with formal service and a large array of Vietnamese-style dishes. The **Southida Guesthouse**, Chao Anou, one block from the river, is also good value and does a reasonable western breakfast.

Savannakhet *p374, map p377*

Several restaurants on the riverside serve good food and beer. The market also has stalls offering good, fresh food, including excellent Mekong River fish.

🍴 **Sakura**, T041-212882, near the church (signs read Khampa Café). This is a bit of a shock find – in a good way. A very atmospheric lantern-lit garden, with a country and western meets Oriental

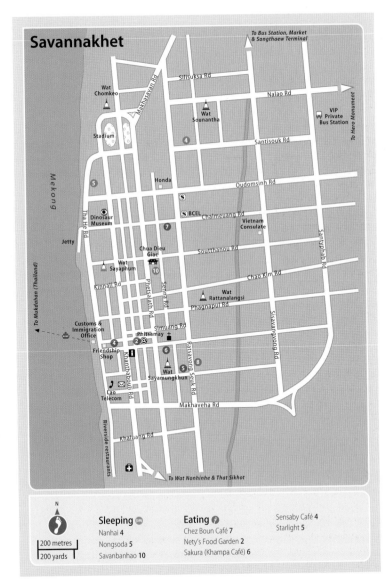

Savannakhet

Sleeping 🛏
Nanhai 4
Nongsoda 5
Savanbanhao 10

Eating 🍴
Chez Boun Café 7
Nety's Food Garden 2
Sakura (Khampa Café) 6

Sensaby Café 4
Starlight 5

200 metres
200 yards
N

sukiyaki feel. Acoustic guitarists often perform here. Good sukiyaki fondue and basic Asian fare like fried rice but it's the atmosphere that makes it special.

¶¶-¶ Chez Boun Cafe, opposite the big trade centre. A tiny little café; you could easily walk straight past it as it isn't sign-posted. Great steak, pizza, espresso and cappuccino. Good for brunch.

¶ Sensaby Café, next door to the derelict Santyphab Hotel. Cozy little café run by a young Chinese-Lao woman. Good atmosphere at night. Choice of western food including salads, muesli and ice cream at very cheap prices, best milk shakes in town.

¶ Starlight, opposite Wat Sayamung Khum, on the corner. BBQ, deep-fried dishes and spicy salads. Cheap and cheerful, and favoured by many westerners. The owners are a delight and speak good English.

▲ Activities and tours

Savannakhet *p374, map p377*
Savannakhet Provincial Tourism Authority, T041-214203, savannakhet guides2@yahoo.com. In conjunction with the NGO, **SNV Netherlands**, the tourism authority runs excellent ecotours in the area. There are 14 keen, English-speaking guides who take tourists out to see the local culture and sights. 1- to 3-day treks have been established, with proceeds filtering down to local communities.
Savanbanhao Tourism Co, Savanbanhao Hotel (see Sleeping), Mon-Sat 0800-1200, 1330-1630. Tours and trips to most sights in the area.

☺ Transport

Thakhek *p370*
Bus/truck
Thakhek's bus station is 4 km northeast of town. Daily connections northbound to **Vientiane**, 0400, 0530, 0700, 0830, 0900 and then hourly until 2300, 346 km, 6-7 hrs, 40,000 kip; the VIP bus also dashes through town at 1300, 60,000 kip. Southbound buses to **Savannakhet**, every hr, 1100-2200 daily, 139 km, 2½ hrs, 20,000 kip; to **Pakse**, every hr until 2400, 6-7 hrs; also to **Sekong**, 1030, 1530 and 2300, 60,000 kip; to **Don Khong**, 1600, 60,000 kip. To get to **Mahaxai**, take a songthaew from the bus terminal, 20,000 kip, or charter a tuk-tuk, which makes it easier to reach the caves en route. To **Dong Ha** (Vietnam), 0800 Sat, 80,000 kip.

Motorbike
Bikes can be rented from **Thakek Travel Lodge**, US$15 per day; the **Chansathid Hotel**, T052-212208, US$10 per day, and from the no-name rental shop, on the left-hand side, near the traffic lights, US$8 per day (ask for Mr Na).

Mahaxai *p373*
Songthaews leave from the market in the morning. The last bus back to Thakhek leaves Mahaxai at 1500.

Savannakhet *p374, map p377*
Bus or truck
From the government terminal, northbound buses depart daily to **Vientiane**, 0530, 0600, 0640, 0720, 0800, 0840, 0920, 1010, 1100, 1200 and then hourly until 2200, 8-9 hrs, 55,000 kip. Most of the Vientiane-bound buses also stop at **Thakhek**, 125 km, 2-3 hrs, 25,000 kip. There are also scheduled buses to **Thakhek** at 0730, 0915, 1015 and 1130 daily.

Southbound buses to **Pakse** depart at 0700, 0630, 0900, 1200 and 1430 daily, 6-7 hrs, 30,000 kip; buses in transit from Vientiane to Pakse will also pick up passengers. To **Don Khon**, 0700, 9-10 hrs, 50,000 kip.

Eastbound buses depart daily to **Xepon** and **Lao Bao** (Vietnam border, see p159), 0630, 0900 and 1200, 4-5 hrs, 30,000 kip. A bus also departs at 2200 daily for destinations within Vietnam, including **Hué**, 13 hrs, 90,000 kip; **Danang** 508 km, 15 hrs, 110,000 kip, and **Hanoi**, 22 hrs,

200,000 kip; there are additional services at 0700 and 1800 Sat and 0700 Sun. Luxury Vietnam-bound buses can also be arranged through **Savanbanhao Hotel** (see Sleeping), T041-212202, US$12.

Car, motorbike and bicycle
Car and driver from the **Hoong Thip Hotel**, Phetsalath Rd, T041-212262, US$50 per day, and from the **Savanbanhao Hotel**, prices vary. The latter also has motorbikes, US$10 per day. **Xayamoungkhun Hotel** (English sign just reads 'Guest House'), 85 Ratsavong Seuk Rd, T041-212426, rents bicycles for US$1.

Songthaew or pickup
The songthaew terminal, near the bus station and market, serves countless provincial destinations; most services depart at 0630-0700. To **Thakhek**, 0800, 0900, 1030, 1130, 1350, 1440, 1530 and 1620, 3-5 hrs (depending on the number of stops), 20,000 kip. Songthaews to the **Vietnam border** depart with more frequency than the buses (see above) but are much slower.

Tuk-tuk
Most tuk-tuks charge around 5000 kip per person for a local journey. A tuk-tuk with good local knowledge and exemplary English is **Amphone**, T020-5440821.

ⓘ Directory

Thakhek *p370*
Banks Banque Pour le Commerce Extérieur, Vientiane Rd, just across from the Post Office, will change cash and TCs and does cash advances on Visa. **Lao Development Bank**, Kouvoravong Rd (eastern end), exchanges cash but doesn't do cash advances. There's an exchange counter at the immigration pier.

Post office Kouvoravong Rd (at crossroads with Nongbuakham Rd); international calls can be made here.

Savannakhet *p374, map p377*
Banks Lao Development Bank, Oudomsinh Rd, will change most major currencies. Banque pour le Commerce Exterieur Lao (BCEL), Chalmeaung Rd, will exchange currency as well as do cash advances on Visa/MasterCard. There are exchange counters around the market, any currency accepted, and at the pier (bad rate). **Embassies and consulates** Vietnam Consulate, Sisavangvong Rd, T041-212737, Mon-Fri 0730-1100, 1400-1630, provides visas in 3 days on presentation of 2 photos and US$55. Thai Consulate, Kuvoravong Rd, open 0830-1200 for applications, 1400-1500 for visa collection, visas are issued on the same day if dropped off in the morning. **Immigration** Lao customs and immigration, Tha He Rd, at the passenger pier, for exit to Thailand and Lao visas, 0830-1200, 1300-1600 daily, overtime fees payable Sat and Sun. **Internet** Internet cafés here haven't really clicked onto net calls yet but it's only a matter of time. Phitsamay, Chaluanmeung Rd, is quite a decent internet café and shop in a convenient location. **Medical services** Savannakhet Hospital, Khanthabuli Rd, T041-212051. **Police** A block back from the river, near the tourist office, T041-212069. **Post office** Khanthabouli Rd, daily 0800-2200y. **Telephone** Next door to the PO is Lao Telecom Office, for domestic and international calls. There are also plenty of IDD call boxes scattered around town (including 1 next to the immigration office at the river).

Far south

The far south is studded with wonderful attractions: from pristine jungle scenery to the cooler Boloven Plateau and the rambling ruins of Wat Phou, once an important regional powerbase. The true gems of the south, however, are the Siphandon (4000 islands), lush green islets that offer the perfect setting for those wanting to kick back for a few days. Don Khong, Don Khone and Don Deth are just three of the many islands littered across the Mekong right at the southern tip of Laos near the border with Cambodia. There are roaring waterfalls nearby and pakha, or freshwater dolphins, can sometimes be spotted here between December and May, when they come upstream to give birth to their young.

⊘ **Getting there** Plane, bus, boat, car, songthaew
⊖ **Getting around** Songthaew, bicycle, walking, hired car with driver, motorbike
⊖ **Time required** 4 days
⊚ **Weather** Hot and sticky in summer, very wet and muddy in Jun-Jul. The Boloven Plateau can be very cold Nov-Dec.
⊖ **Sleeping** A few mid-range hotels in Pakse, Siphandon and Savannakhet; also many backpacker options.
⊘ **Eating** Limited to Lao and generic, Asian meals. More choice in Pakse. Fantastic coffee.
▲▲ **Activities and tours** Trekking, river trips, elephant trekking.
★ **Don't miss...** Mekong Islands of Siphandon ▸▸ *p386 and p387.*

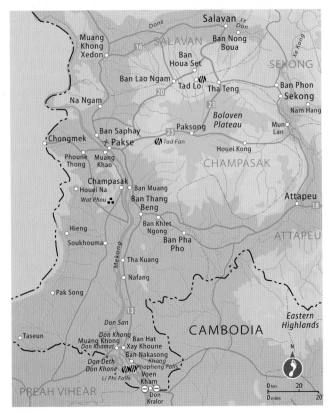

Pakse (Pakxe) and around 🏠🍴☀️🔺📷🌙 ›› pp391-402

Pakse is the largest town in the south and is strategically located at the junction of the Mekong and Xe Don rivers. It is a busy commercial town, built by the French early in the 20th century as an administrative centre for the south. The town has seen better days but the tatty colonial buildings lend an air of old-world charm. Pakse is a major staging post for destinations further afield such as the old royal capital of Champasak, famed for its pre-Angkor, seventh-century Khmer ruins of Wat Phou. Close by are ecotourism projects where elephant treks, birdwatching and homestays are possible.

Ins and outs

Getting there Pakse is Southern Laos' transport hub. The airport is 2 km northwest of town; tuk-tuks will make the journey for around 15,000 kip. There is a small café and BCEL exchange in the terminal building. International flights, as well as domestic flights to/from Vientiane, run several times a week. There are three official bus terminals in Pakse: the Northern terminal (Km 7 on Route 13 north, T031-251508) is for buses to and from the north; the Southern terminal (Km 8 south on Route 13, T031-212981) is for buses to and from the south, and the Central market terminal is for northbound VIP buses. Tuk-tuks wait to transport passengers from terminals to the town centre; you shouldn't have to pay more than 5000 kip but they will wait until the vehicle is jam-packed. A public passenger boat from Champasak to Pakse leaves at 1400 having come from Don Khong. But, do check on all times. 🚌 ›› p399.

Getting around Tuk-tuks and saamlors are the main means of local transport and can be chartered for half a day for about US$5. The main tuk-tuk 'terminal' is at the Daoheung market. Boats are available for charter from the jetty at the end of the new road by the river. Cars, motorbikes and bicycles are available for hire from some hotels and tour companies. The town's roads are numbered as if they were highways: No 1 Road through to No 46 Road.

Tourist information National Tourism Authority Champasak ⓘ *No 11 Rd, T031-212021, erratic hours but try Mon-Fri 0800-1200, 1400-1600.* Some patience is required in dealing with officials here but, once you get past the initial bureaucratic difficulties, you will find they have some fantastic ecotours on offer to unique destinations (some are offered in conjunction with local travel agents, such as **Champa Mai**. Mr Na, a guide at the office, speaks very good English and is probably the best person to speak to.

Wat Phou

ⓘ *The site is officially open 0800-1630 but the staff are happy to let you in if you get there for sunrise, even as early as 0530, and you won't get thrown out until 1800. Admission 30,000 kip goes towards restoration. There are foodstalls at the gate.*

The archaeological site of Wat Phou is at the foot of the Phou Pasak, 8 km southwest of Champasak. With its teetering, weathered masonry, it conforms exactly to the western ideal of the lost city. The mountain behind Wat Phou is called **Linga Parvata**, as the Hindu Khmers thought it resembled a linga – albeit a strangely proportioned one. Although the original Hindu temple complex was built in the fifth and sixth centuries, most of remains today is believed to have been built in the 10th to 11th centuries.

Most of the ruins which date from the fifth and sixth centuries, making them at least 200 years older than Angkor Wat. At that time, the Champasak area was the centre of power on the lower Mekong. The Hindu temple only became a Buddhist shrine in later centuries.

Archaeologists and historians believe most of the building at Wat Phou was the work of the Khmer king, Suryavarman II (1131-1150), who was also responsible for starting work on

Angkor Wat, Cambodia. The temple remained important for Khmer kings even after they had moved their capital to Angkor. They continued to appoint priests to serve at Wat Phou and sent money to maintain the temple until the last days of the Angkor Empire.

Ins and outs Most songthaews run from Pakse's Southern bus terminal on Route 13 to Ban Lak Sarm Sip (which translates as 'village 30 km'), where they take a right turn to Ban Muang (5 km). Here, people sell tickets for the ferry to Ban Phaphin, 2 km north of Champasak, 5000 kip. From the dock, you can catch a tuk-tuk to Champasak or the archaeological site for around 10,000 kip. Public boats from Pakse make the journey to Champasak in 1½ hours, docking at the landing near Ban Lak Sarm Sip, from where you can catch a songthaew to Ban Muang. You can also charter a boat from Pakse to Wat Phou, which makes sense for a larger group; expect to pay about US$50-60 for boat hire for 15-20 people. The boat will probably dock at Ban Wat Muang Kao, 4 km downstream from Champasak; take a bus or tuk-tuk from there. ⊟ ▸▸ *p400*.

Exploring the site The king and dignitaries would originally have sat on the platform above the 'tanks' or *baray* and presided over official ceremonies or watched aquatic games. In 1959 a **palace** was built on the platform so the king had somewhere to stay during the annual Wat Phou Festival (see p397). A long avenue leads from the platform to the pavilions. This **processional causeway** was probably built by Khmer King Jayavarman VI (1080-1107) and may have been the inspiration for a similar causeway at Angkor Wat. The sandstone **pavilions**, on either side of the processional causeway, were added after the main temple and are thought to date from the 12th century (most likely from the reign of Suryavarman II). Although crumbling, with great slabs of laterite and collapsed lintels lying aesthetically around, both pavilions are remarkably intact. The pavilions were probably used for segregated worship by pilgrims, one for women (left) and the other for men (right). The porticoes of the two huge buildings face each other. The roofs were thought originally to have been poorly constructed with thin stone slabs on a wooden beam-frame and later replaced by Khmer tiles. Only the outer walls now remain but there is enough still standing to fire the imagination: the detailed carving around the window frames and porticoes is well-preserved. The laterite used to build the complex was brought from **Um Muang**, another smaller Khmer temple complex a few kilometres downriver, but the carving is in sandstone. The interiors were without permanent partitions, although it is thought that rush matting was used instead, and furniture was limited – reliefs only depict low stools and couches. At the rear of the women's pavilion are the remains of a brick construction, believed to have been the queen's quarters.

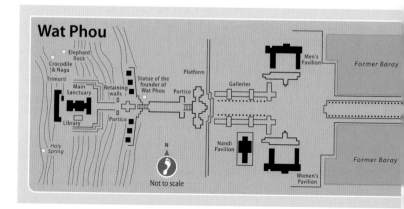

Wat Phou

Elephant Rock

Crocodile & Naga

Trimurti

Main Sanctuary

Retaining walls

Library

Holy Spring

Statue of the founder of Wat Phou

Platform

Portico

Portico

Galleries

Men's Pavilion

Former Baray

Nandi Pavilion

Women's Pavilion

Former Baray

N

Not to scale

A monk worships at Wat Phou

Above the pavilions is a small temple, the **Nandi Pavilion**, with entrances on two sides. It is dedicated to Nandi, the bull (Siva's vehicle), and is a common feature in Hindu temple complexes. There are three chambers, each of which would originally have contained statues – these have been stolen. As the hill begins to rise above the Nandi temple, the remains of six brick temples follow the contours, with three on each side of the pathway. All six are completely ruined and their function is unclear. At the bottom of the steps is a portico and statue of the founder of Wat Phou, Pranga Khommatha.

The **main sanctuary**, 90 m up the hillside and orientated east-west, was originally dedicated to Siva. The rear section (behind the Buddha statue) is part of the original sixth-century brick building. Sacred spring water was channelled through the hole in the back wall of this section and used to wash the sacred linga. The water was then thrown out, down a shute in the right wall, where it was collected in a receptacle. Pilgrims would then wash in the holy water. The front of the temple was constructed later, probably in the eighth to ninth century, and has some fantastic carvings: apsaras, dancing Vishnu, Indra on a three-headed elephant and, above the portico of the left entrance, a carving of Siva, the destroyer, tearing a woman in two.

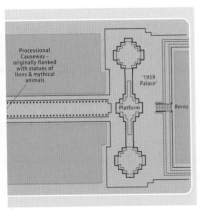

The Hindu temple was converted into a Buddhist shrine, either in the 13th century during the reign of the Khmer king Jayavarman VII or when the Lao conquered the area in the 14th century. A large Buddha statue now presides over its interior.

Champasak

The agricultural town of **Champasak**, which stretches along the right bank of the Mekong for 4 km, is the nearest town to Wat Phou and, now that it has enough comfortable accommodation, is a good base from which to explore the site and the surrounding area.

From Pakse follow Route 13 and turn left at Km 38 onto Route 18b. Continue for another 13 km and you will reach **Ban Khiet Ngong**. This village has a community-based project which offers trekking and homestay accommodation on the edge of the **Se [Xe] Pian Wetlands**, which are rich in bird life and one of the most threatened land types in Laos. The provincial authorities are trying to promote ecotourism in this area, so please take this into consideration if you visit.

From Khiet Ngong, elephant treks can be organized either through the **Se Pian National Protected Area** or to the amazing fortress of **Phu Asa**. Located 2 km from Khiet Ngong at the summit of a small jungle-clad hill, this ancient ruined fortress is an enigmatic Hindu-Khmer site. Unlike Wat Phou, it isn't really intact but it does have over 20 interesting 2 m-high stone columns arranged in a semi circle – they look a bit like a scaled-down version of Stonehenge.

There are several eco-tourism two- to three-day trekking/home-stay tours offered in the area, contact the Provincial Tourism Information Office in Pakse and ask for Mr Sulichan. Other tourism operators in Pakse can also organize tours to the area. ▲▲ ▶▶ *p398*.

▶▶ *pp391-402*

Boloven Plateau ⊕⊘❀▲⊜❶

The French identified the Boloven Plateau, in the northeast of Champasak Province, as a prime location for settlement by hardy French farming stock. The soils are rich and the upland position affords some relief from the summer heat of the lowlands. However, their grand colonial plans came to nought and, although some French families came to live here, they were few in number and all left between the 1950s and 1970s as conditions in the area deteriorated. Today the plateau is inhabited by a colourful mix of ethnic groups, such as the Laven, Alak, Tahoy and Suay, many of whom were displaced during the war and (to a lesser extent) by recent dam-building efforts. The premier attraction in the area is the number of roaring falls plunging off the plateau. Tad Lo and Tad Fan are particularly popular tourist destinations.

Ins and outs

Tourist infrastructure is limited. Trips to Tad Fan and other attractions can be organized in Pakse through the **Pakse Hotel**, **Sabaidy 2**, **Champa Mai Travel** and **Lane Xang Travel**. Alternatively, the best base on the plateau is Tad Lo (see p385), which can be reached by bus or songthaew from Pakse, alighting at Ban Houa Set (2½ hrs from Pakse). There is a blue sign here indicating the way to Tad Lo – a 1½-km walk along a dirt track and through the village of Ban Saen Wang. You can usually get a tuk-tuk from Ban Houa Set to Tad Lo for around 5000 kip. All the guesthouses in Tad Lo can arrange guided treks to Ban Khian and Tad Soung. Before you set off, pop in to **Tim's Guesthouse & Restaurant** for a quick chat to Soulideth (Tim's English-speaking husband). A great source of free and friendly information, he is the foremost authority on all there is to do in the area and is unbelievably helpful. He seems to be able to arrange tours and excursions with less hassle and more local involvement than anyone else. He'll also give you a map which you can copy, www.tadlo.laopdr.com. ▲▲⊜ ▶▶ *p398 and p400*.

Paksong (Pakxong) and around

The main town on the Boloven Plateau is Paksong, a small market town 50 km east of Pakse. It was originally a French agricultural centre, popular during the colonial era for its cooler temperatures. The town occupies a very scenic spot, however, the harsh weather in the rainy season changes rapidly making it difficult to plan trips around the area.

> ## Tahoy festival
>
> **Background**
>
> The Tahoy village of Ban Paleng, not far from Tha Teng, is a fascinating place to visit, especially in March (in accordance with the full moon), when the animist Tahoy celebrate their annual three-day sacrificial festival. The village is built in a circle around the *kuan* (the house of sacrifice). A water buffalo is donated by each family in the village. The buffalo has its throat cut and the blood is collected and drunk. The raw meat is divided among the families and surrounding villages are invited to come and feast on it. The head of each family throws a slab of meat into the *lak khai* – a basket hanging from a pole in front of the *kuan* – so that the spirits can partake too. The sacrifice is performed by the village shaman, then dancers throw spears at the buffalo until it dies. The villagers moved from the Vietnam border area to escape the war, but Ban Paleng was bombed repeatedly: the village is still littered with shells and unexploded bombs.

Just 17 km from Paksong are the stunning twin falls of **Tad Mone** and **Tad Meelook**. Once a popular picnic spot for locals, the area is now almost deserted and the swimming holes at the base of the falls are an idyllic place for a dip.

Not far from Paksong, 1 km off the road to Pakse, is **Tad Fan**, a dramatic 120 m-high waterfall, which is believed to be one of the tallest cascades in the country. The fall splits into two powerful streams roaring over the edge of the cliff and plummeting into the pool below, with mist and vapour shrouding views from above. One of the best viewing spots for the falls is the **Tad Fan Resort**'s restaurant, which offers an unobscured view of the magnificent site.

Tad Lo and around

Tad Lo is a popular 'resort' on the edge of the Boloven Plateau. There are now numerous places to stay in this idyllic retreat, good hiking, an exhilarating river to frolic in (especially in the wet season) and elephant trekking. In the vicinity of Tad Lo there are also hill tribe villages, which can be visited in the company of a local villager. The **Xe Xet** (or Houai Set) flows past Tad Lo, crashing over two sets of cascades nearby: **Tad Hang**, the lower series, is overlooked by the **Tad Lo Lodge** and **Saise Guesthouse**, while **Tad Lo**, the upper, is a short hike away.

There are two Alak villages, **Ban Khian** and **Tad Soung**, close to Tad Lo. The Alak are an Austro-Indonesian ethno-linguistic group. Most fascinating is the Alak's seeming obsession with death. The head of each household carves coffins out of hollowed logs for himself and his whole family (even babies), then stacks them, ready for use, under their rice storage huts. This tradition serves as a reminder that life expectancy in these remote rural areas is around 40 (the national average is a little over 50) and infant mortality upwards of 120 per 1000 live births; the number one killer is malaria.

Katou villages such as **Ban Houei Houne** (on the Salavan-Pakse road) are famous for their weaving of a bright cloth used locally as a *pha sin* (sarong). This village also has an original contraption to pound rice: on the river below the village are several water-wheels which power the rice pounders. Tours to the village are run by **Saise Guesthouse**: at 150,000 kip per tour, it's best to set off in a group. **Tim's Restaurant** can also make arrangements for you to get there, negotiating directly with the tuk-tuk driver to keep the price down.

Don Khong ⬤🚲❄🚌🏦 ▸▸ *pp391-402*

Don Khong is the largest of the Mekong islands at 16 km long and 8 km wide. It's a tremendous place to relax or explore by bicycle. Visitors might be surprised by the smooth asphalt roads, electricity and general standard of amenities that exist on the island but two words explain it all – Khamtay Siphandone – Laos' president, who has a residence on the island.

Ins and outs

Getting there In the high season songthaews depart Pakse's Southern bus terminal hourly between 0800 and 1200. The occasional bus will also ply through but songthaews are the most common transport option. Some depart direct from Pakse airport. The journey to Ban Hat Xai Khoune should take between four and five hours and cost US$3; in most cases the bus/truck will board the car ferry (3000 kip) at Ban Hat (1 km south of Ban Hat Xai Khoune) and take you right across to Ban Naa on Don Khong (1 km south of Muang Khong). There are also motorboats from Ban Hat Xai Khoune to Muang Khong (5000 kip, dependent on the number of passengers). If there is not a bus directly to Don Khong, catch a bus bound for Ban Nakasong and jump off at Ban Hat Xai Khoune. If by chance you get dumped at Nakasong, you can arrange a boat to Don Khong from there; although this is a very pretty route it is time-consuming and not the most efficient way to get to the island. If you travel all the way from Pakse or Champasak by boat, alight at Ban Houa Khong on the northern tip of the island and arrange transport from there to Muang Khong (buses and tuk-tuks wait here). The boats often continue to Ban Muang Saen Nua, although they may arrive here considerably later, as they tend to visit neighbouring islands first.

Getting around All of the guesthouses can arrange bicycle hire for 8000-10,000 kip per day. There are a few tuk-tuks in town but they are hardly required around tiny Muang Khong. It is, though, possible to charter a tuk-tuk for the trip to the far side of the island, load on a bicycle or two and then cycle back. ⬤ ▸▸ *p399*.

Around the island

Don Khong's 'capital' is **Muang Khong**, a small former French settlement. Pigs and chickens scrabble for food under the houses and just 50 m inland the houses give way to paddy fields. There are two wats in the town. **Wat Kan Khong**, also known as Wat Phuang Kaew, is visible from the jetty: a large gold Buddha in the mudra of subduing Mara garishly overlooks the Mekong. Much more attractive is **Wat Chom Thong** at the upstream extremity of the village, which may date from the early 19th century but which was much extended during the colonial period. The unusual Khmer-influenced sim may be gently decaying but it is doing so with style. The wat compound, with its carefully tended plants and elegant buildings, is very peaceful. The naga heads on the roof of the main sim are craftily designed to channel water, which issues from their mouths.

Most people come to Muang Khong as a base for visiting the **Li Phi** and **Khong Phapheng Falls** (see p389 and p390) in the far south. (Dolphin-watching trips are much easier to arrange from Don Deth or Don Khone.) However, the island itself is worth exploring by bicycle and deserves more time than most visitors give it. It is flat – except in the interior – the roads are quiet, so there is less risk of being mown down by a timber truck, and the villages and countryside offer a glimpse of traditional Laos. Most people take the southern 'loop' around the island, via **Ban Muang Saen Nua**, a distance of about 25 km (two to three hours on a bike). The villages along the section of road south of Ban Muang Saen Nua are wonderfully picturesque.

Ploughing the paddies on Dong Khong

Tham Phou Khiaw is tucked away among the forests of the **Green Mountain** in the centre of the island. It's a small cave, containing earthenware pots. Buddha images and other relics and offerings litter the site. Every Lao New Year (April) townsfolk climb up to the cave to bathe the images. Although it's only 15 minutes' walk from the road, finding the cave is not particularly straightforward except during Lao New Year when it is possible to follow the crowds. Head 1½ km north from Muang Khong on the road until you come to a banana plantation, with a couple of wooden houses. Take the pathway just before the houses through the banana plantation and at the top, just to the left, is a small gateway through the fence and a fairly well defined path. Head up and along this path and after 300 m or so, there is a rocky clearing. The path continues from the top right corner of the clearing for a further 200 m to a rocky mound that rolls up and to the left. Walk across the mound for about 20 m, until it levels out, and then head back to the forest. Keeping the rock immediately to your right, continue round and after 40 m there are two upturned tree trunks marking the entrance to the cave.

About 6 km north of Ban Muang Saen Nua is a hilltop wat which is arguably Don Khong's main claim to national fame. **Wat Phou Khao Kaew** (Glass Hill Monastery) is built on the spot where an entrance leads down to the underground lair of the *nagas*, known as **Muang Nak**. This underground town lies beneath the waters of the Mekong, with several tunnels leading to the surface – another is at That Luang in Vientiane. Lao legend has it that the *nagas* will come to the surface to protect the Lao whenever the country is in danger.

Don Deth, Don Khone and around ◉◉◎◎▲◎◉ » pp391-402

The islands of Don Khone and Don Deth are the pot of gold at the end of the rainbow for most travellers who head to the southern tip of Laos, and it's not hard to see why. The bamboo huts that stretch along the banks of these two staggeringly beautiful islands are filled with contented travellers in no rush to move on. Travelling by boat in this area is very picturesque: the islands are covered in coconut palms, flame trees, stands of bamboo, kapok trees and hardwoods; the river is riddled with eddies and rapids. In the distance, a few kilometres to the south, are the Khong Hai Mountains which dominate the skyline and delineate the border between Laos and Cambodia.

In the area are the Li Phi (or Somphamit) Falls and Khong Phapheng Falls – the latter are the largest in Southeast Asia and reputedly the widest in the world.

The French envisaged Don Deth and Don Khone as strategic transit points in their grandiose masterplan to create a major Mekong highway from China. In the late 19th century ports were built at the southern end of Don Khone and at the northern end of Don Deth and a narrow-gauge railway line was constructed across Don Khone in 1897 as an important bypass around the rapids for French cargo boats sailing upriver from Phnom Penh. In 1920, the French built a bridge across to Don Deth and extended the railway line to Don Deth port. This 5-km stretch of railway has the unique distinction of being the only line the French ever built in Laos. On the southern side of the bridge lie the rusted corpses of the old locomotive and boiler car. Before pulling into Ban Khone Nua, the main settlement on Don Khone, Don Deth 'port' is on the right, with what remains of its steel rail jetty.

Ins and outs

A number of companies run tours to this area, especially from Pakse. To get to Don Deth or Don Khone independently from Pakse the bus/songthaew will need to drop you off at **Ban Nakasong**. This is not the most pleasant of Lao towns and several travellers have complained about being ripped off here. However, it has a thriving market, where most of the islanders stock up on their goods, so it's worthwhile having a look around before you head off to the islands, particularly if you need to pick up necessities like torches, batteries and film. It'a 500 m walk from the bus stop down to the dock. The 'ticket office' is located in a little restaurant to the right-hand side of the dock. However, you can ask anyone that's jumping across to the islands for a lift, at a dramatically reduced rate. The boats take about 15 to 20 minutes to make the easy trip to the islands and cost around US$2 to US$3 per person. Prices will be higher (US$5-6) if you are traveling solo. A boat between Don Deth and Don Khone costs 20,000 kip; alternatively you can walk between the two islands, paying the 9000 kip charge to cross the bridge (also used as ticket to see Li Phi Falls). Both islands can easily be navigated by foot or bicycles can be rented from guesthouses for US$1 per day. ▲▣ ▸▸ *p398 and p401.*

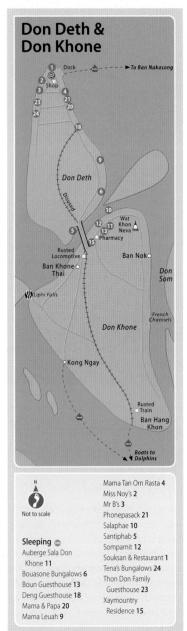

Don Deth & Don Khone

Sleeping ●
Auberge Sala Don Khone 11
Bouasone Bungalows 6
Boun Guesthouse 13
Deng Guesthouse 18
Mama & Papa 20
Mama Leuah 9
Mama Tan Orn Rasta 4
Miss Noy's 2
Mr B's 3
Phonepasack 21
Salaphae 10
Santiphab 5
Sompamit 12
Souksan & Restaurant 1
Tena's Bungalows 24
Thon Don Family Guesthouse 23
Xaymountry Residence 15

Dolphin spotting near Don Khone

Don Deth

The riverbank here is peppered with cheap-as-chips bamboo huts and restaurants geared to accommodate the growing wave of backpacker travellers that floods south to stop and recoup in this idyllic setting. A good book, hammock and icy beverage is the order of the day here, but those with a bit more energy should explore the truly stunning surroundings. It's a great location for watching the sunrises and sunsets, for walking through shady palms and frangipani trees and for swimming off the beaches, which attract the hordes in the dry season. Away from the picturesque waterfront, the centre of the island comprises rice paddies and farms; you should take care not to harm crops when exploring the island.

The national tourism authorities have been coordinating with locals to ensure that the beautiful island doesn't become 'Vang Vieng-ified', so you'll find no *Friends* videos or 'Happy' shakes here. The island has no electricity (except for a generator supply 1800-2200), no cars (except for the odd truck) and no other modern conveniences. Internet has amazingly made its way to the island, however, and it's possible to get mobile phone coverage.

Don Khone

From the railway bridge, follow the southwest path through **Ban Khone Thai** and then wind through the paddy fields for 1.7 km (20 minutes' walk) to **Li Phi Falls** ⓘ *aka Somphamit or Khone Yai Falls, 9000 kip paid at the bridge*. These are a succession of raging rapids, crashing through a narrow rocky gorge. In the wet season, when the rice is green, the area is beautiful; in the dry season, it is scorching. From the main vantage point on a jagged, rocky outcrop, the falls aren't that impressive, as a large stretch of them are obscured. 'Phi' means ghost, a reference, it is believed, to the bodies that floated down the river from the north during the war. It's best to visit Li Phi around June or July, when all the fishermen are putting out their bamboo fish traps.

The Mekong, south of Don Khone, is one of the few places in the world where it is possible to see **freshwater dolphins.** They can be spotted in the late afternoon from December to May, from the French pier at the end of the island, not far from the village of Ban Hang Khon. The walk across Don Khone from the railway bridge is some 4 km. Bicycles can be hired. It is easier, however, to catch a glimpse of the dolphins if you're in a boat, as they reside in deep water pools. In 1996 there were thought to be 30 dolphins, after which the numbers

Khong Phapheng Falls

seemed to decline and, according to local data, there were fears that only four or five were left, although a new calf has recently been spotted. The problem is that the Laos-Cambodia border transects the dolphin pool and the Lao boatmen have to pay US$1 to the Cambodian authorities in order to access the waters in which the dolphins reside. Cambodia gets a bit tetchy about these 'border incursions' and may, on the odd occasion, deny access. ▲▲ ▶▶ *p398.*

Khong Phapheng Falls

ⓘ *Near Ban Thatkho. US$1. Guesthouses organize trips for around 60,000 kip per person (min 5 passengers) and will usually be booked in conjunction with a trip to see the dolphins.*

About 36 km south of Ban Hat Xai Khoune at Ban Thatkho, a road branches off Route 13 towards Khong Phapheng Falls, which roar around the eastern shore of the Mekong for 13 km. One fork of the road leads to a vantage point, where a large wooden structure, built up on stilts, overlooks the cascades for a fantastic head-on view of the falls. When you see the huge volume of white water boiling and surging over the jagged rocks below, it is hard to imagine that there is another 10 km width of river running through the other channels. A perilous path leads down from the viewpoint to the edge of the water. Unsurprisingly, the river is impassable at this juncture, as an 1860s French expedition led by adventurers Doudart de Lagrée and Francis Garnier discovered. Another road leads down to the bank of the Mekong, 200 m away, just above the lip of the falls; at this deceptively tranquil spot, the river is gathering momentum before it plunges over the edge.

Sleeping

Pakse *p381, map p392*

A-C Champasak Palace, No 13 Rd, T031-212263, champasak_ palace_hotel @yahoo.com. This is a massive chocolate box of a hotel with 55 rooms. It was conceived as a palace for a minor prince. There are large rooms and 40 more modern, less elaborate rooms, which were added in 2000. Despite the gaudy plaster additions of recent years and general lack of maintenance, some classic touches remain: wooden shutters, some art deco furniture and lovely tiles. The restaurant is the most atmospheric place to eat in town, set on a big verandah overlooking lovely frangipani trees and manicured gardens. Friendly staff, a good terrace and the best facilities in town, including a massage centre, and a great position above the Xe Don.

B-C Champa Residence (Residence du Champa), No 13 Rd, east of town near the stadium and museum, T031-212120, champare@laotel.com. Modern-style rooms, with a/c, mini bar, hot water and satellite TV. Very clean and with some character. Attractive terrace and lush garden, Visa accepted and tours arranged. Includes breakfast.

B-D Pakse Hotel, No 5 Rd (facing the new market), T031-212131, www.hotelpakse.com. Recent renovations have rendered this one of the nicest places to stay in town with 65 rooms. The French owner, Mr Jerome, has integrated local handicraft decorations and tasteful furnishings into this slick hotel. Good restaurant attached, with the best pizza in town. Wonderful views of Pakse from the roof.

D Salachampa, No 10 Rd, T031-212273. The most characterful place in town. Choose a room in the main 1920s building: huge with wooden floors, large, en suite bathrooms with warm water showers; the upstairs rooms with balconies are best. There are also some additional, quaintly rustic rooms in a 'new' extension and a nice garden area between the two. Recommended for those looking for a touch of colonial elegance and friendly service. Tours organized from here.

E-F Sabaidy 2 Guesthouse, No 24 Rd, T031-212992. A wide range of rooms on offer, from dorm rooms through to rooms with private bathroom and hot water. The rooms are quite basic but the service here is exceptional. The proprietor, lively Mr Vong is a regular 'Mr Fixit' and offers tours, information and visa extensions. Mr Vong's grandfather, Liam Douang Vongsaa, was the first governor of Pakse and this building was the governor's residence, where Mr Vong was born in 1944.

Champasak *p381*

D-F Anouxa Guesthouse, 1 km north of the roundabout, T020-2275412. A wide range of good accommodation from wooden bungalows through to concrete rooms with either a/c or fan. The concrete villas are the best, with a serene river vista from the balconies. The only drawback is that it is a little out of town.

F Vong Pasued Guesthouse, 450 m south of the roundabout. A firm favourite with the backpacker set, this small family-run guesthouse offers pretty reasonable but basic rooms (mosquito nets, thin walls and cold water) in an old longhouse. Good restaurant, perfect for a natter with fellow travellers.

F Khamphouy Guesthouse, west of Dokchampa. Delightful family-run place. Fine bright rooms in the main house with shared facilities and 1 cottage (in the garden) with 2 rooms and en suite shower. Clean, comfortable, friendly, relaxed. Bikes for hire.

Ban Khiet Ngong *p384*

F Boun Home Guesthouse. Very basic guesthouse with wooden rooms and shared facilities.

There are also a few basic wooden bungalows geared towards foreigners. Homestays can be arranged through the **National Tourism Authority** in Pakse (see p381).

building has a cabin feel and is surrounded by coffee trees, corn fields and a flower garden. The simple rooms are bright (pink floral sheets) and clean with en suite bathrooms but no hot water. Very friendly owner speaks English.

Paksong and around *p384*

B-C Tad Fan Resort, T020-5531400, www.tadfane.com. Perched on the opposite side of the ravine from the falls is a series of wooden bungalows with nicely decorated rooms and en suite bathrooms, with hot showers. The 2nd floor of the excellent open-air restaurant offers the best view of the falls and serves a wide variety of Lao, Thai and western food. Great service. Treks to the top of falls and the Dan-Sin-Xay Plain arranged.

F Borlaven Guesthouse, Route 23 about 2 km north of the market, beyond Paksong town. The new brick and wood

Tad Lo and around *p385*

B-C Tad Lo Lodge, T031-211889; also through **Sodetour** in Pakse, T031-212122. Reception on the east side of the falls with chalet-style accommodation (13 rooms) built right on top of the waterfalls on the opposite side. Rates include breakfast and hot water. It is an attractive location (during the wet season) and the accommodation is comfortable – cane rocking chairs on the balconies overlook the cascades on the left bank. Good restaurant serving plenty of Lao and Thai food. Elephant rides are available (US$10

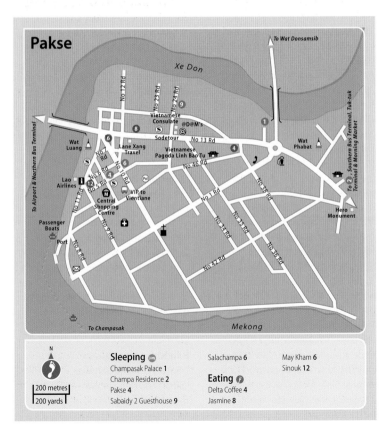

Pakse

To Wat Donsamsib

Xe Don

No 12 Rd · No 23 Rd · No 24 Rd

Vietnamese Consulate · @D@M's

Sodetour · No 13 Rd

Wat Luang

Lane Xang Travel

Vietnamese Pagoda Linh Bao Tu · No 46 Rd

Wat Phabat

To Airport & Northern Bus Terminal

No 7 Rd · No 5 Rd

Lao Airlines

VIP to Vientiane

Central Shopping Centre

Passenger Boats

Port

No 9 Rd

To Champasak

No 1 Rd · No 38 Rd

No T Rd

No 24 Rd · No 35 Rd

No 42 Rd · No 8 Rd

Hero Monument

To 2, Southern Bus Terminal, Tuk-tuk Terminal & Morning Market

Mekong

N

200 metres
200 yards

per elephant for a 2-hr trek; each elephant can carry 2 people).

D-E Saise Guesthouse (aka Sayse Guesthouse), T031-211886. The guesthouse, comprises 2 sections: the lower part sits near the restaurant at the foot of Tad Hang and consists of rooms and bungalows, all with hot water and fans. The more attractive and peaceful option is the so-called **Green House** (the roof's a giveaway) above the falls. This is a wooden chalet with 6 huge rooms, 4 with en suite shower and toilet, and 2 of those with balconies overlooking the river. The beautiful garden restaurant offers Lao and Thai food, but service is poor and the menu features protected wildlife.

There are also a number of small guesthouses near the bridge on the east side of the river, including:

F Tim's Guesthouse & Restaurant, down the bridge road, T031-214176, soulideth@laopdr.com. Twin and double bungalows with hot water, fans, and lock boxes. Also internet access, international calls, room service, laundry, book exchange, a substantial music collection and CD burning, bike rentals (8000 kip per hr or 30,000 kip per day) and just about anything else you could ask for.

Don Khong p386

A-C Auberge Sala Done Khong, Muang Khong, T031-212077. This traditional wooden house, the former holiday home of the previous regime's foreign minister, was once the best place to stay on Don Khong but although the exterior is still stunning the rooms just aren't worth the price. There are 12 tastefully decorated, large rooms with a/c and en suite hot water bathrooms; the best are in the main building on the 1st floor where there is an attractive balcony overlooking the Mekong with comfortable deckchairs. Clean and professionally run, tours arranged, bicycles for hire, good food – very relaxing. The best of the upper price-range places. Slightly cheaper rate in the low season.

B-E Souksan Hotel and Bungalow, northern end of Muang Khong near Wat Chom Thong, T031-212071. A range of rooms, from well-designed a/c rooms with en suite bathrooms to simple rooms with fans and shared facilities, all set around an attractive garden. The rooms in a separate building, with bizarre river landscape paintings, are nicely decorated and comfortably set-up with desk, cane chairs, tiled floorboards and hot water. Much better value are the bungalows, with wooden floorboards and hot showers. Like most places, discounts are offered in the low season. The manageress, Mrs Khamsone, will arrange boats to visit the falls or see the freshwater dolphins, also motorbike hire (US$10 per day). She also runs one of the most popular and best-value guesthouses on Don Deth.

E Mekong Guesthouse, Muang Khong, T031-213668. Beautifully simple and spotless rooms with fans, some overlooking the Mekong and all with comfortable mattresses. Some rooms have a/c and hot water showers (US$20). Also cheaper rooms with shared facilities (equally clean) in a wooden building.

F New Pon Guesthouse and Restaurant, Muang Khong, T031-214037. This establishment has been renamed to reflect the massive renovations undertaken in recent months. The fan rooms are very good value, with hot water showers, mozzie nets and comfortable beds. For an extra US$10 you get a/c. Mr Pon, who speaks French and English, is perhaps the most helpful of all accommodation proprietors on the island and can offer an endless supply of tourist information. Motorbike rental US$8 and bicycles US$1. He also runs a minivan service to Pakse for US$6 per person (minimum 10 people).

F Phou Kong Guesthouse, just near the bridge, Muang Khong, T031-213673. Very cheap rooms with tiny bathroom cubicles (cold water). If you can draw the owners away from the television for a second, they will organize tuk-tuks to the Cambodian border and boats to Don Deth and Don Khone. Restaurant serves the standard quasi-Asian fare.

Don Deth *p389, map p388*

Many people tend to make their choice of accommodation on the basis of word-of-mouth recommendations from other travellers; this is as good a way to choose as any, as the accommodation is all cheap and usually much of a muchness. It usually consists of spartan, thread-bare bungalows with bed, mosquito net and hammock, and shared squat toilets (unless otherwise stated). Always opt for a bungalow with a window, as the huts can get very hot. The wooden bungalows don't provide as much ventilation as the rattan equivalents but tend to attract fewer insects. Always check that the bungalow has a mosquito net. Other things to consider is the distance from the toilet to the bungalow, the state of the hammock, whether there is a restaurant attached and whether generator power is provided. Note that there may be a small price hike in accommodation in the near future to ensure that tourism benefits all of the islands inhabitants, including the farmers. Costs are likely to double once the island gets electricity.

The accommodation runs across the two sides of the island, known as the **Sunset Side** and **Sunrise Side**. There is a large conglomeration of accommodation towards the northern tip, which is a good option for those wishing to socialize and hop between the various establishments' restaurants/bars; this is also the most common drop-off point. As a general rule, if you want peace and quiet, head for the bungalows towards the mid-point along each coast; ask the boat drivers to drop you off directly at the bungalows as it can be a difficult hike with baggage.

Sunset Side

D-E Souksan Guesthouse and Restaurant, T031-212071, Houa Deth at the northern tip of the island, at the pinnacle of the Sunset and Sunrise strips. 20 or so twin and double rooms built from wood and bamboo with shared shower and toilets, not to mention a legendary Chinese restaurant. There are also a couple of concrete bungalows that are slightly more expensive. The beautiful garden is home to hundreds of butterflies, with little paths linking up to the restaurant. It's a cracking place to chill out as you sip one of the many cocktails on offer. Water volleyball is a popular option in the dry season. Electricity daily 1800-2200; internet 1200 kip per min (10 mins minimum). This is the hands-down winner on the island and more than worth the extra few bucks.

F Miss Noy's. Very close to the island tip and a small hike from the main drop-off port, this place offers an excellent view of the sunset. Clean but very basic bungalows overlooking the river. Restaurant in a prime position.

F Mr B's, follow a small trail past Miss Noy's to reach Mr B's (signposted). The owner and staff here are tremendously friendly and the restaurant offers a semi-diverse range of options (it's all relative here!). The bungalows and grounds themselves are a bit lacklustre and the enormous pigs swilling around the backyard don't make for the most pleasing surroundings. However, the river views and the helpful staff make this an outstanding option.

F Tena's Bungalows (aka Sunset Bungalows), located further along the same path. Nine rattan bungalows with mozzie nets. The restaurant is more of an attraction and is a popular meeting spot.

F Thon Don Family Guesthouse and Restaurant, further along Sunset Boulevard and right down a little lane. Bungalows with outside toilet. Rickety restaurant that's a very popular nighttime chill-out joint. The owners are exceptionally friendly. Good for hanging around and swinging in a hammock.

Sunrise Side

F Bouasone, riverside midway along the Sunrise Side, T020-5833001. Secluded bungalows with shared facilities. Restaurant with guitar for those that want a jam session, which may be difficult above the loud Lao music blaring from the premises. Six threadbare bungalows with hammocks. It's difficult to get to from the main jetty, so ask the boat driver to drop you off right in front of the establishment.

F Deng Guesthouse, next door to Oudomsouk. Three wooden bungalows on stilts. Very popular with those who want to laze on a hammock overlooking the water. Scenic position.

F Mama Leuah, on the south side of the former French concrete port towards the centre of the island. Several bungalows that seem a bit newer and jazzier than most. Shared squat toilet facilities.

F Mama and Papa, on the northern peninsula just up from **Paradise**. Typical thatched bamboo bungalows with mosquito nets and shared facilities. Nice shady position. The restaurant has battery-powered lights for the night-time blackout and serves a pretty exceptional lentil curry.

F Mama Tan Orn Rasta Café. This place has had numerous names but the atmosphere remains unchanged. There is a beautiful view from the communal balcony and the effervescent Mama is good value, with her jovial demeanour and back-slapping, cheeky quips. The place is somewhat run-down, with rattan huts and communal facilities but is a popular place to hang out in the hammocks.

F Phonepasack Restaurant and Guesthouse, northern end of the island, 650 m from the port. Five rooms in a wooden waterfront shack. Popular, perhaps due to the lively proprietor rather than the standard of accommodation.

Cheap restaurant with meals at around US$0.50. Lovely fishing from hammocks hanging over the water.

F Santiphab Guesthouse, far end of the island, facing Don Khone. Seven basic rattan bungalows right beside the bridge, most have the quintessential hammock. Idyllic setting, flanked by the Mekong on one side and rice paddies on the other – a friendly, timeless place. Good for those who want to be secluded. Very cheap restaurant serves tasty fare along with buckets of atmosphere.

Don Khone *p389, map p388*

Although Don Deth attracts the vast majority of tourists, Don Khone holds its own by offering some very pleasant accommodation alternatives and close proximity to most of the attractions.

B-C Salaphae, along from Auberge Sala Don Khone, T031-217526, www.salalao.com. This the true stand-out accommodation in the whole of the Siphandon area. 3 rafts are managed by ex-lawyer Leusak and hold 2 bungalows per raft. The rooms have been decorated perfectly, with all the minor touches that can make accommodation outstanding. A wonderful deck, with seating overlooks the stunning river scenery. Fantastic restaurant. Solar power heating.

B-D Auberge Sala Don Khone, Ban Khone Nua, T020-5633718, www.salalao.com. A former French hospital built in 1927, this place is one of the nicest places to stay on the island. Two traditional Luang Prabang-style houses have also been built in the grounds, with 6 rooms, all with en suite hot water shower and toilet, some with a/c. The restaurant, across from the guesthouse, is one of the best places to dine on any of the three islands, with an unobscured waterfront view from the comfy deckchairs and a unique cuisine selection that offers great relief from t he menus found in every other establishment. Generator daily 1800-2200. Reduced rate in low season.

Southern Laos Far south Listings

Organizes tours and boat trips. The manager is very informative and speaks excellent English.

F **Boun Guesthouse**, next door to Auberge Sala Don Khone. Mr Boun has built a couple of basic thatched bungalow with shared facilities and a few, newer wooden ones, complete with en suite bathrooms.

F **Sompamit Guesthouse**, across from Boun Guesthouse, on the riverside, T020-5733145. Threadbare rattan thatched bungalows with mosquito nets and shared bathroom facilities. Also a couple of basic rooms with en suite bathrooms.

F **Xaymountry Residence**, towards the bridge, T020-5735755. This old wooden villa with polished floorboards does not live up to the grandeur of its exterior. Tacky linoleum floor covering but clean en suite bathrooms. No riverviews but magnificent old building.

ⓞ Eating

Pakse *p381, map p392*

♥♥-♥ **Jasmine Restaurant**, No 13 Rd, T031-251002. This small place has outdoor seating and is a firm favorite with travellers. Offering the standard Indian fare and a few Malaysian dishes, it's reasonable value.

♥♥-♥ **Delta Coffee**, Route 13, opposite the **Champasak Palace Hotel**, T020-5345895. This place is a real find for those craving some western comfort foods. The extensive menu is tremendously varied and offers everything from pizza and lasagna to Thai noodles. The coffee is brilliant and staff exceptionally friendly. It has an unusual ordering system in place, where you write down orders by number.

♥♥-♥ **Sinouk**, opposite Lao Aviation, T031-212552. This is without a doubt the most tastefully decorated place in town, with tables adorned with glass-top coffee bean arrangements. There is a very reasonable breakfast and exceptionally good coffee. A creative menu is offered,

which includes tomatoes stuffed with pork, ribs and a few other fusion-inspired meals, but coffee is its real forte.

♥ **May Kham**, No 13 Rd, close to the bridge across the Don River, 100 m from Wat Luang. Many locals maintain this serves the best Vietnamese and Lao food in town, a/c restaurant but no pretensions, superb steamed duck with black mushroom and sweet and sour fish and morning glory stir fry.

Champasak *p381*

Most restaurants are located in the guesthouses; all are cheap (♥). **Anouxa Guesthouse** has a small but delectable menu; opt for a fish dish.

Ban Khiet Ngong *p384*

Eating in the village is very basic and you will have to rely on the local food. *Feu* and noodle soup can be made on the spot; most other meals, such as *laap*, will need to be ordered in advance.

Paksong and around *p384*

♥ **Khihtavan Restaurant**, on the road between the bank and market, across form the Kaysone Monument, T020-5769874. 0800-2100. Quiet place with very friendly service. Britney Spears poster turned menu board is only in Lao. Standard Lao food and good coffee.

♥ **Borravan Plateau**, Route 23 about 1 km from the market towards Tha Teng. The owner is very friendly. Standard selection of Lao dishes in an indoor setting, safe from the weather. Unfortunately there is no menu and no English spoken – so opt for something easy like *feu* or *laap*.

Tad Lo *p385*

♥ **Hath Restaurant**, behind the **Sailomen**, has a wide selection of western and Lao food, including sandwiches, fish and chips, vegetarian dishes and freedom fries for US$1-2; also international call services.

Don Khong p386

The majority of restaurants only serve fish and chicken. In the low season most restaurants will only be able to fulfill about half of the menu options. Special dishes such as a roast or *hor mok* will also need to be ordered a day in advance to ensure the proprieters have the required produce in stock. Although many other towns and areas also make such a claim, Don Khong is renowned for the quality of its *lau-lao* (rice liquor). Local fish with coconut milk cooked in banana leaves, *mok pa*, is truly divine and makes a trip to the islands worthwhile in itself.

††-† **Souksan Chinese Restaurant**, Muang Khong. This attractive place on the Mekong has a stunning, unobscured view of the river. It serves mostly Chinese food, including good local fish and tasty honeyed chicken. In recent years a number of western specialities have been added to the menu, including the US$5 roast (beef, chicken or pork with potatoes and gravy), which needs to be ordered a day in advance.

† **Done Khong Guesthouse**, Muang Khong. The restaurant attached to this guesthouse produces good food – nothing flash, just simple single-dish meals. It does a good line in pancakes.

† **Mekong Restaurant**, attached to the Mekong Guesthouse, Muang Khong. This restaurant is pleasantly positioned near the bank of the Mekong and provides legendary fare at seriously low prices. Good *feu*.

† **New Pon's Restaurant**, Muang Khong, T031-214037. Good atmosphere and excellent food, try the fish soup.

Don Deth p389, map p388

Most people choose to eat at their guesthouses, which all have pretty much the same menu, however, a couple of standouts are:

††-† **Souksan**, see Sleeping. Excellent Chinese-inspired dishes in addition to well-cooked fish. The restaurant is in a

prime location to take in sunset and the chef will cook up a roast for US$5 with advanced notice.

††-† **Mr B's**, see Sleeping. Italian bruschetta, rice pudding and a famous selection of burgers, including chicken and pumpkin. Service is faultless.

Don Khone p389, map p388

††† **Salaphae**, see Sleeping. The best choice on the island, with a selection of scrumptious and creative dishes.

†† **Auberge Sala Don Khone**, see Sleeping. There's a beautiful view from the restaurant and some fine options on the menu, such as tuna and orange salad and steak salad.

† **Channihoummas Restaurant**, further along the track towards the bridge. Basic, limited options – fruit shakes, coffee, baguettes, open from 0700.

⊛ Festivals and events

Wat Phou p381

Wat Phou Festival lasts for 3 days around the full moon of the third lunar month (usually **Feb**). Pilgrims come from far and wide to leave offerings at the temple. In the evening there are competitions – football, boat racing, bullfighting and cockfighting, Thai boxing, singing contests and the like.

Tad Lo p385

Buffalo ceremony This traditional Tahoy ceremony (p385) takes place in a nearby village on the first full moon in **Mar** and is dedicated to the warrior spirit, whom the local tribesmen ask for protection. Villagers are happy for tourists to come and watch (5000 kip per person). The spectacle kicks off at about 2000, with dancing; the buffalo is sacrificed the next morning at 0500. Throughout the day, the entire village shares the meat of the sacrificed animal, as well as leaving some choice pieces for the spirits of the dead warriors in the Ceremony House. **Tim's Guesthouse**

(see Sleeping) is the best place to go for information about this event.

Don Khong *p386*

Dec A 5-day **boat racing** festival takes place early in the month, on the river opposite Muang Khong. It coincides with National Day on 2 Dec and is accompanied by a great deal of celebration, eating and drinking.

○ Shopping

Don Deth *p389, map p388*

There isn't much to buy here. A small grocery store across from the port has a few essential items and snacks but is not very well stocked. If you're in desperate need of any items, make a quick trip to Nakasong and pick up things from the market there. Most guesthouses go to Nakasong on an almost daily basis and will usually buy things for you if you pay them 5000 kip or so.

▲ Activities and tours

Pakse *p381, map p392*
Tour operators
Most of the hotels in town arrange day tours to Wat Phou and Tad Lo; of these the best is the **Pakse Hotel**. There are a number of tour agencies in town, all of which will arrange tours to local sites.
Champa Mai Travel, T031-212930, sonethida02 @yahoo.com, has teamed up with the NTA to offer a diverse range of unique ecotours for the benefit of local communities. Although you can approach the NTA directly, it is probably best to go with Champa Mai.
Lane Xang Travel, opposite Jasmine Restaurant, T020-2255176. Offers a variety of tours and useful tour services (including a minivan service to Siphandon, 55,000 kip).
Sabaidy 2, see Sleeping, T031-212992. Mr Vong and crew offer a wide range of tours around a variety of top-notch provincial sites, very good value and recommended

for visitors who are only around for a day or two (US$15 per person, 4 people min).
Sodetour, No 13 Rd, near No 24 Rd, T031-213431. Arranges adventurous tours to the Boloven Plateau, and to other destinations in the south.

Ban Khiet Ngong *p384*
There are several 2- to 3-day trekking and homestay trips offered in the area; contact the **Provincial Tourism Information Office** in Pakse, T031-212 021 and ask for Mr Sulichan. These tours are designed to ensure that local communities reap the rewards of tourism in a sustainable fashion and are highly recommended. Other tourism operators in Pakse also runs tours to the area.

Elephant treks
Elephant treks to the **Phu Asa** take about 3-4 hrs, US$13; the elephant baskets can carry 2 people. If you wish to travel independently to this area, you need to allow enough time for the elephants to be organized by the *mahouts* (elephant keepers) once you arrive. Contact **Mr Peua**, T020- 5731207 (no English spoken) in advance. Otherwise, when you turn up in Ban Khiet Ngong, ask for **Mr Bounsome**, who runs the only bona fide guesthouse in the area. Although only minimal English is spoken in the village, most of the locals will understand the purpose of your visit.

Tad Lo *p385*
Elephant treks
This is an excellent way to see the area as there are few roads on the plateau and elephants can go where jeeps cannot. It is also a thrill being on the back of an elephant. Contact any of the guesthouses for information (50,000 kip per person; 2 people per elephant).

Don Deth *p387, map p388*
Almost every guesthouse on the island can arrange tours, transport and tickets. The best way to book yourself onto a tour

is through the new 'whiteboard' system. A couple of whiteboards have been placed around the island (the most popular one is at the northern end, near the port); simply write your name down next to the tour or trip you wish to take.

Dolphin watching boats from Don Deth depart when they have enough passengers and charge about US$6 per person; put your name on the noticeboard the day before. Rates are highly subject to change as they are based on petrol prices and the individual boatman's prerogative more than anything else. The best bet is to gather a group of 4 or 5 people together and then approach a boatman.

For boat trips further afield, see Transport, p401.

Don Khone *p389, map p388*
From Don Khone, it is possible to hire a boat for the day, to visit the islands and go fishing or dolphin watching. Boats depart from Kong Ngay, US$7, or from the railway bridge, US$4. For boat trips further afield, see Transport, p401.

Swimming
There is a sandy beach on Don Khone where many travellers like to take a dip. In the wet season this can be dangerous as there is a nasty undercurrent and tourists have drowned here, so be careful. The other thing to consider is the nasty parasite called schistosomiasis.

⊖ Transport

Pakse *p381, map p392*
Air
To **Vientiane** and **Siem Reap**. A flight between **Bangkok** and Pakse is being planned; check with **Lao Airlines** for latest information; it has offices at the airport and by the river in town, T031-212252.

Boat
A public passenger boat leaves at 0800 daily for **Champasak** and **Wat Phou**,

1½-2 hrs, 40,000 kip per person, depending on numbers; boats can also be chartered for around US$50-60. In the dry season the public service continues to Ban Hua Khong on **Don Khong**, 8 hrs total, US$8/100,000 kip. Be warned, though, that the turnaround time is speedy, and by the time this boat leaves Champasak, it's usually full to bursting and not apt to wait for any stragglers. In Ban Hua Khong you can catch a tuk-tuk to Muang Khong on the main part of the island. During the wet season, it is almost impossible to find a scheduled boat, in which case you can charter boats to Don Khong for around US$130 one way from the jetty at the end of No 11 Rd. Note that, even if you're chartering a boat, the boatmen will not make the journey in the dark, so embark before 0900 if you want to get to Don Khong in one trip.

Mr Bounmy, T020-5631008, will charter his speedy 30-seat, longboat to Champasak and Don Khong for slightly cheaper rates.

Bus or songthaew
Songthaews for **Paksong**, 50 km, depart from another small bus terminal at Km 2 on the other side of the bridge, every 15 mins from 0800, US$1. Make sure you stipulate where you are hopping off.

From the Northern terminal Hourly departures 0600-1500 to **Savannakhet**, 250 km, 4-5 hrs, 30,000 kip; to **Thakhek**, 6-7 hrs, 60,000 kip; to **Lak Sao**, 8-9 hrs, 75,000 kip; to **Vientiane**, 13-14 hrs, 85,000 kip.

From the Southern terminal Regular connections with **Champasak**; stay on the bus if you are travelling to Wat Phou (see p381). Ask for Ban Lak Sarm Sip ('village 30 km'), here there is a signpost and you turn right and travel 4 km towards Ban Muang (5 km). In the village there are people selling tickets for the ferry 7000 kip. Also songthaews to **Champasak**, 1000 and 1300, 1½ hrs, US$1.50.

Occasional buses to the **Siphandon** area but these can't be relied on; a cartel of songthaew drivers have some kind of scam that ensures buses won't operate while they are around. Note that buses are twice as likely to depart in the high season, usually at 1000 and 1200. Consider yourself lucky if you catch a bus but, if you do end up on a songthaew aim for a seat on the inside, in case of rain, and try to find some padding for the seat as it can be a painful trip. Note that some songthaew wait at the airport to take travellers direct to Siphandon. Price depends on numbers but a group of 5 can expect to pay US$5 per person. To **Don Khong/Muang Khong**, 0800, 1000, 1200, 1400 and 1600, 140 km, 4 hrs, US$3; to **Tad Lo**, 0700, 0900, 1000 and 1200, 85 km, 2 hrs, US$2 (ensure that the bus is taking Route 20 and not the alternative Route 23 via Paksong); to **Tad Fan**, 0800, 0900, 1000 and 1200, 50 km, 1 hr, US$1.50; to **Tha Theng**, 0900, 1100 and 1200, 15,000 kip; to **Ban Khiet Ngong**, 1000 and 1200, 56 km, 2 hrs, US$1; to **Don Deth/Don Khone** (via **Ban Nakasong**), hourly 0800-1300, 144 km, 4 hrs, from 25,000 kip. A more comfortable alternative, in the high season, is to take the minivan service to **Don Deth/Don Khong** offered by Lane Xang Travel, 55,000 kip.

Local buses coming through from Vientiane provide the main means of transport to other destinations down south, so can be slightly off kilter. Buses depart for **Salavan**, 0700, 0900, 1000 and 1200, 110 km, 2-3 hrs, US$2. This is a good alternative for those wishing to head to **Tad Lo** (20,000 kip), just make sure that the bus is taking Route 20 (not Route 23) and that the driver understands you want to get off at the junction.

From the Central market These buses are a much quicker northbound alternative. KVT Buses, T031-212228, depart at 2030 for **Vientiane**, 10 hrs non-stop, US$16. **Laolee VIP** buses depart at 2000 for **Vientiane**, US$11, via **Savannakhet**, 5 hrs, US$6, and at 0700 for **Thakhek**, 7 hrs, US$8. Sengjadut VIP buses depart for **Vientiane** at 0800, 10 hrs, US$11 (US$13 with toilet), via **Thakhek**, 7 hrs, US$8.

Motorbike and bicycle
Sabaidy 2, see Sleeping, rents motorbikes with insurance for US$8 the first day and US$7 for consecutive days. The **Lankham Hotel**, off Rd 13, rents out bicycles (US$1 per day) and larger dirtbikes.

Tuk-tuk or saamlor
A tuk-tuk to the northern bus station should cost 5000-7000 kip. Shared tuk-tuks to local villages leave from the Daoheung market and from the stop on No 11 Rd near the jetty. Tuk-tuks can also be chartered by the hour.

Champasak *p381*
Boat
Boats coming upstream from Don Khong arrive at Champasak at about 1400 and continue on to **Pakse** but always check in advance that the boats are running. There's also a morning connection downstream to **Don Khong**, leaving 0930-1000, 8000 kip (see also Pakse Transport, above).

Tuk-tuk
A tuk-tuk to **Ban Thong Kop**, the village opposite Wat Phou costs around 10,000 kip; direct to **Wat Phou** is US$5 return.

Paksong and around *p384*
Regular connections to **Pakse**, 0630-1200, 1½ hrs, 10,000 kip.

Tad Lo *p385*
There are buses from Ban Houa Set (1½ km north of Tad Lo) to **Pakse**, 0830, 1000, 1100, 1300 and 1400, 17,000 kip. You may also be able to catch the daily service to **Vientiane** on its way north, 0930 and 1430, 85,000 kip but don't expect it to be on time.

Don Khong p386

Boat

See also Ins and outs, p386. **New Pon's** (reliable and recommended) and **Souksan Guesthouse** can arrange boats to **Don Deth** or **Don Khone**. There are also several boatmen on the riverfront who are more than happy to take people for the right price. Fares tend to fluctuate according to international fuel prices but the going rate at the time of publication was US$15-US$20 for up to 10 people, one-way. Most leave around 0800. Day trips can be tailored to suit (for example, to visit both waterfalls, or the dolphins and one fall). It is also possible to alight at **Ban Nakasong**, from where you can charter a tuk-tuk (50,000 kip round trip) to the **Khong Phapheng Falls**. On the return trip, boats leave the falls around 1600-1700, although check with your boatman, and be aware that they do have a habit of setting off without conducting a head count. It's a great time to come back as you get a tremendous sunset thrown in.

Public passenger services going upriver from Don Khong leave around 0700 towards **Champasak** and take over 8 hrs to reach **Pakse**. Chartering a boat to or from Pakse costs around US$100-US$140 (maximum 20 people).

Bus or truck

A bus to **Pakse** departs from the intersection near Wat Kan Khong at around 0800 daily but it's worth asking the guesthouse owners for the most recent transport information; for earlier departures to **Pakse**, cross to **Ban Hat Xai Khoune** and pick up a bus heading north from Nakasong (from 0600 onwards). To reach **Ban Nakasong**, walk to Route 13 from Ban Hat Xai Khoune and try for transport south.

Ban Nakasong p388

Boat

To **Don Deth** and **Don Khone**, 15-20 mins, 30,000 kip per person. To **Don Khong**, 2 hrs, US$15 (divided between the passengers).

Bus or songthaew

Decent buses depart from Nakasong's market at 0600, 0700, 0800, 0900 and 1000 northbound for **Pakse**, 30,000 kip; some continue onwards to **Vientiane**; get off at **Ban Hat Xai Khoune** for the crossing to **Don Khong**, US$1. Note that there is a scam in operation on the Pakse-bound bus. Songthaew drivers, in collusion with bus staff, get on the bus at a halfway point and tell foreign passengers they have to continue by songthaew to the terminal. This is not true. There's also a pickup to Pakse at 1030, US$5 per person. Buses to **Voen Kham** (for the Cambodia border; see p274) depart in the morning, 13 km, US$1; alternatively, you can charter a songthaew for US$3, or hire a motorbike.

To **Khong Phapheng**, take a tuk-tuk or motorcycle taxi for around US$6-7 return.

Don Deth and Don Khone p387, map p388

Boat

Guesthouses organize boat trips around the area every day; the following rates are susceptible to change: to **Ban Nakasong**, US$2, divided by the number of passengers; to **Khong Phapeng Falls**, 60,000 kip, minimum 5 people; to **Pakse** by boat and bus, 0600, 0700, 0800, 0900 and 1000, 40,000 kip; to **Voen Kham** (for the Cambodian border, see p274), 0800 and 1300, 30,000 kip, min 3 people (for around US$3-4 they will stop off at the **Khong Phapheng Falls** on the way). Otherwise you can do the border trip yourself from Ban Nakasong (see above).

There are two ways to get to **Don Khong**, either by boat from Ban Nakasong, 2 hrs, US$15 (divided between max 5 passengers), or by bus from Ban Nakasong (see above); motorbike taxis also make the trip for US$3. Although it's slower and more expensive, the boat trip is recommended; it is one of the loveliest trips you can do in Laos.

🅘 Directory

Pakse *p381, map p392*
Banks BCEL Bank, No 11 Rd, changes US$ and most currencies (cash) and offers a better commission rate on cash exchange than other banks, also Visa/MasterCard cash advances at 3% commission, Mon-Fri 0830-1530 (with 1-hr lunch); Lao Development Bank, No 13 Rd, T031-212168, cash and TCs.
Embassies and consulates Vietnam, No 24 Rd, Mon-Fri 0800-1300, 1400-1630, visas for Vietnam, US$50, 3 days to process. **Internet** Expect to pay around 200 kip per min. D@M's Internet & Email Service, No 13 Rd; Lankham Hotel has about 5 computers.
Medical services There is a huge hospital between No 1 Rd and No 46 Rd, T031-212018, but neither the English skills nor medical service will suffice for complex cases; in case of emergencies you are better off going across to Ubon in Thailand; there is a pretty good pharmacy at the hospital which stocks most medicines. **Police** T031-212145. **Post office** No 8 Rd, overseas telephone calls can also be made from here; express mail service available; note the ashtrays made from defused (one hopes) unexploded shells. **Telephone** Telecoms office for overseas calls on No 1 Rd, near No 13 Rd; all of the internet cafes have internet-call facilities which are the cheapest option.

Paksong and around *p384*
Bank Lao Development Bank, east side of No 23 Rd, opposite the Kaysone Monument, open 0830-1530, exchanges baht and US$.

Don Khong *p386*
Banks Basic Lao Agriculture Promotion bank in town; hours are erratic and it accepts only US$ or Thai baht; guesthouses will also change cash at rates slightly poorer than market rate; New Pon's Guesthouse will change most major currencies and TCs but a photocopy of your passport is required.
Internet Alpha Internet offers internet and internet phone at 1000 kip per min; it also burns CDs, hires canoes and does laundry. **Post office** The post office is opposite the jetty in the centre of town, unreliable and slow mail service; international dialling available here.

Don Deth *p389, map p388*
Banks There are no banks; a foreign exchange service near the port will change most major currencies; Mr B of Mr B's guesthouse will also organize the cashing of TCs, but the commission here is quite hefty, so you are better organizing your cash from Pakse. **Internet** Small internet café across from the port junction, 1000 kip per min; calls can also be made, 10 min minimum. Souksan also has internet at 1200 kip per min.
Telephone The best way to make a call is via the net, though most guesthouses will let you make calls from their mobiles, which can be incredibly expensive, up to US$4 a min. **Visas** The Riverside Restaurant can organize Cambodian visas, 3 working days, US$55, or 5 working days, US$45.

Don Khone *p389, map p388*
Communications There's no post office and no telephones on the island, although some guesthouses will allow you to make international calls from their mobile phones, up to US$4 per min.
Electricity No mains electricity but most places run generators daily 1800-2200.

Glossary

A

Amitabha the Buddha of the Past
Ao dai long flowing silken tunic worn over trousers by Vietnamese women

B

Bodhi the tree under which the Buddha achieved enlightenment (Ficus religiosa)
Bodhisattva a future Buddha. In Mahayana Buddhism, someone who has attained enlightenment, but who postpones nirvana to help others reach it.
Bot Buddhist ordination hall, of rectangular plan, identifiable by the boundary stones placed around it; an abbreviation of ubosoth
Brahma the Creator, one of the gods of the Hindu trinity, usually represented with four faces; often mounted on a hamsa

C

Caryatid elephants, often used as buttressing decorations
Chao title for Lao and Thai kings
Chedi from the Sanskrit cetiya (Pali, caitya), meaning memorial. Usually a religious monument (often bell-shaped), containing relics of the Buddha or other holy remains. Used interchangeably with stupa

D

Deva a Hindu-derived male god
Dharma the Buddhist law
Doi moi 'renovation', Vietnamese perestroika

F

Funan the oldest Indianized state of Indochina and precursor to Chenla

G

Ganesh elephant-headed son of Siva
Garuda mythical divine bird, with predatory beak and claws, and human body; the king of birds, enemy of naga and mount of Vishnu

Geomancy the art of divination by lines and figures. Geomancers were responsible for the position of a palace, tomb or other auspicious building.
Gopura crowned or covered gate, entrance to a religious area

H/I

Hamsa sacred goose, Brahma's mount; in Buddhism it represents the flight of the doctrine
Harihara a syncretic deity combining Vishnu and Siva
Hinayana 'Lesser Vehicle', major Buddhist sect in Southeast Asia, usually termed Theravada Buddhism
Ikat tie-dyeing method of patterning cloth
Indra the Vedic god of the heavens, weather and war; usually mounted on a three-headed elephant

J

Jataka(s) the birth stories of the Buddha; they normally number 547, although three were added in Burma for reasons of symmetry in painting and sculpture; the last ten are the most important

K

Kala (makara) literally 'death' or 'black'; a demon ordered to consume itself, often sculpted with grinning face and bulging eyes over entranceway to act as a door guardian; also known as kirtamukha
Kinaree half human, half bird, usually depicted as a heavenly musician
Krishna incarnation of Vishnu

L

Laterite bright red tropical soil/stone commonly used in construction of Cham monuments
Linga phallic symbol and one of the forms of Siva. Embedded in a pedestal (yoni) shaped to allow drainage of lustral water poured over it, the linga typically has a succession of cross sections: from

square at the base through octagonal to round. These symbolise, in order, the trinity of Brahma, Vishnu and Siva

M

Mahayana 'Greater Vehicle', major Buddhist sect

Makara mythological aquatic reptile often found with the kala

Meru sacred or cosmic mountain at the centre of the world in Hindu-Buddhist cosmology; home of the gods

Mondop from the sanskrit, *mandapa*. A cube-shaped building, often topped by a cone-like structure, holding an object of worship like a footprint of the Buddha

Montagnard 'hill people', from the French

Mudra symbolic gesture of the hands of the Buddha

N

Naga benevolent mythical water serpent, enemy of Garuda

Nandi/nandin bull, mount of Siva

Nirvana release from the cycle of suffering in Buddhist belief; 'enlightenment'

Non lá Conical straw hat

P

paddy/padi unhulled rice or an irrigated field in which rice is grown

Pagoda a Mahayana Buddhist temple

Pali the sacred language of Theravada Buddhism

Parvati consort of Siva

Prang form of stupa built in Khmer style, shaped like a corncob

R

Rama incarnation of Vishnu, hero of the Indian epic, the Ramayana

Rattan Forest creeper that is woven into baskets or furniture. Sometimes mistaken for bamboo

Rong the Bahnar rong house is instantly recognizable by its tall thatched roof. The height of the roof is meant to indicate the significance of the building and make it visible to all. It is a focal point of the village for meetings of the village elders, weddings and other communal events

S

Sakyamuni the historic Buddha

Sala open pavilion

Sampan a small wooden boat, traditionally made of three planks of wood

Sim/sima main sanctuary and ordination hall in a Lao temple complex

Singha mythical guardian lion

Siva the Destroyer, one of the three gods of the Hindu trinity; the sacred linga was worshipped as a symbol of Siva

Stupa dome-like Buddhist monument. Originally a topknot of hair, the building symbolises variously the upper part of the head, a tree's stem and a tower reaching up to heaven

T

That shrine housing Buddhist relics, a spire or dome-like edifice commemorating the Buddha's life or the funerary temple for royalty

Theravada 'Way of the Elders'; major Buddhist sect also known as Hinayana Buddhism ('Lesser Vehicle')

Traiphum the three worlds of Buddhist cosmology – heaven, hell and earth

Trimurti the Hindu trinity of gods: Brahma, the Creator, Vishnu the Preserver and Siva the Destroyer

U/V

Ubosoth see bot

Vahana 'vehicle', a mythical beast, upon which a deva or god rides

Viharn from Sanskrit *vihara*, an assembly hall in a Buddhist monastery; may hold Buddha images and is similar in style to the bot

Vishnu the Protector, one of the gods of the Hindu trinity, generally with four arms holding a disc, conch shell, ball and club

W

Wat Buddhist 'monastery', with religious and other buildings

Index ▸▸ Entries in red are maps

Credits

Footprint credits

Editor: Claire Boobbyer
Managing editor: Sophie Blacksell
Editorial assistants: Angus Dawson, Nicola Jones
Proofreader: Stephanie Lambe
Map editor: Sarah Sorensen
Picture editor: Claire Benison

Publisher: Patrick Dawson
Editorial: Alan Murphy, Sarah Thorowgood, Felicity Laughton
Cartography: Robert Lunn, Claire Benison, Kevin Feeney
Sales and marketing: Andy Riddle
Advertising: Debbie Wylde
Finance and administration: Sharon Hughes, Elizabeth Taylor

Photography credits

Front cover: Superstock (Dragon)
Inside: Alamy, Claire Boobbyer, Corel Professional Draw, Jamie Marshall, Jock O'Tailan, Superstock, Travel Ink,
Back cover: Alamy (Beach at Nha Trang)

Print

Manufactured in Italy by EuroGrafica
Pulp from sustainable forests

Every effort has been made to ensure that the facts in this guidebook are accurate. However, travellers should still obtain advice from consulates, airlines etc about travel and visa requirements before travelling. The authors and publishers cannot accept responsibility for any loss, injury or inconvenience however caused.

Publishing information

Footprint Vietnam, Cambodia and Laos
1st edition
© Footprint Handbooks Ltd
December 2005
ISBN 1 904777 56 2

CIP DATA: A catalogue record for this book is available from the British Library
® Footprint Handbooks and the Footprint mark are a registered trademark of Footprint Handbooks Ltd

Published by Footprint

6 Riverside Court
Lower Bristol Road
Bath BA2 3DZ, UK
T +44 (0)1225 469141
F +44 (0)1225 469461
discover@footprintbooks.com
www.footprintbooks.com

Distributed in the USA by

Publishers Group West

Advertisers' index